STUDIES IN EQUITATION

The complete book on the art of riding horses

by

Tony Silverman.

Pre-press by F.E. Burman Ltd, London
Printed and bound by Polestar Wheatons, Exeter

A TONY SILVERMAN INSTRUCTIONAL BOOK.

First published in the UK in 2002
Copyright © Tony Silverman 2002

Photographs, Drawings and Diagrams copyright © Tony Silverman
Except for plates i ii iii and iv.

Tony Silverman has identified his right to be identified as the author of this work in
Accordance with the copyright, Designs and Patents Act 1988.

A catalogue record for this book is available from the British Library

ISBN 0-9543307-2-2

Published in the UK 2002 by
Tony Silverman,
19 Lake View,
Edgware,
Middx. HA8 7RT.

The information in this book is given without prejudice or responsibility. The author does not accept liability for any incident
that may arise as a result of information or opinions contained herein, being put into practice.

Front cover drawing 'Tony's Jeeves' by Kate Harrison. Commissioned by the author while Kate was a
student at Suzannes. She is now a well-known and extremely talented artist.

Revised and updated 2005

Contents

Chapter 17 Introducing jumping.

The policy of the school.
The correct horse.
The ability of the rider.
Confidence.
Going forward.
The open and closed positions.
Trotting poles.
Horses that play up.
The horse preparing to jump – trot – canter.
The bascule.
How does a rider jump? - Approaching a jump.
The first round.
Running out or refusing - cantering when it should be trotting.
The 2nd round.
Jumping with the eyes closed.
The 2nd – 3rd and 4th lessons.
Advanced jumping.
Teaching children.

Chapter 18 Things to avoid and dealing with problems.
Clients.

Difficult clients.
Professionals and Captains of industry.
The quid pro quo.
Clients who complain. - Clients who 'do their own thing' - riders with dubious explanations.
Parents who push their children - parents who interfere.
The social ladder.
Giving clients problems too difficult to solve.

Horses.

Reporting odd behaviour. - Misbehaviour. - Bad behaviour.
Young stock
Putting in a buck.

The weather.

The effect of wind on sound and vision - on your voice – on temperature – on balance.
Snow - the bitter cold.
Teaching in the rain.

Chapter 19 New Technologies.

The video camera.
The mechanical horse.
The mobile phone.
The tension or position alarm.
The plastic horseshoe.

Chapter 20 Hacking Out.

Introduction.
The Instructor.
Equipment.
The horses
The riders.
Planning the route – emergency meeting points.
The clients.
Types of hack - during the hack – giving commands.
Avoiding difficult situations –leaving the road – proceeding across country.
The experienced hack – the instructional hack – exercises – special points.
Further thoughts.
The novice hack – the private hack.
Returning.
Difficult situations
Horses that continually try to eat grass.
What to do if… - A rider has been told by another client that a horse is known to be 'a bit of a handful'.
A rider suddenly panics – there is a thunderstorm – a horse goes lame – a client is taken ill – there is an accident -
A horse declines to be caught - Conclusion..

Chapter 21 Playing Games.

A suitable type of pony – utilising an area – working out in a field.

Maintaining control – by area – by gait.

Setting the rules – using rhymes.

Setting the parameters for all gaits – the accent on safety – the benefits.

Maintaining discipline and safety.

Team games and choosing team leaders – choosing teams – uneven numbers – helpers.

Cheering on a team – dealing with cheats.

Your contribution.

Riding and leading races.

The components of a 'race'.

Bad weather.

Chapter 22 Liveried horses.

Why should an owner have problems? – Providing simple answers for simple problems.

Problems through simple incorrect choice - horses that are simply disobedient – bad habits – standing for hours on end.

Over horsed and under used – horses that will not stand still – horses with bad habits.

Horses that are fresh – young horses.

Providing a higher target for the owner of a liveried horse.

Dressage or jumping? – General schooling – jumping for liveries.

Final thoughts on instructing livery owners.

Experimentation – working liveries.

Dealing with private clients – giving a demonstration – teaching how to develop creativity.

Chapter 23 The reasons why.

Chapter 24 Care of the arena.

Chapter 25 Games list.

Chapter 26 Stories to entertain.

Bibliography.

Explanation of terms used.

Glossary of commands.

Index.

Photographs/ coloured illustrations.

DEDICATION

To my daughter Emma who rides so well (No I did not teach her)

And all the hundreds of children and dozens of adults from whom I have learned so much.

To all those clients and students who agreed to pose for photographs both in the correct and incorrect position!

To Margaret Thompson (the author Margo Lawrence) my neighbour, Valerie Holcombe and Caroline Davis all of who read my manuscript.

To Julian and Suzanne Marczak for whom it has been such a pleasure to work all these years.

Finally to Jeeves who taught me while I taught him.

For this printing, to my wife Benita who proof-read this revised version and having absolutely no knowledge whatsoever regarding equitation made me rewrite some of my more convoluted paragraphs.
To my grandsons Sebastian and Cameron who are now living in Perth - Australia. They might grow up to have an interest in the noble art.
To my sister-in-law Valerie who made me get on with the job of finalizing this impression and especially to Rob King who was so persistent in removing all the glitches in the PDF files.
Many thanks. **T.S.**

Some references.

Foreword.

I have known Tony Silverman for many years, during which I have constantly been aware of his enthusiasm and vigour for the subject at hand.

It comes, therefore, as no surprise to me that in writing *Studies in Equitation* Tony has endeavoured to give his all in sharing with his readers his detailed thoughts on equitation, approaching the subject often from a different perspective to that seen before.

Tony is a long-standing teacher of riding who has always proved highly popular with his pupils for his clear and concise methods of communicating which come through in this book.

To have all the information produced in CD format, as well as book form, will surely add to the appeal of Tony's writing and diagrams and I have no doubt that students, as well as true enthusiasts of horsemanship, will find them stimulating and thought-provoking.

I can recommend *Studies in Equitation* to those seeking knowledge in this fascinating world of horses.

Julian Marczak. ABRS (Prin. Dip.) (TC) LCGI LGSM.

T.S. says.

I am extremely grateful to Julian for being so kind as to write a foreword for this book.

Julian and his mother Suzanne run a very large and efficient riding school in Harrow Weald. I consider Julian to be a superb instructor with the patience of a saint. However despite the pressure of commercial considerations, there have been occasions where I have heard him tell a client, who has bloated ideas as to their ability and who won't listen when instructed, to take their business elsewhere! At Suzanne's the well-being of the horses are paramount.

As I mention in my dedication, I have had great pleasure in working for Julian. In fact it is getting on for nearly twenty-five years.

List of illustrations.

List of illustrations. (Note all coloured Photographs and the drawings for chapter 20 are now placed at the end of this book).

Photographs.

Drawings. (Note Drawings and Diagrams are shown at the end of each chapter to which they apply with the exception of drawing nos. 12, 27 and all those for chapter 20 which are coloured and thus placed at the end of the book).

List of diagrams. (Note all black and white Drawings and Diagrams are shown at the end of each chapter to which they apply. Coloured diagrams are shown at the end of the book).

14

Addendum.

Additional diagrams.

Plates of pictures reproduced.

Explanation of symbols used in diagrams.

Segment of exercise at walk.   ....

Segment of exercise at trot sitting.   – – – – – – – – –

Segment of exercise at trot rising   •••••••••••••••••••••••

Segment of exercise at canter   – • – • – • – • – • –

Thus transition point from trot rising to canter ••••• – – – – – – • – • –

Direction of movement   – • – • – • – • – • –▶

Any movement irrespective of gait.   ————————————————

You the Instructor.

A marker cone

Horses on different reins.

Explanation of symbols used in diagrams

Introduction

This book is not intended as a guide as to how to learn to ride. It is more an instructional manual on how to create a degree of unity and co-operation between two types of mammals, humans and horses!

Now it is possible that the occasional rider or livery owner picking up this book might well wonder if, since it is mainly directed towards those hoping to become qualified as instructors, there is anything in it for them? My reply is that in order to be able to teach it is essential to have a deep and thorough knowledge of everything that has to do with ones subject. In this case how to ride a horse. Thus it follows that even those who do not ride regularly will find the answers to most of the problems that they may come across and will improve their riding skills accordingly.

When I originally started to consider this undertaking I had thought of writing two books. One for teaching adults and the other for children. Time has passed. I do not now think that that is necessary. I have learned more. Teaching both generations demands almost the same skills. However there may be times when special consideration should be made for youngsters and also for older riders and in order to provide for this I have added a special section, where required, at the end the pertinent chapter.

I have been at this teaching lark for around forty years. I owe my teaching career to playing bridge! I had acquired my first hunter the 'Buccaneer' so named because his sire was a thoroughbred named 'Pirate Chief'. He also had a propensity for dislodging, once and once only, anyone who rode him. As soon as my bridge-playing friends, those with moderate riding experience, learned that my great passion had now become riding, they nagged me to arrange a hack for them. I duly did so and was asked to provide the escort; this developed into a regular outing. As we progressed around the countryside I started to give them advice. My approached was influenced by my bridge teacher, the great Victor Mollo, who when I was having a lesson would hover behind my back looking at the cards that I held and exclaim with a shout, such things as, 'Never play away from an ace'. The Master of course knew what he was talking about, but I didn't, at first, have the slightest idea. Thus when I started to teach equitation I decided that my pupils had to understand exactly what I meant.

Occasionally, much to my pleasure, I meet up with attractive young women instructors who throw their arms around my neck and give me a big hug. I am then challenged as to whether or not I can remember their names, for had I not taught them to ride when they were children! Then there are the parents who bring along their offspring and ask if I will teach them to ride as I have taught Mum or Dad. I have to say it makes me feel ancient.

I would describe myself as a journeyman-riding teacher. I am not a specialist. It has been my job, throughout these years to try to impart the basics of equitation to urban dwellers that wish to ride, for pleasure, mainly at weekends. It is to the instructors of this particular group of riders that this book is directed. I assume that most of my readers are quite young so please use my advice as a means of acquiring knowledge that has taken me many years to learn. I have tried to make the distinction between the teaching of 'Equitation' and the 'Teaching' of people. One may well qualify and pass numberless exams for the former but without the ability to pass this on to the latter you will never become a 'Great' instructor. Further more I have tried to give you as many 'tips' as I can remember. I say 'remember' because, when teaching, some of the finer points of instruction are performed almost subconsciously but they do tend to make the difference between success and something less than that. This is especially so when teaching beginners.

My clients are, generally, not people 'born in the saddle'. Thus the sport of riding does not always come naturally to them. Most of them will never become real experts. Some of you may wonder why one should bother about them at all? It is a reasonable question. The reason why I am so concerned to see this part of equitation flourish is because, not only does it provide thousands of people with light exercise, combined with relaxation from the pressures of the weeklong servitude, but it also helps to maintain or even increase the overall horse population. I write at a time when diversity in the animal world is shrinking fast under the pressure of an ever-expanding human world population. (At present it stands at 6.0 billion. I wonder what the figure will be when you read this book in time to come?). It is my belief that noble efforts to prevent the extinction many species will fail unless animals become part of the economy of the peoples whose land they share. This is just as true for horses. At the time that I write increasing numbers of riding schools are being forced to close due to the pressure of regulation and the demand for payment of ever-higher rates. When they close what happens to the horses that have served them so well? Of course there will always be a minority of those with sufficient funds to indulge in competition riding and so forth but horse numbers and the variety of breeds will suffer. One should also not forget that the sport of riding for pleasure provides employment for the thousands of young people who work in these yards.

Therefore this is a book about teaching the basics. In these pages you will find neither the secrets to 'Haute Ecóle' or training the horse. I try to avoid using terms that require quite extensive explanation such as 'direct or indirect rein of opposition' when something simpler will do. It is my view that all horses used for riding schools should *already* have been trained or as they say in the profession 'schooled'. It gives a false illusion to imply that someone who has not mastered the art of equitation, whose seat is somewhat less than 'good', has the ability to teach a horse his work. It should be the instructors' aim to enable the pupil to elicit from the horse, the very best of that which it is capable. Further more I must make it clear that this book is definitely *not* for those who only judge an instructor by their success in competition. I am referring to those who, when asked what they consider to be the fundamental difference in approach between say Charles Harris and Daniel Plevner, reply 'who? I don't recall having read anything about them in the results of recent dressage competitions!'

Let us be clear about one thing. There is nothing mysterious or arcane about riding a horse. All that is required is the absolute fundamental of being able to stay on its back without falling off and the ability to get it to go from one place to another according to the will of the rider.

That, being so you may well wonder why I have adhered so strongly to the principals of 'Classical Equitation'? I admit that there are many riding teachers around today who specialise and do not consider that this way of riding has any importance at all. They consider it to be outdated. Well if I may use an analogy, I am reminded of the poet John Betjman who wrote to Mary Wilson, (the wife of Prime Minister Harold Wilson) who also wrote poetry. She did not have a very high opinion of her own work because she thought that the fact that it all rhymed somehow diminished her work. Critics had said that it was mere doggerel. Betjman did not agree, he thought that her work was very good and he compared her critics with abstract painters, who having never learned perspective accused classical artists of being mere photographers. I feel the same way about classical equitation. Establish a good foundation and then and only then explore where you will.

The reader will note that I have been fairly detailed in my descriptions of many things, for example the 'aids'. Now this may seem rather strange in view of the fact that this book is not about *learning* to ride but about *teaching* people to learn to ride. So why such detail? Surely you the reader are already well aware of these matters. This may be so but knowing about the practice of a particular profession and putting this knowledge into words clearly understood by the layman, are entirely different matters. That is why the descriptions are so specific. This does not mean that you need to use my exact words. The only criterion for you is to be sure that your clients have understood *your* meaning. Sometimes when I have finished a lesson, I have had the friends or parents of those who have been riding in my classes come up to me and say 'I watched your lesson and though I do not ride I understood every word that you said'. One cannot ask for more than that!

You will also note that I sometimes make mention of certain aspects of equitation in chapters where you might not expect to find them. This tendency to overlap has to do with the changing circumstances in which you may find yourself. For example I do mention the canter both in the chapters dealing with beginners and novices. For the former chapter the emphasis is on teaching riders on the lunge on a one to one basis. Thus you start with someone who cannot ride and end up with someone who can. The chapter on novices and indeed intermediate riders is based on the assumption that you are teaching a class. This being the case you may have pupils joining you whom are already *presumed* to have had some experience though in fact this may prove to be somewhat ephemeral. Should this be so then you must know how to adjust your lesson to fit their actual ability. In this book I do, sometimes, refer to 'clients' rather than pupils. The reason for this is that in this profession we do often talk about them in this way, especially those who are freelance instructors. One builds up a client list as it were. This is especially so for those who tend to have private lessons which they share with no one else. Further more some 'advanced' riders prefer to be addressed in this manner. Also, please note that in later chapters I may appear to be quite scathing about some riders. Take this with a pinch of salt it is simply my way of keeping myself on an 'even keel' when dealing with riders who insist that they know better than I do.

All that I write in this book arises from practical experience in the ménage and the study of the masters of equitation whose views I have tried out and found to work. Like so many before me I occasionally draw a comparison between the mechanics of the interaction between horse and rider with those of machines. In this respect I may have some slight advantage for a period of my life was spent, first as a work-study engineer and then as a consultant in manufacturing industry, so I really do know how machines work! What this has revealed to me is; that, in practise, the complicated dynamics involving the motions of horse and rider are not to be compared with that of machines!

As I look over the thousands of words that lie ahead I am reminded of the fact that, as there may be so many of them, I need to try to make the reading of this book a little easier. I will do this by presenting the information in an order that makes it easily accessible. You should be able to 'dip in' as it were and, hopefully, find the answer to any question or problem that you may have. This being the case I have taken the liberty of repeating certain fundamental points. You will find references to 'position' in several different chapters. The reason for this is that, when simply glancing through the text, you will not overlook, what I consider to be, the very foundation of good equitation. I hope that I will succeed.

It is often said to many would-be riders that 'you won't learn to ride by reading a book'. There is some truth in this remark. However it is also true that they will *learn* if they have a *good instructor*. Good instructors become so through a combination of learning the job thoroughly, experience and studying the masters whom have gone before. A good instructor will turn a rider with natural ability into a superb horseman. A mediocre rider will become a competent and above all safe rider. A *good* instructor is the instrument through which *all* riders learn to maximise their enjoyment of the sport.

In chapter 20 I have included a slightly revised version of the little booklet 'The Instructors Guide to Safe and Interesting Hacking' that I published in 1995. I originally wrote this in order to help those who are given the responsibility for taking clients out hacking. I am delighted to say that it has been included as recommended reading for the teaching exams of the ABRS.

Horses behave in an entirely different manner when they go out. Even some very skilled instructors may not have much experience when it comes to taking out between 8 and 10 riders across country. My remark is not intended as a criticism, for even as brilliant a teacher as F Baucher (French School around the middle of the 19th century) was rumoured never to have to have ridden outside an enclosed ménage. *36. Since hacking out requires different abilities from both horse and rider I have decided not to alter very much. This means that you may come across remarks that I have made elsewhere in this book. Forgive me for being repetitive.

Finally I hope that I do, eventually, get this manuscript finished! During the intervals between typing, I venture forth to give a lesson or two. Every time I do so I return to the keyboard and unscramble a scribbled note that I have made during that time. For as I teach I realise to my horror that something that I consider being significant has not yet been recorded. Further more I have polished and re-polished my notes. Still unsatisfied I do need, eventually, to reach a point where I place them in the manuscript. You may find fault and disagree with my views. If you do, well, that's life and I do make the point that there are many different ways of going about teaching people to ride. You may create your own, unique way of doing this but when you do I hope that you will reflect that that which I have written may have influenced you.

Chapter 1

Evolution

This may be considered a rather strange subject with which to open a book simply concerned with the teaching of the art of equitation. For me the matter is fundamental. If your clients are, eventually, become good riders they will do so through understanding the mental processes of the horses that they ride.

At this point I have to make my own position quite clear. I do not accept the view, generally prevailing, at the time I write, that genetic change is simply a result of error or chance. Neither do I accept that somehow or other all other creatures are our inferiors and that we alone have an understanding of the universe and that therefore by some mysterious means we are the sole masters or custodians of this planet. I do believe in the Darwinian view of the survival of the fittest, in so far as any creature will be judged by the way in which it manages to produce progeny better suited to the environment in which they will have to live. However I believe that in this matter all life forms exercise free will. Some degree of luck may be involved but it is intelligence that will, ultimately, produce a more successful offspring. Choose the right path and you win - the wrong path and you loose, for we are talking here about genetic immortality.

All living creatures deal with the problem of survival in different ways. Primarily they have to decide what sort of young they should produce that will be best suited to the changed conditions that *will* prevail during the life span of the next generation. They try to preserve their species by developing distinctive markings and yet they try to bear young ones that will be sufficiently different to take advantage of the changed conditions that they believe *will* exist after their offspring are born. This, to my mind, is what evolution is all about.

There are learned scientists around today who would take exception to my forgoing statement. Richard Dawkins is their High Priest. He insists that evolutionary change is pure chance. A chance error in the way in which DNA replicates itself. If the change accidentally produces, says Dawkins, a creature better able to succeed in the current environment, then, according to Darwin's laws of the survival of the fittest; that creature will survive and multiply and, eventually, it will supersede all those of its kind that have not made such a change. I accept the point regarding the survival of the fittest but I do not believe that one can put this down to pure chance. In the first place it eliminates free will and a belief in the Almighty and whilst I do not picture a man sitting on a throne in the vastness of heaven I do believe in the unseen force that we have over the millennia called G-d. Freedom of choice is open to all living things and it is a measure of a creature's intelligence as to the manner in which it chooses to use that freedom.

If one accepts Dawkins' view that every change is purely 'accidental' then, it seems to me, that we would never have made much progress because an 'improvement', through DNA error, in one generation might well be cancelled by another 'accident' in the next.

In fact there does not seem to be any proof that mutation occurs in only *one* offspring in any particular species and that this *single* creature eventually affects the whole species. It may well be that as soon as one life form becomes aware of a change that has proved to be successful in the offspring of one of its relatives, and then it too will try to reproduce a similar change in its own progeny. There has been no epidemiological (in the sense of mutation by error) survey, as it were, that proves things one way or the other. The problem lies in the fact that though there have been millions if not billions of creatures that have lived and died, the few fossils that we have found sufficiently preserved for our study are numerically minute compared to the number of those that have gone before.

I suppose I should go back a bit. For here I am rattling on about intelligence. What exactly is intelligence? So far as I am concerned there are two basic rules that govern the definition. They are: -

Rule 1. Any organism that has the instinct to survive by successful reaction to stimuli.
Rule 2. The ability to produce offspring that are so changed as to be better able to succeed in the environment, which the parent believes, will exist when they are born.

The first rule is self-explanatory. After all an organism that doesn't search for an energy input (food), move away from an object that causes pain or obey any of the hundred and one reflexes that have developed to, instinctively, help to keep it alive, will die. So far as the second rule is concerned, this is where the free will element comes in. A creature may not necessarily make the correct choice and if it is wrong then, its offspring will probably not survive long enough to have issue. Immortality, in genetic terms, ceases.

Dawkins makes this very point. He writes that, if there is one certainty in this uncertain life, it is that there is an *unbroken line*, from you, running back through your ancestors; to the moment that life was created. If there had been a break, then you wouldn't be here.

This causes some difficulty for both the believers and unbelievers in the Almighty. Personally, I don't have a problem with this. Though I must admit that my view does to some extent lessen that feeling of self-importance that man has had since his dominance over the rest of the mammalian species on this planet.

Note I said dominance over mammals. I did not mention insects, bacteria or viruses. This is because, in truth, our sojourn, so far, has not affected any of these life forms in any way whatsoever. We have managed to suppress, temporarily, a small number but for sure they lie in wait simply awaiting for our attention to wander before staging a return that might well produce a catastrophe. We are creatures that have elected to evolve by handing on our accumulated knowledge by either the spoken, or when the body of knowledge became too great, by the written word. By becoming extremely specialised, we have become vulnerable to any deadly pathogen that attacks before we are able to find a way of neutralising it. We may still retain the ability to develop resistance, in our own bodies, but we do not use this mechanism, in its original form, very often these days. However should a disease such as Ebola escape its confines and make its way via infected human hosts crossing the Globe so quickly by air, then, it is possible that a near mortal blow to our dominance of this planet might be inflicted upon us.

The reason for this is that we have become so *extremely* *specialised* that the decimation of our species on a large scale would certainly shake our grip upon the world. I suppose that the forgoing sentence may seem rather dotty, but stop for a minute and consider your own life and to what extent your daily existence depends *entirely* on the specialised work of others. Farmers grow your food, its freshness depends on daily deliveries, a small glitch in the transport system and there is none available. Stupid I hear you say, what about the food in the freezer? Fine so long as the electricity supply does not breakdown! I could go on indefinitely with other examples but enough is enough. Amused I watch the more flamboyant supporters of the Green Lobby belting out heavy metal or rock songs at music festivals. Specialists in electronics make their instruments and the sound is amplified to umpteen watts by electricity produced by other specialists and there they stand telling us all how we are destroying the planet!!!

Please do not misunderstand me I am not against mans' domination of the planet. Neither am I against specialisation. I have simply been pointing out that it can have shortcomings. We are vulnerable and should anything catastrophic happen to our species, the planet, apart from being destroyed by the sun going nova or some other disaster of cosmic proportions, will still continue on its merry way and some other life form, quicker to adapt, will become dominant. The majority of other living creatures are, by and large, able to survive with minimal help almost as soon as they are born. Their survival instincts are inborn. Ours are no longer. We don't have to save the planet but we might have to save ourselves.

Male and female.
Up until now there has been nothing in that which I have written that consists of anything more than an opinion and the same may be said for Richard Dawkin's views. I agree that for mutation to take place the DNA must change. My argument is that it does not happen by chance. What arguments may I put forward to make my view more substantial? One would be the development of two sexes. This is certainly a fundamental step for most life forms in their striving to produce mutations of themselves otherwise why bother?

In the biblical Genesis it says that the earth was created in seven days. Man was created before woman and for a time, they both lived happily in the Garden of Eden. Some of those of a religious persuasion will only accept this explanation: anything else is a heresy. Professor Dawkins doesn't have much time for those who hold this biblical view. Those of his ilk prefer the exact moment of all creation as the 'Big Bang' from which all else has flowed. If you ask them what was before the 'Big Bang' they answer that of course there was nothing and proceed to get very annoyed with you. I suppose that the truth lies somewhere between.

In the first place one has to realise that the writer of the Old Testaments' first chapter 'Genesis' was trying to provide some account of how we came to be on this planet and our part in the scheme of things. He did not have access to the scientific tools that we have available today. The ideas are expressed by analogy. He did not expect to be taken absolutely literally. I believe that he, whoever he was, did an excellent job. Consider the order of things. First there was a void, and then there was light, after that land then living creatures and so on. After all even today we are finding it harder and harder to describe, in scientific terms what exactly is an absolute truth. The more we learn the more difficult it becomes. In Victorian times the earth was considered to be 20 million years old. This view progressed to a point where 200 million years was considered a likely figure. Today 4.5 *billion* years is considered reasonable.

For me the Female was created the moment that a Male evolved. Prior to that there was no specific sex. Dawkins says that there is a 'Mitocondrial Eve' In other words there is part of the female egg that hardly evolves at all and at that, extremely slowly. Further more females are *born* with the totality of the eggs that they will issue during their years of menstruation and this does seem to present problems when it comes to changing a part of their basic structure. Males on the other hand continually make sperm. Up to 500 million for one ejaculation. Further more the testes are always partially exposed to the elements and are, ideally, two to three degrees colder than the rest of the body. (Do bear in mind that it is changing climatic conditions that is of the greatest concern to all living creatures). It is my view that the reason for this is due to the fact that part of the DNA structure of sperm is continually changed as it is made. By choosing her mate with great care the female endeavours to choose a male with the ability, most likely, to pass on improvements that she considers vital to survival of her offspring. In particular those that apply to staying alive in the conditions into which they will be born.

Dawkins points out that there appears to be 'redundant' DNA in sperm and he wonders why? I would suggest that it is not redundant at all but might simply a part of a mechanism, at present not understood, that is responsible for shuffling the genes around in order to facilitate change.

It seems to me that the extraordinary and vast variety of species abounding on the planet today cannot have arisen simply through mere chance. One has only to observe the manner in which all of them have evolved either by developing markings that serve to camouflage, to change colour as required by the background, or as in the case of plants to attract insects and birds that will spread their pollen. The variety is infinite. Can this incredible diversity utilising sophisticated poisons, protective colouring, or the ability to prosper on food that is not in such short supply, be put down to a happy co-incidence?

Some people would argue that we are the *custodians* of the planet but I do not think that we are *that* important. Life will go on long after mans' dominance has been shattered. Other species will come into their own as happened over 200 hundred million years ago when the supremacy of Dinosaurs was toppled. It's all a question of adapting to changed conditions quickly enough. Let us as a species be satisfied that, whilst we were at the top of the tree, we dealt reasonably with all the rest of the creatures with whom we share this world. To do that we need to review our relationships with animal life constantly. For are we not near that point where the very success of our species actually threatens, not only ourselves but also much of mammalian life in general?

I hope that I have made my point. It is possible that I will have aroused, in some minds, great rage. There may be exclamations such as 'absolute rubbish' and 'the man doesn't know what he is talking about'. Should this be the case, then I will know that to some extent I am probably correct in my views.

Commonality.

I make this point about evolution in order to pose the question. If, as mammals we have a great deal in common with one another, for example the DNA and bone structure, then is it unreasonable to believe that there is a great likelihood that our brains may work in a similar manner? Surely we are in fact very alike?

Do not all creatures, each in its own way, have something to offer the stream of life? Therefore though one species may appear to dominate another, in fact there is an equality as each species plays its part in the overall environment. Is not the social cohesion even greater with animals with which we work especially horses and dogs? In their case we are certainly not dealing with mindless creatures that have no self-awareness. On the contrary they have a good intellect and generally speaking, finding themselves in a situation where, when they have to have a symbiotic relationship with man, they try to make the partnership work.

Having made this point it is also worthwhile pointing out that though the brain of a horse is, biologically, not that different from our own, none-the-less the manner of thought does differ. By this I mean that whereas we tend to generally think in sounds and words, it is my view that horses tend to think primarily in a visual way.

The horse from ancient times.

The Horse has existed in one form or another for approximately 50 million years. Of course its form was not that which we behold today. In the beginning its size was only that of a large dog and it had five toes to each limb and what is more it was a leaf eater. The first of this species we have named Eohippus. As a class it was quite successful. Unfortunately that very success must have created problems due to an expanding population and a limited food supply. The main problem with being a dog sized leaf eating creature is that only leaves on bushes up to a height of about three to four feet are available and once these leaves have been cropped they do not grow back all that quickly. Observe in your own garden, if you have one. Look at a trimmed hedge and you will see that the leaves are quite slow to grow back after they have been clipped. The horse would no doubt have tried to get the last few remaining top leaves, normally out of its reach, by standing on its hind legs. The effort required, probably consumed as much energy as the nutrition the food provided, leaving nothing over to sustain basic life requirements. It had to think of another way.

Evolution
All mammals started from a common ancestor. Generally, the structure of mammals is basically the same (we all have seven cervical bones). However these basic building blocks have simply developed differently over the millennia. Giraffes are a good example having developed longer neck bones (not more of them) enabling them crop leaves at the very top of trees. Nature does not seem to invent, it adapts. It is my opinion that horses chose to develop first by standing on their toes as they tried to reach the higher leaves. They eventually dispensed with all toes except the central one on each foot. When this was taken to the limit of efficiency in terms of percentage energy input/output, they had to look for another more readily available means of obtaining sustenance. Growing slightly longer neck bones, adapting the size of the mouth, the shape of teeth together with longer intestines, made the eating of grass a reasonable food source. Grass, as we know from mowing the lawn grows the more quickly for being cropped.

This was a successful development. Though grass does not have the nutritional content of the more choice leaves; stronger and bigger teeth (to aid pre-digestion) and the longer gut took care of this problem. The modern horse Equus Calabus (evolving about 10 million years ago) is still a grazer, moving slowly from place to place on the, one remaining, extenuated middle digit of both front and hind legs. It only moves at speed in order to escape danger or else to show off.

We know from the study of discarded bones that for many centuries in the past horses provided a food source, one that was, readily, plundered by human hunters working in packs. In North America, where a plethora of prehistoric horse fossil bones have been found, the species had become extinct a considerable time before the Spaniards first started to explore the hinterland. Therefore the stories suggesting that early Indians were first seen riding across the prairies on horseback is a myth. In fact they did not learn to ride until *they* had seen the Spanish riding horses and caught some that had escaped. The Mustang: that breed of feral horse natural to the plains even to this day is in fact the progeny of those horses that, having got loose, successfully re-adapted to living in the wild. You may well be thinking 'Surely the indigenous hunters would not be so foolish as to hunt the prehistoric horse to extinction'? Well I have no doubt that a changing environment played its part. It is quite likely that apart from over-hunting, pressure was also brought to bear as the world went through a periodic warming. Forests would have spread over the grasslands, leaving the horse with less and less living room. The Indians probably did not appreciate what was happening and so no attempt was made towards conservation. Even today we have not learned the lesson and I would ask you to ponder as to why it is, at the time that I write that we with all our modern knowledge and technology, are so over-fishing the seas that we are in danger of causing some species of fish which are a food staple to crash to the point of extinction?

Excavations of ancient settlements in Europe have revealed that this diminution of the horse population was also proceeding there *21. Bones found by the remains of campfires show an ever-decreasing numbers of horse bones as decades passed. This may surprise you as surely that noble animal would have been appreciated for its fine qualities, and at the very least used for ploughing and pulling carts.

You have laboured for many weeks baking in your kiln wares that you intend to take to market. Are you likely to put your delicate goods in a crude cart and attach this to an animal that is quite likely to take fright from something either seen or unseen? A creature that believes that it can only escape from danger by speedy flight, taking with it the accumulated product of your months of toil, down a path that is far from smooth? I think not: better to use a plodding old ox.

So how was it that a close association between men and horses developed? Well it is possible that it has to do with the makeup of the horse herd. The dominant mare will choose the stallion that she considers has shown those characteristics, which she requires in a mate. All the other males are then banished to live alone or in small groups, but they are *herd* animals and do seek company, so it is quite possible that in seeking good grazing the rejects came upon humankind and were quite prepared to live in close contact.

24

You may wonder why horses did not immediately flee at the sight of men whom they knew might kill them? This might have had to do with the conservation of energy. Most quarry do not take flight upon seeing a predator, they only do so when they realise that the animal is hunting. Speed of movement by the predator triggers flight by the quarry. That is why it is so important for those working in stables not to run around shouting loudly.

Domestication.

The Oxford Dictionary of English defines domestication as to 'bring (an animal) into subjection or dependence on man. I would not entirely agree with this definition. To my mind the word might be used to denote the 'loss of fear of man'. In other words the horse obtained food and some degree of companionship by hanging around early campsites, this subsequently encouraged it to develop a symbiotic relationship with man, which suited it very well.

Fortunately in Asia, the diminishing horse population was arrested by the discovery that with a bit of pluck it was possible to mount and to stay on the back of a horse. I would even speculate that the ability to ride probably arose out of games played by early camp dwellers. Out of boredom and to demonstrate their great courage, young men probably had bets with one another as to whether they could get on, and for how long they could remain, on a horse's back. The rest follows….if you could stay on, the creature calmed down and eventually, realising there was no, immediate, real danger acquiesced to being ridden. Then followed the discovery that on horseback one could travel considerably greater distances at a higher speed than it was possible to do on ones own two legs. Imagine the thrill of this newfound method of locomotion. And not only that; but you could use this creature as a weapon of war!

Originally these 'weapons' were utilised by lining them up in a row and charging at the foe who were expected to break ranks and scatter, thus being more easily be taken on by foot soldiers. Control, such as stopping, was probably as a result of the horse getting tired and simply doing so of its own accord. It was ridden bare backed. As time passed rough rope halters became leather bridles and a rope through the mouth evolved into quite a severe metal bit with long cheek pieces acting as levers on each side to accentuate the effect of metal on tongue. Oh the poor horse's mouth! Saddles followed. Then the discovery that a long wooden pole could be effectively used as a lance thus extending the point where contact was made with the enemy. To avoid being thrust backwards when that contact had been made, stirrups were invented.

In the main, this business of simply charging through ones enemies and then going home for tea, as it were, lasted for several millennia. (Though some early cavalry did actually ride a loop in front of the enemy during which time they shot off about three arrows before galloping out of harms way). It wasn't until the sixteenth century that, as part of Oliver Cromwell's development of the 'New Model Army', the cavalry were taught to turn after a charge and repeat the action. The Cavaliers of Charles I were not trained in this tactic and it was one of the reasons why they lost the civil war.

Now please do not misunderstand dear reader, there were many instances prior to that time when men had shown remarkable control of their mounts. Julius Caesar was just one example. He is reported to have ridden his horse for the entertainment of his troops by demonstrating such movements as flying changes. However, generally speaking, throughout most of history, the horse was regarded to a greater or lesser extent, with fear. Nothing changed until the Renaissance. Until that time control was exercised through barbaric bitting, sharp spurs and long whips. An engraving from Antoine de Pluvinel's beautifully illustrated book 'Instruction du Roy' shows a rider holding his whip in front of him in a vertical position. This was to indicate that the horse was considered to be completely schooled and *subservient*. Even at this time men still handled horses with a brutish lack of feeling but things were beginning to change and a greater understanding of horse psychology started to emerge.

So throughout much of fairly recent history this excellent animal has, continually, proved its worth. In the past the horse was considered of value as a weapon and heavier breeds were used for ploughing and for providing the power for a huge variety of machines. Surprisingly the horse population expanded even with the onset of industrialisation. The arrival of the steam locomotive encouraged larger numbers of the public to travel, but they still needed to get from their homes to the railway station. The breeding of the 'Hackney' carriage horse fulfilled this need. Not only that, but the increasing wealth of the middle classes brought about the owning of horses and carriages, on a scale not previously thought possible. Of course all that changed with the invention of the motorcar but, today, industrial progress has provided us with ever better standards of living. With more disposable income, many people are able to take up as a pastime which was, usually, denied to their ancestors – the riding of the horse simply for pleasure. Yet perhaps there is something more, for now we reach out to the stars in the hope that we are not the lone intelligence in this universe. We search for other beings with whom we can communicate and yet we already have, with horses and dogs, conversations that may be more intimate than we may ever have with any alien!

Chapter 2

Personalities.

1. THE HORSE
The correct type of horse
The best type of horse is the one most suited for the work it has to do. Thus a racehorse is trained only to win races. A dressage horse has great athletic ability, which, together with good looks will win dressage competitions. Both these types do not necessarily have kind temperaments, they are trained to do particular jobs and they try to do their best. But these are not the qualities best suited to a riding school horse. Indeed both the former will probably not have the patience to deal with the lack of co-ordination and balance of the average riding school client. The client may have a mental image of themselves as well horsed and looking good but, unfortunately, if placed on the back of anything other than a good schoolmaster, they are likely to find themselves sitting on the floor. This applies not only to novices; for even fairly advanced riders, mounted on horses with a high degree of knowledge, are quite likely to come unstuck should the horse consider that they are taking advantage of its good nature or simply boring it to death.

By a good schoolmaster I mean one that has the knowledge and ability to perform all the basic and probably most of the advanced movements that a horse can perform, but who will also have a great deal of patience. A horse that will both try to take care of those riders who are nervous and afraid and yet will put up with being pulled in the mouth. My old friend Jeeves was one such character. He has been variously described as the ' perfect civil servant' and the 'finest schoolmaster in southern England'. He obtained these accolades due to the fact that, since I spent many weeks abroad on business, I used to allow clients ride him. This saved me money through not having to pay for him to be exercised and thus he always had enough work to keep him fit and mentally occupied. 'How on earth do you allow your horse to be ridden by in-experienced riders?' I used to be asked. 'Surely this will ruin him?' they went on. Well my Jeeves was no fool and he was quite capable of knowing when he had to perform to the highest standards. The knowledge that I gave him was available to anyone who had the correct key to unlock it. If they were unable to so do, which was usually the case, it had no detrimental effect on his performance when I rode him. He and I were real pals and now that he has passed on, I miss him dearly.

Horses, like humans, do have individual personalities. Some may be rather docile and need to be pushed on, while others may be rather pushy characters and need to be contained. It is up to you as instructor to assess these individual traits and act accordingly. It does not mean that because the horse acquiesces to a second rate rider, that it has neither a mind of its own nor that it has permanently submitted to domination by human beings. My Jeeves, on being turned out for the first time in the spring would not allow any of the students to catch him for the first day of his freedom. You could see the laughter in his eyes as he demonstrated his independence. Thereafter, having proved his point he was never a problem.

It must be born in mind that the majority of horses may try and take some form of initiative. Even if they are complete dullards, they may try to take a liberty. This may be due to a bad mood or simply the idea that they can get away with it. This will range from simply refusing to go forward, cutting corners, and dashing off at a gallop around the arena or, possibly, trying to dislodge the rider. I have watched horses that I have worked well with my clients, many of them novices, become totally uncooperative, in someone else's class when ridden by some charming older ladies who had been riding at the yard for many years. One of them commented 'I suppose that I am getting him rather confused'. 'Indeed you are Madame' I thought silently to myself, as she, violently, booted the poor animal with her legs trying to get – was it a turn on the forehand? – Yes indeed, after watching for five minutes I came to the conclusion that that was her object. The instructor allowed such abuse to continue without comment!

Horses are very intelligent. They will, like human beings form an opinion about the people with whom they are asked to work. Should a riders' approach be unkind, should they use harsh words, when a kind one would be better, then a horse will respond accordingly and may end up being completely unhelpful. Recently I escorted a hack on my young five-year-old mare whom I hadn't ridden for about three months. On returning one of the student instructors asked me 'how I got on'. 'She went brilliantly' I replied. 'In fact I sent the ride away from me at a canter and she stood motionless on a long rein'. My answer was heard with surprise and amazement. 'When we hack her out she carts us all over the place'. ' I suppose that it's because she was out with "Dad"', she went on. This is probably true for I am not suggesting that the students were unkind, or particularly inept, rather the opposite, but it is I who am *especially* kind. I take the trouble, even when not riding to go to the box and upon entering, tender a titbit, spending some 10 minutes or more gently patting the mare and having a gentle and soothing conversation with her. Further more perhaps I am the one who insists on just that little bit of extra discipline.

Another factor that should not be overlooked: is the effect of diet. The horse is one of those creatures that quickly respond to the amount and quality of the food that it eats. It has the ability to translate food into energy with remarkable efficiency. A feeding regime that involves high-energy feeds may be utilised by the trainer of racehorses. However if there is not going to be any immediate outlet for this energy, a similar diet could be a positive disadvantage for horses working in a riding school. A horse that seems to be rather difficult may, in fact, only be suffering from a surfeit of energy. This is a factor about which you should have knowledge and if you believe that you have such a horse in one of your lessons you should inform the yard manager. With horses that are at livery this may arise due to the fact that the owner wishes its little darling to have 'nothing but the best' whilst not realising the effect that this may have over their somewhat inadequate control.

On the other hand where you have school horses in lesson that are fed correctly, they generally go quietly. This being the case it is unreasonable for you to expect them to perform movements that are energy sapping in the extreme.

Above all just as with human beings, horses *must be capable of performing the work that is asked of them.*

Mares and antisocial horses

One needs to take special care with horses that wish to 'have a go' at others in the ride. It's all very well you simply telling the rider to be constantly vigilant but this may not be good enough. The rider may well *know* what they have to do to keep both themselves and others safe but they may not have sufficient riding skills to be able to so do with a determined horse. You must adjust your lesson accordingly. Suppose, for example you proceed with an exercise involving an individual canter, going large, from the front to the back of the ride, you then develop this into a canter past the ride. If you have a mare that is in heat, you would be well advised not to ask the rider of this animal to perform this part of the exercise, for it reasonable to assume that the rider may not have the ability to ask the mare to go past at a sufficiently safe distance. The mare will probably, decide that she is only going to go from front to rear. The rider may well try to insist otherwise, but this will become an unbalanced battle of wills. The rider may temporarily get the upper hand but it is a sure bet that they will not, at the same time, be able to concentrate on keeping the horse on the correct inner track. As both stagger past the ride somewhere between a trot and a canter the mare will so position herself as to be able to take a swing at one or more horses. In fact she may well be at that strategic point, where she appears to be a reasonable distance away but none-the-less is able to make contact at the very limit of the extension of her kick, thus achieving maximum impact.

Similarly with a horse that has shown an inclination to be anti-social by, for example, whipping around and trying to bite other horses; again you need to use your discretion. If you ask such a horse to perform a canter with, even, an intermediate rider on board, then it is quite likely that it will use the opportunity to unpredictably spin around, as it has a go at another horse. Your pupil, loosing balance, lands needlessly on the ground. In earlier years such a happening might well have been regarded as one of the normal hazards of equitation. At the time that I write, with insurance premiums climbing all the time, such an *event* is one that you can well do without.

The social order.

Horses have a very strict observation of social order. They not only relate to other horses but also include human beings. In your classes you must use your powers of observation to decide what that order is. You must place the horses in a suitable position in the ride, before trouble breaks out. Watch out for ears being laid back and tails swishing. In a novice class the male horses that you have should be geldings. The reason for this is that riding an entire could prove to be difficult and dangerous for most riders. However you must also pay attention to mares for it is a fact, frequently overlooked, that in horse society, though there is only one stallion for a given herd, he shares the leadership with the dominant mare. In the wild it is she who decides in which direction to lead the herd as they move from pastures old to new. The stallion will, frequently, remain behind to protect from predators. Thus if you have included in your class several mares you must note with what regard they hold each other and place them in your ride accordingly.

You must also take special note if a mare is in heat. For it is in their nature to react, sometimes quite violently with the hindquarters, against *any* male whom they perceive is in a mood to make advances on them before they are ready.

Being challenged.

You may, occasionally come across the odd horse that resents *your* authority and wishes to challenge you. You must watch out for this. A horse may suddenly, for no apparent reason, start to cart its rider in your direction. It usually means that as it passes you it will try to kick out. If you are observant you will, clearly, see the intention in its eye. You have to be prepared to promptly move out of harms way.

Many years ago an old pony mare once caught me out. She had been eyeing me for some time during a lesson and half way through she put in a buck that partially unbalanced the child riding her. As the child started to slide sideways off the mare I ran forward to prevent her from falling to the ground. As I pushed her back onto the saddle, the mare realised that my attention was elsewhere and wheeled round and kicking me on the thigh: propelling me through the air for about five feet. I got up and asked the child to dismount, quietly growling all the while (so that the mare would not loose the mental connection between her action and my response). I led her to a corner away from the class and delivered her three short, sharp and deliberate taps, with the handle end of my whip, on the side of her nose. At the same time I told the mare in a quiet low voice that if she ever did that again she would get more of the same. She never did!   Having delivered my remonstration, I helped the child to remount. The class had all looked on aghast when I flew through the air. Now I realised they were looking to see what effect that this had had on *me*. There was no way that I was going to allow the incident to affect *them*. Turning back I said in a very calm low voice, 'Well now that we have sorted that out lets get on with the lesson'. Several hours later after I had finished my work, I returned home and took off my breeches. The trauma on my thigh was quite considerable.

Time of year.

One factor that will certainly have an effect on the type of lesson that you give is the time of year. In winter you may have to create lessons that are composed mainly of exercises suitable for a whole ride. After all on a freezing cold day it is not a good idea to have riders and horses standing around in the cold, while each rider is asked to perform a movement individually. Those who have to wait their turn will start to chill and will not enjoy themselves and, if the horses are sweated up from previous lessons, they may well catch a chill.

So in winter it is a good idea to have nice quiet and controlled lessons – as a ride. In spring you will have to contend with horses that are looking to establish their dominance. Since horses tend to regard both humans and horses as different species but of the same herd (Since we all intermingle constantly), this will apply as much to riders as to other horses. My own horse Jeeves, a brilliant schoolmaster, could be relied upon *just once*, in the spring, to try and 'take me for a ride', simply to see if I still was able to have the last word.

Being stabled for long periods.

It is also worthwhile bearing in mind that during the winter months one may encounter a problem that does not occur at other times of the year. I am referring to the fact that some horses get absolutely fed up with being in their boxes for prolonged periods, even though they may be getting plenty of work. In the arena this can result in behaviour rather like that of a prison riot. They all watch one another to see which one will have the courage to take the lead.

Any excuse will do; the sound of the wind; a door banging; a wheelbarrow being blown over or even the very familiar sound of a tractor passing by. Sometimes the outburst occurs at the very beginning of the lesson and at other times towards the end. Quite suddenly and without any warning (should you be seen to be unprepared) one horse starts to belt around the arena bucking vigorously. The rest follow suite almost immediately. At this time do not loose your cool. In a firm but quiet voice tell everyone to take hold of the pommel of the saddle and to hold on tight. At the same time, in a very firm voice speak out to the motley crew '**oih you lot what the devil do you thing you are doing? Cease at once!** I have never known this to fail. All the horses stop and look at you. As they do so, ask everyone if they are all right and get them back in good order. Proceed at once with a prolonged period of energetic but quiet trotting.

The Instructor.

Those involved with the use of horses for commercial purposes may be placed in three groups.

1. Those who train.
2. Horse Masters.
3. Those who teach.

I have not met many Trainers or Horse Masters who had the patience to teach ordinary people to ride, especially if those that they had to deal with were 'weekend' riders. Whereas an instructor *should* be able to ride any horse quietly, I haven't come across many instructors who are also Horse Masters.

What exactly is the difference between each of these categories?
The trainer.
This obviously speaks for itself. It is quite simply someone who teaches the horse its work. This may range from the earliest job of breaking it, to teaching it the movements of advanced dressage.

The Horse Master.
By Horse Master I mean someone who is able to sit on a horse and within a very short time establish a relationship that will encourage the horse to give of his best. Further more they are able to communicate the subtle aids needed for an intricate movement, without the horse getting itself all worked up.

Horses, however, are not stupid. I have come across many that, having 'played up' for a client and been 'sorted it out' by a Horse Master, revert to their previous behaviour as soon as the client remounts. Sometimes it goes even further, acquiescence to the Master; promptly followed by dislodging the client out of sheer irritation.

The instructor.
What then is an instructor? I hear you ask? Well... the majority of instructors that I have come across certainly know their stuff. That is to say they are very capable of instructing clients as to the precise aids that should be given. They are also excellent at noting whether or not the horse is moving correctly, but I have seen one or two go to pieces, when asked to sit on a horse that is a bit shirty. However this did not necessarily mean that they were not effective instructors.

Ideally one would like to have all three specialisation's combined in one person. This seldom happens. For me one such personality was Henry Wynmalen *7 who, was not only brilliant in all disciplines but also the possessor of the one overriding quality that is so important: ***Compassion***. I quote his feelings as he turns out a foal and for the first time teaches it to be led.

'It will begin by just wandering around the mare and her attendants for a little while. Very soon it will react to the feeling of the warm sun on its back and to the softness of the turf underneath its little feet; it will sense liberty and the lure of the wide-open places, that will one day be its destiny; it will suddenly jump, plunge and rear in little orgies of athletic extravagance; it will suddenly stop dead and stand as still as a mouse, in obvious and enchanting wonderment.' These are the words, of someone who passionately loved these animals. As I read them they bring moisture to my eyes.

I have four of Wynmalen's books in my library and, if you are able to obtain copies, I heartily recommend you to read them all, in detail, if you wish to develop a ***true understanding*** of horses and the training thereof. In those texts you will discover all three attributes that I have mentioned above. Not only are they extremely informative but also they are written in the superb English that only Continentals seem to achieve, for Wynmalen was a Dutchman!

Though I have attended many courses and watched countless demonstrations, I have, personally, only *met* one person whom I consider embodies all these qualities and that is Mr. Charles Harris. To hear him give a demonstration, lecture or a 'teach-in' is to experience real pleasure. Not only does he have a deep understanding of the horse but he also has the ability to disseminate his knowledge in a clear and lucid manner. Further more, when teaching, he has eyes like a hawk and misses nothing.

Obviously there is room for a whole variety of characters and personalities in the business. By that I mean one may be of a fairly diffident nature and another rather more outgoing. None-the-less it would be true to say that the personality of any teacher has a great deal to do with their success or failure. Personality, together with the desire to be of a mind driven to know ones subject very thoroughly, and I mean *thoroughly*, breeds success. You must have an intimate knowledge of the horses physiology and mentality. You should be teaching from the top 10% of this knowledge. You must have the ability to put across the information in a manner that can be easily understood by the pupil that will entertain, stimulate and ultimately result in an improvement in riding technique.

In a nutshell.
The essentials are a deep understanding of the subject and a command of language in order to be able to put this across.

There are other traits that are desirable in the making of a good instructor. Some of them are listed below: -
1. You must invariably be polite. I am not only referring to the duration of your instruction but also at any moment when you come across someone who looks as though they may need some help. For example a potential client wandering around the yard and uncertain as to where they should be going to obtain further information. You should smile and in a friendly way ask if you can help, direct them to the office or, if it is past office hours tell them when it will re-open. Alternatively give them the telephone number. Should you be asked for information concerning fees only impart this if you are in possession of an up-to-date price list. If you give out information that is incorrect then this may cause embarrassment at a later date.

2   You must be able to adequately ride every movement that you are teaching on any horse that has the ability. If any animal does not have good enough confirmation for advanced work, it should not be used to teach movements that are beyond its capability. This does not preclude, for a young horse, the introduction to a movement that it may not have previously undertaken.

With regard to things equestrian your education should have covered far more than a simple ability to ride all the various movements that you will teach. You should have a good knowledge of the horse's anatomy. You should be able to name every bone in the horse's body, most of the muscles, tendons and internal organs. You should also have a thorough knowledge of stable management. You should be able to recognise most of the more common bits, saddles and bridles that are used today (and include some that are not). Further more you should be able to talk about all of these matters in an informed manner.

'Why'. You may well be thinking. 'If all that I am required to do is to teach people to ride?' The answer is that a client may well ask you a question and you should always be able to provide the correct answer. The other day as I was about to leave, after having finished my lessons for the day, I was accosted by a livery owner (not one of my clients). 'Excuse me Tone.' He said 'But what is this depression just here above the eye and why does a bulge appear in it when my horse is eating? Is there anything wrong with the horse?' 'The Supra Orbital Fossa.' I replied and then went on to explain how it was derived from the Latin and also to explain that the reason that a bulge appeared in it as the horse worked its jaws was due to the action of coronoid process of the mandible. And 'no there is nothing wrong with your horse, you just haven't noticed it before'. As I was about to go on my way I said 'why on earth did you stop *me* to ask that question?' 'Because I knew that you would be able to give me the answer'. He replied.

3   Beware of taking verbal shortcuts. Using jargon the client does not understand. If you use a particular term, then follow this up in plain language until the meaning is well understood by the pupil. A simple word can be more effective than its technical equivalent. Thus in cantering when I can see that the horse is going to break to trot, I call out to the client 'with your inside leg, touch him….touch him…' I have found this to be more effective than 'Keep your leg on', because very often the client hasn't got the slightest idea what that means.

4   Do be short and precise in what you have to say. Don't stand there for ages and ages waffling on and waving your hands and body about and using the word 'OK' as a form of punctuation.

5 Your job is to inspire confidence in the client. You should not talk down to the clients or treat them as some form of mental delinquent simply because they are not, immediately, familiar with the terms you use or do not have the balance or reflex response to counter a horses' sudden movements or evasions. I have come across pupils who, having ridden at other yards with very well known instructors, have told me how they were continually shouted at. The interesting point about this was that it didn't seem to have improved their riding at all! Generally speaking your pupils will be extremely intelligent people and very successful in their jobs or professions. If they were not, then they wouldn't be able to afford riding lessons. Sarcasm is out. Patience is in.

6 While it is unnecessary to be a Sergeant Major on the parade ground bawling commands at your riders, it is very important that you are heard clearly. If you ask your ride to keep at a horses' length from one another you must accept nothing less. I have seen instructors telling their class to close up. A minute or so later someone is still riding with a gap of three or four horses' lengths between themselves and the horse in front. I will not accept that state of affairs. It is sloppy riding and I tell my pupils so. What I am requesting is not unreasonable. If I had asked for a perfect half pass this might prove to be a problem for some of them and impossibility for others. I could shout my head off until kingdom come - it would not produce success. However asking a rider to keep the correct distance simply requires their concentration.

7 It is a great advantage if you spend a little time studying public speaking. Learn to vary the pitch of your voice. You may be one of the most brilliant instructors that the world has ever known but if you, continually, speak in a monotonous drone your clients will become bored, fall asleep and probably fall off! As you address the class allow your gaze to travel so that you have eye contact, for a few seconds, with every member of the class. Stand tall and act as though you were giving a performance on a stage with the audience in front of you.

   On the other hand try not to babble all the time throwing out streams of words that your pupils will be hard pressed to keep up with.

8 Presentation is very important. Choose the words that you wish to use with care. The correct choice can make all the difference between presenting a new exercise, as something special and exciting rather than mundane and dull. This is especially the case when dealing with young teenagers who are making the transition from the junior to senior school. Youngsters taught by me were always given a combination of straightforward flat work combined with 'games'. On going up to the seniors, something that they had longed for, they found themselves suddenly facing strictly formal teaching with other instructors and became somewhat bored (or so parents have told me). 'Do you not take classes in senior school?' I have been asked. 'Yes I do but they are full' I have replied. 'And what is more I only teach late teens to adults in my senior school classes. I do need a change of emphasis.

9 You must be extremely observant. Every error of position, every aid given incorrectly or not at all, must be observed and commented upon. This is particularly true when teaching advanced riders. You may be thinking to yourself 'Surely this chap is overdoing it a bit'? I do not agree. How are your clients to learn if you do not point out their faults at the very second that they occur?

   Trust – Your clients must have confidence in you. They must know that when you give them advice it is not given lightly and you will always have their well-being and safety in mind. Furthermore that you will not ask them to do anything that will put them in danger.

Finally it is a great help if you are possessed of a sense of humour. It is through laughter that you will, probably, be most successful. However if I were asked to sum up in only three words I would say that you need **'Knowledge and Flair'.**

Correct dress.
At the time this book is being written we are travelling through a period where dress is very casual. That is not to say that people do not dress attractively or for that matter expensively. They are still influenced by

fashion but formality is almost non -existent. If one goes to the theatre, opera, ballet or concert one will see people dressed in garments that range from formal attire to sweatshirts and jeans and all sitting next to one another. I have no particular view about this, though, personally, I do like to change out of clothes that I wear during the day for something that is obviously more formal when I go out of an evening.

There are professions where it is decidedly an advantage to be dressed in a manner that clearly underlines ones position. An airline pilot or a policeman comes to mind. I believe that the same applies to the riding instructor. No matter where you are, either walking around the yard or entering the arena, people should know from your dress that you are someone who is in authority. There are several ways of achieving this. A riding school may provide specially embroidered sweatshirts in a colour that may only be worn by instructors who have achieved a given level of expertise. At the School where I teach this is black for senior instructors. Students wear blue shirts, green ones by clients. Whatever the uniform, be it sweatshirt or hacking jacket; you should have a change of clothing at hand so that you always look clean, tidy and presentable. Whether you wear full-length riding boots or Jodhpur boots these must always be polished. Your clothing must also conform to safety requirements. (See photo no. 2 now page 433)

If I manage to finish writing this book before the fashion changes, yet again, you may well wonder why I make so much of this matter. After all you may reason, what difference does it make how you are dressed, provided that you know your job and do it properly? There are two reasons. In the first place, there are certain requirements, regarding correct dress, made by the bodies that govern our profession, to which you must conform. Secondly, even if this were not the case, you are responsible for the safety of the pupils and animals in your charge. Your appearance should highlight your responsible position.

Your Personality interacting with people.
One of the things that might affect your ability to be a successful instructor is your own personality – that with which you were born and has developed, as you have grown older. Should you be brash, then, you may well not get along with pupils who prefer a quiet sort of person. On the other hand if you are timid you may well not be very effectual in helping those with ingrained problems, to overcome them. Generally I don't think very much of those who stand and bawl or shout at their class - Oh no- I don't think much of that at all! To my mind there is absolutely no reason why you should not be able to put across your point of view in a quiet and yet purposeful manner. I never shout at my pupils – haven't done so for years! I do make my point clearly and back it up with logic. I expect, and am very pleased, when a rider asks me to explain in greater detail a point about which they are not clear. It demonstrates that they have been thinking about what I have said. Many people do not do this; very often they just sit there and don't give any real thought to what you are saying. Needless to say this doesn't get them very far. A good personality trait should be persistence. You must learn to recognise those who are simply switching off. When you spot them, you must ask them questions in order to reveal whether or not they are actually absorbing what you have said. Sometimes pupils will not like this, for they feel that they may make a fool of themselves. You must talk to them in such a way that they are able to put aside these fears.

Relationships.
I would not say that a person with a somewhat bland or retiring personality would not make a good instructor. However it is in the nature of things that if one is successful then this will probably be not only as a result of ones deep knowledge of the subject but also ones ability to communicate this to your students. This may mean that there are occasions where the very inspiration that you create, leads on to something more. You may find that a pupil may wish to develop this relationship into something much more personal. It may start simply as a result of being asked out for a drink after the lesson is over. A discussion about the finer points of the lesson as it were! Now I am not saying that an instructor should not socialise with members of the ride after class but do take care. It is much better for everyone if a professional distance is kept. Anything else, in the context of interpersonal relationships, requires a great deal of skill on your part. Maybe it's best not to flirt with a client when that could lead to great difficulties later on.

Grooms and helpers.
I do not think that it is at all acceptable to remain aloof from those who work or help around the yard. You depend upon all these people to ensure that your horses are properly groomed and tacked up. You should make it your business, almost as soon as you start to work for a new yard, to ensure that you know everybody's name and the level of their expertise. This, to my mind, is simple politeness. If you get to know

everyone properly, then you should be able to ascertain who really knows their job and whom you need to keep an eye on.

The interaction between instructors and horses.

One must not overlook the interaction of personalities between instructor and horses. Horses are just as likely to respond to your personality and will sum *you* up in the same manner as they do the clients sitting upon their backs. Your posture, as you enter the arena will be noticed by everyone present – humans and horses. The horse judges you as they would their own kind. A 'horse with class' is the one that carries himself erect with head held high, his very posture telling everyone that he considers himself to be the best. For a punter (one who likes the occasional bet) like myself this can be very useful in divining the likely winner of a race. It has even been suggested by Stephen Budiansky *30 that this 'dominant stance ' could effect the outcome of a race because horses that are actually faster may 'defer' to slightly slower but more dominant individuals. I am not sure that I agree, for the other 'dominant' factor must surely be the jockey.

Coming at the matter from another point of view we have Monty Roberts the so-called 'Horse Whisperer'. An American who has become very successful at breaking horses with a minimum of trauma – for the horse. He uses his body language as part of his system.

In the same way when teaching a class your body language has its effect. If you 'walk tall' and stand confidently when you have entered the arena this will enhance your 'presence'. (See photo no. 3).Other factors that influence horses are how do you pitch your voice? Or for that matter how do you move?

Take the trouble as you inspect tack at the beginning of the class to give each horse a kind word and a pat on the neck before you start your lesson. The horses will assess you and decide whether or not they have to get on with the job or if they can have a bit of fun and generally mess about? As I have said previously, horses are not mindless creatures. Oh no, those required to present themselves for the next hour to carry your riders around and around, up and down or wherever, do have minds of their own. They decide what sort of a person you are and act accordingly. If you are afraid or do not like any of them, they will sense your feelings and react accordingly. It is a decided advantage if you are able to develop 'charisma'. This will encourage your horses to go well for you.

I have frequently been paid a compliment by being told that horses go well for me – while for someone else they play up. However beware, if you have a strong personality, you must take care. For example should you be standing close by a horse and ask the client to canter, it is possible that the horse, hearing your request and being respectful towards you, may well leap forward and in so doing unbalance your pupil.

You are the Master of the Ring.

So we have discussed the importance of personality and presence. As I have said horses know from the very beginning of a lesson whether or not they have to listen to you or lark about. This is important so far as maintaining discipline amongst the horses is concerned. The result is that you are not that far removed from a Circus Ringmaster for the horses may be doing your bidding alone and not listening at all to the people who are riding them. Such a situation does not help your pupils to become good independent riders. In order to do that you must be successful in transferring the power that you have over the horses to your students. This is realized by devising exercises in which the *correct* performance can only be as a result of an initiative, which stems from the rider alone. The measure of your success is revealed by the exact and correct manner in which the client and horse acting as one unit carry them out.

The Voice.

A good manége will measure twenty metres by 40 metres or even larger. You will need to be heard quite clearly throughout that area. Therefore you need to have a voice that carries. This however does *not* mean that you must, necessarily, shout. Yelling, from the top of ones throat as though one was a Sergeant Major on the Drill Square is to my mind, not acceptable at all. A really deep breath enabling you to speak from the depths of your chest is sufficient. Your pupils are neither deaf nor imbecilic. If they do not understand what it is that you require them to do, then the fault, probably lies with you for not explaining yourself clearly enough. Of course I do acknowledge that there are some people for whom any number of explanations do not work. This is due to the fact that they have in their minds a prefixed idea as to either the standard of rider that they are, or as to the manner in which their horses should be ridden. They simply are not listening to what you say. It is a measure of your success as an instructor to be able to break through this idée fix (as the French would say). Through your own, quiet, persistence you will get your pupil to follow your advice, eventually, they reach a point where they have successfully performed that movement, which has been causing them such extreme difficulty. I have been down this path on so many occasions. At the end of the movement so well performed I finish with the words, 'I presume I have made my point'. The rider flushed with success will gratefully agree.

The other matter concerning the use of a loud voice is that the horses do not like it. They will become tense and afraid. An example of this may be found in 'Flyers and Stayers'* 29 by Margo Lawrence (my neighbour incidentally). In the Chapter dealing with Alexander the Great subduing the horse, Bucephalus, Margo points out that Alexander realised that the horse was afraid of its shadow. He overcame this by turning the horse's head away so that it would not see it. However this was not the only reason, for he also realised that, standing near by was the dealer whose harsh voice the horse associated with cruelties that had been inflicted in the past. When he sent the man away the horse became calm.

Sharing an arena.
A clear voice is all very well but when sharing an arena you must take care that you do not drown out your colleague. In these circumstances it is a good idea to have your clients fairly close to you whenever you have something, at length, to say. If you do have to address an individual at a distance then keep your remarks quite short.

Assessing new horses.
When you have a new horse in the class you must take extra care to observe it and ensure that it does not get into trouble with the other horses. The problem, if there is one, will, probably be due to the fact that horses, being herd creatures have not yet accepted the newcomer. You may get very little warning of an impending confrontation and in any case you may be giving your wholehearted attention to your pupils. So be vigilant.

Welcoming a new client to the class.
When someone new joins your class be sure, first to introduce yourself, then ask the pupils' name and find out how much riding they have done and whether they are able to ride all the normal paces, that is walk, trot and canter. You should also ask them if they are joining you on a temporary or permanent basis. (Ideally the office should already have informed you of all the foregoing but sometimes things happen at the last minute). Finally introduce them to the regular members of the class being sure to mention everyone by name.

THE CLIENTS.
Liquorice assortment.
It will no doubt have been noticed that occasionally I refer to those attending my classes as pupils, students or simply riders. But this section is the headed Clients. The reason for this is that in the world of teaching equitation we do tend to refer to those coming to us for instruction in this manner, and for the remainder of this section I shall refer to them in this way. Clients come in as many different varieties and sizes as the ice cream you will find in an American Ice Cream Parlour. It is extremely important to assess the type of character, with whom you are dealing. Personalities have to be taken into account for they will reflect the way that different types of people react to both you and the horses. Another consideration is that of their physical build. You must learn to make allowances for some people. Those for example, who are rotund and have short fat legs, probably have more difficulty in achieving good balance than those who are thin with very long legs that they can wrap around a horse achieve.

Taking account of clients' health and those with hearing difficulties..
Another matter that should not escape your attention is a clients' general health. Adjust your program for those who may be out of condition or suffer from allergies. Make an allowance for those wearing hearing aids, especially when a tractor is passing by.

The client's mental attitude.
Another aspect is that of the client's own mental attitude. Some, who wish to ride, do so because they are daredevils and relish the idea of going across the countryside at speed, until they fall off that is! Others are quite introspective and deduce from every movement that the horse makes, an underling antipathetic motive on its part. Usually the later so afflicted would probably not be averse to a degree of psychoanalysis . A top-

notch instructor should know how to deal with people who may suffer in this way, but, generally, speaking very few instructors have the ability, time or the training, to do this and it is advisable that they do not try. None-the-less you need to be aware, as to where, your client 'is coming from' to use the modern parlance and I don't think that it will do any harm if you try to find out why it is that your clients want to ride in the first place.

Should this effect the content of your lesson? Well, it is obvious that you should be looking for any sign of fear or tension. Equally you should engage your clients in a few words of conversation and note if they have spent the previous night 'celebrating' and have been up until dawn. The effects of activities undertaken previously could certainly have an influence on their ability to perform whilst on the back of a horse. Whether or not a heavy hangover is or is not conducive to good equitation is a matter for speculation! On the one hand the ability to think clearly when having to deal with a pounding headache may be a problem. On the other hand the remains of an alcoholic haze might be conducive to a state of relaxation that will benefit the rider!

The interaction between client and horse.

How should the client behave so far as their interaction with the horse is concerned? It is very important that from the beginning a client understands that they are not dealing with an inanimate object such as a motorcar. The horse is a living creature with feelings and emotions. It will react to the personality of the rider, either giving or withholding its co-operation. I would say that the first thing that you suggest is that the client makes friends with their steed. Before they mount, even before they have checked the girth, they should be encouraged to gently touch the horse's neck and speak kindly to it. Throughout the lesson the client should be encouraged to compliment the horse whenever it carries out their wishes. Few clients do this, or if they do, then not soon enough. They very often say that this is because they are concentrating so hard themselves that they forget. This may be so but it is not acceptable. Further more some clients will frequently blame the horse for their own lack of ability.

Unreasonable clients

Up to this point I have, of course been talking about reasonable clients. Alas this is not the way things usually workout – oh no – many clients think that they are much better riders than they really are. Then there are others who, though they love to ride are, quite frankly, petrified of either the horse or the very act of riding. They all have to be dealt with satisfactorily so that they enjoy their lessons with you and also make progress.

I suppose that if there is one problem more difficult than any other it is to persuade the client that any movement induced in the horse is entirely as a result of the rider's action. In the early stages this should not be too difficult. They may, at first as novices, experience extreme frustration even in getting a horse to move in a particular direction at either walk or trot. They may well ascribe this to the horse's obstinacy and there may well be some element of truth in this because the horse will feel their imbalance and decide to act accordingly. Of course the other reason is that again, due to this lack of balance the rider is simply not able to give the horse clear signals as to what they require. With your help these problems are soon to be overcome. More advanced movements, such as the half pass, are sometimes quite difficult for a horse. They are certainly athletically more demanding, and can frequently be a problem for the client because they do not understand that, not only does the request for such a movement issue from the rider but that they are responsible for the resulting correct execution.

Whereas a client may sit upon a 'schoolmaster' and appear to execute various lateral movements, it may well be that these movements do not arise because the rider has given the correct aids. On the contrary it is very likely that the horse will try to divine what it is that the rider is asking and then give its interpretation of those instructions. How often have I observed 'advanced' riders sitting upon extremely well schooled horses and performing what they – the riders- believe to be a correct half pass! Whereas in fact, most of, the horses are simply crossing the arena on a diagonal straight line.

Becoming an excellent rider requires the ability to give precise aids and *to ensure that their execution by the horse be carried out correctly*. A rider well taught will be able to accomplish this on **any** horse irrespective of its experience (assuming that it does not suffer from such a poor confirmation that it is thus prevented from so doing). The 'quid pro quo' for the rider is that he or she must not ask the horse to continue for so long that in the end the horse is forced into disobedience because it is suffering *prolonged* physical discomfiture.

Now I have already mentioned that the instructor should really only be teaching around 10% of their total knowledge. It is really quite simple; therefore, to reveal to an arrogant rider that they are, perhaps, not quite so good as they believe themselves to be! How does one do this without giving offence? Well one of the ways is through exact analysis. This may take the form of asking for an accurate description of the aids required to perform a particular movement. I mean *exact*. The action of every part of the body and the reasons therefore to be explained. It is unlikely that a weekend rider will be able to do this. If this is not forthcoming one may well inquire how it is that the rider is going to get the horse to obey if they do not themselves know the signals? You then tell them that it is one of the reasons that they are in your class. Generally this should have a sobering effect.

Nervous clients.
With clients who are nervous a different course of action needs to be taken. Clients do not become more reassured as a result of being shouted at or by being told 'not to be silly'. The attitude that you should take is one of reassurance. In the first place you must make the client understand that it is your job to prevent anything untoward from happening. The client must have faith in *you*. Of course we all know that when working with horses it is really not possible to prevent an incident from occurring, but we do not tell that to the client. What we have to do is to reduce that possibility as close as conceivable to zero. Thus we are constantly alert for anything that may either startle a horse or give it an excuse for 'playing up'. If working outside be sure that a gate or stable door left open nearby and likely to bang about in the wind, is secured. If in the arena, pick up any scraps of paper that may have blown about. Sometimes it is the thoughtlessness of onlookers who, constantly open and close large umbrellas (ask them to stop it). It is through being vigilant that we can avoid many unnecessary mishaps and in this way our clients will become more relaxed and start to loose their fear.

Sometimes you may have a client who has suffered a nasty fall prior to their coming to you. In this case you must acknowledge their fear but tell them that when that happened it was in different circumstances and is now in the past. It is very helpful if they arrange to have lessons with you on a one to one basis. You will then be able to concentrate on getting them to relax which in turn will help them overcome any residual anxiety.

Difficult clients.
I have had clients harangue me for a good twenty minutes before the start of a lesson because they felt that the horses that they had been allocated were not of a high enough standard to enable them to practise the lateral work on which we were about to embark. 'I pay a lot of money' one would say 'and I am thoroughly fed up with being given horses that are not in the top rank'. No amount of persuasion on my part would change their minds. I tried explaining that riding advanced horses does not reveal to the rider whether or not they have given the correct and precise aids. Neither would they accept the explanation that these very horses were sometimes so fed up with doing lateral movements that they became 'crabby'. 'Lets get on with the lesson' was my suggestion. 'If you are unhappy with your progress at the end of the lesson, then I will personally ask for you to have different horses the next time'.

The lesson starts. The quiet old horse that had been accused of not being able to raise a trot - never mind about anything else, produces the best shoulder-in to half pass that the client has *ever* ridden. The same applied to the much younger horse, though it took a little longer for it to understand what was being asked of it. The clients had the revelation of putting the question to their horses and not permitting any movement to take place unless that movement – even if only one stride – was correct. Towards the end of the lesson that one stride had become half a dozen. All of them correct! They say to me 'that was an *extremely* enjoyable lesson but I suppose that the horse knew the movement all along' I simply reply 'It is beside the point. It is possible that the horses may have done this work before; on the other hand they may not. But one thing is for sure they certainly haven't done it recently and they only did it now because you asked for it correctly and were good enough riders to have your question answered precisely'. ' I think that I have made my point' I say as we finish. 'You certainly have' is the reply. No more complaints are made in the future.

The psychology of an adult.
An essential part of, successfully, teaching adults to ride does depend, to a great extent on your ability to understand what it is that motivates them. Why do they want to take up riding in the first place? If you are able to do this, then, though you may be unable to change the way that they think or for that matter

overcome their basic fears, you will at least be able to shape your lessons so that they are able to get the maximum benefit. They will not be so restricted by emotions that serve to interfere with the enjoyment of their chosen sport. Now it should be quite clearly understood that I am not only referring to such fears as falling off or being carted. There are those who do not suffer from these shortcomings at all. Their fear may simply be that they might be 'shown up' before other class members. The result is that they become very aggressive riders and this may not always encourage the best co-operation from their horses. None-the-less this aggression is simply a means of concealing fear.

I have noticed that some riders resort to the hard use of the whip without cause. This is unacceptable behaviour and I as have mentioned above frequently is the result of the rider's own fear. Should the horse respond, to what it regards as a quite unreasonable punishment, by giving just the smallest of bucks as a means of showing irritation, then the rider immediately 'falls apart' fearing to do anything at all and will frequently end up by asking if they can ride another horse!

Motivation.
It does help considerably, if you wish to have clients who *are satisfied with the work that you do for them*, to find out why they want to ride. This information can be used most effectively for clients who have private lessons with you. I have come across reasons as varied as, a mother who is having problems with a teenager, to a middle-aged man who had racehorses and wished to obtain a licence to ride in a race before he became too old! If you bother to learn what motivates these people then you may provide them with the lessons, the content of which will not only improve their equitation, but will also go some way to providing a short period during which they are taken out of themselves. In the case of the mother, who was in any case a very good horsewoman, the lesson sometimes took the form of multifarious changes of direction. She became so absorbed in riding these accurately that she completely forgot about her problems at home.

On Reflection.
I suppose, in a word, an instructor should strive not to be boring. You must improve your client's skills, but must never compromise safety for the sake of innovation This means that you must, constantly be examining the content of your lessons. You must reflect 'Have I left such and such an exercise neglected for too long? Is it time for a period of riding without stirrups and so on?

WORKING WITH CHILDREN
So called problem children.
You may sometimes come across children who, through their natural disposition or having had an unpleasant experience such as being carted as beginners, have developed a fear of riding and in particular cantering. You may well believe that these children are going to be very difficult to teach. In practice this is not, usually, the case. The reason for this is that by making their fears known, they are actually admitting them. Once a problem is out in the open, it is much easier for you as an instructor to form a plan, which will help to overcome a problem that is, in reality, not at all unreasonable.
'Real problem' children.
Oh no the really difficult children (and this applies to adults as well) are those who do *not* admit to any fear at all. Very often they see themselves as expert riders disdaining to ride quiet ponies. Insisting on riding faster animals but lacking the mental maturity and ability to apply the aids correctly that, in turn, will give them the necessary control. And what happens then? Why as soon as the pony starts to move at anything faster than a trot or tends to jiggle about a bit, then the child lets out the most almighty and continuous scream. This is a problem because in the first place the poor pony wonders what on earth is happening to cause this outburst and may then dash off in mild panic. Secondly this may also affect other ponies in the class who react, as do most herd animals, and also prepare to make off.

If you are fortunate, the rest of your riders will have the common sense and ability to maintain control, and this will give you the opportunity to call out to the screamer and ask what on earth they are screaming about. On hearing your voice (provided it has sufficient authority) the child will stop screaming and the pony will calm down at once without any real problems occurring. At this time I give a stern lecture. I tell them that I will not tolerate children who scream (I call it squeaking) whether or not they are in a state of fright or for that matter simply having fun. They have to learn that when working with ponies it is essential to be quiet. This precludes team-mates from giving encouragement from afar in a competition but even then this should be muted.

Being manipulated

Adults generally do not to try and impose their will on you as an instructor. However this is not the case with children and you will need to very quickly assess not only some children's inflated opinion as to what they are capable of, but also to divine when they are trying to manipulate you. You will frequently get the 'May we canter, please, please, please'. If you are not happy about either their ability to cope or the prevailing conditions *do not consent*.

Dealing with fear.

A very important aspect when dealing with either young children or come to that with adults is helping them to come to terms with their *fear*. It is essential that any youngsters who are fearful need to be told that this is *nothing to be ashamed about*. Anyone who does not suffer from some form of apprehension is to my mind – a fool! What young people have to be taught is how to deal with that fear and learn to control it. You can help by adjusting the format of your lesson or allowing them *not* to have to perform a particular gait at a given level. The problem may arise out of having to trot without stirrups or simply it may be a canter. By showing some compassion and consideration and by offering encouragement you will be able to help them overcome their problems. Don't forget they are already under pressure from their peers. This very pressure does serve to help them make progress. The important thing is for you to control this so that over a period of time the fear will subside in an entirely natural manner. In the end, if you are able to provide a continuous environment in which 'incidents' are minimal, you will produce a young rider who has skill, knowledge and rides with confidence.

Chapter 3

Going about ones business.

Getting qualifications.

Now it does not necessarily follow that one must be qualified in order to be a good instructor. In fact I have come across several *highly qualified* instructors who were quite diabolical. In the past, many good instructors were likely to be a product of experience. Their wisdom was acquired over many years - though without any paper qualifications to prove it. The principals of equitation have largely remained unchanged or if they have it is probably more due to the influences of fashion than anything else. Today, however, it is unlikely that you will obtain employment unless you are qualified. This means that you have taken and passed a series of exams with either the B.H.S or the A.B.R.S. The reason for this is due to the fact that the insurance for riding schools designed to protect against third party claims may be void if an accident arises when an unqualified instructor is in charge.

Of course there are riding establishments that run courses that will teach you and help you to pass your exams and as part of the curriculum you will start to instruct clients. These schools should have insurance in place that will cover you for third party liability while you are studying. For the purposes of this book I am starting from the premise that you have passed whatever exams are required for the practise of your chosen profession. If you are freelance then you will certainly require cover and this will not be forthcoming unless you can show that you *are* qualified. **Do remember that if you teach equitation without adequate third party insurance cover then you will not have any protection should you be sued for negligence.**

Is your qualification enough?

Some instructors, having taken and passed their teaching exams, breathe a sigh of relief and never bother to try and further improve themselves. I believe that ***passing an exam is only the first step*** in *your* ongoing education ***in the teaching of equitation***. You never stop learning; every lesson that you give should teach you something new about your subject, as you indeed are teaching your clients. The only difference is that you are approaching it from a different angle. I strongly advise every one of you to try and attend as many demonstrations and lectures as you can afford and that your time allows. From my own experience and having been teaching, regularly, for nearly half a century, I would, long ago have reached very sterile ground indeed if I had not sought out and attended the many courses that have refreshed my ideas.

Finding a good establishment.

Having passed your exams. The very first thing that you need to do is to try to obtain employment with a *good* riding school. Much easier said than done. In the first place, unless one comes across a school that needs an emergency replacement, it may be quite difficult to find any work at all. Rather like acting, this is an occupation where though the pay is not very high when you start, none-the-less would be practitioners are spurred on by a sense of vocation and, as with acting there are more applicants than there are jobs. Here I am not referring to working as a groom; usually it is not too difficult for anyone to find work in that area. My metaphor drawn on actors is quite appropriate, for indeed when you stand in the centre of an arena with up to a dozen people awaiting the delivery of your accumulated wisdom, it does help if you are able to pass this on with panache. There is a certain element of the thespian.

What do you look for?

The next question must be what constitutes a good riding school? You can make your decision by observation and asking questions. My list below is quite long but by no means covers every question that needs to be asked. Start as you would when buying a horse with a general impression, and then become more specific.

1. What is your general impression of the yard as you enter it? Is it clean?
2. Are the directions to the various parts of the school well sign-posted?
3. What is the office like? Does it emit an aura of efficiency? Are the staff friendly? Are the records of the yard on computer?
4. Are clients able to hire riding crash hats and are these up to the most recent safety standard?
5. Does the stable have insurance for all the instructors, be they on the payroll or freelance?
6. Are the tack rooms well appointed? Do they have adequate heating and drying facilities? Are they well

ventilated? Is the tack clearly marked for each horse? Are there spare tack, cavesson, and lunging whips, brushing and overreach boots and so on? Above all, *is the tack clean especially the bits*?

7. Are the fire precautions adequate?
8. Are the stables well constructed and in good condition? Are they well ventilated? Are they large enough to comfortably house their occupants? Is water available at the point of consumption? Are the horses predominantly kept in good-sized boxes or are stalls used instead of boxes?
9 What is your overall impression of the stock? Are there any that look mean? Do you see the odd stable door banger or weaver? How many are school horses or liveried? Are the horses of sufficiently varied in size and strength to accommodate a variety of riders especially where weight carriers are needed? *Above all do they generally look healthy, happy and contented?*
10. Are the common areas large enough to accommodate the movement of horses as they are taken from their boxes to the mounting areas?
11. Are there any special areas designated for mounting and dismounting? Are they large enough to ensure that there is room for both un-mounted riders to walk safely and mounted riders to move away to the appointed arena or ménage? Are there mounting blocks of varying heights?
12. How many arenas are there? Are they covered or open? What size are they?
13. What type of surface do they have? Are they of a good quality all-weather type that will ensure safe use even during the worst winter months?
14. Are the droppings collected in the arenas or are they allowed to lie for long periods?
15. Are the toilette facilities kept spotlessly clean?
16. Is there any jumping equipment? Is it in good condition? Is it stored away safely when not in use?
17. Is there land available for horses to be turned out during the summer?
18. Are the feed stores secure and free of rat infestation?
19. Is the staff, generally, of a friendly and cheerful disposition?
20. Does the office staff have available, prices for lessons and client declaration forms. Do they know how to fill in a RIDDOR form (Reporting of Injuries, Diseases and Dangerous Occurrence Regulations)?
21. Are there signs, prominently displayed, that warn the public as to how to behave when in the proximity of horses?
22. Are instructions for dealing with a fire clearly displayed?
23. Are meals and accommodation provided? If not then are these easily available nearby?
24. Is there adequate parking for all clients?
25. Finally and perhaps most important of all. Is the establishment B.H.S or A.B.R.S approved?

Why do I think that you should be asking all these questions?
The reason is that if *you* are to give of your best then you should have the best facilities available to *you*. You may be young and inexperienced but you should have self-respect. Your decision may be dictated by the urgent need to earn a living but on the other hand you may have more than one offer open to you. When you go to new jobs you will, to some extent, be judged on where you have taught in the past. That is why one needs to pay attention to all these details and many more?

An efficient yard usually means well-managed clients and stock. If both of these are properly maintained, then your employment is placed on a more secure foundation. If you teach at a yard where the horses are standing in boxes all year round without ever having the opportunity to be turned out, then it is possible that they may be getting soured or stale They will be more likely to have a 'tantrum' and dislodge a client. This is much less likely with horses that do enjoy a break out in the fields. The same applies with regard to the surfaces of the arenas. It is no use obtaining a job at an establishment where, when winter arrives, the ménages become unusable due to bad weather. If you are unable to teach then you will not be paid! The discipline applied to clients by the office is also important. A badly run yard may allow them to cancel at the last minute, without penalty! They may also allow clients to ride in a class that is beyond their ability.

Remember some of the things mentioned above can contribute to an accident. It may simply be an accumulation of small details unattended to: badly maintained tack, which can break; too many horses in a class that don't get on well with one another; slippery surfaces in an arena - I can go on forever but I'm sure that you get my point. If the culmination of some of these small details contributes to a member of your class having a fall or sustaining an injury then it is *you* who are the last link in the chain and it is you who will be held responsible. And all this arose out of the fact that in your enthusiasm to get employed, you

41

settled for second best or simply because you didn't know any better. Things may get so bad that you decide to leave and this poor judgement on your part will reflect badly on you when you apply for your next job.

How does one deal with a state of affairs that is less than satisfactory?
Now I must admit that this can be quite tricky. In the first place it is unlikely that you will find a school where everything is run to your satisfaction and further more *you* may well be regarded as a bit 'green'. You may make yourself very unpopular if you go around 'laying down the law' as it were! In practise you will need to compromise. If you do see something that is simply not acceptable, say, for example, the centre of the arena absolutely littered with poles and uprights for jumping then, in the nicest way, you should mention the problem to the owner of the school. Tell them that you would not, safely, be able to teach unless they were stored away properly. In most cases they will not get upset with you but instead you will be quietly admired. Suppose that they reply that they have always worked like this and do not have any room to properly store such apparatus? In that case do not work for them, for should there be an accident and you are the one in charge, then the unsafe conditions in which you are teaching will be held against you. It is your responsibility, as an instructor, to insist that safe conditions prevail in your work place. It is your employer's job to create them.

Negotiating with the School.
The conditions under which you will work must be, clearly, specified, (pay, meals accommodation etc.) Everything should *always* be in writing.

Documentation.
You should always have copies of your certificates of competence available. You will need these whenever you apply for a job. I suggest that you keep everything in a leather or plastic folder. As you progress from job to job you may add the references that you have been given and also any kind comments clients have made to you, in writing. You should also keep a written copy of any comments that you have made to the management concerning unsatisfactory conditions or horses that have played up. Note well that I have said *copies*. Keep originals at home or in a safe place.

Keeping a log.
It is my view that every instructor should keep a log into which such details as the name of the establishment where the lesson has been given, also the date and time of the class, the names of all riders and horses that they rode, together with *short* comments as to any problems experienced, by individuals of any movement or gait that has been undertaken. (It is not necessary to write a book about every class). In this way you will be able to keep a check on the progress of your clients and also, should the unthinkable happen, have a note as to whether or not a client had undertaken, successfully, that movement previously. You should also note your impression as to the overall success of the lesson.

How to do it.
Ideally this log is best based on a loose ring folder. With this system, you may, should you so wish, attach plastic sheets, which will help to keep your pages dry in inclement weather. Another advantage is that you take with you only those sheets that appertain to the classes that you are going to take on a given day. This avoids the necessity of going around with an enormously heavy folder. In order to keep writing to a minimum, develop a sort of shorthand or have a code which will clearly indicate to you (and no one else) the exercises that your clients have done and how well they got on (see drawings 1 and 2).

There are two ways in which an instructor may undertake the business of teaching others to ride. The first is as a member of the staff of an established riding school. The second, as a freelance.

So far as the former is concerned the rules governing the criteria for every class, in any properly established school should be quite clearly delineated. The classes will be arranged according to ability and specialisation. It is the instructors' job to be sure that the curriculum is clearly understood and followed to the letter. A well-run school will probably have a printed introduction as to their requirements. This is the most satisfactory way of going about things, since the instructor may study these at length and, should anything be unclear, this may be queried and further clarification obtained.

For example one must be quite clear, by observation, as to the standard of pupils in any class that one is given to teach and that one must also be sure as to what standard the school expects you to be teaching. Without establishing these parameters it is not possible to observe whether or not ones pupils are making satisfactory progress. It may well be that on taking over a class you may consider that one or two riders do not have the required ability for that class and it might be advisable to ask if they can be placed with another group. Do not necessarily expect this to happen. Riding schools are businesses and have to do their best to accommodate the free time that a client has available and not the other way around. If it is not possible to relocate substandard pupils, then, make changes to the format of your lessons and only allow those clients whom you feel are quite safe to undertake the more difficult movements. For the others, simply make an exercise easier for them, so that they may take part and enjoy the pleasure of achieving their maximum potential. With exercises presented in this manner it is surprising how quickly the weaker riders will catch up as their confidence grows.

As a freelance one does not always have the luxury of taking clients or classes with which one is familiar. This means that one must be meticulous in adhering to the basic safety rules before proceeding with any lesson and also take care to make progress *slowly*.

The Riding School Secretary and staff.
Now I have already mentioned that one should be polite and cheerful to everyone but I do think that one should, especially, not forget those who work behind the scenes as it were. A good relationship with the office staff can help you to avoid having unpleasant horses allocated to you. Or, to put it another way they may take more trouble in ensuring that you have horses that are suited to your needs (I have in mind particularly, giving a private lesson on the lunge).

Get your information by asking questions and being observant.
What are we looking for? Well, for a start, it is unlikely, when you first take on a new class, that you will be familiar with either the riders or horses with whom you have to deal. You must ask the clients as to how long they have been riding and what level they have attained, follow this up with a series of very simple but quiet exercises that will provide confirmation of that which you have been told. So far as the horses are concerned, start by asking members of staff as to what are the particular characteristics of the horses in your lesson. You may not always get accurate answers but it may help. You must use your own powers of observation to spot mares that are in heat and likely to kick out at geldings. You must take the class through a series of transitions that will establish how the horses are going. For example the first canter towards the end of the lesson should be very short, from front to rear. If you already know that there is a horse or two inclined to dash off when asked to canter, and if by this time you also suspect that the clients riding them may not be very good at coping, then either ask them to forgo cantering or, alternatively, tell them to trot most of the way around the arena before asking for canter.

Incidentally a further thought crosses my mind when it comes to obtaining information about the horses in the yard. It is a very good idea, if you are to be employed on a regular basis, that you make a list of the boxes where each horse stands. This may be useful to you when you finish a lesson at the lunch hour. It is possible that everyone may have gone off to lunch and there is no one about to take the horses that your clients have been riding. This being the case you are going to have to deal with the matter of putting them away yourself. It does help if you know where they are supposed to go (think about their feeds if nothing else).

A final thought.
Though I have tried to point out many of the things that I think that you should look for when selecting the place where you will work, it is possible that you may find that some yards are to be found wanting. However you should remember, as you read on, that my comments concerning riding schools and the sort of horses that they use, are based on those schools where I have worked and I must say that these were all first class.

If you are to be really successful in keeping the number of clients who sustain a fall to the minimum, it is essential that you try to have all horses selected for their suitability to the clients. By that I mean that you need to *know from your experience,* the clients and horses well enough to be quite sure that every client is allocated a horse to that they can cope with. This might seem to be a rather obvious comment to make but there are so many intangibles that you need to take into account. For example you may have a client who is to a reasonable degree a competent rider -when riding a quiet horse. That same rider may be entirely unable to cope when mounted on another horse that is more forward going. They become seized by a paralysing fear that in turn is transmitted to the horse who responds to what he now believes is an unseen 'danger'. He makes off at high speed and the client 'bales out'. I always inspect my class lists of horses and riders as soon as I arrive at the yard. Should I see that someone has been allocated a horse that, I think is unsuitable then I immediately ask the office for a change. Generally this is not a problem because riders and horses may be changed from the group already selected. Sometimes this is not possible and one is then left with a decision that must be made. Either you simply tell the office that you think that it is quite unsafe for the client to ride that particular horse and not have them in your lesson or alternatively, if you think that matters are not as serious as that, then tell the client what your feelings are at the start of the lesson and give them the choice of either declining to ride the horse or else tell them that for this lesson you will not allow them to canter. I have always found that clients will trust my judgment and, willingly, go along with my advice.

Continuing in the same vein there is another matter that you need to bear in mind and that is the danger of becoming *complacent*. In this case I am referring to that time when you, eventually, become a much sought-after instructor. You will have a list of clients who take lessons with you week after week. By and large they will have become quite good riders who ride with confidence on the horses that they are allocated. However at some point they may be asked to ride a horse that they have not ridden previously and this is the time when you must be very observant. The reason for this is that the action of this new animal may differ from those that they have ridden before. This horse may have a more pronounced moment of suspension, particularly during canter. Whereas your client has sat well to a horse with a fairly flat stride, they may now have difficulty in coping. The first sign that you may notice is that, at the trot, their hands which are normally reasonably still, start to jerk about. This first warning should be sufficient. It tells you that whatever program you have had in mind this must now be changed for something that is less energetic. Failure to do this will, again, result in a client suffering a needless fall.

Finally - Finally. I have mentioned all the things that you should *look* for. However there is one matter that is of paramount importance and this is not immediately visible to the eye. I am referring to ***correct feeding***. Oh yes I am sure that those of you who have already gained some considerable experience before you started to read this book will at once remark 'What is the fool talking about? Anyone with even the most basic knowledge will be able to spot horses that are not thriving'. I am not referring to an animal's well-being. I am now talking about a yard that has someone in charge of feeding who has had years of experience and also the authority to adjust the feeds as and when necessary. 'Surely most yard managers will be able to do that?' I hear you say. Indeed they probably can – after the event! 'What event?' The time when without any warning even the mildest of your horses start to deposit your clients on the floor! 'When is that?' Very often during that difficult period between winter and spring. That time when horses are itching to get out into the fields for a break but haven't been allowed to do so perhaps because there has been a prolonged cold spell which has restricted the growth of grass. The horses only know that the days are getting longer and they begin to show very small signs of truculence, then, without more ado they vent their frustration on the riders.

A good yard manager will anticipate this. The remedy is probably quite simple: substitute a good feed of hay instead of the midday mix. Do this unilaterally across the whole yard and unnecessary problems are avoided. But as I have said it is one of those things that are not always apparent – until after the event that is!

IT MUST BE CLEARLY UNDERSTOOD THAT BEFORE YOU BECOME INVOLVED IN ANYTHING THAT HAS TO DO WITH INSTRUCTING ANY PERSON RIDING A HORSE, YOU MUST FIRST HAVE TAKEN THE APPROPRIATE COURSE IN FIRST AID.

Drawing No. 1.

Private lesson record sheet.
All details of the lesson may be entered before commencing. Comments afterwards.

Establishment *A.N Riding school*		Date 11/10/00	Time 10.00 am	No. in class 1
Riders Names	*Barbara*			
Horses	*Winston*			
Movement	**Gait**	**Remarks**		
Working-in going large. Shallow loops, long rein	*Walk.*	*Correcting rider's position. (toes turn out)*		
Trot rising going large and riding				
Circles of half the arena at A & C and in the centre.	*Trot sitting*			
		U/S even shape and tempo well maintained.		
Resting Shoulder-in Resting	*Walk.*	*F/hand allowed to drift back to the track.*		
Lengthened strides along long sides.	*Trot sitting and rising*	*Good lengthening without increase in tempo.*		
Resting Going large	*Canter going large with diagonal changes and 3 strides only thru X to change the lead.*	*1st attempt 6 strides* *2nd down to four* *3rd – perfect!*		
Shallow loops long rein	*Walk*			
Special Notes. *This rider has really made an improvement over the last four lessons. She is beginning to think more about the horse and the manner of its going. This is reflected in the improved Work that she is doing.*				

Class record sheet.
Obviously you must keep your eyes on the class for the whole duration of the lesson. Therefore it is best to fill in the program (which may have to be subsequently amended according to conditions) and the names, before the start of the lesson., The completetion of the log is carried out afterwards.
It is also understood that between each movement there must be adequate periods of rest both for riders and especially horses.

Establishment A.N Riding school	Date 10/10/00	Time 10.00 am	No. in class 6
Riders Names	Lee, Linda, Claire, Joanne, Gwen, Jackie		
Horses	Spectra, Jeeves, Lady C, Logic , Henry and & Ross.		

Movement	Gait	Remarks
Working in going large. Shallow loops, long rein	Walk.	Correcting everyone's position.
	Walk	V/S even shape and tempo well maintained.
Circles of half the arena at A & C	Walk	Quite good, Ride more or less in line and tempo reasonably maintained.
Resting. Changing the rein, as a ride, cross the long side of the arena. Resting	Sitting trot	First two attempts rather ragged and Linda and Claire allowed their horses to break to walk. Improvement all round at second attempt. Third attempt rather good.
Figure of eight Resting	Walk	Well ridden by all.. Nice active walk.
	Trot rising.	Quite well ridden, some falling in at corners.
Resting Going large	Canter from front to rear.	Nice quiet canters all around the arena. Corners quite well ridden too.
Shallow loops long rein	Walk	Well ridden, good wind down.
Questions		Lee asked what he should do in order to keep his hand still.

Special Notes. Lee needs to practise the aids for a smooth canter depart.

Jackie must, constantly, be reminded to keep her hand still.

Henry's saddle needs reflocking.

Drawings Nos. 1 & 2 Examples of lesson logs.

Chapter 4

Preparing your lessons.
The basic foundations.
A good riding school will have a curriculum. You may consider that the limits placed upon you are somewhat restricted. For example, some schools do not allow jumping to be included as part of a basic lesson. There may be various reasons for this, one being concern about loosing work time through lameness. Others permit jumping but only as a specialised lesson. As a professional you must stay within the parameters that have been set for you. Read M. Guérinière *5 in the 'School of Horsemanship' published in final form in 1733. He wrote 'All sciences and arts have principle and rules, by means of which one makes discoveries leading to their perfection. Horsemanship is the one art for which it seems one needs only practise'. Today the scales have, if anything, tilted the other way. We have so many people providing ' principles and rules' that the art developed through practise seems to have diminished somewhat. None-the-less equitation is an Art, and if one may take the simile further, you should not teach 'abstract painting' when you are supposed to be teaching 'representational painting'. Or, should you not have understood what I have just written, don't teach jumping when you are supposed to be teaching flat work!

May I never go outside the curriculum?
The simple answer is 'No'. Unless, that is, you have first obtained the permission from the management. Suppose that, as a change, you think that it would be beneficial to have a jumping lesson. If the management is agreeable, then you must discuss with them the ability of each client, in the class, to cope with this. You should also delineate the extent to which you intend to involve them in the jumping exercises, i.e. how many jumps, their height and whether or not you are going to end up with a small course. This will allow for suitable horses to be provided, and, if the office are co-operative, to make arrangements for the jumps to be set up in good time for your lesson.

What will happen if I do it on the spur of the moment?
Suppose for example your are persuaded to do a jumping lesson by your clients, whom you have been teaching for quite some time and who you have got to know really well, ? You see some poles and uprights just by the arena and you set-up a small course? Everything goes well but towards the end of the lesson one of the horses, who hasn't done very much jumping gets a bit fed up and, as it lands, after a jump, it puts in a buck? The client is thrown and is injured. If you have instituted the lesson without permission and the client accuses you of being negligent, a subsequent inquiry by the Insurance Company may result in your finding that your third party cover has been nullified.

Think before you act!

Preparation.
If you wish to develop into a really good instructor you should take the trouble to prepare your lessons during the week preceding the time when you will give them. If you do keep a journal then you should refer to this as you devise each new lesson. In this way you will be able to introduce movements, which will make sure that the basics are still being taught while not being obviously repetitive. Thus without your clients becoming aware that this is the case you also provide them with the opportunity to make progress. Even if you are dealing with advanced riders you need to be sure that, every so often, you *revert to basics*. You need a lesson that will ask the clients to define the paces, describe the aids or to ride transitions from letter to letter, while counting down to the moment of execution ' 3 – 2 – 1 '. It is surprising how often clients forget how to do these simple things. It is not satisfactory to simply appear in the arena and then to devise a series of exercises ad lib as it were. Of course should you be asked to take someone else's class in an emergency, then you will have to think very quickly 'on your feet' as it were.

What do you do if you have been called in at the last minute?
It may well be that you have been asked to take over a class at short notice. You may not have had any time to prepare a specific lesson and you may know relatively little about either the clients or horses. In these circumstances you will need all your experience to assess them all - quickly. However you do have a means

of obtaining information that can help. *You simply ask the clients.* Chances are that they will have ridden the horses before and will know all their little foibles and physical difficulties. Of course some of them may tell you that certain horses will not do this or that but this may only be a reflection on their own lack of ability. However you will have useful information with which to work. In any event you would be advised to keep the work fairly simple and straightforward.

At the start of a lesson you should decide if you are about to utilise horses at livery or school horses. It is my view that school horses should be given a certain consideration. By and large they know their business and are trusted members of the team. They must therefore be treated accordingly. For example you will not allow any excessive use of the stick, when the fault plainly lies with the rider and not the horse.

The components of a lesson.
Whatever the case, your lessons as I have already said, must be constructed strictly according to the syllabus that applies to the course that you are teaching and must be at a suitable level for the standard of rider who will attend. Further more you must take care not to be repetitive. This is where your logbook will come in useful. One of the most often heard criticisms of riding instructors is that they become boring, teaching the same movements week after week. It may be that those instructors will reply that it is their job to repeat the basics until the student has mastered them. This is quite correct, except that you must have clients *attending* your classes if you are *to be successful*. That won't happen if they get bored and no longer turn up.

The answer lies in the *presentation* of those basics in a manner that continually surprises and interests your pupils, by so doing they do not realise that you are simply presenting them with the same basic principles. It does not matter whether you are teaching an absolute beginner or an advanced rider, all must be stimulated and enjoy what you teach. Your pupils should leave your lesson with a greater understanding of the horse and an advance in their skills. I am reminded of a Pony Club instructors' course that I attended some time ago. The instructor was Yogi Breisner. His presentation was extremely good and furnished me with yet more new ways in which to present *the basics*. However, for me, the most significant thing was his recounting of a conversation he had had, during the lunch break, with a lady who did not ride at all. She was a ballet teacher. What she had apparently said was to the effect that 'You may give them gold but they will not accept it unless you gift-wrap it'. I find that a very interesting remark when taken in the context of repeating the basics.

Set your targets.
It is also important to set reasonably achievable targets. By that I mean that ideally, the clients should succeed handsomely in the tasks that you have set for them but should they fail to gain perfection, then, they should not finish the lesson in a state of depression. I suppose the phrase ' Always finish on a high note' is most apt. It is your job to have improved the riding skills of your clients in at least one or other particular aspect. What that will be is up to you, but by the end of the lesson, even if the clients have only managed to make small improvements, you should point out what they are and they should feel pleased about it.

The formula for success is; that no matter what you teach, *keep everything simple*. A client, whom I had, temporarily, taken over, while her regular instructor was on holiday, once paid me a compliment. 'I have understood more in this one lesson,' she said, 'than I have in the last six months. You make things so clear and I can follow everything that you tell me'. She then went on to say that she would like to change and have me as her instructor, at which point I had to demure and point that, as much as she might desire this, it simply was not acceptable etiquette.

Allow for the type of horse that will be used.
You must take into account the kind of horses that you will have in your class. It is no use devising an extremely arduous lesson based, to a great extent, on lateral work when you have horses that are generally used for hacking. If you *do* wish to teach this sort of work, then you must make sure that you build up the movement progressively, each movement leading on, logically to the next, so that both horse and rider achieve success in the execution of whatever you ask of them.

The element of fatigue
All lessons that you create must include *clearly defined periods*, which will allow both riders and horses *to rest*. I make special mention of this because if you do not do so, then you may find that you become so

involved as your lesson progresses that you forget this very important point. You must not loose sight of the fact that whereas riders, if properly taught by you, will have no qualms in telling you that they are getting tired, your horses cannot do so as easily.

Allow for the build-up of muscle fatigue.
Continuous movement involving changing states such halt (at attention) to forward movement do not allow a horse to breakdown the products of muscular chemistry as easily as they would if, for example, they were proceeding at a nice steady but prolonged canter. The chemical mechanisms change slightly and, at the higher gaits, become more efficient. You must never loose sight of the fact that muscle fatigue produces at the least discomfiture and very possibly pain. Time must be allowed for the horses to recover.

The time factor.
All successful lessons depend on the correct allocation of time. You must make provision for the warming up period and then for **all** your class members to perform correctly *each movement* that you set for them. This means that they should be able to ride each exercise at least twice. They will need the first attempt as a means of getting the feel of the task that you set. When this has finished, there should be a short period of discussion during which you point out what went well and what didn't. You should explain how difficulties might be overcome. If you are successful, then the second attempt will be an improvement on the first. You must congratulate your clients when this is so. It may be that all are agreed that a third go would be beneficial, to add an element of polish, as it were!

Taking extra care with children.
You should be extremely careful when taking a children's class for the first time. You may well be filled with the desire to give them an entertaining lesson, but do not do so at the expense of dispensing with calm and controlled conditions. You may not realise that those apparently confident youngsters have only reached that state due to the effort made by their previous instructor to keep everything within certain fixed parameters. (For example suppose you are working out in a field and they beg you to let them go away from you say all around the perimeter of the field, should you agree, do not be surprised if all the ponies dash off at high speed entirely uncontrolled by their little riders). Several of whom will fall and much of the confidence built up by your predecessor is destroyed.

Always have a back-up routine in order to take the weather into account .
Of course even a well-prepared lesson must have one or two back-ups or variation on a theme to allow either, for unforeseen weather conditions or horses that are playing up. For example it is not satisfactory to have devised a lesson, which, during a freezing spell will have your clients standing around for longish periods while you go into great detail regarding the mechanics of a particular movement. Neither is it a good idea to give a lesson involving the class in mass participation of an exercise at the canter when one or two of your horses have shown a desire to dash madly around the arena. You must also take into account the way in which the arena surfaces that you use stand up to extreme conditions. Though you may not be able to predict the weather accurately you should have a good idea if you listen to the weather forecasts.

Very dry conditions.
Sometimes one has to make an allowance for an excessively dry period. It may well be that you are working on a prepared surface. In dry weather even the best-prepared surfaces get very dusty. I do not think that it is very much fun, or for that matter beneficial to either horse or rider if you persist in continuing with a lesson, (albeit a quiet one), if everyone is coughing and spluttering in clouds of dust as soon as they all start to trot. (Yes I do realise that dry surfaces should have been well watered before the lesson but what are you going to do if this has not been done?)

This is the time to switch quickly to a lesson that involves less dashing around. Ideally one should revert to exercises that allow riders to participate one at a time whilst the remainder stand in the shade (if there is any).

Wet conditions.
You must also be prepared to adjust your lesson if there has been a lot of rain. Even the best all-weather surfaces may eventually become partly waterlogged. This may result in a reduction of the usable area and if

this is the case, then you must change those components of the lesson that would involve using a great deal of space. Furthermore should the ground surface become boggy, you should mark out that part in which you do not wish your class to ride. You must also be quite strict and make certain that no one wanders casually into an area that is unsuitable to ride over.

Cold but bright winter days.
Sometimes in the winter we experience a day that has an alpine brightness. There has been a light frost on the ground and everyone feels rather good. Or at least they do until their horses start jumping around a bit! For the fact is that in the same way as humans feel the elation engendered by the increased oxygen that results from anticyclonic conditions, so do horses! There they stand having been clipped out to varying degrees and anxious to get going. This is an occasion when it is advisable to do just that, keep the working in period at walk fairly short and then proceed to a fairly extended period of steady trot. This does not mean that you should then induce a feeling of boredom in your horses by simply going large around the arena lap after lap, introduce movements that are mentally stimulating to both rider and horse. These may be quite simple such as medium half circle and return, reverse half circles and so on. This is the time to make use of such exercises as turning across the arena in twos and similar but quite simple variations. You are thus giving your riders something to think about and concentrate on the manner of their horses going and this in turn leads to the horses themselves starting to focus on what they have to do.

A windy and blustery day.
In these conditions, (in which it may not actually be raining), the wind may in fact be quite warm but with strong gusts. Here you need a different approach. So far as the content of your lesson is concerned it may be very similar to that which I have suggested in the last section. However this time it is advisable to *carry out all these exercises at a walk* for the greater part of the time. The reason for this is that some horses are ill at ease in high winds. The wind gets 'up their tails' as we say. Further more, as I mention elsewhere, a strong gust can tend to unbalance a horse, especially at a pace that has a moment of suspension, as in the trot and to an even greater extent the canter. If you find this concept difficult to comprehend then simply imagine yourself leaning into a strong wind. Are you likely to be jumping off the ground, I doubt it. Instead you are going to place one leg firmly in front of the other and thus ensure that you are on a firm foundation. A horse has a much larger skin area than we do thus; despite its much greater weight it is quite likely to find the wind causing problems that eventually disturb its mental equilibrium.

Allowing time for preparation when using equipment.
You must allow sufficient time if you wish to use equipment or to set up a course (not necessarily jumping but perhaps simple obstacles). You should be on hand early enough to do this before your class arrives. Of course this may not be possible if the arena is occupied. Provided you don't leave your arrival until the last minute, you can use the time between changeovers to prepare. This will avoid your having to keep the class standing still longer than necessary, for you may not turn your back or take your eyes off a class while a lesson is in progress. You will also avoid providing an opportunity for those horses whom, wishing to get up to mischief, do so when you are not looking at them. They are not stupid you know? They will observe that second when your concentration is elsewhere.

The Leitmotif
The object of this book is not so much to provide complete lessons but rather to illustrate the various components that need to be included in a lesson and the exercises that will allow for this. It may not be possible for you to include all aspects of equitation in every lesson. Rather you should select a particular theme for your clients to concentrate on. This needs to be varied from lesson to lesson. I always believe that it is a good idea to explain, at the beginning of a lesson, the elements that will be included on that day. *Further more each should lead on, logically, to the next one.* Having explained the movements that are going to be ridden, you should ask your clients if they are able to tell you what is the leitmotif (the underlying theme) that runs from movement to movement. In other words can they guess what it is in each section of the lesson that will connect all the parts of the lesson together?

The overall strategy.
Once in a while it is worthwhile spending a few minutes discussing what has been achieved over a period of

time and the progress that you and your pupils will be aiming for in the future. You may say that for the next four weeks the class is going to concentrate on smooth transitions or going on the bit. You make your decision according to their ability. It may well be that some of them are not really interested in making significant progress but that is up to them. So far as you are concerned you must *present the opportunity* and it is up to them to *take advantage* of it if they will.

The charter.

If all lessons are to have a sound basic construction, then it is very important to have a good foundation upon which to build. For me it takes the form of a charter. This is mine: -

THE ART OF EQUITATION

TO SIT UPON A HORSE IN AN ELEGANT AND WELL-BALANCED MANNER AND WITHIN THE LIMITS OF ITS CAPABILITY, CAUSE IT TO MOVE IN SUCH A WAY AS IS IN COMPLETE ACCORD WITH ONES' OWN WILL.

THE FIVE BASIC RULES.

1.   RIDING IS THE ART OF BALANCE AND NOT GRIP.

2.   THE RIDER MUST BE COMPLETELY RELAXED SO THAT THEY MAY BE ABLE TO GIVE CLEAR AND PRECISE AIDS. (SIGNALS).

3.   THE RIDER MUST NOT ASK THE HORSE TO PERFORM ANY MOVEMENT THAT IS UN-REASONABLE.

4.   THE RIDER MUST BE CLEAR IN THEIR OWN MIND EXACTLY WHAT IT IS THAT THEY ARE GOING TO ASK OF THE HORSE.

5.   THE RIDER, PROVIDED THE ABOVE FOUR RULES HAVE BEEN PROPERLY APPLIED, MUST BE DETERMINED TO BE OBEYED. THIS WILL BE BY GAINING THE HORSE'S RESPECT, FOR NOTHING OF REAL QUALITY IS EVER ACHIEVED THROUGH FEAR.

THE FINAL RULE FOR THE CLIENT.

ALWAYS LISTEN AND DO EVERYTHING THAT YOUR INSTRUCTORS TELL YOU. IT IS YOUR SAFETY THAT IS PARAMOUNT IN THEIR MINDS.

BALANCE AND AIDS

IN ORDER TO PRODUCE A MOVEMENT DEMONSTRATING THE PERFECT HARMONY, BETWEEN HORSE AND RIDER. THE RIDER'S BODY MUST BE IN TOTAL BALANCE, THE TORSO AND LIMBS WITHOUT TENSION - FREE TO GIVE PRECISE BUT LIGHT AIDS. THE HANDS MUST REMAIN STILL. THE FINGERS MOVING ALMOST AS THOUGH THEY WERE PRODUCING MUSICAL NOTES. IN FACT THE WHOLE THING MAY BE LIKENED TO PLAYING A FUGUE ON A CHURCH ORGAN WHILST SITTING ON A TWO LEGGED STOOL.

Rules for yourself.

1.   Always have your lesson well prepared in advance.
2.   Always take into account the level of ability of your clients.
3.   Always arrive on time.
4.   Always finish on time.
5.   Never allow the horses in your class to become sweated-up or over-excited. By the end of the lesson they must be cool and calm and have sufficient energy left over to continue with further work.

Sometimes it will help in the preparation of your lesson if you know, before hand, whether or not you have to share the arena with one or more instructors.

The very basic foundations for success.
* Watch the weather.
* Know the horses.
* Understand the clients.
* Ensure that they achieve the tasks you have set for them.

Believe me there is no greater pleasure than having your clients leave your class at the end of a lesson having succeeded in riding, correctly, whatever movements no matter how simple, that you have set for them. They will be brimming over with satisfaction and will return for further lessons.

Final thoughts.
A lesson that suits.

A good riding school will endeavour not only to ensure that riders of similar skills are placed in the appropriate class but will also try to have people of a similar background riding together. By that I mean that you may find that you have been asked to take a class of riders who are, mainly, middle-aged ladies. Alternatively it might consist of young teenagers from a nearby school. If you wish to be successful then you should devise a lesson that befits the outlook of each specific group.

If for example we take the ladies, it is quite likely that a number of them, though fairly capable riders may tire easily. This may mean that they will probably enjoy having included an exercise, such as a turn on the forehand, performed individually. During the time when the some members of the class are showing the movement the remainder will use this interval to rest.

Now let us consider the youngsters. They probably belong to the school riding club. During the summer they hack out with you but in winter this is not possible because it is dark during the period when they are free to ride. They will not be encouraged to continue with the clubs' riding activities if you now proceed to give them lessons in which they are asked to continually concentrate, for example, on some long winded explanations. Droning on for ages over such matters as 'the effect of horses' confirmation on its ability to give a lengthened stride'! For these lads you need to engage their interest through movement. Drill rides are excellent for this purpose. Of course you do have periods where you explain and encourage questions but a drill ride suits very well because no young man likes to be shown up in front of his mates. They will try like mad to ride with great accuracy and also thoroughly enjoy themselves.

Now you may well ask 'Why should I bother?' The answer to that is that in a riding school environment the front office, grooms, grounds-men, all the other instructors including you yourself are part of a team. It is the team's job to create an environment, which will help the school to prosper, and that means increasing the number of people who wish to ride there. Therefore you not only need to improve your clients riding abilities but also to induce in them a feeling that having a riding lesson is perhaps something more than simply sitting on a horse's back for an hour.

What is in it for you?

What should you be getting out of all this; apart that is from being paid? From your personal point of view you should have derived pleasure from knowing that you have been able to successfully look into the minds of all your pupils and to understand their motivation. You should have acted in good time to prevent them from suffering needless fear. You should also end with the satisfaction of knowing that after the lesson, *all* your pupils, be they adults or children, have found their time with you enjoyable and stimulating. That they have learned more about equitation than they knew at the beginning and have improved their riding abilities.

Your pupils should depart the class with smiles on their faces and with a degree of animated chatter. If they have really enjoyed themselves they will come up to you afterwards and tell you so. Sometimes there may not be enough time for you to receive such compliments. I have often had to quickly depart for another arena only to find myself walking behind a little 8 year old whom I have just finished teaching. The parents are on either side each holding a hand and I hear an animated discourse from the child. 'Well you see there I was cantering around the arena when my pony broke to the trot. Weeeell I started to rise but of course Mr Silverman told me always to try and sit when that happened. I did so and got the canter back again…….' Ah the pleasure!

Chapter 5

Before commencing a lesson

As I have already mentioned in chapter 4, it is helpful if, before you prepare a lesson that you have some idea as to the size of the area in which you will be working.

Sharing an arena.

Quite often one may be asked to share an arena. (If you are asked to do so), before you start your lesson, speak to the instructor with whom you are going to share.

Utilising the arena by splitting.

You both should decide if you are going to split the arena with each instructor sticking to his or her chosen end, or to use the whole arena with your clients simply avoiding the other ride. If you are working with clients who are comparative novices, then, it is probably better to keep your clients in one half. You may help them to visualise the extent of the area allocated to them by putting cones across the centre i.e. from B to E. (See fig. 1) Another factor to be considered is the character of the horses that you are using. Are there any basically unsociable by nature or mares in heat? If the answer to both these questions is 'yes', then definitely stick to you own end. However you must discuss these matters with your colleague. You must also inquire, if you don't already know, as to whether *they* have any horses that are likely to give trouble. This might be by dashing off when they see the other horses going in a different direction or, if they are simply bad mannered, likely to try and take advantage of what could become a difficult situation.

Using the whole arena.

This, to some extent, depends on how many clients each of you have to work with. If you have agreed that both rides are capable of controlling their horses to the extent that they will not collide with one another when going large, then all the clients must be made aware of the rules that apply to working in this manner (some of which are discussed below).

The rules for sharing an arena.

1. Always ask permission to enter an arena if there is an instructor already using it. Do the same before you leave. This is very important because the other instructor may need time to take hold of the bridle of the horse with which they are working, in order to prevent it deciding that it too has come to the end of its work and try to depart with the other horses. Thank the other instructor for sharing with you.

2. If sharing the whole arena, all the slower paces must be ridden on an inside track, thus leaving the outside track available for anyone wishing to ride at a higher gait. Thus someone who is walking must use the inside track and one who is trotting or cantering should use the outside track. This is irrespective as to which direction they are proceeding.

3. Should both rides be working at the same pace in opposite directions, then, the rides *must pass left hand to left hand at all times.* (See fig. 2)

4. When rides do have to pass one another, then those on the inside *must* leave sufficient room for those on the outside to proceed. Its no use your clients taking what they believe to be the inside track, whilst in reality the horses approaching them find that they are being squeezed up against the wall or fence. If this is allowed to happen, then you will probably have a kicking match.

Of course, having made clear to your class what is required of them, you may *not* leave it up to them. I am frequently amazed by the number of people who seem quite incapable of going, correctly, either on the left or right rein as they have been instructed to do. You *must* control them the whole time, think ahead and anticipate what may be going to happen and, if necessary, quickly apply a corrective command in a very strong voice. If they still don't react, then bring them to halt at once.

Splitting the arena and, later, using the whole area.

You may well start your lesson by working at one end, but you may prefer not to continue in this way for the whole lesson. If you find that things are going well and that all the horses are well behaved, you may then approach the other instructor towards the end of the lesson and ask them if they would mind your clients going large for the last few minutes. Further more should you intend to include a canter during this period, you should not do so until you have made certain that the other instructor is quite happy about this. My rule is - When in doubt don't!

Your voice in a shared environment.
In an earlier chapter, I have written about the necessity of projecting your voice in order that you may be clearly heard. When you share an arena you do need to exercise a degree of tact. Should you be blessed, as I am, with a voice that can be projected over at least two fields (no I don't mean that I shout, my voice *carries,* or so I have been told!), then you should take care to keep your voice low. Failure to so do so may drown out the voice of the instructor with whom you are sharing. Should you have a class of younger clients, you should also avoid games that, in a state of excitement may cause them to shout out in support of their team-mates.

What sort of exercises should you *not* embark on in a shared arena?
When you share an arena you should not embark upon any type of work that may cause problems for the instructor with whom you are sharing. I have in mind for example jumping. You may ask 'Why should this present a possible problem? After all you could insist that the jumps only be low ones and approached at the trot?' My reply is that though this is all very well in theory, in practise this may not be the case. Some horses, as soon as they see a jump, think only of canter and all too often the rider is unable to prevent this. Thus we have a possible scenario where the horse rushes at the jump and because the rider is trying to prevent this, it gets its stride wrong. The horse stumbles, dislodges the rider and goes dashing off into that part of the arena being used by your colleague who might be teaching a novice or someone of a nervous disposition!

A useful exercise for a shared environment.
When you do have to share an arena it is a good idea to have exercises in mind that lend themselves to a restricted area. One such is the change of rein through a circle (see chapter 15 - Exercises to form a lesson). It is possible to produce a quite comprehensive lesson based on this movement because one may introduce elements from walk through to canter which are mentally quite stimulating for a client and yet which will not entail the necessity of having to ask your client to go large. One may also use this type of movement when the area is restricted due to poor surface conditions, such as after extensive periods of heavy rain.

At the end of the lesson.
Do thank the other instructor and clients if it is you who have been allowed to join the arena.

Working according to conditions.
It is extremely important that you work the horses in your class according to the prevailing conditions. This applies both to the weather and the condition that the horses are in when they come to you. Now it is obvious that, during a hot day in the summer, it is not acceptable to give the class exercises that are so strenuous for the animals that they end up dripping with sweat. This is not fair to the horses nor the next instructor who may have to use some of them. For though in an ideal world, a horse that has just done an hours work may be expected to have some time off for it to recover, in the environment of a school, especially one catering for weekend riders, this may not always be practical. Several horses might be out of work due to lameness or colic. In which case others may have to work two, maybe even three hours, without a break. Therefore you must make allowances and adjust the work according to the conditions. If you do not do so, then you hand on a problem to the colleague who has to follow you. Even if the horse does not continue to work, you will still present a problem for the groom who must walk the horse until it cools down in order to avoid it getting a chill. I have sometimes had a sweaty horse passed on to me and my clients know what to expect – they are not going to do very much until that horse has cooled off. In the case of clients going out hacking this is particularly unfair but you may be sure of one thing - *all* my horses, out on a hack, no matter in what condition they are at the start, return cool and dry.
Does and don'ts
Don't keep children (or for that matter adults) standing around on a cold day, while you give them a long

lecture about what it is they are going to do. If you do have to explain something and you are using an outdoor ménage, then try and use a part that is sheltered by an outbuilding or hedge that will shield everyone from the wind. On a cold day it's no good proceeding with a routine that you have previously worked out but which involves work with minimal movement such as turns about the forehand or rein back. You need, particularly, to watch out for children who are not warmly dressed. Try to get every thing going quietly but briskly. After a very short period at the walk go to a trot for a period long enough for them to warm up. You must tailor your program to suit the weather. When the weather is cold have games that involve everyone taking part at the same time. Cowboys and Indians for example or games where all those taking part, simultaneously, compete against everyone else. During the summer, when days are warm you can have games that involve a member of one team competing, individually against one from another whilst the remainder wait their turn. In very warm weather this will enable you to avoid the ponies getting too hot and tired as a result of the heat.

The voice as an aid to producing a good lesson.
When you are in the arena you are centre stage. It is almost as if you are the ringmaster of a circus. If you have good presence and a high degree of simpatico with the horses then they will listen to your instructions rather than those of their riders. As I have said elsewhere, they will go well for *you*. However it is your job to provide exercises that will pass control from yourself to each individual in the class. The manner in which these exercises are ridden will be an indication as to the degree of success that you and your clients are achieving.

Inevitably you will still remain the main actor in the spectacle that you are helping to create for indeed if you are successful it is a *spectacle* that will provide the finish to your lesson. By that time all the riders will have answered the questions, no matter how simple, that you have set for them. They will have ridden all the movements smoothly and precisely. There should be a general feeling of satisfaction all round, both in horses and riders.

Your voice and the manner in which you speak are one of the essential components of this production. When addressing the class make sure that your vary the tone of voice. If you maintain a constant pitch, then, it is very likely that it will sound boring.

Listed below is a synopsis of the main points of interaction between you and clients.

1. Do not shout at clients but speak to them calmly and politely.
2. Ask them if they understand what you are saying.
3. Encourage them to speak up if they do not.
4. **When answering a query, never show impatience or imply that the client is rather stupid because they did not understand. The fault will probably lie with you for taking a mental short cut or through speaking in jargon.**
5. If you do use technical terms, make sure that *all* the clients understand your meaning. Ask them if they do! If they don't: then explain!
6. When addressing the class, as a whole, be sure that you use your diaphragm so that your voice carries and you can be clearly heard by everyone. If you have a client who is slightly deaf, then turn to face them so that they can see your lips moving. (Many deaf people lip-read).
7. I do not like using the word 'OK?' as a punctuation mark or as a means of eliciting a response from clients that shows that they understand or agree with you. For me using such a word indicates a slapdash mental attitude in so far as that it is imprecise. It can have a multitude of meanings and each client may place their own interpretation on that word – none of which may be correct. Rather say 'Have I made myself clear?' or 'Is there anything that you do not understand?'
8. When speaking to an individual move up close to them and speak in a quiet voice. This is especially important if you have to give them a correction or remonstrate for an act, on their part, that is not acceptable. After all it is your job to instruct but not to embarrass.

Safety and etiquette when using an arena.
It is essential that you arrive sufficiently early to be able to check any arena that you may have to use. You must make sure that equipment that has been used for a previous lesson is stored away. I mean that it has been completely moved from the arena and not just moved to the side. In particularly I have in mind,

jumping equipment. I suppose that poles placed along the *very edge* of an arena would not be too much of a problem but uprights do constitute quite a hazard. Should a client become unbalanced and suffer a fall, from which they suffer injury as a result of their landing on top of an upright, you may leave yourself open to an accusation of negligence. It may well be that you had no control over the client's loss of balance but you should have made sure that the only thing with which they are going to make contact is the ground and that is hard enough.

Of course giving a jumping lesson is another matter. In this case you must make provision either to have had the course constructed before you started or, better still, allow sufficient time and have assistance available to be able to construct the required jumps at the point in your lesson when they will be needed. At the end of the lesson be sure that everything is properly stored away.

Removing droppings.

The efficiency of most all weather surfaces depends on the ***removal of droppings as soon as they fall.*** You should leave an arena, as you would *like* to find it. That means free of droppings. However you need to take precautions before you go merrily on your way to picking them up. Obviously if they are left on the ground your class will probably trample them into the surface and this will make their subsequent removal more difficult. But you must ensure that the class is standing still quietly at halt before you start to pick them up, for it will not be possible for you to both pick up droppings *and* keep your eye on the horses at the same time.

Taking extra care especially with children.

This may particularly apply to freelance instructors. If you are earning your living in this manner you may be more likely to be asked to take a class with whom you have not worked before. I have no doubt that you will be able to assess the competence of your students as soon as you see them ride. You will also ask them, individually what experience they have had. Some people have a rather inflated idea as to their ability. In these circumstances make sure that you, truly, find out what this is. It is especially important if you are to work with children and be required to take them out to the fields. I mention this particularly because, occasionally, when I go off for a holiday the instructors designated to take out my classes sometimes get themselves into difficulties. The trouble is that they do not realise that, due to my experience, I get to teach many youngsters who are rather nervous. I overcome this by keeping everything under strict control. However in order to avoid having to walk on foot my stand-ins will usually be mounted and will take my class along the route that they usually take their own classes. Alas their pupils may be more confident and experienced than mine are and very shortly, it is possible, most of the ponies dash off with great glee and several riders are thrown or bale out. The parents are not best pleased.

Older riders having private lessons and sharing an arena.

Quite frankly this is a matter that should be dealt with by the office. However it is a problem with which you should be cognisant. Some older people, quite frequently, do not like sharing an arena with other riders (It puts them off). That is one of the reasons why they spend extra money on booking a private lesson. Should this be the case then have a word with your colleague in order to avoid causing unnecessary irritation.

The accident book.

It is imperative that whenever someone takes a tumble, then you must fill in the accident book. Make sure that you have a clear description as to what, exactly, happened and ensure that the client signs the form with you. The form should be completed in the office with a member of the management present.

The completing of an accident form is not intended to apportion blame it is simply a record of the incident and is filled in as much for your protection as for any other reason. Since this may, subsequently, form the basis of any claim by a client that may be made against you or the school it must be filled in *accurately*. For example, if a horse that you are using suddenly turns in off the track and, by so doing, causes the client to become unbalanced and fall, it is not advisable to state, in your report that the horse napped. Though you may use this term casually a lawyer will seize upon it and claim that a horse that was nappy was used for a novice client and that therefore the school was guilty of being negligent. In reality this may not have been the truth at all! The horse may simply have reacted to an instant flash of light against the stable wall caused by the reflection of sunlight from the windscreen of a passing tractor? Or possibly it was simply responding to an involuntary touch by the rider's outside leg, neither of which you were able to see!

56

Diagrams

Sharing an arena.   Figure 1

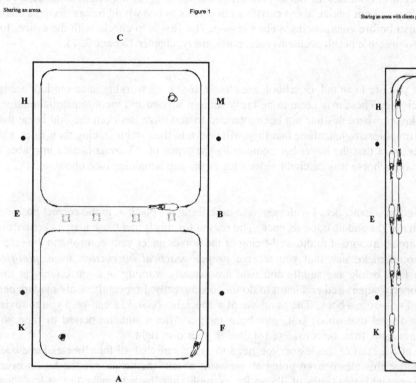

Figure no. 1. Sharing an arena.

Sharing an arena with clients going large (passing left hand to left hand).   Figure 2

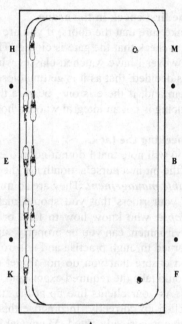

Figure no. 2. Sharing an arena with clients from both rides going large (passing left hand to left hand).

57

Chapter 6

Carrying out checks.

I consider the matter of checking both tack of horses and clients dress to be so important as to deserve a chapter of its own. In this chapter I am talking about carrying out checks as one would before giving a client a lesson on the lunge and also before commencing a class lesson. The first is to check, with the office, for previous assessment and also possible health problems (see, particularly, chapter 18 page 337).

The first check in the arena.

Make sure that the doors, if you are in an indoor school, are closed. If you are working in an outdoor arena, then check that the gate is closed. These may seem to be fairly straightforward and inconsequential matters. However I have watched classes where this has not been attended to and there has been the odd horse that has decided, that as it is getting close to lunchtime that they will return to their stable, taking their rider with them and, if there is one, be sure that the lower bar completing the fence of the arena is also in place. If fencing is not an integral whole a horse may catch the rider's leg in the gap remaining (see photo no. 4).

Checking the tack.

You will note that I do not go into exact detail with regard to describing the placing, in the correct position, of the bit in a horse's mouth nor the saddle upon its back. The reason for this is that these matters are part of *stable management.* They are so important to the well-being of the horses under your control and the safety of your riders that you should make sure that you receive *proper practical instruction* from *qualified people,* who know how to fit a bridle and saddle and who are actually working in a yard. Only in that environment can you be properly supervised and learn to do the job correctly. I repeat these are matters best learned through practise and not from a book. The purchase of a specialist book *15 can help you to revise and ensure that you do not forget that which you have been taught. After a suitable period of time you should take the required exams and, then, be considered skilled in your own right.

As your clients line up at the start of the lesson you need to make sure that all their horses have been tacked up correctly. In practise this means even going as far as to check whether or not the bit on every horse is correctly fitted. Many stables, at times of illness for example, may have to make use of less-then-completely-experienced staff. Ideally all their work should have been supervised but it is always possible that something may have been overlooked. It is up to you, and you alone, to carry out the final checks. *The responsibility lies with you!* Also be meticulous about checking girths, (both sides) even with clients whom you know well and trust. As you carry out your checks, don't forget to stroke the neck of each horse in a gentle manner, thus showing them that you mean them no harm.

Do bear in mind that as you check tack you should, at the same time, explain to your clients what it is that you are doing so that they may also learn. You must teach them to carry out these checks for themselves. After all it is not very satisfactory for you to teach clients to ride to an ever-improving standard of *equitation* if they do not know how to ensure that their horse has been tacked up correctly. What might happen to them when they ride at another establishment where the job has not been done correctly and no one bothers to check properly?

Lining up at the start of a lesson.

This is a matter that would appear to be fairly free of potential problems, but one does need to make sure that the safety parameters are clearly understood. In large yards you may find that in the interests of efficiency riders are already mounted when they enter the arena. If this is the case then proceed with checking as mentioned below.

I usually have the class line up along the centreline A – C. this is not necessarily a fixed rule (see addendum fig. 1.1). Should you be sharing an arena it might be better to make use of one end. It all depends on the space that you have available. As the riders line up, check that they are a safe distance apart. This, again, will depend on the size of the arena. There are two distances. The first is to have sufficient space (a good horses' length) to avoid one horse making contact with another should they kick out. Alternatively if space is at a premium have them lined up very close to each other with, say, just enough room for you to get between each horse in order to check the girths. Many people do not understand that horses standing close to one another do not have the room to develop a kick that can do any real damage. The disadvantage of this approach is that whereas they may not kick, they may well try to bite. In this case the rider can exercise some form of control with the reins but I consider that the safest way of dealing with such an animal is to take it out of the line and make it stand in front of and well away from the others.

However some schools do have the riders lead their horses into the arena before mounting (let us hope that they have been supervised during this short journey!) In this case I feel happier with a good horses length or slightly more. The reason for this is that many riders tend to forget about the horse as they concentrate on getting up. Horses become aware of this lack of concentration and use that moment to challenge the horse next to them, especially if they think that their personal space is being infringed. They may well whip round and as they do so the poor rider is caught in between.

Checking the girth and mounting.
Now ask the riders if *they* know how to **check the girth before mounting.** It is part of their tuition that they learn how to do this. If they do not know then you **must show them.** Then ask them if they know how to mount and that they are aware of the fact that the girth must *always* be checked before even a foot is placed in the stirrup. If they do not then you must assist them and arrange a demonstration so that they learn to mount correctly unaided. Even if they tell you that they do know, watch them carefully, being ready to correct any errors.

Check *all* tack.
With the horses in line make your approach from one end and ideally towards the near side. This should be from an angle of about 45 degrees. (See photo no. 5) Walk slowly and quietly and look at the rider and not, directly, at the horse. (Many horses don't like to be looked at in the eye. It is for them, a form of confrontation).

Walk down the line, as you do so first have a quiet word for each horse. Then talk to the rider asking their name or using it if it is already known to you. Ask after their health. As you reach the horses head start by reaching out and, gently, touching its neck, as you do so say its name. Look at its muzzle. Is there a discharge from the nostrils? If so the horse may have some form of chest infection and you will have to remember this during the lesson and be prepared to make allowances in its work.

Checking the bridle and reins for a client about to work on the lunge.
The bridle (*3)
In this case the horse will have a *Cavesson lunge bridle* (This is a special bridle used when you are teaching with the horse on a lunge rein) as well as the usual bridle. You must make sure that the nosepiece is tight enough to prevent the bridle twisting but without pinching. It should be placed at the same height as the normal noseband). The jowl strap should also be tight enough to assist in preventing slipping. There also should be a neck strap and, possibly, side reins. For novices I do not, usually, attach the side reins to the bit. These are used, when correctly adjusted, to produce a rounded outline in the horse. I do not think that one has to consider outline when one is simply teaching someone to sit tall and learn to balance. The job is hard enough, for the horse, as it is. Best to either not have them fitted or, if they are, then to leave them securely attached to the rings on the side of the saddle. Now you are casting your eyes over the bridle proper (this, generally, have been fitted with the normal noseband removed). You make sure that the bit is placed correctly (both sides); browband should be level etc. check that all the straps have been placed in their keepers. Pass on and check (if fitted) neck strap and breastplates**. The reins of the bridle proper should be twisted so that they are shortened and secured by the throatlatch (see photo no. 6). Until such time as your client is going to pick them up, they must remain secured.

Checks of a bridle for clients about to receive an ordinary lesson in a class.
These are essentially the same as those for the client about to have a lesson on the lunge. In this case, of course, you will not have the lunging cavesson fitted and the bridle will probably have a noseband and, possibly, a martingale, neck strap and rein stops. You do need to check that the client is holding the reins correctly. The rein should not be twisted and lie flat against the horse's neck. The *spare loop should rest under the bit rein on the off side.* Now your gaze travels down the neck and over the withers.

The saddle
The saddle must be checked to ensure that it is a proper fit for the horse. Do not assume, that, simply

because the horse has been tacked up before being delivered to you, that the correct tack has necessarily been used. Oh bless you no! It is perfectly possible for someone acting as a temporary helper to have taken the wrong tack. If it is incorrect, then, send the horse back and have it changed. Let the person responsible, *out of your clients hearing*, have a piece of your mind, Even if it is the right tack for the horse, you still need to ensure that the saddle is placed properly on the horses' back (neither too far forward nor back). Sometimes it has been placed so far forward so that the horse's shoulder is not free. If this is the case, ask the client to dismount, undo the girth and refit the saddle yourself. To do this place the saddle on the back almost over the lower part of the withers then allow it to slide down the back (under gentle hand pressure) and settle in its correct position but not too far back. (See drawing no. 3) Doing it this way not only ensures that it lies correctly but also makes certain that all the hairs underneath are all lying in the same direction.

Be sure to check that it is the correct fit and not pinching or inclined to rock. Above all be sure that the saddle does not sit so low so that it is pressing against horses' spine. There should be space for at least three fingers placed on top of each other between the saddle arch and the horse's spine (see photo no. 7). If there is not enough room to do this, it is possible that the saddle may have been dropped and the tree broken. In such a case there will be no way that the clients' weight will be distributed correctly over the muscles running *alongside* the spine. Instead their weight will be directed on to the top of the bones of the spine, which may prove to be extremely harmful and painful to the horse. (See drawing no.5.) I have a specimen of backbone, acquired after a post-mortem had been carried out. The exostosis (bony deposit), in the area underneath where the saddle would have rested is so bad that I am sure that during life the poor horse suffered periods of acute pain (see photo no. 8). If you receive a horse into your class tacked up with a badly fitting saddle, then have it returned to the yard so that it may be changed.

If the saddle also has a numnah, this should be lying, evenly each side and flat without any wrinkles. It should have been lifted, in the centre, slightly off the horses back so that it reflects the shape of the gullet of the saddle. (See drawing no. 6) If it is lying flat across the horse's spine then this can cause just as much injury as a badly fitting saddle. If it is not correct then attend to it!

The girth
Your hand is now sliding down the neck, over the shoulder and down to the girth. You check this again ensuring that you can just get two fingers, but no more, between it and the horses' side. All the time you are talking quietly to the rider, telling them what you are doing. If the girth is loose ask the rider to move their leg forward and hold up the saddle flap for you while you tighten the girth (one strap at a time). At this time glance at the girth and ensure that no part is worn and in danger of breaking. Check the buckles and see that they are not bent out of shape (carry out these checks to both sides).

If the girth is done up to the top hole on each side, and your experience leads you to believe that though it appears to be tight but the horse is inclined to blow out, have the client dismount immediately. Summon a groom to bring you a new girth of the correct length, or else have the horse taken away to have this done. Similarly if the girth, girth straps or stitching is worn and you think that that one might possibly break have someone come with a replacement. Apologise to the client and explain that this is for their safety. As you carry out your safety checks explain to the client what it is that you are doing and why. Tell them to learn the drill themselves for they may not always be riding at a stable where the standards of safety are as high.

The horse's legs and feet.
Now let your eyes travel down to the legs and feet. If boots have been fitted make sure that they are put on and done up correctly. Now look at the feet. Are the clenches of the shoe nails tight or are they starting to rise. In the case of loose shoes, again, have the rider dismount and have the horse taken away and replaced with the a spare horse. I am in two minds as to whether or not you should allow sufficiently experienced clients to lead the horses away, by themselves. If they have passed a stable management exam in which they were required to demonstrate leading correctly and they are always in your sight, then I suppose that this may be acceptable. If this is not the case then don't take a chance. Hold the horse for them and ask them to go on foot and summon assistance from a groom. *You must remain* with your class at all times. Do not leave them unattended.

** Note I have not gone into detail as to the exact checks for fitting these accoutrements because it would take forever. You should refer to B.H.S. The Manual of Horsemanship *12.

Checking the clients' dress.

People just starting to learn to ride may wear all manner of clothing. I do not pay too much attention to this provided that they are not wearing items that could prove to be positively dangerous. I have in mind such items of jewellery as earrings that are worn through pierced ears At the time that I write the fashion has gone even further and people have nose rings, lip rings and heavens knows where else). None of these items are acceptable in any form whatsoever. You may find that a client turns up in tracksuit bottoms or similar clothing. Since one may never be sure that clients may decide not to proceed with the sport, it is unreasonable to expect them to invest in jodhpurs, riding jackets and so forth, before they have had a chance to make a decision as to whether or not they will continue. But there are two items of clothing that *must be of an acceptable standard* and these are the crash hat and footwear.

The office should have intercepted problems of this sort, *before* the client even goes out to meet the horse. If the client does not own a helmet, then the office should have a supply and will provide one of the correct size. The client may hire this for the duration of the lesson. Whatever the case riding *helmets must be manufactured to the required government safety standard*, and you must still carry out your own checks. It's no use, after a fall, saying that you thought that the matter had already been dealt with. Pay special attention to those clients who *do* have their own helmet. They may have borrowed this from a friend and even if it does fit correctly, then it may well not be of the standard required by the current regulations. Shoes or boots must have a *proper heel* in order to prevent the foot from slipping through the stirrup and *smooth soles. Trainers and shoes without heals are completely unacceptable*. Finally, at an early stage of their riding career a client does not need to carry a whip of any sort whatsoever.

The contents of pockets.

One point that must not be overlooked is to ask whether your clients are carrying, in their pockets, any item that might cause an injury were they to sustain a fall. I have in mind a sharp object such as a ballpoint pen. Even the aerial of a mobile phone could cause a nasty depression in someone's' side if it were in an awkward position were the owner to land on the ground.

Mobile phones.

Believe it or not these days you must even remember to ask all clients if they are carrying mobile telephones. I mention this because it is not simply a matter of the carrying of an object that could hurt but also because *they may well not have remembered to switch them off!* Just imagine the effect of the first bars of Beethoven's 9th Symphony or Mission Impossible blaring out shortly after your client has just embarked on a canter!

All such items should be switched off and given to you for safekeeping but don't forget to return them at the end of the lesson!

Now pay attention to the riders' position.

Finally turn your attention to the rider and, gently make any corrections that you may deem necessary to their position.

This means that they should be sitting tall, the **head balanced on the neck**, with shoulders back and chest out, sitting on their seat and *not* the fork of the pelvis, elbows tucked loosely into their sides. The hands are carried as a pair and are *soft and motionless.* Each thumb is pointing to the horses opposite ear. The line running from their elbows through the wrist and on down to the bit is straight. The knee is bent only sufficiently to help the thigh being brought to bear against the horse's side, to lend support to the body. The toes turned in further encourage this. The heels being pushed down must remain springy. The head is held high and the rider always prepared to look where they wish to go. The whole body is in a state of *complete relaxation.* 'Wait a minute I hear you say' or if you haven't then you should jolly well do so now 'If the rider is to sit motionless how do they accommodate the forces produced by the horses movement, especially when it comes to trot and canter?' Well now that's a very good question and one that I am glad that you asked. There is *one part* of the body that does move and in fact *must move* if all else is to remain in place. That is the *pelvis just below the small of the back*. (See drawing no. 7). *The support derives from the abdominal muscles* flexing slightly for every movement, be it walk, trot or canter. For this is the component of the body that acts as a shock absorber both enabling the upper part of the rider's body to remain still and also allowing the seat to remain in firm and in constant contact with the saddle.

The greatest need to absorb the shocks of movement, naturally occur during the gaits that have a defined

61

'moment of suspension' such as trot and canter. One way of overcoming this for the trot is simply to learn to 'rise'. However your clients must also *learn to sit to the trot*. If their backs are rather stiff and inflexible or the horse has a pronounced elevation each stride, then the rider may not be able to absorb this upward force. Even with a flexible spine any residual energy may be also absorbed by springiness in the heel. (See drawing no. 8)

You must make the points very clear to your pupils, for these are the very foundations upon which all else will be built.

Don't forget latecomers.

There is one time when you may be prone to overlook carrying out a check and that is when someone joins your class after it has started. You may be concentrating on the way in which your class is carrying out your first exercise. Or else you may consider that if the person has joined you from another class, then they will have, already, been subject to a check. Never take anything for granted. It is always possible that the checks have not been carried out thoroughly, if at all! Suppose for example that the girth is loose or has become loose because the horse was blown out when previously examined? The rider joins you and proceeds with the movement in hand and then they fall due to the fact that the saddle has slipped. What do you say when you are asked 'did you check'? - Of course it should not happen because if you do your job properly the saddle will not slip.

Always try to be aware. (Horses that bite and stamp).

In this case I am referring to your own safety. Some horses may try to bite you; others may stamp down very heavily with a foreleg, on your toes. If you are positioned incorrectly you may be hurt. This may seem to be unnecessary advice for those who have already spent some time around horses and you will most often be very well aware of the little foibles that some animals develop. You may even treat an attempted nip as a bit of a joke. However no matter how careful you may be, there will be those moments when you are concentrating on carrying out your checks and when your attention is concentrated on your client, that is the moment a wily horse may try to take a nasty lump out of you (a padded jacket is a help because the padding will be nipped and not you!). Never treat an attempted bite or treading on your toes casually. Deliver, with your hand, a sharp, staccato, slap on the neck immediately.

Retribution must be delivered at once.

I am very particular about punishment being received immediately it is deserved. In this way the horse associates it with its misbehaviour. If delayed then the association is lost. It is doubly important because many horses only become antisocial after they have been clipped out and you will not want to allow a casual misdemeanour to develop into a vice.

A final consideration.

When you have thoroughly checked all horses and riders, you now need to consider them as a whole. By that I mean that you allow your eye to roam over the whole class and as you do so you make a note of anything that you might have to keep in mind while the lesson proceeds. This may be a rider whom you feel is a little anxious about the horse that they have been given, or, you may have noted that one of your riders is quite heavy.

All this information is very important and it depends entirely upon you taking the trouble to take note. So far as the first example that I have given is concerned I need comment no further, but for the second example, the overweight rider, the dangers are not so obvious. The client may well have been given a 'weight carrying' horse but even so you must not forget to make due allowance during your lesson. Carrying weight does cause a horse stress and may also result in a back injury that will only show at a latter time. The fact that the horse appears to be big and strong enough to do the job may not be enough if, for example, one of your riders sits very heavily and you have decided to do a prolonged canter. The hurt engendered by your not making due allowance and modifying your programme, even for that one individual alone, may result in the horse having a sore back the following day. This may be especially so if the animal is young.

Keeping an eye on the changing weather.

Watch what sort of clothing your clients are wearing. On a hot day but where there is a possibility of rain, some people will start off the lesson wearing very thick rainproof jackets. You should monitor them and ask, during the lesson if there is anyone who wishes to discard a layer or two. Should they decide to do so, then, there are rules to be followed.

1. ***Do not allow a rider to remove any clothing until either you or a helper is holding their horse***. Simple jackets and bodywarmers may be removed whilst the rider is still mounted provided you know that the horse is not head shy, even then you must tell the rider to take care for even the quietest horse may become alarmed if a garment is flapped around its head.
2. A rider must dismount, should any article of clothing need to be removed over the riders' head or involve the removal of the rider's helmet.
3. If you are a male instructor and the only person around to hold the horse whilst a female rider discards unwanted garments, then do not look at them directly as they are doing so. If you do, you may unwittingly cause them some embarrassment.
4. All discarded garments must be taken and placed safely out of the arena in an area where they will be sheltered and not likely to flap in any breeze that may spring up.
5. At the end of the lesson be sure to remind everyone to return, after dismounting, and collect his or her belongings.

Body armour.

These days many riders choose to wear back protectors. I think that this is very sensible since an injury to the spine can lead to very restricted mobility and, possibly, considerable and continuous pain. However as far as you are concerned as an instructor you must ***beware*** when asked to give ***advice***. I have in mind hot weather. A client may ask you if you think that it is all right if they remove the protection. I personally do not wear a back protector unless I am jumping. My personal view is entirely beside the point and you need to be careful with your reply. You should tell the client that (at the time that I write) there is no legal requirement to wear body protection for ordinary riding. The removal of such protection is therefore entirely up to the client and that they should think very carefully before so doing. They need to be sure that any accident policy that they may have is not nullified by what the company holding cover considers to be 'A failure to take reasonable and adequate precautions to avoid injury'. Should they still decide that they wish to remove the protector, and then you must tell them that you will not accept any responsibility for any injury that may occur should they sustain a fall. Finally they must dismount before taking the garment off. Whatever the case, if a client is wearing protection of this sort, you must carry out a check to ensure that it has been properly fitted.

Now is there anything else that you need to check?

You might be thinking to yourself that we have thought of just about everything? But there is just one more thing that can affect the safety of your class and that is a thoughtless ***spectator***. Now with the best will in the world no matter how carefully you carryout your checks of horse and rider in order to maintain the highest standards of safety, no matter how well you have chosen your exercises to suit both your clients and horses, all that can be rendered as nought if you overlook the effect of thoughtless acts by people who have come to watch.

These may be Mums and Dads, friends or simply people who stop by chance to observe. There is no reason why you should not encourage people who are not riding to take an interest, but what you must remember and make an allowance for, is that they probably have absolutely no idea how to behave when in close proximity to horses.

Remember that your horses have almost a 360-degree ability to see what is going on around them. It is one of their basic survival strategies. Even though they are no longer living in the wild, a sudden movement seen out of the corner of an eye can startle them. You may have paid no attention to the people who are standing around watching. They simply do not figure in your scheme of things. Your attention is entirely given to the clients in your class for whom you are responsible. However the removal of say a brightly coloured raincoat accompanied by much flapping about as the garment is taken off or the opening and closing of an umbrella, can cause even the most quiet of horses to shy. This may set in motion a chain reaction in which other horses become alarmed even though they may not have noticed the original event. It is in the way of horses – flee first – check up afterwards. As a result you may have several people sustain a fall through a very simple matter that could have been avoided.

What to do?

Simply be observant. If you see that you have, even one spectator, remind them not to make any sudden moves, put up an umbrella or shout out when they see a friend approach. It is a seemingly insignificant matter but it can save a lot of trouble. Similarly you must make sure that children, especially young ones are kept quiet and under control.

Maintaining your standards.

After all that I have written above, you must remember that none of these checks will be effective unless you carry them out! By that I mean don't just read the words and pay a mental 'lip service' filled with good intentions. You must meticulously practise carrying out these checks until they become second nature. Even then you must constantly carry out checks on yourself to ensure that you have not grown casual. *It's all about really looking and really seeing. Your greatest enemy is complacency!*

There is one other matter with which we need to deal. This concerns your knowledge or lack of it with regard to the horses that you will be using during a lesson. *If you are unfamiliar with any of them, do ask the office* before you take the class. It is no use having a 'near miss' as one horse kicks out at another simply because you did not know that that horse was inclined to do so. Forewarned is forearmed!

Final thoughts on safety

I am referring here to the safety distance between each horse, especially during the time when horses are lined up and tack is being checked. You may well have tried to ensure that the **distances are correct** as each horse stands beside the other, however you must make certain that your *clients understand* that **this must be maintained**, especially when you have moved on to check other horses. They alone are responsible. Casualness in this matter can lead to a kick, which, in turn, can lead to a broken bone and possible death for the unfortunate recipient. If the clients are novices and therefore incapable of such control over their horses, then, they should have an assistant to help them.

In the interim, since the first printing of this book, third party claims have grown considerably (see also chapter 8). It is now my view that, with novices, you should always have a helper to hand who, strongly, holds the stirrup leather on the offside while mounting takes place. This is to avoid the possibility of an animal breathing out (some horses are very good at doing this,) as the client starts to mount and the saddle, as a consequence, slipping, (the helper should also hold the rein near the bit to prevent any movement by the horse). You are then free to be on the near side to supervise the pupil and help them if necessary. With more experienced riders, who do how know how to mount, you should still hold the leather and rein yourself. Thus you must assist every rider in turn. (This obviously does not apply to giving a leg up but this may only take place with an experienced rider). *Remember also to check girths and straps for broken stitching or fraying and make sure that stirrups are large enough so that the client's boots or shoes do not get stuck in them.*

It is now becoming prevalent for all mounting to take place from a mounting block. This is a very sensible idea since a mounting block both avoids strain on the horses back, the saddle and also makes things much easier for those who may be either not very athletic or small in stature. For example a short person is mounting a large horse or a small child a pony. * Now what is really important is, are the mounting blocks easily accessible and are they of sufficient height? In other words are they so made as to enable someone suffering from, say, arthritis in the back to be able to mount without undue pain? Of course the exception is remounting while out hacking after having opened and then closed a difficult gate, for example one that has come off its hinges. This should, in any case, be carried out by the instructor or escorts.

* Pointed out to me by Louise Hickman a colleague at my present yard.

Drawings

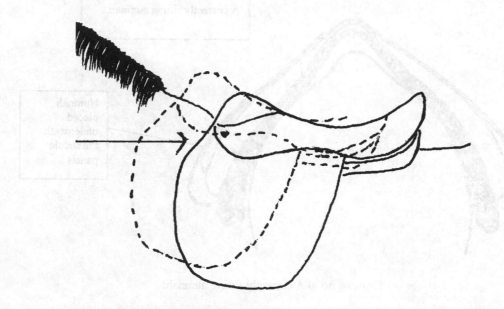

Drawing no. 3.

Placing the saddle in the correct position.

Drawing no. 3. Placing the saddle in the correct position.

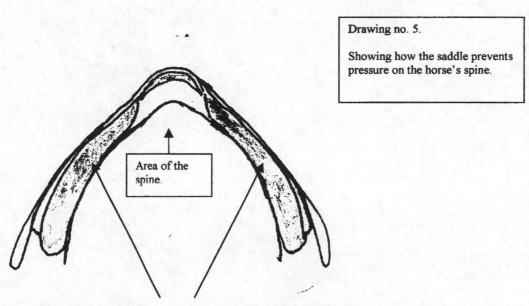

Drawing no. 5.

Showing how the saddle prevents pressure on the horse's spine.

Area of the spine.

Panels (Looking at the knee rolls as seen from the front of the saddle) redistribute the riders weight.

Drawing no. 5. How the saddle prevents direct pressure on the spine.

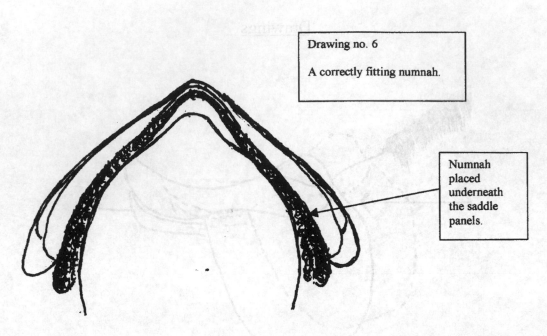

Drawing no. 6

A correctly fitting numnah.

Numnah placed underneath the saddle panels.

Drawing no. 6 A correctly fitting numnah.

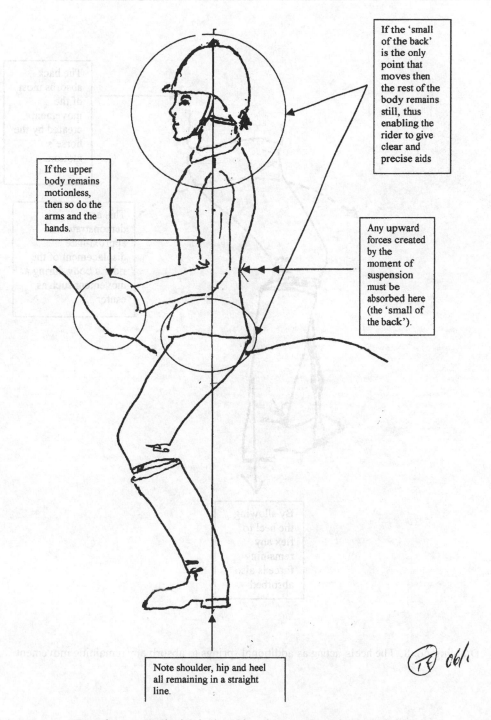

Drawing no. 7

The back absorbing the moment of suspension.

If the 'small of the back' is the only point that moves then the rest of the body remains still, thus enabling the rider to give clear and precise aids

If the upper body remains motionless, then so do the arms and the hands.

Any upward forces created by the moment of suspension must be absorbed here (the 'small of the back').

Note shoulder, hip and heel all remaining in a straight line.

Drawing no. 7. The back absorbing the 'moment of suspension'.

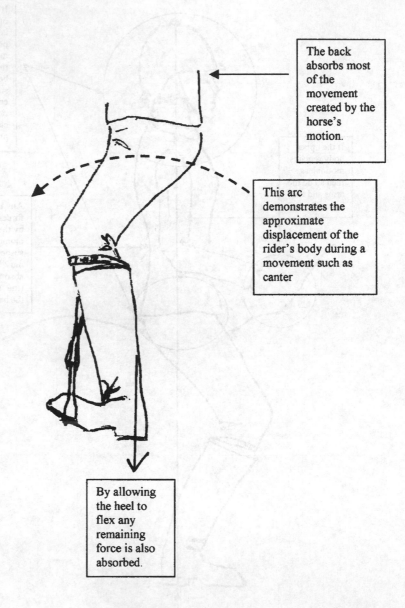

Drawing no.8.

The heels acting as additional springs to absorb any remaining movement.

The back absorbs most of the movement created by the horse's motion.

This arc demonstrates the approximate displacement of the rider's body during a movement such as canter

By allowing the heel to flex any remaining force is also absorbed.

Drawing no. 8. The heels acting as additional springs to absorb any remaining movement.

Diagrams.

Figure 1.1.

Addendum

Advancing every other rider two horse's lengths so that the ride is in an open order
format thus providing extra room for mounting in a small arena.

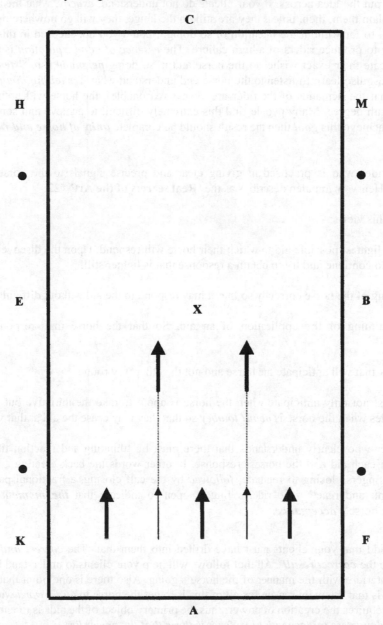

Figure no. 1.1 Making room for safe mounting in a small arena

Chapter 7

The basic aids.

The aids are the foundation of communication between rider and horse. This is so fundamental that it is my view that the means of describing and teaching them requires a chapter of its own. I have separated it from the chapters that deal with teaching people in a class because the understanding of the aids depends entirely on *your ability* to put the idea across. If your clients do not understand, *exactly*, what the aids are, and you do not *clearly* explain them, then, unless they are still on the lunge, they will go nowhere on their mounts or alternatively go all to far without the intention of so doing. Should you not succeed in this endeavour, you will never be able to produce riders of a high calibre. The *essence of good equitation* is the ability of the rider to communicate their exact wishes to the horse and in so doing *persuade it to listen* to them. At the same time they must also learn to listen to the horse and understand what it is *telling them*! The goal being that, (providing that the demands of the rider are always reasonable), the horse will both understand and obey them to the nth degree. Many people find this extremely difficult to achieve and some of them never do so. If they can achieve this *goal* then the result should be complete *unity of horse and rider*.

Your Target.
Is to produce a rider who is practised in giving clear and precise signals to the horse. Someone who understands what Henry Wynmalen describes as the **'Real secrets of the Art'** *22.

Below a précis of his views: -

1. To detect the lightest possible aid to which their horse will respond. Upon the discovery of this lightest possible aid, to continue and try to obtain a response that is lighter still!

2. The positioning of the horse correctly so that it may respond to the aid without difficulty.

3. The correct timing of the application of an aid. So that the horse may respond smoothly and immediately.

4. A quick reflex that will anticipate the horse and not the other way round.

5. The rider must not only anticipate when the horse is about to take the initiative but also be one who also appreciates when the horse is *about to obey* so that they may cease the aid at that very moment.

6. Finally a rider who clearly understands that there must be 'thinking and reaction time' between the application of each aid and the horses' response. In other words the back creating a pressure through the seat, the fingers closing to regulate, *followed* by the calf closing, a fractional pause to allow the horse to 'think and react'. The rider's fingers open to indicate that *the moment is now* as they *anticipate* the horse's *acceptance*.

I would humbly add that your clients must have drilled into them that 'The *correct and consistent aids*, generally, produce the *correct result*'. All that follows will help your clients to understand how to give clear aids that do not interfere with the manner of the horse's going. Also there is one point that they must never overlook and that is that the main reason for all of this is to get the horse to go *forward* with great accuracy and energy. This requires the creation of power; thus the primary object of the aids is to encourage the horse to *engage his hindquarters underneath him, for it is there that the power lies*.

Helping the client to overcome their instinctive reflexes.
The greatest obstacle to making progress is that of fear and the instinctive reflex. It is to this end that you must direct your efforts. It may be helpful if we adumbrate some of the problems.

1   Many people are afraid of the horses even though they like to ride. This is very understandable since horses are generally very large creatures. Unfortunately they have a highly developed sense of smell and will pick up on that fear.

2   This fear sometimes manifests itself, at the very least, in a lack of consideration or even disdain.

3   Most riders instinctively feel that pulling on the rein will stop the horse. Though there are, undeniably, occasions where it may be necessary give several quite **strong** half halts if the horse decides to take a firm hold, pulling will have the opposite effect to that intended – the horse will try even harder to get away from the discomfort.

4   While it may be true that it is sometimes necessary to 'kick on' this is not a good rule for general equitation. Continuously kicking a horse with one's heals, for no real reason, usually results in the horse becoming 'dead to the leg'; in other words it learns to take no notice.

5   Frequently the wish to go forward is expressed by the rider by *leaning forward* instead of sitting down and upright in the saddle.

6   Rising *before* the horse has started to trot.

Your paramount job is to deal with these problems before they become bad habits. If you have clients attending your class whom, unfortunately have already developed them, it may be quite difficult for you to produce a change. But you must persist until you succeed.

Playing the notes and producing a tune
In order to get the difficult concept of the correct aid across it may help to create, in the inexperienced riders' mind, an analogy. One example is playing the piano.

There will be times when your clients, though convinced, that they have given the aid correctly still fail to get a good result. One reason is that even though an aid may be applied in the correct sequence –back /seat – hand - leg to hand or what have you, the horse still fails to comply. This may be due to the fact that though the **sequence may be correct, the timing may not**. In order to help your client understand, perhaps you may draw a metaphor from playing the piano. If one is told the exact position of various notes on the keyboard and also the sequence in which they may be pressed to obtain a series of tuneful notes, the application of this information, by someone without any piano playing experience, will not necessarily produce a tinkling tune. The reason for this is that even though one has been told where the notes are, there is a degree of hesitation before actually placing ones finger on the correct spot. The result is the production of a sound that is not fully formed. With practise the time delay shrinks as the student learns where those notes are. An experienced player will sit down and their fingers will run off the same notes in the correct order and with good cadence so that what emerges is a beautiful melody. They barely have to think about it. No more in fact than you are thinking about reading this book. So it is when giving the aid. It all depends upon the sequence, the cadence and the clarity of the message that will persuade a horse to co-operate and obey the riders' will.

Developing independent use of the body and limbs.
It will be obvious from the last paragraph that it is important that a rider learns to improve co-ordination. In chapter 8 'The Novice class' I have listed some exercises that clients should practise in order to improve their application of the aids. I suppose that they are not that different from practising scales on a piano. Your target must be to enable your clients to give **aids that are always consistent**. This is not a skill that is easy to learn because, generally speaking, many horses try to interpret the rider's wishes and in most cases they succeed, irrespective as to whether or not the aid has been given correctly. This allows the rider to get away with aids that are imprecise. One may say 'Well does this matter, so long as the rider gets where they want to go, in the end?' My reply is that it most emphatically does matter. If the rider learns to be consistent, then, no matter what horses they ride either during a lesson or at another time, all those horses will appreciate the clarity of their aids and give pleasure to the rider by giving a prompt and smooth response.

71

The convention.
In the paragraphs that follow I have described some aids in detail. As I have said elsewhere, it may well be that you have been taught in a different way. However aids are but a convention and there is no unalterable law that demands that horses be ridden through only one strict form of communication. It would be fair to say that, as time passes, new techniques continually evolve. Sometimes they are simply a passing fashion. Whatever the convention used, once a horse has been schooled in a particular way then the rider should use those aids in order that the horse understands what is being asked of it.

For the sake of further discussion the sequence that I mention is – *Back/seat –hand – leg – hand*. Why in this order? Why do I always prefix my aids with bracing the back? There are two reasons. The first is that, for me in the giving aids to the horse, the *back is the foundation for all future progress.* Secondly, any movement of the hand tends to restrict. This is particularly so when it comes to heavy handed riders. If the rider uses the action of the hand *first* in the sequence when they wish to go forward it is quite likely that this may be interpreted by the horse as a signal to stop. Therefore it is my view that it is *beneficial* for a rider to always apply an aid by first *bracing the back muscles*. This is a *signal* to the horse to provide an *increased impulse*. It is a movement of the riders' body that Wynmalen describes as an aid by 'association'. (*32 Dressage). It also assists the rider to place him or herself deeper in the saddle. Without the fingers closing around the rein the horse simply either goes faster or extends or both (it will be influenced by its confirmation).

However the closing of the fingers around the *outside* rein indicates that the impulse is to be regulated and used for some other purpose (a message that something else is to follow). What *follows is* the use of the *riders' leg or legs*. These now indicate the manner of the change e.g. both closing simultaneously behind the girth indicates a trot. They also reinforce the impulse created by the back. Finally the rider's *fingers* holding the outside rein *open* and by so doing tell the horse that '*the moment is now*'. These are but an example, for the language of the aids are developed by many combinations of the above and the horse will have learned these during its education.

Now I must make it clear that what I have just written is *my view of these matters.* Others may have different opinions. I have simply written this in my way because this is the logic that I see that should apply to the giving of aids. You, as instructor must be able to satisfactorily answer any question that a client may put to you with regard to your reasoning. Should you have your own ideas as to how aids may be explained, then so be it, but your answers must be able to stand up to questioning, for you should not expect your clients to accept your word simply as some form of mystical 'Holy Writ'!

For example a question that a client may ask.
In preparing for canter what is the logic in the form of leg aid, where the rider's inside leg requests energy and the outside leg indicates the lead? This is a very reasonable question. Are you able to answer coherently? Perhaps you might reply that as far as you are concerned these form part of the aid combination that you were taught? 'Ah yes', replies your client 'But *why* in that combination'? Have you given thought to this? Could *you* reply at once? My reply would be that there is logic for using the *inside* leg acting almost on the girth to create energy. A horse learning its work on the lunge receives the signal for greater impulse from the trainer who is standing on the *inside* as the horse *goes around him*. He therefore becomes familiar with this. The riders outside leg, following on behind the girth reminds the horse to strike off with the leg on that side. There is a logical symmetry to the whole thing.

By using the pressure of the back, together with another aid, an expert rider may almost invisibly, communicate without recourse to the rein at all. I used to ride my old friend Jeeves in this manner. Simply a light bracing the back muscles and a gentle touching with a leg behind the girth was sufficient to ask for and obtain canter from halt. So you may be saying to yourselves 'why bother to teach a combination of the back and leg at all? Why not simply touch the horse behind the girth?' My reply is that this might very well work, for we are talking about aids by 'association', but if one were to develop these to the extent that only one aid was required, then what would happen when the inexperienced rider, as so many do, touched the horse by accident? There might be an unsought-after response! At least by using a combination of two or more signals the likelihood of that happening is somewhat reduced. Furthermore of the two signals that I have mentioned the use of the back is something that most riders will have to think about first. However I feel that, perhaps I am taking you down a path that has no relevance here. For we are not discussing expert riders and all that I wish to do is to justify my particular point of view.

It is up to you to be sure that you be *exact in your description* of the various parts that form a complete aid.

You must leave nothing out. It is so easy to miss a small but significant element; one which if not applied may result in a poorly performed movement by the horse.

Make sure that your clients have understood.
You must also create a climate in which your clients are so stimulated by actually taking part in your classes that they question you. If they do not do so then you must question *them* in such a way that they feel compelled to give you an answer. It may not be the correct answer but it will be one that tells you whether or not they understand that which you teach them.

Having a standard by which to measure progress.
You need to have some way of observing the progress made by your clients. I would consider that this is best measured by *noting the fluency* with which your clients use the aids. Do they have to stop and consider what they have been asked to do? Or are they able to proceed without even thinking about it, thus leaving themselves free to turn their attention entirely to the horses' way of going? If I may use a simile to discuss this matter further. It is rather like dancing, not the variety practised by the majority of people at the time I write – Disco Dancing. In this milieu people generally stand facing one another (sometimes they dance entirely by themselves) and they move in an entirely freeform manner that may or may not be in time with the music. It's a case of anything goes. No- the dancing to which I am referring is now known as Ballroom Dancing. For nearly four decades, during which time I entered my teens, it was the excepted manner of dancing. There were many different rhythms such The Waltz, Quickstep, Foxtrot, Tango not forgetting Boogie- Woogy and Jive.

In this discipline the novice, say a young man, would approach a girl and ask her if she would like to dance. On approaching the dance floor he would inquire as to what sort of a dance was being played. 'I did think that it was a waltz' he would say 'I think that I know how to dance a waltz'. Upon receiving confirmation from the young lady that he is correct, he then starts to count out, quietly and laboriously to himself 'One, two, three' - 'One, two, three'. Taking the girl, firmly, in his arms he ventures onto the floor trying to place his feet in the manner that he believes is correct. By the time he has thought about it the music has moved on. 'Do you come here often?' he stammers and having no real sense of rhythm his feet occasionally tread on her toes. But by and large the pair manages to circumnavigate the floor without too much damage to either party.

The intermediate rider should be comparable to the dancer who asking the lady to accompany him onto the floor does not have to inquire of the rhythm. He knows simply by listening and as he stands tall and elegant his partner, placing her body close to his, receives the information for each proposed step simply by the pressure of his hip on hers and by the touch of his hand in the small of her back. As she responds so the couple proceed in graceful harmony around the dance floor changing rhythm as the session demands. Three time, two time, and four time – whatever - as the band plays on. The, *verbal,* conversation between them need only concern appreciation of one another. 'You do dance divinely' he breathes in her ear as she yields her body to his every touch. Their steps are clear, simple and straightforward.

Now the advanced rider. This fellow is the one who asks for a dance when no one else is on the floor. Why? Because they are playing a Tango!!! This is a dance that is perceived to be way beyond the ability of most people (the fact that this may not be entirely true is beside the point). It is a dance in which the steps are quite formal and yet there may also be a considerable degree of improvisation in their sequence. It is a response to a primal rhythm that requires great athletic ability and absolute simpatico between both partners. He guides his partner who responds with a flow of energy that derives from his lightest touches, each of which releases a series of steps that, while being the product of the moment, are, previously well rehearsed by both partners. Ultimately these produce a complete series of movements bound by the overriding cadenced rhythm. This is a dance of supreme sophistication and controlled passion. The dancers move with the artistry of precisely controlled movement. Every step will demonstrate a perfect interpretation of the signal given by one partner and understood by the other. It is a creation of the 'Haute Ecóle' of dancing. The spectators simply stand around the floor filed with admiration at the perfection of the whole presentation.

And thus it is with equitation in its various forms that start with the rider scarcely able to give the aids without taking sometime to think about what they have to do, through to the more accomplished rider who can now ride and uses the aids almost instinctively. Finally the advanced rider who through delicate touch and perfect balance, is able to elicit from his horse movements almost beyond its physical capability.

I am sure that you realise that my comparison derives from the end of that period extending back through centuries where the role of male and female were different and yet complimentary. If you consider this to be chauvinistic, then I can only reply that there were always ladies invitation dances.

It's like having different frequencies and bandwidth.

Are the aids for the partnership of the dance so different to those that we require for communication with the horse? I have used the above subtitle for this section in order to remind you, once again that the signals established between rider and horse is purely a convention. In the words of Henry Wynmalen. 'One may just as easily give a signal to a horse by attaching lengths of cotton thread to his ears'. As with broadcast *electrical* signals the rider and horse need to be on the same frequency. The manner of sending the signal or the bandwidth may differ. To simplify my meaning. As you watch your television you may select to receive signals that are sent to you by the TV Company through selecting the *frequency* on which they have been broadcast. But the bandwidth depends on whether you use digital or analogue means of reception. In other words satellite, cable or ordinary aerial.

The result of all this is that if the signals are in a language that you *understand,* you end up with information that either informs or entertains you, depending on the programme you have chosen. Both may well result in provoking a response from you. So it is with those riding horses. Information is passed from rider to horse via an *intricate language of signals.* But these signals are produced as a result of the stimulation of the horse's nerve endings, be it either those in its ears or those around its body or in its mouth.

The next problem for clients is that they don't realise that horses also have thought processes, which are very similar to those that we have ourselves. They are not mindless beings simply waiting for the ignition key to be inserted and the engine started. An intelligent horse may well try to take the initiative at some time and try to do so in an entirely innocuous manner. It may start to walk on as soon as the rider has mounted or it may proceed towards the fields instead of the arena. The horses' attitude towards the rider is shaped by the rider's reaction to this and the overlaying of his (the rider's) own will.

What the rider has to establish from the very beginning, even though they may be in-experienced, is a **private language** between themselves and the horse. Further more this language must override any thoughts about different matters that the horse may also have going on in its mind.

We are talking about good balance, speed of reaction and a kind response.

A good seat.
1. Achieved by developing perfect balance.
2. Perfect balance derives from an elegant position
3. The rider must be clear in his or her own mind that the object is to control the horse and to *enable* it to do the rider's bidding. All requests must be reasonable.

Balance, Deportment and Elegance.
Nowadays people, even off the horse, do not stand or move with elegance. This is especially so at the time that I write. Whereas in the past clothing tended to help with good posture (Corsets, starched collars and so forth), the casual look worn today does not promote this. There are occasions when some people are sufficiently self–aware to try and remedy this fault. On holiday - when they enter the hotel for the first time, board their cruise ship, or attend a public function such as a film premier, whenever they believe that they may be the subjects of public scrutiny they carry themselves accordingly. Walking tall, shoulders back and head held high. I know I have watched them. Unfortunately this good deportment lasts but a short time. I tell my clients to imagine that they are of noble decent that therefore they must carry themselves accordingly. Not only when they ride but also when they are off the horse as well. After all one does not see the Queen of England walking around with a slouch!

So far we have focussed the rider's attention on the need to get the horse to do their bidding. In most cases they already possess this desire. It is the reason that they have taken up the sport. However they may not be aware that the foundation of this obedience derives from the ability to maintain good balance and that this is aided by good posture. What we refer to as a good seat.

Why?
There are two reasons for balance being the foundation of communication. They are: -

1. If the rider's body is in good balance, then, it will remain quiescent. Involuntary movements, that distort the signals that the rider may give with seat, leg or hand, brought about by lack of balance, will be reduced to a minimum.
2. A motionless body will assist the horse as it tries to perform its given tasks. For it does not have to deal with the constantly changing dynamic which would occur if the rider were swaying about the whole time. (Before you ask about rising trot, the answer is that though the rider utilises the horse's motion to send the body slightly forward every other stride, it still remains in balance and *relatively* motionless).

Elegance should lead to tact.
No matter how well schooled the horses and riders are - because they may be more demanding - it is very important that they learn the correct way of introducing themselves. A period which may be a mere twenty minutes or even as much as two or three lessons, provide a time during which the new rider establishes with the horse their own particular means of communication, their standards and required manner of the horses going. Assuming that the horse has both the mental and physical ability to obey, this gradual approach will result in co-operation of the horse and satisfaction for the rider. To fail to do this simply induces a horse to set his jaw and to resist any request that the rider may make. (See photo no. 9). You must be prepared to make provision, in your lesson, for this requirement should it be necessary.

I have seen some riders reduced to tears as they try to get a well-schooled horse to go on the bit, simply because they hadn't bothered or been allowed to make a proper introduction.

Tact is the start of understanding.
This is the description of a born horseman by Waldemar Seunig *6 'A real horseman must not only be an expert – he must also be able to think and feel like a horse, that is, to realise that a horse is not equipped with *human* understanding. Such a horseman should be both horse and man – a centaur, not only physically, but also psychologically – anthropomorphic and hippomorphic'.

The word Centaur is probably a very good analogy. For a good horseman rides, in the main, by using his body and thigh. The lower leg (the calf) and the fingers through the reins do have their part to play but only in so far as that they are responsible for providing very refined signals that assist in regulation.

Teaching the aids.
I have described the aids listed below exactly as though I were standing in front of a class and about to ask them to perform a particular movement. Not only do I try to mention every part of the aid, I give the reasons why and also the possible errors that may occur should an aid be given incorrectly or the horse try to evade them.

The descriptions that follow are given purely as a guide. A means if you like, of organising your own thoughts so that you may impart the information to your clients in a manner in which *you* believe is most suited to their ability to understand. Nothing that I am about to write is necessarily 'Carved in Stone'. As I have previously said, the way we communicate with our horses is based on convention. This convention may vary from country to country. You may take my information in any order that you like. You may, for instance, consider that you wish to start off a novice by allowing them to take a feel of the reins from the very beginning. *It is entirely up to you.* I am simply creating my list in the way that seems to me to be logical.

A language from the horses' point of view.
Though this is not a generally held belief, horses, in common with dogs have a well-developed language of their own. This is quite usual for most animals that live in herds or packs. Without this language the structure of the herd could not be maintained. It is therefore not so fanciful to expect that a *different*, language may be learned by the horse when it deals with human beings. However it is a little harder for them to show their pleasure at meeting a rider whom they like, certainly not in a manner immediately recognisable to the weekend rider. They do not have the facial muscles for smiling and they are not given to wagging their tails and using the other signs of joy, as do dogs. But they will put their heads over the stable door and give a welcoming whinny. The rider should try to ensure that few or many meetings, when not

mounted, should result in the creation of friendly feelings. I repeat again that the language is a personal one for the horse is quite capable of distinguishing between each individual with whom they have to work. I sometimes ride school horses as against my own, when taking out a hack. As I send the ride away from me my fellow will shows signs of wishing to follow. Why not? This is his usual practise. I tell him, kindly, that I wish him to stand still so that I can view everything that is going on. We may meet again two or three weeks later. Again he indicates his desire to follow but less strongly this time. The time after that he stands still on a long rein!

Horses use different ways of expressing their feelings of displeasure as they perform the tasks requested by the rider. You and your clients should learn to recognise them. For example they cannot say in a loud voice 'Oih! How long is this exercise going on, I'm getting tired!' The most that they can do is to put back their ears, swish their tails or, as a last resort, catch the rider at a moment when they are unbalanced and dislodge them.

It follows that lines of communication should not be all one way. The rider must learn to note the signals that the horse is giving and to react *before* it is either inclined or forced to disobey. They have to learn to become *proactive instead of reactive.*

Different types of Aid.
These will be either natural or artificial.
Natural aids.
Natural aids are those signals given by the means of the voice, the influence of the body, seat, thigh and the lower leg. The hands through the fingers

Artificial Aids.
Reins, saddles, stirrups, whips, spurs, martingales etc. There are some who would hold that the voice is an artificial aid but when dealing with weekend riders I am not inclined to agree.

The manner of creating the language.
As I have already intimated. The language is mainly developed through touch and voice.

The upper body and seat.
The prime means of communication is the riders' body. The rider must learn to 'speak' to the horse with body followed by the hand, the leg and hand again. When in training or competition (not dressage for in dressage tests one is not allowed to use the voice at all) the horse may also be encouraged and praised with the voice. However horses are also tactile creatures and they appreciate a touch on the neck just as much.
The torso and back muscles.
The first part of the body to consider is the torso (the part of the body excluding head, arms and neck) and in particular the abdominal muscles and those in the region of the small of the back. Despite the fact that a rider is usually sitting on a padded and relatively heavy saddle, most horses are sufficiently sensitive to feel that moment when the rider braces the muscles of their back. This brings pressure to bear on the rider's seat, tending to move it forward, (as though they were trying to sit deeper in the saddle). This is the foundation of all movements. Likewise the turning of the rider's body either to the left or right can also be made to have meaning for a horse. If the rider turns their head solely through the neck there will be little communication. By turning the whole torso, the horse will feel the rotation through the hipbones.

The bracing of the back, to a greater or smaller extent, precedes every movement. Thus back – hand (fingers), leg (thigh) - hand (fingers).
The legs.
The upper part of the leg (thigh) is instrumental in supporting the torso. It also serves as an extension to the upper body, especially when the rider is about to ask the horse to turn.
The lower part of the leg (the calf).
Used in conjunction with the abdominal and back muscles , closing behind the girth to encourage forward movement, or almost on the girth to contain that movement. Each position and relative sequence of leg use has a different meaning for the horse. Even from an early stage the client should be taught that there are two ways in which the leg aid may be applied.

1   The short pressure, which ask to horse to go forward or away from the leg.

2   The continuous pressure which will encourage the horse to seek support from the leg.

During a movement the *target* for the rider is to learn to *only* apply the leg when they wish to give a specific instruction for a change or when the horse is about to *depart from the gait or tempo* that the rider has asked for. Otherwise the leg should remain passive (this applies to most aids). I mention this point, which is discussed in greater detail in advanced aids chapter 12, only to remind you to plant the seed of the idea in your client's mind. In the early stages of their riding experience pupils are usually reactive and not proactive in their responses to any change in the horses' stride. The result of this is that as they try to get the horse to do their bidding, novice riders may use their legs with great energy. It is a point that you must watch very carefully, for if you do not correct this tendency your clients will join that merry throng continually banging their legs against the horse for every stride. One sees them all the time especially amongst so-called advanced riders. I tend to ask the question 'Is your horse *deaf* to your leg?'

Having just made that point and it is one to which I will continually return, there are certain times when it is necessary to dispense with finesse in order that the horse obey the rider no matter what other ideas it may have in mind. Riding *the last three strides over a jump* on a horse that has previously declined to oblige is an example. In this case you must tell your client to use what we used to call the old pony club 'leg on'. In other words the leg swinging out from the horses' side and giving a really good thump for each stride especially the last one.

The hands.
I have mentioned the hands last in this list. The reason for my so doing is not due to the fact that the hand is necessarily the last to act. On the contrary it is second in a sequence of aids. It is simply due to the fact that in the mind of many riders the power of the hand assumes an importance that is out of all proportion to that required. For example it is a riders' *instinct* to *pull* hard on the reins in order to get the horse to stop. For me to say that this will not be effectual would be absurd. For if indeed your riders do give almighty yanks on the reins, horses will most often stop. At the same time they will also, probably, suffer pain or at least some form of discomfiture. If their mouths have not become deadened to the pain, through past abuse, then there may well be occasions when, instead of stopping they seek to dash off.

So what are the hands for?
You should ask this question of your clients. You may get some correct answers and if you do, then your work has been effective, but it is unlikely that you will get a precise and comprehensive answer. You must provide it. The hands are for giving signals through the reins for the horse to *pay attention, act upon a command, and regulate a movement. They may also encourage him to bring his quarters underneath him* by regulating and storing the energy (power) that he has created as a result of the riders' signal from the seat and leg. They are also for bending the horse's head in a particular direction thus helping him to proceed in a desired direction and in more advanced work, for raising and lowering the position of the head.

But let us be clear about one thing, reading the above paragraph, it might seem that the effect of the hands is fairly minimal. May be flexing the horse this way or that, perhaps regulating tempo? The truth is that hands can be the most destructive part of the riders' anatomy. As dangerous in causing pain as an AK 47 machine gun in the hands of an inexperienced and frightened Afghan rebel. For why you may well ask? Because they are in contact with that most sensitive part of the horses anatomy – The mouth! – The mouth – wherein lie all those sensitive tissues and nerve endings. The area so easily destroyed by the heavy hand.

And yet used sensitively and correctly the *fingers* of those hands seemingly doing so little, in fact actually do a lot. They should be continually 'playing' on the rein giving ongoing tiny signals. Helping, when required, to correct for any imbalance that the horse may have to deal with in its forward progression. Note *fingers* not elbows or wrists but *fingers*. Elbows and arms that row, wrists that turn inward and fan back and forth should not be encouraged. Even the fingers may not move involuntarily but must flex in accordance with the messages that the rider's brain receives about the horses' manner of going. The hand in co-ordination with the leg, properly applied, will encourage a horse not simply to trot but to do so in a manner that has the whole of his hind quarters involved in that activity and not simply his legs. Swinging quarters *through* the movement as some would say, creating power!

Of course there will be those who will challenge me and why not? My remarks are hardly carved in stone. Oh yes I can hear you now 'why shouldn't the arms row or wrists move back and forth as a rower at Henley, or, seaweed in the ocean, so long as they are assisting in the manner of the horses going?' 'What difference does it make as long as there is no unremitting tension in the reins?' Well as I have said before there is nothing absolute in the manner of giving aids or for that matter any way in which one may get a horse to obey. Yet I must have a reason for pressing the point. For me, it is only the fingers that open the portal to real *elegance.* It is difficult for any rider to reach that state of near perfection – that one in which the rider's body is *motionless* – if the arms are continually swinging back and forth. It is only through the use of the fingers that one will get real *sensitivity.* Imagine if you will someone playing the violin. From whence will the most delicate and sensitive melody arise – the one who grabs the bow in his fist or the one who holds it between his forefinger and thumb? That is my analogy and only the fingers satisfy my point of view.

A manner of explaining the use of the fingers.
I find it very useful to demonstrate the way in which the rein should be held and the fingers used: - Have the rider standing at the halt. Go along side the horse, standing at the shoulder. Ask the rider to *hold* the reins, only between the *forefinger and thumb* of each hand, with the other fingers gently closed around the reins but *not actually holding them.* Then with your own fingers take a rein and gently draw it away from the rider towards the bit. As you do so instruct the rider to allow their fingers to open (Accept for the first finger and thumb). Then move the rein back towards the rider to its original position. As you do so the rider's fingers should close. **Keep repeating until the rider is able to follow your movements rhythmically** (see drawings nos. 9 & 10)

You tell the client that what you are demonstrating is the nodding motion of the horse's head as it goes forward. Different gaits have a greater or lesser degree of motion. It is up to the rider to be sure that *whenever that movement occurs their fingers respond* so that there is *never any pressure* on the rein unless it is applied specifically in the giving of an aid. You may go on to say that this is one of the ways by which a good horseman may be recognised. Unfortunately it is also one of the subtlest movements that are *seldom ever practised.*

You should from time to time remind your clients about this matter and occasionally test their reflexes by taking the rein while they still hold it and continuously applying erratic little movements with it. Your pupils should be able to **follow the movements that you create without ever** losing the *elastic* feel on the rein. It should never ever become either too tight or too loose and this may mean that the degree of movement required in the fingers is no more than a slight flexing of the knuckles.

An exercise in giving the rein, using the half halt.
I have already mentioned the benefit of using transitions to obtain ever-lighter touches on the rein. However one can easily demonstrate to a class as to whether or not they have made any progress in this matter. Simply ask them to halt one by one working from the rear of the ride, as each passes a letter. Thus with a class of four riders on the left rein say, *the last* rider will be asked to at 'B' the next at 'M' and so on. As they do so watch them carefully and see whether or not they actually *have ceased the aid a fractional moment before the horse has halted* or do they hang on and pull the horse back to halt. In other words are they still maintaining the rein aid after the horse has obeyed them? In all likelihood the latter mode prevails. In which case ask them all to ride from letter to letter as a ride and to halt at each one for the count of three. Their bodies must be level with the letter, they must utilise the bracing of the back as part of the aid and you should ask them to exaggerate the ceasing of the aid by showing you a slightly loose rein *before the horse has halted.*

Of course for the first two or three halts some horses may not listen. Who can blame them? They are generally pulled back to halt for most of their work. Ask the riders to help themselves by using the voice and to learn to give the horse 'thinking time'. Watch the smiles of satisfaction and delight appear on the faces of your riders as their horses begin to understand and obey!

In a nutshell.
Just in case my previous comments have created any erroneous ideas in your minds with regard to the use of the hands. Let me make the idea that I am trying to get across quite clear . It is that the rider must learn that contact with the horses mouth through the rein, must be always present but also quite neutral, unless the rider wishes to pass part of a message to the horse. In this way the rider may learn to develop 'good hands'.

Of course 'educated' hands are quite another matter, but this may not come about until the former have been perfected.

In the books that I have read one of the most succinct descriptions is given by Harry D. Chamberlin *42 Training Hunters, Jumpers and Hacks. 'Note: "Good hands" are able to maintain soft, continuous contact with the horse's mouth at all gaits. Due to co-ordination and a good seat the rider, after he has acquired good hands, does not jerk or flop his reins accidentally at each unexpected movement of the horse. "Educated hands," beside being "good hands," are highly skilled in resisting, with exactly the appropriate amount of force, any resistance of the horse; also in immediately softening and decreasing their resistance when the horse ceases to resist. They provide instantaneous reward for good behaviour; instantaneous punishment for bad.'

The half halt.
A *taking* and giving with the fingers. (Some say a taking and giving with the hands but I do not agree with this form of words for it implies a degree of unnecessary movement at a time when the one thing that you are trying to do is to get your pupils to keep their hands still). This is the main signal, used for initiating a change and should usually be given by the *outside rein (relative to the movement)*.
Why?
Because the horse has been schooled in this way and it leaves the inside rein available for producing a bend, or other signals, if required. It must be clearly understood that no matter how light or how minimal the intended effect of the half halt, it should always be a part of the whole. Back, seat, hand, leg and hand.

The fingers close momentarily. The duration of their staying closed, however, is of great importance, especially when the rider is progressing to more advanced movements. For a simple request to pay attention or to steady up slightly, then the closing is only momentary. For a transition from halt to trot, or better still to canter, then the fingers remain closed for a slightly longer moment after other aids are given. It is rather like playing the same note on a piano but with a different intensity each time. 'Oho' I hear you say. 'If this is so then what are you going on about when you write of the great part played by the riders back, seat bone and upper thigh?' The answer lies of course in the very in-exactitude of the practise of equitation. For all normal purposes an ordinary horseman will be required to give a 'prompt' or signal to 'pay attention' to their horse. However an expert horseman will not, necessarily, need to do so when he is riding a horse with which he has established complete unity. The animal will be waiting for the slightest of aids and these will be so expertly given that the rein action together with the other aids will be rendered invisible. This is the target that we set for our pupils –they may never get there, but at least they will have been taught to the correct manner and sequence in which they should be given.

Leading away.
This is simply a very small movement where the rider displaces their hand sideways away from the horse's neck. It is a useful aid for the rider to learn. For example when riding a corner or a circle with a horse that has a tendency to fall in, the rider will either try to point the horse's head into the corner thus producing an incorrect bend. Or else they may actually cross the inside hand over the horses neck, which is quite incorrect (see photo no. 10). What they need to do is to anticipate the fault, correcting it by using the inside leg a little before they approach the corner and *then* to reinforce this by leading away with the outside hand thus inviting the horse to keep moving, correctly, in the desired direction.

The most common problem for the novice rider.
Is to be able to judge the duration of the aid. Despite the fact that it has been carefully explained that the half halt is a momentary signal, many riders keep their fingers closed for far too long a time. This is very often evident when they are asked to go forward from walk to halt at a particular letter. They find that despite having given what they consider to be quite clear aids, the horse seems to go wandering on. The reason is very often due to the fact that because their fingers remain closed the horse starts to lean on the bit. The more it walks on, the more pressure they apply to the rein. Usually the horse does eventually stop but not before having walked on for at least half a dozen strides and suffered much pulling on its mouth for so doing.

'What am I doing wrong?' is the usual question. The answer that can be seen quite clearly by you as you watch the fingers close and remain closed waiting for the horse to obey. You explain 'you kept your hand closed for too long. Try again and if you perceive that your aid is *not* going to be *obeyed* immediately, *repeat but more firmly* but *not for a longer period*. And don't forget to brace the back'.

Much to the riders' surprise and pleasure after two or maybe three rapid half halts the horse responds promptly. As they continue, the half halts are reduced to only the one.

Reacting to pain.

I have seen this happen in a class. Without warning, whilst proceeding at trot or even a walk, a horse will, suddenly, break into a canter and it will go around and around the arena. The rider is, ineffectually, heaving on its mouth and the more they do so, the faster the horse goes on until one of three things happens. It may get so out of control and in such a state that it becomes unbalanced and falls over, the rider gets such a fright that they either become unbalanced and fall off (or bale out) or the horse eventually gets tired and stops of its own accord. During this period it is very unpleasant for everyone involved. Not only for the rider in question but also the other members of the class whose own horses may be getting restive. The answer to the problem is very simple. Having instructed the rest of the class to halt, the instructor tells the hapless rider to sit tall or hold the pommel of the saddle for support but *essentially* to let the reins go long and gently touch the horse's neck. Miraculously the horse stops! Everyone is amazed! Of course we know that there is no reason for amazement. The horse has stopped because the pain has ceased. Not only that but also most horses slow down as soon as they feel the rein go long. It is a matter to which they have become accustomed.

Use of the voice.

I must make my position quite clear. With the exception (for the simple reason that the voice is not allowed) of Dressage Tests, I favour the use of the voice. I can see no reason whatsoever for remaining silent when working with a horse. After all the creature is quite intelligent and does understand you're meaning. In which case then, why on earth should you not utilize this additional aid? There are other disciplines that are enacted without words. Ballet is a good example. During the performance the principles do not speak. However this is not so during rehearsals. If no word was spoken at that time, then how on earth would the participants make known their views as to the shortcomings or otherwise of their partners? The use of the voice does have its place. It is the first form of communication used in early training and later in the equine dictionary it is the last. In the distant past, I mean over 6000 years ago, nomadic horsemen were apparently given to riding without any bridle, controlling the horse by voice alone. *37 (Felton).

The voice is an extremely useful way of clarifying the somewhat crude message of the novices' aids. A rider may utilise the already extensive vocabulary that the horse possesses. Many of the words, if I may use computer technology, will have been loaded on to the 'hard disk' of the horse's brain during it's early training on the lunge. It will readily understand. 'Walk', 'Trot', 'Canter' and 'Halt'. So that from a novice rider's point of view, the use of the appropriate word will help enormously when the rider, either through their lack of skill or balance, has given an aid, that is unclear. There is one other advantage in having a client speak to their horses – it helps them to breathe! More than anything this fault is an underlying cause of tension. So many riders concentrate to such an extent, or are so nervous, that they forget this absolutely basic requirement. Air must flow over the larynx in order to speak. Thus one cannot have a conversation with a horse unless one breathes.

Finally and perhaps the most important use of the voice, is to praise and to thank the horse for a task well done.

The use of the whip.

These days many riders carry incredibly long whips. As long as they understand that these may not be used for giving punishment - probably undeserved punishment at that, for in all probability the rider has given an aid that has confused the horse - I do not object to whips being carried by *experienced* riders. It is sometimes useful to be able to *touch* the horse at one of its extremities for example a hind leg, without, first, having to remove the rein from that hand. In order to be able to do this one must have a long whip. A rider who, at the slightest whim strikes a horse sharply should be admonished.

But let us be quite clear, in the third paragraph of this chapter I did mention that it might be necessary for the rider to *reinforce* the aid given by the leg with a *light touch* of the whip. I must go on to place a caveat on this remark. In the first place I believe that a horse should *never* be struck with the whip. As I have just said I am not against a touch but that is *all*. So far as I am concerned the whip should only be used as a form of reminder. In these circumstances it should always be used when carried in the *inside* hand.

' Ah' you may well be saying to yourselves 'what about reinforcing the other leg then'? Most horses are quite intelligent enough to be able to distinguish between a tap that is used as a reprimand and that which is given in order to reinforce the leg. If an aid has been given and not acted upon and a light touch of the whip follows with the aid repeated then the horse will understand, irrespective as to where the touch is placed.

There are some horses whose personalities are such that, when the stick is used, they dig in their toes. Upon meeting such animals I have seen some riders using the stick harder and harder without effect. In some cases, quite rightly in my opinion, the horse, eventually, bucks them off. Whilst others, miserably, simply endure the pain. If you come across a rider meting out such punishment, I suggest that you ask them if it is having any effect? If the reply is 'No', then I suggest you tell them to stop. There is always another way of getting a horse to do ones bidding.

So far as novices are concerned, on reflection, I think that it probably much better if they carry no whip at all. This will avoid the use of the whip in a manner that takes matters beyond their control. If, in a moment of irritation, they strike the horse hard, it may well leap forward and in turn unbalance the rider to such an extent that they fall off. You must use your discretion in this matter, for it will, of course, depend on the horse. For some horses the absence of a whip in the riders' hand is a signal to be sluggish and uncooperative, while the mere sight of a whip in hand, immediately obtains co-operation. Others may put in an objection in the form of a small buck, because they know, from past experience, that this frequently results in the use of the whip ceasing. For those horses that do resort to such behaviour, a touch on the shoulder is very often effective.

Different whip lengths.
Whereas I have mentioned that a long whip enables a rider to use this without removing the hand from the rein, the same cannot be said for short whips or crops. Before using a short whip the rider must first place the reins, as a double loop, in the other hand. You should watch every rider carrying a short whip to make sure that they do so.

A question that a client may ask.
Having just discussed the use of a whip, an intelligent client may well pick up on the fact that you allow them to use a long whip without, first, placing the reins in the opposite hand. You must be ready to explain that if they tried to use a short whip while still holding the rein in the same hand, then, they are going to give the horse two opposing signals. The first is that the horse listens to the riders' leg, reinforced by the whip. Unfortunately if the rein is still held in the same hand, they will, at the same time, be forced to pull on that rein. Pulling on the rein gives the horse a second signal, telling it not to go forward! Two opposite signals. (See photo no. 11 and drawing no. 11)

How to change a whip from one hand to the other correctly.
Short whip (see photo no. 12 a & b page 436) Long whip (see photo no. 13a, b &c page 437)

A synopsis of the aids.

It should be clearly understood that what is to follow is intended merely as a *guide*. I freely acknowledge that there are many ways of teaching a rider to give signals to their horse. What follows here, for good or ill, is my view of a convention through which the aids may be given.

Is there any basic logic as to why we have developed the signals that we use?
The answer is that 'yes' there is. Of course, much of it has to do with the horse's ongoing education. At first a dialogue is created through the voice and this is confirmed by showing the lunging whip. At this time the horse is learning to move without the weight of the rider on it's back. Then, as we have discussed, these same commands are adapted to have meaning through pressure of the, now mounted, riders' seat, leg and hand.

However there is a bit more to it than that and it is bound up with the horses' confirmation. The answer lies in the elbow, the locking joint known as the Olecranon process (see Stories to entertain page 408). This has influenced the type of aid that we use for communication, for it is obvious that if we touch a horse with our leg just behind the girth the first leg to move will be the hind leg on that side. (If one is using diagonal aids, then the riders opposite hand will regulate that movement). This is followed by the foreleg on the same side and then the hind leg on the other side followed by the foreleg on that side. The support is two legs and before the horse can fall over by three legs, then two legs and back to three legs and so on. (See drawing no. 12) There is no moment of suspension at the walk.

So in a nutshell.
So in the paragraphs that follow you will read 'Back (brace)/seat (pressure), to hand (fingers close) – seat (continued pressure) and leg (touch) to hand fingers (open). So how does that sequence fit in, logically, with what I have written above? Let me make it quite clear – it is *my view* of the sequence; other instructors may have different views. As I have mentioned elsewhere, Wynmalen says one might just as well use, as reins, cotton thread attached to the ears.

Preparation.
Your command will always be 'Prepare to.....' Your meaning is that the client should assemble all the required aids, for a particular movement, in their minds – in the correct order. This not only allows them to prepare but also to deliver those aids in correct sequence and with the correct timing so that the horse also has time to think about what is being asked of it. Thus as the rider braces the back and shortens the rein, so the horses ears flick back slightly to show that it is listening.

The logic for the sequence that I suggest is as follows. The back bracing is a signal for the horse to start to create energy but as it does so, the fingers close to regulate. The horse is provided with thinking time. The leg closing on or behind the girth not only provides a second signal to continue but they also tell the horse *what sort of movement is required*. Finally the fingers open saying 'Now'. I suppose that one might make a comparison with turning on the tap for a garden hose. The water flows through under pressure but nothing really happens (apart from the hose getting more solid) until one picks up the nozzle on the end and having pointed it in the required direction, presses the trigger. In this case everything is controlled. If one didn't bother and the trigger was already open, water might be flying around all over the place!

The aid to go forward to walk.
Your command. *always*, **'Prepare to go forward to walk'.**

The horse is standing at the halt.
1. The muscles of the rider's back brace.
2   The rider closes their fingers around the outside rein– This signal is one that says 'Pay attention'. *It says nothing more!* The horse does not know what the command will be. The horse's ears will, frequently be seen to twitch back slightly; this is a reversion to the days when it was first schooled by the use of the voice. It is waiting. The inside rein is ready to bend the horse, if required, in the direction in which the rider wishes to go.
3   The muscles of the rider's back continue to brace.
4. Both legs closing (squeezing) *almost* together behind the girth follow this. As the horse is **about to obey**, the fingers holding the outside rein open. The horse walks on! (in other words the action of the fingers indicates '**Now**')

Upon obedience the riders' whole body relaxes and follows the movement. (Relax does not mean collapse! It simply means that the fingers follow the movement of the horse's head and the rider's lower back follows the movement of the horse's body). The rider must of course be aware of any, potential, change in tempo. Generally, with many school horses this will be a tendency to slow down and the impulsion should be maintained by the rider squeezing, behind the girth, alternately first with one leg then the other. As soon as the tempo returns to that required this should cease. The trouble with many riders is that they do not have the confidence to allow this to happen. Instead they keep on banging away with the leg until the horse ignores them.

With novices it may be that the horse is not inclined to obey. The rider must repeat the signal and at the same time say in a firm voice the horse's name and 'Walk on'. When the horse obeys they verbally reward 'Good boy (girl)'.

Walk on a free rein.
The rider allows the horse complete freedom to lower and stretch its neck. * 43. Only a light contact is

maintained (don't forget this is a *long* rein not a loose rein). The rider must sit motionless and the horse is to go forward with a long stride and no loss of tempo. The rider must avoid the temptation to nag the horse with the leg.

Going forward from walk to halt.
The rider has been, correctly, allowing their fingers to open and close neutrally as required by the balancing movement of the horse's head. If this action is being performed correctly, then, the horse should carry the bit without discomfiture. Correctly performed the rein should have a nice elastic feel to it.
1   The muscles of the back brace.
2   The fingers close.
Why? They are telling the horse that there is about to be a change. He does not know what this may be.
3   The back muscles continue to brace.
4   The legs close *almost on* the girth. (it helps if you tell them to close the thighs on the saddle)
5   As the horse is about to obey the fingers open.
Why?
This is telling the horse I wish you to obey **now!**
Upon obedience the riders' whole body relaxes.

What do you watch out for?
1   The rider must not tip forward. There must be no movement at all, apart from the fingers opening and closing and these should be practically invisible to the observer. Novice riders sometimes appear to be incapable of performing a transition without almost standing up in the stirrups.

2   The rider must avoid the almost irresistible temptation to pull on the rein. What is known as pulling the horse back to halt. It is a habit that many riders find difficult to overcome. This is partially the response to instinct but more often than not it is the result of poor tuition earlier in their riding career.

Standing still at the halt.
I was asked recently by a client who was out hacking with me 'How do you make a horse stand still? I replied that one simply braces the muscles of the back – allow a tiny pause- and then close the fingers of the hand for a second and then relax. I demonstrated on the horse I was riding. He was very full of himself, but upon my command he stood absolutely at attention. A client may also reinforce this aid by accompanying the action with the voice saying, firmly but quietly 'stand still'. I was then asked 'What happens if you do pull on the rein to stop the horse walking forward'? I demonstrated. He stepped back!

In practise, after a short while any horse is going to be inclined to fidget or at the very least to change its weight from one leg to another. This is the time when the rider must learn to use only the subtlest of pressures in order to keep the horse motionless. Perhaps the lightest pressure from the back, the slightest closing of the fingers around the rein. But we should note that it is unreasonable to keep a horse at attention for a prolonged interval, like ourselves it will get stiff and tired.

The aids to go forward from walk to trot.
Almost exactly the same as those given for the walk except that *both legs close simultaneously* behind the girth. However should a verbal command be required then the rider will say 'Horses name and trot on'. And of course the verbal reward.
Going forward to a rising trot. Sitting on the correct diagonal.
The trot may be ridden either sitting or rising. It is, usually, more comfortable for a rider to use the rising trot, this is discussed in greater detail in the chapter dealing with lessons on the lunge. However the rider does need to be taught to sit on the correct diagonal. This is achieved by asking them to glance down at the *outside* front shoulder and to try and ensure that they are sitting as this is coming underneath.
Why? Because the horse, at the trot, is moving with diagonal pairs of legs. It pivots as it goes around corners or bends on its *inside hind* leg. The rider in order to give the horse a sense of security and as an aid to good balance needs to be firmly sitting down as this inside hind leg takes the full weight of the horse. The rider cannot easily see the hind leg but since they know that the legs are moving in diagonal *pairs* glancing down at the front leg and noting its movement also indicates when the hind leg is also moving underneath

the horse. Of course the rider must, eventually, learn to detect the correct diagonal by feel and *not* looking down.

What do you look for?

1   In all these transitions be they trot to walk or to canter or any variation thereof. ***The change must be smooth.*** If for example it is an upward transition from walk to trot then all that you, as the observer, should see is that one moment the horse is moving four-time and the next instant it is two-time.

2   The rider's body must be motionless. There must be no tipping forward.

The aids for a downward transition from trot to walk.

Should the rider be engaged in a ***rising trot***, this ***must cease*** and the rider goes to sitting deeply at trot. As far as the horse is concerned this simply means that the rider is doing nothing more than a sitting trot. The only time that the horse knows that there is to be a change is when the half halt is applied.

1   The back is braced.
2   The fingers of the hand holding the outside rein close (the first part of the half halt).
3   *Both* the riders' legs close simultaneously almost on the girth.
4   As the horse is ***about to obey***. The fingers complete the half halt and open.

A Problem that might occur.

Sometimes horses will execute a transition to walk immediately that a rider starts to sit to the trot. The reason for this is that they are frequently allowed to do this. They begin to take the sitting trot as an aid by association. In other words, for them, sitting trot means walk. Do not permit this to happen. Warn the pupil and tell them to be ready to squeeze with the legs behind the girth in order that the transition only occurs when the rider has completed the aid.

The aids for going forward from *rising* trot to canter.

First a simple reminder as to what we are asking when we tell a rider to prepare for canter.

The canter is a three-time movement; the sequence is inside foreleg (the leading leg) lifting the horse's body into the air and as it does so the outside hind leg (the strike off leg) comes forward under the horses body propelling it forward (the first beat). This is followed by the inside hind leg and outside foreleg acting together (the second beat), finally reverting to the inside foreleg (the third beat) once again throwing the horses body, pronouncedly, through the air (the moment of suspension). This is known as cantering with the correct lead.

The sequence of the aids.

The period of rising trot should be used to produce a well-balanced trot with good ***impulsion*** (the rider uses the inside leg to do this). The ***rider ceases to rise*** and starts to brace the muscles of the back, in order to be in a position to be better able to create impulsion (energy/power). The ***inside leg*** is gently ***squeezing*** almost on the girth helping ***to create this power.*** *(*For a novice who really has a problem simply keeping the leg still, suggest a series of short double taps so that the signal is quite clear). There is a slight pause (The thinking moment) and then: –

1   The rider then closes the fingers on the ***outside*** rein (the half halt)– telling the horse that there is to be a change.
2   The inside rein is slightly shortened.
       Why? By shortening the inside rein slightly, the horse is positioned so that its head is slightly flexed to the inside. The rider's hands are kept level.
3   The muscles of the back continue to brace as the rider's ***outside leg brushes back*** to touch the horse about three inches behind the girth thus giving the signal that what is required is canter with the horse's inside foreleg leading.

Fractionally later –

4 The fingers of the outside hand open, thus telling the horse 'I wish you to canter **now!**

Upon obedience the riders' whole body relaxes and follows the movement.

84

Of course the verbal command to 'canter' may be uttered by the rider as well as a verbal reward when the horse obliges.

Things for you to look for.
As instructor your telling the rider to use these aids is all very well but if they do not sit absolutely still, then the aids will probably be ineffectual. The horse will become unbalanced and unable or unwilling to carry the rider forward to canter due to the shifting weight of the riders' body. You must also watch to ensure that the horse has departed with the correct lead. You must be sure that the horse is giving a correct canter in so far as that it is proceeding with a clear 1 – 2 – 3 – 'and' (the moment of suspension) rhythm

What do you do if a horse departs with an incorrect lead?
You should have a good idea as to why this happened because you were carefully observing the rider as they asked for the canter depart. Immediately ask the rider to go back to trot, steady it down, and try again. Frequently the problem lies in the fact that the rider does not have complete control over their limbs as they struggle with the twin problems of giving the aids in the correct order and at the same time keeping their balance. If you think that this is the reason, as you ask the client to try again, tell them to be sure to brush back the outside leg clearly. You may also tell them to give an additional defining signal to the horse by *raising the inside hand* slightly. Another way of helping is to cause the horse to use his desire for being balanced to ensure the correct lead. To do this, ask the rider to canter as they ride a corner.
Why?
Because as a horse goes through a corner it will have a greater tendency to place its weight on the inside hind leg (part of the diagonal pair) in order to assist its balance. This means that the order of the leg sequence will correctly follow. We must not forget that the correct leading foreleg is only observed as an indication that the weight is correctly placed over the inside hind leg. (The leg on which a horse has to pivot as it turns).
Raising the inside hand slightly can also help.

Another, frequent, reason for the incorrect lead is that the rider has neglected to bend the horses head slightly to the required leading leg (the inside foreleg). In fact they may actually have twisted it towards the *outside.* In which case the incorrect lead will surely follow.

Point for you to watch.
Sometimes, in their effort to get a horse into canter, the rider will twist the animal so awkwardly that it becomes disunited. Should this occur then ask the rider to cease canter immediately, since a disunited canter is a lateral movement and the horse may fall over.

Questions an intelligent rider may ask.
Why does one use the outside leg to ask for the inside leading leg?
Answer - because the horse is trained to move the leg on the same side as that where he has been touched. However he also knows that this is a signal for canter and therefore he will produce the 'silent moment' when he is in the air followed by the strike off with the hind leg on the same side as that touched.

Why is it considered that the inside foreleg as leading leg is correct?
Answer – (again in more detail) because as the horse strikes off into canter he, first, throws his weight on to the leading leg (the inside foreleg) and lifts himself into the air (the silent moment - the moment of suspension). He immediately follows this with the strike off leg (the outside hind leg - beat 1). A diagonal pair moving simultaneously follows this (the inside hind leg and the outside foreleg – beat 2). Finally reverting to the leading leg (inside foreleg beat 3). This is followed once again by the moment of suspension (all the legs in the air). Now the *key* to the reason for having the inside foreleg leading lies in the 2nd beat (the inside hind leg moving together with the outside foeleg) for as a horse navigates a curve or turn it is on *his inside hind* leg that he *pivots* and where he feels his security of balance.

Riders with a problem in initiating the canter depart. (See also exercises to form a lesson page 267).
Sometimes, in an arena, one may have a pupil who, though very proficient in initiating changes from walk to trot and vice versa, and who is also able to ride circles of all dimensions, has a problem when it comes to going forward to canter. They may well be able to do so for a few strides, especially if you are behind the

horse urging it on, but inevitably the canter dies and the horse reverts to trot or even walk. The reason for this frequently lies in the rider's mental attitude towards the gait. They are slightly nervous of it and, without realising, either do not produce sufficient impulsion to help the horse or, if the horse is very willing, as soon as it starts to canter, they hang on to the rein and actually tell the horse to stop. They will frequently admit that this is so. So what are we to do in order to help them?

One answer is to use a superb schoolmaster. (Such as my old friend Jeeves) An animal in this category will be able to divine the rider's wishes and carry them forward no matter what. Even if the rider does give conflicting aids then the mention of the word 'canter' will be sufficient. They are then carried around the arena for a sufficient length of time to be able to become used to the motion.

If such a horse is not available, then the other possibility is to seriously consider going out for a quiet *private* hack. You will both be mounted. Of course the horses used *must*, not only, *be* very *well behaved* but also be possessed of a nice smooth action. In this case we are going to ask for canter, not at a spot where the horse does not expect it, but at the place where it *has* cantered previously. This should be a very short distance to start with and you giving the lead may initiate the canter. You must look back frequently and ensure that your client is coping. However, if the groundwork has been properly prepared, then the client will be able, for the first time, to enjoy a prolonged canter, without any struggle and this should help them to overcome their fears.

I freely acknowledge that in my booklet 'Safe and Interesting Hacking' (now included in chapter 20), I make the point that one does not take a client out hacking, until they have demonstrated the ability to sit to the canter. Despite what I have written above, I still hold this view. However the particular case to which I am now referring is that in which you have complete confidence in the client's ability. In the arena you have asked them to sit to the trot with legs raised and stretched out each side and they have remained perfectly still (see photo no. 14). In other words they have a good balance but *their difficulty is that they have a psychological problem with the canter* and this needs to be overcome. We must try to create a situation, with the client's agreement, where their instinctive pulling on the rein is actually neutralised by the horse. In a field you may suggest that the rider place the reins (as a double loop) in the outside hand and with the free hand hold the pommel of the saddle. You give the lead, the clients' horse follows. When you cease to canter the clients' horse does the same. What if it doesn't? I hear you say. My reply is that you *must* have a quiet well-behaved horse that knows its job so that there will be no problem, for this is not simply taking a client out for a hack, we have an end in view and that is to overcome their fear.

What to do if a client establishes canter but the horse breaks to trot?
You must be the sharp observer. You should have noticed anyone of the following points.
1. The client may have become unbalanced and the shifting weight of their body is, in turn, unbalancing the horse. (They are very probably leaning forward).
2. The client is not be able to keep their hands still and has inadvertently given the horse a half halt, which it has mistaken as a command to trot.
3. They may simply be unable to sit deeply enough and the bouncing of their seat, heavily, on the saddle is causing the horse much discomfort.
4. The horse may have become unbalanced and simply unable to sustain the canter.
5. The horse may have decided that it has cantered for long enough and will change the gait of its own accord. It may simply do this because it has become its habit when being ridden by clients who don't have the skill or mental determination to be obeyed.

In the last example you can be of considerable help. Due to the fact that, since you have the experience, you will be able to spot that second *before* the horse is going to change. In which case you call out to the rider to *touch* the horse *with their inside leg*, that very second the horse starts to think about a change. I find that this works very well and even the most novice rider is able to complete, a good circuit of the arena and then, to initiate a change to trot themselves.

Whatever the reason, if they do become unbalanced you have no option but to ask them to go forward to walk and thus allow them time to get reorganised. Having had the reason for the failure correctly pointed out by you, the pupil should be asked to continue by going through a steady but active trot to ask, once again, for the canter. As they do so you must guide them through their previous difficulty. When they succeed the most important point is that, should a downward transition to trot occur again, they *should not acquiesce to the changed gait by rising.*

The downward transition from canter to trot.

The aids for the downward transition are similar to those used when asking for the upward transition.

5   The back is braced.
6   The fingers of the hand holding the outside rein close (the first part of the half halt).
7   **Here is the difference** – **Both** the riders' legs close almost **on** the girth.
8   As the horse is **about to obey**. The fingers complete the half halt and open.

What do you watch out for?

1   Because the horse may be running onto its forehand (due to the fact that it was probably on its forehand during the canter), the rider must **not go forward to a rising trot** until the horse is rebalanced. The rider sitting deeply with a slight bracing of the back and the application of two or three half halts brings this about. Then and only then may they go forward to rising trot.

2   In order to assist in a smooth downward transition the rider should mentally count out the rhythm of the trot being sure to do this independently of the horse's tempo. This will ensure that the trot then proceeds at a steady tempo that will assist in storing energy and allowing for sufficient impulsion should the rider desire to go forward to canter once again.

3   Throughout the movement the inside hand simply maintains flexion and bend and continues so to do until the horse is given a long rein and is invited to rest.

4   If you wish the rider to continue with a downward transition from trot to walk. You must remind them to go sitting trot before they prepare to give the aid.

Learning to shorten and lengthen the stride.

Now I must, once again, make my position quite clear. I am not going on to describe the *training* of the horse to make changes in the length of its stride from the normal one established during a working or ordinary trot. I am making the assumption that the horses in your class know perfectly well how to respond to a correctly executed request from the rider to change that *normal* stride to one that is either shorter or longer. Of course the degree to which the horse is *able* to comply will depend on its conformation. For example a horse with an upright shoulder will not be able to give a lengthened stride that will compare with that shown by a horse with a sloping shoulder. I am not going to go into the mechanics as to why this should be. Should you wish to find out, then, I suggest that you read 'The Horse in Action' by R.H Smythe. *27.

It may well be that the implementation, by your pupils, of that which I write below may, *subsequently*, result in a horse showing some improvement but that is by the by. Our object is to give instruction that will enable your pupils to perform these to changes satisfactorily. For many intermediate riders these two movements sometimes present great difficulty. This is due to the fact that they do not have a mental picture of exactly what they entail. The result is that shorter strides simply become slower and lengthened strides, faster.

Why?

The reason for this is because the exact definition of the movement has not been made clear. The client only has some vague mental picture in their mind as to what it is that they are expected be asking for. This, no doubt, will have something to do with the fact that they have been told that it is necessary to store impulsion for a shorter stride and to allow impulsion to flow for a longer one. But apart from that, things are rather indistinct and when they do try to put this into practise, say at the trot, they find that when they restrain with the rein (storing impulsion?) they simply get a slower pace or worse still a downward change of gait to walk. Similarly when asking for a longer stride, the trot gets faster or the horse changes gait to canter. The fault must lie with the rider, for the horse is obviously trying to obey otherwise why does it change, if incorrectly, at all? The problem lies with the fine balance between leg and hand.

Making it clear.

Your job is to produce clarity out of confusion. In the first pace your clients need to understand, exactly what is happening. For the sake of analyses let us use the trot as an example.

87

If one refers to the Manual of Horsemanship *4 as distributed by the Pony Club, you will find that speed is described as 'miles per hour' at which the horse is travelling. This is of course quite correct but when teaching the shortening or lengthening of the strides you must take great care that there is no confusion in the minds of your clients. If rhythm describes the actual pace i.e. four time for the walk, two-time for the trot and so on, then there is no change in this or with the regularity of the pace. The tempo is the actual speed of the sequence of each footfall. Again as the rider asks for shortening or lengthening the *tempo remains the same*. Now this where the rider sometimes has a problem and the reason for this is that though the tempo remains unchanged; the *actual movement* of the legs does become *slower for a shortened stride and quicker for a lengthening stride.* The reason is that for a shorter stride the horse has less ground to cover while for a longer stride at the *same tempo* the legs have further to travel and will therefore have to move faster over the given distance. The effect upon the horses progress is that the shorter the stride at the same tempo, the more *slowly* the horse will *progress over the ground* until in the case of piaffe (trotting on the spot) it will not make any forward progress at all! For a lengthened stride obviously the reverse with the horse covering the ground at quite considerable speed whilst the tempo remains unchanged. However in both movements it is obvious the horse must produce a great deal of extra energy (impulsion) in order to keep up the pace, for both are rather special movements.

The clients need time to be able to visualise this. If un-mounted I usually do a little demonstration, which I call my Basil Fawlty trot. I jog around the arena counting as I go '1 – 2, 1 – 2' and so on, this is to represent an ordinary trot. As I proceed still counting at the *same tempo* I then *jog on the spot* and subsequently returning through my original jogging to *a lengthened stride* which still at the same tempo *covers much more ground*. The clients are thus able to see more clearly, what they are going to ask their horses to do.

Sometimes I refer to a musical term. This is a good idea for anyone with an interest in either listening to or playing music. The term I use is 'Allegro Vivache'. One may see the instruction against a Mozart piano score. Many people think that it means play faster but it doesn't. What it does mean is with 'great energy'.

How does the rider put this successfully into practise?
Shortening the stride
This of course is the tricky part. Still using the trot as an example I start by asking them to sit to the trot and to close their fingers very slightly, on the outside rein, as *though* to slow the trot down but at no point may they allow their horses to change down to a walk. This means of course that if they fix their hands the horse will almost be sure to change. Instead the knuckles have to **close and open fractionally all the time**.

But how are they to produce the required energy needed to sustain the elevated action that is such an essential part of the shortened stride? As with everything to do with the creation of energy (and these movements are about the creation and specific release of power), the signal originates from the riders' back muscles and seat. Followed by the closing of both legs behind the girth. In order to make certain that the horse understands that the rider is giving an aid and not simply letting their legs bang against the horses sides, it is a good idea to ask them to use a double squeeze with the leg. (A tap, tap with the calves) The effect of this should be to cause the horse to engage its hindquarters more effectively underneath its body and thus produce the required energy. As the rider gives this aid and allows the fractional pause, so the fingers whilst still flexing open and closed, *stay closed for a fraction longer* than they remain open. Much to the riders delight after one or two attempts the horse will begin to respond giving the rider that superb feeling of sitting to a more collected trot.

The lengthened stride.
I have mentioned the shortening of the stride before the lengthening due to the fact that, there is less risk of the horse becoming unbalanced if a shortened stride is asked for before a lengthened one. The rider still needs to produce impulsion with the seat and the legs. So how does the horse know that a change is being asked for? The answer, again, lies in the *fingers*. For instead of closing for a fraction longer, on the outside rein, than they would for a shortened stride, now they *open* for a fraction longer than they close. For this movement a rising trot can be useful because it helps to inspire the horse and also helps to prevent the rider's seat from blocking the action of the horse's hindquarters.

What about the inside rein?
As for any other movement this rein is used for producing bend. Now if this is required the riders fingers

must still not be fixed even after the bend has been acquired, they have to open and close, *neutrally,* following the movement of the horses head, otherwise, if fixed, the hand will simply cause discomfiture and confusion. The point being of course that the fingers of inside hand open and close at a slightly different tempo than those of the outside hand.

I must confess that when starting to teach movements of this sort I do not dwell on the difference in tempo between the two hands. It is usually too much for the average rider to cope with and I am quite satisfied with an opening and closing of the fingers of both hands, in the same tempo, in the struggle to co-ordinate seat, leg, and hand. In practise the rider should be able to produce shortened and lengthened strides even if the hands that are asking, lack something in accuracy. For the aids to 'Going on the bit' and lateral aids, then that is an entirely different matter.

I have heard some instructors suggest that it may also help a rider if they go forward to rising trot and, perhaps, rise slightly higher than they would for an ordinary trot, squeezing with the legs each time they sit. Since this is a matter of communication, one needs to try whatever works. My personal view is that it is easier to produce impulsion when sitting. One of my reasons for this view is that when the rider rises the foundation provided by the seat is less effective and furthermore other difficulties such as hands dancing about may occur.

The aids for the leg yield.
What is the movement?

The horse is required to move, on two tracks that is both *forwards and sideways*. He is *not looking in the direction* in which *he is moving.* and the horse just begins to cross both inner legs in front of the outer ones. This movement is sometimes considered as a suitable introduction to lateral work, though there are some who think that it is an unsatisfactory movement since it encourages the horse to go on the forehand. We however are not discussing the horses' training here but the introduction of the rider to the idea of a lateral movement and in this respect I think that leg yielding can help. I point out to my pupils that the movement is the source of some controversy. Before embarking on this exercise it is important that you choose the correct part of the arena for this to take place. This is a movement that may require a period of time for the less experienced rider to check that the horse be correctly positioned before asking for the movement. I suggest that you use the long side of the arena. This will give the rider plenty of 'thinking' time'.

A good way is to ask the rider to turn in on an inner track. A three-quarter line is very suitable. The horse remains 'positioned' to the inside as he is turned in. During the turn the rider's inside leg was moved almost on the girth. (There it remains for the duration of the movement +). The outside leg stays behind the girth. The bend at the horses' poll remains positioned to the inside as it was coming round the corner. You ask the rider to ensure that the horse is otherwise *quite straight throughout its body*. The distance required to ascertain this, say from the beginning of the track as they turn down an inside track to the letter in the centre of the long side (B or E). At that point the inside leg provides a gentle 'on' 'off' touching pressure just behind the girth, asking the horse to 'Move over'. The fingers of the outside rein provide a half halt for each stride. The combination of the two aids (*with a fraction of a second delay between them but as one complete component)* tells the horse that he is to both move forward and sideways. Sometimes it helps an inexperienced rider, who may be using rather crude aids to say the words 'Move over'. The horse will have heard this word many times from its groom as it is asked to move sideways, in the stable.

Some instructors teach that the inside leg should be moved *behind* the girth in order to commence the movement. *I do not agree*. It is my view that the rider's inside leg should always remain nearly on the girth. An inexperienced rider *may* control trailing quarters if the leg is brushed back but this is still incorrect. The reason that I take this view is because I believe that when a horse is bent the 'support' arises from the inside leg. Therefore the inside should remain mostly where that support is required: almost on the girth. I do not see how a rider can supply this when they have the inside leg continually halfway up the horse's flanks. Some may argue that it is the only way that a rider can successfully make a horse move over its quarters. I do not accept this because a horse is trained to recognise aids which are combinations of signals. If one has to resort to 'pushing' the quarters over then this begins to depend on a degree of *physical force* and as far as I am concerned that has no place in my teaching.

I would go further, straightening the horse in this way merely serves to bring the weight back onto the forehand. Much more satisfactory all round is simply to use the outside leg to straighten up.

89

Possible problems.

Generally the most frequent difficulty is for the rider to *know when the horse has lost its straightness*. This will usually take the form of the horse letting its hindquarters trail. The reason that it does so is because if uncorrected the horse will be able to cease the movement. In other words it will not bother to cross over its legs at all and simply moves in a straight line along the diagonal. Thus a rider may have become quite good at obtaining directional control in front without having any idea as to what is going on behind. The leg yield is a good exercise in teaching riders to be aware of this.

The turn on the forehand.
What is the movement?

I prefer to have this movement only performed at the halt. The horse is required to turn about its forehand. That is to say the inside front leg is simply raised and lowered *almost* on the same spot. The outside front leg describes a small circle passing around the inside front leg. The hindquarters describe a large circle around that being made by the forehand. The inside hind leg moves over and crosses in front of the outside hind leg that then moves away, these steps continue until the movement is complete.

This movement is not much favoured by horse trainers due to the fact that it is likely to encourage the horse to stay on his forehand. I do agree but since we are training riders and not horses, I think that this is a good movement for encouraging a rider to learn to use their limbs independently. The great advantage for the rider is that, apart from changing direction the horse isn't going anywhere!

Position and giving the aids.

Now I must, once again remind the reader that this is not a lesson in schooling the horse. This is a lesson in which the rider learns more about bending and touching the horse in a manner that shows that the horse is listening to them. I therefore ask the class *to perform the movement one step at a time*.

Start by having the ride line up, at the halt, along an inside track of the arena, with a reasonable distance between each rider (say two horses lengths). Let us assume that the ride was proceeding on the right rein. You are going ask them to make a 180-degree turn on the forehand – to the *left*. That is to say that the horse is going to swing its hindquarters to the right.

1   The first thing that the rider must do is to sit tall, deeply on their seat bones and turn their torso to look in the direction in which they wish to proceed. As this is to be a movement to the left then that is where they should be looking. They must now make the horse look in the same direction. Shortening the left rein until there is a little flexion in the horse's neck to the left does this (until they can just see the corner of the eye, what is known as seeing the 'shimmer' of the horse's eye).

2   The rider must now ask the horse to move his quarters over to the right. This is achieved by touching the horse with the left leg (the inside leg relative to the bend) gently, almost on the girth. (The rider should be holding the whip in the left hand just in case a slight touch is required to back-up the leg).

3   A fraction of a second later the fingers of the of the right rein (the outside rein relative to the movement) close. This is a half halt. These two signals tell the horse two things the first is to move the quarters and the second is an instruction *not to step forward*. The horse, obeying will step with its hindquarters moving towards the right.

4   As it does so the rider closes the right leg (the outside leg relative to the bend) behind the girth and *catches the movement* as it ends. The horse is now stood at attention for a count of three. The aids are repeated in the same manner until the whole movement has been completed, one step at a time.

5   Upon completion the horse is asked to walk on and is touched on the neck as a thank you.

You may consider that this is not the stuff of advanced dressage and you would be correct but as I have pointed out we are teaching riders to learn to give the aids correctly. In the above lesson the rider has learned several things – To use each limb independently, to develop a light touch, to react with the next aid quickly and finally to have the satisfying sensation of having a horse's complete attention and obedience.

Further more both rider and horse have been given sufficient time in which to think about what is being asked for.

I always allow the class to perform this movement in their own time. Sometimes, if conditions are favourable, I ask them to do so one at a time so that the rest of the class can watch and make comments afterwards.

Problems that may occur.

Generally speaking difficulties arise not because the horse is trying to evade, after all so far as it is concerned this is, physically, not very demanding. It is usually the rider who causes the problems for the following reasons: -

1   The rider is not sitting on the seat but rather on the fork. As a result they may be unwittingly apply an incorrect signal with the leg due to the fact that it is being used to help keep the rider in position.

2   They may not be looking where they wish to go and have not flexed the horse's head correctly so that it too is looking in the correct direction. The result of both these errors is that the horse may not turn on its forehand but about the centre.

3   The rider may use the leg aids too strongly and instead of precise clear steps, the horse will rush through the movement.

4   Finally the rider may use the half halt too severely or not at all.

The result of the former being that the horse starts to step backwards, and must, immediately, be prevented from so doing by the rider closing both legs firmly behind the girth. If it is the latter, then the horse may well walk forward.

Since, as I stated at the beginning of this section, trainers do not consider this to be a useful exercise due to the fact that it encourages a horse to go on its forehand, is there any use in teaching it? Well, I think that the satisfaction gained by clients, who, having all performed the movement correctly and together, is well worth the effort. Furthermore it is very useful when out hacking and one wishes to open an awkward gate.

The turn on the haunches.

This movement is, as implied by the heading, similar to the turn on the forehand. However it is a turn that requires the horse to have his weight well on his hindquarters since it is the hind legs that are now going to describe the small circle and the forehand that is going to move around them in a large arc. *The horse is looking where it is going.* This means that this is going to be a collected movement. Without it the horse will be standing with its weight on the forehand and be incapable of executing the turn correctly.

For the rider the aids are not that dissimilar to those used for a turn on the forehand, though there is the additional element in that the rider may now invite the horse to move in the required direction by 'leading away' with the inside hind.

Henry Wynmalen (*26) also mentions the movement as an exercise at the halt. For weekend riders, I prefer this movement also to be learned in this way. Of course we are talking now about a movement that forms part of dressage. It is also carried out at the walk and canter. I have actually read one advanced dressage rider who says that it can also take place at the trot. I must say that I am at a loss to see how this can be, since the movement of the horses legs at that gait would imply an element of tripping it up.

The position and giving the aids.

Since, as I have already stated this movement depends on the horse having its weight directed to the haunches, it is sometimes helpful for a rider to start by going forward from walk to halt. Let me be quite clear about this, I do not mean halt and relax, I mean halt at attention. I have found it helps some riders to, momentarily, have a ***mental picture*** as though about to ask for the rein back. In other words the feeling on the rein is maintained and the riders back is braced.

Now the rider must prepare as for the turn on the forehand.

1   The rider must be sure to *sit on the seat bone* and not the fork. They must look in the direction in which they wish the horse to move.

2   Horse should be flexed so that it too is looking in the same direction

3   The rider slightly braces the spine and applies a half halt with the **outside rein**, as they do so they draw back the their **outside leg** and gently touch the horse behind the girth.

4   Simultaneously the rider opens the inside rein (That is to say that they move their hand, horizontally, about 1" to 2" away from the horses neck). This aid in conjunction with all the others should cause the horse to oblige them stepping smartly sideways by crossing over its outside leg in front of the inside one.

5   The hind legs perform in a similar manner except that the circle is much smaller. So small in fact that the inside hind leg is almost marking time on the spot.

6   As soon as the step has been completed. The rider's inside leg, acting almost on the girth, closes gently to catch the movement, the inside hand returns to its original position and the horse halts at attention. After the count of three the riders asks for the second step and so on until the movement is complete and the horse is asked to walk on.

Problems that may occur.
Generally the problems are not that dissimilar to those for a turn on the forehand. However we do have to contend with an extra element in this movement and that concerns the horse's weight, which must be transferred from front to rear, before the movement starts. This means that there are two further matters that concern us.

1   The horse must be schooled to the point where it is physically capable of performing a collected movement.

2   The rider must have learned the rudiments of asking for a degree of collection. (Shortening the stride?)

3   Any tendency for the rider to lean forward or to shift their weight to the fork will result in the horse having difficulty in performing the movement correctly. *They must sit on the rear seat bones.*

If there is a problem in either of these areas, then instead of turning about the hindquarters the horse will either turn about the middle, or worse still, describe the large arc with the hind quarters. In other words it turns the movement into a turn on the forehand. 'My my', the number of times I have seen that befall, even advanced riders! Should this occur ask the rider to cease the movement immediately and start again. This time you, who will have noted why the error happened, will talk the rider through the movement so that it will be successful.

Final thoughts on turns at the halt.
There are many other views as to how these movements may be performed. In some books on dressage one may find those who prefer to have the horse *not* looking in the direction that it is going. It may even be suggested that a turn *about* the forehand may be performed at the walk. That is all very well when one is writing about *training* the horse but, as I have stressed so many times before, we are talking about *training the rider*. Therefore I believe that it is essential that those we instruct should, first of all, become practised in executing these movements in an, essentially, basic manner. When the rider becomes well versed in every movement they may try as many different variations, as they will. For they will then be in a position to *train the horse*.

Since the turn on the haunches requires a degree of collection, you may well be wondering why I have included it in this chapter, dealing as it does with basic aids. Why have I not placed it with advanced aids? The reason for this is that while in the first place I suggest that you do not encourage novices to perform the movement, I do think that it is quite suitable for intermediate riders. It is a way of introducing them to a slight form of collection without the difficulty that would be involved if there were any forward motion.

On reflection.

Now despite everything that I have just written concerning turns at the halt, many riders do have a problem in performing these movements with great accuracy. The horse very often shows a desire to turn about the centre or to step forward instead of pivoting about the required leg. Why is this so? The reason lies in the imprecise way in which the aid has been given. In fact the rider has probably always been giving aids in an inaccurate manner but has been getting away with it.

Let me give an example. A rider asks their horse to go forward to walk. They use the leg but do not brace the back or give the half halt. The horse walks on. Though the aid is imprecise the rider makes the assumption that they have given the aid correctly, after all hasn't the horse obeyed them? Now we come to the turns on forehand, haunches or for that matter any lateral movement.

The rider gives the aid correctly with the leg but they either do not give the half halt or it is applied too late, by which time the horse has already stepped forward. Upon being asked why, they reply. 'Well I was waiting for the horse to obey my leg. I didn't want to give the half halt until it did so'. Now everything becomes quite clear because the rider is not able to react quickly enough to apply the half halt before the horse moves forward. I hasten to explain. 'Give the leg aid and half halt as a **complete component** even though the fraction of a second time lapse between each part is still maintained'. 'But surely I shouldn't give the half halt until the horse starts to move away from my leg'? I reply '***The very fact that you give the leg aid and half halt as two parts of the same component tells the horse what it is that you require'***. The rider tries the movement gain, this time giving the aids as instructed - the horse turns perfectly! As one of my pupils said to me 'I suppose that what we are learning is to use joined up writing?' Very well put!

The Rein back
What is a rein back?

It is a two-time movement in which the horse moves backwards. Correctly performed the horse steps backward with its legs moving in diagonal pairs. Unlike the trot there is no moment of suspension between each stride. It is probably a good idea to start teaching this movement with the horses lined up along the sides of the arena. The ride should be in open order so that everyone has plenty of room.

This in an excellent exercise in teaching a rider to learn balance between seat legs and hand. When many riders try to perform the movement they, instinctively, simply pull on the reins until their horse obeys. In all honesty I have to say that this sometimes works. This is because the poor horse has, correctly divined that this is the required answer to such a crude message. *However it is not the correct message* and usually it results in resistance on the horses' part.

The correct aids for a rein back are as follows. The rider braces the back – slightly and as they do so the rein is shortened, the fingers close around the outside rein as contact is established. The horse comes to attention. The rider may ask for a little flexion of the jaw with the inside rein. The bracing of the back continues and both the riders' legs close behind the girth. The horse is waiting for the fingers to open and thus it thinks that it will receive the aid to go forward to walk. But the fingers do not open, they remain closed for an extra fraction of a second. The horse now realises that it is being asked for a rein back. *As it is about to do so* the rider rewards it by opening the hand. The aids are repeated for each step. The steps must be measured and not rushed. The horse must not resist the rider. As soon as the required number of steps has been completed the horse should be asked to walk on.

Generally speaking, in an exam or test, a rider will be required to show three clear steps backwards.

Problems arising from the rein back.

1   The rider may be too severe with the use of the rein and as a result the horse may stiffen and resist.

2   The horse may not step back in a straight line. Or, if it does so then it will move with a hollow back. It will therefore be up to you to correct the rider immediately this error is about to occur.

How can you assist?

If a rider has continual difficulty in getting their horse to obey, place the horse alongside a wall or fence of the arena, stand by its forehand facing to the rear. Now sensitively taking the rein in your hand and, using a verbal command such as 'come back', assist the rider by using a long schooling whip in the other hand. With this you may touch the horse and by applying the correct gentle aid to the rein and preventing the quarters from swinging inwards, the horse will step backwards without objecting.

You may have noted that I have left the rein back to the end of this first chapter on giving the aids. The reason for this is that it is essential to ensure that a client has first been successful in making a horse go *forward* before learning to ask it step backwards.

General problems that riders may have in the giving of these signals.

One of the most difficult problems for many riders is the failure to appreciate that the *giving of signals* is the basis of *communication* with horses. Many people find it difficult to understand this concept. It seems logical for them, and their instructors often encourage this, to believe that violent booting with the heels and heavy tugging on the reins is the way to go about things. To some extent this is understandable because the correct application of a *light* aid may have to be reinforced, if required by a touch of the whip. This may be met by an objection from the horse in the form a little buck. The reason for this is simply that this has been the horses' response in the past and it is usually successful - the rider ceases to use the whip and the horse does not have to comply! That is why it is essential that from the very beginning that a good seat is established and this is best achieved by several sessions on the lunge.

However the application of an aid may be likened to an artist applying a brush stroke to a canvas. Light but dextrous. Carried out by feel rather than measurement. *Above all the rider must not look down.* If they do look down then, apart from not being able to see quite clearly where they are going, the actual weight of the head will have an effect on the rider's ability to balance.

Another problem that is frequently seen is the opening of the rein or leading away. A rider using this aid say for example to encourage a horse to yield to the leg or to perform shoulder-in will, either, open the rein too far (usually an inch is quite enough) or, having done so, forget to close it. (The hand stays fixed.)

You may now select any of these movements together with those listed in chapter 16 'Exercises to form a lesson' and create the foundation of a lesson.

Your job in a nutshell.

Some years ago when attending a trade show in Newcastle, I found myself passing a second-hand bookshop. Now when it comes to second-hand books I am rather like Jonathan Gash's, Lovejoy. I am a bit of a 'Divi' when in the proximity of a good book on equitation I get the 'feeling'. So sensing 'vibrations', as it were, I entered the shop and inquired as to what books they might have on riding or equitation. 'On the back shelf' said the shop owner. I looked but found nothing remarkable. 'Real collector are you?' said the man. 'Well come up stairs'. At the end of the corridor on the first floor, lying alone in its own glass display stand, was a first edition copy of Wm. Cavendish's book 'A General System of Horsemanship'. This very book had first been published in English, in 1658! I was allowed to examine it and spent quite some time doing so. In fact I became so absorbed that the whole morning went by and I was late in attending the trade show. 'What will you take?' I inquired. 'Two thousand pounds' he replied. Now this was in 1982 and that sum was a bit much for me at the time but how I have since regretted not buying it.

Years later a similar thing happened when my wife and I, having just come to the end of a cruise to Alaska, had a short time to spend in Vancouver before leaving for the airport. On this occasion I did buy a book from those presented to me but the feeling that this was not the one that had drawn me into the shop did not go away. The owner returned and offered the same Cavendish book, a slightly different edition perhaps, smaller when compared to the one I had seen in the U.K. 'How much?' 'Four hundred dollars'. I hesitated; it had been an expensive trip including as it did a trip through the Rockies. Perhaps the book was not 'quite right' I thought? On return home I wrote to the shop offering to buy, but did not receive a reply.

The point about this little tale is that in these books William Cavendish, the first Duke of Newcastle wrote the following – more or less. 'It takes a time for a boy to learn his ABC, longer to learn to spell and longer still to learn to read. Why do some people expect a horse to learn his lessons in only a very short time and then only by beating him?' He then went on to explain that one would seldom get the better of the horse by losing ones temper. He pointed out the teaching a horse was not dissimilar to a lad learning to play the lute. The animal had to learn its lessons so well that as an expert lute players' fingers touch the notes without thinking about each one individually, so a horses reactions to the aids would be similar. All this takes time and patience. This was a turning point in the 17th century when men started to think more deeply about equitation and to become more enlightened in the way that they trained their horses.

But we are not talking about training horses, so why have I bothered to mention this matter? How does this apply to your pupils? Well I would *change the subject* of these comments and *instead apply them to the rider*. I offer them as a confirmation of my views, arrived at independently, and expressed elsewhere in this book. *What you have to do is to repeat and repeat the basic aids until your pupils are able to give them, correctly, with finesse, and without having to think about them. Above all you must persist in preventing bad habits from forming and doing your best to remove those already established in your pupils prior to their attending your classes.* Only in this way will you produce a good rider.

Drawings

Drawing no. 9.

Holding the reins correctly and using the fingers to maintain an elasticky feel on the reins. As the horse's head nods forward and back so the fingers, by opening and closing keep a neutral feeling on the rein until such time as the rider wishes to give a half halt.

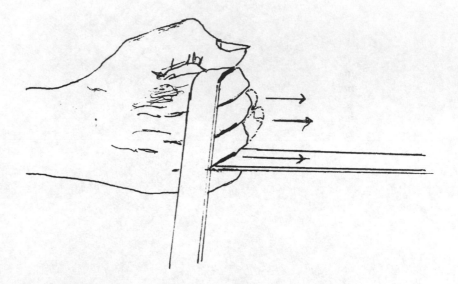

Drawing no. 9. Holding the reins, correctly with the fingers acting as springs.

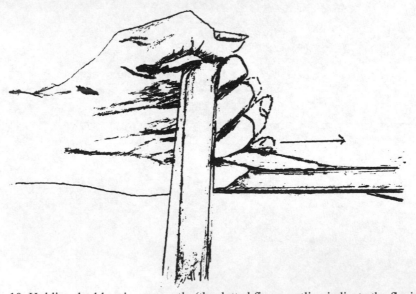

Drawing no. 10. Holding double reins, correctly (the dotted finger outline indicate the flexing motion).

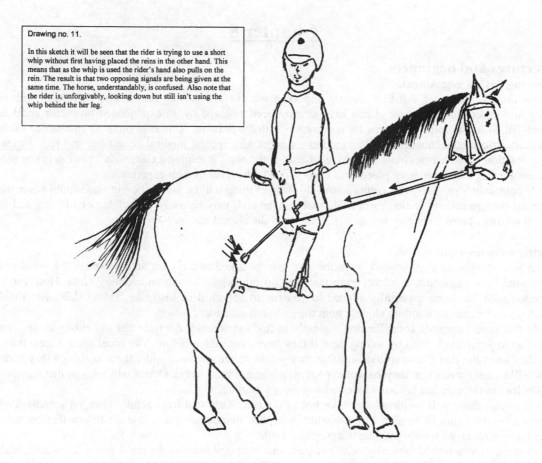

Drawing no. 11.

In this sketch it will be seen that the rider is trying to use a short whip without first having placed the reins in the other hand. This means that as the whip is used the rider's hand also pulls on the rein. The result is that two opposing signals are being given at the same time. The horse, understandably, is confused. Also note that the rider is, unforgivably, looking down but still isn't using the whip behind the her leg.

Drawing no. 11. Using a short whip.

In this sketch it will be seen that the rider is trying to use a short whip without, first, having placed the reins in the other hand. This means that as the whip is used the rider's hand also pulls on the rein. The result is that two opposing signals are given at the same time. The horse, understandably, is confused. Also note that the rider is, unforgivably, looking down but still isn't using the stick directly behind her leg.

Chapter 8

Overtures and beginners.

Carrying out an assessment.

As mentioned in chapter 6 it is extremely important that, before starting *any* lesson, you check with the office and make sure that *new* clients have already been assessed by an experienced instructor and have already filled in the required forms for registration with the School. This is in order to ensure that all the necessary information about the client (address, next of kin, special medical conditions and requirements e.g. a reaction to antibiotics have all been recorded). If the pupil is joining a class with other riders you must also ensure that they have been placed in a class suited to the level of their experience.

Of course in a properly run riding school this sort of thing will be automatic but one should never take anything for granted. It is always possible that regular staff may be away on holiday or off sick and the person who has taken over may not be as familiar with the correct routine.

Taking an assessment lesson.

When you become an experienced instructor, you may be asked to carry out an assessment. I have already mentioned how important it is to ensure that you do this whilst taking an ordinary class. However for someone who has been especially allotted to you for an appraisal of his or her riding skills you should proceed in a manner that differs slightly from the giving of a standard lesson.

At this time your sole consideration is simply to find out whether the rider has any riding ability at all and if so to what level. Start by asking them if they have ever ridden before. The usual answer from men is that they have but that it was so long ago that they would prefer you to consider them as though they hadn't (this will usually mean that they have never sat on a horse in their lives). Others will tell you that they have ridden for many years but have not received any formal training.

Of course there will be those who have been riding regularly and have simply changed schools. From these replies you should be able to know what to expect. Remember that it doesn't follow that because a rider has not received formal training that they can't ride.

Proceed as you would normally, with a request that the pupil work-in the horse going large at the walk. At this time you may give advice as to the sort of thing that you would like to see; correct position for example - but do not be too detailed or expect too much. All that you require is that the rider proceeds quietly around the arena and is so able to control the horse that it does not wander into the centre unasked.

If they do this correctly then ask them to change the rein through a diagonal. Any rider who has had some experience of riding horses should be able to manage this though they may never previously have had a formal riding lesson and thus sit appallingly. If the rider is incapable of this control during a simple walk then do not ask them to trot, simply spend the rest of their allotted time helping them to establish the walk, obtain directional control and possibly learn to go forward to halt.

If the rider does demonstrate reasonable control at the walk, then ask them if they have ever trotted before. Should they reply in the affirmative then ask them to do so covering similar ground as before. You may now ask for a series of transitions upward from halt to walk, trot and then downward. At this time ask the rider to describe the exact aids that they are going to use. Continue with the riding of large circles and observe carefully how accurately they are ridden.

If all goes well now ask the client if they have ever cantered. They may already have told you that they have at the beginning of the lesson. None-the-less ask them again if they would like to canter at this time. If they tell you that they would, first ask them to describe the action of the canter and also what aids they would employ. If they cannot do so (many people are unable to do either) describe the canter and tell them the aids yourself. This is important at this time as much for the benefit of the horse as the rider. Now ask them to try to canter along one side of the arena. If they are un-able to do so do not continue.

End the assessment by praising the rider if they have done well or encouraging them if they really are novices. Reward the horse! Have the horse taken away by a groom and accompany the rider to the office. Ask them to wait for a moment, outside and immediately report your conclusions to those in charge. When you have done so ask the client to step in and leave them to book further lessons if they so wish.

Beginning with beginners.

This chapter and the preceding one together with the next are probably amongst the longest in this book.

The reason for this is that in these sections I have tried to cover most of the absolute basic requirements that form the foundation for teaching pupils to becoming good equestrians. All else that follows is simply a means of honing the skills that were acquired during these first lessons.

The target is position *and* relaxation.
Before we begin it is absolutely essential that we have a clear idea as to what is our target. At this stage, with the client starting off on the lunge, we must, firstly, teach our clients the ***correct position*** and how to maintain it. Secondly to instil in them the need for ***complete relaxation***. At a later stage when the client is riding no longer tethered, as it were, they will then have to cope with the third problem and that of course is how to make the horse go in the required direction and at a pace that they desire. If the two, previously mentioned basics have been well learned then the third will be much easier to achieve. You must remember that a sign of your success will be that the client will carry out your instructions correctly and succeed handsomely without putting in so much effort that they return to the next lesson complaining about muscle stiffness resulting from the last one.

Position and balance.
Building on the part of the foregoing (correct position) the rider creates the foundation from which perfect balance and thus a truly independent seat arise. This will then enable the rider to use their ***limbs independently***. In turn the rider may then be able, once they have learned the correct combinations, to give a schooled horse signals that will leave it in no doubt as to their wishes.

Relaxation.
But it is all very well going on about position and balance if the rider does not also realise that these must be achieved without any rigidity in the body whatsoever. This might seem to be so obvious as not to invite any further discussion. For example one may consider that gripping strongly with the thighs precludes the ability to move the leg with delicacy. One may go further; the human head weighs about ten pounds! It therefore follows that if the rider continually looks down, then the musculature around the area of the neck will be under strain and this in turn will be transmitted to the shoulders, the back and down the arms, the hands even the rider's very fingers! Tension of any sort adversely effects the riders' ability to give the lightest of aids.

So how does the rider maintain position whilst incorporating all these essentials? The answer is that they have to learn to rely on the force of gravity. In other words if the body is maintained in the vertical then gravity will assist in keeping the rider firmly in the saddle. Looking ahead helps the rider to carry their head in such a position that ***gravity alone*** plays a major part in helping to keep the body in place. Making this simple point will contribute to an overall lessening of the resultant fatigue that is concomitant with tension and that in turn will lead to the achievement of the desired goal – an independent seat.

The machine connection.
Some great writers on equitation have drawn attention to the connection of the rider's back and seat. Springs have been used in diagrams to show where flexibility is required. I am tempted to do the same but as I mentioned in my introduction, having spent some considerable time in an industrial environment my view on the mechanics involved are perhaps more specialised. Thus when discussing the absorption of the force produced by the arc of any motion involving a moment of suspension, I would tend to think of the wishbone spring rather than the helical variety (see drawing no. 7 chapter 6). The top part anchored to the upper part of the torso and the flexing movement occurring at the other end where the spine meets the pelvic girdle. In this way the upper body does indeed remain motionless.

Working with the very best material!
In my opinion, the very best pupil that one may have is an absolute beginner and of beginners - children are the finest. Some instructors do not share this view. They regard teaching beginners as beneath their dignity. I do not agree, for if one starts with someone, who has absolutely no idea of how to ride, there is no more, ultimately satisfying, challenge than to teach him or her to become excellent horsemen. The rider will not have developed any bad habits, in the first place and, under your tutelage, will not do so.

Sometimes I get close to the point of despair, when trying to cure fairly experienced riders of ingrained bad habits. Those bringing the inside leg halfway up the horse's flanks as they try to ride a lateral movement, allowing the outside leg to drift so far forward that you can actually see the rider's toe sticking out past the horses shoulder, even though viewed from the other side. Then there are those who ride with their hands dancing about in the air and whose idea of a downward transition is to give an almighty pull on the rein.

On the other hand working with a complete beginner, you have the pleasure of seeing someone progress from novice to advanced rider (given time). Presuming, that is, you are successful in maintaining their enthusiasm and they, in turn, do have at least some penchant for the art of riding. Even if they don't, after a short while you should have produced a rider who, though not a master horseman, is able to safely enjoy the pleasure of horse riding and who can then go off and have much fun.

Before you start.
You must remember that for pupils riding for the very first time even the entry into the yard and going to the office can be a quite an unsettling experience, never mind about getting on the horse, . You must try to put them at their ease so that by the end of their first lesson, which may be only half an hour, they are full of enthusiasm and wish to come back for more. You do this by being kind and in taking your time to explain quite clearly what they have to do in order to get the horse to obey them. Do not be overlong and spend too much time on the details, feed them a little information at a time and then, while standing along side let them put it into practise.

It is essential that you teach your pupils the basics of safety around horses.
Don't forget novices may have absolutely no idea about matters that you take for granted and don't have to think about any more.

1. Never ever walk around the hindquarters. You are bound to get some know-it-all who asks 'What then does one do when going into a horses' box and it has its tail turned towards you'? You should not waste time with a prolonged discussion about something that has to do with stable management. Your answer should be 'don't go into a horse's box or stall without a qualified member of staff attending. They will ensure your safety'.

2. Never shout or wave their arms about when they are anywhere near horses.

3. Never run when in the proximity of a horse.

4. Never feed a horse without permission and under supervision by a member of staff.

5. Never leave a stable door unbolted.

Of course these are by no means all the rules that need to be followed when dealing with horses, but they will serve as a simple guide with which to begin.

The lunge rein.
A good way of introducing a person to horse riding is by giving the first lessons on the lunge. This is a long rein used, together with a Cavesson lunging bridle. The horse should be one that is familiar with this form of tack and work. Similar equipment was probably used during its early schooling. With this bridle and perhaps with long reins, the trainer would have taught the horse to respond to, basic, verbal commands. At that time it would, probably, not have carried the weight of a human on its back. You will now use these same commands. Remember a horse working on a continuous on a circle with someone on board, finds this quite demanding; therefore lunging should never exceed a maximum of half an hour. It is also my view that the instructor should always have a small tasty reward in his or her pocket to give when the work has come to an end. Some instructors do not bother. I do!

However no instructor should attempt to give lessons on the lunge unless they have had considerable practical experience. I would suggest that you read 'The Fundamentals of Riding' by Charles Harris. *23. Also Sylvia Stanier's book 'The Art of Lunging'. You must have learned how to control the horse between the 'triangle' created by the lunge rein running from your hand to the horses head, its own body length and of course the lunge whip that you hold in your other hand, (this directed when required towards the quarters) (see drawing no. 13.).

A suitable horse.

Before you start you must make sure that the horse you are about to use will go well on the lunge. Some horses find this type of exercise not to their liking and may well break into a canter, or even put in a buck, as soon as they are asked to go away from you. Needless to say this must *not* happen whilst your novice client is in the saddle. Obviously you should check with the office and ensure that you have been allocated a suitable animal. I do not think that this is sufficient. Unless you really know the horse well, lunge him, without the rider, for about five minutes on either rein. By doing this you give the horse a chance to get rid of any pent-up up energy. Many horses are exercised in this manner when they have been standing in their stables for a considerable time, for example as a result of lameness. Thus it may well think that this is just another chance to do the same thing. Ten minutes in total should be sufficient to get it going on quietly. It is best to do this before your client arrives; otherwise they may become apprehensive as they see you at work and you will also be wasting time that they have paid for.

Horses may well try to evade your control, especially if they are stiffer on one rein than the other. That is why you must have practised this work and have perfected it, long before you are unleashed on unsuspecting clients! Just imagine what a fool you will look if, every time you wish the horse to go on a different rein, it persists in ducking out and going back in the original direction. It all depends on the suitability of the horse, how quickly you read the messages it sends you, your speed of reaction, and finally, how much the horse respects you!

Checking for basic safety.

The arena must be checked to ensure that it is clear of any object that could course injury were there to be a fall. I have in mind such objects as jumping uprights and so forth.

Showing the client how to approach a horse.

The correct approach to a horse can mean, for both horse and rider, the difference between a happy co-operation and one that is not. The client should be shown how to move towards the animal in a quiet manner. From the front but slightly to one side of the horses' head, on the near side. As they do so they should speak quietly to the horse saying its name and gently pat it on the neck.

Checking the stirrups for correct length.

You need to show the client how they should check the stirrup for correct length. You ask the rider to do this by standing quietly on the near side next to the horse, as one would in preparing to mount. They take down the stirrup and then stretch out the right arm until it touches the buckle of the stirrup leather. With the left hand the rider then takes the stirrup and lifts it until, if it is the correct length, it will rest under the armpit of the right arm (see photo no. 15). If the length is not correct then it should be adjusted. Of course this rule is simply a guide. It may well be that your client is a little short in the leg or is about to mount a big horse, in which case it will be necessary for you to show the client how to lengthen the stirrup so that they can mount more easily. Of course after they are in the saddle, you will have to show them how to readjust the stirrups while mounted.

Preparing to mount

The first thing that a client needs to know is how to get up on the horse. Ideally this should be attempted from a mounting block, since it easier for the client and less of a strain on the horse's back. Sometimes a block is not available, in which case one can mount just as easily from the ground. Whichever way it is very important that the correct procedure be followed.

Before showing a client how to mount it is probably useful, though not essential, to have a helper at hand to hold the horse, by the rein near the bit on the offside. This person, standing by the foreleg of the horse, will also run down the stirrup for you on that side. They will place their left hand on the iron so that, by pushing down, there will no tendency for the saddle to twist over the horses back as the client mounts. It may be thought that this is unlikely since you will have checked the girth yourself and ensured that it is tight. However one cannot be too careful, as some horses do have a tendency to blow themselves out and manage to resist the best efforts to tighten the girth.

Demonstrating mounting procedure (From the near side).

Tell the client that you are going to give them a demonstration/or instruct them. You may mention that you understand that they may have mounted before but that you are going to show them the *correct way*. You may either proceed to mount yourself or you may ask the client to do so. Either way you must proceed step-by-step telling the client what to do and why. At this stage it is best to make use of a mounting block. Be very particular. Show them how to face to the rear and even at this early stage, how to **check the girth**. You recheck yourself in case the horse was blown out the last time that you checked it. If it is loose then ask the client to step behind you and further tighten it yourself. *All the time explain clearly and precisely what you are doing and why.* Bring the client back and once again show them how to stand facing towards the haunches on the near side. Show them how to hold the rein in their left hand, as a *double loop*. If you do use the mounting block, then, have the client stand on the top of the block. With their right hand they should reach forward and taking the *trailing edge* of the stirrup leather, turn this towards themselves, whilst lifting their left leg and placing this in the stirrup. (You should have adjusted the stirrup beforehand so that this movement is easy for the client). Then tell them to place their right hand on the **seat** of the saddle and with their left hand, still holding the reins, to grasp the mane just in front of the withers. Then to hop around with three small bounces until they are facing the horses' side and then to press down on the stirrup and spring lightly up over and onto the saddle, *gently* lowering their weight onto the horses back (see photos no. 16a, b, c etc.).

The explanations.
It is not enough simply to tell the client what to do as described above. You also need to tell them why.

1. Holding the rein as a double loop. (Even if a helper is also holding it).
Why? This is important as it allows the rider a better control over the horses' head should it, for example, try to turn its head and take a nip out of the rider, or start to walk on.

2. Taking the trailing edge of the stirrup leather.

Why? This will ensure that the leather lies flat against the rider's boot after mounting and thus avoid discomfiture.

3. Placing the hand on the seat of the saddle instead of grabbing hold of the cantle (as so many riders are inclined to do).
Why? This avoids twisting the saddle across the horses back thus causing discomfiture for the horse.

It is not enough to make the points once only. They must be repeated time and time again until they become second nature for the rider.

The alternative mounting procedure (from the near side).
If a mounting block is not available, mounting with the aid of a leg up is another way of helping a client to get mounted. Proceed as before but stopping at the point where the client is about to take hold of the stirrup leather. Instead have the client turn to face the side of the horse and ask them to bend their left leg at the knee. Place you hand under the middle of the lower leg and on the count of three have the client spring up onto the horses back whilst you give them a little extra boost. (If you are dealing with a small horse and a short person, take care not to give them such a boost that they go clean over the other side. – I've seen it happen!)

When the client is mounted

Re-check the girth.
You should encourage a client to always re-check their own girth as soon as they have mounted (see photo no. 17). You must also check for yourself that they have done so correctly.
Stirrups.
Check stirrups to ensure that they are not twisted and that the leathers are lying flat against the rider's legs. You should also check that they are level. It is amazing how many riders will embark upon a lesson with one stirrup much longer than the other. This problem will often occur when they have mounted from the ground and the stirrup has been lengthened to enable them to do so more easily. However they forget that

this was done and will very happily ride around the arena in a lopsided manner (see photo no. 18).

Checking for the correct length when mounted.
Ask your client to take their feet out of the stirrups. The lowest part of the stirrup (the bars where the sole of the foot rests) should lie just above the client's ankle. This will mean that when the client has their feet in the stirrups their thigh will be at the correct angle to give support to the body (see photo no 19).

One must, however, bear in mind that the, correct, length of the stirrup is dependent on the clients physiognomy. Even when dealing with someone with a tall willowy body and long legs, *in the early stages,* it will help if they do not ride so long that they are denied *good support from the thigh*. This means that a slightly greater bend at the knee may be very helpful in providing greater support to the upper body. The same would apply to those with rotund upper bodies and short legs (see photo no. 20).

Adjusting the stirrups while mounted.
You must make sure that clients are taught *not* to take their feet out of the stirrups when they wish to adjust them. This will avoid the stirrup accidentally banging against the horse's side and, perhaps, giving it an erroneous signal to move. Another advantage is that should the horse be startled then the client is less likely to become unbalanced because their foot remains in position.

Keeping the foot in the stirrup also helps when making an adjustment. If they simply wish to make the stirrup shorter, then all that needs to be done is for the skirt of the saddle to be lifted. This will reveal the buckle of the leather. The foot is lifted, slightly, and the free end of the strap is firmly held in the rider's hand, released from the buckle prong and pulled through the required number of holes. To lengthen, the foot is simply pushed down on the stirrup and the hand allows the strap to slide through. Because the foot is in the stirrup the whole time the rider will have a better idea as to when they have reached the length that they require. The final adjustment is simply to bring the buckle back up under the skirt where it will be prevented from rubbing against the rider's thigh. This is achieved by the rider again momentarily lifting the weight of their foot off the stirrup and taking hold of the underneath leather and pulling it downwards causing the buckle to move up. Or more simply by taking hold of the top strap of the leather below the buckle, lifting it and at the same time pushing the foot down onto the stirrup. Both ways will have the same effect (see photo no. 20a).

Caution when checking the client's position.
Before a client even starts to ride you must check their position. Start with the head and move down through the body, ending at the feet. If you wish to straighten the back or reposition the leg, tell the client that you are going to do so and ask if they have any objection.

Why?
At the time that I write we have reached a situation where any unannounced physical contact between an instructor and pupil may be misinterpreted as a form of assault. Even if I have informed a client that I intend to make a correction, I usually do so by touching them, gently, with the handle of my whip.

Not only must you check and correct position but you should also make sure that the client knows how to hold the rein. Even an experienced rider *apparently* holding the reins correctly may not really *understand* how they are should be held.

Holding single reins.
When the client is ready to hold the rein, these should be held, initially in both hands. The rider's right hand holds the rein on the right side and the left hand the one on that side. The thumb and forefinger actually hold the rein. The rein then runs down the palm of the rider's hand and passes between the third and little fingers where it travels down to the bit in the horse's mouth. With the thumb and first finger acting as an anchor, the other fingers, closing *around* the rein should not become fixed but remain spring-like; so that they may open and close as the horse gently swings its head up and down as it moves. In this way the rider establishers an elastic feel to the reins so that, as soon as the fingers are closed, even momentarily, the horse will detect the change (see drawing nos. 9 & 10.)

Holding the rein correctly is, perhaps, the one thing that is most difficult for a rider to learn. It will set the foundation for the creation of– 'still hands' – 'soft and sensitive hands' - 'good hands'.

Of course if you are continually making this point, then there may be a 'downside'. This is that the rider holds the reins so softly that the anchor point ceases to be effective and the horse gently (sometimes not so gently) and subtly pulls the reins through the rider's fingers. It is a very common fault and one that you must watch out for. It is no use you trying to teach your class to give aids correctly if half the time control is virtually absent because the horse has quietly adjusted the rein to suit itself.

Explaining to the client the reasons why?
Pupils, frequently have a preconceived mental image of themselves as they start to learn to ride. Whilst some are very thankful to be on the end of a long rein that they perceive as a means of preventing the horse from dashing off into the great beyond, others do not share this view. When asked to go on the lunge, they see themselves as being made to look slightly ridiculous. For their approach derives from cowboy films and they picture themselves roaming free around the countryside from the word go.

You must explain, to both groups, that work on the lunge has very little to do with the horse dashing off. In these circumstances it has to do with relieving the rider of any necessity to give the *instructions* that ask the horse to move at a required gait. You should tell them that the giving of these *aids* is your responsibility. Thus the rider is allowed to concentrate *entirely* upon the twin problems, of keeping their bodies and limbs in the correct position whilst at the same time remaining perfectly relaxed. You should go on to explain that this sort of exercise is beneficial, from time to time, for all riders, no matter how experienced they are.

One day after I had come to the end of a lesson, a rider of intermediate standard, asked me as to how they could give the aids more precisely. Your problem, I told him is that you remain unable to keep your upper body absolutely still. Were you to ride with a German Horse Master, you would probably work on the lunge, daily for six months before even being allowed to pick up the reins! The reason being that you would be expected to develop and strengthen all the muscles that are required to give you a firm but relaxed seat. It is interesting to note that Charles Harris, who was the only Englishman ever to complete the full three-year graduation course with the Spanish Riding School of Vienna, wrote of the following regime. Lunge lessons for *20 to 30 minutes five times a week* passing through *four separate stages*, each of which *is of 3 months duration!*

Unfortunately, those learning to ride in the environment about which I write will probably not have the time available for such a concentrated approach. So we the poor instructors have to do the best that we can.

What you should already know before you start the lesson.
Your communication.
You command the horse with your voice. Back this up with a gentle motion of the whip, flicking the thong just behind the horse's flank. Thus you proceed. 'The horses name let us say that for the benefit of this description it is 'Jeeves'. So 'Jeeves walk on' your voice sharpens as you say walk *on.* As the horse obeys you immediately respond 'Good boy'.

The commands are as follows: -
Having attached the lunge line to the cavesson,
(Hold the line at shoulder height with the remainder of the rein coiled securely in the other hand.
Ask the horse to 'Move out' (say on the left rein)
You may help by pointing your whip at the horse's shoulder. As it moves away let the lunge rein loops flow through your left hand.

The name - then **walk on.** (The voice sharp. The point of whip slightly raised)

The name - then *whoa halt.* (The voice soft, at the same time lowering the point of the whip towards the ground and to your side)

If the horse does not obey you and keeps walking on then repeat the command and either flex your wrist so that there is a momentary increase of tension on the rein. If that signal is ignored gradually draw in the lunge looping the spare rein in your hand again. As the circle gets smaller so forward movement will become more difficult for the horse and it will be more inclined to halt. You may also obtain obedience to this command by pointing your whip just in front of the horse's shoulder. Should you decide to use this latter method, then, do so with care for a horse that suddenly sees someone thrusting a long whip directly towards it may get entirely the wrong impression.

104

The name - then **walk on**. then trrrrot **on** (The voice sharp. The point of whip raised)
Remember for upward transitions your voice is sharper on the last word of command. For downward transitions your voice should be soft and gentle.

The name - then waaalk (The voice soft. Lowering the point of the whip towards the ground)
Whenever obeyed then 'good boy' *every time.*

At some time, if required. The name - then can**terrrr.** (The voice sharp. The point of whip raised)
(For more about canter see below).

The name then Trrrrrot. (Gently - the point of whip lowered) I have written an elongation of the word trot to help you vocalise. It should not be read as troot! And so on back to walk or halt.

The tempo of the paces.
For each gait keep the tempo firmly in your mind. Thus: -

The Walk – 1-2-3-4 slight pause 1-2-3-4- and so on a consistent unvarying tempo all the time. (About 3/4 centi seconds from beat 1 through to 4).

The Trot. – 1-2- 1-2- 1-2-. (About 2/3 centi seconds from beat 1 through to 2)

The Canter – 1-2-3- and 1-2-3 **and** (the *and* is the moment of suspension when all the legs are in the air about 3 centi seconds from the first beat through to the moment of suspension).

These are the commands that you will use as you introduce your client to their early riding lessons on the lunge.

The technique
If your arena is being used by others this may be a quite restricting space. Lead the horse to the centre of this area and prepare to help the client to mount. Before you do so place the lunging whip, on the ground, in the centre of the area that you intend to use (You may also place the lunge line with it).You must take care not to trip over it but it is much better to have it out of the way, for it will avoid you accidentally, touching the horse and giving it a fright whilst you are concentrating on helping the client.

Proceeding with the lunge lesson.
The first lesson for a novice.
Explain the target.
Before you start you must establish in the rider's mind the target. At this stage and forever more (though there may be additions) it is the development of a good seat.

What is a good seat?
A method of riding in which the position of the rider's body and limbs is sustained in such a way that there is no interference with the manner of the horses going. In order to assist in this, you, ideally, should not allow the rider to hold the reins for the first two or three lessons. When they are not holding them, the reins should be twisted around one another and secured through the throatlatch (see photo no. 21). However some clients do want to experience the sensation of holding the rein, without which they consider that they have not truly ridden the horse. Therefore I do sometimes make a special allowance and, having freed the reins, I allow the rider to hold them correctly for the last five minutes of the lesson, but only at the walk.

Avoiding the horse having unpleasant associations.
Having said that, it is most important that you explain to your client why you do not allow them to hold the reins from the very beginning. One of the reasons is that without still hands, with the best will in the world, there is no way that the rider will not inflict on the horse some pain through involuntary movement. They will, probably, instinctively, use the reins to try and maintain their own balance. To overcome the craving to

hold on to something the horse should be correctly tacked up with a neck strap and the rider should use this whenever they feel the need for support.

When holding the reins the rider may regret any discomfiture caused but what they will not realise is that the *horse will remember*. When they eventually come to ride that same horse at a later stage, they may be somewhat surprised when the horse suddenly stops or starts at something that is not there. Of course all that it is doing is looking for a pretext to avoid the pain that it imagines will soon be forthcoming.

Continuous checking.

As you read on you may notice that I repeat some paragraphs in other chapters. This is one of them. The reason for this is that I consider them to be of such fundamental importance that I do not want you to forget. Even if you haven't forgotten, I still wish to refresh your memory without having to revert to a previous chapter.

It is your job to *constantly check* your clients' position throughout the entire period of the lesson. The rider must be examined in detail and the position commented upon. This means praise as well as criticism. You are looking for: -

1. The head held well balanced on the riders' shoulders.
2. The chin tucked in.
3. The rider looking ahead and not down at the horse.
4. The shoulders back and chest lifted up and open.
5. The back straight but flexible.
6. The rider clearly sitting on the seat bones with just a hint of the weight being placed on the rear part of the pelvis.
7. The elbows tucked gently into the waist (Not pushed forward as though wheeling a supermarket trolley).
8. The hands carried as a pair (and perfectly still) with the thumbs on top each one pointing at the horses' opposite ear.
9. The fingers opening and closing to allow for the movement in the horses head.
10. The toes turned up and to the front, (bringing the knee on to the saddle).
11. The heels pushed down but not so far that the ankles cannot remain springy.
12. Finally the whole position held whilst the rider is in a state of *complete relaxation*.

With regard to point no. 10. It is frequently said that the heel position should not be pushed down to the point of exaggeration. The reason being that this may cause stiffening in the calf and thigh muscles that can be translated to the riders' spine. I agree, but to my mind the position should be relative to the rider's experience. By that I mean that, in the beginning it will probably be quite difficult for a rider to obtain any downward position of the heel, this being due to the fact that tendons do not stretch very much. However they do lengthen, gradually, over a period of time. And it is my opinion that this is what your pupils should aim for. If they do not do so, then they will never be in the position where they are able to maximise the spring in their heels. Whilst talking about heels, it is worthwhile considering that fashion does change. When I first learnt to ride the favoured position for the lower leg and foot was with the ankle 'broken' that is to say turned out slightly. The idea being that this was an effective way of bringing the calf and thigh against the horses' side. Today one rides with the leg almost wrapped around the horse. I don't think that I could return to the old position, even if I wanted to.

It is my belief that *every time* you note an error in the client's position you should point it out immediately. This means that *you* have to concentrate 100 percent on the job in hand. Your eyes should miss nothing. It may well be that, as novices, they may have difficulty in making the required correction. One could argue that since their very state of unbalance is responsible for many of these errors that they are not worthwhile mentioning or even bothering about at this time. I do not agree. I believe that the *client should be told whenever there is something wrong with their position.* You do not have to do this in a demanding or nagging manner; you should simply point out the error in a calm low voice. Sometimes a rider will apologise. If they do so tell them that there is nothing for which to apologise after all they are with you to learn. In this way an intelligent rider will make much quicker progress than they would if they were left in a state of ignorance.

106

Proceeding with the first movement

Having assisted the client to mount correctly, as already mentioned, you pick up the lunge line and attach it to the top, central, ring of the cavesson. *Very quietly* pick up the lunging whip. *Keep your eyes on the horse the whole time* as you get yourself organised. If you are starting your lesson with the horse moving on the left rein, then be sure that the whip is held in your right hand, dropping down towards the ground. The spare loops of the line should also be held in that hand. The line should then pass through your left hand and you should hold it at approximately shoulder height. If you allow it to drop then it may become so slack that there is a marked loop and the horse may well trip over it.

Your position.

Some instructors prefer to remain fairly close to horse. I imagine that they think that this will give them a more effective means of control. This means that as the horse describes say a twenty-metre circle, the instructor will walk one of ten-metres.

My view is that one should remain in the centre of the circle with ones feet placed slightly apart. If proceeding on the left rein then the left foot should be forward. As your weight moves back and forward from one foot to the other so this leg will be the pivot around which the right leg moves. The whole time your eyes should be on the horse and rider. (When going in the opposite direction everything changes the other way).

The walk.

The clients' position.

The very first thing is to ensure that the client is sitting correctly. You must be very clear in your instruction. Thus: -

'Sit tall and look *ahead*. Chin tucked in, shoulders back, chest out, elbows resting, lightly, by your sides, hands carried as a pair each thumb pointing to the horses opposite ears'. **The hands should be positioned as though the client were holding the reins**, (even though they are not) about three or four inches above the withers and about the same distance apart. The legs should stretch down being helped by the heels pushing down and the toes turned up and to the front'. – All this to be achieved without any tension in the body. The words sitting elegantly (or arrogantly) come to mind. (See stories to tell – Antoine de Pluvinel.)

Give the horse the command to walk on. Immediately the horse obeys you, you must turn your attention back to the rider. You need to recheck the position. As the dynamics of the walk alter the horse's centre of gravity, so the rider will, initially, loose their position as they try to maintain balance. It is usually the head that drops as the eyes are lowered to look at the horse. This is one of the greatest faults amongst the majority of riders – no matter how skilled they are. It is a form of psychological reassurance and it is very important that you do not allow this bad habit to be confirmed in your novice student. Rounded shoulders and a slumped position then follow. Heels start to lift and so on.

Beware of giving too much information at one time.

You should constantly, firmly but gently, correct any error in position. Now having made that statement I am about to contradict myself. You do need to go through the whole 'check list' as it were, in which you mention straight back, sitting tall, hands, heals etc. etc. but you should also bear in mind that most people have only a limited ability to absorb and act upon *everything* that they are told. Thus having made these points it is a good idea to, sometimes, select one in particular upon which you will concentrate more than any other, for a part of that particular lesson. Thus you may say to your client 'For this lesson we are going to concentrate on sitting tall and trying to prevent the upper body from swinging about'. Though you may mention hands and heels from time to time you do deal mainly with the upper body, to such an extent that every slight wobble is pointed out. The client will not always be able to apply a successful correction, but they will be made aware of the problem and even after they have finished the lesson and go away, they will continue to think about it.

By the way, don't forget to keep your eye on the horse or as soon as it perceives that you are giving your attention to the rider it may well start to slow down or even stop. You *must* anticipate this and give it a little encouragement, if required. Throughout the lesson you must talk to the rider and help them to overcome any feelings of apprehension or tension. There are several ways that this can be done.

Exercises to induce a feeling of relaxation in the rider (and the horse?)

In between the instructions that you issue, insert short periods of conversation. Start by asking the rider what they do for a living or if a child, what school they attend. Be prepared to continue this conversation, intelligently. As this develops the rider will start to feel less tense because they are concentrating on answering you. **Another way is to ask them to close their eyes** (reassure them that nothing untoward will result) and imagine that they are revisiting somewhere pleasant, for example a place to which they went on holiday. If you are truly skilled you will find out where this was and you will help them to recreate in their own minds the image of this place. For example, lying on a sandy beach with the sun shining on them. You help to create this mood with your voice that is speaking to them in soft calm tones. Starting at the neck ask them to try and induce a feeling of relaxation running down through the neck and shoulders. Speak as though the *feeling* were a fluid, flowing down their arms to the fingertips. The fingers should be gently flexed and relaxed. Return to the neck. Ask the client to *imagine* the flow of relaxation moving down, through the torso, towards the hip and onwards down the legs to the very toes. Your voice is deeply calming almost hypnotic.

You tell the client that they also need to keep their bodies in the correct position. Then you ask them to keep this feeling of soft calmness in their minds and to slowly open their eyes. I have been told by many of my clients that they find this exercise very helpful and that when they do open their eyes they actually feel mentally refreshed.

You may also ask the client to perform some simple exercises that will also help to induce relaxation. These can take the form of the following movements: - (Note that I start with the top of the body and work down. However I have not mentioned the riders' head. This is because some doctors have said that rotating the head could be harmful. Though I don't see any reason why one should not turn it from side to side, I would advise *against* any exercise involving the neck in case the client has a problem, which could be exacerbated by their carrying out your instructions incorrectly).

For all these exercises the client should not hold the reins, which should be knotted over the wither or twisted and secured by the throatlatch.

Starting with the shoulders (relaxing).
Alternately rotating the shoulders) –
Rotating both shoulders together (shrugging).

Now passing down to the arms (stretching and relaxing).
Raising the arms, one at a time, so that they describe a full circle reaching as high as possible above the riders' head. All the time the fingers must be totally relaxed. The arm should be lowered slowly and gently to the rider's side (see photo no. 22). This movement may be repeated with both arms moving together.

Arms held out horizontally in front and then both arms swung back at shoulder height to end with hands clasped behind in the small of the back (helps with position) *39.

Taking the above a stage further. Arms folded behind the back with each opposite hand clasping the other arm as they are then pushed into the small of the back. I have found this to be one of the most effective exercises in helping clients to sit tall, especially for those with a tendency to slump in the saddle or to pitch forward as they try to adjust to the walk or trot. The effect is that the shoulders are pulled back and the sternum is raised. It also encourages the client to look up and ahead. When performed at the sitting trot the client is helped to flex the lower spine in order to absorb the moment of suspension, (see photo no. 23)
Caution.
Do remember to tell the rider that should they feel unbalanced, they should cease the exercise, immediately, and take hold of the neck rein or the pommel of the saddle.

For all the following, feet out of stirrups and stirrups crossed. (*Remember; first ask the client if they are prepared to ride in this manner. If they are not, then don't proceed***).**
Onward now to include the leg, (stretching and relaxing). One arm circling in an arc as high as possible. As it starts to descend the leg on that side is moved back and bent at the knee until the rider can touch the heel (see photo no 23a).

Lift, first one leg, then later both legs out sideways as far as the rider is able. Hold for a few seconds and *gently lower* to horses' side (see photo no 23b).

Arms and legs together (stretching and balance and co-ordination).
Marching movement with arms and legs together *39. Take care that the rider does not move both limbs, on the same side, at the same time. Make sure that the rider does not bend the leg at the knee (see photo no. 24).

Finally the ankles and feet (stretching and relaxing).
Toes drop down and feet are revolved both clockwise and anticlockwise.

Note well: for all these exercises, where the rider is using only one limb, all *the others must remain still.*

Breathing.
One must not overlook one of the most important aids to relaxation -correct breathing. Whether riding with the eyes open or closed ask the client to take in slow but deep breaths, to hold them for a second or two and then to release the breath slowly. As they do so, this will also help the feeling of relaxation flowing over them, but of course, you must go on reminding them that they must still maintain the correct position. It can also help if you ask them to recite something quite complicated for example a tongue twister (see stories to entertain).

Correct breathing is something to which you must revert, constantly, throughout your teaching. It is a matter so easily overlooked. I have seen the odd cross-country competitor or two, arrive at the finish of a course so out of breath that they are blue in the face and near a state of collapse. This had very little to do with their physical exertions, for the course was a purely amateur affair designed to accommodate weekend riders and liveries. Its duration was probably not more than 5 to 10 minutes, so the breathlessness of the rider was probably due to the fact that in concentrating on getting around the route they had been holding their breath.

An exercise in awareness.
It is never too soon to start an exercise that will make clients aware of how the horse is moving. Without developing the ability to feel what exactly is going on underneath, the client will never make really significant progress in their control of the horses movements. Therefore you should start on this early. An excellent but none-the-less simple exercise is this: -

Ask the client to tell you, without looking down, when one of the horse's legs is moving underneath them. You may choose any leg you wish but the inside foreleg is a good one to start with. Ask the client to try to feel the horse moving beneath them. Ask for a ***count*** of every ***fourth footfall***. They should use a word such as 'Now'. If they are correct, then tell them so and say 'well done'!

Asking and being asked questions.
Be sure that you ask the client, throughout the lesson whether they have understood what you have been saying and whether they have any questions for you. You might take it as a compliment should the client not question you. However a really intelligent rider will, for sure, pick up some gaps in your narrative that need to be filled in. This should be encouraged.

Your replies.
When you receive an answer that may not be quite correct or you reply to a ***question***, never do so in a voice overlain with sarcasm. ***Your clients*** are, after all, with you so ***that they may learn***. If you put them down, then, they will be less forthcoming when they wish to know the answer to something that they really don't understand. I am sometimes quite amazed to find with new clients that as I encourage them to ask questions it becomes evident that they have been riding for years with a complete misconception about the correct manner of going about a particular movement,
Repetition.
From the very beginning and continuing forever more you must be sure to *repeat the basics* – time and time again. Only by constant practise will your clients be able to make them a part of the foundation of their own riding. Even then they will need to become self-correcting, as indeed do the very best dressage riders.

What am I talking about? At this stage I am referring to such basic requirements such as: -
Sitting tall and relaxed.
Good posture – head up, elbows softly tucked into the sides.
Hands held correctly and still.
Sitting on the seat.
Legs stretched with heels down and toes turned to the front and so forth.
The word here is good posture – good posture – good posture!!!!!

I have seen several instructors make all the above points at some time during a lesson but their clients having paid little attention revert to their old bad habits almost immediately. What is worse, they are not, subsequently, corrected; it is as though the instructor might not have spoken! Now one must be careful here. I do not mean that you should be so repetitive that you are in danger of becoming a bore, but you must make your point and ensure that some improvement results.

The duration of an exercise
Do no more than two or three minutes continuous walking, then stop and ask the client to rest. During this period ask them what they are thinking about. Ensure that they do not loose their position. Continue for another five minutes then stop, put down your whip, approach the horse and turn it around so that it is proceeding on the other rein. Always turn the horse away from you.
Why? So that there is less danger of the horse treading on your foot.
Continue as before. Throughout the lesson you should not only praise the horse but also the client. This is very important to the clients self esteem. If you wish them to return for further lessons you must always be encouraging!
Walking without the rider using the stirrups.
After the initial period of walk of about ten minutes duration in all, ask the rider, if they are willing, to quit (remove their feet out of) the stirrups and then cross the stirrups over the withers. (If they are not then don't continue with this exercise) Even at this early stage the client should be shown the correct manner of so doing. That is to say that the right stirrup is always crossed first, to be followed by the left (the near side). As they do this be sure that the buckle of the leather is not revealed and pressing into the client's thigh. If this is likely to happen, simply ask them to take hold of the buckle and pull it down three or four inches. This will move it well out of harms way.
Why?
You must explain that since the near side is the normal side for mounting then should the rider wish to remount in a hurry, they have only to uncross the stirrup on that side in order to do so. You should endeavour to get them to make a habit of doing this correctly every time.
　You now ask the rider to try to keep their balance, without stirrups, whilst sitting on a horse that is walking forward. It is my *opinion* that during this exercise whilst the correct position must be maintained it is not necessary for the rider to keep the toes turned up. The reason for this is that, for most clients, the fact that they have given up the security of stirrups does tend to produce some tension. It is one of those things that they do instinctively. By allowing the lower leg simply to hang down one is able to reduce this. Anyway this is a matter for you to decide yourself. What is required is that the legs are stretched downwards as far as possible and the thigh lies against the horse's side *without any tension.* Without stirrups the rider's seat is encouraged to sink lower into the saddle and this helps them to develop a good position. This part of the lesson should last about 3 to 4 minutes on each rein. At this time you may introduce or repeat the eyes closed session. You may also ask the rider to rotate the ankles and feet to help induce this feeling of relaxation (see drawing no. 16).The object of these exercises may seem obscure to the rider; therefore you must explain that everything is directed towards the development of those muscles that will help to keep the riders' body in the correct position. Position is everything.

Why? (Again!) Because it enables the horse to move without the riders' constantly changing weight upsetting it's balance. Without the ability to keep the body still the rider's limbs will constantly touch the horse or its tack at inappropriate moments, thus giving erroneous signals. Everything, especially the hands, must remain still. If the rider has to maintain their position by either gripping or supporting themselves with reins they will never become really effective in communicating with the horse and thus getting it to do their bidding.

110

How to hold the reins.
Towards the end of the lesson, you may free the reins and show the client how to hold them. The reins should be held, in each hand *between the forefinger and thumb,* with that part of the rein attached to the bit curving upwards between the third and little fingers. All fingers (except the thumb and forefingers) should curl around the reins so that they open and close as the horse moves forward (see drawing no. 9).
Why? Because, as the horse moves, it balances itself by moving its head up and down. A fixed hand (i.e. one in which the fingers do not open and close in time with the nodding head) will, at the best, give the horse an irrelevant signal, at the worst will cause it discomfiture.

From the beginning you must make the novice aware as to how important this is. You demonstrate as described in chapter 7. You must make it clear that the majority of riders do *not* ride with such finesse and it is a compliment to the horse that it puts up with such poor treatment and still gives good service. The main thing for the rider to concentrate on is *keeping the hands absolutely still.* They must also be positioned correctly –about three inches apart with each thumb pointing at the horses' opposite ear.
When the elbows are tucked into the waist and the hands held as a pair, at the correct height, then a ***straight line*** should run from the rider's elbow, through the wrist and on down to the bit.

The spare loop of the rein should lie *underneath* the section attached to the bit, out of the way down the *offside* of the horse (See photo no. 25).
Why? *Underneath* so that the weight of the loop does not give an unwanted signal by resting on that part going to the bit.
Offside. (The right-hand side).
Because tradition has it that, in the past, a rider would carry his sword on his left side. He would wish to avoid the hilt getting caught up in the spare loop as he went to draw it from its scabbard.

Considering the possibility of the client giving the aids for the horse to move forward whilst still on the lunge?
I do not recommend that you encourage clients to do this.
Why?
Because the client is unlikely, as yet, to be able to give accurate or effective aids. This may confuse the poor horse, and what with being restricted by the lunge rein may well cause an unfavourable reaction.

Praise at the end of the lesson.
At the end of the lesson have a short discussion. Ask your client what they thought of their first attempt to ride. (Did they enjoy it?) For your part you should use this time to mention any areas of weakness that you may have noticed. These may be, loosing position, heels rising, or hands moving about excessively.

Always finish up by being very *very* encouraging. Tell the client how well they have done. Before the client dismounts be sure that they make much of the horse.

Demonstrating the dismount.
Before asking for the dismount, you should first place your whip on the ground by your side. You may gently encourage the horse to come to you or you may walk up to it. Whatever approach, make sure that the lunge rein is taken into neat coils in your hand. Undo the lunge and place it safely out of the way.
Why?
So that the horse knows that the lesson is at an end. At this time you should give the horse a small reward such as a polo mint or slice of carrot and a pat. Coiling the rein as you go will avoid the possibility of you, the horse or your client getting tangled up in it. With the lunge and whip placed in a safe place you will then be unobstructed should you have to assist the client with their dismount.

The dismount is normally carried out on the near side. The rider should place the reins as a double loop, in the left hand and simultaneously swing their legs behind and upwards. At the same time they swing the upper part of their bodies, forward and twist around so that the offside leg comes high enough to clear the back of the horse. They then land lightly on the ground facing the horses' near side. Be close by, in order to hold the horse and ready to support the client in case they stumble as they land. You should now be responsible for making the stirrups secure (show the client how you do this), remove the cavesson and arrange for the horse to be put away. Generally a groom should do this. Should none be available then you must allow sufficient time to do this yourself, especially if you have another lesson following on immediately. In either case the client may be encouraged to accompany the groom or yourself to the horsebox, but *under no circumstances should they be allowed to put the horse away by themselves.*

At the end of the lesson.
Give the client a copy of page 413 'Explanation of terms used' which explains the various gaits. Ask them to study it and learn them by heart. I also give my clients a copy of my definition of the 'Art of Equitation' Chapter 4 page 51.

The second lesson.
Introducing the rising trot.
Ideally this lesson will introduce the pupil to the rising trot (first ask the client if they are willing). Proceed as for the first lesson, ensuring that they sit correctly and keep their hands still (even though they may start off by not holding the reins). Lessen the duration of time during which the rider exercises at the walk. This will depend on the progress that they have made with regard to maintaining a good position. You will decide what that duration will be.

At the appointed time have the horse go forward to halt. Then, ask the rider to try to stand up in the stirrups, it helps if you tell them to push down on the balls of their feet. Having stood up they should try and hold the position for a few seconds. Should they wobble, you encourage them to try to help support themselves by holding the mane or the neck strap (see drawing no. 18). Now ask them to sit down again. As they do so they must lower their bodies *softly down onto the saddle.*

Why softly? Because one doesn't want to cause the poor horse discomfiture during this learning period. If one neglects to point this out to the pupil and they continually allow their seat to drop heavily back into the saddle the repeated shock may, eventually, have an effect on the horse's spine or kidneys. Even when the rider has mastered the rhythm of the rising trot, monitor their performance and make certain that they do not forget this important point at all times.

Repeat this movement three or for times in quick succession and try to get the pupil to establish a rhythm i.e. 1-2. 1-2. 1-2 rising and then sitting down, rising and then sitting down, in the correct tempo which you count out loud so that they can follow. Pause and let them rest, then repeat.

Why the need for a rising trot? You may now explain that this is known as the 'Trot 'a l'Anglaise' (see alternative paces). It was devised as a method of absorbing the moment of suspension, that moment when the horse is momentarily in the air as it hops from one pair of diagonals to the other.

Now ask the horse to walk on and ask the pupil to perform the standing up exercise at the walk. After three or four attempts they should have got some idea as to what is required. Continue with a nice steady trot. Allow the rider, at first, to try only sitting to the trot. After they have experienced this movement allow them time to recover and continue but this time ask them to try and rise. At first they may not be able to do so and instead will remain sitting. This does not matter but ask them to hold the mane or the neck strap or even to hook their fingers around the pommel of the saddle if they feel very wobbly (they should be encouraged to do this whenever they feel unbalanced). They must also try to keep the hip joint flexible as though it were made of rubber. Now tell them to push their heals down and at the same time to allow their bodies to spring forward as the motion of the horse dictates. *If the client shows any tendency to loose their balance, cease the trot and go forward to walk immediately.* Try again as soon as the rider has rested. It does help if your pupil is possessed of a natural sense of rhythm. At first as they try to rise they will lose the rhythm and bounce around helplessly. An audible rhythm against which to move assists in overcoming this. You can provide this by calling out, again, 'forward and back, forward and back' in the correct time or simply 'one – two one – two'.

Usually it is but a short time before they have got the hang of it. As soon as they start to improve, give them much praise with a 'Well done'. It is a pleasure to behold the smile on a pupil's face as they succeed. After the rising trot has been successfully established in terms of the correct rhythm, you should turn your attention to the way in which they rise. At the start novices will tend to rise as high as they are able. This needs to be corrected and you should tell them not to rise so high but to utilise the horses' energy to, just lift their seat about two or three inches out of the saddle. The movement should not be 'Up and down' but

'*Forward and back*'.* Further more remind them that the seat must be *lowered with a feather-like touch* into the saddle. Beware, even when they appear to have mastered the gait, their balance may only be superficial and a sudden movement on the horses part may un-seat them.

A question a pupil may ask.
Why is it important not to rise too high? **Answer.** Because it uses up a considerable amount of energy unnecessarily (don't forget 'let the horse do the work'). Another reason is that rising higher may be useful at a later stage for encouraging a horse to lengthen its stride so one might as well save that aid until it is needed. End the lesson as before.

Final thought.
When teaching the rising trot in this manner care needs to be taken to ensure that the rider does not get the idea fixed in their mind, that in order to ask for a trot, they must first start by rising. I have had many pupils who have come to me having already received several lessons from another instructor. As soon as I ask them to trot they start going up and down in the saddle before the horse has commenced the gait.

The third, fourth and fifth lessons and so on – Introducing the sitting trot without stirrups.
Proceed as above. According to the progress made - so the duration of the different exercises may be varied. In other words as the pupils' musculature develops so you may (if the pupil is willing), extend the period at which they ride without stirrups. This is especially the case with regard to the sitting trot. Sitting trot without stirrups is a very important part of learning to ride. Through this exercise the rider will learn not only to keep the body in perfect balance but also to absorb, through the hip joint and spine, the tendency to bounce about, especially when riding horses that have an elevated trot (they spring high into the air with each stride).

To learn to sit well the rider must try very hard to keep the hip joint flexible. That is to say that the lower spine acts as a spring. At the same time ask them to try and imagine that they are pushing their hips right through the saddle at the very moment when the dynamic of the horse's movement is trying to push them out. Not only that but they must also try to keep the legs and upper body still so that the shoulders, that foundation to which the arms are attached, remain motionless. This in turn will assist in keeping the *hands still* with only the fingers opening and closing with each stride.

The hands.
I cannot stress, sufficiently, how important it is that the art of keeping the hands still must be *thoroughly* learned, from the very beginning of the riders' education. How often have I seen people who have been riding for years, incapable of doing this? They jerk up and down and all over the place thus causing their poor horses much confusion and considerable discomfiture.

An exercise in keeping the hands still.
Give the pupil a plastic cup half full of water and ask them to hold it between their two hands. In the beginning it may be easier for them not to have to hold the rein at the same time. (If you decide to go down this path, then make sure that the reins are secured). You then initiate a walk, which, if all goes well may be followed by a trot (rising or sitting). The object of the exercise is, obviously, to keep the hands still enough not to spill any water. Don't fill the cup to the brim, you do not want to soak the rider or, for that matter, the horse.

The cup should be made out of Styrofoam which is not likely to fracture. As it is very soft it will also teach the client not to grip too tightly.

Another exercise. This time in looking ahead and not down!
The easiest way of preventing really bad habits from being confirmed is to nip them in the bud before they start. One of the most common is that of looking down. If you can prevent your clients from doing this, then you will be well on the way to establishing a good position. The main problem is that they are *not aware* that they are so doing.

In the early stages I like to demonstrate the problem, graphically, in a similar manner to carrying a cup of water. In this case the Styrofoam cup is truncated i.e. you cut off the top two thirds. I also cut the front lower than the back (see drawing no. 19). The bottom part remaining is then attached to the top of the rider's crash hat with a knob of 'Blue Tack'. There are two reasons for cutting the cup down. The first is that it has less surface area and will not be so likely to get blown off. The second, that the contents will spill the more easily as a result of quite a small head movement. However I do not think that water is a good medium to use when one is considering placing an object on a rider's head! It is fairly certain that some water will be spilt and this will cause unnecessary discomfort to your pupil as it runs down the back of their neck. Instead I use the little light plastic balls that are used as packing material. If they are coloured, then so much the better. The fact that they are light means that they will be blown away as soon as they are free of the constraints of the cup. When they land on the ground, like water they are harmless. You may of course use other materials. Rice is quite satisfactory.

Don't forget all that you are trying to do is to help your clients and not have fun at their expense. Cutting down the cup does not make the client feel so ridiculous. Further more you should ask your clients if they mind doing these exercises before they have to carry them out.

Thinking about coming off the lunge.

The numbers of lessons, required, on the lunge are dictated by the client's progress. *You must make the decision yourself.* Beware of getting too ambitious with clients who appear to be making good headway. When in doubt – don't! On the other hand, you may introduce exercises that will help to develop a good seat and at the same time help to build confidence. I have in mind the sitting trot with the client holding out their arms to either side. When your client has received sufficient lessons on the lunge to have established a reasonable seat it is time for them to start riding around the arena on their own. They may do this either by joining a novice class or they may continue to have private lessons. Their pocket, the times when the arenas are free or for that matter their own disposition with regard to being sociable, may dictate the choice. I think that it is a good idea to join a class for therein lies a greater challenge.

A transition period.

Do bear in mind as I have already said, **lunge lessons should not exceed more than half an hour.** It is therefore possible to develop a transitional phase, during which the pupil is given an opportunity to ride free of the lunge line. This may be taken as a preparation prior to entry into a class. It will serve to give the client confidence.

From the lunge to going large.

For this stage it is essential that you do have horses that are very well behaved. When you consider that the client has developed some sense of balance you may suggest that the lesson be extended to an hour's duration. For the second half of the lesson you may relieve the horse of all the accoutrements required for lunging (but be sure to place everything safely out of the way) and give the client the opportunity to go large, by themselves, around the arena. Many clients will be very keen to do this. They should start simply by walking. But you must be sure in your own mind that they have sufficient balance to be able to stay on board if, for example, the horse misinterpreting a signal from the rider and catching them unawares, suddenly starts to trot or even puts in a few strides at canter.

How best to proceed as the client attempts their first 'solo'?

The first thing that they should try to do is to walk around the arena simply following the track. Tell them to look where they wish to go and, if they wish to turn to do so by turning their torso in the desired new direction. They must then make the horse look in the same direction. Now they have to give the command to the horse to walk on. You must remind them of the correct sequence of aids and above all tell them to endeavour to avoid any tendency to try and initiate the walk by leaning forward. They must sit still and use the aids as they have been instructed. They may also use the voice giving the required verbal command.

Thus 'Jeeves **walk on**'. Provided my clients do as I tell them I have never known them have any difficulty in achieving their first walk alone. I do point out that the horse is perfectly aware that they are inexperienced and in order to counteract this they may have to imply a certain urgency when using the leg. They are delighted when they go off around the arena by themselves. Of course they are not aware of what the horse and I both know and that is that I am not going to stand for any messing about and also that after the lesson is over there will always be a rewarding titbit.

If the horse does show any tendency to turn off the track towards the middle of the arena, then it is up to

114

you to give a helping hand. One way in which you may do this is by taking up and pointing the lunge whip at the horse **but be careful how you do this**. Should you brandish it threateningly, the horse may start to move away at speed. Simply stand in a similar position to that which you would have adopted if the horse were still on the lunge line and use the whip in a similar manner. It is also a good idea to *keep hold of the end of the lash* **in the same hand as holds the whip.**

Do try and keep your interference to a minimum. This is the point where the client should be left to struggle alone for a short while. Usually, if you help simply by reminding them as to the correct aids, they will find that they succeed and gain great satisfaction from this. When they have managed to go large for a lap or two, the difficulty may be up-graded by asking the client to dispense with the support of the arena walls and to ride down the centreline. At this stage it does help if you give some simple explanations as to what is going on. You may start by pointing out that horses do tend to use the wall of the arena as a means of helping them to keep their balance and thus go straight. A jockey seeking the rail when he is urging on his tired horse to win a race is a good example.

When proceeding down the centreline they no longer have this advantage. The client may well wonder why the horse does not go straight of its own accord. I explain this both by pointing out that in the first place the horse does not *know* that the rider wishes him to go absolutely straight. Secondly since it probably weighs about 500 kgs. and that weight is supported on four sticklike legs, it is quite likely that the horses' tendency to become unbalanced may cause him to wander off course. The rider has to correct this by consciously using his own legs to correct these deviations.

If it is possible to see the tracks that the rider has made, then point these out and ask them to go round again and try to improve the straightness of the line. Remind the rider how the horse will move away from the leg and how they must utilise this to keep the horse straight. When all goes well, the next movement that I will be asking for is – obtaining- and sustaining a rising trot. However I usually refrain from doing this during the first 'solo' because one must realise that the pupil is putting in a considerable amount of emotional and physical energy.

Creating a simple programme.
You need to have some idea as to what you are going to ask the client to do. As I have stated the first move away from you should simply be going large. Thus, as I see it, the program should be something along the following lines.
1. Going large, at the walk, once or twice on either rein. (Resting in between each circuit).
2. Riding changes of gait. (Walk to halt etc).
3. Changing the rein, at the walk.
4. Riding down the centre line.
5. Going large at a rising trot. Once around on either rein. (Resting between each circuit). Don't forget that a circuit or two ridden by yourself may seem to be inconsequential – to you. For a novice it can be quite exhausting.
6. Riding changes of gait at the trot (Trot to walk to halt and so on).
7. Changing the rein at the trot.
8. Riding shallow loops at the walk.
9. Riding circles at walk and subsequently at trot.

You should make up your own program. You must, however, take into account the time available. Be very careful not to be too demanding for it is important for both the riders' and your own satisfaction that, whatever problem they are given to solve, be it riding a simple change of rein accurately or going forward from halt to walk – whatever – by the end of the lesson they should succeed handsomely. This may mean that, sometimes, you shrewdly, tailor the exercise to the propensities of the horse.

The lesson that introduces the canter.
When you are *completely* satisfied that the client has developed a reasonably well-balanced seat, then and only then can you consider introducing a few strides at the canter. It is extremely important that you use a horse that not only goes calmly and quietly into the canter but it is also advantageous to have a horse that canters with a fairly flat canter (in other words without a high moment of suspension). It will also help to have a horse that responds well to the voice. (You may need to lend a hand by simply asking the horse to canter through a vocal command).

In my experience a client may well not canter until they have been riding for about a year. (This is dependent on their natural ability and how regularly they ride). They may well have managed to cope with riding in straight lines, in circles or even around obstacles after as few as half a dozen lessons but then there follows a plateau during which the muscles that maintain their balance are developed. This may take several months. The client will also need to develop their reflexes with regard to the horse's, possible, evasions. Of course it does depend upon the frequency of the lessons and also the honesty of the horse, but as I have already pointed out, this book is basically about teaching weekend riders; thus this period could be quite considerable.

Beware.
For many clients the one thing that they really want to do is to canter. When they come to you they may imagine that this will happen after a very few lessons. You must, tactfully, disabuse them of this notion. They may well press you to let them try. Unless you are confident that they have developed a seat able to deal with this gait, do not consent.

The canter moment.
If you are satisfied that the seat is reasonable then, *towards the end of the lesson* **ask the client** if they feel confident enough to try a few strides of the canter. If they say that they would rather not, then do not proceed and leave the exercise for another time.
Why? Because should the client become un-balanced and sustain a fall, then it could be said that you did not take sufficient care. That you asked them to canter before they were ready. It may well be that nothing untoward appeared to have contributed to their departure from the saddle. But it is not beyond the bounds of possibility that the client got such a fright at the unfamiliar motion that they 'baled out', i.e. decided to throw themselves off for safety. You as an experienced rider may find this point of view quite extraordinary but then you are not the novice? Are you?

If the client does agree and this should be the case if they have sufficient confidence in you, then you may proceed.

Using an analogy.
Sometimes a pupil really does have a problem in initiating the canter depart. There may be several reasons for this, such as grabbing the rein as a means of support and therefore unwittingly telling the horse not to perform the transition. More often than not it is simply due to the fact that the rider throws their body forward. In these circumstances I have found that it very useful to ask them to imagine that they are climbing a mountainside. On their back they carry a heavy backpack. They are about to step from one ledge to another but in order to so do, it is necessary to make a small jump through the air. At that very moment they do this, the backpack slips. How would they feel about this state of affairs? The answer is always that they would feel extremely uncomfortable and revert to their secure starting position. 'Your horse feels exactly the same' I say 'When at the very moment that he propels himself forward to strike off at the canter and you fall forward over his withers'.

Learning to sit to the canter.
Tell the client to be sure to try and sit tall the whole time. They may also hold the horse's mane, a neck loop or even the pommel of the saddle. The most important thing is that they keep looking ahead. This will play a very important part in helping them to keep their body upright and still. Another essential is to tell the rider to be sure to allow the hip joint to follow the horse's movement as though they were *trying* to polish the saddle with their seat bones (note the seat doesn't actually move). You will note that I have suggested that the client may hold the pommel. Some may disagree with this, however so far as I am concerned that is far more preferable than the sight of a client being thrown high in the air at every stride, where they balance precariously in the stirrups and the slightest of unanticipated movements will send them shooting forwards or sideways through the air and down to the ground.

If you are satisfied with this first attempt, ask the client if they would like to repeat the exercise on the other rein. If you are not – don't. If they do not wish to – don't! There are going to be many occasions when the client will have the opportunity to canter. Do remember – should your client loose their balance and fall off, then, it is you who are responsible. Oh I know that one is inclined to say 'well they are very inexperienced and everyone is going to fall off sooner or later.' Its up to you to try to ensure that it is unlikely to happen.

Cantering on the lunge?

I am very wary of introducing pupils to canter whilst they are still having lessons on the lunge. It seems to me to offer the temptation of taking a short cut. One might be tempted to think to oneself 'oh well, perhaps I will try and introduce the client who is obviously making good progress, to just a very short session at canter, perhaps no more than half a circle'. This is not a good approach for it is very easy to forget that in canter the forces involved are greater than at any other pace. The gait has such forward motion, that allowance must be made for the effect of centrifugal force. That is the impetus that will tend to throw out the horse's hindquarters or cause him to lean in. A pupil who seems to have been making good progress may suddenly be facing forces that are beyond their ability to deal with.

Does this mean that one should never introduce a pupil to canter on the lunge? Well of course not. There may be occasions where it will help a rider to get over that first hesitation or else to improve their position at canter through a lunge lesson. *All that I am saying is take care*. If you do intend to do so with say a novice of many months' experience, you must ensure that you have a horse that goes kindly on the lunge, at the canter. I always make it a point to lunge the horse first without a rider, in order to satisfy myself as to the suitability of the animal. You must also bear in mind that, when asking for canter, since the horse is enclosed in the triangle of lunge line and whip the element of impulsion may be quite considerable. It is therefore a good idea to use a horse that goes with a fairly flat stride without a pronounced moment of suspension, a horse that can carry himself correctly while cantering on a circle.

If you do decide that all the above matters have been taken into account, then, remind the pupil to hold the pommel of the saddle if they so wish, give the command to canter very quietly and firmly but **be careful not to over do showing the whip.**

Why?

Because the horse may suddenly leap forward and what you require is a *smooth* transition.

After a very few strides at the canter have the horse go back to walk through the trot. Keep the trot fairly short during the downward transition, because the client may loose their balance as this takes place. As soon as walk is established, halt and then congratulate the client. They will feel absolutely delighted. For if there is one movement that a client wishes to aspire to when it comes to riding a horse – it is the canter. Remind them that it is essential to remember to breathe! Frequently and on many subsequent occasions they will forget to do so because they concentrate like mad on what they are trying to do.

Further thoughts on the lunge.

Reading the above one might get the impression that lunge lessons are only for complete beginners. This is not so. Experienced riders can obtain great benefit from the occasional half-hour. That is why I do not have a problem in encouraging canter for those in this category. It enables them to dispense with the need to keep part of their mind on the manner of the horses going and to concentrate completely on deriving a good position and in inducing relaxation. Many experienced clients of mine have told me how pleasant and relaxed they feel after this short session.

On the other hand, despite what I have mentioned previously about the benefits of the lunge, it is not always essential to start off novices in this manner. I have had several clients who, for one reason or another, did not wish to start in that way. I never had a problem in starting them off on their riding careers by riding freely around the arena. In this case the one matter that needs to be born in mind, is that since they have not had the benefit of strengthening their muscles on the lunge, they will tend to interfere with the forwardness of their horses through their lack of position. This can be overcome by a more urgent and vigorous application of the leg aids. You must also keep on at them not to loose their position and you must urge them to use the leg proactively instead of reactively. You have to constantly call out 'sit tall and squeeze or tap or even double tap with your legs and *keep on doing so* until the horse obeys you, then cease- look where you want to go – tell the horse what you want him to do.' and so on. So far as this latter command is concerned be sure that they use the correct word. It is no use their calling out 'move' or 'come on' when the word that they should be using is 'Trrrrrot **on**'. In fact if the horses that you use have respect for you, you can control the situation by using your own voice, just to help out if required. Working in this way I have had many riders who were well on their way, having achieved successful directional control and rising trot after only two lessons.

Final thoughts on going solo.

Sometimes a client may be impeded in their efforts to ride by themselves simply because they are nervous. No matter how much you reassure them that their horse will not dash off, they have a quite understandable fear that this may happen. In such a case it is a good idea simply to walk along side of the horse by its shoulder, close enough to hold the rein if so required but without actually doing so. This will not only reassure the client but will also help them to get their horses going, for it is frequently a part of a horses' early schooling that it has been taught to follow the trainer wherever he or she goes. Of course you may think that this will detract from the clients efforts to get the horses going forward by themselves but this does not need to be the case for you may ask the client to execute a turn without its being forced upon the horse by a corner, say across the arena, from 'B' to 'E'. Keep watching and reminding them of the correct aids before they do so. As they make progress you may step slightly further away and to drop behind a little so that your influence on the proceedings is lessened.

Final thoughts on cantering.

Sometimes novices have difficulty in riding the transition from trot to canter when going solo. In such cases I have seen some instructors, take a lunging whip and use it to encourage the horse to perform the transition. Despite what I have already said about cantering on the lunge, I do not agree with this practise when the rider is going large. It is very dismaying to see a young instructor running around the arena brandishing a lunging whip. The poor horse is, probably, already showing willing by trotting ever faster but is unable to canter because the riders' position and/or their aids are, actively, preventing the desired transition. Frequently the result is that the horse will put in an objection in the form of a buck and this may result in the client becoming unseated and suffering a needless fall. After all one should be working with an animal that with a more accomplished rider on its back will canter willingly. Therefore one must ask oneself why this same animal will not do so with a novice. The fault obviously lies with the rider. Therefore the horse considers, quite rightly, in my opinion, that being shown the whip is unreasonable and accordingly puts in quite a strong objection. It is much more satisfactory to improve both the clients' position and aids until such a time as they alone, are able to get the horse to execute the change. It may take longer but it is much safer.

Third Party Legal liabilities.

During the ensuing years between this impression and the first one, the problem of third party liability, (see chapter 20) which has always hovered in the background, has now started to have a very serious effect on the financial viability of riding schools. Insurance premiums have tripled and quadrupled as insurance companies deal with an ever-greater rise in the number of claims for negligence. Frequently these claims are found to be unproven. None-the-less the costs of defending such actions are exceedingly high and these are simply passed on by the insurers in the form of increased premiums. Many cases are simply settled out of court because the insurers feel that it is cheaper to settle a claim for say £10,000 than take it to court where the costs might rise as high as £50,000 or even more.

When a novice first starts to learn to ride the danger of a fall is quite minimal but as the pupil makes progress the possibility increases. Balance is an integral part of equitation. If the riders loose this then they may fall off. However as things stand today it is my view that it is incumbent on the instructor *to point out the possibility* of such a situation arising before a client starts to learn to ride. As they make progress to higher gaits they should be, constantly, reminded of this possibility. In which case they will not be able to claim that they really had no idea that riding a horse could be quite so hazardous, when, at a later date, they do, unfortunately take a tumble. This of course is a matter that you should discuss with your employers before you proceed along this path. They may well take the view that if you do mention this, then, the client will be put off. To my mind this is akin to putting ones head in the sand, but if they do tell you that they do not want you to proceed in this manner, then get them to put their instruction in the form of a memo.

* Sometimes an experienced rider will have difficulty in correcting the rising trot (i.e. they cannot stop going up and down excessively). The answer to this is to ask them to ride sitting and then to cease the flexion in their backs but to allow their hips to move forward. I have found that this affects an immediate cure. All my clients have then told me how much more comfortable they feel riding in this manner.

Drawings

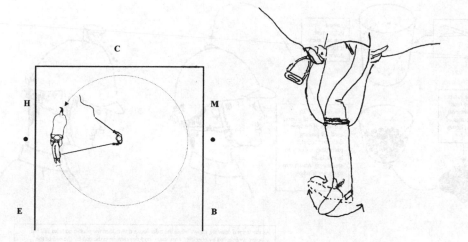

Drawing no. 13. The correct position for lunging.   Drawing no. 16. Rotating the feet.

Drawing no. 18. Standing up in the saddle as a practice for rising trot.

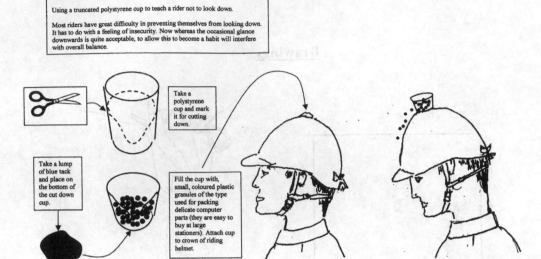

Drawing no. 19.

Using a truncated polystyrene cup to teach a rider not to look down.

Most riders have great difficulty in preventing themselves from looking down. It has to do with a feeling of insecurity. Now whereas the occasional glance downwards is quite acceptable, to allow this to become a habit will interfere with overall balance.

Take a polystyrene cup and mark it for cutting down.

Take a lump of blue tack and place on the bottom of the cut down cup.

Fill the cup with, small, coloured plastic granules of the type used for packing delicate computer parts (they are easy to buy at large stationers). Attach cup to crown of riding helmet.

As the second drawing shows when the rider looks down, then the plastic nodules fall out. Success is observed by checking how many nodules remain in the cup by the end of the session.

Most riders are quite willing to perform this exercise, fully realising that it can be very beneficial but one may get the odd rider who considers that it is beneath their dignity and object. If they do then don't insist. It is their loss and they will continue to ride with a less-than-perfect position.

Drawing no. 19. A truncated polystyrene cup used to teach the rider not to look down

Chapter 9

The novice class lesson.

The primary target.

It is important that an instructor sets a target that is tailored to the abilities of each rider or group. In the case of teaching novice riders this should be – *Simply to ask the horse to proceed, with a reasonable degree of vigour, accurately from one place to another either in a straight line or on a circle.* You must try to ensure that the rider does this while keeping absolutely still and relaxed. You are aiming for a correct and elegant position. Now the foregoing sentence may seem like 'going over the top'. I can well hear friends of mine in the business, should I be lucky enough to have them read my words, 'Saying how typical of Tone, always coming on a bit strong'. But I stand my ground for this simply must be *your target.* I have seen so many riders over the years, inflicting pain and discomfort upon their horses because they have *never been taught the basic foundation* – a good seat! On the other hand I have been paid the compliment by other instructors who ask me if I have ever taught so and so as a child. When I confirm that I have, they say 'Thought it was one of yours, they sit well'

In the early stages of a riding career, sitting still and relaxing are a tall order for any would-be riders. Some instructors like to talk to the student in terms of schooling the horse. They suggest that the client should, somehow, try to improve the manner of the horses going in terms of creating something that was not previously there. It may well do no harm to mention such things but I think that most novice riders will be unable to react quickly enough to be effective. A quick reaction is after all dependant on the rider sitting still in the first place. The most that they can hope to achieve is to exert some influence on direction, tempo and transition. Not only that, but in teaching riders in this category, or at any other level, it is incumbent upon you also to ensure *that all your horses enjoy their work.* Not an easy thing to do when you have to deal with people who at this stage may, say through pulling on the reins, unintentionally or otherwise, cause the horse much discomfort.

With regard to the last point where we are dealing with novice riders, I should make my position clear. Over the years I have come to the conclusion that, whereas it is important to mention the correct handling of the reins at all times, in practice I have found that, if a client tends to ride with a rein that is *slightly* loose, then this is a better situation than one where the client holds the rein under constant excessive tension. Thus if I notice that a client has a bit of a 'droop' in the rein I do not make too much of it. The reason for this is that without having established a secure seat most pupils will find it almost impossible to keep their hands still. If they jerk the reins about then they interfere with the horses' forward movement.

You may consider this to be a sacrilegious comment. For are we not being told all the time to have proper contact, and how important it is to correctly place the horse in such a position that he is able to obey? My answer to this is that for most ordinary movements, it is quite possible to ride the horse without touching the rein at all. The most *important thing* is for the client to *learn to keep their body still*. Only when they have learned to do that, is it time to start thinking about keeping a constant contact on the rein. Should there be a slight loss of directional control, I usually say 'Look where you want to go. Use the correct leg and shorten such and such a rein so that the horse is looking and bent in the direction where you wish to go'. As they do so the horse is immediately brought back on track.

Your secondary target.

You should also have a secondary target. This is to produce 'A calm and confident rider to whom, in turn, the horse will give his confidence and co-operation'. And also 'An observant and sensible rider who will be sensitive to the effort that the horse has made and be quick to reward work well done, by praising him and ensuring that he has a few moments relaxation immediately this is due. These two requirements are unlikely to arise spontaneously. It is you, the instructor, who will be responsible for their creation. You must also try, from the very beginning to encourage your pupils to think for themselves. Bear in mind that despite the search for kind co-operation, in the final analysis your endeavours are to be directed towards creating in the rider an ability to *persuade the horse to do their bidding instead of following its own desires.*

Who is most suited for the job?

It has been said that the top instructors should teach novices. (Usually they would rather die than suffer such an indignity). However we do need to define a good instructor. Is it one who has many letters after their name, and will only teach those willing to pay an inflated fee? Or is it someone who is extremely knowledgeable, observant and quietly persistent? One who will spread this knowledge to *anyone* prepared to listen? My view is that it is the latter.

The school for horse and rider technique.

I have alluded above to a manner of teaching known as 'School for Horse *and* Rider'. And I have already said that, except for livery owners, I do not think that this is a proper way for an instructor to teach weekend riders. I revert to what I have said previously, I do not accept that any rider is capable of 'schooling' a horse if they themselves do not have an independent seat and a good knowledge as to how a horse should move. It is unreasonable to expect a rider whose hands bob up and down in the air to ask a horse to go 'on the bit'. Where the rider is at a stage where they are, as yet, incapable of describing, more or less accurately the basic movements at various paces, it is unreasonable to talk to them in highfalutin terms about the manner of a horse's going, and the finer points of dressage. Nor do I see any reason for putting up a pretence that a rider has come to the riding school in order to teach the horses a 'thing or two'. It is simply pandering to the client's vanity. There are many pupils who like this sort of treatment. They like to delude themselves that they are not going to a riding school to learn to ride; they are simply attending a 'clinic' that will help them iron out a few little problems! I do not go along with this affectation! On the other hand I do not set out to, deliberately, deflate those who have been subject to this sort of instruction in the past. I introduce them gradually to my way of going about things and I do so by asking them quite basic questions to which any *experienced* horseman will have a correct answer and without which the client soon begins to realise that they are not.

Does this mean that the novice rider does not influence the horse at all?

The answer is, of course they do. But whereas one would expect an *advanced rider to actually improve* the manner of a horses' going, what we require of our riders is that, at the beginning of the lesson, the horse is scarcely paying them any attention at all. By the end of that lesson, the rider will become aware of the fact that the horse *is now listening to them*. This is part of your target.

The object of your exercises.

Since, as I have already said, we are not talking about training horses, this means that you are free to choose exercises that will have a twofold effect on your pupils. The first is fairly obvious, to choose exercises that will help the rider to develop control over their muscles until they reach the point where corrections to balance become a reflex. The fact that I make this point in this chapter does not mean that I expect pupils to achieve that state of affairs so early on in their riding careers, it is merely that you should be devising activities that will always *lead in that direction*. The second is that you should also teach movements that encourage a rider to think ahead. I have in mind an exercise such as riding medium circles natural and reverse at every letter (fig. 3, 3a & 3b). This type of movement helps the rider to both concentrate on more than one thing at a time as well as thinking ahead.

Dealing with a basic problem.

We would all like to think that we will be teaching in an ideal situation but this is seldom the case. For whatever reason be it a horse's bad mood, part of its nature, the time of year or a simple desire not to co-operate, we may have a situation where we not only have to deal with the rider but also the horse. The horse may not simply be being naughty; its behaviour may arise from having to deal with a rider whom, it perceives is totally without any redeeming features at all. (Yes indeed horses do sense the feeling of their riders towards them and react accordingly). In practise this usually means that the horse refuses to go forward. By that I won't go so far as to say that it is actually being nappy, I mean that it goes everywhere except in a straight line. The problem frequently arises because the rider perceiving that the horse is deviating does not use the correct aids in order to turn it back to its appointed path. They twist their bodies in awkward positions, look down at it and use the incorrect leg. The rider is now in a quandary for try as they might the horse still keeps wandering off anywhere but in the direction where the rider would like to go.

Therefore the most important thing that the rider must do is just that – *Make the horse go forward in a straight line at a good regular tempo.* It will not matter if this is only at a walk but forward it must go. In the beginning you may help the rider with this, if they are having a problem. You do so by simply leading the horse back to the track or by pointing (with great care) a lunging whip at it. However the only really successful solution to the problem must arise from the rider himself or herself. You must tell them to *fix their gaze* upon a point in the arena immediately in *front of them*, make the *horse* look *where they are looking* and finally to *use both legs, equally strongly behind the girth*. Since you will be using horses that are suitable for novices the riders will, much to their amazement, find that they are obeyed.

Of course it is necessary for horse's good manners to be preserved. By that I mean that the instructor should *ensure* that any horse's attempts to deviate from the movement required of it, must ultimately be corrected, even if a pupil has been allowed to struggle for a short while. It is possible, that, when working with novices some might tend to overlook a degree of naughtiness on their horse's part. But poor behaviour should not be allowed to go unchecked, even if it means that you do, eventually, have to lend a hand from the ground. For it is only through a horse knowing that it will be corrected, *every* time, that well-mannered horses remain so.

What to do about liveries?
What does one do when teaching riders who are mounted on their own horses? I must make my position clear. I do not think that it is a good idea for a novice to own his or her own horse. However we do not live in a perfect world so I will cover this particular point in the later chapter that deals with livery owners. I do believe that a rider will only be truly effective in *schooling* a horse when they have reached that point where they are considered to be a rider of intermediate to advanced level.

Before we start anything.
As with the lesson on the lunge it is essential for *every* class that you are about to take, that you carry out thorough checks of horse, equipment and rider as soon as they arrive in the arena. Also do not forget that, even in the most well run yards, horses may have been tacked up by helpers, who may not be very experienced in this job. *You need, personally, to be certain that every detail is correct.* You cannot, for example, rule out the possibility that someone may have, *accidentally tacked up with the wrong bridle* or saddle!

Otherwise these checks will be very similar to those explained in the last chapter. However we are going to assume that with a novice class you will have to deal with several riders. Whether you do or not is really beside the point but if you have more than one or two riders you must exercise a degree of efficiency in your approach. If not, you will spend a substantial part of the lesson simply carrying out the various checks and thus be short of time to put across the content of your lesson. However safety cannot be compromised!

Fitting riders to horses.
You may, occasionally, find that a rider of small round stature has been allocated a very big horse. Despite the fact that we are dedicated to teaching our pupils to ride well on any horse offered (provided that is, that it is within their ability to control it), sometimes the shape of the horse may so discompose the rider that it is good idea to allow them to change to a smaller horse, provided that you find a willing volunteer with whom you may make the change and that the policy of the school permits this.

Size alone may intimidate.
Sometimes, irrespective of the physical make up of the rider, a large horse, even one of a kindly temperament, may engender fear in the rider. There are very few horses that will not, to some extent, take advantage of the this diffidence to try and have a relaxing hour in which they do as little work as they possibly can.

The only horse that I know of, who would not do this was my old fellow Jeeves, who could, frequently, be observed taking the most nervous riders quietly around the arena, without their having to make any undue effort. Bear in mind, that though the above remarks appear in this chapter dealing with novices, you might find the same problems occurring when you are dealing with intermediate and even advanced riders.

Safety is an ongoing matter.
This attention to safety must continue during your lesson. You must continually watch the manner of your horses going and ensure that no lameness has appeared after the lesson has started. Beware: some horses can have some fun with you, especially if you are new to the job. My old friend Jeeves would regularly

pretend to be lame as soon as he worked in the class of a new instructor!

Remember names

It is very important to ensure that you remember all your pupils' and the horses' names. If like me, you have a problem with this then write them down. Above all do not refer to pupils by the names of the horses that they are riding since this is bad form.

Using the client's name as a trigger.

One of the most important jobs that you have to do is to prevent bad habits from becoming permanent. You may have a pupil who through previous poor instruction or an absence of any at all, has very poor posture. You need to correct this (a hard thing to do). In this case, instead of having to tell the client every time that they are incorrect, which may become somewhat ineffectual, you should have *the client tell you* their particular problem *every time you call out their name*.

Let us suppose that you have a rider called Janet who continually looks down. What you do is to say to Janet. ''Janet every time I call out your name, you will say to me 'I must not look down'.'' It is surprising how effective this can be and in a short time the problem diminishes.

You may apply this to almost problem. Below is a list of some examples.
'I must keep my heels down'.
'I must keep my toes to the front'.
'I must sit tall'.
'I must keep my hands still'.
'I must relax'.
'I must look where I want to go'.
'I must flex my lower back'.
'I must soften my hands'. And so on and so on.

In the beginning.

As I have said in the last chapter, the very best pupil for you to teach the art of equitation is one who comes to you without ever having ridden before. If you take care, then, no matter whether you have someone who is nervous or without any natural talent (by that I mean, for example, a good sense of balance and an immediate ability to understand the horse's mentality), in time you will be able to produce, a rider of skill. To my mind this is the most satisfying thing in the world. Of course none of this is possible without your time and dedication.

The private lesson.

When your client first started to ride it is to be hoped that these lessons were given on the lunge. By its very nature the lunge is a private lesson . Since you are able to give your whole attention to just the one person it is obvious that your pupil should have a better chance to improve. The lunge is a one to one lesson, but even when the necessity for lunge lessons has diminished, should the pupil be able to afford to continue in this manner, then they should not be dissuaded from so doing. However private lessons are not necessarily without shortcomings. Though you may be able to concentrate on the failings of this one person to the exclusion of everything else, there are advantages in learning to ride with a class. Even though there may be others using the arena during a private lesson, it is not quite the same as having to learn to ride with, say, 8 to ten other people. In class your pupil will get the experience of having to interact with other horses and riders. They will learn, for example, to keep the correct distance from other horses, enjoy the company of other riders, be able to observe others performing the same exercises as themselves and judging how well they are doing by comparison. Not only that but pupils will get much comfort through watching other riders and after the lesson is over, it is not unusual for members of a class to meet and discuss the results of their labours.

Having said all that, it is worthwhile remembering that there are some pupils who do not aspire to and as a result will never achieve great advances in their horsemanship. It may be that they are a little fearful of riding with a class and much prefer the quiet intimacy of the one to one relationship. I do not see that there is any harm in your accommodating riders in this category. By that I mean, that as zealous as you may be in getting some positive improvement in *all* your riders, there may be those occasions when you have one who merely wishes to spend a quiet and relaxing hour riding a horse. Sometimes these are people approaching middle age and it is up to you to discern what they really want. I say discern, because if you come right out with it and ask them, they will of course reply that they wish to make great progress and will be satisfied with nothing less. In practise this, sometimes, is not the case and if you continually push them further than they are prepared to go, you will find that they start to make excuses and do not turn up for their lesson.

In such cases you should set a fairly moderate standard and stick to it. This does not mean that your lessons need become boring in fact quite the opposite, they should be, mentally, quite stimulating, but they should not leave your client in a state of physical and mental exhaustion. You may well be saying to yourself, 'there is no way that I am going to lower my standards'. My reply is that if you wish to be truly successful as a teacher you must become a consummate professional and that means that you should be sufficiently flexible to succeed with anyone who comes your way.

The basics.

Having thoroughly made the point as to how ideal it is to start with several lessons on the lunge, it does not follow that a client will always be able to book this type of lesson. This may simply be due to the fact that there is not enough room in the ménages for these to take place. There is no reason why complete novices should not *start* by attending a class. In the event, you do need to take special precautions. It should be remembered that you are probably dealing with people who have never been on a horse in their lives. This being so you must have no expectations of them whatsoever. If someone falls off it is no use your saying, 'Well what do you expect they are only novices'. It is up to you to ensure, to the best of your ability that this does not happen and the one way of minimising any possible mishap is to have a *leader for every horse*. These people *must* be experienced in handling horses. Furthermore they must also be knowledgeable in attending to beginners. This means that as well as looking where they are going; they must also keep a constant eye out for the rider and ensure that they do not loose their balance. This is especially important when you are teaching young children. It is also worthwhile pointing out that while it is correct to always lead a horse away from oneself, say when turning a corner, in the context of an arena this is not practicable the reason being that it would mean that the leader would have to be on the outside and thus exposed to the possibility of being crushed by the horse against the wall.

If you do have a class that includes pupils who have not received the benefit of the preparatory work on the lunge, then you are going to have to take them through all the basics. *You should proceed with leaders until you are satisfied that the riders have reached a high enough standard to be able to, reasonably, control a horse so that they may ride through the most fundamental movements without endangering safety in a class environment.* I suppose that I must consider that odd occasion when you *do* have a class full of novices and you do *not* have enough leaders to look after each one individually.

The answer is that you should not feel compelled to have your riders going around the track the whole time. Some instructors think that their pupils will not be happy unless they are constantly *doing* something. Always pushing forward. For beginners this is not so important, they will still enjoy themselves (and probably be a little relieved) if you have them all lined up along the centre line and ask them to come out one at a time. You ask them to try making their horses walk away from the others, and go large around the arena. Where it is necessary, they should be led, otherwise you ask them to try on their own. You may make a bit of a competition out of it by asking those waiting their turn to judge their fellow riders' success. However for this chapter I am going to assume that this groundwork has been done and that by and large they are all able to manage on their own.

As an instructor your teaching will be drawn from a large reservoir of knowledge. Your pupils will have, in most cases, no knowledge at all. It is therefore unreasonable for you to expect them to be able to absorb all the outpourings of your accumulated wisdom over a short period of time. Certainly not in one lesson. Therefore it is essential that you concentrate on the essentials that your pupils first need to acquire. You must ensure that these have been clearly understood and successfully put into practise, before moving on to more advanced exercises. The basics are only achieved by constant repetition. But this means that your approach must be varied in such a way that your pupils will not become bored to death.

For example: It is no use telling your pupils that they must keep the horse ***moving straight*** throughout its body, before they have learned to use seat, leg and hand independently. Neither will they be able to make a significant improvement in their skills as a result of your telling them to 'lighten the forehand', when they do not, clearly, understand what this means. They may have a guess and think that you wish them to lift up the horse's forelegs a bit more, but how to do this? Do they heave upwards on the reins? Before you present them with such esoteric questions, you must ensure that they understand *all* the basics and are able to put them into practise. As we proceed from the novice to the advanced rider the same basic preparation will need to be repeated.

You need to explain without the use of jargon, that a horse uses ***its hind legs to produce forward going power.*** What we call *impulsion*. As your pupils progress you may introduce the term 'engage the hind quarters' but you must not take it for granted that they will automatically understand your meaning.

The meaning and understanding of words.

In fact you may need to go even further in order to make certain that your pupils *really* do understand what you have said to them. Let us take for example a real beginner sitting upon a really quiet horse. One of those whom you use especially for novices. Even this dear old thing does have a mind of its own. Every so often, responding either to erratic movements of the riders body or simply through a desire to be a little mischievous, it leaves the outside track along which it is supposed to be walking, ,and makes for the centre of the arena. It may have covered several metres in spite of the rather feeble efforts of its rider to prevent this from happening. You say to the rider 'Use your inside leg and bend your horses head in the direction in which you wish to proceed'. There is little or no result! In the first place the rider has probably disregarded all that you have told them and is leaning inwards and forwards with the inside leg pressed against the horse's side. They are also probably looking down and as for the pointing the animal in the direction in which they wish to go, the horse has probably taken the reins through their ineffectual fingers and there is no rein contact at all. Your temptation may be to go up to the horse and point your whip at it as you tell it to move out. Alternatively, you may take the bridle and lead the rider back to the track only to have a repeat performance a few minutes later. It is all rather exhausting. I do know of some more mature instructors who decline to take classes of absolute beginners because they 'no longer have the energy for all that running around'.

I am sure that we have all suffered similarly at one time or another. So what is the answer? The first thing that you must say both to yourself and the rider is; 'Is this a reasonable horse'? In other words can its will be bent to that of the rider without too much difficulty? The answer should be 'Of course it can'. That is why it was consigned to the rider in the first place.

Approach the rider standing disconsolately in the centre of the arena going nowhere. First correct their position and tell them to look back to the track. Let us suppose that it is necessary to go to the right. So they turn their whole torso so that they are now looking to the right. Ask them to shorten the right rein so that the horse's head is now slightly bent to the right. (They must now hold that rein quite firmly and resist all attempts by the animal to turn its head in the opposite direction). Having asked the client if they would mind your touching their leg, you now move their left leg two or three inches *away from* the horses' side and tell them then to close the leg against that side again in a clear movement so that the horses ***clearly feels them touching it***. Now ask the rider once again to use the aids that you have taught them for going forward to walk and ***watch them all the time.***

As soon as you perceive even the slightest tendency in the rider to lean forward - correct it – any changing of the direction of the torso – correct it - any tendency to let the rein slip through lifeless fingers – correct it. As horse and rider reach the track tell the rider to turn the torso and look to the next corner towards which they are now riding. Now they must continue to touch the horse with each leg alternatively. You call out 'Use your legs – touch the horse -left leg – right leg -left leg – right leg' in order to keep the walk going forward. You keep your eyes fixed on the rider. Now you say 'At the very first ***tendency*** for the horse ***to deviate*** from the track to the inside, stop using both legs and ***use the inside leg only*** (in this case the right leg) – Don't look down – look where you want to go – ***touch*** the horse with your inside leg and *feel* the outside rein – touch him - touch him - touch him'.

The rider, now understanding your meaning quite clearly does as you ask and – surprise surprise the little horse now receiving aids that have some determination about them, obeys!. The client walks around the whole of the arena without any deviation on the horse's part. They have made their first successful attempt at bending the horse's will to their own. They are delighted! You have helped them to do this without running around the arena like some sort of demented coot!

Now dear reader, I can feel the thought running through your mind. Why has this obviously inadequate rider not been started on the lunge? A very reasonable thought, but in practice, life doesn't always work out in such a convenient way. For example, you may have been asked to take several classes of University riders. They all belong to the University riding club. Up they come, most of them with the idea that they are pretty sharp equestrians. After all are they not reading law, philosophy, history or media studies? With all that under their belts, riding should be a doddle. In any case they have all ridden before! Oh yes, there is the charming young girl who tells you she has actually done jumping yet is incapable of riding a transition from walk to trot!! She is a novice rider. Then there is the charming chap who tells you that he has ridden lots of times, but as soon as his horse makes any movement whatsoever he freezes with fear. The pre-arranged groups into which they had been placed have disintegrated and you find that you have a *complete* beginner in a class of novices. What are you to do? Ask the beginner to leave? They are all much of a muchness anyway and you should be able to cope by going right back to basics and **ensuring** that **everyone understands clearly** what you are telling them. Order emerges from chaos and, with your sense of humour; they all have an enjoyable hour!

Physical ability and mental maturity.

You must realise that your pupils do not start with the same muscular development that you may have developed over the years. Even if they are physically fit and well developed it is quite probable that none of their muscles will be those that are needed to support their bodies in the position required for good equitation. Do not push them too hard or they may well suffer such discomfiture after a lesson that they may be deterred from continuing. I would go further and say that I am not *particularly* in favour of classes of mixed ages. This is not due to the fact that I consider that there is some form of barrier between the young and the old. On the contrary when it comes to equitation the only assessment that is of value to you, when taking a class, is the *ability* of all those taking part? Are they all of a similar standard?

The point that I am getting at is that every age group may require a slightly different regime. With youngsters, just out of the junior school it is not satisfactory to; subject them immediately, to over long and deeply serious discourses on the theory of equitation. But there is no reason why you should not be very strict about, accurate transitions from letter to letter.

For though in the last chapter we were talking mainly about having one client only, the same rule still applies when you are teaching a large class. You allow your eyes to roam over the class and as you note errors you correct them without this interfering with the flow of your dialogue. For example you may be talking about tempo whilst your class are working at the trot. You note that one client's hands are moving up and down excessively. In the middle of what you are saying and without any preamble you say 'try and keep you hands still, Janet' and then you continue to talk about tempo. Note that I used the name last. This not only reminds the rider of a continuing fault but since you do not start the comment with the name, for a few seconds, every member of the class thinks that you are referring to them. It also tells the class that you are extremely observant and determined to get them all to improve.

Middle aged and older riders.

With middle aged riders you should bear in mind that though they may *appear* deeply interested in learning about the components of the higher forms of dressage, they really desire no more than an hour's pleasant diversion. When asked, they may not be too keen to engage the posture required for a really serious attempt at riding the more difficult movements. The reasons may be no more than that they suffer an occasional bout of sciatica. When you request them to use the back, preparatory to cantering they may not attempt this because they anticipate possible pain. As a result the canter depart that you have requested at a certain letter may take place several strides later. It is not necessary to jump up and down about these shortcomings. Indeed you should allow them to proceed at a pace that they find comfortable. I recently started to teach a man of 65 who had only briefly been on the back of a horse in his youth. Now this gentleman, though enjoying short periods where we do nothing more than have a bit of a chat about this and that, has over a quite a short period developed into one of my most promising riders. The reason for this is twofold. In the first place he had no bad habits that needed to be eliminated, secondly he is very self-critical and constantly strives to improve.

Another aspect of teaching older people is that they may already have fixed ideas as to how to go about the art of riding. You need to be flexible in your approach. If you are persistent, tactful and do not loose interest yourself (through lack of apparent progress) you will succeed in getting these older riders to change their ways but you must above all remember to approach any problems with a sense of humour. On the other hand you may decide that teaching of pupils in this category is not for you.

Pupils are not usually morons.

Your pupils are always entitled to know the reason why. And you must be able to explain your reasons for asking them to perform any movement or exercise. Riding is nowadays, not simply a means of getting from place to place, but can evolve into an intimate form of communication between rider and horse. The horse being a willing partner.

At the start it is my policy in teaching to concentrate on the rider and to develop his ability to get the horse from A to B accurately. I do not bother the novice with such matters as pointing out that the horse is unbalanced due to its confirmation. and that they need to apply a remedial correction. It is my view that this sort of thing can come later, when they have greater skills. It is after all not the job of a novice to carryout schooling on a horse but rather to learn to unlock the ability, which is already available in every good school horse. But one must not forget that some school horses will tend to show some disrespect as soon as they perceive that they are to work with a rider of limited ability. However it is your job to reveal to the rider that it is, for example, his or her own poor posture that is causing the horse to react as it does. They have to learn to correct this so that the horse, in turn, will oblige them. An example would be a rider who continually looks down. Amazement follows when you give the instruction 'look where you wish to go and make the horse look where you are looking' and the horse proceeds to move in that required direction.

To my mind riding a horse has to do with intelligence. It therefore follows that the more intelligent person, with good instruction, has a greater likelihood, to become a good rider. This point should be made very clear to your pupils so that they realise that by using their own intellect they will eventually gain complete co-operation from the horse and become more expert.

When anyone joins a class, the instructor must ensure that they are familiar with the basics. That means even such matters as how to approach a horse or pony and how to mount. *Always put the pupil through the basics especially a reminder to 'never walk behind a horse'.*

The Contract.
On reflection, I suppose it could be said that you are responsible for helping the rider and horse to create a contract between them. The rider's part is to promise to be still and be well balanced so that they will not interfere with the horse's manner of going. They are also responsible for giving clear and precise aids and not to ask for movements that are beyond the horses' physical ability.

Further more the rider must learn that no matter how determined they may be *in trying to obtain the horses' obedience*, they must *not resort to abuse either verbal or physical*. You must point out that, generally speaking, horses are born gentle creatures and though they may be sorely tested they usually manage to retain their 'Sang-froid'. However if continually subjected to bad treatment then that kindliness may be lost forever.

The horse's part of the contract is to obey the rider's wishes to the limit of its capability. So what we are looking for is a feeling of mutual respect between both horse and rider.

Getting Pleasure
We must clearly understand that when working a horse there must be an element of fun for both the rider and the horse! Pupils should finish a session be it either in the ménage or out hacking with a feeling of great stimulation. Horses relaxed, but with a feeling of enjoyment. This does not mean that the pupil may have had to work very hard the whole time. It means that they have been required to use the 'Grey matter'. If at the end of a session your pupils have achieved, to some extent, the targets you set for them and they also tell you that they have thoroughly enjoyed themselves and if your horses are still cool and calm, then, you may consider that you yourself have been successful.

Don't start difficult exercises at the end of a session.
In order to be fairly certain of achieving your ends avoid trying new and difficult exercises at the end of a lesson. Instead, place these in the middle of the routine after the horses have limbered up and with enough time to be able to repeat a movement should this be necessary. In any case I always like to start a new movement at the walk (this gives pupils time to mentally visualise the different elements) and then to follow this at the trot. If a new movement has been somewhat indifferently performed then return to an exercise that you know that has been ridden successfully. In that way even if the foregoing work has not been all that effective, at least your pupils will end the lesson with some degree of satisfaction.

The essential qualities of the instructor must be patience, kindness and understanding of both horse and rider. These coupled with a determination to ensure that improvement is made; one must never resort to sarcasm or short temper. Bearing in mind that many pupils have responsible and demanding jobs or occupations it would seem to be fairly obvious that, if a rider fails to understand the instructions that have been given, then the fault will lie with the instructor. The problem arises because you have probably made the fundamental error of either using jargon with which the client is unfamiliar, or else of not using words that will adequately explain your requirement. You have failed to create a mental image in the mind of the rider as to what it is that they have to do.

Providing continuing interest and a desire to improve.
One problem that an instructor may face is that though the pupils may all enjoy their lessons, they may have absolutely no ambition to really improve. They arrive week after week and, obviously, enjoy their time spent with you. They probably show some improvement during the lesson but when they return a week later, you notice that despite all your exhortations they have slipped back into their old bad habits.

How does one deal with this problem?
One way is to become more authoritarian and shout at them a bit. I do not, in general, favour that approach. I do know of many instructors who do. The problem is that unless you have a class that are emotionally strong enough to withstand a bit of bullying, you may all too easily go 'over the top' and end up causing much distress and perhaps the loss of a client. I do not deny that there have been the odd occasions where the 'Sergeant Major' had crept into my voice and I am told that my voice is very powerful. But it is my view that this approach does require a great deal of skill and one must be an expert at both increasing the pressure and then, quite abruptly lowering it if one is to be successful.

My approach is to keep in mind the faults of previous weeks and to correct them as soon as I see them occurring again. I keep on about them, never letting up. It's all done in the friendliest of ways, don't you know? Suppose, for example, you have a client that has the very bad habit of riding with the heels coming up or the toes turning out. I say 'Heels Anne, please keep them down' if that is the pupils name. I will continue 'Heels Anne' throughout the lesson immediately I see a return to the bad posture. I may then say to the class in general. 'Heels and toes everybody. Keep them down and to the front'

A dressage test provides a target.
Sometimes it is a good idea to provide a target for excellence and I believe that setting a dressage test is a very good way of going about it. The test selected must be at a level that is attainable by your pupils. I try and select a test that will include elements on which I wish my pupils to concentrate. As an example for clients who seem to be incapable of riding a circle correctly, I choose a test that contains at least two circles. You should provide a test sheet for each class member. You must also allow enough time for the test to be learned and, possibly, practised (if not the whole test then at least parts of it). An associate should be prevailed upon to be judge (if you do it yourself you may be accused of bias). Rosettes should be given down to sixth place. I personally try to provide *prizes* down to third place. Whether or not you are able to go that far will depend on your pocket or your ability to persuade the management to cough up the money.

Let the lesson commence.

The leading file.
Before sending your ride out onto the track you must have them in a good order. Several factors will govern this. They are: -

1. Generally, you need to have the larger or more forward going horses in front. This will avoid the frustration engendered by closing up on smaller and thus slower moving horses in front of them.

2. Having said that you should not have the lead taken by a horse whose only thought is to dash from front to rear. A nervous rider who is hanging on the reins like grim death may well fuel this desire. You may well tell such a person that they need to relax and 'soften their hands' but very often instinct will get the better of them and they will not listen to you.

3. You should also make provision for mares or for that matter any animal that is particularly unsociable. I would suggest that, it is better if such horses are put at the back of the ride; out of harms way. The reasoning for this is that others in your ride may themselves not be sufficiently in control and, as a result, unable to stop their own horses from getting too close.

4. For a really satisfactory lead you should have a horse that is forward going and a rider who is reasonably in control. The horse may *not* be the one with the greatest stride but a smaller horse ridden by a competent rider will very often provide an excellent lead file.

Finally your lead file must be made aware of the fact that they are required to set a nice steady pace for the rest of the ride. Therefore they need to be reminded to glance behind them every so often to ensure that the other riders have not been left behind. This may be due to one of the horses desiring to stale or simply due to the fact that it is refusing to go forward properly. Whatever, the lead file cannot simply go merrily on their way without any concern for the other class members.

It is also up to everyone else to try to ensure that they stay in touch. The correct distance, for a close order ride, is one horses length. At this distance the rider and horse are safe from being kicked by the horse in front. The rider judges this by seeing only half of its tail when looking in between their own horses ears. If they see less than half, then they are too close; the whole tail and more, too far away.

One of the ways in which you can instil some discipline into your ride is by insisting that the rider pays attention to the correct distance and maintains it at all times. Variations creep in because the rider simply looses his or her concentration. Another reason may be that some horses are lazy. This means that the rider will gain a valuable lesson in keeping their horse forward going by using their seat and legs.

The structure.

You should initiate a lesson by starting with movements that allow both horse and rider to limber up. You then continue with exercises that in turn, logically, lead on to the next. These may increase in terms of difficulty for your riders but at no time should exceed their overall ability to cope. By this I do not mean that you should always avoid doing anything that will slightly stretch them. What I am saying is that you should not go so far that you might unwittingly precipitate a situation where an accident may occur.

The climax of the lesson should be reached about 15 to 20 minutes before the end. You then introduce movements that descend through quiet trot and finally walk on a long rein. This will allow sufficient time for both horse and rider to 'unwind' and finish the lesson in a cool, calm and relaxed state.

Every lesson that you give should have this same basic form. Do not forget that there are an infinite variety of ways of getting the same basic message across. However you should beware of trying to teach too many different things all in the same lesson, if you do, then you may end up with riders who have not really learned anything in depth.

Suggested exercises are to be found in chapter 16 'Exercises to Form a Lesson'.

The fundamental importance of position.

Be they adults or children the foundation for success throughout the riders' 'riding life' will be the entrenchment of a good position. More than anything else it is up to you, from the very beginning to ensure that this is established. Now as I say throughout this book, in equitation, there are many ways of achieving a desired result and most of them have some merit.

So far as position is concerned I would refer you to Dr. HLM van Schaik the famous dressage judge in his book *8 Misconceptions and Simple Truths in Dressage. He is but one of many who all make the same point. I will quote him verbatim because, even though he is a judge at the very highest level of dressage, he covers so many of the problems that we as instructors at the very basic level have to deal with. He writes: -

'The position is functionally correct when the rider does not disturb the horse, and when he is able to give the aids in a discreet but emphatic way, at the correct moment, to the correct spot, at the correct strength. The rider will not disturb the horse when he has an independent seat. He does not have to use the reins to stay on the horse; his hands are totally independent of the movements of the horse; he never has "dancing hands" and he never yanks the horse in the mouth because of an unexpected movement.

Having an independent seat means also that the rider is able to move in unison with the movement of the horse, and to keep his own centre of gravity as much as possible in line with the horse's centre of gravity. The rider sits at all times as lightly as possible on the horse, for it is evident that the less of a burden a rider is for the horse, the better the horse can perform'. I do not think that many have put it better.

The first thing that everyone has to learn is that horses are creatures with whom one can communicate very successfully. Secondly there is the prime fact that riding is essentially a mental process accompanied by good balance. I suppose one could say that it is about 75% mental and 25% balance. On the other hand it might be 100% mental and balance combined! Whatever way one looks at it, it is not about the use of force. The pupil needs to know from the very beginning that one cannot force a horse to do ones bidding. If it is sufficiently determined it may well rather die than give in to you. On the other hand if you have developed a bond it may well die for you in its attempt to do as you ask.

I have no doubt that there will be the odd reader or two who will have knowledge of the past where in fact horses were forced by cruel treatment to obey. We have moved on. The average weekly rider is not going to have the time, equipment or temperament to engage in the practises described and I must say condemned by Sydney Galvayne*24 who then goes on to describe his own "interesting methods of 'bending a horses' will to his own". *It is essential that a horse be mentally relaxed if it is to go well.*

The very basic basics of movement.
For this section we are assuming that the members of your class have learned to sit reasonably well as a result of lessons on the lunge. Now however they are faced with the problem that they are, to some extent 'going solo'. In other words there is, apparently, no one else there to either make the horse go forward or for that matter in the required direction. Whilst on the lunge all those problems were removed from the rider's responsibility. Now they are on their own, so to speak. It is therefore very important that they are made aware of the basic essentials that are required. They are as follows: -

1. The rider must always look in the direction in which they wish to proceed (they must not look down).

2. The rider must make the horse look where they are looking.

3. Should the rider wish to turn the horse, they must do so by first looking in the new direction themselves. This is achieved by their heads being turned solely through the movement of their whole torso into the direction in which they wish to go.

4. The rider must bend the horse so that it is looking in the new direction.

The usefulness of exercises.
As with any sport, exercises play a useful part in helping riders to limber up at the start of a lesson. You should allow at least five minutes, after you have warmed up the horses, to give your class some of these exercises to do (see photos 22 to 24 incl.)

Turning the ignition key and *gently* touching the accelerator.
Quite often this can become a moment of frustration for some riders. The reason being that they ask the horse to go forward and it takes absolutely no notice of them whatsoever! They try kicking hard with no effect. So far as you are concerned this should not be at all surprising. After all the horses have already assessed your pupils and they know full well that they are all novices.

How?
Because they have already smelled the odour of apprehension that your pupils have probably emitted when they first met. If there were no apprehension, then as soon as they are mounted, the horses would know as they felt their new, temporary 'masters' momentary imbalance.
Teaching the aids.

Giving the aids correctly.
The answer to the above problem is that from the very beginning pupils are taught how to give the correct *signals* to the horse that will tell it what they wish it to do. Note I have mentioned the word signals. You must explain that *aids are signals*, which horses will understand if given in the correct sequence. If they are given with authority and precision the horse will very likely obey.

The voice.
I repeat that I am very much in favour of pupils being encouraged to make use of the voice.

131

Why so? Simply because during its original breaking the horse will have been trained to respond to the trainer's voice. It therefore follows that this natural aid may be used to form a basis of communication between rider and horse. The advantage of going back to basics, as it were, is useful for several reasons. In the first place a rider even in the intermediate or advanced stage of their riding experience may still give the animal signals that are unclear. It is one of the great mysteries of life that never ceases to fascinate me. Despite the fact that so many riders ride badly for years on end: the hands jerking this way and that, the legs kicking, the bodies slumped in the saddle, in spite of everything, their servants, the horse, still look after them!

One of the problems that you will have to overcome is to instil in your pupils a purposeful determination. *It is a question of becoming proactive rather than reactive.* To explain; very often the horse will catch out a rider. The animal may decide, of its own accord to leave the track. The rider only reacts after the horse has done this and, by then is well away from the place where it should have been. You must teach your class to learn to anticipate this sort of thing. Very often the horse is simply having a bit of fun. This is all very well but if the rider is caught out and unbalanced, then you may have a fall to report!

A rider needs to learn how to balance the resolve to get the horse to obey their will without letting it slide into aggression. Many horses love to get a reaction from the rider and will attempt to develop this. The rider must learn how to get obedience by quiet determination. In fact it could be said that, with the instructors help, a pupil should contribute to a horse's good behaviour by the simple means of ensuring that they correct any digression immediately. This is seldom the case.

Points to watch continuously.

When giving a lesson you should pay particular attention to your pupil's position. Check their bodies from head to toe as it were. People tend to sit with rounded shoulders and in a slumped position. That is to say with the spine curving out backwards. There is a great tendency to do this whilst at the halt. If not corrected then they will be unable to absorb the forces generated by the horse in motion, especially at the higher gaits. With the spine curved correctly (see drawing no. 20.) a shock-absorbing unit is created and this allows the rider to maintain the body in balance. One has to make sure that the rider keeps their whole body as close to their centre of gravity as possible. If they do not do so then, more energy has to be used by the muscles simply to keep the rider in place. Generally speaking it is the muscles of the back and thigh that are the foundation of control. But even then they cannot do the job well if the rider persists in sitting on the fork instead of their seat (see drawing no. 21)

Another problem that many riders experience is the inability to use their limbs independently. So often I have seen a horse move in a direction other than that apparently required by the rider. Close observation reveals the reason for this. Out of sight, in other words on the far side of you, they will be using a leg at the same time as they use their other one. The poor horse does not know what to do.

Maintaining the position of the leg frequently gives many problems. Outside legs may be seen to come so far forward that the toe can be seen in front of the horse's chest. Then again inside legs are drawn so far back that they are almost level with the knee.

Now it may well be that what I am about to say, may not be generally accepted, as the basis for instruction of the beginner. However it is my *method,* if you like, and I have found it very successful. It is my view that a pupil must learn, from the very beginning that it is the horse that moves and not the rider – a very difficult thought to instil since most people instinctively feel that if one, for example moves ones upper body forward, then the horse will, itself move. Of course this is the very opposite to that which actually happens. *The rider has to sit still.* The only real movement that takes place is a flexing of the spine. In fact movement on the part of the rider, of *any sort* reveals to the horse that there is, sitting upon his back an object that *can be moved.* If he considers this to be so, then he may be inclined not to obey and may even take action to remove that weight should it plague him. Therefore the rider must learn that movement from the horse occurs as a result of giving signals. If these signals are not obeyed then the horse will be touched with the whip and it is at this point more than ever that the rider must, always, keep his body upright and absolutely still.

Exercises to improve co-ordination.

It is a good idea for pupils to practise using their limbs independently not only when mounted but also when they are at home. One of the problems that many a novice and indeed intermediate riders have is the inability to use their hands and legs independently. When they should be using only one leg at a given point during a movement, they seem to be incapable of separating them and use both together. It is as though they

132

are tied together with string. One exercise that can be done at home and which improves the independent use of hand or leg is to sit upon a chair and to practise using one leg at a time, creating a series of movements, which involve different combinations of leg use. Similarly the same may be applied to the hand. This will require the assistance of a friend and consists of a piece of cotton thread being tied in a large loop to either side of the back a kitchen chair. The rider then sits on another chair in front of the person who is holding the first chair with the thread attached and holds the loop in both hands as they would the reins. The 'helper' then moves the chair back either back and forth or side to side, whilst the rider tries to keep an elastic tension on the thread following the movement of the chair back but without the thread breaking. ** (See drawing no. 22) This is of course not an original idea. You may see something very similar illustrated on the dust jacket of McTaggart's 'The Art of Riding' *13. Here the author is shown riding a horse with paper reins. What you see, in the photograph, is a loop of paper passing through the author's hand; as it progresses around the neck it seems to disappear and then reappear. What has happened is that the middle section has been removed and the ensuing gap joined with cotton thread to the final ten inches or so where paper again continues to the bit. – A wonderful exercise for developing good hands.

*Taught to me by Sheila Freeman, of Catlips Farm. My first riding instructor.

An exercise to be performed in class.
It is obvious from all that has gone before both in this and previous chapters, that a high degree of limb co-ordination is essential for the development of the ability to give clear and accurate aids. I have seen an instructor demonstrating the idea by patting their head with one hand while the other described circles of the tummy. Both hands were doing slightly different things. This does serve to make a point but to my mind it is more advantageous if you give your pupils an exercise that actually helps them to develop movements that are within the context of equitation.

An example of one such exercise would be as follows: -

1 Sitting on the horse the rider flexes the horse to the right and to the left alternatively.
2 As they do so the fingers of the opposite hand only close and open.
3 Both hands move alternately, laterally, about 2 to 3 inches away from the neck and back again.
4 The heel of the each foot is lowered and raised slightly but remain unmoving against the horse's side.
5 The legs are moved, alternately away from the horses side and back again to their original position **(without actually touching the horse)**.
6 All the above movements are combined in varying degrees.

Your class should spend two or three minutes continuously practising these combinations first with one hand and then on the other. So far as responses to the rein or leg are concerned, the horses' only reaction would be to yield its jaw. If the horse does move away from the riders' leg then the exercise should, momentarily, cease and continue when the horse has been straightened up once again.

This is but one example and you should devise similar exercises of your own. I repeat, so much depends on *good communication and co-ordination*. I acknowledge the fact that some pupils never bother to learn and, sometimes, are never taught, a way of improving these skills. If *you* are to become really successful then you must endeavour to ensure that *your pupils* do become expert at these sorts of exercises.

Acute observation.
In this paragraph I am referring to the instructor and not the client. What I mean by this has already been mentioned in the previous chapter. *You must note every fault in all your pupils* as soon as they occur. It may well be that by the time you have gone through them all, their positions have changed in relation to yourself. This means that you are no longer looking at the client first observed, because your eyes have moved, say to the back of the class. Let me give you an example. You give the ride the command to change the rein through a long diagonal. You do this well before the leading file arrives at the required letter. As you give them the command you are looking at each one in turn and noting any faults, but since you are already giving an instruction it will only confuse matters if you point them out at that time. Then as they carry out your command and your attention is focused on them riding, correctly from letter to letter, this is the time that you now point out the faults. They may be actually passing right behind you. Thus ' Heels

down Roger, hands still Mary, look up Tim, thumbs on top Bridget, toes turned in Carlos' and so on. Note that I mention the fault *followed* by the rider's name. The reason for this is that if you mention the fault first, the whole class thinks about it before realising that the comment does not specifically apply to them. Since you may not at that moment be actually looking at the rider, they wonder how on earth you have spotted them!

Understanding the manner of the horse's going.

Even at this fairly early stage in the pupil's riding career it is important to encourage them to understand what the above heading means. As instructors we know what to look for. For a novice this is best achieved at the walk. Start by asking them to 'walk on'. As they do so, they should, immediately, be made aware of the quality of that walk. ***You will need from the very beginning and forever more,*** to constantly, mention this ***for every gait***. You should ask them to imagine that they have an imaginary metronome in their minds counting out the rhythm, 'One - two, three, four. One - two, three, four. You should ask them to count out this rhythm, one at a time, out loud, so that you may correct them if their tempo is wrong.
This will serve to have a twofold benefit: -

1.   In the first place they will have been provided with a target at which to aim. To achieve this they will have to learn to use their seats and legs.

2.   The horses will listen to this rhythm being established and be more likely to co-operate even though they know that the riders are novices and therefore suitable to be taken advantage of.

Learning to relax the horse.

From the beginning your pupils must start to learn how to ride in a manner that will help their horses to relax. They may have many other things claiming their attention, but if they are left to continually ride around the arena with, say a rein that is too short, before long the poor horse is going to get 'wound up'. You must be sufficiently observant to prevent this from happening. Correcting the position is an essential element in avoiding possible problems. Many riders, who are seen to continually, stick out their arms in front of them do so because they see a short rein as a means of maintaining greater control. In other words the longer the arm, the shorter the rein. When you ask them to tuck their elbows into their sides, they are bemused because they cannot do so without lengthening the rein and this, in their minds, means loosing control.

In fact what may happen is that the horse, protesting at the manner in which it being 'strangled' by the rein, may start to tense up. The rider feeling this happen makes the rein shorter still. They are probably also riding with their heels up, at the same time. In order to try and stay secure in the saddle they clamp their legs against the horse's sides. The horse thinks that he has been given a long awaited signal to escape. Heels dig in even more, the horse goes even faster?????

Going large, warming up and riding corners.

Riders must learn the essentials and you must be meticulous in teaching these fully and correctly. The very first thing that you may ask your class to do is to go large at the walk. In other words you simply ask them to ride in a straight line from the centre line where you have been carrying out your checks, to one of the long sides of the arena. This movement alone forms an exercise in itself, for as the class goes forward to walk you tell them to fix their eyes on a point on the wall of the arena directly in front of them so that they may proceed in a straight line. Further more, taking their dressing from the lead rider they also have to try and keep level with one another. As they reach the track, depending on your instruction, proceeding either to the left or right, things are momentarily easier for them. If you have a willing and forward going horse in front, then the others will follow without too much difficulty. Having the side of the arena to support them, the class is free, momentarily, to concentrate on keeping their horses going forward at a pace that will avoid too large a gap forming between themselves and the rider in front (or too close a gap come to that). At this time they must also be asked to check their own positions. You should remind them that they will not be able to accurately ask anything of their horses if their own positions are not first corrected.

All lessons should basically have a similar structure: that is to say that horses must be allowed a short period during which they are worked in. This means that you should always start your lessons at the walk on a long rein. Please note a ***long*** rein is not a loose rein. For the former the rider maintains contact but allows the horse to stretch the neck and with the rider's encouragement, start to track up. The latter means that the rider holds the rein by the buckle only. Tracking up means that the horse is engaging his hind quarters and if this is happening, the rider will, if they glance down, note that the hoof print of one hind leg falls in front of that made by the foreleg - on the same side. At this stage the horse will not be ridden too deeply into the corners of the ménage.

The reason for this manner of proceeding should be explained to the rider. You should briefly describe how the horse has evolved. How the tendons have grown longer and, as a result need a period in which to warm up. It is no different for a human athlete. In both cases - horse and human - if the tendons aren't warmed up they may be subject to sprains.

If you also wish to keep the interest of your ride during this period, you may give a short discourse as to the differences in the efficiency of energy conversion, in the horse's muscles between anaerobic and aerobic chemical reactions. (See chapter 23 and also read up the subject. *33 Stephen Budianski).

Riding corners

After the warming up period the pupils should be asked to take up contact. That is to say they shorten the rein slightly whilst, at the same time, asking the horse to continue to walk on with impulsion. They should also begin to ride the corners of the school. This is the next problem for the riders to overcome. How many times have I watched *advanced* classes riding around an arena and *not* riding the corners correctly? (See fig. 4)

Why is this important?

Because if the corner is not ridden correctly and by that I mean deeply, then the rider has handed over the initiative to the horse.

Why so?

Simply because the horse sees the corner coming and, having no wish to bang into the wall it turns the corner of its own accord. The rider has not asked it to do so. 'So what!' I hear you say. The answer is very much 'so everything'. Since it isn't stupid the horse will then try and shorten the distance that it has to travel by coming further and further in.   If the pupil expects the horse to obey them throughout the lesson, then why on earth hand over the control for something as simple as riding a corner?

The corner must be ridden correctly. The object for the rider is to make sure that the horse is ridden *through* the corner. Its head should be flexed to the inside and its body is bent throughout its length. The hindquarters should follow in the same track as the forehand. In order to assist in this process, on entering the corner the rider's inside leg comes forward to lie almost on the girth. It is stretched down as though it was a pole stuck in the ground and thus gives support. The riders outside leg is behind the girth to control the horses' quarters and to prevent them from moving out, which due to the centrifugal forces created by the movement might tend to happen. The rider's torso is turned with the outside shoulder coming forward in the direction of the bend. Obviously as the rider's body turns so does the head so that they are now looking in the new direction. The horse is flexed in the direction in which it is proceeding but the riders' hands are kept level.

This is one of the early movements where the rider has an opportunity to effectively influence the horse. It should be apparent to any rider that a really well schooled horse will not turn until the rider gives the aid. 'So if the rider does not give the aid then will the horse actually bang into the wall?' Yes indeed it might but it will do so only once for if the rider were to allow this to happen they will have lost the horses' confidence, which it will not be in a hurry to return! In practise, of course the horse takes the initiative away from the rider.

Problems with corners.

Now having made the point in such detail as to the correct way of riding a corner what do you do help a pupil who is riding a horse that persistently falls in on every bend? It is a problem that may be experienced by riders irrespective of level of skill. The answer is quite simple. The problem lies not so much with the horse as with the rider! As in everything to do with riding horses the rider must be *proactive and not reactive*. That is to say that even though the rider *knows* that the horse is going to fall in as it goes around the corner, they *don't do anything sufficiently early to prevent this happening*.

What happens with pupils who do try really hard with little effect?
You will have some pupils who as they ride the corner do keep kicking the horse and further more they

twist the horse's neck to the outside in order to correct the track. It has little effect. Sometimes they try to obtain a result by crossing the hand over the horses' neck (see photo no. 10)

My pupils say to me 'This horse is a naughty boy. He keeps on falling in on the corner and I don't seem to be able to do anything about it?' I reply 'Your problem is that even though you know what is going to happen you don't react until you are actually riding around the corner and by that time it is too late! If you know that your horse falls in then you must **prepare** for this ***well before you reach the corner*** by using the inside leg to indicate your wishes to the horse, you may also assist the leg by leading away with the outside rein. That is to say you move the outside hand about two to three inches away from the horse's neck as you enter the corner and this avoids the temptation to twist the head in the wrong direction. If you take action with a gentle nudging of the inside leg all the time as you approach, then by the time you ride the corner the horse will have obeyed you'. With a horse that does not want to respond, your pupils may also touch the neck with their stick on the inside. They may also slow down the walk or even ride to a halt until the horse has obeyed and is back on the track where it should be.

Oh the satisfaction to be seen on riders' faces as they deal with the problem successfully. Of course at this point we are talking about riders learning to cope with a difficulty at the walk. Alas it may well return at the higher paces where things happen more quickly, but the problem is still, fundamentally, the same and should be dealt with in a similar manner.

Riding a change of rein.

The next suitable movement is to ride a change of rein through the *long* diagonal. The class must be given the instruction *in good time*. You will probably need to point out the significant letters, i.e. H to F or K to M or vice versa. This is essential for the riders already have a great deal to think about and unless their attention is specifically drawn to the letters they will probably have ridden past them before they are aware of having done so. (See fig. 5)

Using transitions.

Sometimes even though the rider tries to give the aids correctly, the horse does not listen. A method of helping the rider during this period is by asking them to make the horse do a series of transitions in quick succession. Halt to walk, walk to trot and then downwards again. As the exercise progresses ask the rider to make the transitions more quickly.

Riding circles.

Even during the early stages of learning to ride, pupils should be introduced to the idea of riding circles. There are several advantages to be gained from circular movements. In the first place the rider must learn to give up the comforting support provided by the arena wall. Like the horse, they have been using this as a reference point with which to guide themselves around the arena. A drift from the track is very easily spotted almost as soon as it starts. Even when you have asked for a change of rein along the long diagonal the rider still has the letter on the other side of the arena to use as a target towards which they have to aim *in a straight line*. Now, when asked to ride a circle everything changes. There are the main reference points but in between the true path is slightly more intangible. Not only that but surprisingly enough the horse does not seem to be able to oblige the rider, it may wander to the outside of the designated path or, more likely, consider that since the shortest distance between two points is a straight line, take it!

When you explain that the horse does not go on a circle as though on railway tracks and that the rider is solely responsible for having it follow the intended path then, from these exercises alone the client will learn a great deal about using each leg independently.

Always start with a large circle. As the rider grows more experienced the size may be reduced to a medium circle and then a small circle. As the circle grows smaller so the number of things for the rider to think about, increase. Now there is not only the size which having been reduced gives less 'thinking' time but there is also the matter of maintaining impulsion.

As the lesson progresses.

You should have constructed a lesson using such movements as are shown in chapter 15 - Exercises to form a lesson. When you are satisfied with the standard achieved by the class, at the walk, you may proceed with an upward transition. Usually this will be the trot. The initial trot should be rising.

Continuous checking.
It is your job to *constantly check* your pupils' positions throughout the entire period of the lesson. Each rider must be examined in turn and the position commented upon. This means praise as well as criticism. You are looking for: -

1. The head held well balanced on the riders' shoulders.
2. The rider looking ahead (with chin tucked in) and not down at the horse.
3. The shoulders back and chest thrown out.
4. The back straight but flexible.
5. The rider clearly sitting on the seat bones with just a hint of the weight being placed on the rear part of the pelvis.
6. The elbows tucked gently into the waist (Not pushed forward as though wheeling a supermarket trolley).
7. The hands carried as a pair (and perfectly still) with the thumbs on top each one pointing at the horses' opposite ear.
8. The fingers opening and closing to allow for the movement in the horses head.
9. The toes turned up and to the front.
10. The heels pushed down so that the ankles are springy.
11. Finally the whole position held whilst the rider is in a state of complete relaxation.

Not too much to ask is it?

The state of balance.
What is seldom made clear to our pupils is the exact, meaning of some of the terms that we use. For example we say when riding on a circle 'the inside leg is, almost, on the girth providing impulsion, whilst the outside leg is just behind the girth, controlling the quarters'. All very well as far as it goes but this does not serve to help the rider in understanding that, as a horse proceeds around a circular path its very dynamic may serve to unbalance it and thus cause it to veer off the correct path. Neither does it help in understanding that the horse, having a mind of it's own, may well decide that it is ridiculous to go around a circle when it is much simpler to cut straight across. This means that the rider must use both hands and legs, independently, touching the horse either inside or outside, as required, to keep the horse on the true course. We may do this instinctively but a novice may not. Only when you point out this out will they understand. If you do not do so then they will simply sit in the saddle rather mystified about what is happening?

Awareness
After balance and learning to use the hands and legs independently. The next problem that the rider has to overcome on their way to becoming really expert is - awareness. Most often riders are unable to place their horses in a correct position due to the fact that they are not aware when the horse *is not* in the correct position or for that matter moving at a satisfactory tempo. You should spend some time on exercises that encourage the rider to 'feel' what is going on below them. For example you may ask them, at the walk. – without looking down – to tell you every time the horse places its weight on it's inside foreleg, or any other leg for that matter. The pupil should call out 'One' or 'Now' every time that they think that the designated leg is moving under them. The front legs are easiest because when you do allow them to look down they can see for themselves whether or not they are correct.

You must explain to the client that it is very hard to make good progress and make corrections if one isn't aware as to how the horse is moving in the first place.

Explaining each new section of the lesson.
Before a class embarks on any exercise, no matter how simple, you must explain exactly what it is that you are going to ask them to do. I am belabouring this point because so many instructors forget that pupils may not have the same comprehension of the movements and an understanding of the terms involved, as we do. All to often an instructor will explain movements in terms of a. c. d. g. leaving out the essential b. e. f. In other words their thoughts take a mental short cut. This may mean that the class has not understood. Very often, they will either be too embarrassed or nervous to ask the instructor exactly what they mean.

Prefixing a comment.
I prefer to make my comment and then to use the rider's name – thus 'reins Angela'. The advantage of this

is that it alerts the whole class before being specific. With children I like to have a generic name for a fault. So 'Widow Twankies' means that the reins are being held so loosely that they represent washing lines. The metaphor is of course drawn from pantomime where Aladdin's mother first appears on stage. She is a washerwoman and is hanging up the washing on a droopy line. Children remember this sort of thing very well.

Jargon and explanations.

The master horseman Colonel Mario de Mendoza trained me, for two years. He had, for many years been the Chief instructor of the Portuguese Military Academy. He was also a great personal friend of Nuno d'Olivera. Colonel Mendoza came over to the U.K. in order to improve his English. In the beginning his lack of command of the language caused him great frustration in getting his ideas across. However in a short time his English was excellent. In all that time I never heard him use a word that was not readily understandable to a layman.

Further more Colonel Mendoza would, sometimes carry on about a book he had been reading. I remember him once complaining about a tract written by a well-known German instructor. 'His instructions (the German's) are so complicated that I think that, in fact, he is writing about the setting up of a video machine and not riding a horse'. Riding is, indeed, an art form but it does have basic fundamentals. These are the immortal words of François Robichon de la Guérinière ' Every science and profession has its principals and rules that lead on to greater discoveries, why is it, in equitation alone, that practice is considered to be sufficient?' Today it is frequently the opposite, all is Principal and Art is forgotten.

Obviously you should use the correct terms, otherwise your pupils will never learn to understand their meaning, but you should also make sure that you give an adequate explanation in ordinary language so that they do not remain deeply ignorant about what you are really saying. You will need practise at turning the technical jargon into words that everyone can understand. It does not matter what words you use so long as you are *understood* and you will only find out if this is so by questioning your riders one by one (though not all at the same time!) and listening to their replies.

Covering the intervals.

There are those moments when you wish to allow the horses and riders a moment's rest. This is a very good time to have laid-by a store of stories that are pertinent to the exercise that you are about to move on to. For example you may wish to explain the mechanics of the canter and it is well at that time to have a little diversion, as it were. This may be achieved by recounting the first capture, on film, of the moment of suspension. This is also an opportunity to point out to pupils the need to become more closely acquainted with the visual signals given out by the horse. Draw attention to the difference between the ears being laid back close against the head as opposed to the turning of the ears towards the rider as they wait, at the alert, for instruction. *44 (See drawing no. 23)

Observation overall.

During any lesson, especially those where you are working with several horses you must never concentrate on any one rider to the extent that, no matter how momentarily, you forget about the other horses and riders in the class. You must continually keep an eye open so as to ensure that all the horses are the correct distance away from one another i.e. a horse's length. At the beginning of the lesson you must explain exactly how your pupils can recognise whether they are too close or too far away. Too close and they can only see the top of the tail and the croup of the horse in front. Too far away and they can see the whole tail and even ground. The correct distance: half the tail only should be in their view. No matter how strongly you make this point, you may be sure that, some of, your class will allow their attention to stray and the distances between horses will get wider or closer. If it is the latter, you must correct it. 'Watch your distance John'. Its no use waiting until someone's horse receives a kick, by then it's too late!

They used to say 'manners maketh man'. With a horse it could read 'Horse manners are made by the rider'. In which case, since the instructor is during a lesson involved in the behaviour of both horse and rider, it is obviously up to you to ensure a horses' continuing good behaviour by not allowing an exhibition of bad behaviour to go uncorrected.

Horses that are a little fresh.

Of course it is important not to forget that horses may simply be a little frisky, especially after they have been clipped out and when the weather turns colder. A rider may also be a little over zealous in the use of the aids. The horse anxious to get going – may break into a canter – the rider may have been told that when this happens to ride a circle – they do so but the circle is too small – the horse losses balance, falls and as it does so it rolls on the rider. Thus something quite innocuous can result in a serious accident. I have seen this happen to a student studying for a B.H.S qualification. It is most important that you deal with this sort of problem with skill. You must be sure that your pupils are told how to proceed and the last thing that they should do is to ride the horse on a small circle. Much better to allow it to go large for a few strides before telling them to use the back muscles together with the voice and then the most gentle contact with the rein.

Focusing on the problem in hand.
Now I have already mentioned the importance of having previously prepared the lesson that you are going to give to a particular class. However sometimes things do not always go according to plan. You may have a client who is experiencing difficulty in getting their horse to settle, in other words to go around the arena in a calm and relaxed manner. You must be on the lookout for this sort of problem and the moment that you spot it you must deal with it *immediately*.

Dealing with fear.
Many pupils probably have to deal with their innate fear engendered by actually sitting on a horse's back. Frequently they will be the last to admit this. But their mental attitude may play a very considerable part in subsequent difficulties. Fear that is not admitted is never faced up to. A rider who in reality is petrified may pass this fear on to the horse. As soon as it starts to move forward they tighten the rein creating great pressure on the bit and at the same time in order to provide themselves with what, they believe is a secure seat, they grip like mad and end up digging their heels into the horse's sides. No wonder the poor horse is in a state of high anxiety. For here we have a rider who, on the one hand is telling the horse to go forward with their heels whilst on the other hand telling him not to go forward with the rein. Is it any wonder that the quiet well-mannered horse that you were pleased to see had been selected for that particular client is now sweating up and showing every indication that it wants to dash off with them?

Generally this sort of thing occurs with a novice, especially when they start to trot, but may also happen when you are teaching a more experienced rider for the same reasons. Put aside the exercises that you have prepared and deal with the matter directly. Having made your own assessment, ask the rider how they are feeling. You will probably be told that the rider thinks that the horse is on its toes, or they may readily admit that they are in an extremely nervous state. Having observed closely, you will know the real root of the difficulty and it probably does indeed originate with the rider but look at them closely, how are they sitting? Probably hunched forward, hanging on to the reins and gripping like mad with their knees and thighs – look down further – what are the heels doing? As I have said, they are very likely to be digging in even though the client does not realise that they are doing so. Tell the client to 'sit up' and to take their legs away from the horses' sides.

What to do if things do get slightly out of hand.
It is most important that the foundation of good horsemanship prevails even though this has not yet been established in your pupil.

In order to correct the situation you must first:

1   Tell the rider to sit tall and take the heels away from the horse's sides and go forward to a walk (If they are not walking already). In their anxiety they may not move the leg at all. In this case you walk up to them quietly and gently remove the leg from the horses side.

2   At the same time ask the rider to let the rein go longer. (If they do not do so, again do it for them).
3   Remain at the horses' side gently holding the rein near the bit.
4.   The result will be that the horse begins to relax and so will the rider.
You must try to establish this as a permanent way of thinking by the rider and this will require you to talk he or she through their problem as we have already discussed in chapter 9.

Having reached a state of equilibrium, it is not advisable to simply revert to the exercise that you previously had in mind. If you do, then, it is quite likely that you will have the same problem all over again.

139

Instead confirm the state of relaxation in both horse and rider, even if this means that for the next twenty minutes your class continue to proceed at nothing more than a walk. If you are teaching a large class I am sure that they will understand. However this does not mean that you have to reduce everyone to a state of stupefying boredom.

This is where your flexibility of mind comes into play and I do confess that it takes a fair amount of practise before you are able to do this with great fluency. You must have at your fingertips other exercises that will be stimulating but none-the-less still maintain the state of quiet that you have already created. (See examples of exercises at the walk chapter 10 pages 3 -7) When you are quite satisfied that all is well, then and only then should you proceed to faster paces.

Pupils' physical limitations.

Your pupils may also have physical limitations. After all you probably spend hour after hour, day after day, sitting on a horse's back and suffer nothing more than simple tiredness. This may not be so for them. Physical fatigue arises because they are not used to the horse's movement. It is highly likely that they may well be quite stiff the following day and you should be aware of this and act accordingly.

Watch the horses.

It is possible for those teaching others to ride to concentrate to such an extent on their riders that they overlook the horses. Remember to keep an eye on them also especially the manner of their going. Watch for lameness in particular. One must also be able to recognise if a horse has a real difficulty in moving in a particular direction or in a certain manner. I have sometimes come across a horse that will perform most willingly all gaits, but is unable to perform a canter on a circle. You may be thinking 'Ah well, the horse is jolly well going to obey me'. I would suggest that this is not a good idea if it results in your rider being bucked off and landing hard on the ground. It is up to you to get to know the limitations of any horse and to stop well before that horse is so hard pressed that it revolts!

How can problems be avoided?

1. Horses are creatures of habit. They usually do the same thing in the same place.

2. A horse will, very often signal that it has suffered enough and is about to take the initiative.

3. Pupils need to understand that, when riding, one must concentrate on what the horse is doing 60 seconds out of every minute. The animal will notice the slightest loss of concentration and may try to take advantage. By learning to concentrate the rider will be ready to firmly but gently react to them *before* this happens.

4. Time is usually in your favour for after a while the horse will, eventually quieten down. Most horses, even if they have played up a bit will, in the end, decide that it is really not worth while kicking up a fuss and that it might as well get on with the job.

The reflex reaction.

Having said, earlier in this chapter, that the riders should learn to think for themselves, it is worthwhile mentioning that in this respect you are, from the very beginning, trying to develop 'reflex reactions' in your pupils. By that I do not only mean with regard to the muscles involved in that area concerned with the support of their bodies, but also in their minds when it comes to involuntary movements arising from the horse that they are riding. I have in mind those sudden motions arising when a horse is startled. This may take place in an arena when something untoward happens outside. It might simply be the sound of a tractor starting up. Now most horses are quite familiar with the sounds that arise from normal work being carried out around the yard. However there are the odd occasions when a loud noise may occur or a horsebox with which horses are not familiar may appear on the scene. Some horses will react with a series of darting motions here and there. The effect on the rider is that they too are seized with momentary panic and that they do not immediately realise the source of the problem. Sometimes they become unbalanced and the situation escalates. The riders are sitting there and thinking 'Oh my g-d what is happening!' Of course all that 'is happening' is that the horse has been startled. Prior to that moment it had been doing its work calmly and quietly.

140

You may now be speculating as to why I mention this matter in a chapter that is dealing with the quite early attempts of people learning to ride? 'Surely' I hear you say ' What else do you expect of novices'?
Well my point is that you have to 'sow the seeds' as it were and the best time to do this is right at the start of a rider's education. If you do not do so, then how on earth are they going to learn?

Therefore you must tell your pupils, fairly early on, that this sort of thing may occasionally occur, but if it does then their first thought must instantly be to calm the horse, both by voice and a touch on the neck. At the same time they must try not to loose their position. 'Easier said than done' may be the response. I agree but my point is that if you don't tell them then they are unlikely to think about such things and are therefore unlikely to learn.

Creating a good atmosphere for both pupils and horses.
Fear of showing themselves up in front of the class, should not prevent anyone from asking about something that they have not clearly understood. You must ensure that the prevailing atmosphere is one in which everyone feels that they can ask questions without embarrassment. You are the one who creates this environment.

It all depends on the trouble that you take. When you start a lesson go along the line and whilst you check girths you may ask each rider if they have checked, but do the final check yourself. At this time also have a *quiet kind word* with each horse. Pat it on the neck - caress its nose. Do the same at the end of a lesson. Horses may not 'know where you live' but they will certainly size you up. If you *take the trouble*, then, you should *not experience trouble*.

Slightly increasing the level of difficulty.
When you get to know your pupils well, the time will come to put on a little pressure in order to achieve greater progress. One way of doing this successfully is through drill riding (see chapter 10). In drill rides it is incumbent on all riders to be in the correct place at the same time. This means that, whereas, they may have been sitting on their horse's backs without really trying to get a result and that this may not be noticeable to the rest of the class, in drill rides that lack of effort will become, immediately, apparent.

Repeating an exercise in a subsequent lesson.
Some movements from a previous lesson should be repeated if they were not very successful the first time. It is quite likely that pupils, during the time that they have been away, will have spent some time thinking about what they did incorrectly and you will, usually, find that the subsequent attempt is a considerable improvement on that which went before.

Try to be precise but also be tactful.
This simply means that commands and instructions to the class as a whole should be given clearly and precisely, but when addressing an individual client it is often better to go up close to them and speak quietly. While the whole class is performing a movement instructions given to individuals as they ride should be short and precise. Such as 'push your heels down and turn your toes in - Amie' or 'Try to sit down deeply in the saddle - John'. In cases where a client has real difficulties, I usually ask the class to halt and then approach the person closely. I speak to them in a very low voice that only they can hear. I find that this avoids embarrassment and encourages the rider to respond and may give the key as to what it is that they don't understand.

At the beginning of a lesson and especially with new pupils, I always tell everybody not to be afraid of asking questions if they do not understand exactly what I am saying, or for that matter to challenge any information that I may give. I consider this to be very important. A pupil should not feel afraid to admit that they do not comprehend. It is incumbent on me to make myself understood. If they cannot understand the instructions that I give, then, the fault lies with me and not the rider and I must rephrase what I say, perhaps approaching a problem from a different point of view so that I develop the required mental image in their own minds. It may mean that for a particular movement I have to actually walk through the exercise so that it is clearly understood by all. After all it is unlikely that a pupil will be able to move a horse in a particular manner if they themselves don't clearly understand what they are supposed to be doing. I will only rest and ask the class to commence an exercise when I am certain that they do understand what is required. What is really not acceptable is for a pupil to pretend that they know what you are talking about when, in reality, they do not. **You must be sure that they really do understand.**

Going forward from walk to halt.

This is a simple enough command but one with which many riders do have slight problems. I do not mean that they are unable to get their horses to stop, but that they do not do so in good time. Whilst they have been going around the arena at walk under your instruction they should have been maintaining the correct distance of one horses' length. But as soon as you give them the command to halt they wait until their horse's nose is practically up the bottom of the one in front. The reason for this is that they have, very often, allowed their concentration to lapse. You must watch for this and prevent it from happening. If you fail to do so, then, you are allowing a horse to enter the kicking danger zone. If someone gets kicked, it is your fault. Sometimes the horse simply doesn't' appear to be listening to the rider. There they are pulling on the rein to little effect. However if you suggest that it might be easier if they tried bracing the back muscles which, in turn thrusts the hips *slightly* forward and closing the thighs on the saddle, then they are quite surprised to find that this is much more effective.

Improving balance -Riding without stirrups (only for those willing to do so).

When you ask your pupils to 'quit and cross their stirrups' i.e. take their feet out of their stirrups and cross them over the withers, be sure to show them how to pull down the upper straps of the leather so that the buckle is not lying under their thighs. If you don't do this they may well suffer unnecessary discomfort due to the buckle digging into them.

As is well known periods of riding without the stirrups are a great help to pupils for improving balance. Exercises during which this takes place must be carefully planned in advance. The level of a client's ability must be taken into account. They should be introduced to the idea gradually.

Why? Because most of them will associate the idea of riding sans stirrups with falling off and may tend to stiffen up thus undoing all the good work already achieved.

I would suggest that you start these exercises only at the walk, encourage the pupils to sit tall and maintain a good position. Ask them to go through all the relaxing exercises and above all stress that they should *not* try to maintain balance by clutching at the reins. Proceed to sitting trot only after the relaxing exercises are complete

An exercise whilst riding without stirrups

In order to encourage riders to sit deeply and have their weight distributed evenly over the saddle, I ask pupils to try and lift their legs away from the horses' sides – all the way from the ankle to the thigh. While they do this they must be careful neither to hold on to the reins for support nor to loose their upright body position. You should not ask them to maintain this position for so long that they suffer discomfiture and possibly get cramp in their limbs. When you do allow them to *lower* their *legs* to the *horse's sides* it must be done *gently* otherwise the horses may mistake the resulting 'tap' as an indication to canter.

The advantage.

The idea behind this type of exercise is that it encourages the pupil to learn to *really* sit on their seat bones instead of trying to grip the horse with their thighs.

Beware.

Do not force your class to do these exercises for too long. Don't forget they will not be used to doing this and their muscles will soon become tired. They must be allowed a good period of rest. Always commence with the walk and don't be too ambitious and go to sitting trot too soon.

Sitting trot without stirrups.

When you have allowed the class time to get used to the movement, then, you may proceed to repeat the exercise at the trot – sitting. Unless you have a class with some previous experience I would not advise introducing this gait until the following lesson. When you do ask for trot, encourage your pupils to place the reins as a double loop in the outside hand, and hold the pommel of the saddle with the inside one. This will give them more confidence, and the horses will have less of a problem in dealing with the shifting weight of their wobbly bodies.

Beware.

Should a horse have shown a disinclination to trot you may decide to help things on by approaching the horse and encouraging it with your voice. This could cause a problem, for should the horse be extremely respectful of you, then in order to do your bidding it may well dash forward and even break into a canter catching the rider by surprise and unbalancing them.

Persistence.
Though this is particularly important when teaching the more advanced movements such as getting a horse to go on the bit (about which we will talk later), even in the early stages a horse will at once sense a rider who is quietly determined as soon as they actually mount up. This will help them enormously to get it to do their bidding. A successful lesson is one where a horse starts out with a will of its own but by the end of the lesson has acquiesced to the pupil's desires and goes forward in light and active manner.

You may, eventually, become a good instructor because you have the ability to inspire in your pupils a feeling of confidence and a desire to improve. This will be partially achieved through asking them questions about their jobs or what they do for a living. In this way you get to know them better. You should also be able to make intelligent and informed comments upon that which you are told. In this way you will become better able to build a bond between yourself and your pupils and thus to create a mood that will enable you to better impart to them the art of good equitation.

Keep watch on the level at which you teach.
When pupils appear to be making good progress there may be the temptation to ask them to perform at a level that is quite beyond their ability. This should be avoided. It is so easy to raise your requirement to a point where the rider, through their lack of expertise, may actually cause pain and discomfiture to the horse.

I do not think that novices should ever be asked to show collection because they are usually incapable of keeping their hands still. The horse will become confused because of the riders continually jerking hands as they try to obtain outline. Not only that but pupils need first to learn that impulsion must be created with seat and leg *before* asking for any form of containment of that energy. In other words they must learn to sit on and use, their seat bones thus encouraging the horse to become rounded - going forward *into* the bit but without any excessive use of it.

The disappearing time interval.
By proceeding in this manner the class will have time to mentally adjust to the exercises that you give them. You should not forget that the trot leaves less thinking time for the rider and the canter less still. It therefore follows that most movements should be, first performed, at the walk and then progress to higher gaits.

Decision time for canter?
You may be thinking 'Why on earth does he introduce the subject of canter in a chapter that is dealing with novices?' Generally speaking one would not consider canter as a gait, which one should ask of a rider, deemed to be in this category. But what the office may describe as a novice may in practise turn out to be someone more advanced. You alone must be the judge and a very careful judge you must be. So assuming that you are such a person, and you feel that conditions are right, then I feel that it is acceptable for you to heed the advice that follows even though this chapter is about novices. Don't forget when you go on to read the chapter on *intermediate* riders, you may have included in your class someone who isn't and you must then act accordingly.

However should your client have good natural balance there is really no reason why they should not have a short canter. After all, in reality, the gait is one that is easier to sit to than say for a sitting trot. Therefore it is not necessary to be bound by nomenclature. In other words for you to say to yourself 'this client has been deemed a novice and therefore they should not canter' when you can see that they obviously do have the ability, is hardly logical. It may well be that after one or two lessons with you, a pupil may have quickly evolved into an intermediate rider. Therefore the most difficult problem for you is, in my opinion, *when* to introduce the canter. **You must be sure** not only that the pupil can sit to the gait but that they are *psychologically* able to deal with the increase in inertia and speed that the gait produces. I repeat that it is solely dependent upon the *progress that you judge that your pupils have made*. **If you are in doubt, then don't** This has always been my motto and it has never let me down. Have the dubious ones come and stand in the centre of the arena. This would also apply to any horse that given the opportunity may have a tendency to play up. For riders with ability but riding such animals, then offer them a chance on another horse.

143

Cantering.
However let us assume that we do, finally, allow a short canter. Whether you are working in or out, you should pick your moment with care. Should you start too early on in the lesson, some pupils may have a problem with horses that, full of energy, go dashing off. Riders thus momentarily alarmed loose their balance and suffer a fall. Obviously if the progression to canter is approached by having allowed some energy to be used up at more sedate paces, then the canter depart *will* be more likely to be nice and steady. Above all at this stage we want to get off to a good start with horses that are going quietly.

How much work has a horse already done?
One of the things that will help you to make a correct decision is to find out which horses have already worked that day. If they have not and are very 'fresh', then you must make due allowance. On the other hand if they have already done an hour or two previously then you make take this into account as well. This will also work in reverse for if you are working with horses that are already into their fourth hour of work; you should make life a little easier for them by shortening the duration of the higher paces.

Take into account the discomfiture engendered by a novice rider.
I have already mentioned, with regard to the rising trot, in the last chapter that you must bear in mind that a novice starting to learn canter may not be able ride with a 'light seat'. By that I mean that they may have a problem in simply sitting deeply and keeping their bodies in the correct position. The moment of suspension will, quite probably, cause them to rise off the saddle with each canter stride, and then land with a great thump on the poor horses back. You should subject a horse to this sort of treatment for only a very short period.

The canter.
Now just in case you have simply glossed over the foregoing paragraphs let me remind you. *This movement should not be undertaken until the pupil has developed a good sense of balance, a reasonably independent seat* and the musculature that will allow them to maintain that balance. They must also have the *confidence*. Some riders have no problem with this. In fact they may have such a desire to canter that they wish to so do too early. Others will not be so brave and there may come a time, when *you*, having decided that they are quite capable of performing the movement, will have to encourage the horse with your voice. I mean that you resort to the vocal aids that it learned at the beginning of its career on the lunge. Having warned the rider of your intention, you, in a firm voice, simply command "The 'animals name' and Canter**rr**". (The horse then canters because of course it is listening to you). However you must always take into account every riders' ability, individually.

One of the best ways of obtaining a very quiet canter is to have the class ride, individually, from leading file to rear. The class should, for this initial exercise, be at the walk until their turn arrives. The reason for this is that even at this stage of the lesson the riders should be given maximum opportunity to maintain control over their horses. That is why the transition should be *through* the trot and then the canter out of a corner. This will give the rider plenty of time to prepare and will allow you to make an overall assessment.

How far should they go?
Now I have suggested that a canter from front to rear is a good starting off point. However you need not even go that distance. Should you have one or two riders whom you think are capable of only a *very* short canter, then simply ask them to trot around two sides of the arena before cantering along the third side. However I would go further. The mental attitude of the rider obviously affects the manner of their horses going. If they have displayed any nervousness during the lesson, then do not take a chance by asking them to canter at all. Instead have them go large at a trot. If they perform this exercise well, congratulate them. You may explain that it is far better for someone to have performed a really good and well cadenced trot than to have ridden a poor canter.

Does the horse know?
Pupils have frequently asked me why they have a problem with canter. There may be multifarious reasons, such as poor balance, incorrect aids etc. They then ask me why it is that so and so has managed to canter

successfully when it was quite obvious to the rest of the class that they too have given the wrong aids. A very good question. I have to remind them that there are other factors at play. There is the instructor's vocal command, given to the rider but acted upon by the horse. There is also the time of the lesson. 'Horses' I tell them 'Are not stupid'. They do this same sort of thing day after day and week after week. They know that, generally speaking, when 40 minutes or so of the lesson has elapsed, that it is canter time and they try to do their best to oblige the rider. However sometimes the rider's position is so poor that try as they may, they simply are not able to respond.

Using an analogy.
Sometimes it is difficult to create in a rider's mind the possible effect that their poor balance has upon a horse. Canter depart is a movement that provides a clear example. Since the canter is a bounding movement and depends upon the horse throwing his body both upward and forward from one leg, this is a gait during which the involuntary movement of a rider's body will probably unbalance the horse to some degree. It is readily seen where a rider asks for canter but the horse does not respond, instead it does try to comply by giving a faster or even extended trot. You can create some idea as to what goes on in the horse's mind, if you ask the rider to imagine that they are, say rock climbing. You may use any example that you think will fit. I like rock climbing because even if the client has not participated in the sport personally, it is quite likely that they will have seen it on television. I ask them to imagine that they are actually climbing up the quite steep side of a mountain. On their backs they are carrying a very heavy backpack. They are balanced on a small ledge on one foot and are about to place the other on another ledge that is slightly higher. The distance between the two ledges is such that it is not possible simply to step up; they have to imagine that there is a very slight hop involved. The pack is not completely secure and, at the very moment that they are about to transfer their weight from one foot to the other, the backpack weight shifts (see drawings nos. 24a&b & 25a&b). What are they likely to do? The answer is pretty sure to be that they will not continue with the movement. So it is with a horse and the comparison very often helps the rider to understand what it is all about.

The relaxed canter.
One problem facing many riders is that they canter too fast. This may be due to a variety of reasons. For example the urgent desire, on the riders' part to actually achieve a canter and keep it going, or the horses desire to escape the stricture of 'cast iron' hands – There is altogether too much tension. We may have the creation of a 'double negative' as it were. The client has an urgent desire to succeed and tries so hard that a willing horse then makes off at high speed. Which in turn causes the client some anxiety or a loss of balance, which in turn causes the horse to cease cantering. In order to make progress it is your job to help the client understand that a transition merely means a change from two-time trot or four-time walk, to the three time canter. Once the aid has been given the client must learn to relax and allow the canter to continue. It does not really matter if the canter is so slow and relaxed that the horse actually breaks to trot for a stride or two so long as the pupil does not start to rise and accommodate it.

A slower tempo is best achieved by having the client ride a large circle. Again they may have a problem in that the horse, finding the movement more difficult breaks to the trot but it is up to the rider to develop a reflex that is fast enough to correct this.

Do remember that what I have suggested above is simply to help you arrive at the correct and safe decision. Therefore, in a class, it is important to *always* start with each rider cantering alone (say from front to rear) in order that you may assess their ability. If you are satisfied then, with a ride that *is experienced* (see chapter 14 The advanced class), I do not see why you should not have the whole class going off at a canter one after the other. Though this is something that many instructors are nervous about. I always have each rider depart *individually* but do not wait until they have ridden round the whole school.

Working out of doors.
Another difficult problem for an instructor is, when do you send your pupils away from you 'solo' as it were? My old flying instructor must have had the same problem. The answer is when you are quite sure that the rider is - able to ride at all paces - is fully in control of their horse and are riding an animal that is kindly and will not try and take advantage of them. You should also initiate this first departure in an area that is suitably enclosed. A small to medium sized field is best.

145

Thinking about the weather and time of year. Why have I mentioned the weather at this point? The reason is that you will be far less likely to have any problems with horses dashing off, on a warm day than you will have on a cold one. You may consider, especially, on mild days that it is a good idea to have all the class lined up either down the centre line of the arena or split into two rides, turned in at either end. This type of approach has a great advantage since it will allow the class as a whole to more easily view the performance of each of their classmates. Each pupil is then, individually, being asked to leave the rest of the ride and perform alone and the extent of their ability is revealed to all. With the riders turned in at either end, and well off the track, you may also ask your riders *when they become sufficiently skilled* to perform circles or even figures of eight.

Springtime.
In the forgoing chapters I have mentioned the time of the year in the context of changes in the weather. This of course involves some generalisations such as 'winter gets colder and summer hotter'. These in turn have an effect upon your horses. Apart from heat and cold, there is one other factor that you must take into account and that is the effect of the lengthening days upon the mentality of your horses.

In spring the 'sap starts to rise' in geldings, and in mares the desire to see off unwanted suitors may result in behaviour that is not conducive to you pupil's safety. By this I mean that geldings may show a desire to dash off around the arena just to show off and mares may put in an almighty buck when they spot a male horse 'giving them the eye'. There is more, this is the time of year when horses 'test' the ability of the rider, should the latter become too demanding. It is at these times it may be wise to reduce the level of difficulty that your riders are asking of their horses. Due to the somewhat clumsy manner in which they make demands they may, unwittingly, be generating a challenge that they are then unable to cope with. Ask for too much and the horse may say to itself 'blow you I'm going to chuck you off' and a formerly quiet little horses will put in a really big buck and dump the rider on the floor. It is your job to avoid such situations!

Lining up along the centre line can also be very useful in bad weather.
When the weather is wet and cold, you may have noticed that though there have been no real problems that you can pinpoint, the general mood of your horses is perhaps slightly less than co-operative. This may be due to the fact that they are, generally fed up, damp and miserable, very similar in fact to humans in similar circumstances. When you come to that part of the lesson where you wish to have a short canter exercise, this is the point that the horses may take advantage of any feeling of imbalance on the part of the rider. Even a simple canter from front to rear may be sufficient to set them all off in a general display of irritation, sometimes with unfortunate consequences. By having them line up you help to diffuse the situation. The ones that are lined up will stand quietly and relax. Further more if you allow them to line up with their hindquarters turned towards the wind and rain (even if this means that they stand at a slight angle to the centreline), they will feel more comfortable. The one sent out to do its work may be inclined to go forward quite quietly since it may well decide that it is not going to expend vast energies while its mates are all standing still doing nothing. Of course it might also be likely to object to having to work completely alone. Unless you have a *complete* novice, riding a nappy horse, (when canter exercises should nor be asked for at this level), most riders should be able to get their horses to, at least, go around the arena even if it is only at a trot. They will get great satisfaction from so doing. On the other hand if you have any serious *doubts* about the general *mood* of your horses then completely leave *out* the *canter* part of the lesson that you may have planned.

A final thought on the weather (clothing).
Sometimes when the weather is unseasonably warm, pupils may wish to remove a layer of clothing. Never ever permit them to do so unless you or your assistant are holding the bridle. Some pupils will not understand the reason for your caution. You must explain that whilst most horses do not object to things flying about just at the edge of their vision, this cannot be taken for granted. Further more should anything suddenly catch the horse unawares, for example a car backfiring, then the client caught at a vulnerable moment, say when the sleeves are being worked over the wrists, could lose control and suffer an accident.

Should the garment be one that must be lifted over the head, then the rider must dismount.

146

Comments made during or at the end of a lesson.
I think that it is much better to always start with a word of praise about the positive things that have happened and then to follow it with any criticism. When dealing with advanced riders I do tend to be stricter. Always ask your pupils what are *their* views of the results of an exercise. Frequently they will be very deprecating of their efforts. I think that you should counter this with some form of amelioration so that they are encouraged to do better. You may decide to repeat a movement but change it in a subtle way so that it is easier for your pupils to obtain some success. There is no reason why you should not tell them that this is the case.

Giving praise.
Do not always wait until the end of a lesson. *It is very important to ensure that as soon as a pupil begins to improve in the riding of any movement they are praised for so doing.* If you wait until they have reached something near your idea of perfection, then, they may no longer be attending your classes, having lost heart.

In a nutshell.
Now having gone into such detail in all the above paragraphs what are the *main problems that one will find in the majority of pupils*, not necessarily with novices? They are: -

1. Sitting round-shouldered.
1. The arms are stuck out in front.
3. Riding with loose reins.
4. Riding with heels up and toes turned out,
5. Looking down.
(See photo no. 27) These are, usually, the problems that you need to deal with most often.

After the lesson - leading away.
When the pupils have dismounted, they should be taught, fairly early on, to lead correctly. These are the points that they need to learn: -
1. The rein should slide up the arm into the crook of the elbow thus leaving both hands free to run up the stirrups. Whips should be tucked out of the way under the elbow or, better still placed on the ground far enough away not be trodden on.
2. You must then show all your pupils how to secure the stirrups by taking hold of the stirrup leather in one hand and with the other, sliding the stirrup along the underside of the loop until the stirrup bar stops it. Finally tucking in the loop and spare leather through and under the stirrup footrest.
3. Now, standing in front of the horse, the rein should be gracefully flicked over its head and caught in the rider's hand. (I have noticed that some instructors advocate doing this *before securing the stirrups*. I do not think that that is a very good way of doing this because there is a degree of control lacking should the horse be a mare, for example and rather ticklish. It might mean that as the client goes to secure the stirrup the horse moves away. In so doing its quarters may swing out towards another horse in the line, who thinking that it is about to be kicked may try to put one in first.
4. The rider now must move so that they are standing by the side of the horse at its shoulder. (Ideally this should be the near side but this will depend on which way the rider is going to proceed). The arm nearest the horse should be extended with that hand (knuckles on top) holding both reins close to the bit. The spare loop of the rein should be held at the very end in the rider's outside hand. This same hand should also now hold the whip.
5. The rider now gives the horse the command to 'walk-on'. If the horse does not immediately obey then the rider may *gently touch* the horse with the whip just behind the girth (see photo no 28). The rider must *not turn to look* where they are touching the horse, for it is the riders job to *look where they wish to go at all times.*
6. Finally with the horse walking forward, the rider proceeding at its shoulder, we come to the point where they may have to turn. When this happens, the rider must be sure to turn the horse *away from themselves* so there is no danger of having their foot accidentally trodden on by the horse.

A question that an intelligent rider might ask.

Why is it safest to stand by the horses' shoulder?

Answer. Because the horses' limbs are so made to facilitate mainly forward and backward movements. There is a small degree of lateral movement but it is quite restricted. Further more the very structure of a horses leg with the accent on the elongated mainly bony lower part, means that the relatively bulky body weight has to be balanced at all times. Thus without generating some forward going movement, the development of inertia a horse needs to push someone over sideways is less likely to occur.

The same comments apply to standing by the quarters (as one might for picking out or examining the feet). However in this case the horse can gain momentum by putting in a buck and thus being able to swivel its hind quarters as it places its weight on the forehand.

Learning to un-tack.

It is very important that all pupils should have some basic training in both tacking up and un-tacking their horses. By this I mean that I do not consider that it is good enough simply for pupils to await the arrival of their horses at the appointed mounting block before the lesson and then simply to hand over to a groom at the end of the lesson. When possible, for example, if a horse is not going to be ridden again for an hour or so, a client should accompany the groom back to the box and there learn to un-tack the horses themselves. Later they should be encouraged, again under supervision, to learn to tack-up. In the first place this gives a more rounded education and secondly it helps the pupil to get used to being in the proximity of a horse and to learn how to move about without it getting startled. Pupils will also learn instinctively how to protect themselves by the observance of basic safety rules.

Creating a bond.

I have made much of the fact that this book is not about the training of horses. However the essence of successful training is for the trainer to establish a feeling of trust between himself and his horses. He will do this in several ways. For example he will probably spend some considerable time working with a horse from the ground. Getting the horse's trust until it will follow him at will. Walking at his shoulder when he walks. Halting at his shoulder when he stops. All the time the trainer is quietly talking to the horse and gently patting it. Many advanced movements are taught in this way. The advantage for the horse is that he does not have to carry the riders' weight while he absorbs the new information. I do this regularly with my horses and I get a good response.

Nonetheless trust may be developed between horse and rider on a more casual basis. As an example, when taking out hacks, I sometimes ride horses other than my own. During the summer I use a flywhisk of my own construction. This consists of a whip to the end of which I have firmly bound baling twine all cut to the same length (about 6"). As I start to ride out I gently touch the horse on the neck with the whisk. The horse does not react and as I continue with the hack, I use this instrument to brush the flies away from my horses' face. Pupils passing by on another hack, marvel. 'Look at that strange thing Mr. Silverman is using. His horse does not seem to notice at all. I don't know why the horse doesn't freak out'! The answer is that though I may not ride these horses as regularly as my own, they *do* trust me and know that I will do nothing to harm them. Further more they soon catch on as to the usefulness of the whisk.

Pupils do not have as much opportunity to establish a bond in quite the same way, but they should be encouraged to accompany the groom back to the stable and, after the horse has been un-tacked, to give it a reward. This *will* encourage the *bonding* between that horse and its rider. This must be done inside the stable preferably in the area of the feed trough. On no account should a pupil be allowed to feed a horse over the stable door as this encourages the horse to develop the vice of biting. **Neither should they be left alone in the stable with the horse, at this stage they simply do not have the experience to deal with any sudden movement that it might make.** Some simple reaction on the horse's part such as having an argument with a horse in the next box could escalate into a dangerous situation.

Pupils will need to be told that they should *not feed* horses over stable *doors*. They will also require instruction as to how to *slice a carrot down its length*. Many people do not realise that, chopped through its width, a carrot provides discs that are exactly the same circumference as the horses' throat. If swallowed whole they may get lodged in the throat, leading to the animal choking to death.

Teaching a client to know when a horse has taken to them.

It is useful for a rider to get to know when trust is becoming established. Obviously one sign is that the horse shows no fear as the rider approaches. Another and more subtle sign is when, standing just in front of

148

the forehand and looking in the same direction as the horse, as one might when say putting ones arm under and around the neck, the animal rests its chin on ones shoulder and gently nuzzles ones shoulder with its lips.

Questions that your client might ask you.

It is quite possible that a pupil may query the advantage of bothering to make friends with a horse. 'Why waste the time?' they will say. 'After all, horses are not really capable of recognising human beings are they?' You should ask such a pupil why they think that a horse will go well for one person and yet be extremely uncooperative with another.

The answer is that horses are very able to recognise both one another and individual humans. Read Stephen Budiansky, The Nature of Horses * 17. It would seem obvious that those with whom a horse will, most readily bond will be its groom, trainer and of course the owner (If they take the trouble). This does not mean that it is not worth while a pupil trying to make a bond with each horse that they ride. It is my opinion that a few minutes spent with a horse doing nothing more than giving it a treat and stroking its neck will be very beneficial.

As for recognition? There is no doubt in my mind as to their ability. When I was in business and my time was limited, sometimes the most that I could do would be to pay a short visit to the yard and give my horses a treat. Now it was obvious to me that my voice was recognised, because if I were talking to a groom but concealed from view, as soon as I uttered a word I would hear the welcoming call from either Jeeves or Moonlight. As an experiment I tried entering silently and just poking my head around the corner I was spotted immediately with the same result.

Teaching Children

What sort of ponies are needed?

The very best ponies for working with children are older ones who have been working in a riding school for years. They know their job and, generally get on with taking care of their young charges. However these ponies may have some disadvantages that you should watch out for. Since they are old they sometimes get rather crotchety with one another just like elderly adults. In the case of ponies this usually takes the form of a baring of teeth with the threat of a bite or else the danger of a kick. This may cause the subject of such treatment to back away suddenly thus catching the little rider unawares and unbalancing them. You must learn which ponies do have this tendency and those that are the object of their dislike. Fortunately it is seldom that one pony will take a dislike to *all* the ponies in your class and if you take care where you place them, relative to one another, you should not have any problems.

Why have I placed children in this chapter and not the previous one?

My first reference specifically to children is included at the end of this chapter, which, essentially deals with novices joining a class. The reason for this is because I think that it is in a *class* that they should begin. The advantage in having children in a group is that they can develop a relationship with one another and this will help in their learning to ride.

I do not see any reason why children should not perform similar exercises to those of adults. Obviously one must take into account their age and physical ability to cope, but then one must do that with grown ups, especially older persons. I expect my advanced children to be able to change the rein in line abreast across the arena and to maintain position as they do so. I also expect them to split into two rides or more with precision and finally I expect them to ride the scissors (each ride changing the rein through a diagonal and riding through the other ride) at walk then trot and finally at canter!

At what age should children start?

Children may start to learn to ride from about of five. Well let us be a little more precise, they may be introduced to ponies at that age.

Some may come with great enthusiasm because elder brother or sisters are already learning to ride and they wish to be just as 'grown up'. While there are others who have an entirely different view of the matter! They have only come because Mummy or Daddy wishes them to do so. This may be due to the fact that Mummy or Daddy learnt when they were young and expect their offspring to do likewise! Or they may simply have absolutely no concept as to what riding entails and are taken up with the idea as to how gorgeous little Sarah will look when dressed up in riding gear! These are the parents of whom I am most wary, for they have no knowledge as to what is involved. If the child settles down nicely in a class it will not be long before they approach you and ask when their little gems are going to a more advanced class!

What do you do with those who are unwilling?
So there you are, you have your class of about five youngsters who have been with you for some months and they are joined by a new member who is not only not interested but is determined to make the point by screaming their head off. If your attempts to pacify the child do not work in the first five minutes, then don't try any further. ***Immediately*** take the child out of the arena and quieten him or her down, Tell the parents to make arrangements with the office to bring the child again but for a private lesson. Do spend a few minutes explaining to them that you are *not* rejecting their pride and joy but simply that you need to have the time to adopt an entirely different approach on a one to one basis. If you are really clever you will have already spoken to the child, before the lesson had started and you would have already formed your own opinion as to what was likely to happen.

The Office will then have been prepared to re-book them at a time suitable to you. Ideally this will be when you have time available to spend at least a whole half-hour with the child without too much going on in the yard that may distract. If you have done your job well, there will be no problem in getting the child to come back.

What do you do if they do return?
You should have already set out the conditions for a return between the child and yourself. The understanding will have been that they are ***not*** going to have to ride the pony at all. Oh no no no. They are merely coming back just to say hello to the pony and to tell it that they hope that it wasn't upset when screamed at on the last occasion! After all it hadn't done anything wrong had it?

The day arrives for the child's return and when it does so you take them by the hand and walk slowly and quietly towards the pony that is being held by a helper away from any other ponies. (This is important because the last thing that you want is for your pony to catch some odd expression made by one of its mates to whom it may respond by turning and baring its teeth or whatever). While you approach the pony keep the child in constant conversation about any subject apart from riding or ponies. It can also be an advantage for the child to be lifted and held in someone's arms. This can have the added benefit of presenting the little one from higher up and thus making it feel safer.

When you are standing in front of the pony *you* offer the pony a titbit. You do *not* ask the child to do so. Instead you then reach out and stroke the pony's neck. You ask the child (using its name) if it would like to do the same. If it declines to do so you tell it that you think that the pony may start to cry because it was expecting a little pat from the child to say sorry for screaming when they last met. If you are skilled and patient you will, in the end, succeed with this first step.

As time passes you may ask the child if it would like to sit on the pony's back. If it agrees then pop it up in the saddle but have the helper hold it gently but firmly. After having sat in the saddle for a few minutes to the accompaniment of many little pats of the ponies neck you may then ask if the child if it would like the pony to take a couple of steps. If the answer is 'No' then leave it at that and ask the parents to bring the child back next day or week.

It should not require more than a few visits for the child to get over its fear. This may have arisen as a result of the parents subjecting the child to a very unpleasant riding experience when they were away on holiday or, more likely, when they were put up on Auntie's ever so quiet mare. Oh yes I know all the reasons, for they surface to be talked about when after a month or so that same hysterical youngster has evolved into an enthusiastic and confident young rider. I learn all the dark and unspoken secrets about what went on before. Not that I didn't suspect as much already!

Is there any special technique that one should use for children?
What does one have to take into account when working with children? The most important thing is to establish rapport. Avoid talking down to them and learn the art of becoming 'one of the gang' and yet at the same time remain the leader who must maintain discipline. You must be very strict about this. It is amazing how manipulative some children can be as they try to get their own way for an extra canter. When working out doors I use the first few minutes on our way down to the fields to talk to them about the sort of subjects

150

that I think that they will be learning in school. Perhaps some historical fact or a famous author. On other occasions I use this time as an opportunity to have a quiz about the points of the horse or some associated subject.

You are not addressing an invisible audience.

When you take a class you must learn to *look* at each child in turn. This is extremely important; otherwise you will not know whether or not they have understood what you have said. I expect *all* my youngsters to be able to describe, in detail - walk, trot and canter and also the required aids. This can only be achieved by repeating these questions every lesson. In the end having all class members giving the correct answers, promptly, rewards you.

When you teach children you must give them your constant attention. By that I mean you must keep your eye on each child for at least 15 to 20 seconds and this must form a continuous rotation through every rider for the whole of the lesson. Every fault must be immediately pointed out. It is only in this way that you will be able to prevent bad habits such as toes turning out and heels being raised.

Don't talk *at* children – Talk *to* them.

You may go further. I like, especially with younger children, to allow my questions to take a more general form. I mean that while they are proceeding around the arena at a walk, I may cease to talk about riding matters, instead, I may ask them what is their favourite subject, say at school. The answers are very often quite surprising. In this way one can develop a conversation and this in turn leads to an establishment of confidence in you and thus you will be paid greater attention.

Spotting the beginnings of nervousness.

Little fears manifest themselves in quite innocuous ways. Sometimes these take the form of complaints about imaginary ailments, such as 'Can I not trot without stirrups because I have a headache' or a stomach-ache or even 'I don't like the way Tim's pony is looking at me'. It is of course up to you to judge whether or not the little problems are real or not. It is quite a fine art. Obviously when you are going to trot without irons and you receive the complaint which otherwise should have come at the beginning of the lesson, you have a quite reliable guide. I usually say that I do understand but that the trotting will only last a short while and when it is over the child may retire from the lesson if they so wish. All the headaches magically disappear after the exercise is over. Of course there are those times when a child is genuinely 'under the weather'. In which case you should allow them some respite from the more physically demanding exercises.

Sometimes you may have a flat-out refusal to ride the pony at all. This may occur when a child is about to canter in a field. The child simply dismounts and won't get back up. I do not allow this state of affairs to remain unchallenged and insist that the child remount immediately. Then I inquire as to the reason. Should this be that they are afraid to canter, then I do *not* insist that they do so. I simply have them standing by my side while I send the rest of the class away. This may seem to be a form of compromise, which it is, but also one that is acceptable because you are then able to work out the problem with the child, at another time, one must weigh up the 'pros and cons'. The child has acquiesced to your command by remounting, if you then insist that it goes away at the canter, out of your control it may well decide to bail out, which really isn't a positive answer at all.

It does help if you are able to anticipate a problem *before* it occurs. If you do so then you are very likely to be able to avoid most problems by thinking ahead. So far as children are concerned their attitude towards cantering will very often be revealed *before* any canter work starts, *provided* that is that *you are listening*. One child will say *when* are we going to canter? Meaning that they are looking forward to it. While another may say '*Are* we going to canter'? Clearly revealing that they have some reservations about the matter.

The hidden agenda.

I suppose the following remarks could equally be applied to a grown up. However I have found that children are much more skilled at manipulating one situation in order to succeed in another.

For example I may have a child in my class who has suffered an unpleasant riding experience. Let us imagine that a pony has kicked out nearby. The safety standards set in place worked and nobody was hurt, none-the-less the child starts to cry. Having brought the situation under control, I go up to the child who was completely uninvolved and try to pacify it. I succeed and the class continues.

The following week the same youngster comes up to ride, I ask her if she is all right and she gives me a nice sunny smile. She doesn't ride with me on this occasion because she is being taken down to the fields. On the following week she arrives back in my class in the arena and is full of tears. I ask her what is the problem and she says that she is afraid that the pony that kicked out might do so again. Nothing unreasonable about that. Perfectly understandable in the circumstances. After the lesson has ended I decide that a word with Mum might be appropriate and go into the coffee shop and – to my surprise there is a laughing smiling face eating chocolates and generally having great fun whereas only minutes before it had been twisted in a rictus of anguish.

As is frequently the case with homo sapiens the penny starts to drop. I think back several weeks when I had earlier had a conversation with the same child and gained the impression that though her sister was enthusiastic about riding that she was not. Then my mind returns to the day that she went out round the farm, it was nice and sunny, whereas the week she had been with me it was raining and horrible – you dear reader are begging to get the picture? How do I make sure that my suspicions are correct and that the anguish has nothing to do with kicking ponies but more to do with the state of the weather?

Well being a bit of an actor myself, the next time I have the child in my class and the weather is a bit on the grey side and I see this face with down turned lips working very hard to squeeze out a tear. I go up to her and say 'hang on a minute I see that you are having a bit of a problem with your tears this week, let me have a go'. Whereupon I screw up my face and a flood issues forth. I squint through my half-closed eyes and see this little face busting out with fits of laughter; she's been sussed! Of course you will have to devise your own way of sorting out these little local difficulties.

Changing the pony.
You must judge the situation carefully and be accurate in your assessment of all children. In the previous paragraph I mentioned what I would call the 'fail-safe method'. However it may not be necessary to go down that path. The problem may simply lie with the fact that the child *is* nervous of the particular pony that they are riding. If you judge this to be the case, then ask them if they would like to ride another one. If you deem the one that they choose to be suitable and you have the agreement of the other rider, then you may make the change. This of course is subject to the fact that you consider that the other child will also be able to manage on the pony that they are being offered in exchange. You must also ensure that the policy of the school permits changes of this sort.

There is the other side of the coin and that is that some children insist on always riding a pony that they have become used to. Generally the office will ensure that this does not happen. None-the-less whether they do ride different ponies or not, it is a good idea to, occasionally, have the whole class swap ponies with one another for a short period during a lesson. Of course if you do this, you must be careful to change each child to a pony that it will be able to manage.

Taking age into account.
In an ideal world the children whom you have in a class will all be of a similar ability. It also helps to have them all of a similar age. Even if they are, you may have to use your authority to ensure that the more dominant personalities do not impinge to too great an extent on the quieter members of the class.

Sometimes you may feel that a child in one of your lower classes really has the ability to ride with a more advanced group. If the change takes place this may well mean that you have entering the higher group a youngster who is somewhat junior, in years, to the current class members. If your classes are conducted correctly the more experienced members will not try to dominate the new member, in fact they will be welcoming. But what you should remember is that the newcomer may well feel overawed by those whom he or she *sees* as their superiors. Cast you mind back to your own school days and try to recall the enormous difference that there was between yourself and those say, a couple of years ahead of you. You must find out if your children have any feelings of inferiority and, by talking to them, help to reassure them that they have nothing to worry about.

The tone of voice.
I personally do not favour using a little baby 'squitzy whitsy' voice as if I was talking to imbeciles; I didn't like it when I was young. I do use *softer kindly tones* and I keep my voice fairly low. Apart from that I do not make any concessions in the words that I use. I do ask everyone if they have understood what I am saying and even though I may consider that it is something that they should have known had they been listening, I always praise anyone, who *does* ask a question. I point out that real foolishness lies with those

who do not understand but try to cover it up. In this way youngsters develop a confidence in you and will not be afraid to ask about something that they do not comprehend.

If I think that a child is simply pretending to have understood, when I think that they have not, then I question them in depth and if they are found wanting, I *do not mock them* but instead try to find out exactly where the problem lies. It may have been that they are not used to my choice of words. This is especially so when one has been describing a particular movement such as a shallow loop or perhaps a serpentine. If this is the case then I walk the shape and sometimes invite the class to follow me. As I do so I point out the likely difficulties that may be encountered when the class rides the same shape later on but without me leading them.

Finally I constantly ask questions individually of each of my pupils, if one child does not appear to know the answer, then I do not prolong their agony but ask someone else instead. Sometimes a child knows the answer perfectly well but has a problem in putting it into words. If this is the case, then help and encourage them even if you only receive a half-correct reply. The one thing that one must remember with children is that their attention span is much less than that of adults, so keep your explanations short.

Things not to do.

1. Never be sarcastic to a child or make fun of it if it fails to succeed in riding a movement or providing a correct answer. The self-esteem of a child is very brittle and if severely dented this may have a detrimental effect on it for the rest of its life.

2. Do not allow children to manipulate you. You might be surprised at how skilful children can be in getting you to bend to their will.

3. Do not allow your discipline to become lax.

The element of enjoyment.

So far as children are concerned and adults come to that, it is my view that lessons should be an occasion for happiness and laughter. After all there is nothing so grandiose about learning to ride that an atmosphere of grey concentration should continually pervade a lesson. One does not learn through being humbled or being made to feel inadequate. Your pupils should not have to struggle hopelessly through the lesson with a view that if they return, they might do better the next time. It might give the instructor a distorted view of their exalted position but that's about all.

Every word that you utter, every instruction that you give should be said in such a way that you immediately stimulate the interest of your class. You provide the key that will unlock the child's understanding of the language of equitation.

You may be humorous without being condescending. You may enliven your own dialogue by using the little snippets of conversation gleaned from your pupils that do not necessarily have to do with the subject in hand. For example on one occasion one of my pupils appeared rather tired. Upon my inquiring why this was so, she informed me, that she had been rearranging her bedroom furniture the night before. Her mother who was also a pupil of mine had told me that this had taken place during a dinner party and that loud and mysterious bangs were heard coming through the ceiling. So for a short while I referred to her as the 'Interior Decorator'. 'Will the Interior Decorator please prepare to canter' – Much giggling and mirth all round.

The effects of sound and natural reaction, especially with children.

I have already said that you need to take into account the unpredictable moods of horses and ponies. These *are* affected by the time of the year. For example in spring, as the days grow longer, ponies as well as horses will try to establish a dominant place in the herd that also includes the humans. But one must go further and make an allowance for the combination of the ponies' mood and how it will react to children getting excited as they play a game. I always insist that the vocal side of any competition be kept fairly muted otherwise normally quiet ponies well may get over excited as a result of their riders own enthusiasm.

Keeping parents in touch.

Children's parents' should be kept informed. If you are a keen observer, you can be a source of considerable information as to a child's development. I have taught several children, whose parents thought that their offspring were either dyslexic or backward but my observations indicated that they were, in fact extremely bright, though they did in the beginning exhibit a lack of concentration. This inability was overcome through the riding lessons. So you should not be surprised if parents are very pleased when you talk to them.

Do not imagine that because a child is quiet and appears to be withdrawn that it is because it is not very bright. Generally I have found that they are absorbing all the emotional input that may be entailed in learning to ride. They have to deal with their own fears, and the need not to be shown up in front of their peers. All the time they are listening to everything that you say and taking in all the things that are going on around them. As time passes, one day, they quite suddenly bust into the full bloom of confidence.

Boys are, sometimes, extremely difficult to teach. It's not that they don't have the ability but that, during their pre-teenage years, they can be disinclined to focus. This may simply be due to the fact that they are very busy observing everything that is happening. If they stay with the sport during their teenage years, then a change will be noticed as they start to concentrate with greater intensity. Unfortunately other sports such as football engage their attention and they frequently stop riding, returning only some years later. As an instructor you should derive much satisfaction if you manage to enthuse these young people so that they stay the course.

Personalities - helping to bring out the best.

Children are born with certain personality traits. In childhood these are quite fragile and the way in which these develop depends to some degree on the environment in which the child grows up.

If you are a really good instructor then you may be able to contribute to bringing out the best in the children that attend your classes. They have to learn to become part of a team, to control their fear and to be thoughtful with regard to the pony that they are riding. This is achieved through firm but gentle discipline with much laughter and a lot of praise when things go well.

Praise is most appreciated when it is least expected. Thus when sending a ride away from you, say around the field with instructions to canter at a certain point, the children who have to go last should be the ones to get the most praise. They need to know that you have appreciated their ability to keep their pony at a designated gait and going straight even though it can see its friends in front going off at the canter. This takes a considerable degree of control and the children should be made aware as to how well they have done.

The leading file.

Usually it is best to have a good forward going pony in the lead. Not only that but, as with horses, it is advisable to have the larger ponies with longer strides in the front, after all those riding smaller animals can always cut a corner in order to keep up. However you will notice that some of the exercises mentioned later on in this book do involve a continuously changing leading file. This is a good thing, for children do need to have experience in taking the lead. In fact I would go further, many children consider that it is a privilege to be given the job of being 'leading file'. You should take note of this and, provided that it does not compromise safety or disrupt the progress of the lesson, you should give different riders the task of taking the lead. Should they ride a pony that is less than co-operative, then do not keep them in front for too long. After a short while, tell them that they have done very well and appoint someone else to take over.

Learning responsibility when in the lead.

When you give a child the opportunity to lead, you must also explain the responsibilities that go with it.

1   The lead file must set a good *steady* pace.
2   They must continuously glance back and ensure that the rest of the ride is keeping up with them.
3   If they are not, then they should slow down, change down a gait or even halt for a few moments until the rest of the ride catches up.
4   When riding around a field, in which the class is going to have an opportunity to canter as a ride, from, say the corner of a field; it is the lead files responsibility not to do so until the whole ride has passed the corner. It is up to you to make this abundantly clear.

The psychology of children.

I don't suppose anyone really thinks too much about this subject when teaching children. Frequently it is a case of 'get on the pony – be brave- get on with it'. The fact is that it is very important to understand what goes on in a child's' mind. In the first place the majority of children do not see themselves as such. In their minds they are adult. The fact that they are not is brought home to them when something happens with which they do not have the emotional maturity to deal.

In my experience there are two main ways in which this is demonstrated. The first is that they want to have nothing whatever to do with something that, as far as they are concerned, has proved to be full of danger. Then there are those still willing to have a go, but the willingness may be as a result of peer pressure or shear devilment. Whatever the reasons, if the outcome is a *series of unfavourable events*, then you may have allowed such a loss of confidence to build up that you are unable to deal with it and the child will no longer ride. If you are to become a successful instructor of children, you must learn to discern exactly what lies beneath the surface of those beaming, mostly happy, faces.

Confidence can be a fragile thing.
With children you must keep an eye on those ponies that, in the hands of a nervous rider may tend to take advantage. They may well be the same ponies that in the hands of a competent youngster will give no problem at all. It is up to you to prevent things getting out of hand.

As with all human beings children learn from experience. One does not realise the heat in a flame, no matter how many times one is told, until fingers are burned. Thus you may have a child insisting that it be allowed to canter around a field. If you allow it to do so and the pony, (full of eagerness and detecting that it is carrying a rider, whose control is less than effective) makes off, then the enthusiasm of the child turns from keen participation to complete horror. Screaming may ensue; thus frightening the poor pony whom wonders what on earth is going on when it is having such fun. Bailing out usually follows, thus adding the element of possible injury.

Therefore you must exercise caution. Do not yield to such blandishments as 'Please please, please'. Even when I have children whom I consider are on the borderline I ask them if they truly wish to ride that distance away from me. I stress that there is nothing 'wimpy' in deciding that they should take a shorter route. If I am in a field, then I will send those that I consider very capable around three sides with instructions to *wait at the third corner*. When they are all safely arrived I send the others to join them by going along the fourth side, which is a much shorter distance. You may well wonder why I *wait until the rest have finished?* The reason for this is that if I send the second group earlier, then these ponies spying their friends over the far side may not go where they are supposed to but will, instead, dash across the centre of the field, thus frustrating the plan that I had had in mind. Having made my point, I suggest that you should not, immediately, cast nervous riders into the category of those with whom one should never attempt anything. It is your job to build up confidence – to observe its growth – and to act on it accordingly.

The fragility of a child's' self-esteem.
I have mentioned this before and I do so again. Never be sarcastic when a child fails to perform a movement to your satisfaction. It is your job to help youngsters to surmount the difficulties that will inevitably arise as you take them along the path that will, eventually lead them to becoming good riders.

Putting them down with an ill-considered remark may have the effect of changing their whole concept as to what riding is all about. Instead of looking forward to their riding lessons with pleasurable anticipation, you may well have put them off. All because of a thoughtless word.

Does this mean that you should never have a joke with a child?
Of course you can have a little joke, sometimes at the child's expense, but you must be careful which child that you choose. Always be sure to follow this up with praise. Avoid those whom you think may be especially sensitive. You should also allow them, occasionally, to have a joke at your expense.

A child's' sense of time.
Another factor that should not be overlooked is that for young people time passes very slowly. It is not a good idea to spend more than the minimum time required in explaining what you are going to do or the reasons why. Any time longer than a minute or two is likely to induce boredom and a loss of concentration. Explanations need to be, clear, short and sharp, backed up by questions to ensure that they have been understood. When that is done get on with whatever exercise you have devised. If you are successful a question about 'what time is it?' will only be prompted by a fear that the fun will end.

Working with children and ponies outside.

There is no reason why even little children who are still at the novice stage should not go for a little ride out into the fields. It is very important to have a competent leader for *each* pony and ensure that only quiet ponies are used. You must also be sure that the ponies are placed in the correct order according to their temperaments. Unless you are having short 'races' where the ponies are standing in line, at all other times keep them as a ride.

Avoiding problems with ponies when working outside.

Working out of a manége usually means that you do not have the containing element of walls or rails. This should not be a problem provided you take reasonable precautions. By this I mean that you should try to avoid the tracks or paths that are usually used by other instructors for such gaits as cantering. If you are working with children who are perhaps a little timid you may well say to yourself, 'Of course I'm not going to allow them to canter at this point'. You may even decide that for safety reasons you will not even allow them to proceed at anything faster than a walk. All well and good if all your ponies are being lead, but there does come a time when you dispense with leaders and allow your pupils to exercise control on their own. This is where a problem may occur because it only requires one pony to decide that this is a point where they usually have a jolly good canter and off it goes taking the rest of the class with it. Not only is this dangerous for your charges but if the going is heavy then you may end up with several lame ponies. Ponies can be quite silly when it comes to 'having a bit of fun'. They count the cost afterwards.

So what are you to do? To my mind the answer is find out beforehand where canters are usually undertaken and be sure to avoid this area with your class. Unfortunately we do not teach in an ideal world and other teachers with more experienced riders may have the same ponies that you use and allow their pupils to go careering about all over the place at high speed. They do not give a thought as to the effect that this may have on these same animals when they are out with less able riders. Oh I know that the members of their class love all this mad dashing about – until they have a fall themselves, then it's an entirely different story, especially when recounted to parents!

Discipline.

Do not make the mistake of confusing discipline with regimentation. Your lessons should always include the element of fun and laughter. You should be able to pitch your voice so accurately that you are able to enjoy a jolly good laugh without things getting out of hand. However it is essential that you maintain good discipline throughout. If you do so, then, you end up contributing something more than merely teaching a child to ride a pony, you also teach it to observe the basic elements of politeness, independent thinking and becoming a good team player. Many of my parents send their children daily up to the yard in order to help out. This not only further assists the children in expanding their knowledge of how to work with ponies but it also keeps them away from undesirable elements. So far as riding is concerned instilling discipline with regard to riding ponies does depend on a few basic rules. They are listed below and you must ensure that they are obeyed.

1   Safety must never be compromised. Pay special attention to such matters as- Riding behind other ponies. – Getting too close to the pony in front. Any rider not paying attention to these points must be pulled up immediately. If you leave it and they get kicked then it's too late!
2   Paying attention to what you are telling them. – If you notice someone looking around the arena when you are in the middle of describing the next exercise, then ask him or her to pay attention.
3   General conversation. - During a lesson you must keep strict control of conversations that bubble up spontaneously. In fact, when they start to have a chat, it is usually a sign that children are relaxed and enjoying themselves but they are there to learn and so you must keep this under control. Having said that, if working out in a field with a fair distance to cover when returning, then so long as you are not riding along a road, do not interfere with any conversations at all provided that they don't get out of hand. In fact I encourage my youngsters to ride in pairs - with a friend if they so desire. Pairs of course means just that and no conversation should permit such a lack of attention that ponies or riders wander all over the place!

Focusing the attention.

Sometimes when I am working with children who may be a little diffident, who haven't yet climbed to that plateau of confidence, which in time will come, I sometimes devise a stratagem to encourage them. Where a pony simply is not being very co-operative and the child ineffective, I walk in front and when I am about six paces away, I turn back and 'cock a snoot' at the rider. By that I mean I stick my fingers in my ears and waggle them about. I then carry on walking, jauntily, and at the same time making comments to the air. I say that what with all the wimps that I have following me I really don't need to worry, for I have nine lives and there is no danger of my loosing one by being caught up and touched on the shoulder. Sure enough there is suddenly great concentration and the tempo of the walk will be heard to increase. In a few seconds to the sounds of much giggling I feel a tap on my shoulder. I turn around amazed! 'How as this possible' I protest.

Really bad habits.
As I have already said, the very best pupils that you will get are those whom you teach from scratch. Unfortunately this seldom happens. I find that many children who join me from other riding schools have, sometimes developed really bad habits. The worst of these is the raising of the hands high in the air and pulling like mad as they try to get their pony to turn back to the track if it has decided to have a bit of a wander. This is something that is highly visible but does, sometimes, take quite a while to cure.

Another really bad habit is not always so noticeable and that is the bending forward of the rider's body and the subsequent lifting of the seat out of the saddle every time a change of pace is asked for. It is especially odious when one has given the command to go forward to halt. Bearing in mind that the seat is the very foundation of good equitation it is something that you must never miss and take great pains to correct.

Working on a hot day.
Whether you are working in a ménage or out in the field, very hot weather demands that you arrange your programme so that it is suitable for the prevailing conditions. Hot weather, very often, means hard ground or if in an arena a dusty surface. It also means easily exhausted children and ponies that are likely to suffer stress. In very hot weather reduce the amount of work at the higher paces, For me this is an occasion for the cessation of ordinary schoolwork and in its place games that are specifically devised to both provide entertainment and at the same time allow both riders and ponies to have considerable periods of rest. I have found that the best way of achieving this is by choosing a game that either involves each rider proceeding singly or, at the most in pairs (See games to play for hot weather). The reason for this is that while one or two riders are proceeding, the rest of the ride is standing still. Provided the duration of activity is strictly regulated by the elements involved in the 'game', both riders and ponies will remain cool.

Shade.
If there is any shade then that is where the class should be standing. Out in a field you should be able to find some large trees. In an outdoor arena, maybe there is a wall suitably placed along one side.

Working outside in bad weather.
When you are outside and the weather is bad the first thing is to try and find a sheltered spot. During the summer when it is simply a matter of heavy rain and there is no danger of lightning, then use the protection of any trees that are nearby. Large trees such, as oaks (not during acorn time) will provide excellent cover. Do not misunderstand me, I am not suggesting that you mollycoddle your charges but there is no reason why everyone should have to stand around getting soaking wet while you carry out your safety checks. I am also considering the comfort of the ponies.

Of course there may be no protection whatsoever. Should this be the case then do encourage your class, while they line up, to do so in a manner that will allow the ponies to stand with their quarters facing the oncoming deluge. This is what they would do if turned out and it does afford them some comfort and will avoid well-bred ponies with fine coats from getting fractious.

In the winter there may also be the problem of a wind, which will increase the chill factor. In these circumstances, at the very least, try to make use of a hedge. However when things are really bad do not forget that there is nothing to prevent you from asking the class if they would like to return to the yard, put the ponies away and spend the rest of the hour doing stable management in a stable. Do bear in mind that *everyone* should be in favour. After all there may be those who having paid to ride wish to do so. In which case, unless you consider that conditions are so bad that they pose an element of danger, riders are entitled to ride.

On cold days there are other considerations to be taken into account.
I have already made mention of the need to adjust ones lessons in order to take the weather into account. However in cold times avoid long periods of standing about. Sometimes one should go further. When the weather is *very* cold you should have a fairly prolonged period at a steady trot. This will quickly warm both ponies and riders. Of course one must be careful not to overdo it. By that I mean don't go on for so long that the ponies become sweated up. This can occur very easily when working with ponies that are not clipped out and have long winter coats. If it does happen then it is a devil of a problem to get them dry again. However once the class is warmed up you may still have the problem of cold hands and feet. The discomfort in the extremities can be so easily overlooked. Cold hands certainly are not an aid to improving riding skills because apart from causing extreme discomfort for the owner, they also loose their sensitivity.

Dealing with cold hands.
It is my opinion that one should introduce a short period of activity that concentrates on making sure that the circulation of hands and feet are improved. When concentrating on the hands, one should first, line up the class along a sheltered side of the arena or field (if there is any protection). The class is then arranged at suitable distances that allow both for the movement of extended arms and also to provide a safe distance between each pony. Ask your pupils to knot the reins over the pony's necks. Now proceed with the following exercises: -

Arms extended horizontally and twisting the torso.
All riders must sit tall with their arms lifted up shoulder high. They then twist first to the right and then back again in the other direction. You will encourage everyone if you also take part. By doing so you will demonstrate to the class the correct way to proceed and it will also help to warm *you* up. You should set the tempo of each swing by calling it out. If you call out with great gusto then the class will take part with great amusement and joy. The essence of the movement is not to twist too quickly; a slow and deliberate turn is sufficient.

While the exercise is in progress you should ask the class if they know anything about centrifugal force. If you do not get a complete answer, you should go on to explain. The effect is similar to a conker tied to the end of a piece of string moving outward when swung around in a circle, so does the blood in ones body as the arms are swung about. It is the blood flowing through the fingers that makes them feel warmer. Do not keep the exercise going for too long so that everyone gets tired.

Clapping the hands together.
For this exercise the riders simply clap their hands together above their heads and then lowering them to clap their thighs smartly. Six clap sequences should be enough for this movement to have effect.

Neither of the exercises should be carried on for so long that the ponies are allowed to get cold (drawing no. 26). Also remember that the hands clapping should be light and therefore quiet.

Dealing with cold feet.
Unfortunately feet, being little used when engaged in the practise of equitation, also tend to feel the cold. The answer in this case is to institute a dismounting, leading and mounting race. Don't forget to remind ***all participants to check the girth before remounting***.

Competitions.
I think that it is a very good idea to, sometimes give younger riders something to do while they are away from the riding school. A 'points of the horse' competition is one such. I produce sheets, which show the outline of a horse with the various points marked out by numbers. The children have to supply the correct name for each point. They can do so either by writing the name on the sketch in the correct position or by producing a separate list showing all the numbers and the names side by side. I also encourage those with artistic ability to produce their own drawing and to use colours, if they wish.

Examples of other competitions may be seen in the 'Games to play list'.
Dashing around the fields madly.
When I am away on holiday, other instructors take my classes. These lessons frequently involve a hack, a

section of which seems to sometimes include a voluntary or involuntary mad dash across the fields. Very often these involve several children falling off. Upon my return I am, sometimes, inundated with requests by members of the class, to repeat the experience. I do not do so. Instead I ask them the question 'If during this gallop you had wished to pull up your pony, would you have been able to do so?' The answer is usually a crestfallen look. Now I have no objection to taking young people out hacking but I expect *all of them* to have the ability to remain in control except in all but the most exceptional circumstances. For me this ability is developed by sending the riders away, single file, by themselves first over short distances and then increasing them until they are capable of riding any pony all the way around the four sides of a field at any gait that I dictate. Then and only then do I consider taking them out on a hack.

Since many of the children that I teach are placed in my classes because they may have lost confidence, I object to any outing that may set back all the preceding work that I have done. Do not misunderstand me I have no objection to youngsters be taken out across the fields but it must be done under *controlled conditions*. This means that a leader should accompany any child, who does not have complete control or at the very least the ability to sit no matter what happens.

There is another aspect to this matter of fast traversing of the countryside. This concerns the well-being of the ponies. No matter what pupils may enjoy, one must not loose sight of the fact that we are talking, here, about hard working school ponies. I consider it to be most inconsiderate of any instructor to allow any pony to be involved in a flat-out dash. It may get them sweated up, involve injury and make life more difficult and dangerous for another instructor taking these same ponies out at a future time.

A further thought about really small children.

Nowadays I sometimes teach really little ones, I mean about 4 or 5 years old. I do tell them to sit tall. The word I use is 'Royally' and they know exactly what I mean. I show them how to hold the reins and I also tell them about using their back, legs and voice to ask the pony to walk on. I always have them on a lead rein and remain very close in case they should wobble. But I don't dwell too much on the specifics of riding a pony for most of the lesson. Instead I suggest that we sing a little song or a nursery rhyme as we proceed around the arena. When we reach a letter they are asked to try to get the pony to halt. I then ask them to tell me as many words as they can think of beginning with that letter. I go on to ask them what school is like and what is their favourite subject.

In this way the child associates riding with a period of interest and pleasure and becomes more at ease. I know when this has happened because they will, quite suddenly, start to talk to me about matters that have nothing to do with riding at all.

Safety again!

When you are giving a lesson you will, of course, be paying great attention to the element of safety. The time when you are most likely to be *caught out* is not so much during the lesson but *at the end* of it. The reason for this is that, quite naturally when a lesson comes to an end and the ponies are all lined up, that is the moment when you start to relax. And this is the very point when some damned pony is going to air its dislike or frustration by twisting around and trying to have a go at the pony standing next to it. The child, caught unawares, is thrown! *Take just as much care at the end of a lesson as you did at the beginning.*

Drawings.

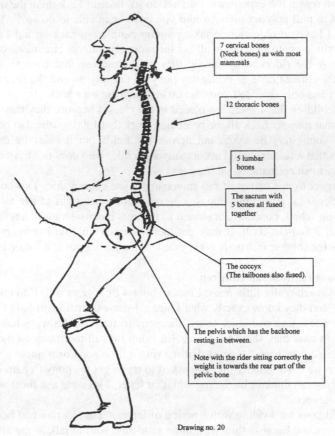

7 cervical bones
(Neck bones) as with most mammals

12 thoracic bones

5 lumbar bones

The sacrum with 5 bones all fused together

The coccyx
(The tailbones also fused).

The pelvis which has the backbone resting in between.

Note with the rider sitting correctly the weight is towards the rear part of the pelvic bone

Drawing no. 20

Sitting with the correct curve in the spine.

Drawing no. 20. Sitting with the correct curve in the spine.

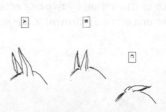

Drawing no. 22. Using cotton thread to develop 'feel'.

Drawing no. 23. The positions of the horse's ears.

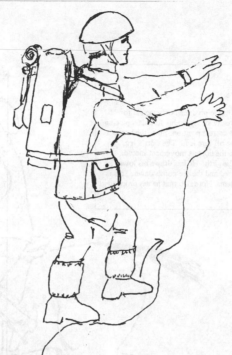

Drawing 24a. The weight of a backpack.

Drawing no. 24(b)

The weight of a backpack shifting.

Drawing 24b. What happens when it un-expectedly shifts?

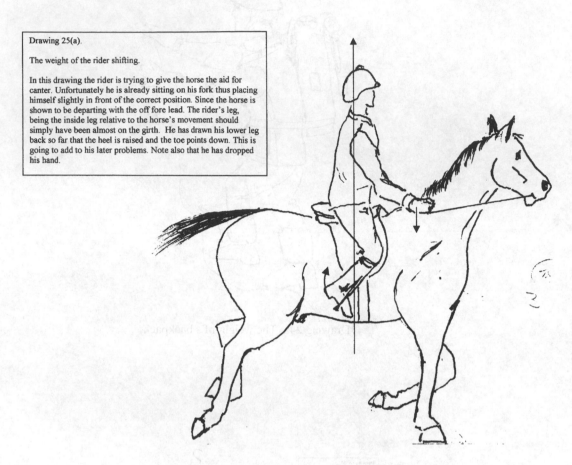

Drawing 25(a).

The weight of the rider shifting.

In this drawing the rider is trying to give the horse the aid for canter. Unfortunately he is already sitting on his fork thus placing himself slightly in front of the correct position. Since the horse is shown to be departing with the off fore lead. The rider's leg, being the inside leg relative to the horse's movement should simply have been almost on the girth. He has drawn his lower leg back so far that the heel is raised and the toe points down. This is going to add to his later problems. Note also that he has dropped his hand.

Drawing 25a. The weight of a rider shifting.

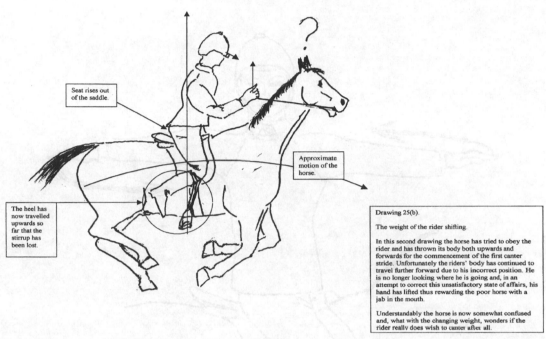

Seat rises out of the saddle.

Approximate motion of the horse.

The heel has now travelled upwards so far that the stirrup has been lost.

Drawing 25(b).

The weight of the rider shifting.

In this second drawing the horse has tried to obey the rider and has thrown its body both upwards and forwards for the commencement of the first canter stride. Unfortunately the riders' body has continued to travel further forward due to his incorrect position. He is no longer looking where he is going and, in an attempt to correct this unsatisfactory state of affairs, his hand has lifted thus rewarding the poor horse with a jab in the mouth.

Understandably the horse is now somewhat confused and, what with the changing weight, wonders if the rider really does wish to canter after all.

Drawing 25b. The rider tilts forward and the horse is unable to deal with this change of weight and most often ceases to canter.

Drawing no. 26. An exercise to warm the hands and strengthen the muscles of the torso.

Diagrams

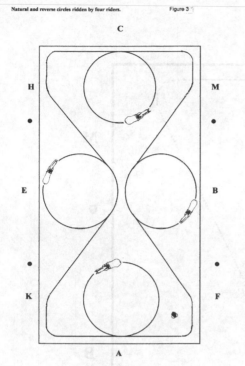

Figure no. 3. Riding natural ands reverse circles around the arena.

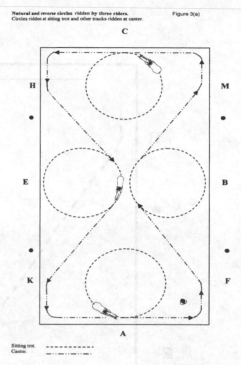

Sitting trot. – – – – – – – –
Canter. – · – · – · –

Figure no. 3a. Riding natural and reverse circle at trot and canter (three riders).

Natural and reverse circles ridden by five riders.   Figure 3(b)
Circles ridden at sitting trot and other tracks ridden at rising trot.

Note the rider halted at H does not start to move until approached by the rider leaving C

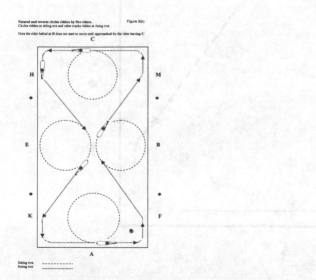

Sitting trot. – – – – – – – –
Rising trot. ············

Figure no. 3b. Riding natural and reverse circles (five riders).

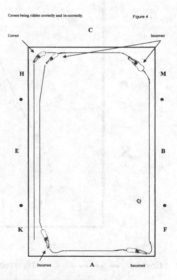

Figure no. 4. Riding corners, correctly and in-correctly.

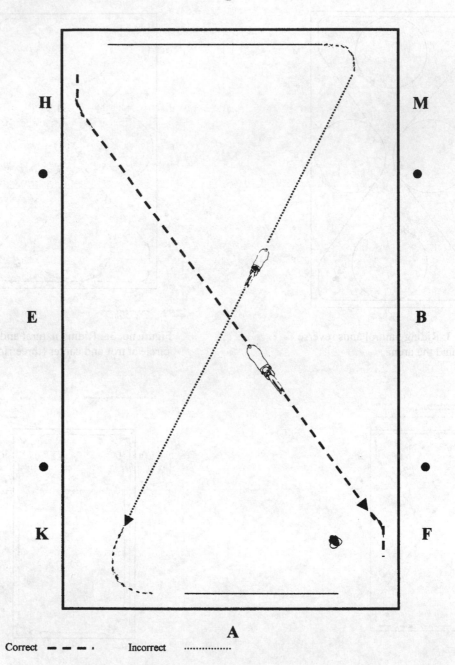

Figure no. 5. Riding a long diagonal, correctly and in-correctly.

Chapter 10

Drill Rides for novices.

I have placed this chapter immediately following that of the novice class because I think that a drill ride is an excellent way of improving the abilities of all your pupils. These should be introduced from the point where they have demonstrated sufficient control to get their horses to go large around the arena, without any real deviations occurring. Of course you must start with movements that are not too involved, for if you make them too difficult then you may end up with your riders going all over the place. Having said that, each subsequent exercise should be at a *slightly* higher level of difficulty so that your pupils have to stretch themselves a little in order to succeed.

Please note that some of the movements mentioned below might be more suitable for intermediate riders and I have marked them accordingly. There are further drill rides for intermediate riders in chapter 12.

What is a drill ride?

Any movement where each member of the ride moves in strict and constant relationship to all the other members, irrespective of any changes taking place.

What are the advantages?

As I have already mentioned, one of the difficulties that most riders encounter is *developing the ability to think of more than one thing at a time*. As an example let us consider and analyse a very simple movement such as riding, *individually*, an *accurate circle* at the walk. This, of course, is not a drill ride, but it does serve to demonstrate the problems facing many riders.

1. The rider must be looking in the direction in which they wish to go.
2. The rider should be checking that their body is in the correct position – sitting tall and turning the torso in the direction of movement.
3. Checking their leg position – inside leg almost on the girth, outside leg behind the girth
4. The hands – inside hand providing bend, outside hand monitoring the tempo - ready to lead away if required.
5. Now the horse –head bent in the required direction, hind legs correctly following the track of the front legs.
6. Horse proceeding at the correct tempo in the correct direction.

By no means does the above list cover every point. But how many riders, especially during the early stages of their riding careers, are actually able to remember all of them and even if they do, are they able to recognise when they are incorrect and act accordingly? As their instructor you will no doubt firmly point out some failings but will your pupil really be aware as to the *full extent* of their shortcomings?

The whole reasoning behind most drill exercises is that all class members must act as one. Therefore it is an excellent opportunity to **highlight** many *faults of individuals.* These will be shown up in stark relationship to the rest of the class – a half circle ridden incorrectly, soon demonstrates any one individual's failings when compared to those who are riding correctly. A loss of tempo is immediately revealed as the rider gets more and more behind the rest of the ride. Therefore by introducing a drill ride we are encouraging every member of the class to develop the ability to think of an increasing number of details all at the same time. I find that riders try much harder when riding in this way; they really use their seats in order to keep their horses, constantly in the correct relative position to the rest of the ride.

Another advantage is gained where you have a large class or one of mixed ability. In such a case the splitting your class into more than one ride and riding drill exercises is extremely useful.

Enjoyment for the pupils.

Thus dear reader, what may seem to be quite a simple riding movement for experienced riders such as ourselves, can also provide much enjoyment for a class of novice riders. Take for example riding a 'scissors' (described below). Even at the walk this movement will provoke great interest. There are so many different matters upon which the rider must concentrate – direction, tempo and so forth, but not in isolation – everything must be kept in the correct relationship to the partner in the other ride.

The other day I watched two student instructors who were sharing an arena. One had two pupils and the other three. All the pupils were, more or less of the same standard and all were novices. After their separate lessons had proceeded for approximately half an hour, the girls (the instructors) got together and decided that they would join together as one class. They then introduced a drill ride, first at the walk and then at the trot. The change in the pupils' attitudes was a pleasure to behold, whereas they had, initially, been doggedly riding circles and trying to obtain reasonable transitions, when presented with the challenge of having to interact with all the other riders, they suddenly became alive. Each rider was watching the other intently, so that they could maintain position. Great efforts were made to keep the relationship correct. There was much laughter and obvious enjoyment.

From the instructors point of view
Embarking on a drill ride may impose an extra burden for the instructor. Perhaps this is why some instructors do not trouble themselves. It is much easier to handle if you have prepared the content of your lesson beforehand. Imagine what you intend to do in your mind's eye and then make a note on a piece of paper in order to ensure that you do not forget the correct sequences.

Splitting a ride into two, with both groups going on in the same direction, should not be too problematical. Provided that you keep the leading files in the same relationship with one another, ensure that the other riders all maintain their distances, you should be able to keep everything going on an even keel. It is still not too difficult when you ask your class to turn across the school, say in threes, change the rein and then continue in single file. The duration in which they are separated is quite short.

However when you get down to splitting the ride into say *three separate rides*, then things can get trickier, especially if you intend to ride movements that are a little more ambitious. In this case you must have your eyes everywhere. You must spot out of the corner of your eye the last ride and check its position relative to that of the first ride. For example if your arena is perhaps slightly on the small side, then you must be sure that when you ask a ride to 'right incline', that you have room for them to return to the track without getting tangled up with another ride. Even if you have only two rides going large but in *opposite directions* then you must ensure that they always *pass left hand to left hand*. Above all you must be sure that everyone understands, clearly what he or she are about to do.

What to do if things go wrong.
The most important thing is not to panic. Stop all movement and get everyone sorted out. Don't get irritated. It is not really a matter of life and death. If you do get upset then your pupils will, in turn, start to get uptight, and that will then be transmitted to their horses.

Proceeding with a drill ride.
Before you start any series of drill rides you must explain *exactly* what it is that you will be asking the ride to do. When you have done so, ask them if they have understood what you have said. Do not simply use what is for me, that pejorative word 'OK'? Actually say 'Have I made myself clear? Is there anyone who does not understand?' You should not be surprised that, if you are a respected instructor, you may well have one or two members of the class who have the courage to put up their hands and ask for a further explanation. Do not necessarily take this, as a criticism of yourself for there may well be members of your class who have a poor concept of things spatial. In these circumstances I have no hesitation in actually walking the movement so that everyone can, clearly, understand what they are being asked to do. In fact as I perform the walk I also point out various elements upon which I wish the riders to concentrate.

Don't make things too difficult.
Do not, at first, ask the ride to perform too many different movements in continuous succession. In the first place they may well forget what they have to do and for this reason alone, never mind about inaccurate riding, render the movement imperfect. Secondly it is my view that one should try and achieve some form of satisfactory performance in one exercise before moving on to the next. I always start a movement at the walk and then repeat it at the trot. Far in the future when the whole class consists of very very good riders, I might even introduce a movement with both rides changing across the diagonal at canter! Towards the end of the lesson you may ask the class to string together several of the movements previously ridden

successfully and allow everyone to have the pleasure of giving, what they all know, is an excellent display.

Create a balanced lesson.
You should remember that, as advantageous as they can be, drill rides should be *performed as a part of the lesson and should not constitute the whole lesson*. I have sketched below a few examples of drill riding but you will find many more in 'Drills and Formation Riding' by Shirley Renowden *18 or The B.H.S. 'instructors Hand Book'. *19

Drill Ride no. 1
You should not commence any movement until the riders are all the correct distance apart. If they are too spread out then there will not be enough room to carry it out correctly.
The command is- 'The whole ride prepare to inwards turn and change the rein'
The executive word of command is– **'March'** (see fig 6). On hearing the word 'March' the whole ride simply turn across the arena and endeavour to keep abreast of one another until they reach the far side of the school. Before that happens you must tell them whether you wish them to change the rein or simply to keep on the same rein. All return to single file. The former will have the same leading file.

Turning across in the school in twos.
This is a good introduction to the idea of riding in pairs. Riders who are able to exercise sufficient control to be able to ride in straight lines may undertake it. The difference between this movement and true pairs is that the riders maintain the same distance between their horses as when riding single file i.e. one horses' length. It is also another of those exercises that ask something of those following behind for as the first group turn away it is up to the leader of the second group to ensure that their horse does not do the same.

What letters should you choose?
You may choose any letter that you like but, as mentioned above, you do need to leave sufficient room so that remaining riders do not impede each of your early groups as they return to going large.

Preparing for the exercise.
Before you start, make sure that the horses in each group are compatible with one another. Have the ride number in twos. Designate a number for each group. Thus 'First group, second group' and so on. Ask every group to prove. In other words call back their correct group number to you. Before you start be sure to explain exactly what each group of riders are going to do. You must choose a point where each group will cross the arena without there being any danger of getting tangled up with other members of the ride.

Commencing the exercise.
Start with a simple movement. On the right rein turn your first group at say **'E'** (see fig 7) when each group reaches the other side they stay on the same rein and proceed in single file. On your command the next group follows. You must watch them all carefully to ensure that the turn is made at the same letter. Alternatively you may use this point in the exercise to increase the distance between each group. This being the case, simply give the command a few seconds later.

Points to watch.
1   Your riders must be sure to keep the same distance apart from one another as they cross the arena. They will be able to do this more easily if they pick out some detail on the wall immediately opposite them as they turn. Eyes fixed on these targets will help to keep them straight.
2   You must not allow anyone to 'switch off' after completing the turn. Correct distances must be maintained at all times.
3   If the exercise is ridden at the trot, it is quite likely that some horses will break to a walk. Do not allow this to happen.

Variations of the movement.
Turning across the school twice on one circuit with changes of rein.
There are many different ways in which this type of ride may be ridden. Apart from turning across the

school in twos you may increase to any number per group, provided that there is room for the whole ride down one side of the arena. If this is not the case then split into two rides. However we deal with this type of ride further on in this chapter. For the moment let us concentrate on riding in twos. On the right rein one may ask the riders to turn across the school in twos say from '**K**' to '**M**' on reaching '**M**' to go large, single file, on the other rein. Then, almost immediately, to turn across in twos at '**E**' and when they reach '**B**' to change the rein again (see fig 8). This does give everyone something to think about.

Riding a half circle in twos.
Assuming the ride is on the right rein. At the letter '**B**' instruct the ride to turn across in twos towards '**E**' but at '**X**' to ride a large half circle in twos towards the right and the letter '**C**'. Both riders *pass 'C' level with one another* and continue now in a straight line until they reach the track before '**M**', whereupon meeting the track together they *continue on the same rein **but now single file*** (see fig 9).

What do the riders learn from this movement?
Since both riders should remain level with one another, this movement introduces the idea of asking the horse to take longer or shorter strides. The outside rider has to do the former and the inside rider the latter.

Increasing the difficulty (more suitable for intermediate riders).
This is simply achieved by asking the riders to change the rein as they reach '**X**'. This means that they will be riding a half circle towards '**A**'. Therefore the bend must be changed to the new direction and when the exercise is ridden at rising trot the diagonal must be changed. Continue as before (see fig 10).

Riding in twos - a means of providing interest for older riders.
The above movement is also useful for those who through advancing years or muscular injury may not be able to carry out a lesson involving the full spectrum of changes of gait. For example let us suppose that you are about to give a shared private lesson to two people of advanced years. One of them has told you that during the last lesson they strained a muscle during the canter and after having tried to ride several strides at trot both rising and sitting, find that this is quite painful.

What are you going to do about it?
Well the first thing is fairly obvious, ask the rider with the infirmity if they feel that they could manage walk for the whole lesson. If the reply is in the affirmative, (which it ought to be otherwise why are they up on the horse at all?), you should now instruct them both to ride a series of movements based on exercises of riding in twos but conducted solely at the walk.

You may now query as to whether or not this will satisfy the able rider? The answer to which is, probably not. But you don't have to keep that rider at the walk the whole time. At a given point simply ask the infirm rider to remain at walk going large and ask the able one to trot going large and then have a short canter. In a normal size arena this should end well *before* that rider reaches the point where they are going to rejoin the other one.

Now carry on with the riding in twos exercise and a while later repeat the trot and canter segment. Two short sessions at canter is usually quite enough for an older person. They find the higher gaits quite tiring and are only too pleased to revert to walk. But just because they are old it does not necessarily mean that they are senile! A client has told me, after having such a simple lesson, that they felt quite mentally stimulated!

Riding to music.
I do not think that it is ever too early to occasionally introduce your classes to the pleasures of riding to music. Come to that there is no reason why one shouldn't do the same for individual pupils. For many years the idea of riding accompanied by music was considered something akin to circus riding. Fortunately that view has changed and today the benefits of this activity are well recognised.

What sort of music?
So far as I am concerned any music will do but it does help if the rhythm is in keeping with the movement being ridden. My personal preference tends to classical music. By that I don't mean only that written during the 17th to 19th centuries. No indeed the term 'classical' does not only denote music written years ago, but any that is deemed to have a quality that marks it out from the dross that was produced at the time that it was created. Thus I would include recent works such as those written by George Gershwin, Abba and the

Beatles. But I suppose that the best is really Spanish or Latin rhythms.

Just to give you an example I might use the following: -

General expression – The interlude music that connects the various 'Pictures at an Exhibition' by Musorsky/Ravel. El Amour Brujo – Manuel de Falla.
Walk/March – The entry of the Montagues and the Capulets from Romeo and Juliet by Prokofiev.
Trot. - The Troika from Lieutenant Kijet by Prokofiev.
Canter – The Argonaise from Carmen by Bizet or the overture to Thieving Magpie by Rossini.

The choice is up to you . If you wish music suggested by your class, then you should also encourage them to bring along anything that they feel that they would like to ride to. Do remember that a royalty must be paid for any recorded music performed publicly. You must make arrangements with your employer for this to be attended to.

Is any preparation needed?
As with all class work it is important to have thought through the material that you wish to use. This may mean preparing a tape onto which you have recorded a series of works that when put together will provide a good five-minute session encompassing rhythms to suite different gaits. Alternatively you may simply provide music that will act as a general background for a period of the lesson. As I have already mentioned you may also play that provided by members of the class and it is also very interesting to discuss, afterwards, what the other riders thought of each piece.

What sort of exercises?
So far as movements are concerned, I would suggest that you use a combination of drill ride movements that will allow you to include the different gaits that you intend to use. However you must take into account the level of ability that your pupils have reached. If your class is not able to safely canter as a ride, it is **not** a good idea to include a canter simply because your music has a good three-time rhythm such as a waltz.

Providing amplification.
If you are lucky the riding school will have suitable equipment to hand. If they do not then you will need to provide your own. A portable tape/disc player will often suffice provided that it has sufficient amplification to be heard clearly. You must also make sure that there is a power source close to hand and do be sure that any cables are tucked out of the way. If there isn't then you must rely on battery power.

What about the horses?
Generally horses do not object to the reproduction of recorded sound. In fact many of them actually 'get in the groove' as it were, swinging their hips to the rhythm. *It is important to make sure that they get used to louder sounds.* You should do this by increasing the volume very gradually and also allowing riders to let their horses pause near the sound source whilst being given a reassuring pat on the neck, until their apprehension ceases. If you find that you have a horse that shows continual fear, then either try and have it changed for another more suited to the work or else abandon this part of the lesson. *Do not continue and hope for the best!*

Diagrams.

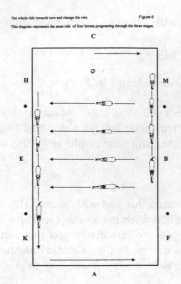

The whole ride inwards turn and change the rein.   Figure 6
This diagram represents the same ride of four horses progressing through the three stages.

Figure no. 6. The whole ride turning across the school and changing the rein.

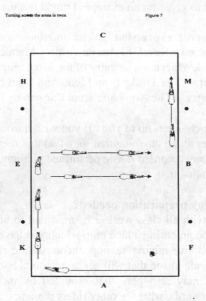

Turning across the arena in twos.   Figure 7

Figure no. 7. Turning across the arena in inwards twos.

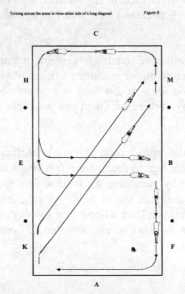

Turning across the arena in twos either side of a long diagonal.   Figure 8

Figure no. 8. Turning across the arena in twos along the long diagonal followed by a turn with a change of rein.

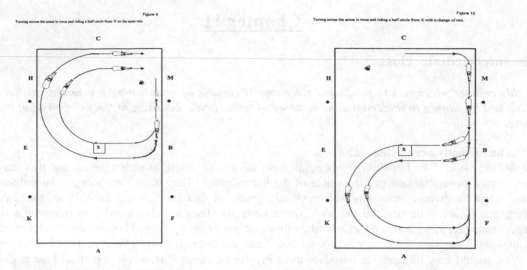

Figure no. 9. Riding a half circle without a change of rein.

Figure no. 10. Riding a half circle in twos but changing the rein.

Chapter 11

The intermediate class.

In this chapter we expect to produce a rider who is capable of maintaining a constant rhythm at all paces and beginning to understand the meaning of 'collection'. Learning to 'focus' + on what they are doing.

What has already been achieved?

By this time it is to be hoped that your pupils have learned to sit still to such a degree that they may now start to pay more attention to the manner of the horses going. They must learn to react immediately the horse starts to diverge from any aid previously given. In fact they should be able to anticipate that divergence *before* it occurs. All the while sitting correctly. They are also learning to ride with a slightly longer iron, except for those occasions when they ride out or over jumps. They should also be capable of maintaining a constant rein feel, which is not over-tense and certainly never a 'Widow Twankie' (droopy).

You should now be ready to introduce more involved concepts. However you should not neglect the basics that your students have already learned. Start to introduce movements that will help to end complete reliance upon you as instructor. By this I mean that the pupil should be encouraged to carry out self-checks of position and the manner of the horses going, without, first being, asked to do so by you.

Our target.

By now every member of your class should be able to ride all the paces confidently and safely. They should also have a reasonable degree of directional control. They should also have developed reflexes and muscles that enable them to hold their body position correctly. If they have reached this stage, then it is time to ask them to start **thinking**, seriously about **lightening** their horses' **forehand.** You may ask 'Should this process not have started to take place in the last chapter'? Well, theoretically, the answer is yes and there is no reason why you should not have attempted to get them to do so. In practise, however, it is unlikely, unless they are remarkably talented, that they will have succeeded. The reason for this is simply due to the fact that it will be very difficult for any horse to engage his hind quarters effectively and by so doing, transfer a substantial proportion of his weight from front to back, while his rider is interfering with that very process. This being due to the fact that they are wobbling about all over the place. This is the main reason that riders, though they may have achieved some considerable success in providing directional control and in changing from one pace to another, frequently have difficulty in establishing canter.

The increased possibility of an accident.

It is at this time when pupils have reached a reasonable standard of riding that the chance of an accident may more easily happen. It is very easy for you to make an incorrect decision.

Why? The reason for this is that at this level of their education pupils are able to take part in movements where things happen much more quickly.

My view is, when in doubt - don't. You may have asked your class to canter one at a time around the arena. You find that you have another ten minutes to go. Perhaps time for one final canter before winding down at the walk. *Avoid this last canter.* This is when accidents and falls are most likely to occur. We instructors with our hours-spent sitting in the saddle may be able to ride without feeling any serious fatigue. With pupils this is not so and though they may not realise it, they are likely to be very tired by the end of a lesson and what is more the horses will know it! This is the time when they may decide to put in a little buck – just for fun don't you know!

+ (See Explanations of terms used page 415.)

Making an allowance for the short-term inclusion of pupils whom may be below the standard of that class.

Since riding schools have to accommodate as many pupils as they are able, in order to remain successful businesses, it may be that you do have the odd pupil who is not of the same ability as the rest of your class. In which case you *must make* an allowance for this, whether riding in or out, and, if required, adjust the content of your lesson. This means that you should have a backup program for just such a circumstance. Should the pupil that you have been allocated reveal that they are nowhere near the standard for your class, you must make a decision. Is the pupil likely to be a danger through their lack of ability, or will you be able to accommodate them for this lesson at least? The decision is yours. If you feel that it may be the former, you should summon help and have the pupil sent, if possible, to another class. If the latter then carry on and make due allowance. *At the end of the lesson you must report your findings to the office.*

Dealing with a pupil who is confident but has been badly taught.
One problem frequently encountered is the pupil who either has never received proper instruction or who, if they have, has been taught badly. These people are those who give you the greatest problems, for bad habits are, sometimes, very hard to correct. In the first place the *pupil* may have **absolutely no idea** as to just how *poor* is their *standard*. But they may get some idea as you introduce them, with the rest of the class to a *safe exercise* that will reveal their lack of ability.

How do you do this? You simply choose a simple exercise that you know that the class rides well and during which you suspect the new pupil's lack of ability will be revealed for all to see. In these circumstances you should be *very tactful*.

Further more in order to make your point you must not allow an element of danger to creep in. In other words don't choose an exercise such as riding without stirrups if you believe that the pupil is so unbalanced that they are likely to fall off! Problems must be dealt with over a period of time. All that is necessary is for you to reveal to the pupil, that their ability is not quite of the standard that they had imagined it to be. Do not tolerate any suggestion that the problem lies with the horse and not the rider. If this question does arise then ask a competent member of your class to demonstrate on the pupils' horse.

Method.
Some schools subscribe to the policy of providing lessons that are a school for both horse and rider. I do not believe that that is always a good idea, unless that is, you are teaching *pupils who are livery owners*. It is my view that the majority of horses used in riding schools are already well schooled (if they are not, then they should not do this work). They know their business, though it may well be that they are stiffer on one rein or the other and a rider may have to take this into account. Generally speaking I prefer to concentrate on the rider, teaching them to learn to sit perfectly still, so that they are able to give clear and precise aids.

I have watched instructors going into great detail as to the advanced ways in which a novice or even an intermediate rider may *teach* the horse to be better able to move. Usually there is nothing wrong with the horse, it is the riders' fault, for example sitting on the wrong diagonal or riding too small a circle. What I am saying is: that the instructor by using this form of words ' *to teach'* is to encourage the rider to believe that they are in a position to *school* the horse to move in a correct manner. In fact, the horse is encouraged to move incorrectly due to faults that lie with the rider. How can they *school* when they have not yet learned to sit still? In other words one may be asking for corrections that *depend* on a foundation of good horsemanship that, so far as the pupil is concerned, is yet to be confirmed.

I suppose that I could be accused of being a bit pernickety about the matter. For indeed I suppose that it is purely a problem of semantics. But the exact words are important to me. If one introduces ones class to the leg yield using the words 'We are now going to *teach* the horse to move away from your leg'. This is the incorrect use of words. If riders experience difficulty in producing the movement – even one stride correctly – then fault will probably lie with the rider every time. This may be due to the fact that they have not yet learned to control their limbs and thus produce the co-ordination required to give the *correct* aids for, what is to them, (the rider) a new movement. Therefore it is absurd to say, that they have to *teach* the horse to move away from the leg, never mind about being correctly bent etc. In their first attempts to ride the leg yield, upper bodies will be seen to lean to one side or incorrect legs will, involuntarily, touch the horse. Only the most accomplished Schoolmaster will be able to divine what on earth it is that the rider is asking and even then the rider may accidentally countermand the instruction that they have given.

This does not mean that one should never embark upon the teaching of such a movement to a pupil who has yet to obtain the ability to give a precise combination of aids. It is very useful for a rider to be 'stretched' somewhat by attempting this sort of thing. But one must make sure that the rider is under no illusion that a failure lies with the horse and not with himself or herself. I would instead say ' We are now going to try to *persuade* the horse to move in this manner'. 'Aha' you may well be thinking ' What if the horse really does not know this movement' Well my reply would be that a skilled horseman can cause a horse to move in any manner provided it has the physical ability so to do. If your pupils think that this is not so, then, get up on the horse yourself and show them! If you can't, then don't teach the exercise!!!

The voice as an aid.
We do come back once again to the advantage of using ones voice. The reason for this is that one remembers that horses respond to the norm. So, for example, you may have decided that you wish to give a lesson on going forward from *halt to trot*. Your pupils may try this. It may even be that they give the correct aids for trot and yet their horse's put in one or two strides at the walk before obeying. Why is this so? The reason obviously lies in the fact that they may not be asked to perform this sort of transition very frequently. It follows that if the class is encouraged to say 'trot' as they give the aid, this will help to produce a satisfactory result. This may not happen when first asked for, but it usually works the second time. I have mentioned this transition simply as an example, for we must not forget that the horse must have the muscular development and balance to be able to perform the exercise in the first place.

The importance of success
It is up you to accurately assess the ability of your classes. By that I mean that when you introduce a movement you must be sure that your pupils have the *competence* to attain some degree of success in whatever you ask of them. This is very important because if you do not end up with a, reasonably, successful outcome, then not only is this disappointing for the rider but what is worse you *diminish the performance* of any horse in that it does not perform as requested. Let us take quite a simple movement, say for example the canter. Your pupils may well be able to ask for and be given this particular pace. However, any horse having been asked to go forward to canter may well decide that after, say half a circuit of the arena, that they have had enough and may break to trot without being asked to so do. At this time the rider rises and this is not acceptable. As I have already mentioned in the chapter about aids, the one thing that a pupil should *not do is to oblige the horse by going forward to a rising trot*. If they do so then they are simply acceding to the horses' wishes and it is most important that the exercise be completed according to the *rider's* wishes and not those of the horse.

Obedience and being reasonable.
I for some reason the pupil is unable to make the horse obey, you *yourself* must ensure that the *horse does so* until such time as it is so instructed to do otherwise. Failure to do this means that the horse has learned to take the initiative and this may, eventually, develop into a vice. It may become so bad that the horse will give considerable problems for riders in subsequent classes. Be sure that this does not happen. This is one of the reasons why I insist that you do *not use a lesson* in a riding school environment as a means of *schooling horses* for *movements* that are completely *beyond their abilities*. I repeat we are talking in the context of pupils attending riding schools in order to *learn to ride*. None-the-less it is up to you to ensure that all your horses are subject to a high degree of discipline, so that their performance always retains its sharp edge. The *quid pro quo* is that you must not ask for a movement that the horse is physically unable to attain. Say suddenly being asked to jump a five foot fence when it is only used to jumping 3ft 6".

If a horse during canter does a transition to trot, then the fault usually lies with the rider. Why should the horse decide to change gait? Simply because, if the rider is sitting on his back for a prolonged period with no form of meaningful communication going on between them (not even murmured words such as 'good boy'). In these circumstances the horse, quite understandably, may question as to whether or not it is necessary for him to continue at that energy-consuming gait.

Learning to feel.
The rider must let the horse know that even though he or she is simply sitting still, they are not out of touch. In other words, they must *learn to feel what is happening underneath*, to know the exact moment when the horse is thinking about changing, and before that occurs, let the horse understand by one aid or another that this must not take place. Even if the downward transition does accord with the rider's desire the horse must not take the initiative by himself. However should the rider apply the required aid and the horse fail to respond, then it is the horse who is being disobedient and the rider should act accordingly, by reapplying the aid again but more distinctly.

176

Learning not to be unreasonable.
You should not encourage the rider to be unreasonable. To keep a horse continually cantering for a prolonged period without a break is to invite his disobedience. He will have no choice since he will simply run out of energy (some horses have been known to be so loyal that they gallop on until dropping dead!). It is the instructor's job to have this thought foremost in the rider's mind. If the rider is not constantly thinking about what is happening with regard to the relationship between the horse and themselves, (especially when working independently) then, they will lose touch and the horse will be *forced* to take the initiative.

Horses of quality.
Riding schools may have some horses that are very well bred and light to the touch Very likely only riders of a fairly high standard will ride these animals. Occasionally you may find that one of your pupils in an intermediate class has been allocated such a horse. This may be due to the fact that there are a number of horses lame, and this is the only one available to make up the numbers. The office will usually warn you. Whilst you do not want to frighten the poor pupil out of their wits by warning them that care needs to be taken, you must however, ensure that the pupil rides in a very tactful manner. The trouble is that pupils, even at the intermediate level, frequently, still do not have complete control over their limbs. An unintentional touch may send the horse whizzing off into a half pass or a vigorous canter. The pupil, very much alarmed by the unexpected reaction, will start to grip and pull on the rein like mad and before you know where you are a complicated situation may have developed.

In a circumstance such as that described above, it is my view that you should forget about any *demanding* exercises that you might have previously had in mind and change everything to a simple, straightforward and uncomplicated lesson. Simply concentrate on developing a movement such as the trot until it becomes light and airy. Tell your pupils what you are doing and why. This will help them to relax and all will go well.

A prolonged period of riding without stirrups.
Riders who have reached an intermediate level of skill should be able to start riding for longer periods without the stirrups. They should eventually be able to do this at all the paces. It is good practise for them, since without stirrups they can be encouraged to sit still and maintain good posture with their weight positioned on the seat and not the fork. You do need to remind them of the need to absorb the ***moment of suspension*** through having a *flexible spine*, which in turn will allow the rider to keep their ***hands still***. This is fundamental. As you initiate this part of the lesson you may well hear a not so quiet groan. I always make it clear that this is not a part of the lesson form which I derive some sort of sadistic delight as I perceive the pain and anguish suffered by everyone else. Instead I point out that riding ***without the stirrups*** is a way of ensuring ***greater safety*** for the rider. This is due to the fact that correctly practised; the rider learns to sit more deeply in the saddle. One of the first things that most riders do is to start gripping with the thighs. So, before I commence the movement I always ask everyone to be sure to relax and let their legs hang down without ***any tension***. I don't mind if the toes are pointing down so long as the rider has good upper body posture and is sitting deeply in the saddle. As I have mentioned in a previous chapter I don't object if, for a short while, they place the reins in the outside hand with the whip also held in that hand but lying across the wither so that they free the other hand to hold the pommel. (see photo no 29).

Thus you should make sure that you start with the walk, and correct your pupil's positions one by one. Your instruction: - 'Sit tall chin tucked etc, do not slump etc. etc'. The object for everyone is to learn to sit so still and with such soft hands that the horse will be willing to acquiesce to the their wishes. When you are satisfied that all is well proceed to a quiet sitting trot.

Remember.
For the trot sequence you should have a competent lead file riding a horse that will oblige with a nice steady trot. At the trot these exercises should be ridden both sitting and rising.

Intermediate to advanced riders.
The heading for this section may seem strange. 'Surely' you may ask 'Is there not a clear distinction between the two abilities?' The answer to which is that sometimes there is a considerable degree of overlapping. It is not always possible to designate such and such an exercise for a particular group. One must be flexible. We have started by encouraging our pupils to develop a 'good seat'. By which I mean that

we have assisted them in developing the reflexes that will control the muscles in their abdomens so that they are always able to sit lightly. These same muscles, through constant practise, also have become strong enough to do the job, so that the pupil is able to sit in a vertical and well balanced position. They should now be riding with longer stirrups: not so long that they have to stretch down to find the stirrup but long enough so that they are relying to a lesser extent on support from the thigh, *sitting on the seat and not the fork*.

We must now go a step further and assist them in learning to use their hands correctly.

The hands.
Why is it that one rider may sit upon a horse and ask for a little flexion (bending the head at the poll and yielding the jaw) to be faced with a horse that immediately resists and starts to 'gaze at the stars', as it were? Whilst at the same time it is trying to twist its head in the very opposite direction to that of the riders' wishes? Whereas another may sit upon the *same* horse and with an almost invisible closing of the fingers get it to yield at once? This is the next great climb that a rider has to face before reaching a further plateau of achievement.

All Masters of Equitation write about the need to have '*soft hands*', yet this is the most *difficult concept* to get across to your pupils. In the first place these cannot be easily developed independently of all the other requirements of learning to ride. The reason for this is that, at the start, pupils will have a great difficulty in concentrating on more than one thing at a time. Ask them to make sure that they do not 'block' the horse by fixing their hands and they will do so until you draw their attention to the fact that they are riding off the desired course or have lost the tempo. As soon as they turn their attention to correcting these deficiencies then they forget about their hands and these become fixed once again.

Not only that but you have to try to make it clear just how subtle are the flexions of the fingers. They have to learn that we are not even talking about opening and closing the fingers but actually, in some cases, just flexing the knuckles.

Another problem that you must help your pupils to overcome is their approach. Having reached that particular point where they have good directional control and can ask the horse to change gait at will, they may now ask for paces that are either extended or collected. If they go about this like 'a bull in a china shop' then, only disaster will await them. You have now to teach them how to build up, slowly, to a desired movement.

Checking the position.
In many chapters in this book I have mentioned 'checking position'. Here I mention it yet again but this time the accent is subtly different. For now we are asking our pupils to carry out a *constant check by themselves*. By this time they should be able to concentrate not only on their own position but also that of the horse. 'Haven't you been telling us this all along?' I hear you say. Of course we *have* been *trying* to correct the basic position. The truth is that, up until now most riders have had so much else to think about. Even if you mercilessly and unceasingly 'hammer away' at them, trying to get them to correct every last detail, riding only once a week or so, they are quite likely to be unable to oblige and will probably leave your class out of fear or boredom. But by now they should be ready to take on greater responsibility. They should be able to sit upon a horse and have developed reflexes that enable them to do *several things* at the *same time*. Apart from your telling them what to do, you must teach pupils to, constantly, carry out their own checks *all the time*. This should become part of the routine when riding any movement. They have to build up a series of checks, rather like an airline pilot before taking off.

One might almost describe it as a *litany*. *The pupil must regularly repeat to himself or herself*, a list created by you, for it is only in this way that they will make a constant improvement.
Thus: -
1. Is my position correct? (Am I looking ahead? Are my shoulders back? Is my chin tucked in? Am I remembering to breathe? Are my hands held correctly? Are my toes turned in? Are my heels down?
Later you may add.
2. Are my legs pushed far enough back from the hip?
3. Is my horse positioned correctly?
4. Is he moving in the correct manner and at the correct tempo?

178

5. Am I applying corrections in good time to avoid any deviations that may occur due to his imbalance?
6. If all is well, am I then relaxing and making life easier for the horse?

Don't give your pupils a list that is too long or they will spend so much time struggling to remember the content that they will pay scant attention to what they are actually doing.

Fluency.
The ability of your pupils to perform the tasks that you are now asking of them will depend on the fluency with which they are able to give the aids. By that I mean that they have to progress **past the point** where they have to **think through** each part of the **aid sequence**. Thus let us say the aids (loosely) for the canter from rising trot are: -
1. Sitting trot. (Creating power with the inside leg almost on the girth).
2. Brace the muscles of the back.
3. Shorten the rein. (Get the correct bend and store the energy).
4. Touch the horse with the outside leg just behind the girth.
5. Open the fingers of the outside hand.

These might be the type of instructions that you would give a novice in preparing for and actually initiating a canter depart. However as the rider becomes more adept, these aids should become so fluent that they *almost* meld into one. Or at least that is the way it should be. What you must look out for is the tendency of riders when trying to obtain this fluency to actually give the *wrong* aids! Perhaps the outside leg is not used, possibly there is no shortening of the rein to contain the energy, and very likely the rider forgets to open the fingers of the outside hand.

An analogy.
Let me put it another way - perhaps this will help. Let us assume that you are able to drive. So we start with the example of getting into and starting your car. During your period as a learner driver, you would have had to carefully think through every stage of this process. To get the sequence wrong might mean that your car leaps forward and bashes into one in front. Thus: -

1. You unlock the car and get in.
2. You check that the car is in neutral and that the hand brake is on.
3. You insert the key in the ignition and turn it.
4. As the engine starts you gently tread on the accelerator.
5. If your car is not automatic you engage the clutch and select first gear. (If it is you engage drive).
6. You check your rear and side mirror to ensure that the road is clear.
7. You release the handbrake at the same time as you lift your foot off the clutch and press the accelerator.
8. And finally still checking that the road is clear and also looking where you want to go, you turn the steering wheel and pull away out into the road.

Now if you question a pupil about this, the object of this is not to catch them out in the manner of starting their cars. On the contrary, for they may well forget part of the sequence – when they recount it to you. The whole point is to illustrate that an experienced driver *does all these things* in the space of a few seconds *in the correct order, without thinking,* every time that they drive away! This is what I mean by *fluency* and aids must be given in a similar, fluent and correct, manner every time that a pupil asks the horse to do something for them. How on earth can they ride horses in any other way???

Fluency lost when introducing new movements.
Unfortunately introducing a new movement frequently poses problems for pupils. The reason for this is that as they try to concentrate on getting the horse to move in a manner in which they have not moved previously, for the pupil that is, they tend to *forget all that has gone before*. Hands start to tug and pull, legs slap uselessly against the horse's sides; bodies begin to lean in peculiar directions. This is due to the fact that even at this, intermediate stage of their studies; many pupils still find it hard to concentrate on more than one thing at a time, especially when it is new or unfamiliar.

The problem facing the instructor is how to put the correct image in the mind of the pupil. How to ask for a movement that the horse may very well know but which it hasn't been asked for some time. I have in

179

mind collected and extended paces. It is very important that the pupil is taught to think of this entirely in terms of *communication*. So for a collected walk it is no use their thinking 'I must restrict the forward movement'. Instead, get them to *think* first of an active walk and then gradually whilst using the legs to produce firm and clear tap-tap aids, the hand instead of opening and closing – closes – momentarily. Then as the pressure of the back is maintained an outline is asked for and finally the fingers start to open but they do not simply stay open instead they open partially and with each stride they quickly *close* before opening again. In a very short while the horse understands what is being asked of it and with great pleasure the rider starts to experience steps that are lighter and have more collection and cadence. The basis is similar whether for collected or extended paces and irrespective of the gait.

Giving a demonstration.
Elsewhere I do mention both the advantages and disadvantages of giving a demonstration. I have already said that it does not necessarily help a pupil to improve if you get up on their horse and ride it for them. These remarks were directed mainly at novice riders who really need to find their own way to correct balance; you simply cannot do it for them. However, when they have reached the stage where they have learned to sit reasonably well, it may help in the teaching of more advanced movements, to show that they are actually achievable by getting up on one of the horses, and demonstrating yourself. If you simply allow your pupils to struggle and to depart without ever having witnessed any form of success, they may be of a mind that you are simply being perverse in asking them to produce a movement that they are convinced is impossible with the particular horses that they are riding.

New Horses
Horses that are new to the yard, those that have just arrived and finished their quarantine, do need special consideration. In my opinion it will take a minimum of one month and usually up to three months for a horse to settle down in new surroundings. You may not realise it but humans displaced from their regular routine will also feel a modicum of disorientation. Therefore when you have a newly arrived horse in your class for the first time, ensure that it is being ridden by an experienced rider and do not ask for movements from the horse that are too stressful.

You need to pay special attention to a horse from a different background. Should you have an animal that has spent most of its previous life out hunting, then you must take into account that it's passage from place to place has, generally, been in a straight line. Therefore, should you immediately start asking for prolonged work on ever-smaller circles, you will be subjecting it to a high degree of discomfiture.

Helping pupils to deal with horses that are particularly stiff on one rein.
By this time I do feel that one should start talking to pupils about the fact that horses, like human beings are sometimes left handed or right handed. That is to say that they go more easily on one particular rein. The difficulty manifests itself most prominently during work on circles, though it may start to show when a horse starts to cut corners. The pupil should now be made aware of the reason that their horse is having a bit of a problem and it is up to you to devise suitable movements and explain to the pupil as to how they should use their aids in order to help the horse out.

Sometimes, especially towards the end of the lesson, a combination of stiffness on one rein and a pupil's poor position will make a canter exercise almost impossible to complete successfully. Keep your eyes open and don't just stand there shouting at the pupil to sit correctly. It is very likely that, having experienced an initial difficulty, the riders' position will deteriorate further still. The simplest answer is to change the rein!

The physical condition of pupils.
A quite important factor which you should make yourself aware of is the physical condition of your pupils. You need to observe them as they walk towards their horses and also when they mount. Should this be impracticable, then, you should attend to this matter during the line-up at the start of the lesson, as you go about checking the tack, you should also assess each pupil in turn. Do so with what appears to be a casual glance. The physical condition is to a great extent self-explanatory, but you will need to judge age. For a men and woman of middle age you may have to make an allowance and adjust the difficulty or duration of your proposed exercises. Of course here I am merrily talking about 'middle age'! The remarks that I have just made could apply equally well to a young person who is overweight or for that matter someone in their eighties!

Allowing pupils to work-in by themselves.

By this I do not mean that you should absent yourself from the arena and go off for a cup of tea. You of course are on hand to keep a watchful eye on things and you must also maintain safety. But it can be helpful to introduce a period during which pupils, who have developed reasonable control, should be encouraged to have five or ten minutes in which they *work-in independently*. That is without your having to give them every instruction. This might seem like a fairly strait-forward sort of exercise. After all you simply say to them, 'You have such and such a time to work on your own?' In practise this is much more of a challenge than at first it would appear. The reason for this is that you might expect your pupils to use this period to establish a good rapport with their horses and, perhaps, to find out the extent of their horses education. In practise, I am afraid that this may not work out. Suddenly, working without your guidance, many riders find that they have absolutely no original input. The reason for this is that they have grown used to you being the one that always guides and controls them. The result is that they very often resort to going large, either at walk or trot on one rein forever and ever. The poor horses simply get bored out of their minds.

The challenge is of course for you to help them to learn to make up their own programs. You start the process the week before by telling everyone what your intentions are for the following week. You should also give everyone the parameters within which they may work (don't start with canter work, for example). Ask them to start using their own initiative, to think about such matters during the time before the next lesson so that they have devised some sort of a basic programme, which they can then try to put into practise.

Working outside.

Sometimes you may have no option but to do some schoolwork in a field (as opposed to hacking out). In fact this may be a good idea anyway. Many riders excel in an enclosed arena but as soon as they ride out into the countryside they sometimes fall apart. It is true that horses become more alert and interested in what is going on around them as soon as they venture out onto a green landscape. However for some riders, lulled into a false sense of mastery through many months (years?) of working in enclosed areas, entry into an open space produces feelings of deep insecurity. In essence what is happening is that though the rider does still possesses the ability to, very adequately, control their mounts, they are simply unable to do so because they freeze. In such circumstances you must be aware of these feelings and be prepared to take them into account. (See chapter 20).

Can more involved exercises be performed in the field?

There is no reason why working outside means simply going from A to B in straight lines and in control. This is an excellent time to use the greater usable area provided by a field to take advantage of the space and allow the ride to perform slightly more exacting exercises. I have in mind asking each rider to come off the track as they progress around the field and to try to ride a fairly precise figure of eight. Returning to the exact point from which they originally departed. Many riders, who are perfectly able to ride from one point to another in a straight line, find this sort of exercise quite demanding. The reason for this is that their points of reference are extended over a greater distance. Further more they also have to contend with their horse that, while not intending to be disobedient, does have to rely completely on the guidance of the rider, which of course is not necessarily forthcoming. The change of emphasis can be highly beneficial. Of course you must only do this type of work, which is generally off the track, in those fields where you have permission to do so.

Children who are intermediate riders.

Working outside with ponies.

As I have just mentioned horses and ponies behave in an entirely different manner when out in the fields. How is one to accommodate this change? How does one maintain an adequate level of safety? From my own experience this can be best achieved by sticking to a strict routine. When working out in a field it is very important that the ponies know that when they are in your charge a certain standard of behaviour is required. You may not be able to establish this at once for there is always some cheeky pony who will try you out by dashing off without warning. Never-the-less you must try and establish *your* routine. In a short time the ponies will become used to you and should not give you too many problems.

One does need to keep everything at a level that does not encourage ponies to get over excited. Unless you are very sure that all your youngsters are of a reasonable standard, you should not, at this stage, permit cantering as a ride. This is the time that some pony will decide to dash off in the opposite direction to everyone else. An orderly ride will disintegrate into a mad charge with ponies going all over the place and will result in at least one youngster either becoming unbalanced and falling off or at the very least 'baling out'. By all means send them off one at a time, provided that the remainder are able to sit and give the half halt with sufficient authority so as to wait their turn. Some children may consider that this is unfair and you will have to explain that you have to consider *everyone's* safety.

So often I see instructors with reasonably competent young riders going across field at a flat out gallop. The more able and braver children may well enjoy this, though frequently I know that some of the members of the ride are frightened out of their wits but are afraid to say so in front of their peers. To my mind this sort of behaviour in a riding school is not acceptable. You may well get away without any serious accident occurring during *your* ride but you also need to look ahead and consider the effect that this will have on the ponies when they reach the same spot the next time, *with a different class*. On that occasion the instructor may have riders who are not so experienced. What do you think is likely to happen? And who, ultimately, will be responsible?

This does not mean that you should not send those who *do have the ability* to handle their mounts, *away* from you. What is important is that you do this in a controlled manner. By this I mean one at a time. Of course you may well come up against the problem of the 'nappy' pony that does not like to go away. I do not think that this is such a problem if you consider that the children have the ability to cope generally. They will simply have to deal with the problem. In fact it usually provides them with some useful experience.

The **order** in which the ponies are sent away is ***important***. Those that tend to race should be sent first, to be followed by those that are reluctant to leave. On no account leave a 'puller' until last or it will be sure to dash off past the others and set them all 'alight'. This will certainly result in someone departing his or her mount. As the riders leave you and proceed around the field they must ***be in your sight at all times*** and further more you must watch each rider very carefully. Sometimes you may see a rider trying to ride their pony around in a circle. This is all very well if they simply wish to impose some discipline over the animal. Very often however the rider does this simply because they are frightened at the thought of possibly being 'carted'. This results in the distance between themselves and the rest of the ride getting too great, and in the end, the pony will do the very thing that the child has been trying to avoid and departs at speed, sometimes dumping the rider on the floor.

Take care of their fragile confidence.

What one must not loose sight of is the fact that a child's' confidence can be quite fragile and may change from week to week. For example, the fact that they are on a different or larger pony, may contribute to a partial loss of confidence. This is something that you must watch out for and it is not always that easy to spot. However should you decide to send a youngster away from you then this shortcoming, even though of a temporary nature will be noticed by the pony who may try to take advantage. Frequently the reason for their fear is simply that they have not yet developed the emotional maturity to deal with a problem. One would not expect an adult to have the same difficulties and yet we do, for are we not, after all frequently children at heart?

The effect of distance.

For those children who are not yet ready to go away from you, the most important thing is to maintain a fairly close proximity to yourself. I would say a distance that varies from 25 – 50 yards is the maximum. Within this distance the ponies will still feel that they are under your control. However if you let them go farther afield then you may loose that authority. Of course when your children have achieved a high degree of expertise then they should go away, in fact that is one of the objects of your teaching.

When do you make the decision?

We now come to one of the most difficult decisions that you have to make. When do you decide to send them away from you around a field? As I have already said when they are close, the ponies feel that they are under your influence but when you send them a fair distance away, they may well decide that this is a good time to lark about. If this happens, then, even the most confident of riders may find that their skills desert them.

My advice is to try and do this by degrees. Start by sending them just down one side of the field away from the point where you entered. Use the most reliable rider and pony to take the lead. Have the class walking or trotting away as a ride – nothing more.

Be flexible.

Sometimes you may have a class of, say, eight youngsters, of whom six are extremely confident and two are a little unsure of themselves. In this case, should you be working in an enclosed field, then send away the six who are confident around the three sides of the field. Send them one at a time in a good order. Their leader should be instructed to wait for *everyone* else to join them and you must make it clear that this will include the two whom you are going to sent down the fourth side. Watch main ride depart keeping hold of the two remaining with you. This is more to give confidence to the riders than out of the fear that their ponies will also dash off. When the leader has reached the designated corner, then send the remaining two off, one after the other to join them. It will not be very long before the timid ones get over their fears and the ride all go off in the same direction.

What do you do if they all suddenly dash off?

This is a very reasonable question. No matter how careful you may be, it is always entirely possible that, just at that point when you think that all is well and you start to relax, that is the very moment when with a starburst of exploding energy one pony (usually) takes off and sets all the others going. Of course if your riders have been well prepared then only this one fellow will be successful. But this is not always the case even in the most well schooled class. Through sheer excitement and/or dismay most of your riders will allow their mounts to go where they will. This is the time when ***you must not panic***.

You must try and make the most of a difficult situation. The fact that the ponies have made off should not, necessarily, lead to disaster, even though you may feel that this to be the case. Keep your voice calm and in a voice that, none-the-less carries, remind every one to sit down, if necessary, pulling themselves down into the saddle by holding the pommel with one hand. Above all this is not the time for them to be standing up in the stirrups and pulling on the reins for support and screaming their heads off. As your youngsters should have been told many times in the past, the ***ponies will stop simply because they get tired***. They will also stop when they notice that they have failed to ignite a general state of alarm, have not dislodged anyone, and the little blighters reflect on why on earth they are bothering to expend so much energy, needlessly.

Generally the ponies will make for the gate (going home?). Provided you *have* made sure that all gates are closed securely, they will then stop. In fact they will probably stop quite abruptly and that is one of the reasons for your children to be sure that they are secure in the saddle.

What do you do after this has happened or if someone has fallen off?

Immediately make for the rider, yourself, If you have a helper, then, send them off to secure the pony. Check that the rider is not hurt (for further information; see chapter 20 on Hacking). Get them to remount and summon the class to form a half circle around you. Most of your riders will be full of apologies. You may admonish them gently and humorously. The most important thing is not to allow the incident to develop into to something out of all proportion. I usually say wryly 'Who was the wimp that started that off?' Of course I know full well who it was because I was watching them the whole time. The culprit will shyly own up. I will say 'I think that you are not a merely a wimp, you are a grand wimpo deluxe' as I say this I smile the whole class break out into fits of laughter. I then ask the culprit and the rest of the class what they could have done to have avoided it happening. Riding a circle for instance. The class will be quickly distracted by this discussion and having a quiet game to follow will finalise the matter. The attitude of your ***children*** will be entirely ***dependent on your attitude***. Make nothing of the matter and they will, in most cases, do the same. If a child has fallen and appears to have lost some confidence, then, have a helper stay at their side or if you don't have any assistance do so yourself. Talk quietly and kindly to the child.

Don't forget the time factor.

Don't forget that should someone fall off, then, you must make an allowance for extra time to return so that you can fill in the accident form. Be sure to tell the child not to leave, after dismounting, until they have seen you in the office. If you think that ponies have behaved atypically (whether or not a child actually had a fall) and that this occurred as a result of the manner in which a previous ride with some of the same ponies has been conducted, then you should say so – to the office but not in front of the children. On many occasions when I have been hacking out adult classes I have observed less experienced instructors taking junior school rides in mad dashes over the fields. It's all very well for them but it is quite likely to store up trouble for someone else.

The need to remember to engage reverse.
I teach most of my children in classes on a fairly formal basis. By that I mean that all my youngsters attend my classes regularly term by term. There are now four terms a year. This is a very good way of providing continuity. The children make excellent progress. Their move to the Senior School is governed not so much by their ability but by weight and height. The change usually takes place at the end of term.

When one has children able to ride say, an accurate scissors at the canter, one may consider that the skill factor has progressed satisfactorily. Children from lower classes fill the places of those that move up. This may mean that one week all your pupils are of a similar ability and able to ride exercises involving a high degree of skill and the next you may have two or three youngsters who haven't done anything like that in their lives.

This means that whenever this sort of thing happens you must review your general curriculum and be prepared to go back to basics until you have assessed the new intake. It is so easy to overlook this sort of potential problem, especially when you have had an uninterrupted run of may be up to twelve weeks.

Older riders.
Now I have already mentioned the discomfiture that a horse may suffer when a novice rider attempts a canter. (chapter 9 pages 24. The inability to flex the small of the back and sit to the movement). The same situation may arise when one is teaching older people who may be quite experienced and enjoy cantering. The problem arises simply because they are *unable* to flex the back simply because they are suffering from arthritis or some similar disease. Here you will have a rider quite able to initiate canter but they still bounce up and down in the saddle and , especially if they are a little on the heavy side, with quite considerable force. I repeat what I have said previously. You should only allow a rider with this type of disability to canter when riding a horse with a suitable temperament. One that will put up with the discomfiture. Further more even with a horse of such a generous spirit this sort of duress must only be endured for a very short period. The client may well ask you to allow them to canter for longer but you should refuse. You should give your reasons. You may explain how the very inability to sit to the canter could cause them to become unbalanced and suffer a fall. If they are quite old you must ask them to carefully consider how this might effect them should it happen.

Another thing that you should not overlook is fitness. You may hear an older rider beginning to breathe rather heavily during a trot or canter. They are beginning to have difficulty in coping and may be too proud to ask you to let them have a rest. When you spot this you should, immediately ask them to turn in onto the centreline and have a short break.

As I have said in an earlier chapter, some elderly riders have hearing difficulties. This is frequently compounded by the fact that they will not admit to having a problem. Sometimes they carry on for as long as possible without having to resort to using a hearing aid. In order to do this they try to interpret your commands by guessing what you are saying. This could lead to a possibly risky situation. For example if you ask your class to turn down the centre line at 'C' but one of your pupils does not hear you correctly and thinks that you have said 'B' and turns at the wrong point.

There are two ways in which you can try to reduce the problem. The first is always to try and look, as you speak, at the rider who is hard of hearing . The second is to use the phonetic alphabet such as saying 'turn down the centre line at 'A' for Alpha' and so on. However you must also remember that even when a client has a hearing aid this may not work properly if there is a very loud background sound such as the passing of a tractor.

Chapter 12

Drill rides for intermediate riders.

Splitting into two rides, which proceed on different reins. (But keeping the rides staggered).
Explaining the movement to the class.
This is another excellent exercise for developing riders' attention to detail. As with any movement success entirely depends on *everyone understanding* what it is that they have to do and what part they play in the overall action.

Preparing for the exercise.
I usually do this by numbering in pairs. I then give the class a pre-ride instruction telling them that on my command the 'ones' will go to the right and the 'twos' to the left. If I am dealing with youngsters I ask every other child to 'prove', that is to say all the twos must hold up their *left hands*. This helps young children who may have difficulty in distinguishing between their left and right. You may split the ride at any point you wish but generally the A –C or E – B lines are easiest since the new rides will be balanced relative to each other (see fig 11). You must go on to explain that when splitting into two rides they must be sure to watch the following points.

1   They need to *prepare* the horse or pony for the turn, *in good time*, that is to say several strides before the point where they are going to split up. As they ride say from 'A' and approach 'C' they must start to look in the *direction* that they *wish to go*. The horse must be flexed in the same direction and the riders' leg must be positioned for the turn, i.e. outside leg behind the girth inside leg almost on the girth (both relative to the approaching change of direction). If the *preparation* is correct then the horse will go in the direction desired by the rider. If not? Then the horse will simply follow the one in front. As I tell my classes any rider who allows this to happen is a 'wimp'.

2.   Having split into two rides the next matter requiring attention is to ensure that the *distances are maintained*. Do this by first sending both rides large around the arena so that you may remind them to make any adjustments that are necessary. While they are doing this they *must* pass left hand to left hand. *The correct distance between each horse, in each ride, should now be three horse's lengths,* (some riders may find this difficult to comprehend).

Why?
Because every rider behind the lead file will be *one horses length behind the other*. Thus when every other rider *leaves* to form the 2nd ride *the place that they occupied must remain*, in the first ride. *These distances must be sustained by both rides at all times.* Thus there is room to form one ride again, later on.

As both rides progress around the arena everyone must maintain their correct distance relative to the rider in front and also be sure that they are placed correctly with regard to their opposite number in the other ride. If you have split at either 'A' or 'C' then easy checkpoints are 'E' or 'B'. Thus if the lead file of the first ride passes 'B', then the leader of the second ride must pass 'E' two strides later. The same applies to all the other riders in each ride. The key to success does lie, to some extent with the lead file of the first ride. They must lengthen or shorten the stride in order to accommodate their opposite partner. All the other riders must also do the same thing.

To prove the point, after one or two circuits of the arena, (during which time you make sure that relative positions are correct), you ask both rides to form one ride again, by riding down the centre line, at either 'A' or 'C'. If the distances are correct, riders should become part of a single ride without having to adjust the pace of their horses. In other words if the exercise is performed at a trot no one should have to walk in order to fit in. If you are satisfied then prepare to repeat the exercise again.

Points to watch.
1   You do need to keep on about the *correct distance*. It is surprising how many riders are unable to concentrate on this simple matter for a prolonged period. I watch every rider in turn and bark out commands for correction sharply. Thus 'you are too far behind Amy get a move on and use your legs. Make your horse work for you he is being lazy as a sloth!' or 'You are too close John' and so on.

2   It is also surprising how many lead files forget when it is their turn to pass on the inside track. You must be sure, well in advance that they do so! Further more you must ensure that the ride on the inside leaves sufficient room for the other ride to pass by them.

3   Finally check that all corners are ridden correctly. Having to concentrate on tempo, distance and direction something usually goes by the board and very often it is well-ridden corners.

4   Whenever both rides become one, recheck each riders safe distance from the horse in front, and make sure that they are all correct down the centre line.

As soon as the ride is correct and have joined as one ride, go forward to walk on a long rein and praise *them all warmly*.

Riding a 'Scissors'
This is the movement where the class has been split into two rides during a change from, say, '**E**' to '**B**'. I suggest these two letters since the two rides will be so placed as to be able to execute simple changes of rein across the long diagonals. *Maintenance of correct distances is essential.* As each ride approaches the letter where they would normally ride a change (for their ride), on your command they do so, riding across this long diagonal. As they reach '**X**' each rider passes in front of their opposite number coming from the other direction. (see fig 11(a) stages 1 & 2).

Points to watch.
1   Inevitably in concentrating on their correct distance many riders will loose direction. You must ensure that every change is ridden *from letter to letter*.

2   Having ridden the scissors successfully riders sometimes switch off. This may mean that the ride now due to take the inside track, fails to do so. *You must correct them in good time,* for you do not want to have both rides colliding with one another.

Splitting into two rides in order to ride in pairs.
Many drill exercises may be based on riders riding in pairs or threes and even fours. *I do not recommend these exercises for novice riders,* for *they* will not yet have developed the skill required in maintaining their horses in positions that are safe. There are many other movements that you can ride with novices so why take a chance? Having said that you may well raise a question about the movement already mentioned in chapter 10 and that is turning across the school as a ride 'Surely' I hear you say 'The horses are moving side by side'? They are; but it is not quite the same thing. Turning as ride across the arena does have the horses moving in parallel relative to one another but they still have a *safety distance* between them. Furthermore the duration of the movement is relatively short and everything gets back into order again as soon as they move in single file once more. Riding in pairs, in fact forming a double ride means that the riders are level shoulder to shoulder. Stirrups touch.

Levelling up.
If you intend to ride in pairs, from two rides, you must make sure that the *lead files* of both rides *become level* with one another. Of course as already mentioned group rides in twos may be achieved without the necessity of first splitting into two rides, in that case it is simply a matter of asking each pair numbered one and two to turn in on your command (see chapter 10). You will, however have to pre-set the distances, whereas if the two rides simply become a *double ride* then the distances (three horses' lengths are already programmed into the exercise) (see fig 12).

Exercises based on two rides joining in pairs.
Riding in pairs is excellent practise for making sure that pupils do really *ride* their horses. No deviations should be permitted. Before starting it is as well to make sure that you have arranged your pupils so that you have horses of a similar size meeting up when the rides come together. *Also try and ensure that each horse does get on reasonably well with the proposed partner.* It may well be that you would have no difficulty in insisting on good behaviour from any horse that *you* may ride but the same cannot be said of your pupils who may allow things to get out of hand simply because they become nervous. Having said that you must

make it clear that the safest position to ride with another horse is right up against it. The distance being so close that horses cannot develop the momentum to get in a kick. This means that the pupil can then concentrate on keeping their horses' heads straight so that no biting can take place.

Before you start both rides must be well balanced one against the other. This simply means that you ask each leading file to look across the arena and ensure that they are *level with the lead of the other ride*. The other members should all repeat this check. Choosing a letter say 'E' and 'B' and making sure that each *partner* in the *other ride* is level with them.

You are now ready to start bringing both rides together at a given point. For riders at this level, this is best done at the letter where the ride first split up. You must now tell them beforehand what you expect when they start riding in pairs. It is no use waiting until they are already performing the exercise because, by then, it is too late! I repeat you must make sure that they understand that horses proceeding in pairs are safest when they are close together. So close in fact that the rider's stirrups are making a small tinkling sound as they touch.

Your command.
"As you approach the letter 'A' both rides prepare to turn down each side of the centre line in pairs. Be sure to remain level shoulder to shoulder, stirrup to stirrup". At **'C'** you may then ask for either of the following movements:

1. To turn and proceed on left or the right rein still in pairs but going large as a ride.

2. Alternatively still keeping in pairs have alternate pairs going either to right or left. If you use this option then you should give the command for each of these pairs to turn down the centre line again at **'A'** thus forming ranks of fours. At this stage it is a good idea to have the first rank of four halt across **'G'** with any other ranks halting one horses length behind them. You may then, provided that an altered file will still have horses that are reasonably placed with regard to their getting on with each other, ask all the riders from each rank say of the left file to go forward to be followed by the second file and so on (see fig 13 &14).

3. If you take option 1. Then you should ask the ride to turn down the centre line at **'A'** and when they reach **'C'** again to split into single rides going on left and right rein when they will now *adjust their distances* so that each *ride is staggered* again and they may then form one ride as they finally turn down the centre line again at **'C'**.

The combinations are numerous and the degree of complication depends entirely on the ability of the riders and your skill and quick thinking as instructor.

What do you watch out for?
1   Obviously these are exercises that depend on riders keeping their positions relative to one another.
2   They are movements that need constant attention to maintenance of tempo.
3   The ride must ensure that they utilise the whole area available to them. This means that corners must still be ridden correctly.
4   When going large around the arena in pairs adequate provision must be made by the inside riders (relative to the movement) to allow room for those on the outside.

Riding circles as two rides.
The cogwheel.
For this exercise both rides *remain staggered*. Thus this is an excellent movement to use where you may be doubtful as to the sociability of some of the horses in the ride.
Having numbered in twos split into two rides say from **'B'** to **'E'**. Both rides go large. Immediately they reach **'A'** and **'C'** respectively instruct them both to ride 20 metre circles. Each rider remains on their own circle and passes through **'X'**. This will mean that, ridden correctly, at this point, each rider will be the correct distance behind a rider from the other ride for, *one stride only,* at **'X'**, after which they continue again on their own circle. (See fig 15 & 15a).

Your command.

"Both rides *prepare* to ride a circle of 20 metres, at '**A**' and '**C**' respectively *keep your distances*. Make sure that you *ride through 'X'*. Stay on your own circle".

What do you do now?

You are the judge of the situation. It is usual to ride the exercise until most of the riders are riding their circles correctly. When you are satisfied you may give the next command.

Your command.

'Starting with the lead files, *prepare* for the next time you pass through '**X**' to form one ride proceeding in a straight line to '**E**' then going large on the left rein. (See fig. 16). Of course this is only one way of proceeding. You may command: - At '**X**'

'Form one ride and proceed in a **half** circle to '**A**' or '**C**', then going large'. (See fig. 17)

'Form one ride and ride **a complete circle of half the arena**, then going large at '**A**' or '**C**'. (See fig. 18)

'Form one ride and ride a circle of half the arena. When you have ridden one complete circle, at '**X**' split into two rides once again. Numbers one on the left rein, twos on the right rein and so on ad infinitum. (See fig. 19)

Developing the idea further.

1   Once you are quite sure that everyone is confident about what they are supposed to be doing, you may then introduce the idea of changing the rein (i.e. their circle) through '**X**'. This means that every rider must prepare to change the direction in which they looking (turning from the torso), the bend of their horses' heads and also their own relative leg positions, at least *one stride before* they pass through '**X**'. After they have passed through '**X**' and changed the rein, both rides are now riding circles at opposite ends of the arena to that which they were riding before.

2   Having established both rides on their new circles for a circuit or two you may now instruct them to change back to the original circles. (See fig. 20)

3   Just to keep matters bubbling along nicely and only if you are happy about the way things are proceeding, you may command the class to change the circle every time that they pass through '**X**' (see fig. 21).

What do you need to watch out for?

1   Make sure that everyone is clear as to your commands.
2   Obviously you must *make sure* that *distances are correct*. This means that whatever the gait, the tempo must remain constant.
3   Make certain that riders do not allow their horses to 'fall in'.
4   Watch for true circles and not straight lines, especially when there is a change of rein (the moment you mention a change many people lose concentration and revert to a simple change through the diagonal).

Riding circles meeting at 'X' in pairs.

If you are confident that all your riders are in control and that all your horses are reasonably sociable, you may allow both rides to *level out*. This will mean that when they separate and ride two independent circles each of the two riders will come *together* at '**X**'. The stirrups should actually touch. This will now open a whole new series of movements, for you may now instruct the class to proceed as a *double ride* going in any way that you choose (See figs. 22).

Two rides changing the rein through their own circle but maintaining position with a partner in each ride.

This is an exercise *suitable for even numbers* of riders. The optimum number is really eight riders but it can be performed with as few as two and up to a maximum of say ten (5 in each ride). Again it all depends on the size of the arena that is available to you. If you have a really large class (say 12 riders) and an arena to match, then there is no reason why you should not create three circles!

188

For the sake of an example let us assume that you have eight pupils in your class. You ask them to number in twos and then to split into two rides riding say from **'E'** to **'B'**. You instruct each ride to keep their correct distances, and to ride a circle of half the arena (or a 20 metre circle) starting at **'A'** and **'C'**. You now ask each lead file to position themselves level with their counter-part in the opposite ride. The easiest way of doing this is as they pass either side of **'X'**. All the other riders must do likewise. When they are all organised, (that is forming a pair momentarily at X) you now give the command for every rider, when they reach the correct point, to change the rein through their circle. (see fig. 23). (Of course they do this in single file). Now it follows that if you have too many riders in each circle then there will be no space available for those having changed to proceed on the new rein. (see fig 24).Well of course *it is possible* if those who have changed pass inside those still going the other way but it is going to be jolly untidy.

What does the rider have to think about?
Quite a lot actually.

1   All riders must keep riding a correct circle until the time arrives for them to change.
2   They must be sure that they are also correct with regard to their partner in the opposite ride.
3   When they do ride the change they must be sure that each half circle is accurate and that they
         maintain impulsion so that they do not loose the *relative* position with their partner.

This is an exercise that gives great pleasure to riders, for it is not full of rushing fury, and it may be equally ridden at a walk or a trot. It also demands complete concentration.

Elegant ways of restoring a double ride to a single ride.
Having made sure that the ride is staggered. Instead of having the rides simply form one ride down the centre line as the two rides come together, you may ask your two rides to return to single file in the following manner:
1   Let us assume that both leading files *pass one another* in opposite directions at **'A'**. Ride No. 2 is on
         the right rein and ride no. 1 on the left. According to the rule left hand to left hand, ride No. 2
         should be on the inside track. Command 'Ride No. 2 to change the rein across the diagonal **'K'** to
         'M''. Due to the fact that ride No. 2 Is on the *inside track* then the fact that the distance **'A' 'K'**
         'M' is slightly longer than **'A' 'F' 'B' 'M'** will become insignificant. Provided that all riders
         maintain the *three horses length* distance then at the letter **'M'** ride No. 2 will slot into the
         available spaces in ride No. 1 (see fig. 25)
2   The change may be ridden in a similar manner if both rides *pass one another* at **'B'**. In this case the
         respective positions of each ride in the arena mean that the distances involved will result in ride
         No. 2 joining the track **behind** ride No. 1. (see fig. 26 1st & 2nd stages)
3   The change to one ride may also be initiated when *both rides* are going large *in pairs*. In this scenario
         we will imagine that ride *No. 1. is the outside ride* with both rides going large on the left rein. As
         they pass **'A'** you give the command 'Inside ride *No 2 only* change the rein **'F'** to **'H'** on
         completion both rides continue to go large'. This is followed by the next command 'Both rides
         keep your distances'. ' Ride No. 2. change the rein again **'M'** to **'K''** Ride No. 2 is now able to
         slot into the spaces between the riders in ride No. 1. (see fig. 27 1st & 2nd stages).

Riding a continuous change of rein from trot to canter.
This is not, strictly speaking, a drill ride. However it is an exercise, that while not being one for which you need to create a 'macro' command. It is, none-the-less one in which the class, having been started off by you, continues on their way by themselves until the whole class has ridden the movement.
    As the title suggests the class ride around the arena at the trot. Whenever a leading file arrives at a point where they would naturally ride a change, they do so. The rest of the ride follows. When the lead file reaches 'X' they *alone* go forward to canter, along the diagonal and continue going large all the way around the arena. The new leading file takes the ride around to the next, logical, point for a change and again as they approach 'X' they proceed at canter in the same manner as the first rider and so on until the whole ride has performed the exercise. The question that is so often asked is, how do I know that the rider who has

cantered away from the ride will not get lost somewhere around the arena or else come crashing into the ride as it changes to the new rein? The answer is that, provided the rider cantering large does so at a reasonable pace then, due to the geometric distances involved, they will be in the right position to join the rear of the ride without having to cut in or radically change direction. If the cantering rider does have a problem for example, the horse breaks canter, then they may not be sufficiently advanced as the ride which having changed the rein across the arena approaches their track. In which case the ride simply take the inside track (see fig. 28 1st & 2nd stages).

What use is this for the rider?
There are several advantages to this exercise. I will list them below: -

1. The lead file, as they go forward to canter, asks the horse to leave the ride. It may be reluctant to do so but the rider has to learn to be the dominant partner. Further more the rider must ensure the correct leading leg.

2. The actual direction teaches the rider to ride accurately from letter to letter whilst still on the diagonal.

3. The new lead file has to restrain their horse if it shows any indication that it wishes to follow. They also must ride on the same diagonal track to the letter in front of them.

4. Every lead rider has to be sure to prepare for the canter as they reach '**X**'.

5. This is an exercise about constant and regular tempo. Each subsequent lead file must maintain a regular trot neither faster nor slower.

6. You are handing over the initiative for the exercise to the class. For once you have set the exercise in motion you need say nothing more until it is over. They have to 'remain' awake and be sure to make the change of rein at the correct time.

7. Finally – It's great fun!

What do you watch out for?
1. Obviously the first thing is to make sure that the pupils give the correct aids to canter at the proper time.
2. Once the lead file has initiated a good canter depart you must make sure that they continue to ride towards the correct letter. What sometimes happens is that pupils are so relieved at getting their horse to canter that they no longer concentrate on where they should be going. The usual thing is that they allow the horse to fall-in and fail to ride their corners correctly.
3. The same problem may occur with the new leading file, who suffering the shock of finding themselves at the front with the figure still to be ridden, forget where they are supposed to go. Frequently they miss the next correct change.

Finally.
If you turn to the addendum diagram (1.2 stages 1 & 2). You will see a combination of movements such as turn on the forehand utilised with an open order movement. Very useful when working in a restricted area.

Diagrams.

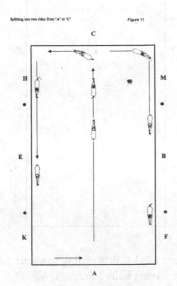

Figure no. 11. Splitting into two rides from A to C.

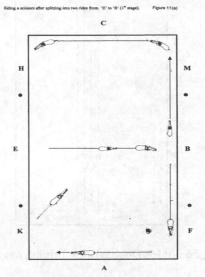

Figure no. 11a. Riding a scissors (1st stage).

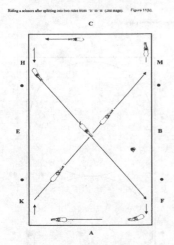

Figure 11b. Riding a scissors (2nd stage).

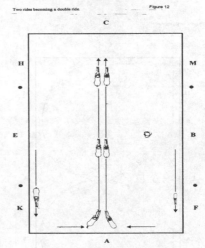

Figure no. 12. Two rides becoming a double ride.

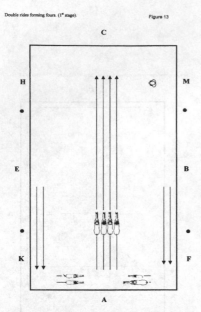

Figure no. 13. Double rides forming fours and halting.

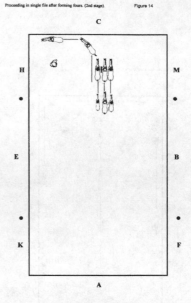

Figure no. 14. Proceeding in single file after having halted in fours.

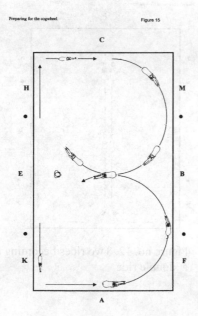

Figure no. 15. Preparing for the cogwheel.

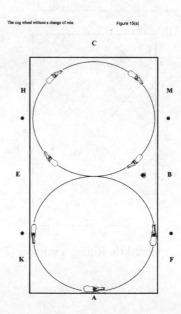

Figure 15a. The cogwheel without a change of rein.

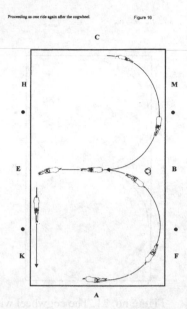

Figure no. 16. Proceeding as one ride again,
after the cogwheel.

Figure 17.

Two rides having, each, been commanded to ride a quarter circle to 'X' where they form one ride and proceed on a half circle, left rein, to 'A' before going large.

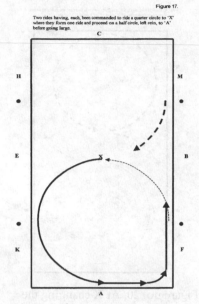

Figure no. 17. Proceeding as one ride
for half a circle.

Figure 18.

Riders on two circles proceeding as one ride at 'X' and then riding a half circle going large at 'A'.

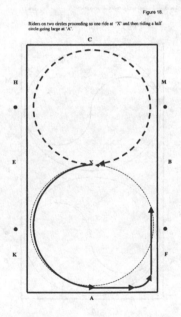

Figure no. 18. At X proceeding as one
ride for a complete circle, and then going large.

Figure 19.

Proceeding as one ride on a circle and then, at 'X', splitting into two rides again.

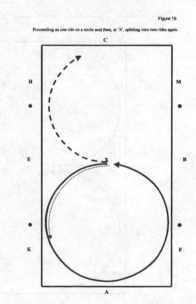

Figure no. 19. Proceeding as one ride
for a complete circle then,
at X splitting again.

193

Figure 20.

At 'X' each ride changing the rein from the circle that they are riding to a circle at
the other end of the arena. (they must all left hand to left hand).

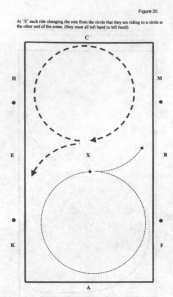

Figure no. 20. At X changing the
rein and riding circles at the other
end of the arena.

The cog wheel with a change of rein.   Figure 21

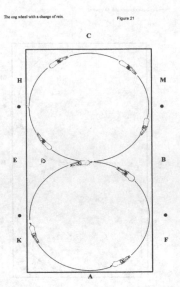

Figure no. 21. The cogwheel with
a change of rein.

Figure 22

Forming a double ride at X.   Ride No. 1 ———— Ride No. 2 ————

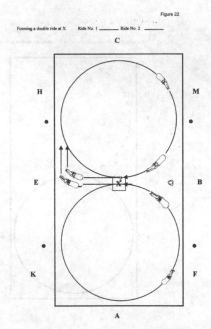

Figure no. 22. Forming a double ride at X.

Two rides changing the rein through their own circles as a drill.   Figure 23

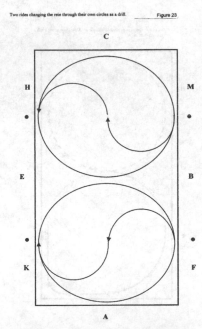

Figure no. 23. Two rides changing
the rein through circles as a drill

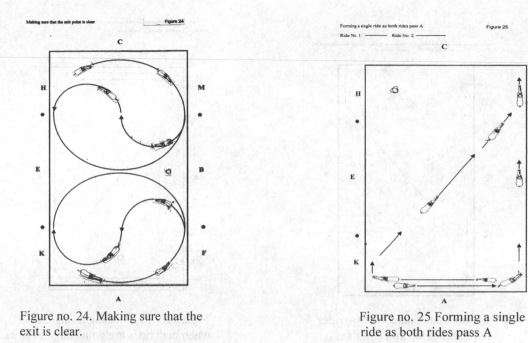

Figure no. 24. Making sure that the exit is clear.

Figure no. 25 Forming a single ride as both rides pass A

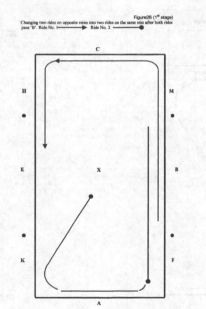

Figure no. 26. Changing two rides as both rides pass A on opposites reins into two rides on the same rein, as both rides pass B (1st stage).

195

Figure26 (a) (2nd stage)

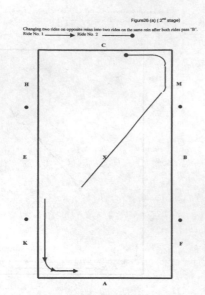

Changing two rides on opposite reins into two rides on the same rein after both rides pass 'B'.
Ride No. 1 ——— Ride No. 2 ———

Figure no. 26a. Changing two rides
on opposites reins into two rides on
the same rein, as both rides pass B (2nd stage).

Forming a single ride when both rides are going large in pairs (1st Stage). Figure 27
Ride No. 1. ——— Ride No. 2 ———

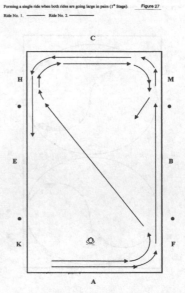

Figure no. 27. Forming a single ride
when both rides are going large in pairs.
(1st stage).

Forming a single ride when both rides are going large in pairs (2nd Stage). Figure 27 Ca.
Ride No. 1. ——— Ride No. 2 ——— Single file ———

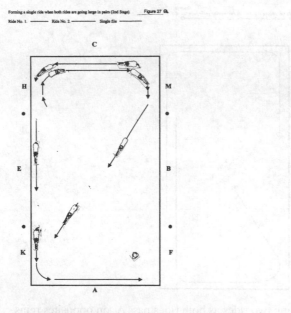

Figure no. 27a. Forming a single ride
when both rides are going large in pairs
(2nd stage).

Figure 28(a).
Continuous change of rein with each successive leading file only going forward to canter at X (1st stage).

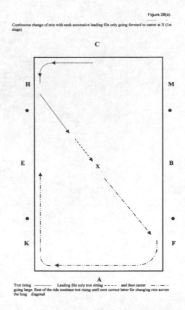

Trot rising ——— Leading file only trot sitting – – – – and then canter — · — · —
going large. Rest of the ride continue trot rising until next correct letter for changing rein across
the long diagonal

Figure 28a. The continuous change
of rein from trot to canter (1st stage).

Figure 28(b).

Continuous change of rein with each successive leading file only cantering at X (2nd stage).

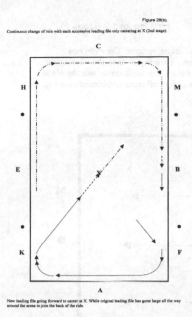

New leading file going forward to canter at X. While original leading file has gone large all the way around the arena to join the back of the ride.

Figure 28b. The continuous change of rein from trot to canter (2nd stage).

Figure 1.2 (stage 1).

Addendum
Advancing every other rider two horses lengths so that the ride is in open order format thus providing extra room for performing 'turns about' from the halt or even dismounting in a small arena. The odd nos. _ _ _ ► remain at halt. The even nos. ——► take several steps forward and halt in line. The whole ride turning 180 degrees about the forehand looks very effective.

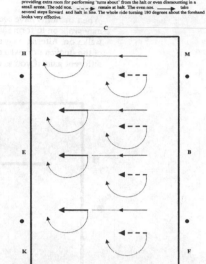

Figure no. 1.2a. Advancing every other rider so that the ride is in open order format and then developing into a drill ride with turns about the forehand (1ˢᵗ stage).

Figure 1.2 (stage 2).

Addendum

When the turns have been completed you then have multiple options. The even nos. may walk on to form a line with the uneven nos. When all are in line then the whole ride walks on. Alternatively as the turns are completed the even nos. walk on to take the place of the uneven nos. who also walk on. You may create many different combinations using different gaits if you so wish.

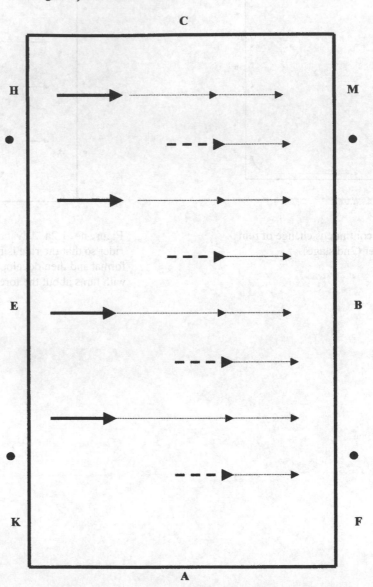

Figure no. 1.2b. Developing the drill ride further.

Chapter 13

Aids for advanced movements.

I originally entitled this chapter 'Advanced Aids'. Then I stopped to think, what exactly did this mean? The simple truth is that aids are aids and there is no difference between those that I have previously referred to as 'Basic' and those that are supposed to be something more.

I will ask the reader to forgive me for boring repetition. 'There is no added complexity in the aids required for advanced movements, only an *ongoing refinement* of their application.' I can do no better than repeat my précis of Wynmalen as quoted in chapter six.

He said (more or less): -

1. To detect the lightest possible aid to which the horse will respond. Upon the discovery of this lightest possible aid, to continue and try to obtain a response that is lighter still!

2. The positioning of the horse correctly so that it may respond to the aid without difficulty.

3. The correct timing of the application of an aid. So that the horse may respond immediately.

4. A quick reflex that will anticipate the horse and not the other way round.

5. The rider must not only anticipate when the horse is about to take the initiative but also **appreciate when the horse is *about* to obey so that the aid will cease.**

Finally a rider who clearly understands that there must be 'thinking and reaction time' between the application of each aid. In other words the seat creating a pressure, the fingers closing to regulate the movement, *followed* by the calf closing, a fractional pause to allow the horse to think about whatever has been asked of it *before* the fingers open again.

Still repeating the basics but also refining them.

Even though, at this stage, one may be thinking more in terms of lateral work, the basic exercises such as transitions from walk to trot to halt and so forth continue. However one is now looking for a greater degree of finesse. One may start with transitions that allow, in the beginning, for several steps at each gait, but as the session continues so the number of steps quickly diminish between each change. The riders must now reach a stage where, for example, only one stride is permitted at walk before trot continues and that stride should appear to be almost a fleeting momentary movement and nothing more! Not only that but the rider's aids should be almost invisible. The horse in turn responds to these touches that become lighter and lighter still, leading on to such a complete union that the horse is trying to divine the riders thoughts without actually anticipating them.

Caution as one continues!

After having made so much about the average school horse knowing his job, what I am about to say now may seem to be rather at odds with what I have said previously. None-the-less when embarking movements that are physically more difficult for the horses *you do need to remember that these horses may not have been asked to do this sort of work for some time*. I have already mentioned that some animals may not have the conformation that easily facilitates advanced lateral work and, if this is the case I do not think that they should be asked to do so. For others it is worthwhile remembering that even though you may be using animals that *are* used to advanced work, your *approach* may be unfamiliar to them.

Let me give you a very simple example. You ask the class to perform an exercise that requires them to ride transitions from letter to letter. You tell them that they must have *ceased* the aid, say for a downward transition, a fraction of a second before the horse obeys. Does this work immediately? Probably not, because the horses have become so used to being pulled back into downward transitions that they might not, at first, understand what the rider is asking. However provided the temptation to pull is eliminated and the aid is backed up with the voice, after one or two attempts the horses will understand and the transitions will be produced correctly.

Here is a slightly more involved example. Let us suppose that you are giving a lesson and the introductory exercises are shoulder-in? Down a long side of the arena this does not pose a problem for any of the horses in your charge. You then ask your class to continue with the shoulder-in through the corner. Now it is possible (not very likely I admit but for the sake of this discussion possible) that these horses have not been asked for this movement for a *very* long time. What are you going to do about it? The answer is to *proceed slowly*. By that I mean that you tell your pupils to enter upon the exercise giving the horses ample time to think about what is being asked of them. Slow and perfect steps are far better than fast and incorrect ones. You should apply this maxim to any work that you do. In this way you will not encourage a state of affairs where the horses, more through confusion than for any other reason, reach a point where they become determined not to co-operate.

To continue.

I still have a slight dilemma for in the following paragraphs there are occasions where I have not only described the aids but have also followed these up with some exercises that will help you to put across your instruction. On reflection it does occur to me that these more properly belong to Chapter 15 'Exercises to form a lesson' but I have left them where they are since, having gone into detail, they do seem to follow on logically and it also avoids the nuisance of your having to flip forward to find out more.

Getting a horse to go 'On the Bit'
The definition.

A horse may be said to be 'going correctly on the bit' when it has self-carriage, it is going *forward from behind lightly into the rider's hand*. The head is bent at the poll. This means that in the correct position the nose will be only *just in front* of a vertical line running from its poll to the ground, (see photo no. 30) a greater angle and it will be considered to be behind the bit).

I must say that I hesitated for a while before deciding whether to place this section in Basic Aids or Advanced Aids. As you will note I finally decided on the latter, and have done so because it is my belief that it is quite counter productive to ask any rider to start giving the delicate signals required without having first developed a completely independent seat and hands that remain still.

Before that, however, it is absolutely *essential* that the rider learn to ask the *horse to go forward willingly and with energy in front of the rider's legs*. This applies to whatever gait is being ridden be it walk, trot or canter and the only way that this can be achieved is by asking for transitions from one gait to another with ever lighter aids.

This is probably one of the most difficult things for *you* to teach a casual rider successfully. It not only depends on getting them to *have the horse respond without resorting to force* but having done so to then develop the fine play of the rider's fingers, (which are effectual only with the use of the back, seat and leg). These, in turn, are not so much asking for bend at the poll as for a **transfer of weight from forehand to hindquarters.** In other words the raising of the neck and subsequent lowering of the jaw assist in this.

And all of this is entirely dependent on you getting to pupils to change their *attitude* towards the horse. When working with a well-schooled horse, it is almost always the *lack of understanding* that causes so many riders great difficulty in getting horses to oblige them. Another problem is that of apathy. Riders are, after all, able to ride throughout their lives without ever once having to bother to learn such a fine art.

The horse part.

One problem lies in the fact that there may be a lack of recognition on the part of the rider as to what exactly the horse is doing as they apply the aids. Many riders think only of using the hands. Their idea - and it is acquiesced to by many instructors - is that one simply tugs on the reins with sufficient force until the horse, seeking a relief from the discomfiture tries more or less to do what it is asked.

However the horse has *not* been asked to *engage its hindquarters*, from which all-else flows. In practise all that happens is that it goes around the arena *bending its neck* and dropping its head until its chin is about three feet off the ground. Round and round the arena go the pupils with arms stuck out straight, hands fixed under the erroneous impression that they have the horse going 'on the bit'. The truth is that the horse is 'behind the bit' and becomes hollow in its back. Alternatively, if its nose is pushed forward, it may be simply leaning on the bit and using the riders fixed hands for support.

The problem may be exacerbated due to the fact that the horse is trying to work with a rider who is not

200

sitting on their seat but *on the fork*. This has *encouraged* the *horse to go on its forehand* and it may be taken by surprise as the rider, upon the command from the instructor, suddenly asks for the reverse of this. 'What' says the horse to himself after all that has proceeded during the earlier part of the lesson 'is this person really serious? He feels no pressure from the rider's back but merely experiences a sharp tug on the reins, and is therefore confused as to what is required. Who can blame him?

The rider part.
Going on the bit is more than simply getting the horse to bend at the poll; for though the essence of compliance really lies in the delicate hands of the rider, *the prime consideration in this matter is a good seat.* This is the foundation. Without it the rider has extreme difficulty in simply keeping their hands still. It will have helped if the correct use of the hand has constantly been a focal point from the start of the pupils riding career. The likelihood for the development of bad habits, such as cast iron hands, may have been avoided. However to return to the matter of the seat. *Without this there is no impulsion and thus collection, without these two there can be no true flexion.*

The rider must also be taught to develop the manual dexterity that will, ultimately, help them to get their horses to oblige by bending at the poll and relaxing the jaw - going 'on the bit'. Some riders simply may never the have ability to develop the finesse required for this type of work. But you must try at least to ensure that they *don't* fix their hands. My view tends towards introducing the rider to working the horse on the bit, only when the rider has learned to sit and knows that *engagement behind and impulsion, precedes* flexion. For we are now talking about a state of affairs where the hand *through the rein* assumes a much greater importance.

One of the greatest difficulties for many weekend riders is to develop the sensitivity in their fingers. I am referring to the rider who rides the hardworking general school horse, who is quite capable of going on the bit, but who, unless *asked correctly*, will not do so. The reason for this is that being seldom asked for this outline, the horse *tends to think that it is some sort of aberration on the part of the rider.*

One may make the comparison. You want to help someone try to find middle 'C' on the piano, while they are blindfolded. You may well place their finger on the note, but if you then ask them to do this by themselves, they will, probably, be unable to do so correctly. Thus it is with many riders. In the first place they may have ridden for years but have *never* even *thought* about asking their horses to go on the bit. When they do ask, they are surprised that they are not obeyed. You may try helping them by going up to the horse and applying the aid to which the horse will oblige – for you -, as soon as you turn away the outline is lost. I do this quite often; walking up to the horse and very simply only using my forefinger and thumb to hold the rein, produce the required result within seconds and not only that but, much to the riders chagrin, I will release my touch for a second or two and the horse will still maintain the outline.

In this category I am even including 'advanced' riders sitting upon high school horses. Well-schooled horses are accustomed to the signal asking for outline, even though it may be given in an incorrect or desultory manner. *They will oblige, at first,* in the full expectation that the 'thank you', the yielding of the rider's fingers will follow. They will, very often, continue to hold the position for short period of time, after which, unyielding hands cause such discomfort that, they then throw their heads about in irritation or even put in a buck.

The problem for so many riders is that they *forget* that *the horse must be ridden for 60 seconds in very minute!* By that I mean that you explain to our pupils how the fingers must play with the rein as they ask for outline. This the horse duly gives them. Having achieved this satisfactory state of affairs they then *stop thinking*, switch off and allow their hands to become fixed. They forget that the fingers must *continually* be passing little messages or simply achieving a neutral effect. After a few minutes the horse starts to throw its head about and become stiff throughout it's body, and the rider wonders why? 'What on earth can be wrong with this horse' they say to themselves forgetting that their cast iron grip is now causing the horse much discomfort.

Putting theory into practise.
Now the first thing that we have to remember is that a horse will not be able to oblige unless its musculature and flowing from this, its balance, have been developed to a point where it is *able* to carry itself in an outline. In other words it is able to engage its hindquarters sufficiently deeply to produce real power and remain in balance at the same time. What we are talking about here is, *good posture* but in horse terms

rather than human. Instead of slouching about or strung out like a beanpole as we say, the horse is being asked to carry himself 'tall'. Provided that the rider has asked for and **obtained** the **impulsion,** then there should be little difficulty in asking the horse to bend at the poll and yield its jaw. The message from the rider to the horse must first be sent via the rider's **seat and legs**. The seat and legs *stimulate,* followed by the hand that produces a very short and slight vibration on the inside rein that then asks for the resultant energy to be used to produce good deportment. I have seen many riders using their fingers, opening them and closing them to no avail. The reason is that the **aid has no form**. If it is to be at all effective, then, **it must deliver a message.** In this particular case it is a vibration that takes the form of a series of short but clear pulses a 'ddddit' as it were. The fingers open and close with increasing rapidity but ever ready to cease; for the **hand must give the very moment the horse is about to obey**. For what we are talking about here, as with so much in equitation, is the rider's **speed of reaction**. In this context it is more important than in any other. What most riders do not understand is that there must be a **reward as soon as the horse obeys.** In this case it consists of **ceasing the aid**. It means that the vibration on the rein stops and the fingers open and close in neutral time with the horses' movement. For it should not be forgotten that any feel on the rein and hence pressure on the bit must cause the horse some slight discomfiture. It also follows that any ceasing of the application of an aid brings about relief. This is what schooling is all about. The horse has been taught that disobedience brings about a feeling of discomfiture – obedience brings relief. The more expert the rider the shorter the *duration* of the aid. In fact I would go further. At this stage the rider should be able to produce aids that are so gentle and yet persuasive that, if I may be permitted to allude to a romantic analogy, they are as soft as a lovers gentle caress.

A further explanation of the rein vibration.

Some pupils may have extreme difficulty in understanding what is meant by fast vibration. As I have said before it can only arise from the fingers (a rowing motion with the arms may prevent the rider from continuously pulling on the bit but there is no way that the arms can move fast enough to produce vibrations of sufficient hertz, if you like, to have meaning for the horse. Yes hertz is what I have just said for I am now trying to use an analogy about the different speeds of computer chips which, perhaps, will help some riders to understand. Thus a computer that is using a chip of only 200 MHz. will not properly run a sophisticated program that requires a chip of say a 1000 MHz. The images are processed so slowly that everything is practically unintelligible.

The demonstration.

I really cannot, sufficiently, stress the point about the giving hand. Sometimes, when the pupil has a real problem, I get on the poor horse myself. As soon as I mount it immediately comes to attention. It senses my seat sitting deeply in the saddle and feels my motionless balance. It knows who I am. Its ears flick back ever so slightly; it is listening; I pick up the rein. It might even become a little apprehensive; I touch its neck in order to show that it has nothing to fear. I brace my back muscles and give the most gentle of vibrations down the rein. **The horse responds at once. My hand gives at once.** I wait with relaxed fingers for *that very second*, if indeed it is going to occur, where the horse, having given, may now decide to try and take the initiative by coming off the bit. If the resistance does occur my fingers **instantaneously close** again, resisting. I talk to the horse telling it that it is a good boy (or girl). I may actually let go one rein as I touch the neck and gently caress with my fingers. *I am letting the horse know that it has, correctly, done my bidding and that I am pleased with it!* There follows a gentle stasis where my fingers take and give in a gentle vibrato and the horse starts to mouth the bit. Usually there is no resistance and I show my confidence by dropping, both reins completely for a few seconds. The horse still maintains the outline. The pupils are staggered!!!

A Question that a pupil may ask.

An intelligent rider with an inquiring mind may well ask you exactly what is the sequence of the vibrations? Do they have a fixed form? What they are saying to you is 'can I learn by rote the sequence and in that manner become a good rider?' You may well reply that there is no exact sequence and that you do it by 'feel'. This is not strictly true, for though there is an element of 'feel' it is not without form. The whole thing is dependent on the horse being ridden. If I get up on a pupil's horse that has been leaning on the bit throughout the whole lesson, I must first collect it using my back and leg – bring it to attention as it were. Then I apply the aid to indicate my desire. I will start with a gentle signal, which is usually enough but if the horse does not listen, I will *immediately* repeat the signal more sharply. (Your pupils should not confuse the strength of an aid with its duration.) After two or three short but sharp vibrations down the rein the horse yields its jaw. I immediately cease the aids and open my fingers. I am waiting for the horse to react. A horse that has been leaning on the bit all through the lesson will, having submitted this once, try to go back to its original position. Before it can do so, I sense what is to come and immediately close my fingers thus restraining it until I feel it submit once again. I do not wait to find out if the horse has submitted because I anticipate that it will, thus the reward for obedience is already being given. Thus to the onlooker it appears that my fingers are continually playing with the rein in an apparently random manner. In fact it is an intricate interplay between the horse and myself. The result is that the horse is placed continuously on the bit. The essence is all to do with timing. If I do not anticipate a counter move quickly enough then the head is already proceeding skywards and if it gains momentum, before I can react I will have more difficulty in restoring the status quo. Horses being creatures of habit will be inclined to start resisting, once again, after a given number of strides thus, if the rider counts the strides to the point where this may occur, then, if they re-apply the aid in the stride *before* this point they will, probably, be more successful .

Exercises that may help.
Sometimes it may help if a rider, on entering a corner, stretches out their inside arm and having raised it about 12 inches in the air, turns the hand outward so that the fingernails are on top and then opens and closes the fingers rapidly. This will serve to bring the bit into the more sensitive corners of the horse's mouth. On exiting the corner the hand is lowered. Carried out correctly the horse lowers its head going forward nicely on the bit, provided that the riders remembers, immediately, to give with the hand!

I say that this may be done with little difficulty but perhaps that is a bit casual. For even though the horse *may be able* to carry out the riders' request, it may not *choose* to do so, no matter that the aid given is tactful and authoritative. This may be especially the case if a horse is not often asked for flexions of this sort. Sometimes the refusal is due to the fact that the rider has already asked for the outline for too long a period without rest. If this is the case then, the fault lies with you – the instructor!

Sometimes it pays to stop asking.
There are times when even a quite competent rider, has great difficulty in getting their horse to oblige.
I have discussed above many of the reasons why this might happen. However just as with human beings, a horse may shrink from doing something that has caused it much pain in the past. Thus it will resist an action that it already *believes* is going to be difficult.

The answer to all of this is to ask the rider to halt in front of you and cease to ask! Have them ask the horse to stand attention but quite motionless while they still maintain a good but light contact. You now start to talk to them about an entirely unrelated matter. Within 20 to thirty seconds you will observe the horse starting to play with the bit and producing copious quantities of saliva. Quite suddenly and apparently unasked, it yields its jaw. There it is standing to attention with a perfect outline. Quietly draw the riders' attention to this and then ask them to play with the rein being sure that as soon as the horse shows any inclination to raise its head their fingers take and as soon as the horse yields their fingers must give. Thus they begin to develop "feel" and seldom have any further difficulty.

The importance of warming up.
Occasionally another factor may influence the horses' going. That is that its muscles may simply be rather stiff. Reiner Klimke mentions in one of his excellent videotapes on training a horse for dressage, that he always allows his horses a nice *steady* canter *before* entering the arena. 'After all' he says 'This horse has been standing for 23 1/2 hours, surely it is only reasonable to allow it to have a stretch before work commences'. Accordingly he has his trainers start by taking the horse onto a prepared gallop and giving them a short period of free canter.

My dear friend Julian Marczak, the chief examiner for the ABRS. (Julian is also proprietor, with his mother of Suzanne's Riding School with over 300 acres of open farmland to ride over) mentioned something similar to me the other day. He was riding a chestnut and told me that, complaints had been made, by instructors, about the horses' refusal to flex at all. He had had a similar problem with a pupil who rode the horse in his class. 'However', he said 'after I had hacked it quietly about the farm, on return to the arena, the horse behaved impeccably.

Now few of us freelance types have either the time or the facilities to work a horse in this manner but this does not mean that, with a little forethought, we should not allow our horses to 'limber up' in a similar way. 'But haven't you have already mentioned allowing time to work in?' I hear you query. Quite so, but I am now suggesting that there may be those occasions where it is of benefit to construct your exercises in a manner that allows for a more *prolonged* period of warming up, for those horses that require it. In the confines of the arena, I am certainly not going to suggest that you start with a short period of canter. We are not, after all, dealing with professional riders who ride day in day out, week after week and month after month. Our pupils are generally once-a-week riders with perhaps a few extra sessions during their holidays. A canter exercise at the beginning of the lesson with fresh horses could lead to a quite alarming state of affairs. However there is no reason why one should not allow a *prolonged* period of working trot, this accompanied by frequent changes of rein. This will help to keep pupils interested and will also help to create a better framework for the more demanding work that is to follow.

The Surrender of the hands (La descent de Main).

When your pupils do have their horses going forward with a nice rounded outline and are able to do so without nagging the horse every stride, then the time has come, for a brief period, to tell the horse that they are satisfied. Thus, for a few moments, they are going to release him from the bondage of hand and leg. This is known as 'La descent de main'. The complete cessation of any tension on the reins. If you and your pupils have done their work well, then, when this happens the horses will continue to proceed for as many strides as the rider wishes (within reason) *without anything changing.*

A question that a rider may ask.

Do I ask for flexion and bend at the poll only with the inside rein?

Answer.

Now there may be other instructors, trainers and so forth who have their own quite distinct views as to what is correct and what is not. I have always made it quite clear that, as far as I am concerned, in relation to the giving of signals to a horse, the aids are based on convention: a matter of custom and practise. For me, technically speaking, the inside rein is for bend and yield, the outside rein to signal intention and to regulate. However when dealing with relative novices to the art of collection, I do not mind too much if the rider gives the vibrations through both reins simultaneously, provided that this does *not descend into a sawing action.* They must also be watched to ensure that they do not forget that back and seat precede the action of the hands.

Specific aids (these are my preferred aids. Others may have ideas of their own).

The walk initiated from a desired leg.

I am sure that there are some amongst you who are already wondering about this matter (or are there?). Anyway if there are not, then you jolly well should be. For at this level one should be reaching the point where one considers matters of this nature. The manner of obtaining this is quite simple. The horse, trained correctly, will move his hind leg as soon as it feels the rider's leg touch its body on the same side. Whereas you may not have bothered too much about the manner in which your pupils have given leg aids for the walk in the past, you must now be very particular that the horse is touched with the rider's leg on the desired side a second before the other leg acts. (For precision of this sort it does help for the rider to have the horse engaged with a degree of collection from the start).

Initiating a trot on a desired pair of diagonals from the walk.

As we have discussed, the successful application of an aid depends upon its timing. In this case we have to remind ourselves as to what, exactly is happening during the walk. We know that the horse steps forward from a hind leg, (let us assume that this is the near side) this is followed by the lateral foreleg, (support on two legs on the same side). Before he can fall over he has already activated the opposite hind leg (support on three legs). A fraction of a second later the initial strike off leg (the near hind) is already on its way backwards and coming off the ground. The support is now once again reduced to two legs but now instead of lateral support we have *diagonal support* (near fore and off hind). However the off fore leg is already on its way to give three legged support once again and almost at once the near fore has passed on its way thus leaving only the off hind and off fore (two lateral legs on the other side) in support. And so on and on.

If for example one wished to initiate a trot with *off fore and near hind* then the leg aid (both the rider's legs together) would need to be given as the *diagonal support* (near fore and off hind) at the walk was taking *place*. This will give the horse *'thinking time'* in order to realise that the four time is to change to two time (see drawing no. 27) and the next occasion for the diagonal support will now be trot.

Why?

Well really it is quite obvious. Since the walk is essentially a lateral movement, if one requires a trot initiated on a particular diagonal, then one must choose that very moment when a diagonal element of the walk is about to come into play. However one should not expect that diagonal (in the walk) to be acted upon instantly, because a trot has an element of suspension every stride and the horse does need thinking time.

Who is the wise guy shouting out 'I thought you said that the walk was a lateral movement and now you are talking about a diagonal?' Well said that person but do not become confused. The legs do *move* laterally and the diagonal is only a fleeting element of the movement acting as a connection between the lateral movements on either side.

Initiating a trot from halt with a particular diagonal strike off

The first thing to bear in mind is that it is unreasonable to ask a horse to proceed from halt to trot without first having him collected. This will ensure that he is standing with his weight more or less evenly on all four legs but with his quarters under him. Once again we utilise the fact that a horse will move a hind leg on the same side as the riders instructing leg. Let us assume that we require the near hind diagonal and off fore diagonal to initiate the movement. Having, correctly, *prepared* for the transition, the rider has only to touch the horse with *his* left leg to request that the near hind act. Follow this with the right leg *fractionally* later and the horse will trot with the movement starting with the off fore and near hind diagonal, (subject to the rest of the criteria associated with the aid). 'Wait a moment'. I hear someone say. 'Isn't that the same aid used for asking for a specific leg at the walk'? Quite so but as I have said **subject to the rest of the aids required for the trot.** Just to remind you. The back braces the outside rein closes for the first part of the half halt. The legs now apply their signal (almost but not quite simultaneously) but the fingers of the half halt rein which would normally open immediately for walk stay closed for a fraction of a second longer with the back aid still applied. The horse is waiting for the fingers to open and as this is fractionally delayed, he now knows that a trot is required and further more he knows which of his legs are to initiate the movement.

A deeper examination of the aids for the canter depart.

Up until now the whole of the pupils previous learning curve has been directed to developing a good seat and learning to keep the hands still. Once that has been achieved the pupil is free to 'feel' what is going on below him. When they are able so to do, then they are in a position not only to give effective aids for any change but also to do so accurately.

In the case of the canter depart this is especially important, if the transition is to be smooth and immediate. In order to achieve this transition from the trot, the actual aid indicating the desired lead must be given as the **opposite diagonal pair to the required lead is about to strike the ground**. This allows the horse time to think and thus to smoothly strike off with the correct lead followed by the outside hind leg, correctly. If the aid is given as the same diagonal pair as the required lead is in the air, then the horse must wait a stride in order to organise himself if he is not to become unbalanced. *22.

The Counter canter.

The counter canter is a movement similar to an ordinary canter except that the horse is bent in the *opposite* direction to that in which it is going. The leading leg is the **outside** foreleg (Relative to the movement (see fig. 29). This is a more difficult movement for the horse than an ordinary canter because the horse is *pivoting on its outside hind leg* of the diagonal pair in the second stride. A horse may experience some difficulty in performing this movement unless it is well balanced.

What use is this to the rider?

In the first instance this is an excellent exercise in teaching a rider to sit absolutely still. The best way of introducing it is, as usual, by small degrees. Before starting to teach the movement you explain exactly what it is. If your pupils do not understand, then you must find out precisely what it is that is unclear and, through your own words, clarify matters.

The best way to introduce pupils to counter canter.

For the sake of safety, they are to ride individually on your command. Therefore have the class lined up along the centre line facing that side of the school where the counter canter is going to take place. This will enable the class to watch one another perform. You explain to the class that they are going to ride a canter around the arena. This will include a shallow loop of one metres depth. You also tell them where the canter loop will start and finish. They might start from the trot at the 'A' end and prepare to canter as they approach the corner between 'A' and 'K'. As they exit this corner they should be cantering with correct flexion and lead along the 'E' side getting their horses in balance. They ride along the next short side (The 'C' end) and as they exit the next corner and pass the letter 'M' they now ride a shallow loop, and as they pass 'B', they should be one metre in from the outside track. At this point they now proceed to return to the outside track, reaching it by 'F. *The point of the exercise is that during the execution of the movement the horse should not change either his flexion or his lead.* (Should your horses have been, previously, working hard do not have them complete a circuit. It is unnecessary).

In order to make the excise clear; demonstrate on foot or, better still ride it yourself. (For heavens sake do not choose a horse that you know has a tendency to do a flying change every time it is asked to change direction). Ask the class if they understand what is happening. Make sure that *you* ask the sort of questions that will reveal, by the answers given, whether or not your class have fully understood what they are going to do.

You must explain that as a rider starts to ride the first part of the loop there is no problem. Point out that if they were to continue this track, *but slightly accentuate the curve,* then they would be riding a half circle across the arena but still on the same rein. (See figs. 30 & 31) However they do not do this, because they ride the loop until reaching the point where, at an ordinary walk or trot, they would change the horse's flexion and return to the track. At canter the rider does the same thing but when returning to the track they do *not* change the horses flexion. If they were to do so then the horse would most probably change its leading leg. (You must take particular care to explain the reason for this, which is that if this return to the track were extended the horse would, *theoretically* have to pass through the side of the arena and proceed in a curve but on the other rein). And if it were to lead with the *correct* leg (for this new direction) it should change its leading leg. (See fig.32). But this exercise is all about a horse *not changing its lead*, in other words a counter canter.

How does the rider actually ride the movement?
The answer is of course by sitting absolutely still. The relative position of seat and leg does not change from start to finish of the whole movement. As the rider approaches the point where they are about to leave the track they gently ask the horse to move along the first part of the loop by a *gentle touch* of the outside hip and leg. This is the rider's leg, still behind the girth, that initiated the correct lead in the first place, as it is touched so the horse understands that it is being asked to change direction but not the lead. The rider may also 'lead the horse away' in the new direction by, very slightly, opening the inside rein.

As the rider is about to reach the apex of the loop they gently ask the horse to return to the track by gentle touching pressure of the *inside hip* and leg. This is acting, in its position, almost on the girth so once again it is direction and not lead that is indicated. The opening of the outside rein may support this. Of course as the rider's aids become more refined, then the touch of each leg will be supported by pressure from the opposite hip and leg (weighting the hip) thus, at the start, encouraging the horse not only to move away from a touch but to move *towards* pressure. The rein simply maintains the correct flexion but it is sometimes very difficult for the rider not to, accidentally, change the bend of the horses' head and thus, inadvertently, initiate a change of lead.
Questions that intelligent riders may ask.
1.   If one is to sit completely still, does one look in the direction that one wishes to go?
Answer. Yes, but since the rider is not to change the position of their body they must do so by looking out of the corner of the eyes only, and not turn their head or body.
2.   On the change of direction does the rider change the position of their legs relative to the horse?
 Answer. Definitely not. There is no reason to do so since the horse is not changing its bend. Further more any movement of the rider's legs might be taken, by the horse, as a signal to change the lead.

Proceeding with the exercise.
Call out each member of the class in turn. This need not necessarily be in the order in which they are lined up, for it is quite likely that this will be according to the size of the horses. I always like to start with a rider who is reasonably competent. This will demonstrate to the class that it is possible to ride the exercise correctly and sets a standard for the others to try to improve on. I always like to finish with a good horse

and rider who will show the movement to perfection. After each member of the class has ridden the loop, I invite everyone to take part in a discussion during which the performance of the rider who has just performed the exercise is analysed. Always do this in a kindly and constructive manner. It is not part of your job to make people, who may have experienced difficulties, look small.

Your command.
Having called out the rider of your choice by name. You say. "Prepare to go large on the right rein. At 'A' end of the arena, in your own time proceed through trot to canter. Between 'M' to 'F' ride a shallow loop of one metre without changing the lead".

Riding the shallow loop at the canter. What to watch out for.
As the pupil proceeds along the first long side make sure that the canter is established and well balanced. You have plenty of time to give the riders advice as they progress. 'Sit deeply' 'Shorten your reins' and so forth. Make sure that the rider starts with the correct lead and bend. Do not forget good balance is the foundation of this exercise.

Things that may go wrong.
The horse will change its lead.

Reasons.
1. This may be due to the fact that the rider has not managed to keep their body and limbs still.

2. The rider may have accidentally changed the bend of the horse's head.

3. The horse may simply feel uncomfortable performing this exercise.

4. The rider may ride a loop that is too large.

Whatever the reasons you must be sufficiently observant to point out all errors and help the pupil to correct them.

A more difficult exercise for counter canter.
When the class have mastered the art of riding a shallow loop without the horse initiating a change of lead, it is time to introduce them to a counter canter ridden on a half circle. As with the shallow loop this exercise is best ridden individually You must line up the class in arena so that there is room for each participant to ride a change of rein, a half circle and, finally another change of rein (see figs. 33, 34 & 35).

Walk to canter.
Some pupils think that there is some sort of magic formulae for initiating a canter depart of this sort. If one is teaching a livery owner on a one to one basis, then there is no real reason why they should not develop their own special signals for any series of movements. Generally speaking it is best to stick to conventional aids, but whatever the aid, you must bear in mind that horses need time to think about what is being asked of them, especially if they are only occasionally, subject to this type of work. When one is working with an animal that performs this sort of change on a daily basis then all that a rider would have to do would be, after having asked for collection, to simply draw back the outside leg. (Quite enough for my friend Jeeves no matter where I was riding him). So far as we are concerned the rider gives the same aid as they would when asking for a change from the trot to canter.

So how does the horse know that it is being asked to dispense with trot?
1. The duration of the pressure of the rider's back in conjunction with the fingers remaining closed for first part of the half halt. In the early stages of a pupil's attempts to make this transition the aid may be backed up by the voice simply saying 'Canter'.

2. So far as the legs are concerned there is quite a clear distinction. For trot both the rider's legs close behind the girth. For canter we not only require canter but also the correct lead. The inside leg is on the

girth (creating energy) and the outside leg acting behind the girth follows, touching the horse as it is momentarily about to place its weight on the diagonal of the inside hind and outside fore.

3. One may draw an analogy with things mechanical. In this case it is as though the driver of a car has gone from first to third gear missing out second. 'Wait a moment', you may say 'this is quite a strain on a motor vehicle, what about the horse'. Quite so. This is an advanced movement for the horse, never mind about the rider! In order to go forward from walk to canter or even halt to canter the horse is required to throw its whole body through the air from one leg. Yes, this is quite a strain and only a horse that is sufficiently well developed should be asked to do so.

4. It therefore follows that a rider should not be asked to perform this movement until they can sit still. If they succumb to the inertia created by the horse and their bodies move about, then it is quite likely that the horse will not be able to perform as they wish.

Going forward from canter to walk.

The aids are similar to those for canter to trot but there is greater pressure of the riders' back muscles, which are maintained for a fraction longer than before, as is the hiatus between the fingers of the outside hand closing and opening for the half halt. *The rider applies the aid, as the horse is about to strike off after the moment of suspension* In order to help a rider's confidence in the execution of this movement they may be encouraged to give the verbal command 'waaalk'. The horse should be rewarded through the rider's fingers softening the rein and gently touching the neck. Should a rider have difficulty in producing a smooth transition devoid of any strides at trot, things may be improved by using two very quick half halts, the one following immediately upon the other.

What should you watch out for?

1. The rider must engage a degree of collection so that the horse is helped to store the energy engendered by the change.

2. There will be some considerable inertia to be accommodated (think of the effect of changing down in a car from third gear to first, while travelling at a fair speed). So the rider must avoid allowing their body to be thrown forward. It may help if they actually *think* about, slightly, leaning backwards.

3. Under no circumstances should the rider be permitted to carryout the change by yanking on the reins.

4. The rider *must* reward the horse after it has changed successfully.

Canter to halt.

Except for fractional increase in feel and duration, the same as for above but I would suggest those only riders with a really sound independent seat and horses that have the experience attempt this.

The Lateral Aids.

Apart from preparing riders for the more advanced dressage competitions, lateral movements do help riders generally, to refine their aids. Whereas they may have reached a stage where they are able to cause their mounts to go forward with satisfactory impulsion and outline, the aids that they use may still be quite crude. When asking a horse to move both forwards *and* sideways at the same time the rider may very easily block the horses' forward progress if the rein aids are too severe, and the movement may be completely lost if the rider is unaware as to the horse's position underneath them. Where one has livery owners actually teaching their horses these movements for the first time, then it is even more important that the aids given are light and refined.

The aid as a component.

At this point, it is worth while my reminding the reader that as mentioned in chapter 7, for all lateral movements true or otherwise, the aids must be given as a component.

Always bear in mind that all *true lateral* movements *may be ridden from a circle* (see figs. 36 a, b, c & d).

This is a very good way of helping a rider of limited experience to understand the basic elements that form these movements. It is a method often used by trainers of young horses and assists in the lowering of the croup.

Shoulder-in. (Also known as shoulder fore or Epaule en Dedans)

There has been much discussion in the past over the correct form for this movement. It was devised by François Robichon de La Guérinière (1688 - 1751.) The argument has been about the extent to which the inside hind leg crossed the outside hind leg (if at all). I have a translation, from the French, of his book Ecóle de Cavalerie (1731). In fact he does seem to contradict himself at one point stating that the inside hind leg does cross the outside hind leg, while later on he says that it doesn't. However the movement is fundamental for all initial training in lateral movements. Today we seem to have clarified the matter and the movement may be described as follows: -

The position of the horse.

The forehand is brought in, about a 1 to 1.5 feet, (depending on the size of the horse), from the track that is being ridden. This track is maintained parallel with the outside track on which the hindquarters remain for the whole of the movement. The horse's body is placed and maintained at an approximate angle of 30 degrees to the direction in which he is moving. **He is not looking where he is going**. In other words the horse is *bent* towards the inside track *around the inside leg* and he is *moving away from this leg*. The great temptation for the student is to overdo the bend in the head and neck and you must be sure that this does not happen. Ideally one should only just see the corner (shimmer) of the horse's eye, (see fig. 37 & 38).

It should be pointed out to all pupils that lateral movements may be difficult, at first, for a horse to sustain.

Question that an intelligent rider might ask?

Why is a lateral movement so physically demanding of a horse?

Answer.

The reason for this is that unlike ourselves, who are quite able to swing our arms and legs around in any direction, the horse has evolved so that the easiest way in which he can move his legs is forward and backwards. The placement of the shoulder blade on the side of the body together with the forgoing of a collarbone assists this. That is not to say that he cannot move sideways, such a remark would be absurd, but until he becomes sufficiently supple, is difficult for him to sustain the direction. In the main the animal will only do a few short steps, as when we ask it to move over in the stable, when it is showing off or when it wishes to move smartly out of the way of another horses that threatens it. This arrangement of muscle *also* makes it harder for him to proceed laterally if he *is* looking in the direction in which he is going. Thus all exercises that involve sideways movement should be undertaken with due care.

The manner in which the horses legs move during shoulder-in.

The horses' inside foreleg clearly crosses over the outside foreleg. The hind legs do not cross but the inside hind leg is brought well under the horses' body (see photo. no. 31). **The movement starts on three tracks.** If you stand in front of a rider performing the movement correctly, you will see the outside hind leg on the outside track, the outside foreleg on the second track but you will not be able to see the inside hind leg because it will be masked by the foreleg on that track. Finally you will see the inside foreleg moving along the third track. However the angle may be increased, say from 30 up to 45, as the horse becomes more skilled at performing the movement, so long as forward impulsion is not lost

The riders' position.

Sitting tall and deeply in the saddle. Riding more with the pelvis and thigh rather than the leg. The rider is *looking between the horse's ears* and the whole body from shoulders down through hips is turned to follow the same bend as that of the horse. The bend is around the inside leg, which should be almost on the girth. The outside leg is behind the girth.

The aids.

Having brought the forehand off the track into the correct position, the rider gives a half halt with the outside rein - immediately followed by the pressure as they lengthen their inside leg bringing the thigh and pelvis against the saddle - immediately followed by another half halt. The opening (by about an inch only) of the outside rein may assist. (In other words the rider is inviting the horse to move in the direction indicated by their body and hand). *Ideally* if the horse is well schooled it should need the *application of these aids only once* and should continue the movement until told to do otherwise. (Needless to say this must cease *before* it becomes tired and is thus obliged to disobey because it is physically incapable of continuing). Incidentally the movement is easier for the horse at the trot because it is moving its legs diagonally in pairs. This movement is one that will help a rider to use an aid precisely. In this case it is the inside leg. For with a reasonable presentation of the movement the rider will easily feel the horses' inside hind leg being brought underneath it. This may be used to ensure that the rider uses their own inside leg just before the horse does so with its own. In this manner they may enhance the movement. When the movement ends the horse is straightened by bringing the forehand back to the outside track to avoid loosing the impulsion thus created.

A question that is likely to be asked by an intelligent rider.
If the rider is looking between the horse's ears (see two paragraphs above) how do they know where they are going? A very good question because this is one of those few occasions where the rider *and* horse are not looking where they are going. The answer is that the rider looks out of the corner of their eye in order to maintain the correct direction, thus overcoming this difficulty.

One should, I suppose, not forget to mention **Counter Shoulder - in**. This is a similar exercise to that described above except that the horse is positioned so that its head is towards the relative outside of the arena. i.e. with his quarters on the inside track. If performed along a wall, it is a *good exercise for the rider*, as an introduction to the movement, since the wall or fence of the arena prevents the horse from simply moving forward along his axis. This allows the rider time in which to concentrate on sitting correctly and giving precise aids. It is a more difficult movement for the horse because having its head brought so close to the wall it may suffer a slight disorientation. Rather as one might feel if asked to read from a book with your nose only an inch away from the page.

Travers. The quarters- in or head to wall. (La croupe en dedans, la hanche en dedans or La tete au mur)
The object of the exercise.
Following on from the shoulder-in, this is a **truly lateral movement**. The object is to cause the horse to, further engage his hindquarters and also to allow the rider to increase his control over them. It is a good preparation for Renvers also known as tail to the wall. Both these movements are useful introductions to the Half Pass or as it is otherwise known, the diagonal change of rein on two tracks.

The position of the horse.
For this movement the horse is bent and **looking** in the direction **where he is going.** However his forehand is on the outside track and his hind quarters positioned, at approximately 40 degrees, towards the inside of the arena. *He is moving both forward and sideways.* The movement is **quite clearly on two tracks** and both the outside foreleg and hind leg cross over their partners. (Do bear in mind that the use of the words inside and outside are always relative to the way in which the horse is bent, this applies to both horse and rider (see photo. No. 32).

This is a physically more difficult movement for the horse than Shoulder-in and he will find it easier to execute at the trot. You may introduce the movement at walk for the benefit of the rider.
Do bear in mind.
Even though we are talking here about teaching the rider and not the horse, it is worthwhile remembering the following: -
1. Though you may be using an experienced schoolmaster for work of this type, it is quite likely that the horse may not have been asked for this movement for some time.
2. This is a difficult motion for a horse, which, combined with the rider's initial lack of co-ordination, may result in the horse becoming confused as to what is required of it.
3. *Many riders, in their efforts to produce what they see as a difficult 'sideways' movement instinctively start by blocking the horses' forward motion.*

In order to avoid this problem you should not ask for too great an angle or too much bend in the beginning. What I am saying is: even though these are supposed to be movements on two tracks it *does not matter if you start* by reducing the angle so that the horse is only moving on three tracks. It also follows that in order to maintain impulsion simply allow the rider to ask for these movements with hardly any bend at all!

The rider's position.
The rider sitting tall and deeply in the saddle. Riding more with the pelvis and thigh rather than the leg. The rider is also *looking in the direction that they wish to proceed.* This means that whole body from shoulders down through hips is turned to follow the same bend as that of the horse. This bend is around the inside leg, which should be almost on the girth while the outside leg is behind the girth. Thus if they are proceeding on the right rein then their horse is bent to the right. The riders' torso follows this and that means that their left shoulder is forward. The head is turned and they are looking to the right towards the far corner of the arena, to which they are proceeding.

The aids.
Start the movement by, first, asking the pupil to ride a shoulder-in say half way down the long side of the arena. This continues into a ten-metre circle and when the horses' forehand has almost returned to the track the rider gives a half halt with the outside rein. This is immediately followed by the pressure as the riders' *outside leg is lengthened, bringing the thigh and pelvis against the saddle* - immediately followed by a half halt again with the (relative) outside rein and the opening (by about inch only) of the inside rein. (In other words they are inviting the horse to move in the direction indicated by the rider's hip, thigh and hand). The inside leg, giving support, remains stretched downwards almost on the girth where it was placed during the shoulder-in but it is no longer the dominant leg. Again if the horse is well schooled he should need the *application of these aids only once* and should continue the movement until told to do otherwise.

Having said that one must not loose sight of the destabilising effects of the shifting dynamics involved and the rider will, usually, be required to make *small corrections* all the time. *Do remind the rider to always end the movement by bringing the forehand to the inside track* and not vice versa. If this is not done, the horse will bring his weight onto his forehand and thus loose all the benefit that has accrued in terms of impulsion (energy) from behind.

Do not invite disobedience by continuing for so long that the horse becomes stressed.

In terms of the aids this is truly a lateral movement and the rider is asking for the movement with both the outside rein and outside of their body (leg). i.e. both on the same side **laterally.**

Possible problems for the rider.
1. Lateral movements do seem to be a problem for some pupils to visualise. Unless everything is quite clear in the pupil's mind it will obviously be difficult for them to ask the horse to perform any such movement. Not only that, many horses have a problem, firstly because they find lateral movements physically difficult and secondly because, in ordinary riding schools, they may not have been asked to move in this manner for some time. One must be *understanding* about such things.
2. Having to concentrate on more than one thing at a time frequently results in the rider's position going to pot. The rider starts to lean out, as they attempt to encourage the horse to move away in the opposite direction.
3. The moment one uses the word *lateral* the rider tenses up, thinks sideways and forgets about going forward. They shorten the rein so much that the horse is 'blocked', in other words it is unable to move forward and is therefore encouraged to try all manner of things as a way out of its difficulties. Remember that all lateral work involves *essentially forward movements.* Riders are frequently 'amazed' as they respond to my request to 'relax the hand and fingers' to find that the poor horse performs the movement perfectly. So remember if in difficulties tell them to think forward first then sideways.
4. The rider simply has yet to learn to give a succession of aids in the correct order, at the correct time and with precision.
5. The rider either does not realise when the movement looses its form or else they do not react quickly enough should the horse try to be evasive.

In order to help overcome these difficulties I have found it helpful to initiate *travers* by simply asking the rider to ride into a corner (see figs. 39 & 40). As the horse is about to exit, simply ask the pupil to keep the forehand going straight ahead and to concentrate on preventing the quarters from following the forehand. This may not result in a true movement but it does allow for the rider to concentrate on one thing at a time.

211

Exercises for everyone to practice. (See exercises to form a lesson. Chapter 15)
I make mention of practice at this point because these are not simple movements. They are very demanding on both horse and rider. The former may easily become fatigued in which case they will be less likely to obey the latter. The rider has a double problem in that they probably have not yet learned to respond quickly enough to ensure that the horse is positioned correctly and to be able to maintain that position. You as their teacher have only a limited time in which to allow them to practice due to the limits set by the duration of the lesson (and horses getting tired) The answer lies in making these movements part of an overall program and practice the old adage of 'little and often'.

Renvers -Tail to the wall. (La croup en dehors, la hanche en dehors or La croupe au mur).
Similar to the travers. For this movement the horse is moving with its tail to the wall. (See fig. 41)
The only difference between these movements is the position in relationship to the wall of the arena.
Half Pass. (l'Appuyer)
This is a movement that also requires the horse to move both forwards and sideways. He is looking in the direction in which he is going. The movement is carried out, across the arena, diagonally at an angle of 50 degrees. *The forehand must always lead.* It is a movement on two tracks. (See fig. 42)

Avoiding confusion.
To introduce ones class to half pass, the same comments, regarding the rider's posture apply, as have been made concerning the lateral movements mentioned earlier this chapter The horse is asked to *move away* from the outside leg whilst *looking in the direction in which it is going.* – In the beginning this may again induce confusion in the rider as to which of their legs or hands and in what manner they should be using them, since they do not have the side of the arena wall close by to use as a constant reference point. *The rider needs time to sort out what they are going to be asking of their own bodies before they can give a clear message to the horse.*

Introductory Method.
The simplest way to introduce the movement is through a, correctly performed shoulder-in. My reason for suggesting this method is that it relieves the rider of the necessity to reposition the horse. As we have seen the shoulder-in has the horse bent around the inside leg. The animal is moving on three tracks but is *not looking where it is going.* It proceeds along the side of the arena encouraged by the gentle pressure of the riders inside leg, which is supported by the outside rein giving a very soft half halt. This rein may also lead away very slightly, that is to say that as the half- halt signal is given the hand is also opened (moved away and back again from the side of the horses' neck) to indicate and confirm the direction of movement.

When this movement has been correctly established to a point about halfway down the long side of the arena, then there is the briefest of pauses and *without the horse or the rider's position being changed*, the rider now uses the *outside leg* behind the girth. The half-halt with the outside rein is still given but now the leading away is with the inside rein. The inside leg stays at the horses' side stretching down and giving support (if required it may actually touch the horse each stride to maintain impulsion). The horse will now proceed on two tracks at an angle of 50 degrees across the arena (see fig. 43). *Both rider and horse look where they are going.*

Pirouettes and flying changes.
It is possible that a pupil may have queried the necessity for those many paragraphs occurring near the beginning of this chapter that were concerned with collection and outline. I do agree that it is possible for a rider to perform some form of what seems like lateral work without the horse conducting himself in an athletic manner. However so far as the following movements are concerned there is absolutely no way that a horse will be able to carry them out satisfactorily, unless he has transferred his weight from his forehand to his hocks. Not only that but for a really brilliant exhibition of these movements this transfer must have taken place to a degree that the horse is actually lowering his croup. You must therefore have had your pupils perform the introductory work to the required standard. (riding small circles).

The Pirouette at the walk.
The pirouette is not in itself a difficult movement for a schooled horse to perform, provided that it is sufficiently collected, which is sometimes very difficult for the rider to obtain from the horse - correctly.

212

We must start with a clear idea as to the exact constituents of the movement. As with a turn about the haunches the rider is asking the horse to describe a small circle with the hindquarters, while the forehand moves in a large arc about them. All this takes place at the walk. This means that there must be no loss of impulsion. There is no halt; it must be a smooth transition from one direction to another. The whole time the horse's feet are moving in four-time and the movement is so collected that the inside hind leg almost marks time (goes up and down almost on the same spot). The exercise should not be ridden at the trot but it is very acceptable at the canter provided that the horse has the ability and rider is able to give precise aids.

The aids.

1   The rider braces the back muscles and as they do so they turn the torso in the direction in which they wish to proceed.

2   A fraction of a second later the outside fingers give a half halt and it is permissible to bring this rein inwards to that it rests against the horse's neck.

3   This is immediately followed by the inside rein both flexing the horse in the direction that it is going to go and also leading away (i.e. the inside hand is moved away from the neck about 2 inches and then returning). It is also permissible for the rider to raise this rein very slightly.

4   The outside leg gently touches the horse behind the girth for each step of the movement (I mean touch and not continuous push).

5   The Inside leg lies against the horse's side almost on the girth and remains there to give support and also to prevent any desire on the horses' part to step backwards.

Possible problems for the rider

1.   Whereas a *turn on the haunches* provides the rider with fairly lengthy 'thinking time', for the pirouette this is condensed.

2.   The horse may not have sufficient collection in order to freely move its forehand correctly about its hindquarters. This may well occur if the rider does not sit really deeply on the rear part of the seat bone

3.   The rider may forget to turn their torso or to look where they want to go. The may also neglect to flex the horse properly.

4.   The rider may well touch the horse with both legs or the wrong leg or else forget the half halt.

5.   If the horse is too much on the forehand it will probably start to turn about the forehand (This frequently happens during the last step in a sequence when it has lost impulsion).

6.   In any case the rider must be ready for this possibility and be able to slide the outside leg back an inch or two to prevent the horses' outside hind leg from flicking out. (All it needs is a light touch).

7.   Horse and rider must continue to walk on as soon as the movement is complete in order to prevent a loss of impulsion.

The Flying Change.

This is one of the movements to which most riders aspire. For them it visually demonstrates more than any other, the pupils' degree of 'expertise'. Further more it looks very 'swanky'. And so it should, for this is a change that, if it is to be performed correctly, requires exact precision and timing in the application of the aids

What is a flying change?

It is simply a movement performed at the canter where the horse is asked to change from one lead to another without first going through another gait. The change must be true. That is to say that the change originates *from behind* during the moment of suspension and is followed through to the forehand so that there is no loss of the diagonal component of the canter. It is not acceptable for the horse to change in front alone for this would mean that it had become disunited (a lateral movement).

Highlighting possible problems beforehand.

Now the heading for this paragraph may seem to be rather strange. Why mention problems before they occur? My reason for doing this is that as with lateral movements one is going to ask the rider to execute an aid, the components of which have to be quite clear in the rider's mind, *before they start*. Further more since this is an exercise performed at the canter, the time available for the aid to be given, correctly, is very short. By that I mean that the sequence of aids must be complete before the moment of suspension has passed – for that stride.

Obviously I take it as read that you will not embark upon such an exercise without first having led up to it by suitable preparatory movements. Quick transitions through walk, trot and canter, of a short duration. All exercises that will result not only in the horse paying close attention to the requirements of the rider but will also lead up to a high degree of collection. That is to say that the horse will be going forward with a nice bouncy stride in front of the leg and lightly into the hand. It is very important that you read through the aids as described in the paragraph. 'A deeper examination of the aids for the canter depart', mentioned earlier on in this chapter.

Preparation.
Once again I must make it clear that the method that I am about to describe is for *riders* and *not horses*. If I were *training* a horse to execute a flying change I would not go about it in this manner. I will discuss my reasons later on.

Now I have alluded to the necessity for the rider to go over in his or her mind the procession of aids required to cause the horse to acquire a particular lead (see chapter 23 'The reason why'. paragraph 'Cantering with the correct leading leg'. However with the best will in the world it is unlikely that merely thinking through these aids will be sufficient to enable a rider to initiate a flying change immediately that they ask for it. What they need is a way in which they are allowed an extended period of 'thinking time', which in turn will lead up to it, as it were. From my experience I have found that the simplest approach is to prolong the time during which a change is asked for and one way of doing this is by asking the rider to insert a few strides at trot before they ask for the new lead.

Explaining what is to follow.
It is important that you inform the class about all the components of the exercises that are to follow. In this case they are going to be asked to canter going large and, upon your command, to change the rein across a long diagonal. As they ride this long diagonal they are to ride three strides of trot with the second stride exactly on '**X**'. During the second and third stride they will give the correct aids for a canter on the new rein.

Examining the aids closely.
It is useful to take the class through the actual aids used for both asking for trot and canter. I will not reiterate them here since they have been discussed in great detail in chapter 6 (the first chapter about aids).

The exercises leading up to flying change.
These exercises should be performed individually. You may have the rest of the ride going large around the arena at a walk or better still lined up at either end. This will leave plenty of room for each rider to practice.

Start by asking a rider to go forward to canter in the normal manner (through a trot if you wish), however it is advantageous if the rider is able to ask for canter from walk or even halt, since these starting points imply a considerable degree of collection. *When the rider has established a collected canter* going large around the arena ask them to *prepare to change the rein at a suitable diagonal* and as soon as they have done so, to start to prepare for a transition to trot. In order that they have *sufficient* 'thinking' time the rider really does need to *prepare* as soon as they have turned their horse across the diagonal. During the performance of this movement there is no reason why you should not, at first, 'talk' the rider through the aids.

What do you have to watch out for?
1. The rider must think through what they are about to do in good time. If they do not do so then they will be three-quarters of the way across the diagonal before they react. In reality this means that as soon as the downward transition to trot takes place, they must *think canter immediately*.
2. The rider then has to concentrate on looking where they wish to go. (They must ride from letter to letter). They must ensure that the horse is now looking in the new direction. In other words that they change the bend correctly, further more there should be no loss of impulsion.
3. They must be quite clear as to which leg they are going to use to touch the horse behind the girth in order to get the correct new lead.

214

4. Though some might say that changes of this sort depend on the rider changing their weight, for less experienced riders I would be content if they simply turn the torso or just sit still. If you start asking them to weight one hip or the other they are simply going to start wobbling about all over the place.

5 It is possible, even when teaching quite experienced riders that the high moment of suspension resulting from the impulsion created may unbalance the rider who must be able to sit through each stride. If they are thrown forward then the horse not only has to contend with its own instability but that of the rider moving about as well.

Continuing towards the flying change.
It must be obvious to everyone the direction that we are taking. The next development of the exercise is to *reduce* the number of steps at *trot* down to two, one and then *eventually none at all*! The problem for you is to decide when these advances should take place? Should they be ridden during the same lesson? Or should you have your pupils practise riding with a succession of ever reducing trot strides over a period of time?

Only you can be the judge of that. You must weigh up the energy expended in this type of work with the advantage of the horse becoming familiar with what is required of him. I do know one thing, if the exercise proceeds correctly the pupil is frequently quite taken aback and delighted as the flying change, effortlessly, takes place.

A little stratagem.
Sometimes even a quite skilled rider will have difficulty in obtaining a flying change. As soon as they know that they are about to embark on this part of an exercise, they immediately tense up and as a result the horse is out of balance and the aids that they give are either incorrect or incomplete. I have found that it can help if at this stage of the lesson you say absolutely nothing about flying changes at all. Of course the preparatory work has already been correctly carried out. In other words the horse is going forward nicely in a collected and well-balanced canter. At this point I simply say, quite inconsequentially to the rider 'I would like you to ride a circle or half circle of half the arena and as you pass through 'X' and then please change your circle to one at the other end of the arena'? I have never known this to fail. The reason is quite obvious for the pupil has been riding changes of circle for years. All that you are asking them to do is the same thing and it so happens that these are the same aids for a flying change. The delight upon their faces is a pleasure to behold and having once performed the change their confidence is established and they seldom have a problem in future. Why would I *not use this method to teach* a horse changes of this sort? Because by using this system you are assisting a change by using the horses' state of imbalance as it passes through '**X**'. When you train a horse everything is aimed at getting it to move *in balance* so why introduce a state of imbalance simply in order to induce a change? But this is not the place to discuss such matters.

Pirouette at the canter.
This movement is similar to the pirouette at the walk. Well similar in so far as the horse moves around its inside hind leg, which describes a very small circle. The movement is carried out without interfering with the three-time movement.

Provided that a horse is sufficiently physically developed and has been trained to perform this exercise, there should be no problem for an advanced rider to perform the movement. The main problem will probably be that which exists in the riders' mind. In other words they must have really thought through the actual change so that the request flows from them to the horse without any hesitation.

Obviously the horse must be collected and the quality of the canter such that the horse is able to remain in balance at all times. By this I mean that the horse is proceeding with calm quiet steps that none the less develop much power. It is no use expecting a horse to perform a pirouette if it is racing around the arena at high speed. The animal must be correctly bent over its leading leg and the hindquarters well underneath. The unity between rider and horse must be such that the rider is able to drop the contact momentarily without the horse loosing its outline. (Small circles are very important in the preparation).

We are now asking for very refined aids from the rider. Apart from the change developing from the rider's torso, this is a movement, which, more so than many others depends on the distribution of power asked for by the rider and provided by the horse. The rider's inside leg must delicately create the energy and deliver it to the outside rein in exactly controlled amounts.

The aids.
These are almost the same as those used for this movement when performed at the walk. In other words the

back braces as the torso is turned in the required direction. The outside hand applies a light half halt as the rein is brought against the horses' neck. The outside leg touches the horse behind the girth, as the inside hand maintains bend but also leads away a couple of inches (it may also be raised slightly for a second or two). Finally the inside leg, acting almost on the girth, must stretch down deeply giving the horse both support and at the same time maintaining impulsion.

At this level the rider must give the aids in such a manner that though they flow smoothly they also still allow 'thinking' time for the horse. Not only that, if they are to be correctly interpreted by the horse they must also now be rhythmical and yet completed within a similar time lapse as for flying change. I have said that the aids are almost the same as for the walk and yet they are not. For this exercise the aids must have both a clockwork precision and also an artistic sweep to them. The sequence should continue for however many steps are required to complete the movement, and yet - they must also be a contiguous whole. The rider must actually *think* the movement and the horse must be able to respond as though it was part of the rider's own body. We have now reached that stage where the signals of leg and hand have *almost* been suborned to that of the rider's body.

Possible problems for the rider.

1. This is an exercise that should only be attempted by a skilled rider. The rider must be able to keep their body completely still and yet, at the same time, be able to flex it as required. Stillness through rigidity is not acceptable.
2. The thinking about what they are going to attempt may result in even experienced riders lapsing into old bad habits and blocking the movement.
3. The rider must have a reasonably well-developed sense of rhythm.
4. Sometimes the rider has a problem in containing the forward movement of the canter. This may be overcome by asking the rider to raise the outside hand slightly before applying the half halt.

What you must not forget.

This is an exercise that is very demanding of the horse. Do not attempt it if your horses have already been working very hard. Further more make sure that your preparatory work is properly carried out.

Remember that when you have achieved a good result, resist the temptation to try 'one more time'.

Finally.

I repeat once again. The aids that I have described are based on accepted convention. By the time you teach advanced equitation you should be able to articulate your instruction using your own words to express your meaning. The only criterion is that your pupils understand what you are saying.

It is also, once again, worthwhile reflecting on the fact that during *lateral movements* it is essential for the rider to *maintain impulsion* and never to loose sight of the fact that these *are essentially forward movements.* Thus the rider must not overlook the use of the inside leg to maintain that forwardness. This means that in their efforts to produce the sideways element of the movement with the outside leg, all riders must also remember to use the inside leg (acting almost on the girth) to ensure that the horse *does move forwards* as well as sideways. For some pupils this may be a problem for, say, during half pass, they may use the inside leg with too much vigour or alternatively not use it at all.

None of this work will be successful unless the horses are, first, ridden in a state of good collection. One way of achieving this is through riding circles (at all gaits) going from large ones to those of only 5 metres diameter. All the while being ridden accurately and with no loss of impulsion. These will encourage horses to lower their croup by bringing their inside hind legs well under their bodies.

It must also be remembered that throughout any advanced work the horse must remain in a mental state of complete calm.

Diagrams.

The counter canter going large on the right rein.   Figure 29

Observe that the horse is bent to the left. The leading leg which is the near fore (the front left leg) is indicated by the fact that that shoulder appears to be slightly in front .

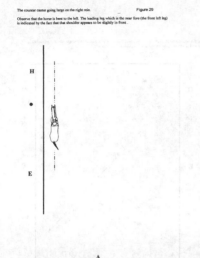

Figure no. 29. The counter canter.

Introduction to counter canter by riding a shallow loop.   Figure 30

Observe that the horse is bent to the right but as it progress through the loop it is for a short while proceeding left. There is little cuve to the loop because this is as much as most riders can manage on the first attempt.

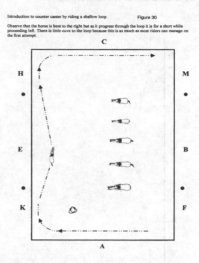

Figure no. 30. Riding a shallow loop as an introduction to the counter canter.

The counter canter from shallow loop (detail) going large on the right rein.   Figure 31

Observe that the horse is bent to the right but but as the rider passes II they go slightly to the left.

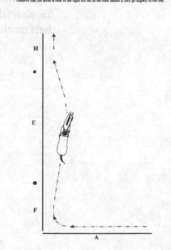

Figure no. 31. Riding counter canter through a shallow loop (detail).

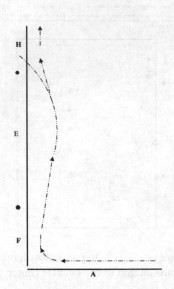

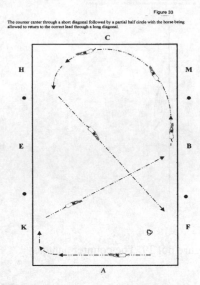

Figure no. 32. The counter canter from a shallow loop with the imaginary new direction.

Figure no. 33. The counter canter through the short diagonal followed by a partial half circle.

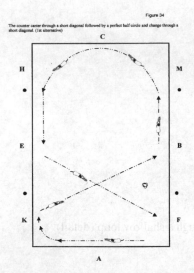

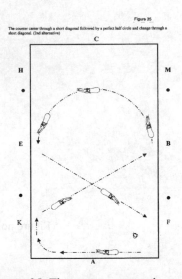

Figure no. 34. The counter canter through the short diagonal, followed by a half circle (1st alternative).

Figure no. 35. The counter canter through a short diagonal, followed by a half circle (2nd alternative).

218

Figure 36

Lateral movements may all be initiated from a circle or part of a circle. (the smaller the circle the greater the angle).
a = Counter shoulder-in. b = Shoulder-in. c = Travers . d = Renvers .
Remember these movements may be ridden anywhere in the arena. They are described by their relative position in relation to the walls of the arena.

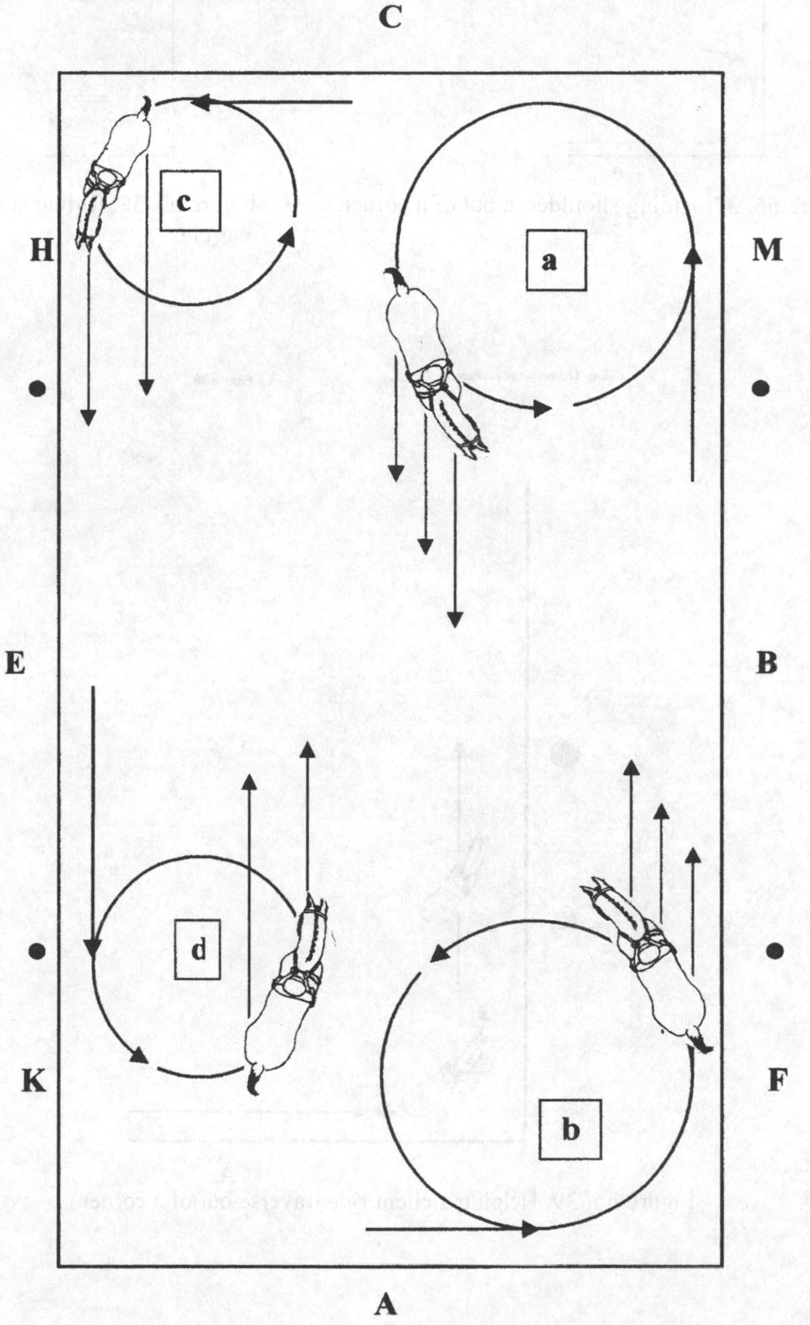

C

A

Figure no. 36. (a,b,c &d). Lateral movements arising from riding a circle.

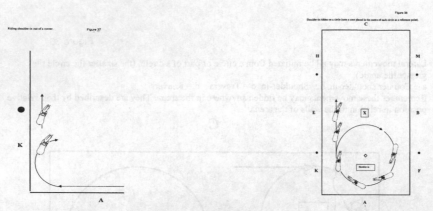

Figure no. 37. Riding shoulder-in out of a corner.

Figure no. 38. Riding shoulder-in out of a circle.

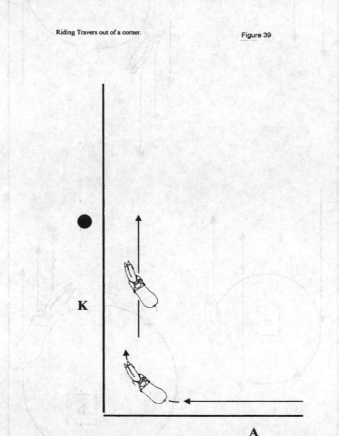

Figure no. 39. Helping a client ride traverse out of a corner.

Figure 40

Travers ridden out of a corner. (head to wall) Note the angle is not too severe about 30 degrees.

Remember the movement is always relative to the wall against which your client is riding. Thus (a) an advanced rider showing the same movment along the three-quarter line about 40 degrees angle.
(Note that in these sketches I have drawn the neck so that it appears somewhat shorter. This is to give the perspective of elevation, similarly the distance from back of rider to tail is also seems to be shorter indicating that the horse is more collected and has his quarters underneath him).

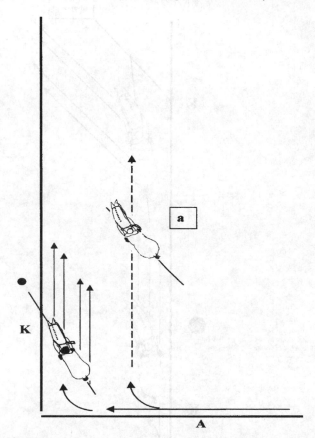

Figure no. 40 A more detailed view of the movement shown in figure no. 39.

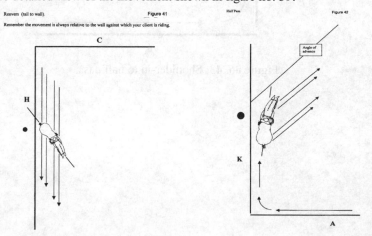

Figure no. 41. Renvers. (tail to wall).   Figure no. 42. Half pass.

Remember the movement is always relative to the wall against which your client is riding.

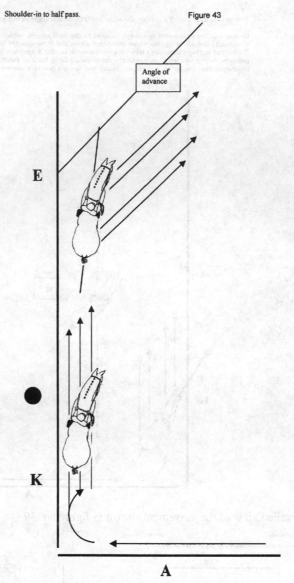

Figure no. 43. Shoulder-in to half pass.

Chapter 14

The advanced class

In this chapter our clients must be able remain completely 'focused' for the whole lesson and to produce and contain 'impulsion'

Advanced Riding.

It may well be assumed that under this chapter one is going to read about advanced riders. Please observe the heading. I am going to talk about advanced riding and not *advanced riders*. Oh bless you no; in fact they are not the same thing at all. There is a vast difference between the two. You will however be required to give advanced riding lessons to people who are not, necessarily, advanced riders. Where this is the case you must be very careful how you go about the matter. It is very likely that you may well be using 'advanced horses'. Your clients will probably expect this otherwise how on earth are the poor lambs going to produce the performance to which they believe that they are heirs. After all have they not paid! Beware – if you work with highly intelligent and knowledgeable horses they may be unaware that money has changed hands and are quite likely to have a very low level of tolerance.

The target.

Despite my carrying on at length about the shortcomings of some horsepersons, we do have a target for *everybody* at this level. By now the rider's seat should be confirmed, to such an extent that they are free to concentrate on *improving* the horses that they ride. Yes that is what I said 'improving'. They should now be able to ride any horse and to make such an impression upon it that by the end of the session the horse will have learned more than it knew at the start. By that I don't simply mean that the horse is just listening to the rider, for we expect that to happen with intermediate riders, no, I mean *improved*, that is to say that its whole carriage and manner of going is better. Advanced riders should be able to do this with most horses that they ride.

At this level your clients are going to learn how to produce movements from their horses that are at a very high level of athleticism. For those students who have been in *your* classes all the while, in other words those whom you have been teaching from the novice stage, there will be little problem in reaching for this next plateau of achievement.

Self-awareness.

Your clients should now have the initiative to impose self-correction most of the time and no longer be reliant upon you to do it for them. They should be able to have most horses going on the bit, with a minimum of fuss. They should be able to ride a simple lateral movement such as a leg yield, correctly. By this I mean that they should be *aware*, throughout the movement whether or not the horse is straight or whether it is trailing its hindquarters.

Seeking to inspire.

We now begin the process where, for your pupils, riding the horse is no longer simply a short period during which they undergo some sort of physical activity. 'No, no'. This is the time where they are now going to enter a world not of virtual reality but actual reality! This will be a world where, when they sit upon a horse, they are transported from the mundane of their other lives. They enter one in which they are able to reveal to everyone else, that in their relationship with the horse they are able to *demonstrate a Unity*. When they sit upon a horse they should be on the brink of being able to give a performance! It will have to do with the way that they think! *The rider is now always proactive*!

In practise this should mean that every movement is as a result of the riders sole decision. For example should they wish to move off to the right turning away at say an angle of 90 degrees? Then the movement should be carried out as a turn on the haunches rather than allowing the horse to slope off and turn around its centre. Even the period of warming up at the walk will be at the tempo *dictated* by the rider Of course the rider should not become too demanding, thus inviting disobedience by the horse, but generally speaking all demands, being reasonable and precise, will be obeyed.

The type of horse

For lessons at an advanced level it is obvious that one requires horses that not only know all the movements required but who are also physically and emotionally developed to be able to deal with this work.

Beware.

You must make sure that you familiarise yourself with the horses that you are going to use *before* the lesson commences. You may do this by finding out their ages, seeing them work with other instructors at which time you may also observe the conformation of each one. The difficulties that they may have in performing certain movements, their manner of going and their attitude to other horses in the class. You may not have all these same horses in your class at any one time but if you go about your work thoroughly, you will then have gathered information that is useful to you. For any horse that is placed in your class about which you know nothing, talk to your clients in a general non-specific manner about that animal and, very soon you will have a pretty good idea of the sort of character with which you have to deal.

Horses that really 'know their stuff'.

Oddly enough this can sometimes work to the disadvantage of a client. The reason being that the horse is *so* well schooled that it reacts to the slightest touch or indication provided by the rider. One sees it happen all too frequently. The lesson proceeds and the client is asked to ride straight down a three-quarter line. Much to their surprise the horse suddenly starts to offer a half pass. The client is much amused and quite pleased. 'Gosh they exclaim I'm riding a half pass!' 'Well you jolly well shouldn't be.' I would reply. 'You are supposed to be riding in a straight line. Either you are unable to keep your leg and body still or you are allowing the horse to anticipate a movement.'

William Cowper may sum up the horse's point of view in the following verse from John Gilpin.

> His horse, who never in that sort
> Had handled been before,
> What thing upon his back he'd got
> Did wonder more and more.

In such circumstances one thing is of paramount importance, the horse must not be chastised. After all he is only trying to do what he believes he has been asked. Good horses deserve respect.

Young stock.

Sometimes you may find that you have been given one or two young horses to work with. This does not mean that they will not know their job but you should take care not to ask too much from them. If you do then you may be asking for trouble. Be sure that youngsters have a sufficiently long period in which to rest between each exercise. If you take the trouble you should have no problems. Don't forget to use your eyes. You will usually have a quite clear warning if a horse is starting to get fed up and is about to throw a 'wobbly'. (Heads will shake and tails will swish).

Knowing when to stop.

Even with mature and experienced horses, you must exercise caution. It is so easy to ask too much. The great temptation is that, having been given excellent renditions of the movements that you require, you ask yet again. 'Perhaps we'll try that once more' you say to the class. My view is 'don't'. The most likely result is that your horses will give something less than perfect, compared with the previous performance and you and your riders will be left with a feeling of dissatisfaction. You will be unlikely to have time enough remaining to carry out corrections and in fact the situation may deteriorate even further. So, *when you get a good performance– stop!*

Considering the position again!

Throughout the foregoing chapters I believe that I have made my thoughts quite clear on the matter. In this chapter however I am opening up the debate. It is my view that advanced riders should ride with a long leg. What I am saying is that I think that the 'classical' seat, that which has come down to us through the centuries is still correct for teaching school riding today.

Some would not agree with me. It has been suggested that this tends to rob the body of a considerable degree of springiness and support. As far as I am concerned most shock absorption arising from the moment of suspension should take place in the riders' lower back. If a little extra be required then a heel well down will provide this. Of course stirrups should not be so long that the rider has, continually, to reach for them. To my mind all riders must by now be able to remain sitting deeply in the saddle with a long iron, unless that is, that they specifically wish to go forward.

Now it seems to me that you should all now be of sufficient experience to question my views? Since we are not able to meet face-to-face as it were, I will assume that this query has been forthcoming from you and I will now try to justify my position. My opinion is based on two fundamentals. The first is that which has resulted from my own experience. While the other is based on that which has gone before. The latter may be open to some doubt since I am referring to times before the invention of movie film or video tape, thus we are left with only the recorded observations of writers, artists, sculptors and photographers over the centuries. Even here one must be cautious for indeed erroneous ideas may be perpetuated through art. Until the photograph captured the motion of the horse at the canter, it was always thought that the proper manner to depict this gait and the gallop was with the horse's legs sticking out as a pair front and back. Today we know differently.

Most prints and paintings of riders, especially cavalrymen, produced during the 17th through to the 19th centuries show the leg almost straight with the heel well down. But the question that one may ask is whether the way in which the rider's leg is depicted correct? Or was this simply the demand of fashion? Further more if the depiction is true is this purely the result of the deep saddles that were so popular, for example, during the 17th century (see plate i). I suppose that there is always the possibility of a slight artistic licence creeping in no matter how honest an artist might try to be. The sitter might after all demand it. But I am, in this case, inclined to accept those representations, because, fundamentally, they do not seem to have changed as time has past. If we look at photographs from the Victorian era we seem to have a confirmation of this – unless that is that the subjects of the photos were asked to lengthen their stirrups before the photograph was taken?

Anyway I don't think that this was so and my opinion was strengthened when, I happened to, recently pay a visit to Messrs Phillips the auctioneers where I came across two superb bronzes by the sculptor Jean Leon Gerome (1824 – 1904). One depicted Napoleon Bonaparte, the other Frederick the Great. Both were mounted on horses. The former is shown riding with a bent knee, the latter with a leg almost straight. Now we know that Napoleon's early career was that of an artillery commander, not a cavalry officer. The position, though flamboyant, is typical of a rider without much experience. In fact it seems to me to be possible that Gerome actually based his work on the famous picture by David entitled 'The first Consul crossing the Alps'. Frederick was taught to ride from childhood. His long legged position similarly appears in all paintings portraying people mounted on horses going all through the 18th & 19th centuries. Of course I could be wrong! (Incidentally the estimated prices were between £12,000 - £18,000 for Napoleon and £7,000 - £8,000 for Frederick -Napoleon is more popular a subject than Frederick.

The point that I wish to make is that if the poses were dictated by fashion, then surely Napoleon would have been modelled with a straight leg as well, for surely the sculptor would not risk offending his fickle public?

However I readily agree that fashion is a very powerful factor in people's behaviour. If you read Charles M Holmes *25, you will find that in the past it was the *fashion* for owners to have the farrier pare away the sole of the horses foot until it was flexible to the touch. In this way countless good horses were lost.

But we should revert to the discussion in hand. This is not simply a matter of what has *not* been observed. Let us go as far back in time to prehistory. I mean to a time when horsemen rode without stirrups because they hadn't been invented. The leg hung down. The rider *had* to sit on the seat bones. Their descendants – The tribesmen from the steppes of Mongolia, may be seen today as they continue to ride as they did thousands of years ago. There are also riders from the fairly recent past who rode with a long leg - Cowboys. There are not many of them around nowadays but those who still ride and their counterparts from the last century all had to develop a really deep and secure seat. Their very lives depended on it, for to sustain a fall during a round up could mean being trampled to death by hundreds of steers. Look at pictures of them as they ride, the leg is stretched down as far as it will go. If you do not have access to old photographs of cowboys, then look at a not so old Western on television , see the leg position of the likes of John Wayne. It says it all.

Mind you the subject of position has been challenged over the years. In 1904, after several years of winning

225

many world class jumping and racing events, Captain Federico Caprilli was at last allowed to teach all his students both foreign and national, his system of 'going forward' (that is riding with a short stirrup so that the rider's body may be easily placed over the withers). At this time many well-known horsemen adopted his methods and threw out the classical position. Of course jockeys had been riding races in this way for many years prior to this but Caprilli persuaded those who still believed in the upright 'Classical' seat. Everything was now about 'Going forward'. Such well known masters as Vladimir S. Littauer actually went into print in order to extol the virtues of the 'Forward Seat' *34. Alas a few years later he had to change some of his views in 'More about the forward Seat' *35, in which he pointed out that while the forward seat was excellent for jumping, for ordinary riding and especially dressage a more classical seat was still needed.

The seat
So dear reader you will now be under no misapprehension that for me it is the 'classical' seat that is still the foundation of all advanced riding. And I hope that you will also realise that I have not taken my position without having giving the matter a good deal of thought. I do not believe that the rider should now have to rely upon the thigh to support the body to the degree that it has previously. The leg will be long. Not so long that this precludes the ability to rise to the trot – but long enough to be able to wrap around the horses body to the extent that leg aids will be given by squeezes of the calf, rather than a kick with the heals.

The weighting the hip.
The ideal, to which we should now inspire our clients to attain, is to ride mainly using the seat and hips. Watch Spanish working riders, riding pirouettes or canter to halt? There is no digging in of the heels or hauling on the reins. In fact the rein contact appears to be non-existent. Every movement is ridden from the hip. The horse feels the riders' body turn or takes note of the change of weight.

This, therefore, is clearly an important aid, but I did not make too much of it, in the earlier lessons, because I consider the use of this aid to be counter productive at that time when one is still trying to get clients to learn to sit still. Even at this stage I am careful about my choice of words. If one for example tells a client to 'weight the inside hip' for say a half pass, unfortunately what frequently happens is that the client starts to lean over in that direction and that is the very last thing that you want. So unless I am dealing with a client who really is an accomplished rider, I usually simply say 'Stretch down your inside leg bringing it against the horses side to give it support. Much more long-winded I admit but it does serve to avoid the development of bad habits. Of course all clients have already been weighting their hips without realising that they have done so. This has arisen as a result of learning to ride a corner correctly. You will recall my advice to the rider to bring forward the inside leg, almost on the girth, as they approach the corner and to stretch that leg downwards riding the horse around it as though it were a pole. What they are really doing is weighting the hip.

Doing they're bidding.
Many of your clients may be either in business or the professions. They may not be their own bosses but they may well have positions of responsibility. It helps if you present information to them in a way that somehow reflects the problems that they may come across in their working environments.

For example the following scenario may represent a scene with which they are familiar. If you are the head of a business or organisation and take on a highly skilled new member of the staff, are you immediately going to launch that person on to some very advanced project as soon as they step through the door? Surely not? You will first pass them to the personnel officer for a general introduction and then allow a period during which they will get to know their colleagues and only after this has taken place do you then ask them to undertake the job that you wish them to do. To cut this process short would be to ask for failure. The reason being that that person will not have had a chance to establish a proper line of communication with their new colleagues. Failing to do this, might result in the rest of the team not accepting them, they may well get fed up and quit. Similarly your clients must realise that they have to initiate a similar process as they go about asking a horse to perform advanced movements.

Dealing with tyros.
Remember this is not a book about training professionals. My whole object is to describe the manner of teaching people who are very definitely not in that category but who ride simply for pleasure. Having said that I am perhaps maligning them unfairly for I have seen some professional horsemen doing dreadful things

to horses, especially in Europe. Owners of riding schools have dozens of clients booking lessons many of whom firmly believe that they really do know how to practise the fine art of equitation. After all don't they belong to some professional services riding club? 'Ho'. 'Ho'. Do they not enjoy a weekend riding across country? Perhaps they have even ridden in the Royal Mews!!!! I regret to say that today's riding schools have to make a living and that means that they cannot always pick and choose their clients. They have to accommodate a huge variety of customers. Sometimes this means that the pompous self-image of many riders is allowed to remain intact.

In the last chapter I have been talking about the horses not obliging the rider and the rider's inability to change this state of affairs. There is of, course, the other side of the coin and that is where the rider *is* provided with a horse that will oblige and goes 'on the bit' without any objection whatsoever. I have watched many an 'advanced' class riding with horses that do this as soon as they are asked but the riders, whose hands are like cast iron, totally and absolutely fixed, do not acknowledge this! The poor horses suffer in silence. 'How come'? I hear you say, that these people are assigned to advanced classes? Surely they should be downgraded? In the harsh world of riding school economics it is easier said than done.

For these riders no communion evolves between themselves and the horse that they ride. They sit grim faced with fixed hands, heels rise upwards, constantly nag, oblivious to the fact that the horse *is doing what they ask.* Indeed the horse is now leaning on the bit – permanently! The rider must surely be aware of this for are they not constantly looking down and the comments flow – 'This horse is lazy', 'this one goes on his forehand the whole time' - yet again 'this one cannot move straight' and so on and on and on. Seldom a kind word for the poor old horse, instead, should the animal hesitate then the whip comes crashing down! This is surprising for many of these types will quote copiously from the books by the Masters that they have read! The trouble is that they only read selectively. An odd dip in here or there. Further more, they frequently do not realise that these books are aimed at people bringing on their *own* horses to a very advanced stage of their education. The rider working a school horse once a week may easily misinterpret these words and, even if they do understand, seldom put them into practice.

It is therefore up to you the instructor to try to improve these clients. For this you need the greatest tact. When you do succeed you will have provided the most valuable service to both the horse and the rider. 'Ah' the pleasure of a client who no longer grizzles, who sits upon *any* horse and shows it off at its best, whose position is always correct, who rides with tact and understanding.

How do you deal with the Glitterati?
I repeat, yet again! The good rider is the one who will sit upon *any* horse and, even for only one or two steps, will cause it to perform a movement correctly. It is to my mind also essential that, whilst mounted, the rider is also elegant. That is real equitation. Unfortunately these days there are many good riders who are not at all elegant. What is more they do not care! How does one get through to these people ? My mentor Col. Mendoza achieved this by projecting his own personality. His whole bearing was elegant either sitting on a horse or standing on the ground. It was the perfection of his waxed moustache, the cut of his jacket and the perfect polish of his riding boots. This told his pupils what he expected. Unfortunately for the less gifted and more mundane practitioners such as myself it advisable to think of an alternative route.

Now you may have noticed that I have become somewhat emotional in the forgoing paragraphs. The reason for that is because I do feel very strongly about those who think that they ride well when in fact they do not. I wouldn't mind if their lack of skill affected no one but themselves but unfortunately it does affect their horses. That it why I do not casually tolerate them.

My approach is to subtly let the clients know that, perhaps their knowledge is somewhat limited.
How? One can do this quite easily by asking a question, which may as basic as 'Describe the walk please', or the trot or canter. I am reasonably certain that they will not be able so to do. Alternatively you may ask them to indicate one of the more esoteric 'points' of the horse, for instance the 'Supra Orbital Fossa' or the 'Submaxilliary space'. This at least has the effect of revealing to the client that their knowledge is, perhaps not quite as comprehensive as they had originally thought. This being the case perhaps it would be a good idea if they listened to what you have to say, and you must seize this moment to kindly and tactfully point out their other failings.

Trying to inspire clients to make progress.
One of the great problems that many people have difficulty in overcoming is the way that they think about horses. This applies irrespective as to whether or not they are novices or experienced horsemen. They are

likely to consider that the horse is simply a mindless beast that has been trained to execute the orders of the rider without due process of thought. In this frame of mind it is unlikely that such a rider will be able to realise the full potential of any horse. The greatest *problem* that you will have to face, unless you are content to have clients that ride with you year after year without any real progress, is ***apathy.*** Clients will be quite content to ride in a class that they consider to be suitable to the level, for what ***they believe*** is their standard of riding. Beyond that, they have no desire of improving whatsoever. Lesson after lesson they go around the arena never changing.

As I have said some riders also consider themselves to be *very* experienced. When they get on a highly schooled horse they expect him to produce all the advanced movements of which he is able, at the 'touch of a button', as it were. There is no process of introduction; no polite formalities are exchanged between rider and horse. These types are those who, generally only ride with the top instructor. (Sorry not instructor - Trainer!) They have paid 'top dollar' for the lesson and they expect the horse to produce the goods! They sit upon the schoolmaster's back and ride the half pass and they think in a very superior way 'Oh gosh aren't I clever, I am riding a half pass'. In many cases they have not asked the question correctly. Usually the horse does perform the movement simply because it has managed to decipher the somewhat distorted signals it has been given, sometimes is does not. Oh bless you doesn't that put the rider out! 'It doesn't know its job, they will complain'

Getting their own back!

You may well have riders such as these; they may have been assessed and considered that for the sake of encouraging future custom it is worthwhile plonking them into your advanced class. The trouble is that many in this category do not ride with kindness in their hearts. They use the stick with much force and irritation. The effect this has upon their horses is to build up a feeling of resentment and this may well manifest itself through the horse taking advantage as soon as it sees an opportunity. So there we have them all riding their shoulder - in and half passes some of them correct but others fairly indifferent. Hands are fixed. Mostly the movements are executed in grim silence. You may see the odd occasional pat on the neck after the movement is finished but seldom will you hear an exclamation of praise at the *exact moment* when the horse is *performing correctly*. Then, when the lesson is over and the rider starts to relax, the horse will pretend to imagine that it has spotted something moving out of the corner of its eye and will shy. The rider caught unawares - because after all it is the *end* of the lesson - will be temporarily unbalanced and thrown. Whereas if they had been riding with joy in their hearts and had passed on a small portion of that feeling, to their mounts, you would not have to spend time filling out an accident form, especially when you are due to be home for lunch!

The demonstration.

When you see someone showing everything, hands tugging, elbows stuck out at awkward angles, arms rigid, biceps bulging and the body bent in an unnatural shape as stomach is pushed out, that client is demonstrating the way they have been taught before they came to you. The answer is for you to get up on the horse before it suffers any real discomfiture. Now you may show how with simple tact and the greatest delicacy, with every aid *concealed*, how you are able to achieve in a few seconds what the client has been struggling, unsuccessfully, to produce for the last fifteen minutes. By giving this demonstration you *may* make the most profound impression. As you proceed you should explain what you are doing and why.

Please do not get the impression that I pop up on a horse's back at the 'drop of a hat'. Oh no I do not! You may have noticed that in the above paragraph I said that you *might* make an *impression*. Unfortunately, very often, after you have worked the horse for a few minutes showing light and airy steps and a nice rounded outline with the hindquarters engaging, you then ask the rider to remount. Despite the fact that you have carefully explained exactly what you were doing and why, it hasn't made the slightest impression at all on the client! I suppose the one thing that it does do is to shut them up! At least they can't moan about the horse being completely useless and unfit for the sort of work in which they wish to engage.

Your regular clients.

However we must return to your ongoing clients. These riders will, probably have been with you for some time, possibly many years. Of course it does depend on their ability and the amount of time that they are able to devote to practice, but they will reach a point where they are able to progress to advanced equitation. Up until now you have been concentrating on honing their ability to point the horse in the direction in which they would like to go and to proceed to that point in the required gait. You may also have embarked upon the introduction to lateral movements – the leg yield, possibly some shoulder-in. Now you have to ask them to aim for movements that are slightly more sophisticated.

The first thing that they have to do is to utilise their newfound ability to *anticipate* the horse's action and to complement it with a reaction of their own. In other words they have to start to influence the horse's dynamic. That is to say they are required to minutely regulate the paces and in doing so correct any tendency towards imbalance that arises as a result of the horses' own imperfect conformation or its wayward desires. You may liken it rather to having the ability to balance a whip on a fingertip and by extremely subtle corrections, prevent it from falling to the ground. It is not an exercise in which you can allow your attention to wander!

Showing appreciation.
I do like to hear, quiet comments from rider to horse for the complete duration of their time together. Not only that but praise should be given *at the exact moment* when the horse does their bidding and not perhaps ten seconds later. Many riders, with whom I have remonstrated about this lack of acknowledgement, say that it is due to the fact they themselves are concentrating like mad. This is probably true but if they are to get the best out of their horses then they must learn not to become so self-absorbed that they miss the moment to give praise, when the horse handsomely obliges them.

Giving the horse thinking time.
Another quite difficult concept for some clients to comprehend is that, when giving a series of aids, for example when asking for, say renvers or perhaps a pirouette or for that matter any movement that is of a lateral or advanced nature, that the horse needs time to consider what exactly is being asked of it. A human being is no different. When you are asked a question of a complicated nature you need a short period during which you consider the matter before answering. Similarly riders must allow the horse 'thinking time'; especially where it is possible that it may not have been asked this question for some while. Aids must be applied *so* tactfully that the horse will eventually understand them without getting in a lather. When a rider has learned to do this and has developed the reflexes to apply small corrections *in good time*, then, they may consider that they have made progress.

Awareness.
At this stage of their education, comprehension of 'what is going on underneath' is one of the most important disciplines that your clients also need to learn. How are the horses moving? If performing say a half pass is *every* step correct? This will depend entirely on your clients' ability to *know* what is happening. If they are unable to do so, then how can they correct an error? Of course you as instructor will probably be pointing out any shortcomings, but that is not good enough, for one must work towards that time when the client is able to recognise any fault for themselves, at the *exact* moment that it occurs. They progress to the point of riding say a half pass, but are they aware to what degree the horse engages, crosses its legs to the extent that is required for a correct movement? If the movement is less than perfect does the client do anything about it? Usually the answer is no. Afterwards and with your prompting they may well express the view that the movement 'could have been better'.

Beginning to really use ones 'Grey Matter'.
On looking back over that which I have already written, I note that I have continually been going on about this particular aspect of equitation. 'Surely by this time', you may be thinking, all that should be a 'fait-accompli'? The answer is quite simply that it should be but most times, it isn't. Despite the fact that at this advanced stage of tuition thinking is more important than ever before.

Why so?
Well…your riders may now pay only minimal and *subconscious* attention to the own correct position, but are they able to recognise a potential deviation at the *very second* that the horse is thinking about it? For example you have constructed your lesson so that it builds up to the point where your pupils ask for a half pass at the walk, but are they ready *to stop* the movement, if they believe that the horse is going to move incorrectly? Do they understand that the horse must then be made to stand still quietly, he must also be given plenty of time to think about what it is that is required and finally, he must perform the steps correctly? It does not matter if he only does one step. *That step must be correct!* What is more it must be undertaken without any tiddleling about? These are matters that demand intense concentration and 'feel'

and it at this point in your clients' riding education where they reach a fork in the road as it were. They have to recognise in themselves whether or not they have a real desire and also the talent to undertake work at this level?

Clients should learn that the matter of paramount importance is that the horse is *persuaded to obey*. This is a process begun by those who broke him and if their work was well done will have laid the foundation for his further education. The most important aspect of the matter is; does he have the physical ability to do what is asked of him? If not, then it is not right for the rider to demand what the horse is unable to give? That way lies the path to *disobedience*. On the other hand most horses are quite capable of *giving* to a very high degree but are not inclined to do so. Their reasons may range from being a bit off colour to downright laziness and disrespect for the rider. We should not loose sight of the fact that most horses will sense immediately that they are approached, whether or not a rider is proficient. They do not have to wait until the rider, sitting in the saddle, confirms this first impression or otherwise. A horse, informed by the manner in which the rider carries himself and the way that he holds the reins will finally verify the respect to be given, and this may eventually evolve into faithful and totally committed service.

All the extra accoutrements.

To my mind it is not 'best practise' to try to control a horse by applying ever more restrictive attachments. The double bridle does have a part to play in so far as it permits the rider to give ever more subtle instructions when positioning the horses' head but to resort to this as a means of exerting greater control, the answer must be no. This is my view regarding the use of martingales and the rest of the leather strap accoutrements. However it is all very well my pontificating about such matters. The fact is that you will have to deal with horses that are tacked up in this way and it is not your job as a teacher to start acting as a trainer. What *you* must bear in mind is that martingales not withstanding, the more intelligent a horse the less it is prepared to tolerate discomfiture. This means not only that an allowance must be made for any gear utilised to strap its head in any one position but that the very exercises that you may be asking of it must be such that it does not explode with frustration as your clients, ineptly, try to force it into position.

The Double bridle.

I once heard an instructor say to a client, after they had failed to get my horse Jeeves going on the bit, 'Never mind we'll soon change that when we put him in a double bridle next time'. There never was a next time. I have already mentioned the fact that due to having to go abroad for long periods, I allowed him to be ridden by any client. However I would not tolerate the use of a double bridle unless it was demonstrated to me that the pupil had developed hands that were good enough and who had the ability to persuade him to go on the bit when tacked up with a simple German snaffle.

Having said that, one may ask, 'is there a use for this form of bridle'? The answer is that of course there is, the double bridle with is two bits the 'bridoon' and the 'curb' is an extremely useful device in the hands of a good rider. However, due to the fact that it is an extremely powerful tool, especially in so far as the use of the curb bit is concerned, you must know how to check that it is fitted correctly. Be sure that you do check and make any adjustments that may be required (especially where the fitting of the curb chain is concerned. Many people have them done up much too tightly).

Obtaining collection.

Sometimes I have clients who though extremely competent in riding in every other way, really do have difficulty in obtaining the correct balance between seat and hand. It is a problem of co-ordination between different parts of their bodies and they can't work it out in their minds. I find it helpful to reverse the imperative of seat to hand. In other words, as an alternative to asking the client to create impulsion with their seat and to store this in the hand, as for any collected movement, I ask them to use the fingers to *slow down* the gait be it either walk, trot or canter. The thought in their *minds* is either slowing down or going faster instead of keeping the tempo the same and shortening or lengthening the stride. Thus the *imperative* flows from the hand to the seat. As far as the horse is concerned it means relatively little to him since all that he is being asked to do is to either go faster or slower. From the riders point of view the difference can be quite significant. They seem to be able to comprehend a slowing of the horses' tempo more easily than they are to feel when the movement is becoming collected. It simply has to do with their inability to feel what is going on underneath them.

Now it may well be that there are instructors who will find fault with this way of going about such matters.

The only thing that I can say is that it has proved to be a useful 'means-to-an-end' and I have found that it works for me. When the mental block has been removed I revert to a more correct use of words.

An exercise that may help.
The exercise proceeds as follows: - I count out the tempo, say for a walk – '1--2,3,4,' and so on. I ask the clients to make sure that their horses are moving at this tempo. They do so by ensuring that every time I count out '1' the inside foreleg is coming under the horse. I then change the tempo by slowing it down, calling out, 'wuuuun – tuuuu, threeee, foooor. The clients now have to slow their horses by closing the fingers on the outside rein until they are walking correctly to this new tempo. The client's goal is to keep the horse walking (trotting or cantering) *without* its deciding that it should stop. (In the case of the trot breaking to walk or canter to trot). They can only do this by using the seat and leg. But they are now learning to refine the application of the aids. For if they overdo either hand, or don't use the seat, then the gait is lost.

So what are we looking for?
The rider must have a clear mental picture of what they require. The horse no longer *strolls* around the arena; instead its steps acquire a certain precision. The horse is going forward rather like a soldier marching. The head is held high, the chin tucked in and each step is executed with vigour. When the rider asks the horse to extend or collect its stride, there is an immediate response. It is also essential that when this happens appreciation must be shown with a kind word.

Before teaching any of the following movements. It is essential that your pupils have developed the ability to produce impulsion in a horse that is going forward in front of the leg and lightly into the hand.
Introducing lateral movements.
Another matter requiring due consideration is the teaching of true lateral movements. Since, once again these may quite difficult for some to comprehend and are also tiring for the horse to perform. If you wish to get some idea as to how a horse feels when asked to perform these movements, then, having first obtained your Doctor's advice that you are fit to do them, I suggest that you try doing some sit ups. Lie on your back and, with your knees bent, place your toes under the edge of a divan or bed. Clasp your hands behind your neck and start to swing your upper body from the horizontal position to the vertical i.e. do a 'sit up'. If you haven't done this sort of exercise before, then you *might* be able to do between ten to fifteen before the pain becomes so great that you are unable to do any more. Personally, at the time I write am able to do 100 and 200 with a break, it depends on my mood. I never do less than 100 and frequently do another fifty after a break of about 30 seconds *but the point is that I have been doing them for years!* Because I do them so regularly, after only a short rest, my muscles have had time to disperse the acids that have accumulated and I am able to continue. It is no different for horses. You should ask your clients to put themselves in the horses' place. As for humans so for horses, not too much at one time, but frequently until they become used to it. As instructor it is *up to you* to ensure that this happens.

Reassurance, especially with regard to the introduction to lateral work.
It is my view that one of the first jobs for any instructor is to reassure the clients that the exercises that they are about to embark on are, generally speaking within their level of competence. This means, of course, that you have already devised a program of movements that they will, provided they concentrate, be able to achieve to a lesser or greater extent. Of course though I have already stated that school horses are usually quite capable of more advanced exercises, such as lateral work, the ability of each horse such as physical or mental make up, must also be taken into account. You must point out the possible limitations to your clients.

A good way of going about things
It is my view that the best way of proceeding with lateral work is to ask each rider to ride an exercise individually. In this way you avoid horses getting on top of one another as the riders loose direction due to the fact that they have something entirely new upon which to concentrate. You are also able then, to correct faults more easily and the rest of the class is able to learn by watching. If you do adopt this approach you must have made sure that all horses and riders have had sufficient time to both warm and limber up. Further more it is essential that you make it clear to everyone that initial failure to perform the movement correctly is not something about which they should be embarrassed.

231

Points to watch.

As you start to teach more advanced work you must pay special attention to two things: -

1.   That the rider always has their own position and that of the horse - *correct*.

2.   That, as they embark on riding these movements, they do not, through such deep concentration, allow themselves to loose that essential relaxation. If riders start to stiffen up, then this will be picked up by the horse, which will then proceed in a similar manner.

3.   The rider must be made aware of the fact that *any* tension spells doom for good advanced equitation.

Providing, simultaneously, work that is suitable.

It does not follow that horses that have never done any lateral work at all should not be asked so to do. What it does mean is that the type of movement asked for should be according to your assessment of the abilities of all the animals in your class. For young horses then, it is better to ask for a leg yield instead of something more strenuous. If on the other hand you know that all the horses in the class have done quite advanced work then you should arrange things so that your clients ask for more demanding movements. You may provide work suitable for horses of differing abilities. This does not necessarily mean that the class must actually be split into two separate parts. You simply tell your clients what movement you wish them to perform and make sure that those movements are not antagonistic to one another. Providing sufficient space helps this.

For example there should be no problem, given sufficient space, for each member of a class to ride either a counter shoulder-in or shoulder-in, in the same line. Similarly when all the class are riding shoulder-in you may ask *some* of the class to translate this into a half pass. For those horses where you think that the movement will not suit either horse or rider, ask them to perform a leg yield instead. Should this be from the track to a quarter line then, they will all end up in the same line. You must be especially careful to ensure that those who are only going to perform a leg yield *straighten* their horses, change the bend and their own torsos before commencing. The rest will be correctly positioned for the half pass exercise.

Above all in any movement, especially the lateral ones, the duration should be only for so long as the horse is able to sustain it without, through discomfiture or pain being placed in a situation where it becomes disturbed or excited. I always say, as have so many before me, one or two steps correctly executed are worth gold. Many steps poorly executed are worthless. So *you* must remind your clients, and guide them so that they too learn to judge when to stop before over doing it. Practically the worst thing that you can do is to allow them to go too far. Believe me, many riders, through lack of sensitivity will often do so. If the horses that work for you learn that in your classes they are going to suffer discomfort, then much to your surprise you may find at some point that their co-operation is withdrawn and you achieve – nothing! *As instructor the fault will always lie with you!*

Now some of you, reading this book, may well have seen great trainers working, and some of them do indeed get their horses all frothed up as they endeavour to achieve higher and higher levels of ability. What is more they keep on until they have obtained complete submission. All I can say is that the really top trainers that I have known have not proceeded along this path. After all one is dealing with creatures that do have self-consciousness and an excellent memory and when you see one of them playing up during a dressage competition, you will probably have a good idea as to why this has happened.

To return to the point, we are not dealing with top dressage riders. Most of the time our clients are people who have yet to develop the quick thinking and reflex reaction that will allow them to deal with the type of problem that arises 'from overdoing it'. What is more as soon as their horses perceive an inability to cope they will probably put in a quick buck and be rid of them. Far better not to allow the situation to occur in the first place.

How does one arrange the structure of the lesson?

Since we are concentrating on rider rather than horse it is important to construct the lesson with a beginning, middle and end. As I have said in chapter 5, each exercise should have an underlying theme that logically leads on to the next. None-the-less one cannot simply dive into advanced lateral movements at the 'drop of a hat' as it were. You must start with exercises that will help your horses to limber up and, above all engage his quarters. These should consist of similar movements to those that form part of less advanced lessons, transitions, circles and so on but on this occasion as you proceed, the circles gradually, get smaller.

Climbing to the peaks.

I suppose that making progress in equitation or any other sport for that matter is rather like scaling the heights of a mountain. There are stages each, of which involves a fairly stiff climb during which skills are developed and then one reaches a plateau where one may sit and rest for a while whilst surveying the extent of ones progress by looking back to the starting point. Then one proceeds to climb the next gradient. These get steeper all the time. As the rider progresses so the vista below gets ever larger and the satisfaction greater. I believe that this attitude is very important for a client for it is only through being able to look *back* that they are able to appreciate the progress that they have made. Thus a client asks the horse to go 'on the bit' and with only the slightest bracing of the back and a 'twitch twitch' of the fingers the horse obeys. This is the moment to remind them of the time say six months earlier where the same request, on the same horse, would have been met with stiff resistance. You are the one who will remind them to look back.

The reward.

I have already mentioned the importance of giving a reward such as a pat on the neck after a horse has performed well. This has taken place as the ride goes forward to a walk on a long rein. At this point it is usual to say 'Make much of your horse'. When we reach the stage of advanced riding, we must take a leaf out of the trainers' manual. That is to say that the rider must learn to give the horse a gentle acknowledgement a *split second* after it has *performed well*.

The riders should not have to be told by the instructor but should recognise that moment themselves and react accordingly. This may be no more than allowing a hand to go forward and, momentarily, gently touching the horses' neck. You may be surprised to hear me referring to a training technique when I am constantly rattling on about this not being a book about training horses but the fact remains that at this level there is no real difference between the way we go about these matters. *It is essential that a horse be informed when he has done well at the very moment that he does so*. He will gain much pleasure from this acknowledgement.

Advanced riders should be given a real mental challenge.
Riding a Passada.

This is simply a lateral movement where the horse is looking in the direction in which it is going whilst the rider asks it to prescribe a semicircle (for diagrams and further descriptions see chapter 16 (Exercises to Form a Lesson). This movement is much favoured in Europe. I personally enjoy riding it for it is a useful way of avoiding boredom, on the horses' part when carrying out schooling.

So far as we are concerned it is an excellent exercise in spatial awareness on the riders' part and also reveals to the rider the extent to which they are able to give really light and subtle aids and also the degree to which the horse is paying attention.

Plate i. Van Diepenbek - for the Duke of Newcastle's La Methode Nouvelle et Invention Extraordinaire de Dresser Les Chevaux. (Kind permission of the British Museum).
The reason for my including this picture is in order to make the point with regard to horses being completely schooled.
Here the rider places his whip in a vertical position thus indicating the complete subservience of the horse to his will. (Note the complete absence of tension on the rein and also the rider's long leg).

Similarly riding school horses should be properly trained for the job that they have to do. The question to be answered is, does the rider possess the knowledge to un-lock that which the horse has imprinted in its memory?

Chapter 15

Drill rides for advanced classes.

The following pages show diagrams for a small number of advanced drill rides. The variety is, of course, infinite and you should try and create your own. Apart from the few that I have sketched, you will find many more in 'Drills and Formation Riding' by Shirley Renowden *18 or The B.H.S. 'Instructors Hand Book'. *19

The only criterion governing any movement is that safety is not compromised and the well-being of your horses not put at risk. Bearing this in mind I advise that *only the most experienced instructors teaching the most skilled riders and horses should attempt exercises at this level.*

The reasons are really quite obvious but for those of a somewhat restricted imagination I will give one or two examples. So far as the instructor is concerned, since several of these movements may be conducted at a canter, one must have developed a quickness of the eye and speed of reaction so as to anticipate any difficulty that might arise. Further more, should a problem occur, then one must always remain calm and be able to issue new and precise instructions that will leave your students in no doubt about what they are to do.

So far as the riders are concerned, they no longer have to give any conscious thought to maintaining their positions. They should be able to concentrate solely on their place and manner of going with regard to the other members of the ride. If for example they find that they have completed a movement, say cantering across a diagonal and then going large, they should automatically now know that each ride should pass one another left-hand to left hand without having to think about it. Thus, those on the left rein will automatically be on an outside track, whilst those on the right rein will be on an inside track. One may be reminded of the simile of getting into ones car and driving away and then going (in the U.K. onto the left lane of the road). For those who do drive, a quite complicated series of actions take place. (Opening the car door, placing the key in the ignition, and so on and so on). . None of which the driver consciously thinks about.

Further more any instructions given by the instructor will not have to be thought about but will be obeyed instantly. Finally we come to the horses, they must all be quiet and forward going and not given to getting overexcited when say they are cantering as a ride.

(See Fig. 44 (also a & b) Riding a 'V' formation. (1st, 2nd & 3rd stages)
(See Fig. 45) Riding a 'V' formation (alternative 2nd stage)
(See Fig. 46) Diagonal changes of rein at the canter.
(See fig. 47) Two rides performing half pass.
(See Fig. 48) Both rides inwards turn and change the rein. 1st three riders to left and 2nd three to right going large etc. (1st stage)
(See Fig. 48 a, b, c & d) 2nd, 3rd, 4th, & 5th stages. Mixing it up.
 (See Fig. 49) Riding in pairs at the trot down the quarter lines and then cantering obliquely to each corner with a medium half circle to finish at trot down either side of the centre line.
(See Fig. 50) Two rides on circles riding a 'Cogwheel' at the canter.
(See Fig. 51) Riding the same movement but changing the rein on the circle with a flying change at X.

Note also that in the diagrams that are provided to illustrate the movements mentioned above, I do not use icons of horses as a supplement to my meaning. If you are not clear as to what is involved by this time then it is not advisable for you to be using these movements at the higher gaits.

Diagrams

Two rides showing a 'V' formation (1st stage).
Sitting trot – – – – – – –

Figure 44

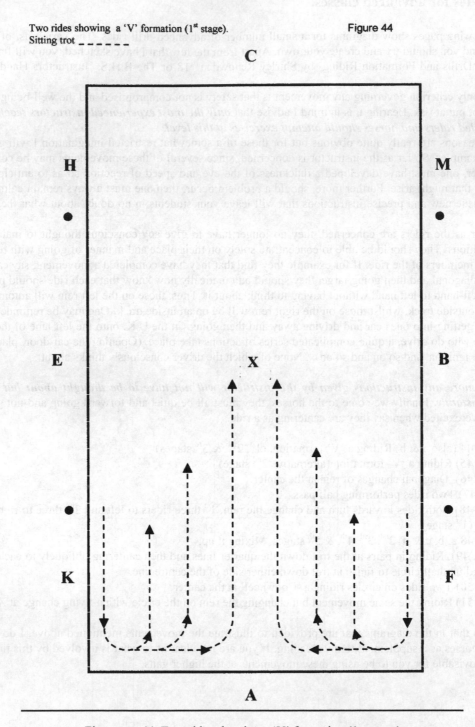

Figure no. 44. Two rides showing a 'V' formation (1st stage)

Two rides showing a 'V' formation (2nd stage).   Figure 44 (a)

Sitting trot _ _ _ _ _ _

Note that there is more to this movement than meets the eye. When the class start the movement they are riding three horses' lengths apart. However its very nature i.e. their positions – relative to one another – especially as they reach the point where they start to go large, mean that they may need to adjust the length of their horses' stride either lengthening or shortening as needs be, so that they all end up going large as a ride one horses' length apart.

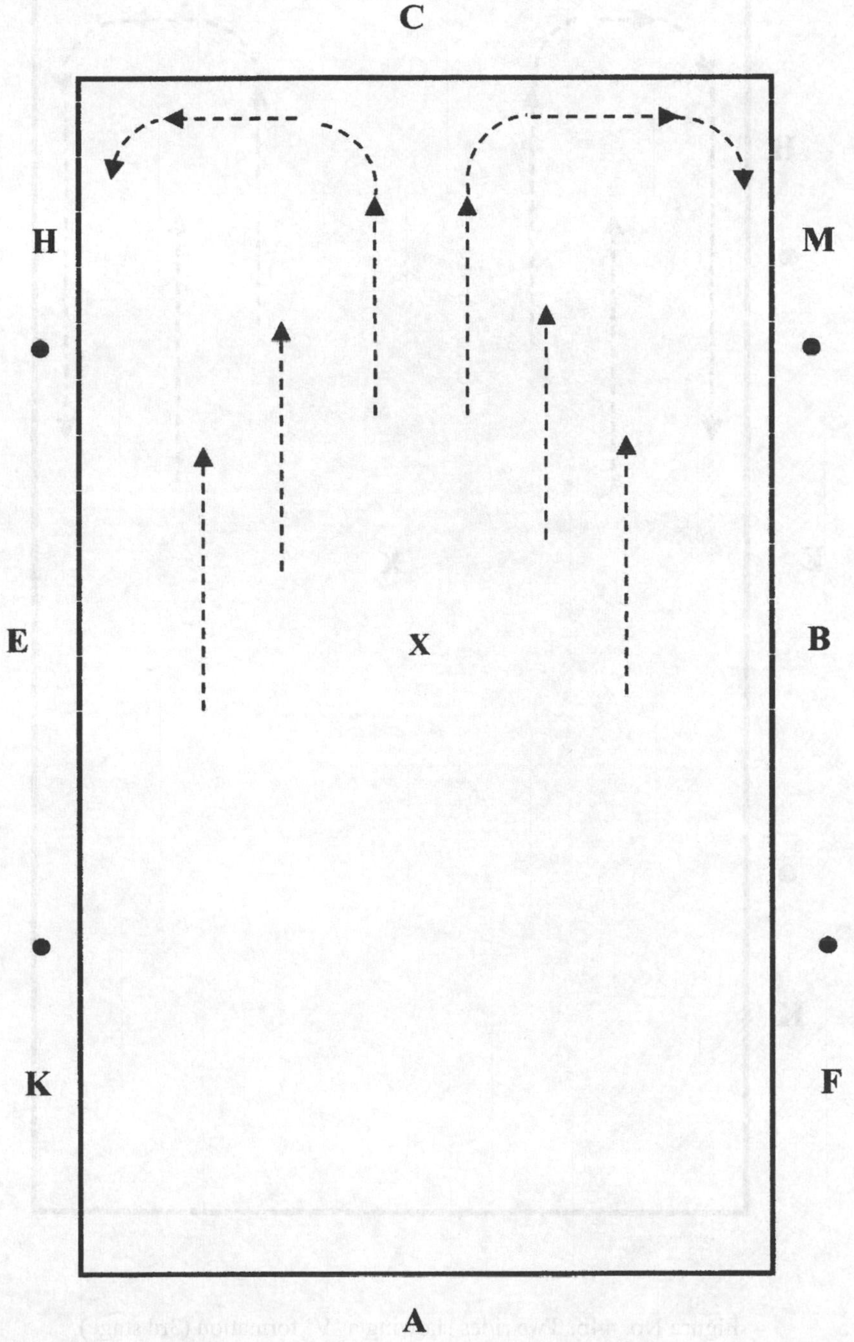

C

H   M

●   ●

E   X   B

●   ●

K   F

A

Figure no. 44a. Two rides showing a 'V' formation (2

Two rides showing a 'V' formation (3rd stage).
Sitting trot _ _ _ _ _ _   Canter _ . _ . _ . _ .

Figure 44   (b)

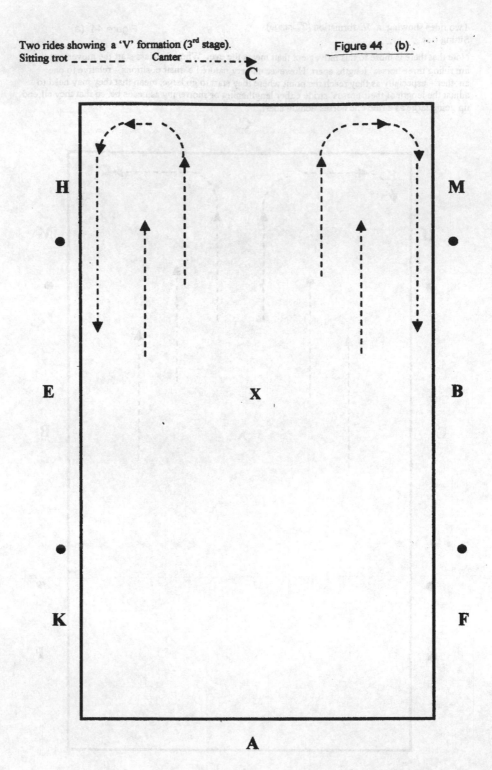

Figure No. 44b. Two rides showing a 'V' formation (3rd stage).

Figure 45

Two rides showing a 'V' formation (**alternative** 2nd stage).
This alternative shows the rides, having adjusted their relative positions so that ride no.1
is one horses' length in front of ride no. 2 . Both ride half pass at sitting trot to single file
and then change the rein cantering going large.
3 horses in ride 1. ▬ ▬▶   3 horses in ride 2. --------▶

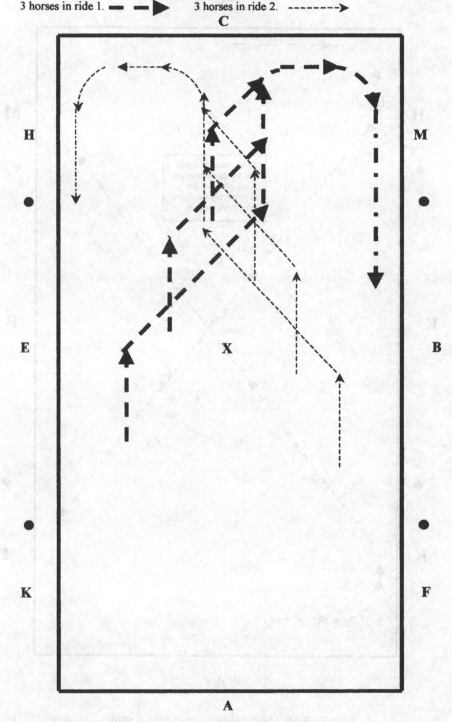

Figure no. 45. Riding a 'V' formation (alternative 2nd stage).

Two rides showing diagonal changes of rein at the canter.
Sitting trot — — — — — —   Canter — · — · — ·   Figure 46

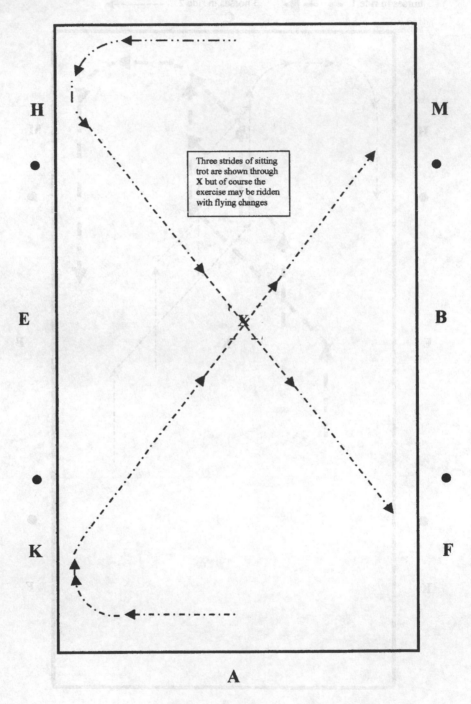

Three strides of sitting trot are shown through X but of course the exercise may be ridden with flying changes

Figure no. 46. Diagonal changes of rein at canter.

Two rides showing Half Pass and then changing the rein. Figure 47
Note Blue ride leads. Sitting trot – – – – –

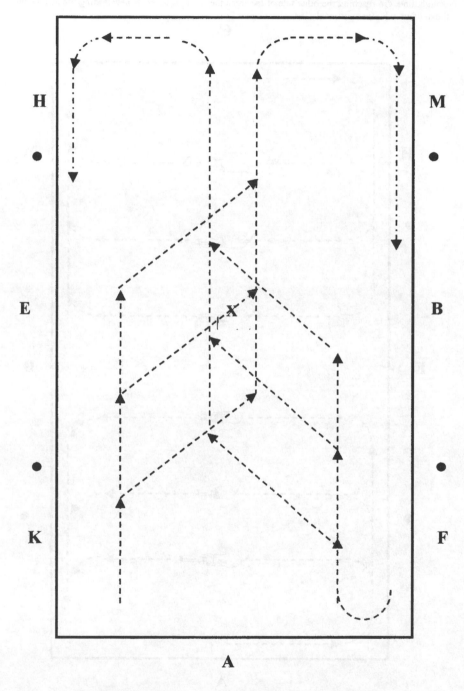

Figure no. 47. Two rides performing half pass.

Two rides turning inwards and continuing on the same the rein (1st stage). Figure 48
As each ride approaches the other, it is left to the leading files to judge that instant when they be one
horses length from one another. At that very moment they turn inwards. The other riders with speedy
reaction note the turn and do likewise so that the whole class now ride across the arena in a perfectly
straight line. On reaching the other side of the arena they split again each new leading file now being
those riders who were originaly last.

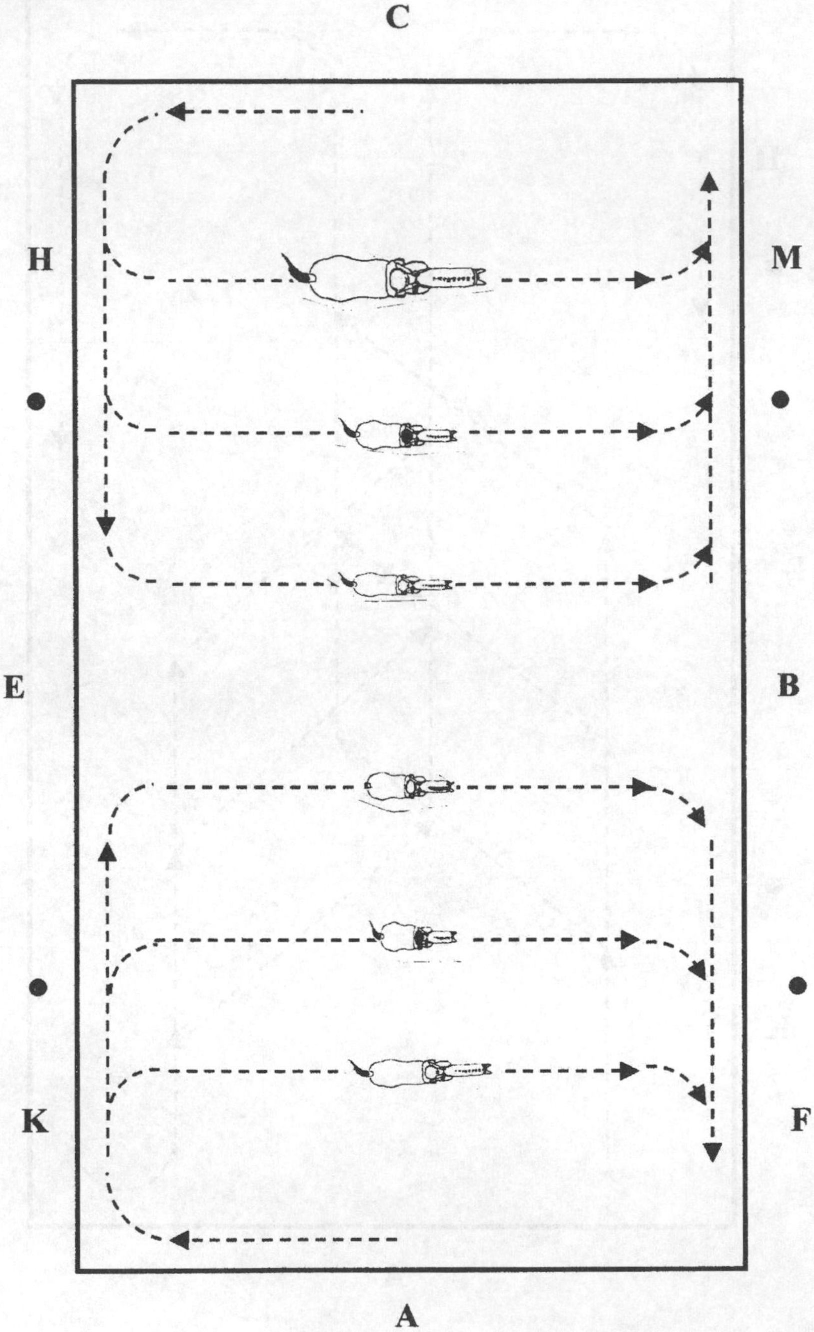

C

A

Figure no. 48. Two rides inward turn and remaining on the same rein (Mixing it up 1st stage).

Figure 48 (a)

(2nd stage).

Mixing it up. The two rides go large and then form one ride 'E' to 'B'. As they reach 'B' they split into two rides once again but on this occasion the first ride consists of the *first three riders* to cross from 'E' to 'B' who now proceed on the left rein while the second group of riders now proceed on the right rein. This means that each ride has exchanged the middle rider with the other ride. These are exercises for riders who are so accomplished that they have time to think, for it is obvious that during each stage of these performances they must continuously shorten or lengthen their horses' stride in order to accommodate the changing position of both rides, relative to one another.

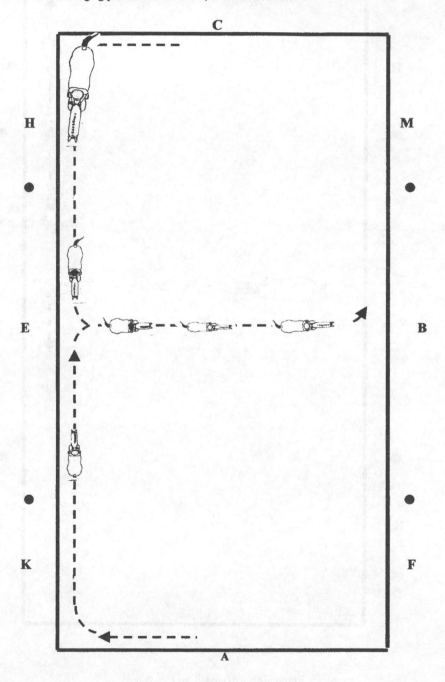

Figure no. 48a. Mixing it up (2nd stage).

Figure 48 (b)

(3rd stage).
Mixing it up. The two rides go large.
Note that the second ride does not turn onto the right rein until the first ride have all completed their turn to the left.

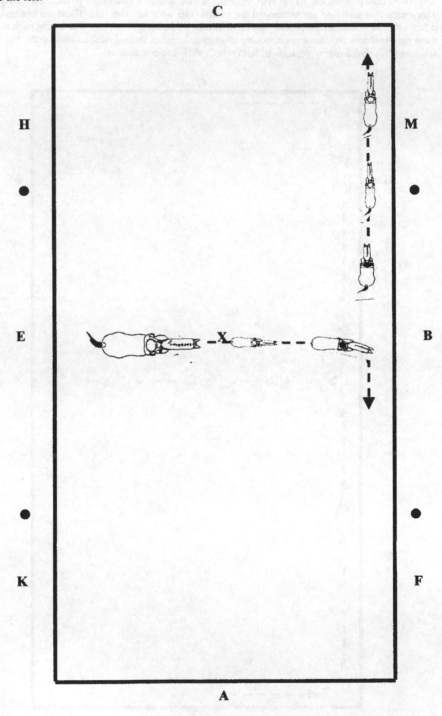

Figure 48b. Mixing it up (3rd stage).

Figure 48 ©

(4th stage).

Mixing it up. The two rides go large.

It will now be obvious that the first ride is now in advance of the second ride. It is incumbent therefore that the first ride shorten their stride, slightly and that the second lengthen theirs, so that they are both, relatively, equidistant as they approach one another along the 'E' side.

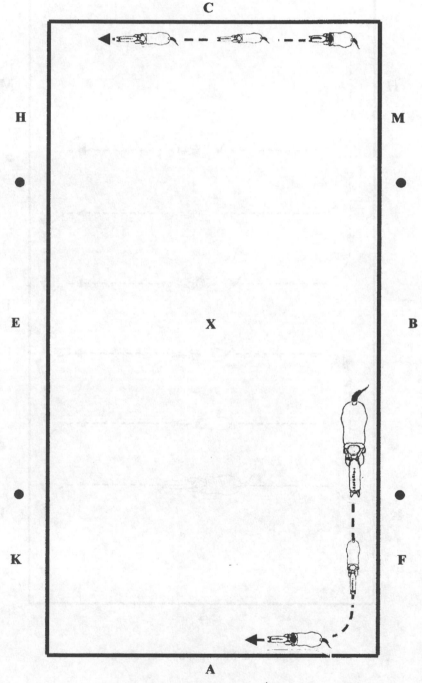

Figure no. 48c. Mixing it up (4th stage).

(5th stage cont.)
Mixing it up. The two rides go large
The two rides now ride towards one another and having turned across the arena as a ride they all now go large on the right rein.

Figure 48   (d)

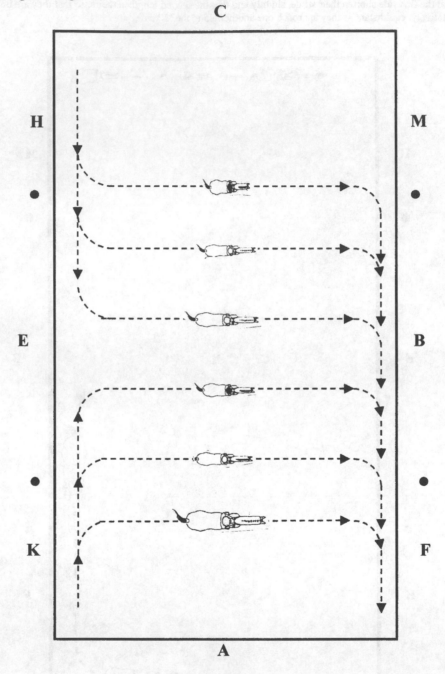

Figure 48d. Mixing it up (5th stage).

Figure 49

Riding in twos at the trot down the   quarter line and then cantering obliquely to each corner with a medium half circle to finish either side down centreline at trot.
Sitting trot   – – – – – – –   Canter   – · – · · – · · – · · – · ·

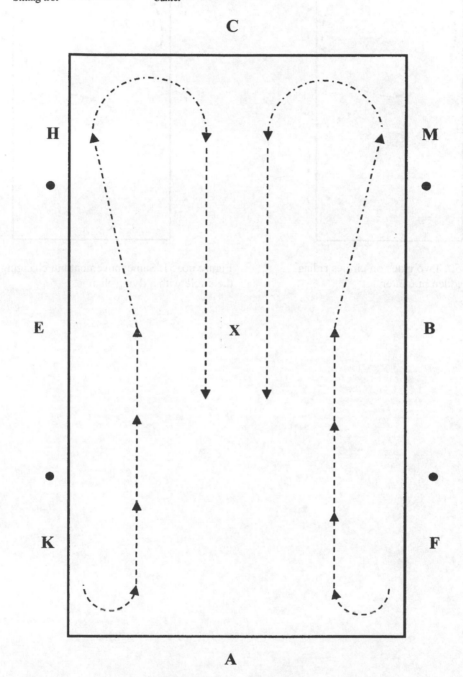

Figure no. 49. Riding in twos down both the quarter- lines and then cantering obliquely to each corner with a small half circle to finish down the centre line at trot.

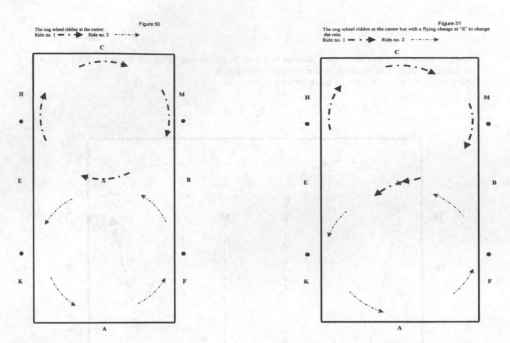

Figure no. 50. Two rides on circles riding
cogwheel ridden at canter.

Figure no. 51. Same movement but changing the
the circle with a flying change.

Chapter 16

Exercises to form a lesson.

Introduction.

Before proceeding with this chapter, I must make my thoughts quite clear. This whole book is devoted to teaching riding to those who wish to do so for pleasure. The approach of the instructor is always made with that thought in mind. Progress is therefore, sometimes quite slow. The *real* satisfaction for me would be to turn out riders who, provided that they are not completely without talent, eventually become *excellent* horsemen and women. Just to be clear as to my exact meaning, I am referring to riders who are *never* seen riding in a slouched position, whose toes never turn out and whose hands are always soft and responsive. Those who have developed such an instinct for the correct position that they have time to think about the well-being and correctness of their horses.

In order to produce riders of a high calibre, in a relatively short time span, it might be necessary to resort to the approach more familiarly associated with an army sergeant major. I do, sometimes, have to contain my irritation, when I tell a pupil for the umpteenth time, not to ride with the toes turned out, the heals sticking up or the elbows pushed out in front of them. I want to roar at them, as I did when, during my initial 'square bashing' on entry into the Air Force, I was put in charge of my squad. I wanted to repeat and repeat any exercise where the standard did not reach that which I considered satisfactory. Not to moving on to the next movement, until the first had reached perfection and had become second nature.

For as much as that approach might well have got quick results in the forces, my pupils, being neither army nor air force, and being free agents, would probably decide to ride elsewhere. However that does not mean that one should go to the other extreme and not really bother too much. I have seen an instructor giving a lesson for the canter. As one pupil struggled ever more unsuccessfully to achieve that gait, so the instructors comments became less and less precise. The pupil resorted to ever greater physical efforts and the poor horse suffered as, due to the riders immense striving, the aids became ever more contradictory. The exercise should have been stopped until the fundamentals had been re-examined. Then the pupil should have been taken through the whole thing step by step with the instructor vocally guiding all the way. After all it wasn't as though the horse wasn't trying, it was proceeding around the arena at a very vigorous trot. But how can I be so sure that the fault did not lie with the horse? Because I had had the animal in one of my classes previously, and its response to every aid, correctly given, was perfect.

The point that I am making, is, 'do not allow yourselves to slide into a habit of not bothering', simply because you do not always make the headway that you would like to see. *Do* be reasonably persistent in giving practical advice to correct faults.

Exercises to form a lesson.

Listed below are movements that have not been included in either Drill Riding or Games to Play. Some of the movements are only mentioned briefly because they have already been described in detail elsewhere. You may choose an assortment from each section to form part of a lesson. When you create your program do not forget that every movement that you include should form a logical sequence. The same basic principal may be practised in various ways, say for example through different changes of rein (see fig. 52). You should also remember that we are making the assumption that the horses know their work. Bearing this in mind you will find in this chapter a series of different exercises, which may be used as a guide to quickly assembling a series of reasonable movements as a basis for your lessons. And also for those times when you are in need of some inspiration.

The exercises are devised to enable the pupils to develop their use of the aids to a point where they are able to communicate to the horse with the slightest touch or pressure from the seat. Do not spend too long on any one exercise, especially those that are more physically demanding of the horses. Remember that as time passes both horses and riders may start to get stiff and tired. Do not forget that, apart from the exercises mentioned below, you may also include those suggested in chapter 14 - Drill Rides and chapter 20 - Playing games.

In general.

You should devise your lessons around the following rules.

1   When constructing a lesson try to include movements that will suit the majority of those who will be attending your class.

2   Always allow sufficient time for the horses to warm up.

3   Try to combine a series of different movements, e.g. exercises on straight lines with those on circles. It is very easy to get stuck in a rut. Always try to use a variety of movements that differ from lesson to lesson. This will avoid both riders and horses getting bored

4   Include a brief period of riding short transitions through walk, trot, walk and halt in fairly rapid succession in order to help riders develop light aids and get their horses listening.

5   Try to have a good balance between exercises ridden as a class and those to be shown individually.

6   Always start with slower paces and work towards the higher gaits.

7   Ride large circles at first working your way down to smaller circles.

8   The same rule should apply to lateral work. Start with elementary movements such as leg yield and work towards traverse, renvers and half pass. (Don't forget that all advanced movements should only be included if the horses have the physical ability to perform them).

9   Be prepared to make adjustments to your programme in order to accommodate any basic change to the conditions that you may find. For example should flooding have reduced a part of the arena area. Or you observe that some of the horses with whom you are about to work have already done some very hard work in a previous lesson. (You should have a word with the office if you, consistently, find that previous instructors have left 'No gas in the tank' and that the horses are sweated up).

10 Allow short periods of time for explanations during which both horse and rider may rest.

11 Make sure that as you approach the end of a lesson that you revert to slower paces so that horses may wind down.

12 Always spend a short time at the end of a lesson discussing with each rider his or her progress throughout the lesson. First praise, then deal with shortcomings and *always end up on a positive note*.

The paces

It should be understood that most exercises, initiated *at the walk*, may be *repeated* at *trot and canter - provided that both the riders and horses have the ability so to do.* It is always advisable to have pupils perform an exercise first at walk and then to proceed to trot. Starting with a walk gives them thinking time. Don't forget that in the early stages your pupils may be unsuccessful simply due to the fact that by the time that they have sorted out in their minds what they have to do, they have run out of space. *All exercises should be ridden on both reins.* Make sure that you allow sufficient time for this

The two main ways of executing a movement.

Divide your exercises into those that require performance as a class and those that are performed individually. Even an individual performance may still involve the rest of the class continuing to be active.

Using exercises in a practical manner

You will note that I *may* mention one pace in particular. I do this where I consider that it is more practical to start at that pace. Thus: - *Going past the ride*. It is quite possible to practise this exercise at a walk. However in order to do so the rest of the class will have to remain at the halt. (Unless of course you are talking about lengthened strides, which will take forever). It is obviously more practical to ride this movement individually at the trot. This will mean that while a member of the class is trotting around the arena past the rest of the ride, the *rest of the class* are fully occupied keeping their horse's going forward. They must maintain an *active walk*, keeping the correct distance from the rider in front and being sure to ride the corners correctly.

So don't forget. Generally speaking start every exercise at the walk, if all goes well proceed to ride the same exercise at trot. (Later on with advanced riders even at canter). Remember each upward transition gives the rider less 'thinking' time.

Riding all sorts of figures.
To keep both riders and horses interested the essence must be variety. Again, provided one keeps the movements within the horse's physical ability, it is up to you to think up as many variations of a movement as you can (safety must not be compromised). Of course, ideally, you should also ensure that each of these follows on and interlocks with the others so as to make a logical and coherent progression.

A completely individual performance.
Pupils need to be stimulated to use their own initiative. One way of doing this is by having riders perform individually. When you wish to do this you must make sure that the rest of the ride is lined up out of harms way. Make certain that there is sufficient room for the person performing the exercise to do so without there being any danger of kicking.

Ride all exercises on both reins.

Upgrading the difficulty of any exercise easily!
This is very simple. You don't even need to bring in a transition. All that you need is to ask your pupils to ride any exercise by starting and finishing at a letter! It is my opinion that it is a good idea to implement this discipline early on in pupils' training.

The walk. - what do you watch out for?
1. When horses are warming up the rider should allow a long rein but not a loose rein. (see photo no. 33 a & b)

2. Corners should not be ridden too deeply in the early stages of the lesson.

3. Even when riding on a long rein the pupils' object should be to get the horse to go forward with a nice regular pace and to engage its hindquarters so that every stride engages the hindquarters ,covering the ground.

4. After the warming up period watch that the pupil takes up the rein correctly (slowly and gently) and now starts to ride the corners more deeply.

The corners.
Most pupils do not give much attention to riding a corner correctly. Whereas on the straight both the riders legs are just behind the girth, as the rider approaches a corner the inside leg should move forward *almost* on the girth and is stretched down. It is as though that leg were a pole around which the horse is bending. To assist in the correct movement the horse's head is flexed to the inside.

Changing the rein through a long or short diagonal.
This is not only an exercise for the rider but is an essential part of your program. Horses should never be ridden for too long on the same rein. The requirement is for the class to ride a corner and as they approach the next letter to look across at the letter lying diagonally across the arena (For example on the right rein from **M** to **K** (see fig. 53) and to ride towards it. The aids are almost the same as those for riding a corner. It is simply a matter of degree. Always ride a change after a corner and *not* before one. Start with the long diagonal and later work towards a short one say **M** to **E** (see fig. 54).

Your Position.
Some instructors prefer to stand in the middle of the arena. The disadvantage of this position is that you must continually turn in order to keep the class in view. If the class does ride behind your back then they may be out of your sight for too long. You should be standing inside the track at one of the corners of the arena. You should be sufficiently far in so that you will not be kicked as the ride goes behind you. In this

spot you have the ride in your view for most of the arena. By turning your body slightly you also minimise the black spot behind you.

What do you watch out for?

1. Some riders will allow their horses to cut the corner and turn before reaching the starting letter.

2. When they ride across the arena they do not do so in a straight line.

3. The ride may have a poor aim when riding towards the letter on the far side. You need to tell them to ride slightly one side of the letter so that at the exact moment when they ride past, their bodies are level with the letter (If changing from **M** to **K** the ride should aim slightly to the right of the letter **K**. It is a good idea to ask for each *letter to be touched* as every rider reaches it.

4. The corner following the change should be ridden correctly. So often one sees a class ride a good change only for it to be spoilt by allowing their horses to fall in as they ride the next corner. The reason for this is a lack of concentration. Having ridden the change riders tend to switch off.

Don't forget that there many other ways in which your class can be asked to change the rein. They are discussed either below or under the section dealing with drill rides.

A sort of figure of eight.

Once your class has mastered the art of going large around the arena, the time approaches for something a little more ambitious. A sort of figure of eight movement is a good start. This is very similar to a change of rein, which they should already have ridden successfully. In essentials it is a double change of rein. Having already ridden one change they must immediately ride the next at the first appropriate letter. What is required from the rider is continued concentration. Previously the whole ride, with perhaps the exception of the lead file, has been content to follow the rider in front. They have only had to think about riding the corners correctly. Now they must concentrate on riding a corner and then changing the rein. And all of this has to be ridden accurately with the changes from letter to letter (see fig. 55).

What do you watch out for?

Well, obviously the same problems as have been mentioned regarding an ordinary simple change across a diagonal. They are: -

1 Turning by the letter (I sometimes ask each member of the ride to touch the letter as they ride past).

2 Not riding the next corner correctly.

3 Losing position with regard to the rest of the ride (Either getting too close or too far behind the horse in front). The reason for this is that pupils have difficulty in thinking about several different little problems at the same time.

4 Losing the tempo.

Changing the rein down the centreline.

This is an excellent movement for ensuring that pupils learn to keep their horses going straight, without the benefit of the wall of the arena acting as a guide (see fig. 56).

Your command.

'The ride, prepare to turn down the centre line at '**A**' (or '**C**, whatever) in single file. Change the rein at ('**C**'). You should give this command as the ride is just making its way down one long side of the arena. The reason for this is that you are going to give a further command. As the leading file approaches the quarter-marker you now issue your second command. 'As you approach '**A**' you will turn your torso and *lock your eyes* on the letter '**C**'. You will flex your horses head so that he is looking where you are looking

252

and you will bend your horse around your inside leg so that you ride accurately down toward '**C**''.

Your position.
Standing at the far letter. As the ride approach you should see one rider only. – The leading file. Now you may think that I am being a bit fussy going to these lengths about a simple change of rein. But this is your opportunity to put across the idea of '*looking where you want to go'*. For this is a movement that will, instantly reveal any deviation as the ride proceed down the centreline. If they are not dead on line, then they will be either to the right or the left and you must be hawkeyed and quick to point out any errors.

What do you watch out for?

1. Riders at the front of the ride tend to overshoot due to the fact that they do not prepare early enough and thus make due allowance for the centrifugal force acting on the horses body (This is especially so when the exercise is ridden at the trot or canter (see fig. 56).

2. Riders toward the rear of the ride tend to allow their horses to fall in and cut the corner (see fig. 56).

3. When actually riding down the centreline, riders allow their horses to drift to either side (they have to learn how to use the leg to avoid this happening).

Using a medium half circle to change the rein.
Another exercise that will help riders to ride more accurately is the medium half circle. This may be utilised in a very simple form as a half circle and return (see fig. 57). Or reverse half circle (see fig. 58).
These may be further developed (see figs. 59 1st & 2nd stages. Fig. 60). All these exercises must be ridden accurately - that is from letter to letter and with the correct shape for the half circle. The size of the half circle may be varied as the rider's ability improves.

Exercises utilising the halt.
Going forward to halt from the rear of the ride (repeat individually for the whole class).
Having started to learn how to use the aids for steering the horse around the arena in various directions, the next exercise that needs to be learned is how to stop and start, especially when the horse may have ideas of its own. For absolute beginners an excellent exercise is simply to have the class going large around the arena at the walk. When the walk has been correctly established you ask the rear file (the last rider) to prepare to go forward to halt in their own time. The rider should then, correctly, prepare and execute a halt. Horse and rider must remain absolutely still until the ride begins to approach them from the their rear. The rider must observe the approach, not by turning the head but by glancing out of the corner of their eyes. They must also ensure that their horses are going forward at the correct moment and in such a manner that they take up the lead file *as* the ride are closing up. The ride must continue, without interruption and with the *correct distance* maintained between every rider.
What do you watch out for?

1. The application of the aids must be correct. There must be no pulling on the rein.
2. The rider must keep their body in the correct position.
3. The halt must be square.
4. The change from halt to walk must be smooth but decisive.

How to deal with difficulties.
1. **Problem.**
   The rider fails to get the horse to halt. The reason? (a) They have not used their seat correctly and given a clear half halt. Very often a rider can be observed to actually stand up in the saddle in the last seconds of trying to halt. (b) Another reason may be that as they are about to halt they tip forward.
2. **Answer.**
   (a) You must remind the pupil to be sure that they sit deeply in the saddle, bracing the back   muscles and closing the legs almost on the girth. This is then *followed* by a clear half halt. In my opinion the bracing of the back is far more important than the half halt. When I school my own horses I always start with a short

253

period of transitions holding the rein by the buckle end and using only my back muscles.

(b) **You** must be sharp-eyed and watch for and correct any errors.

One final point – Don't forget to remind your pupils that, if in difficulties, the voice can work wonders.

Actually I very much like this exercise. It is most revealing at the trot. You would be excused for thinking that it is one that you might, more likely, utilise for novices. But do try it out at the trot with advanced riders holding only the buckle end of the rein. Watch Tyros, as they struggle vainly to get their horses to halt. It is a very humbling experience for them.

Going forward to the halt down the centre line.
An exercise of increased difficulty is one where the whole ride is going large, single file, at the trot rising. As the leading file approaches the markers 'A' or 'C' they only are asked to leave the ride and turn down the centre line. They must then ride downward transitions from trot to walk and from walk to halt, remaining stationary at 'X'. (See figs. 61 for 1st stage).

As the lead file leaves the ride the next rider takes up the lead and it is up to them to keep the ride going large at a nice steady pace.

The rider who has halted at 'X' must ensure that their horse stands still, at attention. The rider must now carefully judge the progress of the ride. As the ride begins to pass in front of them at the opposite short end of the school, so they must judge the point where they ask the horse to walk on. Progressing to trot they should reach the track at the exact point where they will join the rear of the ride the correct distance from the last rider. (see figs. 62 for 2nd & 3rd stages)

The exercise continues until all the members of the class have completed the movement.

What do you watch out for?

1   As the lead file leaves the track you must be sure that they are riding exactly on the centre line. (You should place yourself so that you can step onto the line in front of 'X' in order to see them clearly).

2   Watch the transition from trot to walk (say as they pass the quarter line) and make sure that it is carried out smoothly. Pay special attention to ensure that the rider performs a *sitting trot* before they ask for the transition to walk.

3   Make sure that the halt is square and exactly at 'X'. Above all watch to see that they have given the horse 'thinking time' and that the aid has ceased a fraction of a second before the horse has halted. It would seem such an innocuous series of movements but it is surprising how many riders have great difficulty in keeping to a straight line and halting at the correct point.

4   Finally make sure that each rider prepares to go foreword to walk in good time. Ensure that they are walking on for three or four clear strides before they start to trot. They must make sure that they do not deviate from the centre line as they make their way to join the rear of the ride ending up exactly one horses' length behind the last rider in the file.

Points to help the rider.
1   Frequently the riders' problem in riding a straight line is due to the fact that they do not keep their eyes fixed on a specific target head of them. (In this case the letters 'A' or 'C'). They also imagine that all they have to do is to simply sit on the horses back and it will do everything that is required. Without the side of the arena wall to help guide it, a horse may have difficulty in 'going straight'; therefore it is up to the rider to ensure that deviations are prevented by the use of the legs.

2   The problem with the transition very often arises because the rider, having to contend with the first problem of riding a straight line, is unable to concentrate on the second target of changing from trot to walk elegantly. What one frequently sees is a prolonged trot ending with an awkward shamble through walk to halt and this is not what is required at all! So it is up to you to remind the rider as to each separate action that they should be taking in order to complete the first part of the exercise in an orderly manner.

A more difficult way of going down the centreline to halt at 'X'.
One may up-grade the exercise very simply by asking the *last rider* in the file to start off the movement. This gives the rider two separate problems in addition to all the others that went before.

1   Being the last in the file they must ask their horse to turn away from the ride that is going away from them. If the horse is in the habit of simply following on, then this may cause a little 'local difficulty'.

2   The time lapse available for the rider to perform the various components of the movement is shortened due to the fact that they are going to have to be on track at the ***front*** of the ride. If they dilly-dally, then, they will have to wait for the ride to complete another circuit of the school before they can take their place at the front (See figs. 63. 1st & 2nd stages)

3   It is worthwhile remembering that the duration of the exercise may be shortened, for a large class, if you invite riders to commence the movements at either end of the arena. This being the case they will not be able to halt *on* '**X**' but must do so on either side of it (left hand to left hand). (You should take the precaution of making sure that all your horses are compatible and will not have an argument with one another whilst at the halt). Further more you may have to adjust the point at which each rider both leaves and rejoins the ride. It all depends on the size of the arena at your disposal. Should you be using one that is smaller than standard, then you may have to ask the rider to start the exercise by riding a half circle as they approach the corner before '**A**' or '**C**'. Similarly doing the same as they rejoin the front of the ride (see fig. 64 1st & 2nd stages).

When working with ***advanced*** riders and horses you may perform the same exercise by asking each rider to go forward to canter as they leave the ride and perform a downward transition through trot to halt. Departing from halt to trot.

Upgrading with all sorts of transitions.
Apart from those exercises already mentioned, riding transitions from one gait to another greatly assists the rider in developing ever-lighter aids and also helps in getting horses to listen. Halt, walk and trot have already been mentioned. These should be embarked upon with ever-shorter periods in between each change. This does not mean that the rider should be allowed to dispense with the correct preparation. Thus: -

1   From the halt. Forward to walk for three strides, upward transition to trot for four strides.
2   Downward transition to walk for two strides then forward to trot for three strides. These changes to be repeated several times.
3   Now revert to exercise 1. But in reverse. Repeat the exercise all round the arena.

Now one should start to ask for a slightly different type of change. Listed below some suggestions in order of difficulty. Do not forget that you are now expecting your pupils to be able to use their seat effectively.
Trot to halt and vice versa.
1.   Walk to canter and vice versa.

Now for advanced riders.
2. Halt to canter and vice versa. Don't ask for this combination more than once or twice during a lesson. It is very taxing on the horses and don't forget that these changes can also be as tiring for the rider.

What do you watch out for?
1   Make certain that riders do not loose position.
2   In their endeavours to get the required changes be sure that riders do not resort to booting the horse or pulling on the reins.
Looking to make a transition more accurate still. (Counting upwards and downwards).
When your pupils have reached the stage where they are able to make fairly accurate transitions it can be very helpful to ask them to develop a really sharp edge to any change. One way of doing this is by having

the class going forward at the walk and then asking each leading file, in turn, to go forward to trot *at an appointed letter*. This trot is maintained for two letters and at the following one the rider asks for a downward transition to walk, proceeding at this gait for one letter. In this manner they proceed around the arena until they reach the back of the ride. 'Simple?' you say to the class, 'Very' they reply. 'Well there is just one more additional thing that I would like you do, as you ride each transition, please count down the last three strides 'three, two, one' and as you say 'one' your body should pass the letter and the transition takes place at that very second!' Ah me that does sometimes cause a problem, but it is a very good exercise for introducing an element of extreme accuracy. It also teaches the rider to be able to think about one more extra thing as they prepare to give their aids.

Simply using ground poles and cones.

In search of a means of lessening the use of the outside tracks, you may sometimes find it useful to place poles on the arena floor arranged in a pattern of your choosing. The idea is that you create a design around which your pupils have to ride either at walk or trot. The main criteria as to the way in which you place them is subject only to the requirements of safety, especially with regard any exercise that takes place later on during the lesson. I think that the only really safe way is to remove all poles as soon as this particular exercise is over (for different layouts see figs. 65 & 66). Cones are another way of providing quite safe obstacles around which your class may ride (for different arrangements see figs 67, 68 a -b and 69).

Trotting poles.

I touch on the use of trotting poles. Some readers may consider that I do not go into their use in sufficient detail. Once again; this book is about teaching people and not training horses. Having said that, trotting poles are very useful for pupils to develop both ability to 'feel', (thus to appreciate tempo and rhythm). When the distance is increased between each pole the rider needs to learn how to ask the horse to produce more impulsion and lengthen its stride. Poles are useful for a rider to learn to judge distance.

The poles of a grid should be set up to accommodate the size of the horses being used. For example you will need to decrease the distance if you are working with small ponies. In any case you should set your grid either for walking or trotting. See Manual of Horsemanship *25
The object is that each horse should pass down the centre of the grid without deviating from a straight line. All steps must be in a balanced relationship to the poles. In other words if the poles are set for one step per pole (say 4.5 ft. for a medium size horse), then each footfall should be exactly in the centre between each pole.

In order that horses do not use a sudden approach to the poles, as an excuse for tiddling about, it is a good idea to start at the walk with the poles set up accordingly. Work up to trot (don't forget you must adjust the distances before you have pupils going over them at a different gait). Initially the trot should be rising but with well-schooled horses this may be changed to sitting as the lesson continues. This will enable all the horses to approach the exercise in a calm and relaxed manner. Do not use cavaletti, they may trip up a horse and cause it to panic. As the exercise continues the poles may be altered so that they are either further apart for an increase in the length of stride, or closer together to encourage shorter higher steps. Also remember that it may be necessary to adjust the poles if the horses in the class vary considerably in size (this being the case place large horses in one group and smaller ones in another).

When setting up the grid always use a minimum of four poles. (Anything less and a horse might try to jump them (see fig. 70).

What do you watch out for?
1. Always have a good gap between each rider so that there is time to bring things to a halt should a problem arise. A pole knocked out of position must be replaced before the exercise continues.
2. The riders' approach must always be straight (see fig. 71).
3. The rider must ensure that the approach and traverse of the grid is carried out at a constant, relaxed tempo.
4. The rider must look ahead and not down at the poles. Further more both the entry and *exit* from the grid to the track must be in a *straight line*, unless another grid has been set up that will necessitate a change of direction.

All exercises on a grid should be ridden on both reins.

Riding shallow loops.

The riding of shallow, continuous, ***one-metre*** loops is an excellent exercise for encouraging the rider to use the hands, body and legs correctly. At first this should be ridden at the walk from the outside track to the inside and back again, and then later at the sitting trot. At a rising trot the time lapse is too short and the rider will not be able to change the diagonal correctly and this may lead to the horse becoming unbalanced. The ride should be told the point at which the exercise starts and finishes. For example on the right rein say from '**K**' to '**H**'. The number of loops to be ridden should be specified by you. When making your decision you must take into account the size of the arena and the skill of your pupils.

What do you watch out for?

1. You need to be sure that, for every loop, the rider is looking in the direction that they wish to go.

2. They must change the bend of the horse for every loop.

3. They must be sure to sit upright, turn their torsos and change the leg position for every loop.

4. They must try to ensure that the curve has a constant element, that the horse's hindquarters follow the same track as the forehand and that it does not loose impulsion or tempo. If the curve is too large, the more likely it is that there will be a deviation of some sort.

5   Finally check that every loop is consistently ridden. That is to say, if you ask for a 1-metre loop, then that is what your students should give you. When starting this sort of movement, a novice rider usually tends to over-ride. That is to say they ride loops that are so large that they have difficulty in executing them correctly. The reason for this is that they delay for too long before asking for the new direction. You should help them by pointing out that as soon as they have initiated one loop they must immediately start thinking about the next one.

Don't forget that the inside leg (relative to the bend) should be almost on the girth and the outside leg just behind the girth. Sometimes pupils think that in order to move the legs they must be displaced at least 12 inches or more. You need to remind your pupils that changing the leg position is only a matter of moving the legs back or forward a couple of inches – that is all.

A stage further.
Riding shallow loops without using the reins.

Riding shallow loops without using the rein provides pupils with an excellent opportunity to develop the ability to ride the horse by using the upper body and legs only. At first the torso is supported by the action of the outside leg but as progress is made this leg may cease to play a dominant part and instead the horse should be asked to respond by bending around the inside leg which is stretched down almost on the girth. Most riders are quite surprised to learn that the horse knows perfectly well how to respond to the support of a lengthened inside leg by actually bending around it. They soon learn the extent to which a horse benefits from the support from this leg and that this is one of the important components of lateral work (i.e. moving *towards* a point of pressure).

Riding a larger loop.

When shallow loops have been ridden successfully you should ask your class to ride a single larger loop at walk. This may be from a letter such as **K** (On the right rein) to say two metres inside **E**, returning to the track at **H**. (see fig. 72) After some practise the movement may be ridden at a rising trot. This will provide practise for your pupils to learn to change the diagonal at the apex of the loop. Explain to the class why there is a need to change the diagonal. Demonstrate how the horse first proceeding clockwise is bent to the right. Therefore the rider should be *sitting* as the outside foreleg comes under the horse. However as they reach the apex of the loop they are now, technically, proceeding in a new direction (see fig.73) (as they were for each shallow loop). Therefore the bend of the horse must be changed and with it the riders diagonal. When they reach the track at **H** obviously everything changes back to what it was before.

As riders make progress the size of the loop can be extended to firstly **X** in the middle of the arena (an excellent exercise in spotting the so often elusive **X**) and then all the way across the arena so that the apex reaches **B**.

Riding serpentines.
These are really a series of extended loops. Your pupils must be told to ride the movement, *individually* even though proceeding as a ride. The reason for this is that the rider in front of them may loose the shape and if followed then the rider behind simply does the same. They may be ridden either as a true serpentine (See fig. 74) or with a straight element joining each loop (see fig 75).

Remember.
Serpentines with an uneven number of loops *do not* involve a change of rein. Those with an even number of loops do change the rein.

What should you watch out for?
Since they are large connected loops, it therefore follows that the rules that apply are similar to those applied when riding smaller loops. In the case of the genuine serpentine the loops are more prolonged, and the change of bend for each new direction must be completed as the horse passes over the centre line. Errors usually occur towards the end of the movement when the riders tend to loose concentration and follow one another – their horses taking the initiative, falling in or simply going in a straight line (see fig. 75).

For the serpentine ridden with straight-line connections to each loop, then the change of bend is applied as the new loop is about to be ridden. For advanced riders with horses of considerable ability this movement may be ridden at the canter, with flying changes as they cross the centreline. For *all other riders* only the walk and trot. If the exercise is ridden at the walk or sitting trot, then the rider has only to concentrate on the correct positioning of both themselves and the horse. At a rising trot they must remember to change the diagonal every time they cross the centreline. With regard to changing the whip, obviously they should not do so until and unless they have ridden a change of rein at the end of the movement, otherwise they will be changing the whip every few seconds, which will confuse matters.

How to deal with problems.
(a) One of the most frequent problems for riders is to maintain the correct shape. For both serpentines, they tend to loose the profile of the loop and for a simple serpentine they do not ride across the arena at the correct angle (i.e. a 90-degree straight line to the opposite wall of the arena).

Going past the ride.
This is an exercise that, as already explained, is best executed from trot. It is useful, as are the downward transition movements from the rear, in revealing to the pupil the extent to which they are actually influencing their horses, as against being carried 'Harrods Parcel' like around the arena.

As the class is walking around the arena you ask the leading file, only, to prepare to go forward to trot rising or sitting (the rest remain at walk). However as they approach the rear of the ride they must keep the horse trotting-on past the ride until they have reached the front once again. At this point you then ask them to continue again going large, only this time they may join the rear ride. Alternatively if time is short or you have a large class ask them to ride a half circle to the rear of the ride.

What should you watch out for?
1.   That the horse goes forward to trot with a constant tempo.

2.   The rider must be on the correct diagonal.

3.   The corners must be ridden correctly.

4.   As the rider approaches the rear of the ride they must be on the inside track, looking *past* the ride so that the horse clearly understands what they require.

How to deal with problems.
1.   The horse may not wish to leave the ride. The reason? 'It's all most unfair!' After all are not its friends walking along quietly while it is being asked to trot?

258

Answer.

The rider must look ahead and give clear and precise aids. These may be reinforced, if required by a touch of the whip behind the riders' inside leg. You should also remind the rider that they have one more aid upon which to call – the voice! A clear and determined 'Jeeves or (whatever the name). 'Trrrrot **on!**' Should they still have a problem then you may step in and get everything going by leading the horse away from the rest of the ride for a few strides. Alternatively you may approach the horse from the side and towards its rear (not close enough to get kicked) and use your own voice, which should have enough authority to get the horse to obey.

2.   The horse cuts the corners or tries to return to the ride by the shortest possible route. The reason? Again it does not like to be away from its friends and wonders why should it expend extra energy when it is perfectly obvious that the shortest route is a straight line. Also the rider is looking down. It never ceases to amaze me just how many people ride without looking where they are going. One may compare this with playing the piano. How on earth can anyone play the correct notes unless they are looking at the music in front of them? Of course there may be the occasional glance at the keyboard but that is all that it is. A fleeting look and nothing more. So it is with riding a horse.

Answer.

The rider must look where they wish to go. Furthermore they must make the horse look where they are looking. This may mean that they have to have a firm feel on the outside rein (without changing the bend). The rider needs to use the inside leg to encourage the horse to stay on the track.

3.   The horse heads for the rear of the ride as soon as the rider approaches it. The reason? Well this is so obvious that we will pass on to the correction.

Answer.

Again the rider must be looking well past the front of the ride. The horse must be made to look where they are looking. (It is amazing how many horses are permitted to look where they would like to go and, being uncorrected, proceed to do so. The rider must give aids that clearly indicate that, so far as they are concerned the trot goes forward.

4.   The horse breaks into canter as soon as it is asked to go away. The reason? The rider, being anxious not to fail, overdoes the aids. Another reason might be that, in the past, the horse is in the habit of going forward to canter whenever it has been asked to go away from the ride.

Answer.

The rider simply applies a half halt and continues so to do whenever the horse shows any inclination to canter. Note: - You must tell the pupil that these half halts do not need to be severe. A series of quick, continuous but gentle half halts will generally be very effective. If the horse does not listen, then the severity should be *gradually* increased. But this does not mean that the rider should start to 'haul on the reins!

Riding turns on the forehand at the halt.

At some point in the lesson, especially where you wish to give the horses a breather it is a good idea to have your class ride some turns about the forehand. You may go about this in two ways, either as a ride in which case instruct them to ride in open order, or else to perform them individually. If they are to perform the movement as a ride, open order is very important since it will allow for riders to walk on, as soon as they have completed the movement. Further more they must take the inside track in order to allow room for the turn to take place (see fig. 76). Sometimes I ask a ride to carry out the turn as a ride so that they may get used to the idea of riding the movement, then I ask them to execute the movement individually in front of the other class members. This latter approach has the advantage of allowing the rest of the ride to comment on each individual performance. Constructive criticism is what is asked for! When I am satisfied that everyone is able to carryout the movement correctly, and by that I mean with an established rhythm, I may well revert to asking the class to perform all together and to use this as an element of a drill ride. When one has reached that stage you should have a command as follows:-

The command (a macro command).

'The whole ride take the inside track and prepare to halt then perform a 180 degree turn on the forehand' (to the left or right depending on which rein you are on). The executive command is 'Halt'. You count out each stride in order to keep everyone in step with one another. On completion of the movement the whole ride walks on.

Riding turns on the haunches from the halt.
When the class is sufficiently advanced you may perform similar exercises using a turn about the haunches. To make this part of a drill ride you might ask for a turn from the inside track of say 90 degrees so that the whole class is turned inwards preparatory to riding across the arena as a ride and then changing the rein (see fig. 77).

Riding a diamond shape.
By this I mean that you ask your pupil or pupils to cease going large and instead to ride from designated letters such as 'A' to 'B' to 'C' to 'E' in a straight line (see fig. 78). This movement has two every good uses. The first is that it takes the class off the much-pounded outer track around the arena. Secondly it provides a useful change of target on which your riders may focus.

When using this shape for an individual rider or for that matter when one has a class with no more than four riders, you may use each point of the diamond to ask pupils to perform turns on the forehand or, if they are more experienced turns about the haunches. At first perform this exercise from walk to halt. Later you may include trot, walk, halt.

Incorporating a halt and a turn on the forehand.
Now it is obvious that there is more to this than simply riding from letter to letter. When asking for a turn on the forehand by each letter the rider must go forward to *halt on the **inside** track* in front of a letter. This is in order to leave room for the horse as it turns about its forehand and is then asked to walk on to the next point (see fig. 79).

When performing the movement with a rider at each point of the diamond, you can increase the level of difficulty by asking them all to keep an eye on one another so that they arrive at each new point at the same time as everyone else.

Incorporating a halt and a turn on the haunches.
This variation is suitable for riders who have had more experience. Once again the rider must be sure that they halt on the inside track. On this occasion I like them to halt with the *hindquarters* level with the letter (see fig. 80).

More variations on the same theme.
There are many more ways of utilising this shape. Here are some of them listed below.

1   Ride the movement at trot with one stride only at the walk before the halt and turn and one stride of walk after the turn before trotting again.

2   For more experienced riders, ride trot to halt, turn and halt to trot to continue.

3   For advanced riders on horse with the capability. Canter with quarter pirouette at each point.

I used to ride a similar movement to number 3, on Jeeves, however it was a square and he had such confidence in me that he would not anticipate the turn until I gave him the aid just before his nose was about to brush past the arena rail. But that is taking the exercise to such an extent that I do ***not suggest*** that you ever ask of one of your pupils!

A preparatory exercise for lengthening the stride or shortening the stride.
I have already made clear the principles involved in lengthening or shortening the stride. In practise, for novices, this is not too easy to demonstrate. By that I do not mean that it is difficult for you to show should you be riding yourself. What I'm talking about is getting the rider to *feel* when the stride is being lengthened. A good way of putting this into practise, so that the rider and in fact the rest of the ride can see what is happening, is to ask the *lead file* only to try and obtain a longer stride say at a rising trot. You have already made it clear that the tempo does not change, therefore you will help by calling out the tempo and

making sure that the rider keeps to this. You now ask the rider to give a firm but gentle double squeeze, with both legs, every time that they sit and a fraction of a second later to open and close the fingers. Where a rider has a difficulty in managing their hands correctly you may encourage them to rise a little higher than they would normally (they may not be aware of the fact but this will contribute to giving hands). With novices and intermediate riders the exercise will demand some considerable effort in terms of co-ordination and concentration, bearing in mind that for much of the time riders do not really contribute as much as they might.

Very shortly the gap between the leading file and the rest of the ride will widen. You are still counting 'One Two – One two'. So the horse is not trotting faster and yet the gap is widening. It is very satisfying for the rider (you must ensure that the next lead file behind does not allow their horse to speed up its trot so that it can keep up). In a small arena you may allow the horse and rider to proceed in this manner all the way to the rear. In a large area do not wait for the rider to go all the way round, instead start the next rider as soon as the first rider has covered half of a long side.

What do you watch out for?
1 Obviously, as already mentioned, the tempo is of prime importance.

2 It is imperative that the rider gives effective aids.

3 You do need to introduce, during the exercise a point, where you cease to count and allow the rider to go entirely 'solo'. Never forget that you are the 'Ringmaster'. Believe me those horses will be listening to you but it is your job to *transfer* the control to the rider.

Important - don't forget.
In order to maximise the effect of the exercise and also to ensure that it is not of too long a duration, you must be sure that the next lead does not simply let their horse catch up by simply trotting faster.

Shortening the stride.
By using the above exercise in reverse i.e. you ask the *last* rider to shorten and thus the distance increases in front of them as the ride moves away. Before they proceed you should tell the rider to go forward to a sitting trot so that they may more effectively store the horses' energy. You should allow the horse to go forward to walk after a dozen or so shorter strides.
Why?
Because the rider at this early stage in their riding career will very likely have 'cast iron' hands and will possibly cause the horse some considerable and unnecessary discomfort. If you do tell them to soften their hands, they will probably overdo this and the horse pulling them forward out of the saddle will then canter to its original position at the rear of the ride.

Riding circles.
For the horses' sake the first circle to be ridden should, generally, be a large circle, at *one end* of the arena. In a 40m arena this will obviously be half the arena or twenty metres in size. In a smaller arena then it should be as large as is consistent with maintaining a truly round circle.

Why?
Because a circle ridden at the end of the arena provides three points of reference for the rider to use as a guide (A or C and the two black dots).

Explain exactly what points mean and where they are situated.
Before you ask the class to proceed with the exercise you must explain exactly what you require them to do. They need to be told that a circle is *round*. This might seem to be stating the obvious but you would be surprised at the number of people who have no cognitive ability when it comes to riding shapes, especially circles. Therefore you should **indicate** these important points that assist in riding the circle correctly. These, as I have already stated, will be the end letters, either 'A' or 'C' depending on which end you choose, the black dot quarter makers and – the most difficult of all for so many riders 'X' in the centre. (See fig. 81) First have your class ride the circle at the walk and later, progress to trot and canter.

Your position.
Well inside the inner track at either 'E' or 'B' so that the ride is coming towards you as they ride through 'X'

Points to watch.
Of course the size of the circle will indicate the distance at which your riders will pass the designated points. It may be *one stride exactly as they go by the letter,* or if it is a very large arena, they may be several metres to the inside of the arena wall or fence on one side. (See fig. 82). The tangent points must be ridden accurately and their position, of course, depends on where you have the circle ridden.

The problem that riders frequently face is that of their horses 'falling in'. This may be due to the horse being unbalanced or simply because it sees that the most simple way of going from point to point is a straight line (See fig. 81). Watch that the horse is moving its hindquarters along the same track as that of its forehand.

Helping the rider to apply corrections.
The *one thing* that a *rider often does* as their horse falls in is to *try and turn its head outwards*. This is quite incorrect and you must show your pupils how they should encourage the horse to move out by using the inside leg and also by leading away with the outside rein.

Using large half circles.
Half circles are very useful as a means of using a different path for the benefit of both horse and rider. They help in preventing boredom on the horses' part and also provide yet another means of asking a rider to use their initiative when changing direction. You may use them for all paces and they are especially useful for canter exercises of short duration and also for lateral work. You may use any part of the arena where they will fit in (see figs. 83). When using half circles it is important to have your class going in open order. That is to say you have at least three to four horses lengths between each rider.

Using this as part of a canter exercise.
With the class going large in open order either at the walk or trot each rider uses their own initiative to ride a half circle at canter when they consider that conditions are right. Thus it is incumbent on every rider to look where they are going and ensure that there will be sufficient space available at the end of the movement for them to rejoin the outer track without there being any danger of colliding with another rider (the use of the words 'eyes up' may serve as a useful warning of the riders' intentions).

More difficult circles
A large circle in the centre of the arena.
When your pupils have mastered the art of riding a large circle at one end of the arena, you should start to ride the same size circle but in the centre of the arena. This is more difficult for them because they now have only two, readily visible, points. Those at 'B' and 'E' (see fig. 84).

Smaller circles.
As the pupils' skills improve and provided that you have horses with the ability (by this I am inferring that smaller circles are much harder for very big horses), you may now progress to riding smaller circles. Always reduce the size gradually. Start for example with a fifteen-metre circle, and then reduce to ten metres and finally five metres. Do not ride circle exercises continuously; your horses will need a break. Periodically they should be allowed to go large and unwind at either a good trot or even a canter. (Provided that this is not too early on in the lesson and your pupils have the ability to canter).

Riding more difficult circles.
When pupils have developed the ability to ride circles (not necessarily of all sizes) they are then ready to be given something else to think about. Riding simple circles evolving into riding a change of rein, through 'X' as one circle is completed. This will be similar to riding a 'change of rein' figure eight but in this case *there are no straight lines.*

Before you ask the class to commence the exercise, you must explain exactly what is involved. That is to say that they are riding *only* circles and must be prepared to give the appropriate aids in order to be able to achieve this.

262

What do you watch out for?

1 Some of the ride will forget what you have told them. They will lose the circle shape and simple allow their horses to ride across a diagonal in a straight line.

2 As already mentioned, it is important for you to tell your class that this is an exercise purely on circles. If you have decided to ask them to ride say, circles of half the arena, then it is obvious that, ridden correctly, at the point of change 'X', each horse will, *momentarily,* be straight between 'E' and 'B'.

3 The riders must prepare for the change not less than one stride before 'X'. That is to say they must look in the new direction, make their horses look where they are looking (flexed in the new direction) and change the relative position of inside and outside legs relative to the girth.

4 All this to be achieved without any loss of impulsion or tempo.

Changing the rein through a circle.
This is a convenient way of making a change; especially if you have to use a restricted area, for example, sharing an arena. It is best performed for novices and intermediate riders through a large 20-metre circle. Essentially it is simply riding an 'S' shape starting on one side of a circle and ending up on the other rein as one reaches the opposite side. It has the advantage in that it is useful if one is working in a confined space. It also teaches the rider to ride smaller half circles accurately. (See fig. 85)

Your position.
You should be standing on the centre line, outside the circle and facing 'A' or 'C'. This places you in the best position for you to observe riders approaching the centre of the circle prior to making the change. You must tell each pupil whenever you observe any deviation from the correct track.

What happens?
Suppose that one has the class riding a circle at one end of the arena. Let us assume that it is half the school at the 'A' end. The ride is on the right rein. In its simplest form you will instruct the ride to prepare for the change as they pass 'A'. The actual change will start as the ride reaches the next black dot. At this point they turn and ride a medium half circle that ends precisely at the centre point of the large circle. One stride before they arrive there they must prepare to change the direction and as they pass over the centre point they should now be riding a medium half circle on the other rein which ends as they reach the circumference of the large circle at the black dot on the opposite side.

Why ride the change after 'A' and not as they approach it?
A very good question. There is no absolutely compelling reason why when under instruction one should not ride the change at any point whatsoever. One could start at 'A' if one wished. Or anywhere else for that matter. However we are teaching riders not training horses. If the change is made at the quarter marker after 'A' then when the movement is complete the class are ready, should you so wish, to go large. If you initiate the change so that they finish up approaching 'A', and then ask them to go large they will then have to contend with corners almost as soon as they have left the circle. These will probably then be ridden incorrectly. There may also be a loss of impulsion and what should have been a well-ridden movement will be spoiled. As you should realise by now, I do not believe in giving riders too many problems to contend with all at the same time. However any exercise that you do give them must, before the end of the lesson, be ridden correctly.
What do you watch out for?

1. That the half circles are of the correct shape. As with all movements involving circular shapes riders do tend to allow their horses to fall in so that they end up riding a series of straight lines (see fig. 85).

263

2. This means that they must *look* where they *intend to go.*
3. For one stride only the rider must be dead on the centreline of the circle. That is to say if you are using exactly half the arena the horse should be lined up '**C**' to '**A**'.
4. There must be no loss of impulsion irrespective of the gait that is ridden. Therefore if it is ridden at a trot then this should be sitting as the ride commences the half circles.

As I mentioned at the beginning of this section, it is very useful to have a movement such as this when you have only a small space in which to work. Apart from the basic change you, may develop the movement in various ways so that almost a whole session may be built around this basic movement.

Increasing the difficulty.

1. You may start at the walk but then ask the rider to repeat at a sitting trot.

2. Having done that you then go on to ask the rider to perform three steps at the walk as they pass through the centre.

3. Repeat 2. But also ask for a halt for the count of three and so on. The permutations through the three gaits are quite considerable.

Riding a large circle at one end of the arena as a ride and then each leading file going large.
This is an excellent movement, which provides your class with several different things on which to concentrate. Start the movement by asking your students to ride a large circle, at the walk, at one end of the arena (they must remain the correct distance apart). Now ask the leading file only, to leave the ride and go large all the way around the arena at a trot (the remainder of the ride stay on the circle at a walk). As the lead file returns to the circle they go forward to walk and join the rear of the ride (see fig. 86). On your command the next lead file repeats the exercise and so on until every one has had a go.

'Now'. You say to your class before the exercise commences, 'Will anyone find this movement difficult to perform?' My pupils are of course a rather suspicious lot and do not readily admit that they think that it is going to be quite easy and so one of them will reply. 'It all depends on what you have got up your sleeve'. 'Quite right' I reply. 'Because you have to ride the movement at a trot of such a tempo that you will return to the circle at the exact moment when the rear of the ride is coming into the position where you may join without any increase or loss of pace'.

Thus we have two problems for the riders to deal with. There is the first already mentioned above but they do not ride in isolation for it becomes incumbent on the new lead file to set a pace that will *assist* the departing rider to return at the correct time. Thus though each rider performs the movement by themselves the rest of the ride are also involved in providing support. Of course those remaining on the circle must still continue to ride the circle correctly, thus everyone's concentration is fully engaged.

You may make the exercise more involved by introducing a medium circle for the lone rider at the other end of the arena (see fig. 87). Of course for more advanced riders the paces may be changed to trot on the circle and canter going large which will also include a large circle at the opposite end (see fig. 88).

Changing the rein from one circle to another and then going large.
This is a combination movement that has either a walk and trot element or a trot and canter element. It doesn't matter whether you have odd or even numbers of riders so long as you have the *same number of riders on each circle*. One may even make provision for an odd rider left over as it were. Essentially this is an exercise with pupils riding *three separate circles*, each one on a different rein. The greater the number of riders the larger an arena is needed.

Setting up the exercise.
The first thing is to have your ride number. Let us assume that in this class you have six riders and that the exercise will start at '**A**'. You now explain to the class your 'macro' command.

Your command (Macro).
"When I give you the executive command 'March' the following will take place. The whole ride single file

264

will start to ride, a *medium* half circle at '**A**'. As riders *1 to 4* complete the half circle passing over the '**A**' – '**C**' line they will *change the rein* creating a new medium half circle. ***Riders 5 & 6 will remain on the original circle.***

As **riders 1 & 2** pass over the '**A**' – '**C**' line for the second time they will change the rein again thus creating the third medium circle. ***Riders 3 & 4 will remain on the second circle***'' (see fig. 89).

The riders stay on the circles that they have been allocated. As they do so they adjust their relative positions so that riders 1 – 3 – and 5 all cross the A - C at the same time (they must of course do this on the circumference that is farthest away from '**A**'). Same thing applies to each of the other riders i.e. 2– 4 –6. (It does help if they all take their dressing from the first rider i.e. the one nearest 'C' see fig. 90). Allow them time to get organised then give them your next command. On your next command rider no. 1 is going to leave the ride, going large down the side of the arena to join the vacancy that will have occurred in the first circle since riders nos. 3 and 5 are both going to leave their respective circles at the same moment and move one circle up. You must explain this clearly to the ride before you start the movement.

Your command.
''On my executive command 'March' rider nos. 1 3 and 5 change' (see fig. 91). Your riders know what they have to do. On your second command 'March' riders 2 – 4 - 6 now change. At the end of this sequence the two riders on each circle will have moved up a circle until riders 1 – 2 having consecutively gone large, are now riding the very first circle at '**A**'. Once started the exercise may continue automatically with every other rider changing when they get to the top of their circle and the rider at the top of circle no. 1 leaving to go large.

By this time, provided riders keep the correct position with their fellows on the other circles, you may now give an executive command. 'Circles 1 and 2 change the rein out of your circle - March'. If your pupils have been listening and you have been quite clear in your explanations, then the movement should proceed automatically every time the riders of circles 1 and 2 pass over the '**A**' – '**C**' line. Now depending on the size of the circles that you are using, (in other words it depends on the capacity of circle 3 to contain the riders joining it) no further instruction should be necessary from you until you finally say 'Go large'. In which case the whole thing unwinds as the rider now leading from the third circle goes large and everyone follows (see fig. 92). Obviously you do not wait until every one has joined circle 3.

As I have mentioned, for riders with less experience, it is a good idea for the work on the circle to be carried out at a walk and each rider going large at a rising trot. However for more practised riders you should have the circle work done at the trot and the rider going large at the canter.

Finally you may have this exercise performed even if you are unable to have equal numbers of riders on each circle. Let us imagine that you have say seven pupils in the lesson. All that you have to do is to ask the last rider to halt at '**M**' before the exercise begins. As rider no. 1 leaves to go large, they only proceed as far as 'M'. Rider no. 7 having already moved on goes to circle no. 1 (see fig. 93).

What does this exercise achieve?
This is an exercise that is essentially quite simple. Every rider has to ride some medium circles before eventually going large. However so far as developing co-ordination and the ability to think about more than one thing at a time, then it is *very* demanding. Consider: the riders must concentrate on the following for the duration of the exercise: -

1   Each rider must ride an *accurate* medium circle.
2   All participants must maintain a *constant* position with regard to one another.
3   The length of their horses' *stride* must be *continually adjusted* as they *leave* one circle to join a rider on another circle. And of course they need the co-operation of the rider already on that circle that they have moved to.

Using a circle to spiral in.
A circle reducing in size is a useful means of encouraging a rider to maintain impulsion and start to get a horse to bring the inside hind leg under their bodies. Proceed by asking the pupil to ride a twenty metre circle and then, gradually, to make the circle smaller by means of a spiral (see fig. 94). For most school horses reducing to a ten-metre circle is quite enough to encourage collection and a lower croup.

What do you watch out for?

1   That the rider maintains impulsion with their inside leg, because the smaller the circle the more difficult for the horse.

2   The size of the circle does not decrease either unevenly or inaccurately. In other words the rider looses the round shape.

3   As the rider concentrates on the twin problems of creating the required impulsion and in maintaining the correct shape, they loose their position.

4   The horse is not allowed to trail its quarters i.e. the hindquarters to not follow the same track as the forehand.

Leg yielding.

This movement as already described is where the horse is moving both forwards and sideways but not looking in the direction that it is going.

Your position.

You should be standing at the end of the three-quarter line so that you may clearly see each rider coming towards you. It is a good idea, but not essential, to have the ride going in open order so that you have a little longer to observe each person.

What do you watch out for?

1.   Any tendency for the rider to lean over sideways or to twist their body

2.   The rider must be looking ahead and relaxed.

3.   The incorrect placing of the rider's legs. (There is always a tendency for the inside leg which should be placed almost on the girth, to move back and with the knee bent start to rise up the horses quarters).

4.   The reins are held incorrectly. (Particularly the inside rein which may tend to cross over the neck (see photo no. 34 & 35.)

5.   The rider does not keep the horse straight. (The quarters either lead or get left behind).

Developing the movement.

The first stage.

Passing 'A' the rider positions the horse's head to the inside and *turns down the three-quarter line* . The first thing if on the right rein say level with 'K', is to *ensure that the horse is straight*. The movement, which will be to the left, then commences at 'E' and ends at 'H' (see fig. 95). If the rider does not make the track on reaching the end of the arena this does not matter so long as each step both forward and yet sideways is correct. (The exercise to be ridden on both reins).

Second stage.

The riders are asked to start the leg yield as soon as they turn down the centre line and end at 'H'. In order to achieve this they ask for a combination of leg yield and then going forward in a straight line. You make your own combinations but I would suggest something like two steps leg yield and then say three forward – repeated. If you wish you may devise a different combination for each horse. It all depends on the abilities of your horses and the size of the arena (see fig. 96).

Third stage.

The class rides down the centre line. You commence the exercise by having the whole ride moving one step of leg yield, say to the left (If they are on the right rein). This followed by two paces forward and then one step leg yield to the right. This will bring them back to the centre line. Repeat- two paces forward and then one step of leg yield again to the right. This moves the ride to the other side of the centre line and so on. The number of steps is dictated by the size of the arena because it is best if everyone has returned to the centre line before going large (see fig. 97). For each leg yield horses must be positioned correctly for the direction in which they are about to proceed. During the steps that are ridden straight, riders must change their own leg position and also the horses' bend in preparation for the next leg yield in the opposite direction. As the ride becomes more skilled you may decrease the number of straight strides and increase the leg yielding strides (provided your horses are not old and infirm). Of course the number of steps is really dependent on the number of riders in the ride and also the size of the arena.

266

One last time.

Sometimes you may create what computer buffs would call a 'macro' programme. That is to say a multiple series of instructions that will come into operation upon your giving a simple command. Where you are dealing with riders well on their way to achieving a reasonable level of competence, you may ask the ride to momentarily form two rides by using leg yield. Before you start this movement it is advisable to have the ride numbered in pairs (see Glossary of commands.). So you now have a ride in single file going on the right rein, with alternate pairs numbered one and two. You will now *explain* the exercise. You tell the class what they will be required to do *before they do it*.

Why?

Because though the movement is quite simple, if you give the full command immediately before the moment of execution it will probably take so long that you will, in all probability, run out of room before it can be executed. Your executive words of command are going to be simply 'The ride leg yield march'. Upon this command the class will already know what they have to do. Those numbered '1' will ride two strides of leg yield to the left followed by two strides forward and finally two strides to the right which will bring them back to the centre line. (Obviously they must change the bend of their horses when executing the final two strides of leg yield). Those riders numbered '2' will do the opposite. (Here again this ride will have to change the bend both *before* they commence and also for the last two strides going the other way see fig. 98).

The movement should be ridden, first at the walk and then, if all goes well, at the trot sitting. The number of riders to form the ride will be dictated by the size of the arena. Should you have a large class, then split into two rides ensuring that as the first ride starts to come down the centreline the second ride is just starting to proceed down a long side of the arena (see fig. 97).

The manner in which a movement of this type may be carried out will depend on how many riders you have in a lesson and also the size of the arena. If you are working with say only six pupils in a large arena wait until the whole ride is moving down the centre line before giving the command for the exercise to commence. On the other hand if the numbers are large and the arena small, then ask each rider to commence as they start to ride down the centre line. In this way you may increase the number of side steps before it is necessary for each rider to go large. Do ask the riders following the lead rider to try and get into synchronisation as they each start their movement.

Really swanky.

Again if you have a really large arena or have split your class into smaller more manageable rides, you may really 'put on a show'. All that you have to do is to ask each ride, still riding in twos, to leg yield one step to the right and left followed by one step straight and then *two* steps the other way which brings them to the *other side* of the centreline (see fig. 99).

The execution of the movement.

If the ride is going large on, say the right rein you will give them the command 'The ride at 'A' proceed down the centreline'. When the whole ride is in line down the centreline you give your next command. 'The whole ride leg yield March'. The ride splits, momentarily into two rides, appears to hover as such and then melds back into one ride. Carried out correctly the whole effect is rather swanky! You must then tell them on which rein they are then to proceed as the leading file reaches 'C'. (You could of course have put this instruction into the original 'macro'; it's up to you).

Caution.

For any exercise where you stand at the end of the centre line facing the riders coming towards you, make sure that the ride turns away before reaching you so that you are not in danger of receiving a kick.

Do remember.

The above leg yield movements are used purely *for the benefit of the riders*. I would not advocate their use for the training of a horse. However you should bear in mind that all these exercises might be adapted, with great benefit, for proper lateral movements such as shoulder-in, Traverse, Renvers and Half Pass.

The canter.

This gait should not be embarked upon until the whole class has developed reasonable balance.

If you do have the odd class member or two about whom you have doubts simply ask them to ride this section at the trot. Don't forget their safety is in your hands but there is always the temptation to 'keep them happy' and to let your instinct be overruled by your desire to please. I always precede a canter exercise by first asking if there is anyone who does not wish to canter. If there is, then I tell them that they are quite welcome to proceed at the trot. You may consider this to be a rather wimpish attitude but I am writing at a time where, should someone sustain a fall, questions may well be asked by lawyers seeking to apportion blame. If you were to be questioned as to the situation leading up to the fall and asked 'Did the pupil say that they would rather not canter'? You will be on the wrong foot if you answer either that you did not ask or if you did, that indeed they declined but you overruled them.

Initially all canter work should start towards the last third of the lesson by which time the horses should be well settled. However not so near the end that there is no time for the horses and riders to rest and cool off before the lesson finishes. For less experienced riders all transitions should be through the trot, going large, leading file only, from front to rear, – the remainder of the ride remaining at walk (see fig. 100). Before starting the exercise remind the class of the required aids. It is also a good idea to ask members of the class for a definition of the gait. You may spread your questions over several riders. Start with say, 'what is the first thing that you should do as you prepare to go forward from rising trot to canter'? This will demonstrate as to whether they have listened to your explanation of the aids. And so on. Don't forget to make it clear that the acquisition of canter must be through a smooth transition based entirely on the rider giving clear signals. Not only that but the downward transitions are just as important as the upward. By this I mean that you should not forget to make clear to every rider that as they approach the rear of the ride they must start the downward transition in good time in order to avoid the horse taking the initiative.

Now you will note that I have suggested that you give the initial command as trot and not canter. The reason for this is that in the early stages it is easier to first have the rider establish a well-balanced trot around the arena before asking them to canter. The reason is obvious for if the rider has not established an active trot, with good impulsion or the horse is out of balance, then it simply will have difficulty in obeying the rider's request to canter.

It does not matter if they have to circumnavigate the arena again; conditions must be right before a canter can be asked for. When you consider that all is well ask the rider to prepare and then canter. If they have given the aids correctly, then that is what will happen.

What do you watch out for?

1. The transition must be smooth with the rider looking where they want to go and with the body upright and the hands still.

2. The horse must go large all the way around the arena and not fall-in at corners. Or, worse still cut across to the rear of the ride.

3. The rider must be aware of the manner of the horses going and try to set a regular and balanced pace.

4. The downward transition to trot should be asked for when at least twelve strides from the rear of the ride. As the transition takes place the rider should first *sit to the trot* and apply a half halt. This will help to bring the horse back into balance, for it is sure to be on the forehand. Then they may rise and again after say five paces sit once more as they prepare for the transition to walk. This is the correct manner in which the downward transition should be carried out. It is unforgivable for any rider to allow the horse to take the initiative and make the downward transition simply because it has reached the back of the ride.

How to deal with problems.

1. The rider fails to get the horse to canter and only ends up with a fast trot. The reason is, usually, that the rider has not given the aids correctly or that they are loosing their balance. Many people also have the fixed idea that in order to canter they must lean forward and this is what they do. Since the horse is already trying to lift his forehand in order to canter, the rider's weight makes this difficult.

268

Answer.
This is clearly not a case of the horse being unwilling for very often it is proceeding around the arena, with a very energy consuming and sometimes, even an extended trot? Ask the rider to stop trotting and re-establish a calm and balanced walk. Now ask them to trot again but this time slowly and steadily. Now ask them to re-apply each stage of the preparatory aids for the canter (see aids for the canter chapter 6). At the same time ensure that they are sitting tall and still. I have found that it helps if you tell the pupil to sit so far back that they *think* that they are leaning backwards. (Of course they are not, they are only sitting correctly).

2. The horse may break canter after only a few strides. The reason? (a) The rider's hands are dancing about and the poor horse thinks that the rider is asking for a downward transition. Which due to the fact that canter is a bounding motion the rider may have difficulty correcting. (b) The rider does not have enough flexibility in the lower spine and support from the diaphragm, to move the seat independently of the upper body. This means that they will bounce out of the saddle for every stride.

Answers.
(a) Ask the rider to place the reins (held as a double loop) in the outside hand and to try and pull themselves deeply down into the saddle by placing the inside hand around the pommel.
(b) Remind the rider that they must have more 'give' in their lower backbone. Sometimes a pupil finds this very difficult to do. The answer very often is to ask the pupil to quit and cross their stirrups and ride, (at the trot for inexperienced riders), for *a short while* without stirrups. (They may still hold the pommel, if they so choose). This is frequently successful, because without stirrups the rider is able to get their seat right down in the saddle. This in turn will provide the firm foundation that will then enable them to flex the spine. If the pupil starts to wobble and appears to loose balance – stop the exercise. (In practise I have seldom found this to happen).

3. The horse cuts the corner or does not go large all the way round but tries to get to the back of the ride immediately. The reason? Probably, that the horse simply wishes to be over and done with something it finds both fatiguing and uncomfortable.

Answer -The rider must look where they want to go and be sure to make the horse look where they are looking. They should try and use the inside leg to discourage the horse from falling in. They should also lead away with the outside hand as they approach the corner.

4. As soon as canter is asked for, the horse immediately dashes off around the arena at high speed declining any request to slow down. The reason is that the rider has been subjecting the horse to such discomfiture through keeping a very short and tight rein or through pulling on the rein the whole time that as soon as a canter is requested the horse sees this as a chance to get away. The fault by the way lies with you for not spotting this early on in the lesson.

Answer - Remain calm and tell the rider to let the rein go until they are only holding the buckle end. The rein should be held in the outside hand only. This will leave the inside hand free to first, gently touch the base of the horse's neck, and then if necessary to pull the rider down into the saddle by holding the pommel. I have never known this to fail. The main problem is to prevent the rider getting in a panic and baling out, thus it doesn't really matter which hand is used to touch the horse's neck provided the rein is loose. You must tell the rider that so long as they sit deeply - if necessary holding the pommel, they will come to no harm, because the horse will eventually stop simply because it is tired. (You might also ask the rider to try and gradually turn in to the centre line, *using seat and leg only,* because horses associate this with ceasing their labours). The rest of the ride should be told to go forward to halt.

The question that may be asked by the rider.
An obvious query that may be made by any intelligent rider is why the release of the rein and the gentle touch encourages the horse to cease charging around. It would seem to them to be quite illogical that one should use the very opposite aid to that which instinct would dictate. The answer of course is that it isn't. All that happens is that the reason for this behaviour is removed. In other words the discomfiture and pain cease. So far as touching the neck is concerned, this is perhaps more fundamental. A mare will lick and nuzzle a colt in this area and thus in adult life a feeling of reassurance is induced when this is done by a human being either mounted or un-mounted. There may be yet another reason, which has to do with grooming. Stephen Budiansky *31 mentions a study by two French biologists. They found that grooming

carried out by humans in the area of the lower neck (near the sight of a bundle of nerve tissue) seemed to reduce some horses heart rate by 11 to 14 percent depending on the age of the horse or foal. This, it is suggested might be an ongoing result of the reduction of tension, originating through mutual grooming carried out by horses in the wild. I do not make any further comment on the matter, except to say that for years, rather than pat the horses that I ride, I simply give them a gentle caress on the base of the neck with my fingertips.

Any other possibilities?

Well I would be quite remiss if I were to suggest that there might never be an occasion when a horse may bolt. It could be a car backfiring or the appearance of one of those huge machines complete with mechanical grab that arrives to empty the muckheap. On occasions such as these, again it is essential for the rider to remain calm and you must help them through your voice, but reassurance on these occasions arises from the rider actually taking hold of the rein. It is probably that the rider was not concentrating in the first place and had allowed the horse to take some of the initiative that added to the problem. If the rider were alert then a simple pressure on the rein and a calm word would be sufficient.

But I must say that that it is something which has never happened to me (thank goodness). I have experienced the odd pony that has been inclined to go dashing off hither and thither but this has always been the result of a child simply just not using any aids at all, sitting there either doing nothing or screaming. In any event they have always responded to my calm request to hold the pommel of the saddle and to cease screaming and the ponies have always stopped.

'So I suppose you say that you have never been taking a class when the muck heap lorry or something similar has arrived'? A very intelligent question I thought you'd never ask. The answer is that of course I have experienced these problems but I take the trouble to find out when these blokes are likely to arrive. When they do show up everyone has already been warned not to get 'up tight' and to relax and keep their horses calm. If I know that one of my class is a highly-strung individual, then I will already have taken hold of their rein myself. I then send someone off to ask the driver to cut his engine until I have finished my lesson.

5. The horse refuses to canter. The reason? (a) The horse may have a physical problem or, more likely (b) the horse may be nappy.

Answer.

(a) If a horse really does have physical difficulty in acquiring canter, then it has no business in a class in which canter is one of the gaits being taught. However if the reason is simply (b) that it is nappy, then you must take care. If you consider that the rider has a reasonable seat then they should give the horse a tap with the whip behind the inside leg. (Remember to remind pupils that the whip *must only* be used in conjunction with the leg). They may have to give a couple of taps. If this is necessary, then they should be ready for a small buck. If you are none to confident in the pupils' ability to sit, then why go looking for trouble? It is a better idea to have another, more forward going horse, taken to the front of the ride, to give a lead.

6. The rider achieves a canter depart but it is on the wrong lead. The reasons? (a) The rider may have accidentally given the horse an in-correct signal by touching it with their inside leg instead of the outside one, or have in-correct bend. (b) The rider may be unbalanced and the horse again takes this to be a signal given by the rider's shifting body weight. (c) Finally, the horse may be stiff on that side.

Answer.

For the first two problems (a and b) the answer is quite clearly, stop and start again. This time you make sure that the rider *does give corrects aids* and sit still. It may also help if they raise the inside rein about 3 inches. This action will give an added signal to help the horse lighten that side of its forehand. (c) An additional help, both for the forgoing problems and also for horses that are stiff on that side is to ride a medium to small circle at the trot. This will assist the horse to balance in a manner that will facilitate the correct lead.

Making progress.

As your pupils gain confidence, so the duration of the canter may be extended. You may wish to ask them to canter individually all the way around the arena. In this case it is wise to have the ride lined up, across the centreline facing a long side of the school (see fig. 101). As progress is made and you start to introduce a change of rein, figure of eight or circular movements, then it is necessary to have the class split into two rides. They each face one another along a short quarter line thus leaving free both the perimeter and the centre of the arena (See fig. 102).

Final comments on canter.

This movement is probably the most daunting for both rider and instructor. In all honesty some instructors do have some doubts as to whether they will get their pupils to perform the exercise successfully. The pupil fears that they will be carted.

In fact, provided that you go about the whole business correctly you should have few problems. When it comes to getting the correct lead, start with the rein on which the majority of your horses feel at ease. This will reveal to the class that cantering is not so difficult and when you come to ask for a canter on the other rein, they will have more confidence. If you have a class with a goodly number of students, then I suggest that you try to start and end the exercise with riders whom you know are able to canter. This gives confidence to the rest of the ride.

When I have satisfactorily taken a pupil through the whole thing and they have ended up going around the arena at a nice quiet canter and the exercise ends, I turn away momentarily from the ride and exclaim to the heavens, *'It never ceases to amaze me, how, when the aids are applied correctly, the horse will obey'!*

Controlling the duration of exercises at canter.

For novices, it is a good idea to have the class at halt down one long side. Start by asking fairly inexperienced pupils simply to have a short canter down the other side of the arena. This means that you are able to control (usually) the duration of the canter by asking the lead file to go forward first at the walk, through the trot and finally to canter. The *duration* of the canter *is dependent* on the *number of strides* that you allow *at the lower paces*. Generally, unless the arena is enormous, the distance cantered will probably be quite short by the time the pupil has managed to get themselves sufficiently organised in order to get the canter established. You may be reasonably certain that if the horses allocated to your novice ride are suitable, they will stop when they reach the rear of the ride!

As your pupils make progress so you may increase the distance cantered, until you have them cantering from the front of the ride to the rear.

What to watch out for.

1   The canter depart must be smooth. The rider must not allow the horse to rush forward to canter. This means that there should be some degree of collection at trot before asking for canter.

2   The circumnavigation of the school should be accurate. That is to say that the rider should try to ride the corners correctly. If the horse does try to cut off part of the end of the arena in order to join its mates, then you should point out what has gone wrong and ask the pupil to repeat the exercise.

3   The downward transition is just as important as the canter depart. As the rider asks for the transition from canter to trot you must be sure that for a few strides they ride at a sitting trot and apply the half halt. This will encourage the horse to come off its forehand and be better placed to repeat the movement should this become necessary. As the rider approaches the rear of the ride they may be allowed to rise and then again to go sitting trot as they prepare for the downward transition to walk.

4   The transition from canter to trot should be performed at a point where it is the aids of the rider that ask for the transition and not simply because the horse has approached the rear of the ride. This means that you must give your command for the downward transition at a point sufficiently far from the back of the ride for the rider to clearly demonstrate the effectiveness of their aids.

We have already discussed going on past the ride earlier on in this chapter.

As progress continues

When you are sure that *some* of your pupils are really making progress and are really now in control, have the ride split up and into two groups and line up either side of '**D**' and '**G**' each facing the other short end of the arena (see fig. 102). This will leave sufficient room for all members of the class to individually ride canter. Ask them to go large, at canter, until you are sure that they have the horse well balanced. At the correct letter then ask them to change the rein across the diagonal and, *through the trot* and before they reach the track on the other side of the arena, to take up canter again with the new correct leading leg. The number of strides at trot may be steadily reduced as progress is made. In the end you will ask them to change without trot at all – The flying change - but that lies somewhat in the future. When this exercise has been accomplished successfully you may proceed to ask for *circles* to be ridden at canter, but I would advise that this be embarked upon in a subsequent lesson.

Beware.

Only allow a pupil to ride these changes of direction and circles if their horses are going forward at a steady well-balanced pace. If any horse shows an inclination to dash off around the arena and the pupil is not able to get them in hand, then forget about any subsequent figures that you may have already suggested be ridden. Instead instruct the pupil simply to go large and then forward to trot and walk. For it is possible that a horse dashing around might not remain in balance and any sudden change of direction could cause it to fall over.

Changes of rein and circles at the canter.

As the class become more and more confident you may then ask riders to leave the ride, canter past the ride, change the rein through the trot, ask for the correct lead on the new rein and even include a circle or two. The criterion that will govern these movements will be the position of the rider relative to that of the class. Unless you are dealing with skilled riders it is safer to ask for a circle at that end of the arena, which is clear of the ride. If you find, for example, that a circle will coincide with the approach of the class, put it off until a more suitable moment occurs. Alternatively ask the ride to go forward to halt until the exercise is complete (see fig. 103).

Taking the forward position.

When the class have reached a point where they have developed a reasonable seat in the classical school position it is fun to allow them to practise 'going forward'. This is the position that a rider would adopt as they are about to jump or when hacking out at a canter across country. Proceed as you would for jumping in chapter 15. The difference is, of course, that you must make it clear that in this particular lesson the class is not going to jump. You may find, especially with youngsters, that as soon as you mention going forward you are besieged with requests for jumping 'Please, please, please'. Since this is obviously not a jumping class, do not be tempted to consent.

Upgrading to truly lateral movements.

Earlier on in this chapter we looked at the most basic of lateral movements - leg yielding. This is not a true lateral movement because the horse is not looking where it is going. Further more the aids are still diagonal. As I have already said elsewhere the leg yield is a *useful preparatory exercise, for the rider* but not necessarily the horse. The shoulder-in (even though the aids are still diagonal) is to be preferred as a preparation for more advanced movements such as Traverse, Renvers and Half Pass. You should remember that when one moves on to these progressively more difficult exercises, you must be sure that the horses have a chance to rest and that you do not ask too much of them. Remember lateral movements are sometimes quite difficult for horses, especially when asked for by in-expert riders.

Shoulder in and Counter shoulder in.

As the class progress you may consider introducing movements with a real lateral element. In the early stages, having first ridden circles from 20 metres down to ten, one may have passed through a short period of leg yield, which in turn lead on to 5-metre circles. Now one should consider shoulder in. Let us be quite clear, neither shoulder-in nor counter-shoulder in are truly lateral movements (since the horse is not looking where it is going). However the horse is bent around the rider's inside leg and it is beginning to be asked to engage its hindquarters to a much greater extent than was the case for the leg yield. It is an exercise that will help the rider to prepare for what is to come.

I have already suggested that all lateral movements may be ridden from a circle (see fig. 36 chapter 13). So it is obvious that pupils *may* find it easier to learn to execute these movements from that shape. Whether or not you do so and what size of circle you decide to use depends on the size and type of horses with which you are working. Generally a 10-metre circle will suffice. However I stress that it is up to you to decide whether to use a circle or not. Should you decide to do so then you should start by riding a series of circles starting with larger ones and working your way down. This will help to get your pupils to ride accurately. After all it is not much use asking for precision in one movement if that which has preceded it was wrong to start with. When you are satisfied with the quality of circles being ridden, then arrange for your students to depart from the circle as described in chapter 13 (see fig. 38 chapter 13). You may do so in a similar way for counter-shoulder in but I have to say that I do not always use this movement as a precursor to other lateral movements (see fig. 104).

Traverse and Renvers.

Only riders who have reached a reasonable standard of equitation should attempt these movements. Avoid the temptation to include them as part of your lesson when you are dealing with inexpert riders. You may be saying to yourself 'I certainly would not do such a thing'. Be warned sometimes when one is inexperienced and inspiration is momentarily lacking, one is occasionally tempted to suggest this type of advanced work. One might also do so in order to satisfy a pupils' vanity and give them the impression that they are making truly remarkable progress, when, in fact, they are not.

All that happens is that the pupils fail and leave the horses with the impression that they are able to avoid such movements if they feel so inclined. This may result in some horses, especially advanced ones reaching a stage where they simply decline to co-operate. It is then left to senior instructors, such as myself, to work them until they see sense once again. Sometimes even this may not work completely because horses are not stupid and they know whom they have to obey and those that they don't.

Utilising circles for lateral movements.

I have already mentioned that a circle may be useful for helping pupils to initiate a lateral movement. You should also remember that one may *ride* shoulder-in, counter-shoulder-in and true lateral movements *on* a circle. I think that they are very helpful in developing a riders' sense of their spatial position in relation to the arena, and to be able to do this with only minimal reference points.

I do, sometimes, suggest that they start with a turn on the haunches to create an indentation in the centre of what will be their circle and use this as a guide or reference point. (see fig. 105).

Riding a Passada.

For really advanced riders with horses that have the ability to ride sustained lateral movements. I do not see any reason why your class should not ride a Passada. For weekend riders I suggest that it be only ridden at the Walk.

What is a Passada?

A Passada is a half pass when performed on an ellipse or medium half circle (see fig. 106).

I consider this to be an excellent movement for a rider and horse. The rider must ensure that the horse always has his quarters well under him and that they do not lose any forward movement. The forehand must always lead. At the same time they have to have developed a good spatial awareness, so that they know, at any given moment, where they are in relation to the arena. It requires the most refined of aids, which must be ready to invisibly correct any deviation no matter how slight. Total concentration on the part of both horse and rider must be absolute and yet no tension must be present.

Personally, on my Jeeves, I used to like to ride a combination of several lateral movements. Thus Shoulder-in to Passada to Renvers to pirouette and finally to half pass (see fig. 107). The sensation of riding a horse that is advancing with light but collected and energetic steps, while at the same time 'with every fibre of his being' waiting to interpret your next command, is to be filled with a feeling of exaltation savoured long after the moment has passed.

A variety of changes of rein around the arena.   Figure 52

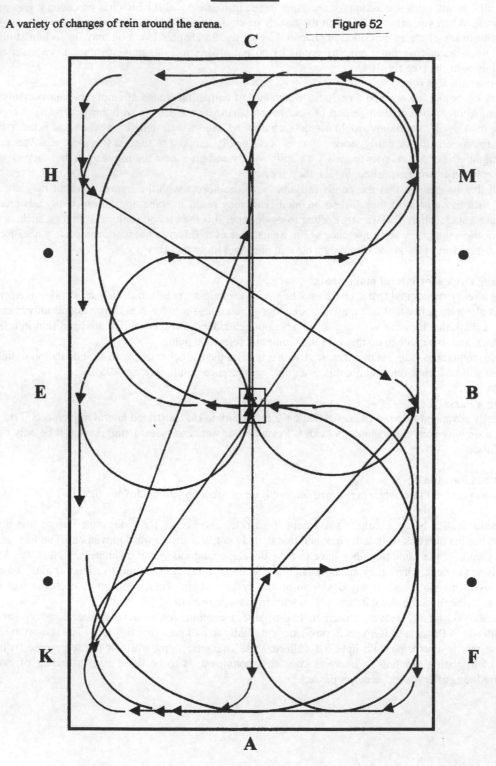

Figure no. 52. A variety of changes of rein around an arena.

Changing the rein through a long diagonal.
Correct _____ Incorrect ....

Figure 53

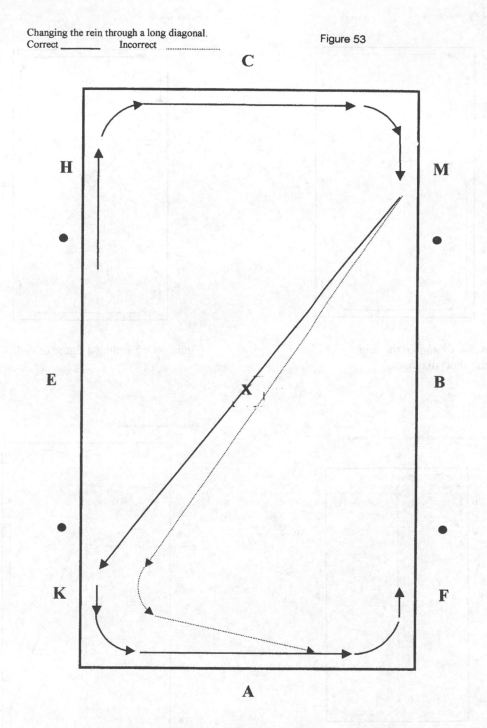

Figure no. 53. Changing the rein through the long diagonal.

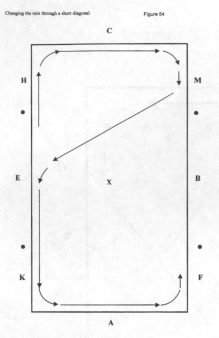

Figure no. 54. Changing the rein through the short diagonal.

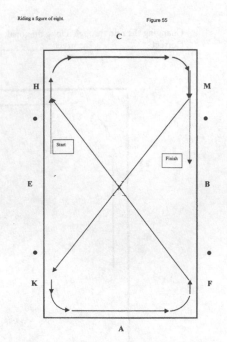

Figure no. 55 Riding a figure of eight

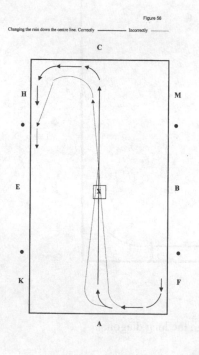

Figure no. 56. Changing the rein down the centre line.

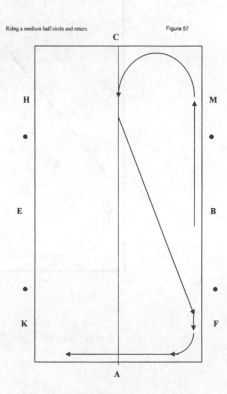

Figure no. 57. Riding a medium half circle and return.

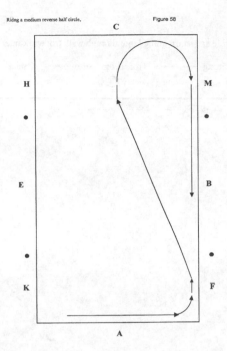

Figure no. 58. Riding a medium reverse half circle.

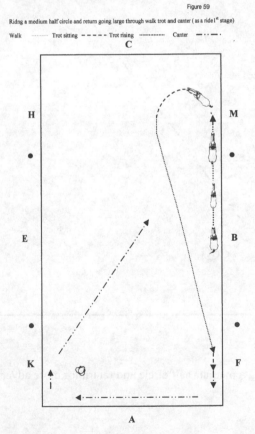

Figure no. 59. Riding a medium half circle and return for more advanced riders (1ˢᵗ stage).

277

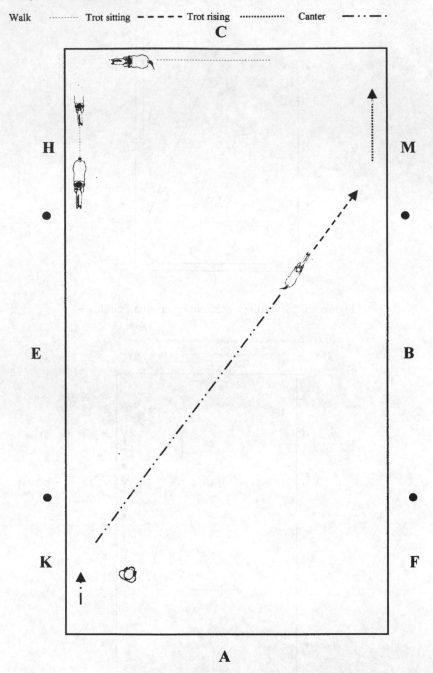

Figure no. 59a. Riding a medium half circle and return for more advanced riders (2nd stage).

Figure 60

Ridng a medium half circle and return going large through walk trot and canter (single rider)..

Walk ········· Trot sitting — — — — — Trot rising ················ Canter — ·· — ·

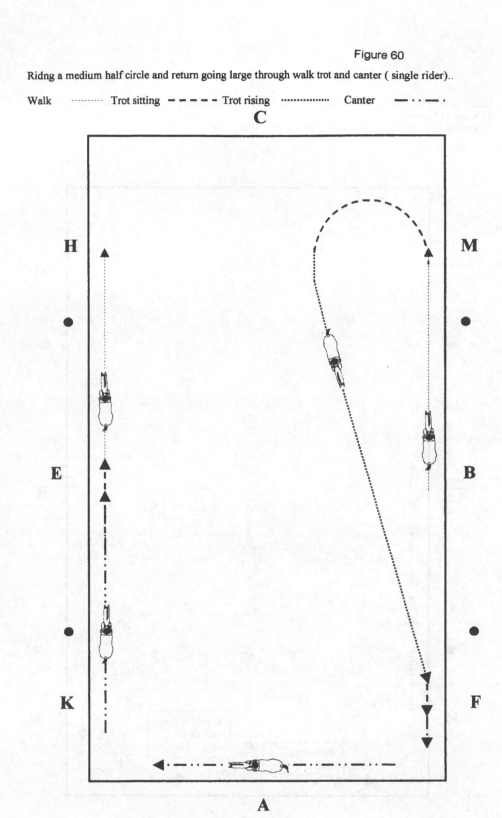

Figure no. 60. Riding a medium half circle and return for a more advanced rider.

Figure 61

Lead file only turn down centre line go forward through trot sitting , walk and halt at X. Rest of the ride go large. (1st stage).

Trot rising •••••••••• Trot sitting ━ ━ ━ · Walk ·····················

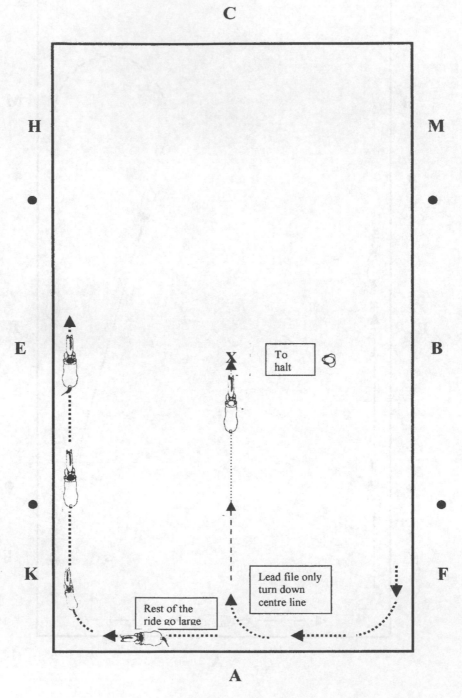

Figure 61. Leading file only leaving the ride to turn down the centreline and halt at X (1st stage).

Lead remaining halt on X. Rest of the ride going large. (2ⁿᵈ stage).   Figure 62
Trot rising   ··········

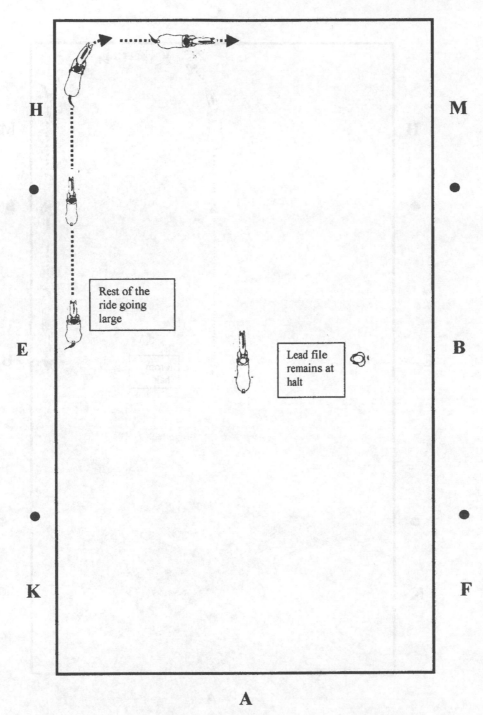

Figure no. 62. Walking then trotting to join the rear of the ride (2ⁿᵈ stage).

281

Joining the rear of the ride from halt at X through walk and trot. (3rd stage).   Figure 62 (a)
Trot rising ••••••••••• Trot sitting ▬ ▬ ▬ • Walk •••••••••••••••••••

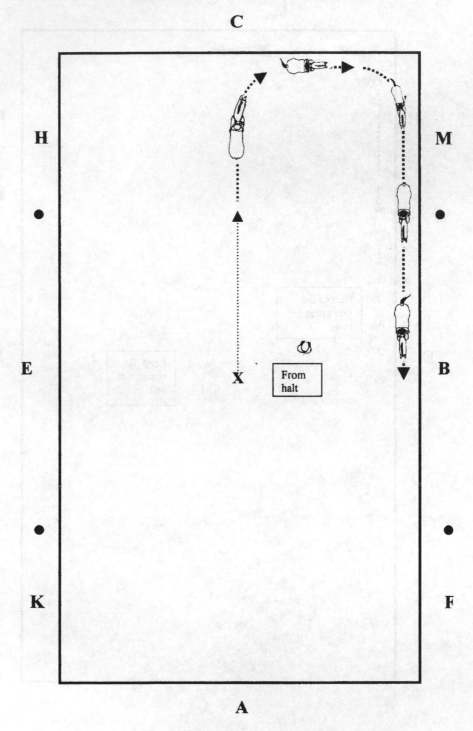

Figure 62a. Walking then trotting to join the rear of the ride (3rd stage).

Figure 63

Rear file only turns down centre line going forward through trot sitting, walk and halts at 'X'. Rest of the ride go large. (1st stage).

Trot rising .... Trot sitting ▬ ▬ ▬ ▬ Walk ....

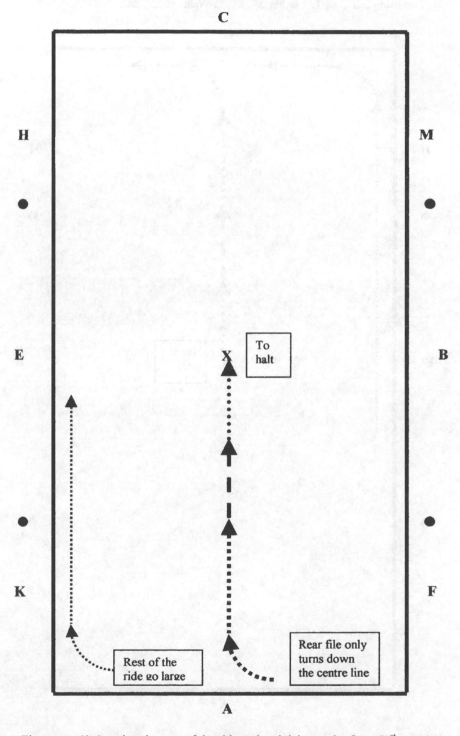

Figure no. 63. Leaving the rear of the ride and re-joining at the front (1st stage).

Figure 63 (a)

Rear file only going forward from 'X' through walk, trot sitting and trot rising to join the front of the ride.(2nd stage).
Trot rising .... Trot sitting _ _ _ _ Walk ....

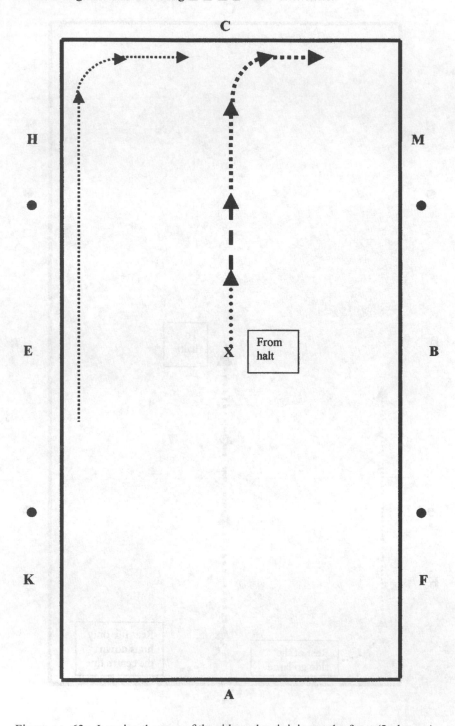

Figure no. 63a. Leaving the rear of the ride and re-joining at the front (2nd stage).

Figure 64

Rear file only turns down centre line going forward through trot sitting, walk and halts at 'X'. Rest of the ride go large. (1ˢᵗ stage **When performed in a small arena**).
Trot rising .... Trot sitting ▬ ▬ ▬ ▬ Walk ....

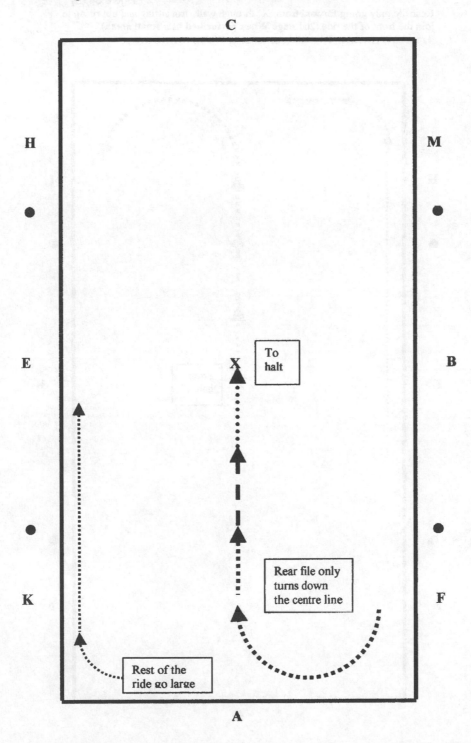

Figure no. 64. Leaving the rear of the ride and re-joining at the front in a small arena (1ˢᵗ stage).

285

Figure 64 (a)

Rear file only going forward from 'X' through walk, trot sitting and trot rising to join the front of the ride.(2nd stage **When performed in a small arena**).
Trot rising .... Trot sitting _ _ _ _ Walk ....

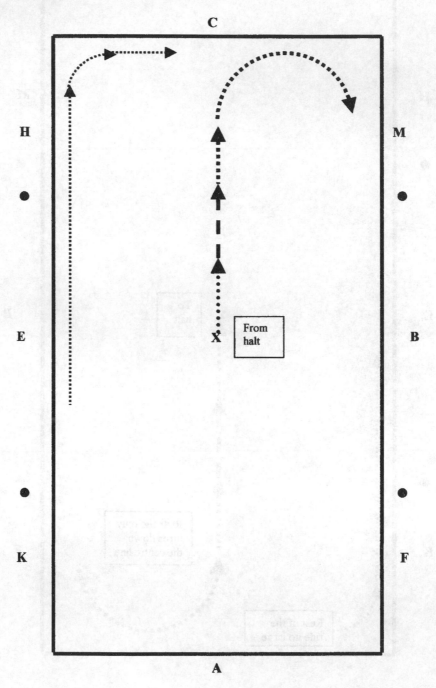

Figure 64a. Leaving the rear of the ride and re-joining at the front in a small arena (2nd stage).

Figure 65

Using poles to provide a course for navigation. A simple three pole arrangement.

Figure 66

Using poles to provide a course for navigation. A series of corridors.

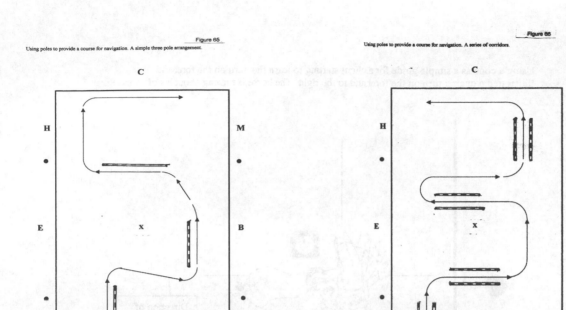

Figure no. 65. A simple three-pole arrangement. Figure no. 66. A series of corridors.

Figure 67

Using a cone as a simple guide for a client starting to learn the turn on the forehand.
Illustrated a quarter turn on the forehand to the right. The horse is turning about his off foreleg.

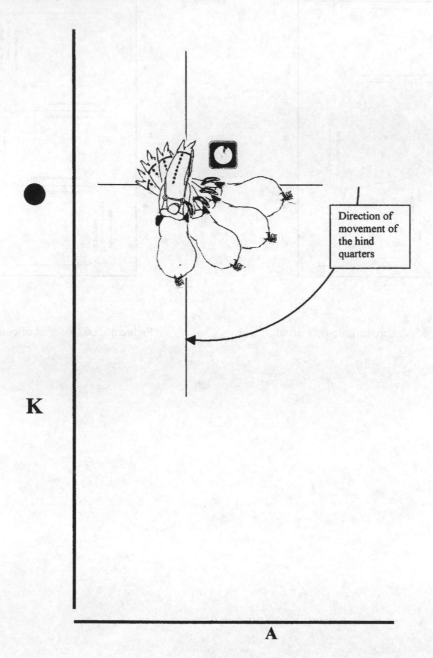

Direction of movement of the hind quarters

K

A

Figure no. 67. Using a cone as a guide for learning a turn on the forehand.

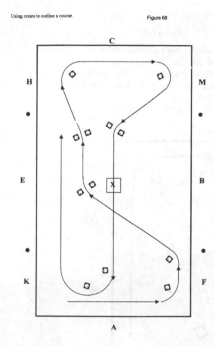

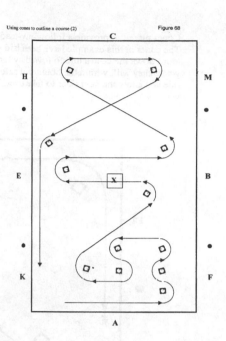

Figure no. 68a. Using cones to outline a course.

Figure no. 68b. Using cones to outline a course.

Figure 69

Cones placed to provide a follow-my-leader course.
The cones in this example have been laid out to provide a course that allows for a series of shallow loops down the centre line followed by loops around a circle. The lead file is at liberty to take the ride where they will, within the bounds of safety. At any point you may tell the leader to join the rear of the ride and allow the next rider to take over. This is a good exercise in helping riders to think in a creative way.

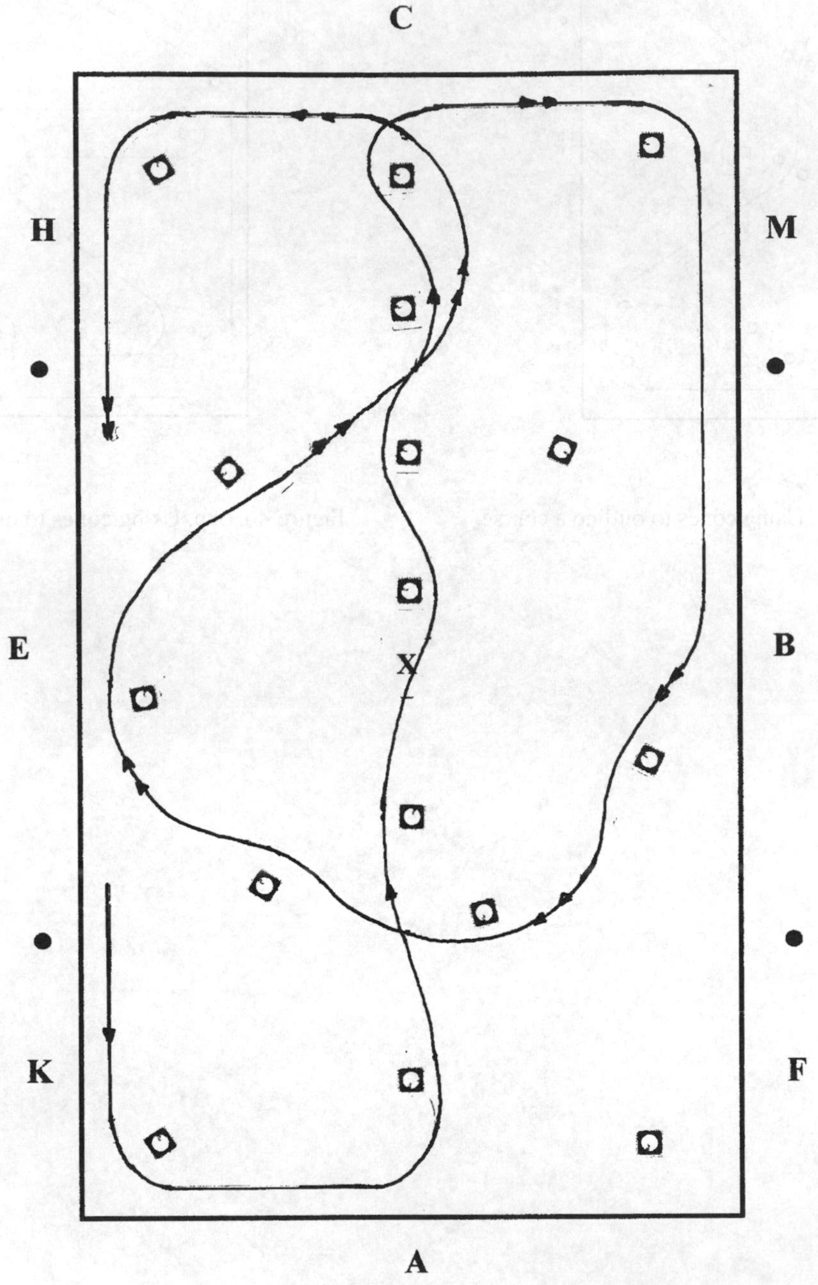

Figure no. 69. Cones set-up as a follow-my-leader course.

Figure 70

Setting up a grid.

Horses may be lined up along the centre line or out of the way along a short end of the arena. The way in which you position them depends on the size of the arena and the space that is available to you. Whatever you decide you must make sure that there is sufficient room for riders to leave and rejoin the ride in safety. In the example shown here the rider nearest the 'A' end leaves the ride and having traversed the grid rejoins at the other end. The rest of the ride have meanwhile moved up one place.

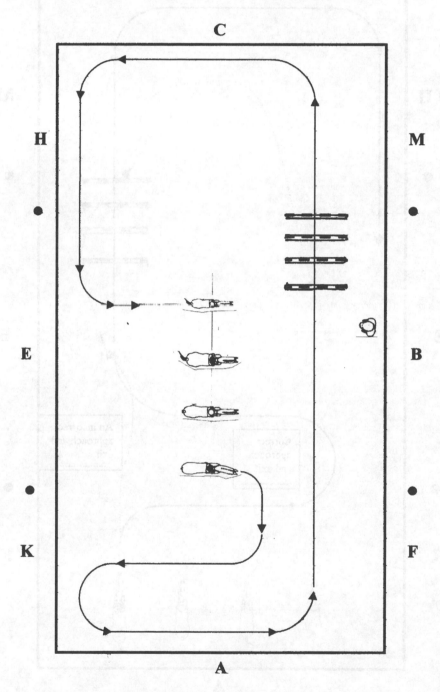

Figure no. 70. Setting up a grid.

Figure 71

Approaching and exiting a grid. (The rider must have sufficient time to get the horse in balance before going through the grid).

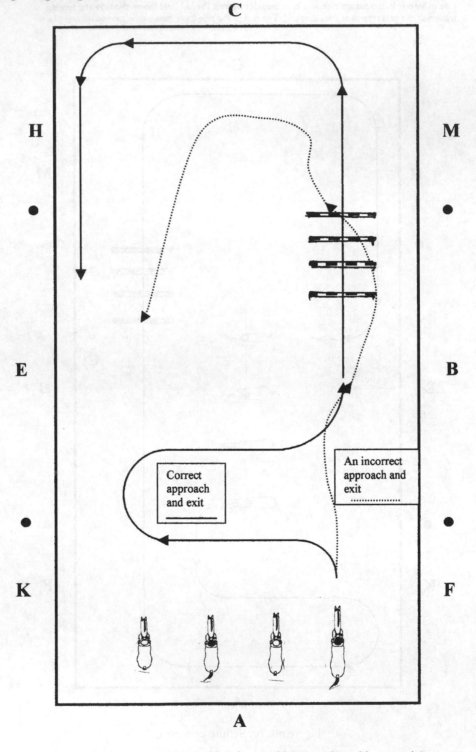

Figure no. 71. Approaching and leaving a grid (correctly and incorrectly).

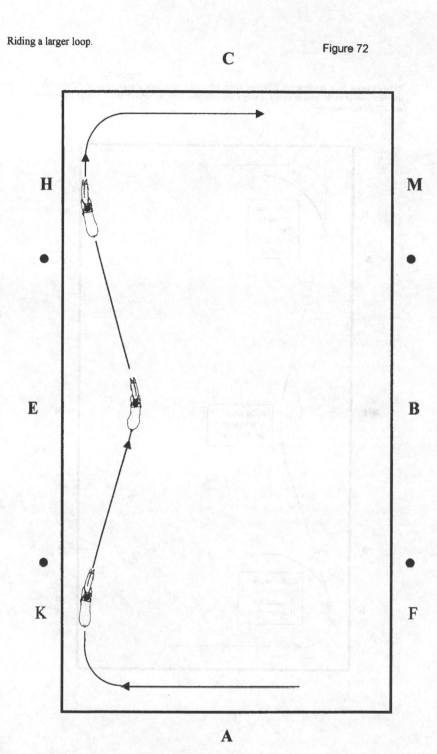

Figure 72

Figure no. 72. Riding a larger loop.

Figure 73.

Riding a larger loop at rising trot. Showing points where the rider must change diagonal. (To do this the rider should sit for two strides) The single line indicates how the bend changes, though the corners are still ridden correctly.

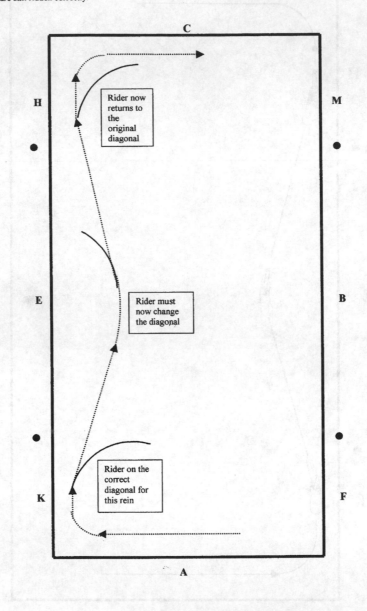

Figure no. 73. Riding a larger loop at rising trot showing the change of diagonal.

Riding a true three loop serpentine.   Figure 74

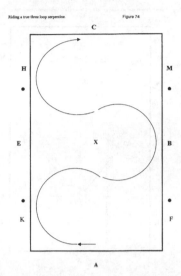

Figure no. 74. Riding a true 3 loop serpentine.

Figure 75

Riding an ordinary three loop serpentine. (correctly ——— Incorrectly ———)

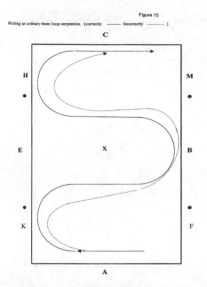

Figure no. 75. Riding a simple 3 loop serpentine correctly and incorrectly.

Riding a turn on the forehand, as a ride, in order to change the rein.   Figure 76

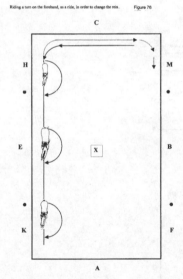

Figure no. 76. Turns on the forehand to change the rein as a ride.

Riding a quarter turn on the haunches, as a ride, in order to change the rein.   Figure 77
Walk ——— Trot rising .... Trot sitting - - - - -

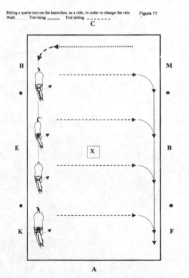

Figure no. 77. Turns on the haunches to change the rein as a ride.

295

Figure 78

Riding a diamond shape using half the arena. This movement may be ridden with simple corners at each angle.

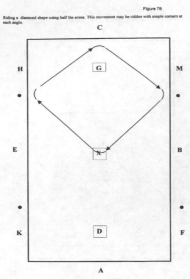

Figure no. 78. Riding a diamond shape at one end of the arena.

Figure 79

Riding a diamond shape in the centre of the arena. With a turn on the forehand at each corner.

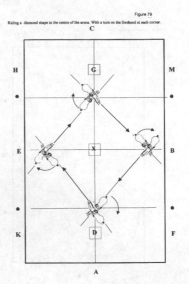

Figure no. 79. Riding a diamond shape with a turn on the forehand at each corner.

Figure 80

Riding a diamond shape in the centre of the arena. With a turn on the haunches at each corner.

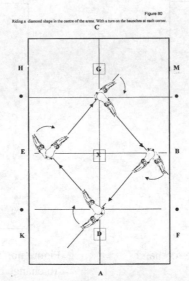

Figure no. 80. Riding a diamond shape with a turn on the haunches at each corner.

Figure 81

Riding a large circle at one end of the arena, starting and finishing at the letter 'C'.
(Note the tangential points – 'C' - 'Black dot - 'X' - 'Black dot' - return to 'C' for the correct circle).
Correctly ———— At the other end. Incorrectly ·············· Also showing how a horse may tend to fall
in . – – – – – .

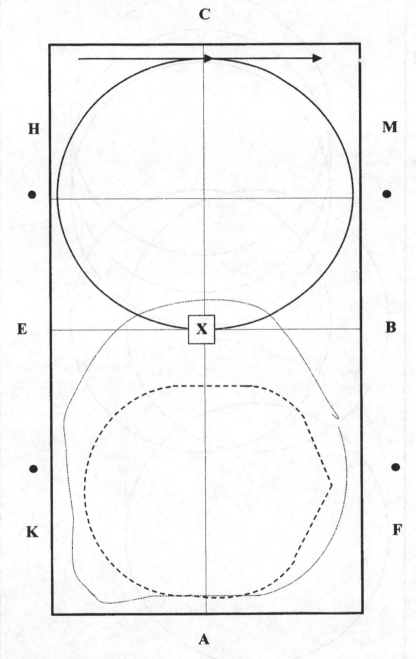

Figure no. 81. Riding a large circle at one end of the arena (correctly and incorrectly).

Figure 82

Riding a 20 meter circle in an arena that is larger than 20 meters. Most of these circles are for quite experienced riders. The reason being that they should be able to pin point the various centres in their imagination and thus to ride any circle of a constant radius in any part of the arena.

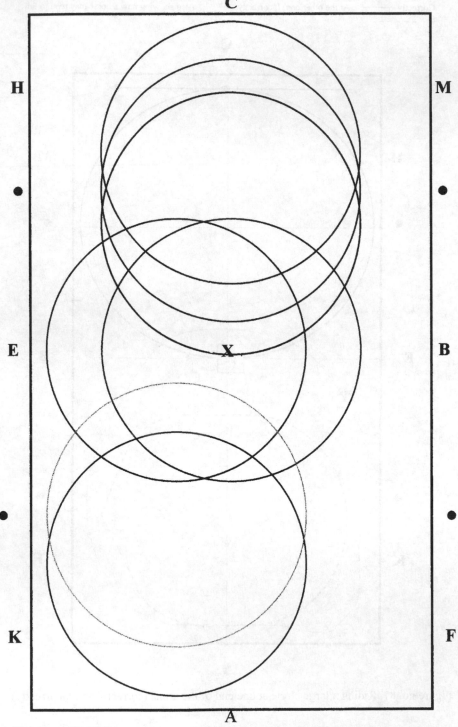

Figure no. 82. Riding a twenty-metre circle in an arena that is larger than 20 metres.

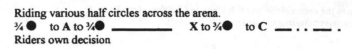

Figure 83

Riding various half circles across the arena.
¾ ● to A to ¾● —————— X to ¾● to C ——‥——.
Riders own decision

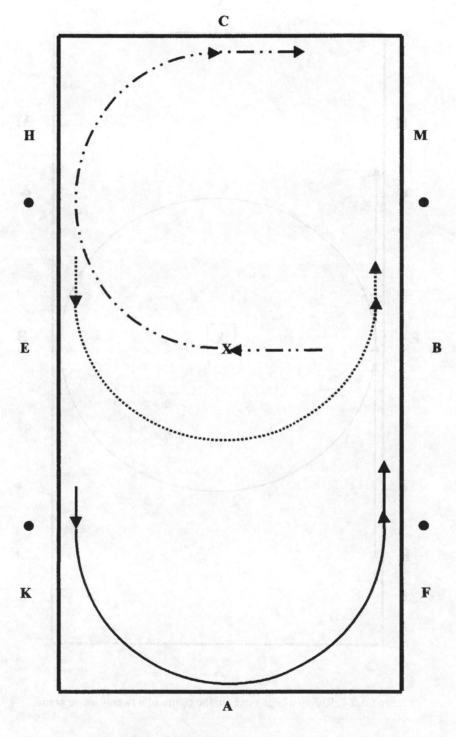

Figure no. 83. Riding various half circles.

Figure 84

Riding a large circle in the centre of the arena. It starts and finishes at the letter 'E'.
(Note the only easily seen tangential points are – 'B' – and 'E'

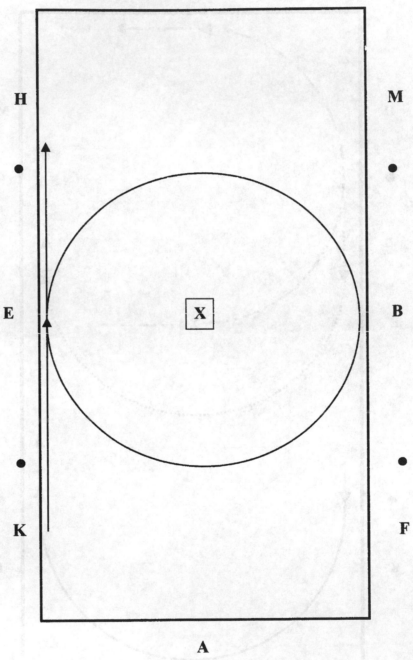

Figure no. 84. Riding a large circle in the centre of a twenty metre arena.

Figure 85

Changing the rein through a circle.
Corectly _____ Incorrectly ....

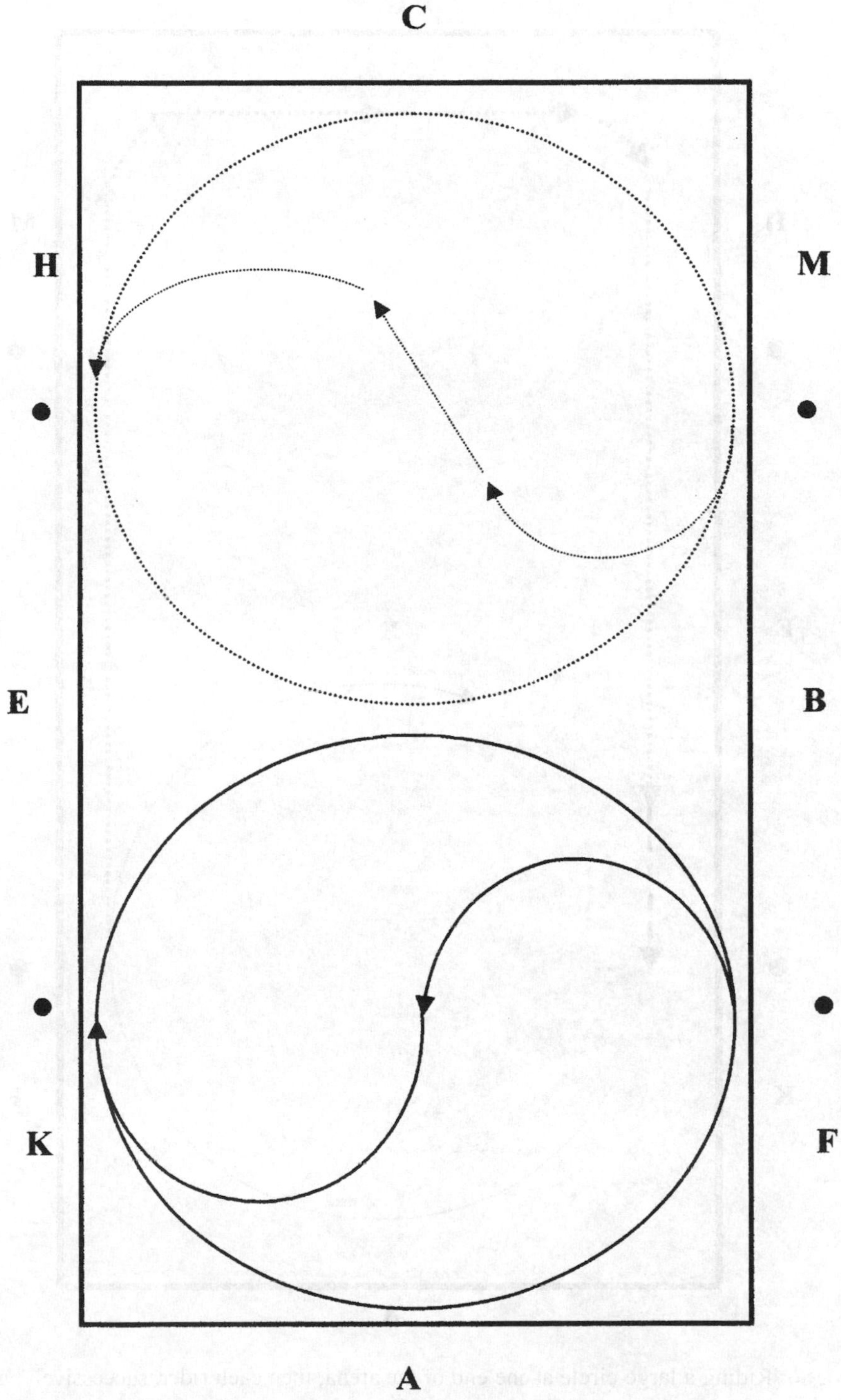

Figure no. 85. Changing the rein through a circle (correctly _____and incorrectly.........).

Figure 86.

The class riding a large circle at walk at one end of the arena while each successive leading file goes large at trot rising, returning to the rear of the ride, through sitting trot to walk. (Walk ⎯⎯⎯⎯ Trot rising ⋯⋯⋯ Trot sitting ▬ ▬ ▬).

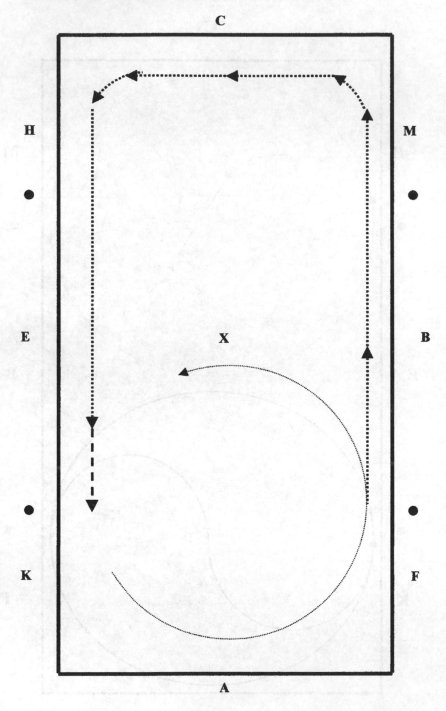

Figure no. 86. Riding a large circle at one end of the arena, then each rider, successively, going large.

Figure 87.
The class riding a large circle at walk at one end of the arena while each successive leading file goes large at trot and includes a medium circle at the other end of the arena before returning to the rear of the ride at walk. (Walk ─────── Trot rising ·······
Trot sitting _ _ _).

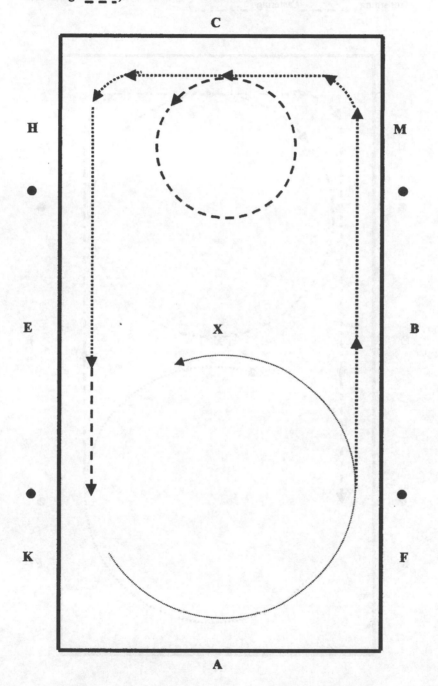

Figure no. 87. Riding a large circle at one end of the arena, then each rider, successively, going large and riding another circle at the other end of the arena.

Figure 88.

The class riding a large circle at trot at one end of the arena while each successive Leading file goes large through trot to canter and includes a large circle at the other end of the arena, returning to the rear of the ride through trot. (Trot rising .... Trot sitting _ _ _ _ _ Cantering _ . _ . _).

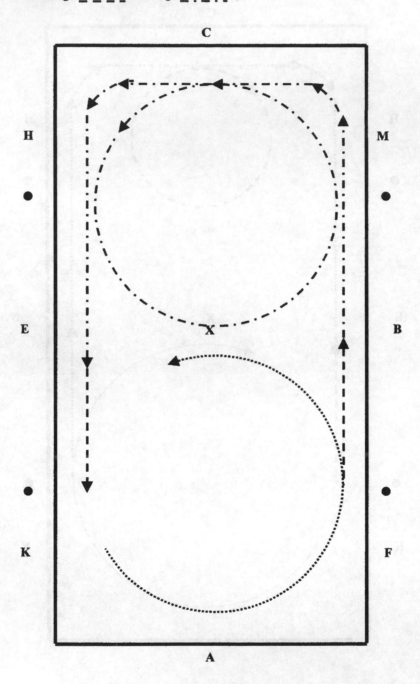

Figure No. 88. Similar exercise but ridden at trot and canter.

Figure 89

Setting up three medium circles for a continous change of rein from circle to circle. (1st stage. Showing six riders taking part).

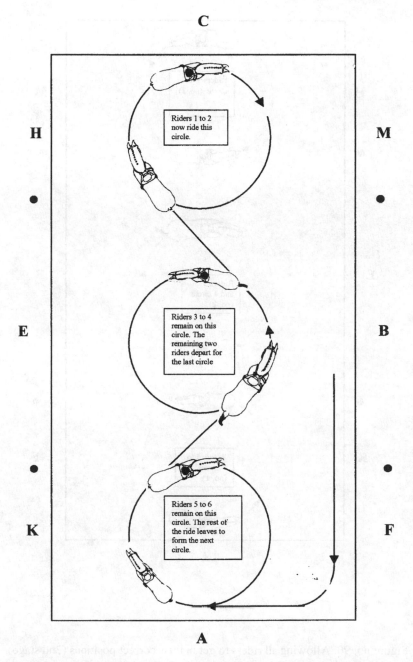

Figure no. 89. Setting up three circles for a change of rein out of a circle (1st stage).

Figure 90

(2nd stage)   The riders in each circle now level up so that they are all crossing the A – C line at the same time.   Walk ·····························

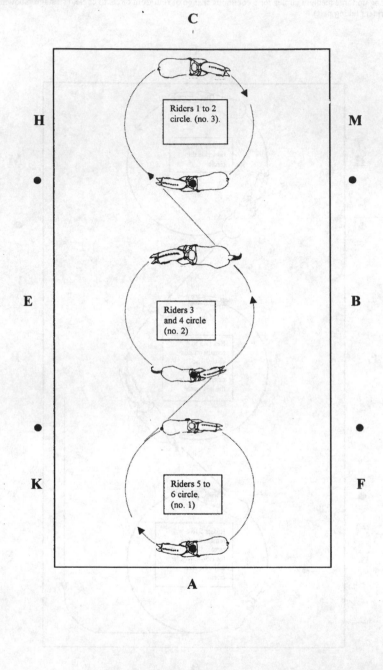

Figure no. 90. Allowing all riders to get in their correct positions (2nd stage).

Figure 91

(3rd stage). **But with 6 riders**. On your command one rider leaves each circle to join the next one. That means that the rider leaving circle no. 3 has to ride down towards circle no. 1. The exercise proceeds with sitting trot on circles and canter for anyone going large.

Sitting trot _ _ _ _ _ _ . Canter. _ _ . _ _ .. _ ...

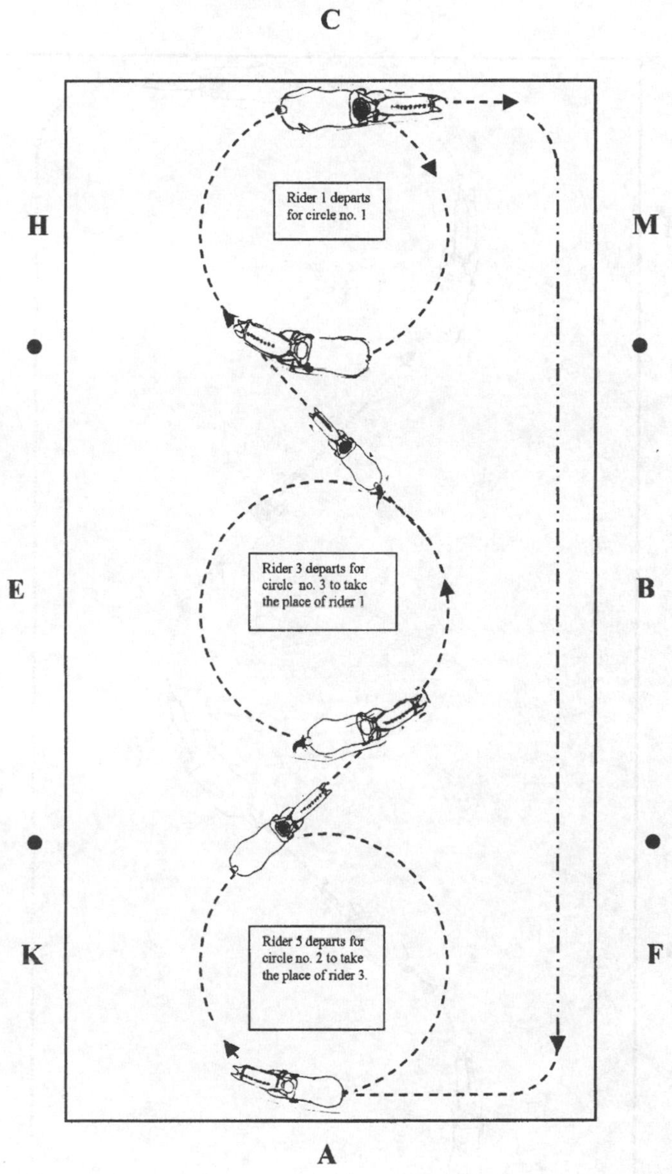

C

Rider 1 departs for circle no. 1

H

M

Rider 3 departs for circle no. 3 to take the place of rider 1

E

B

Rider 5 departs for circle no. 2 to take the place of rider 3.

K

F

A

Figure no. 91. The three circles in operation with the lead rider going large (3rd stage).

Figure 92

(4th stage). Unwinding the movement. This time with only 6 riders at rising trot.

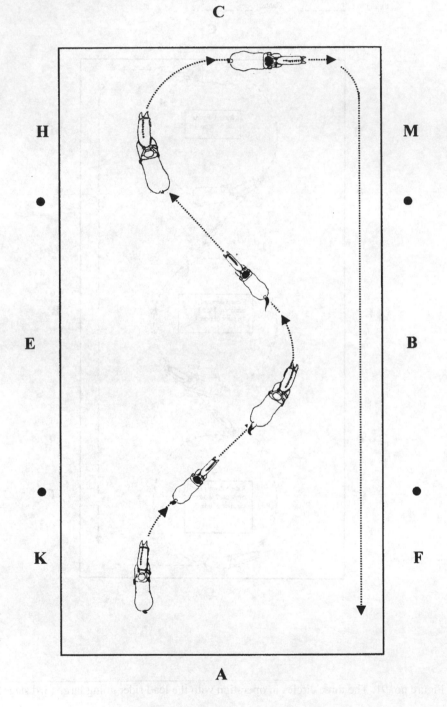

Figure no. 92. The movement unwinding

Figure 93

(3rd stage). **But with 7 riders**. On your command one rider leaves each circle to join the next one. That means that the rider from circle no. 3 has to ride down towards 'M' where they take the place of the 7th rider, who then departs for circle no. 1. The exercise proceeds with sitting trot on circles and canter for anyone going large.

Sitting trot _ _ _ _ _ _ Canter. _ _ . _ _ . _ _ .

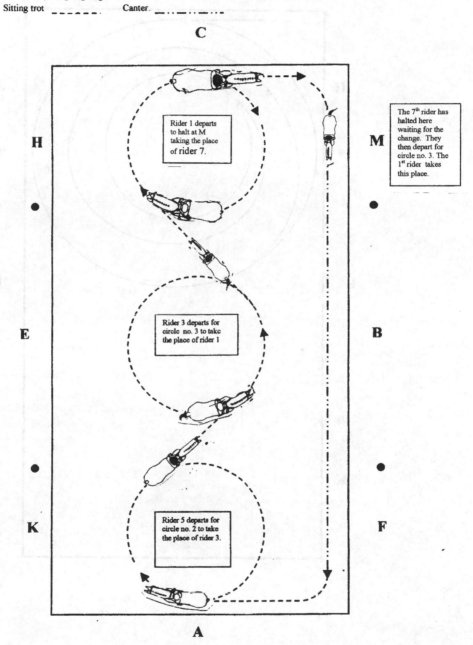

Figure no. 93. The exercise ridden with seven riders.

Riding a spiral as a means of helping to create impulsion. Figure 94

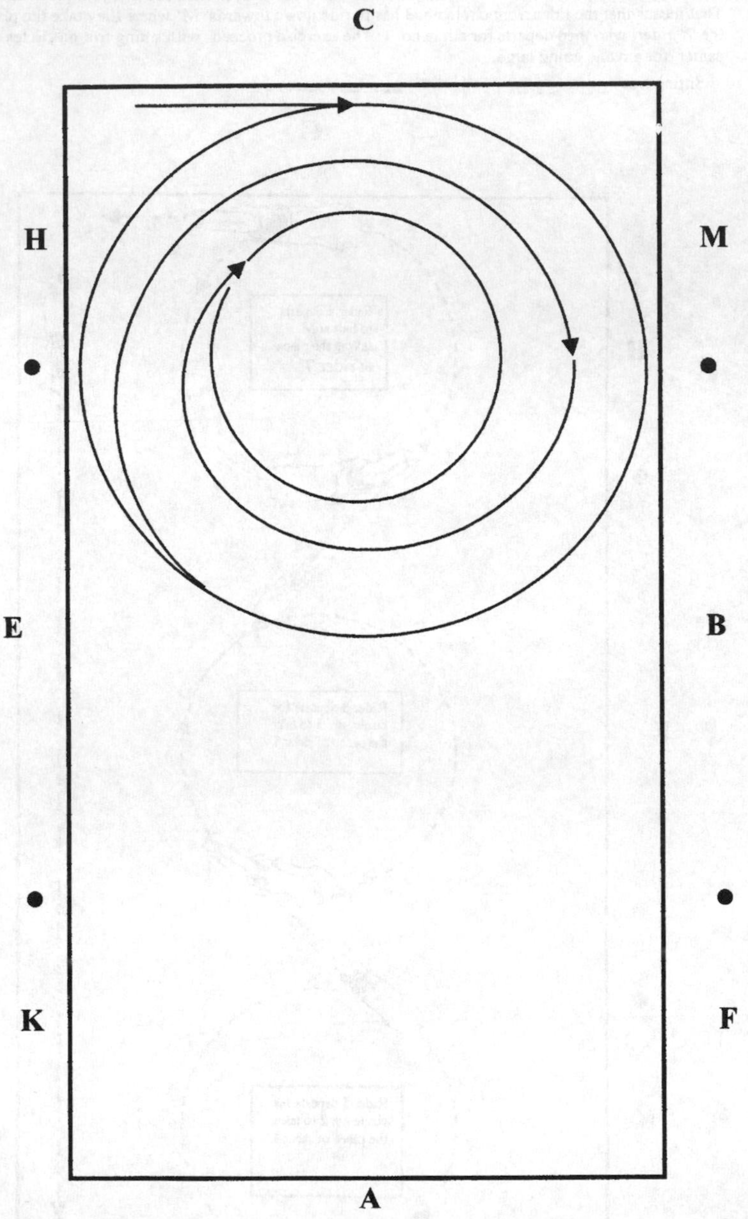

Figure 94. Riding an inwards spiral as a means of encouraging a horse to provide greater energy (impulsion)

Figure 95

Riding a leg yield (on the right rein).
Note that the rider positions the horse right when passing 'A' preparatory to turning down the three quarter line. This position is maintained throughout the movement.

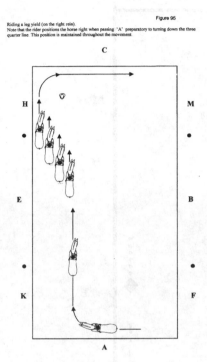

Figure no. 95. Riding a leg yield

Figure 96

Riding leg yields (on the right rein) from the centre line. Including some steps going straight .

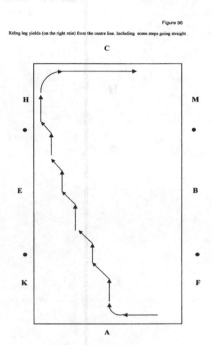

Figure no. 96. Riding the leg yield from the centre line with a series of strides going straight in-between.

Riding a simple leg yield (from the right rein) as a class and then changing the rein. There are two rides each of three riders.

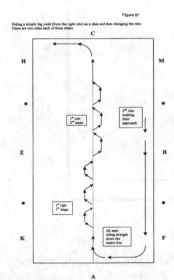

Figure no. 97. Riding simple leg yields as two rides in a class.

Figure 98

Six riding showing more involved leg yields as a class (all riders move simultaneously).

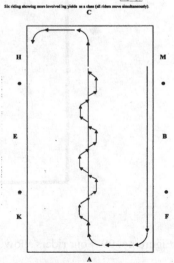

Figure no. 98. 6 riders showing more involved leg yields

Figure 99.

Four riders showing really swanky leg yields as a class.

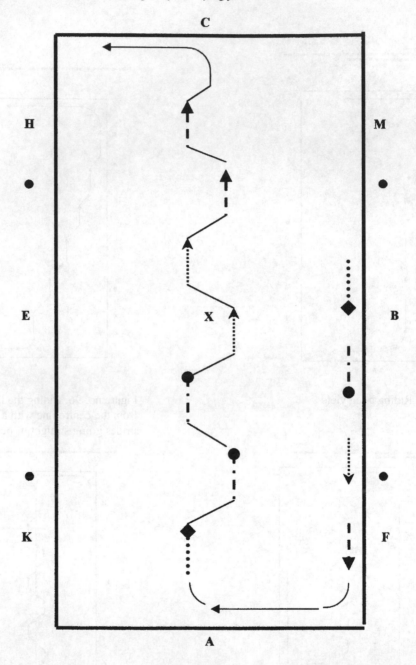

Figure no. 99. Four riders showing really involved leg yields (riders move simultaneously)

Figure 100

While the rest of the ride walk, the leading file only goes forward, through trot, to canter, from the front of the ride to the rear.

Correctly _____ Incorrectly _____

Walk .... Rising trot .... Sitting trot _ _ _ _ _ . Canter _ . _ . _ . _ . .

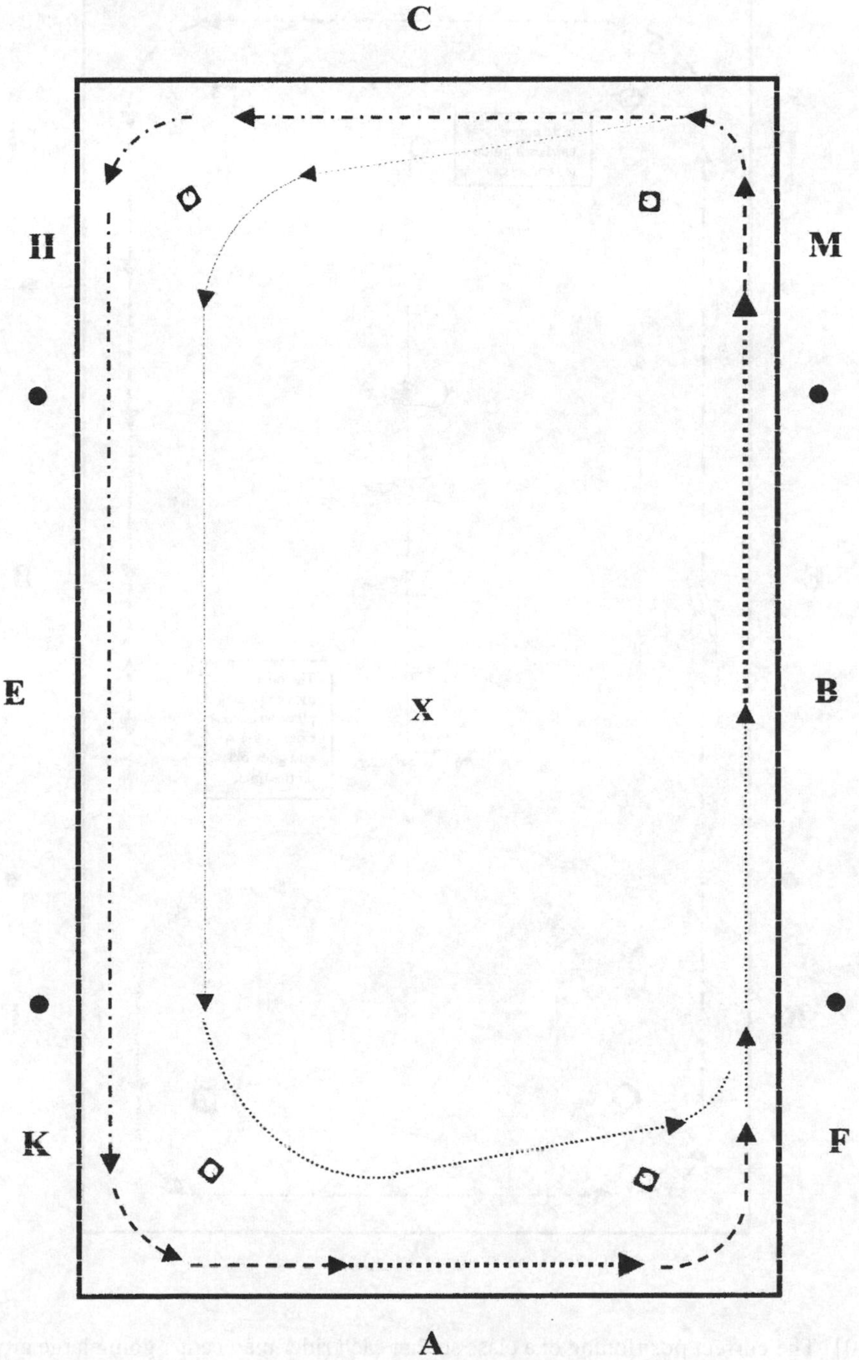

Figure no. 100. While the rest of the ride remain at walk, the leading file only goes forward, from the front of the ride to the rear, through trot to canter and then returning through trot to walk.

313

Figure 101

The correct positioning of a class so that each rider may canter going large around the arena.
Walk .... Rising trot .... Sitting trot_ _ _ _ _ Canter _ .. _ ..

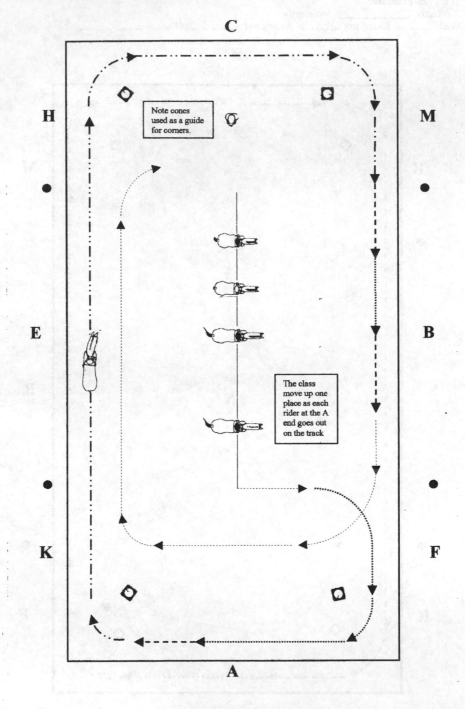

Figure no. 101. The correct positioning of a class so that each rider may canter going large around the arena

Figure 102

Lining up a class so that a canter may be performed individually with a change of rein or a circle.

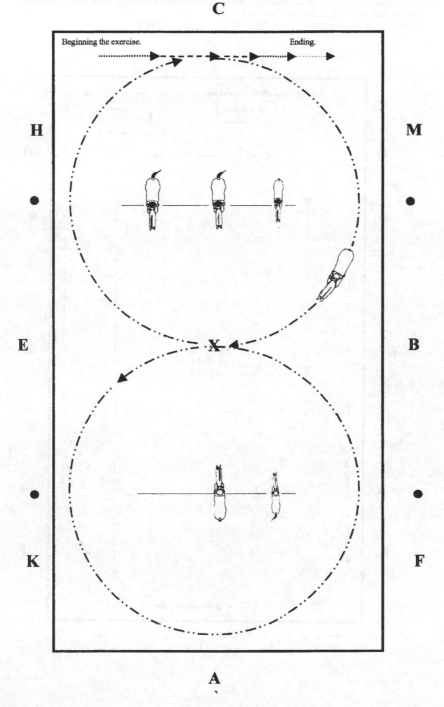

Figure no. 102. The correct positioning of a class so that a canter may be performed individually on circles with a change of rein.

Figure 103

Cantering past the ride.
While the rest of the ride remain at walk, the leading file only goes forward, through trot, to canter.
Since those at walk progress comparatively slowly you have the opportunity to decide if it is safe to
ask the rider cantering to ride a circle as well.

Walk .... Rising trot .... Sitting trot — — — — Canter — . — . — . —

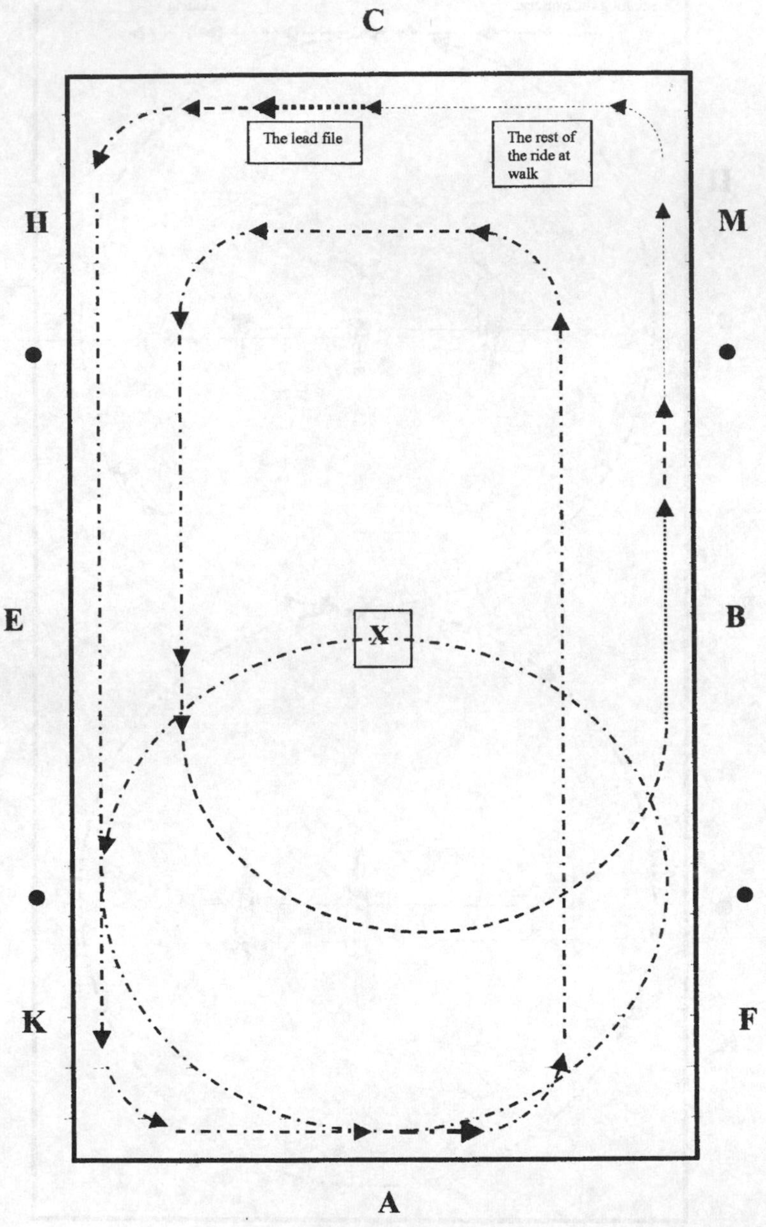

Figure no. 103. Cantering past the ride.

Figure 104

Counter shoulder-in and shoulder-in on a circle (note a cone placed in the centre of each circle as a reference point).

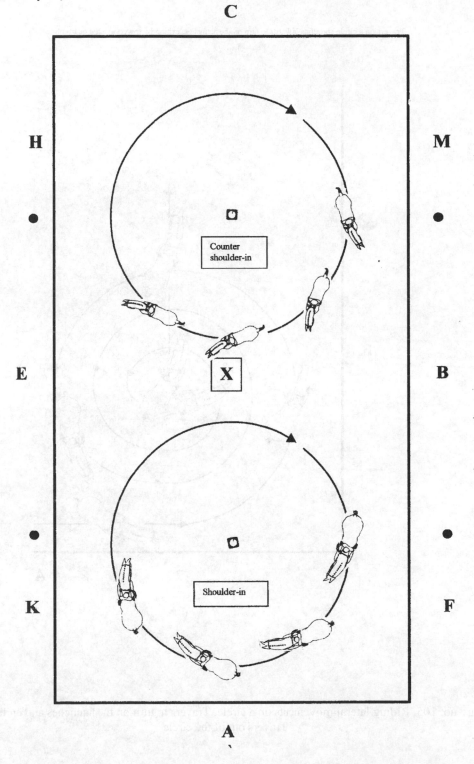

Figure no. 104. Counter shoulder-in and shoulder-in ridden from a circle.

Figure 105

Travers on a circle spiralling inwards to turn on the haunches, exiting by travers along a quarter line.

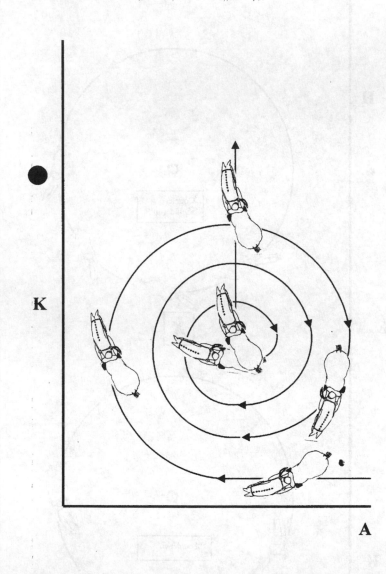

Figure no. 105. Riding lateral movements on a circle. Travers to turn on the haunches and ending with Travers out of the circle

318

Figure 106

Passada.

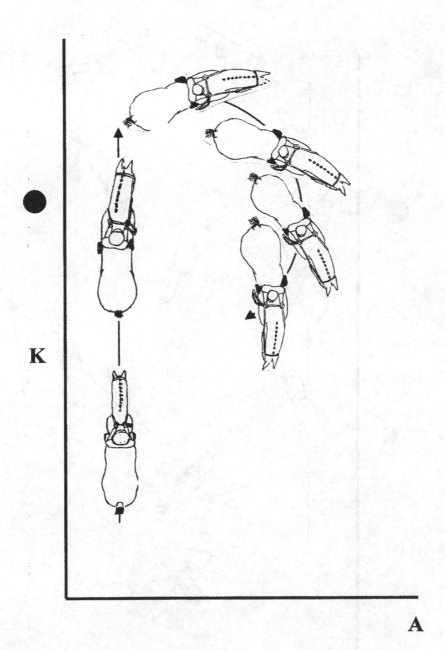

K

A

Figure no. 106. Riding a Passada.

Figure 107

Shoulder-in to passada to renvers to pirouette to half pass.

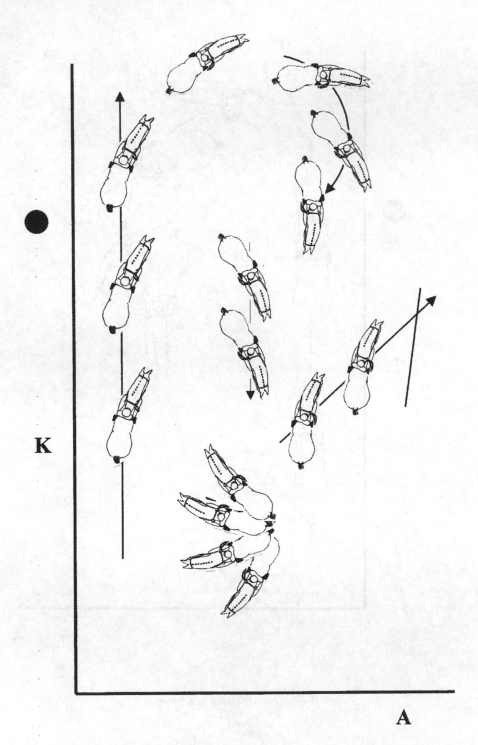

K

A

Figure no. 107. Riding shoulder-in to Passada to Renvers to pirouette to half pass.

Chapter 17

Introducing jumping.

If I may mention yet again this book is about training riders and not horses. This chapter deals with the introduction of pupils to the art of jumping. In order that my remarks are clearly understood I have described some of the mechanics involved so that the position of the rider is clearly seen in the context of the horses' actions. Jumping is a speciality of its own so I am only going to deal with it from the point of view of one giving lessons to beginners and intermediate riders, at which time the foundation is laid for further progress. If you wish to teach advanced jumping then there are other books that deal with the matter most fully. (See recommended reading).

Jumping is one of the aspects of riding that fascinates so many riders. This is not surprising since the motion of the horse through the air as it carries its rider safely over an obstacle is one that has a certain *'frisson'*. I suppose that after cantering indoors and out, jumping follows a close third. However as an instructor it is one aspect of equitation, the teaching of which, we must embark on with great care.

The policy of the school.

The first thing that we must do is to find out exactly what is the policy of the establishment where we are working with regard to jumping their stock. Some riding schools do not allow jumping at all, while others permit it only as a special lesson, at a premium price. This is quite understandable due to the fact that jumping can be quite demanding in terms of horse energy consumed. It is also a sector of the sport where injuries are more likely to be sustained by both horse and rider. Riding schools able to run their establishments without having to resort to jumping are quite likely to do so. A horse that goes lame and is out of work for several weeks, due to the fact that it may have landed badly after a jump, is unable to earn its keep until it recovers.

Proceeding with a jumping lesson.

There are two factors of paramount importance and they are: -

The correct horse.

It has been said that it is not part of horses' nature to jump and that, given the option, they would rather go around an object than over it? If you were in the same position what would you do? Use your judgement I suppose. If the object was wide and unencumbered with obstacles that would impede you going around, then unless you were fleeing for your life you would not bother to jump either.

However I do believe that horses jump naturally. They do not have the flexibility of the spine as do the cat family but from my observations I am fairly sure that it is quite a natural thing for them to do. I have watched a stallion decide to have its way with a fancied mare and jump a five-foot corral in order to be with her and I have watched horses, racing over fences, continuing to do so long after they have lost their jockeys. It may well be that in order to obtained *skilled* jumping over natural or artificial fences that we have to school our horses but I do not think that this is something that is alien to their natures.

Bearing in mind that this is not a book about training horses and in this particular teaching them to jump, it therefore follows that the horses that are made available for the use of your pupils must be schooled and *willing* jumpers. I am not suggesting that they should necessarily have the ability to jump 4ft 6'' or higher, I think that 3ft 6'' to 3ft 9'' is sufficient for most weekend riders. It should be remembered that many pupils, though they want to have the thrill of flying through the air on the back of a horse, are, none-the-less quite apprehensive when it actually comes to doing it. Very often this apprehension may have the effect of inhibiting the horse from going about its business.

The ability of the rider.

I do not encourage any pupil to even think about jumping until they have developed an independent seat. Ideally they should also have reached that stage in their riding careers where they are able to canter going forward. This last point is not an essential but it does help.

Confidence.

Unlike flat work which may be ridden indifferently, jumping has, to use business jargon, a 'bottom line', by which I mean that there is either success or failure. In other words your pupil either jumps successfully, or, alternatively they knock the jump down or have a refusal. There is no way that the rider can blind themselves to these results. Whereas they may have endless discussions with regard to the manner in which they rode a shoulder-in or half pass, when it comes to jumping the result of their actions is there for all to see. This may have a profound effect on their confidence and it is up to you to try and sustain this. If a pupil looses self-confidence then this may have an accumulative effect, for the horse will pick up on it as well.

Balance.

Another, very important factor is balance. Without good balance, and also a feeling for rhythm, a riders' ability to jump may be impaired. We may take these two factors and call them, collectively, ***natural talent.***

The first stage.

I must say that I sometimes utilise a jumping lesson for novices (novice to jumping that is), as a means of allowing horses to have a bit of a rest from their labours when the weather is really hot. This might seem to be a contradiction in terms (jumping and having a rest). But if gone about correctly it is not so. In the first place it is important that you have an atmosphere of calm pervading the whole class.

Why? Because your pupils will probably be getting a little tense if not through fear then through excitement. The horses may not get excited when they *see* the jumps but it is possible that they may do so as soon as they are put at an obstacle.

You will therefore arrange the lesson in such a manner that there is no undue rushing about. Resist the temptation to go at it like a 'bull in a china shop'. By which I mean do ***not*** start by simply having everyone cantering around the arena and then dashing over a series of jumps. Proceeding in this manner may result in the horses getting overexcited and this may precipitate an accident.

First the rider.
Going forward.

Jumping requires a rider to adopt a position that so places their body that it will cause the horse least interference when going over the jump. This means that the rider needs to be as near the horse's centre of gravity. Since this lies approximately just above the shoulder and just in front of the withers, (see diagram…) it is necessary for the rider to try and place their bodies as near as possible to that point. In practical terms this means taking the forward position. This position first advocated by Captain Federico Caprilli, was not, generally, accepted until 1904. *14.

Shortening the stirrups.

At this time pupils should shorten their stirrups. The reason for this is that it will help them to lift the seat slightly out of the saddle as they take the forward position. The number of holes that are required depends entirely on the length of the rider's legs and also the manner in which they were riding prior to the jumping exercise. Thus someone who has been riding advanced dressage with quite long stirrups will shorten them more, than one who is already riding with a degree of bend in the knee. What you must ensure is that they do not shorten so much that they ride as a jockey. It is quite unnecessary and may lead to a fall.

The open and closed position.

For the first part of the lesson the horses should be worked in at walk and trot in the normal manner. At this time be sure to draw your pupils' attention to the tempo of the trot – This should be steady and even. Ask the class to halt and to take the open position. This is an exercise through which the rider finds their balance and, subsequently, learns to go forward.

The open position.

The rider places the reins (held correctly) in the outside hand. They then stand up in stirrups as high as they can. The heels are pushed down and the hips are thrust forward over the withers. You must make sure that your pupils maintain this position for around five seconds. They may hold the mane if they feel a little unbalanced with the inside hand but under no circumstances may they support themselves with the rein (see photo no. 36)

322

Go to each rider in turn and correct his or her position. Make sure that the hips are well over the withers and that the heels are pushed down with the toes turned to the front and not sticking out.

The closed position.

The closed position is one where, from the open position the rider simply pushes their seat towards the cantle of the saddle, by folding at the hip. The position is held with the posterior just above the saddle. I have found this to be the best way of encouraging all riders to obtain a good forward seat. Again check each rider in turn, this time paying special attention to the **back**, which **should be straight** and not curved. (See photo no. 37). Note well that the reins now require to be shortened. There should still be no inclination to hold on to the reins for support. Tell your pupils to rest the inside hand on the withers or hold the mane should they feel a tendency to become unbalanced. In a short time they will be able to hold the closed position without loosing balance at all.

These two positions should then be carried out at both the walk and the trot. If all goes well you may even consider allowing your pupils to knot the reins over their horses' necks and then try, for a short period, to perform the exercises at both paces but with their arms stretched out horizontally either side of their bodies. Should they feel that they are loosing balance, they should, quickly, take hold the mane just in front of the withers. Children love this exercise and it really does help with their sense of balance. It is a useful exercise for what is to follow.

Trotting poles.

I *always* start a jumping lesson with work over trotting poles on the ground (a grid). This grid should be placed *along a three-quarter line* about half way down the arena. The reason for the grid is that, from my experience, I have found this to be beneficial in order to reveal those horses that may like to take advantage of their riders. They sense their riders' slight apprehension and add to this by looking down at the poles and pretending that it is something that they do not like. If one starts with the riders simply walking over the poles and then trotting over them, all these minor problems can be sorted out before the jumping proper begins. When you do start to jump the horses will be forward going, thus enabling the rider to concentrate on position

Placing the poles.

It is essential that your grid consist of at least five poles on the ground.

Why?

Because any less and you may have a horse try to jump them. This may be especially so if later they have been moved closer together. You do not want a horse to anticipate and put in a jump before you are ready. Place the poles on the ground spaced approx. 2.5 to 2.8 metres apart (it depends on the size of the horses in your class) and have the class *walk over them in open order*. Repeat the exercise, say, twice on each rein. When you are sure that all the horses are relaxed you may move on.

After this has been completed successfully then move the poles closer together (say 1. 3 to 1.5 metres) and ask the class to firstly go large around the arena working in as a ride, at walk and trot. At this stage you may wish to put in a few large circles just to limber your horses up. After giving them a short break you then command the class again to go in *open order*. This is important due to the fact that if a horse inadvertently knocks a pole as it goes over them you need to have sufficient time to instruct the following riders to go wide of the grid so that you have time to put it back in its correct position. You should never allow riders to follow on over a displaced pole.

Why? Because the horses that follow on may trip over the displaced pole and there might be an accident.

When they are all organised for the correct distance from one another, instruct your class to ride down the three-quarter-line *over the poles at the trot*. As they pass the letters either 'A' or 'C' they must turn their torsos and look towards the centre of the first pole. The approach should be from the track in a nice quarter segment of a circle. An approach at a sharp angle is not acceptable. As the riders each approach the first pole *they must not look down*. Their gaze is now to be directed to the last pole and before they go over that one they should already be looking ahead towards the end of the arena.

As the riders turn to go over the poles they must ensure that their horses are going forward at a nice and regular tempo. This must be maintained as the horses traverse the grid. The horses should be made to go over the grid at least twice on each rein at both walk and trot. If all goes well and there are no horses playing up then you may ask them to go over the grid once again at walk on either rein and then trot, but

323

this time taking the open position as they turn off the track and the closed position when the are one stride away from the first pole.

Points to watch out for.

1. The riders must *aim for the middle of each pole*.
2. As they **exit** the grid they must *continue in a straight line* down towards the track.
3. You are looking for a nice calm approach by both horse and rider.
4. The rider must be looking up and ahead.

What to do if you have a horse that starts to play up as soon as it reaches the grid?

The riders behind should be instructed to go large. You take hold of the horse by the bridle speaking quietly and kindly to the horse and having the rider pat it on the neck as you, walking along side lead the horse over the grid. The rider then does the same thing again, by themselves and not forgetting the pat on the neck. I must say that in all the years that I have been teaching I have never found this to fail. Of course there is always a first time. In which case try twice more yourself making sure that it is not the rider who, through pulling on the reins due to their own feelings of tension, is causing the problem in the first place. If the horse still gets even more excited then have a groom come and remove it. Try and get the rider set up with another horse or if that is not possible, then ask the members of the class if they will be prepared to allow the dismounted rider to have a loan of one of their horses later on in the lesson.

Why take such a drastic action?

Because this is a jumping lesson and not a lesson about teaching a horse to jump. Your pupils pay to learn to jump and that is what they should get. If you spend a large proportion of the lesson simply trying to get the horse to do something that it should already be quite capable of doing, then your pupils are not going to get their monies worth.

Do not forget you should not embark on traversing the poles or jumping until you are sure that all horses are going quietly.

Now for jumping.

So far as I am concerned, this is the part where the horses have a bit of a rest. One of the reasons for this is that I first spend a few minutes explaining to the class the fundamentals of jumping. I do this whether or not the pupils have had previous jumping experience.

The first thing is to make sure that everyone really understands the mechanics of a jump.

The horse.
How does a horse prepare to jump?

About three strides before the jump a horse first has a good look at it, in order to fix the position and height of the obstacle in its memory. The reason for this is due to the fact that after the last stride it no longer is able to see the jump. It uses its experience from schooling to enable it to clear the jump successfully.

The trot

During the last stride the horse will firstly elevate its body through its forehand and as it does so it is already folding its legs at the knee. This produces a degree of both upward and foreword motion. The neck now shortens as the head is lifted, a fraction of a second later its hindquarters pushing against the ground propelling it forward. The result of these two actions is that the horse goes through the air in a graceful arc known as the bascule. The head and neck stretch forward ready to balance the body as its forelegs reach towards the ground.

The canter.

I have mentioned jumping at the trot in the last paragraph because, as we will discuss further on, this is a suitable pace for a novice. However the most satisfactory pace for a *horse* to approach a jump is at the canter. As we already know the canter is a bounding pace, it has a pronounced moment of suspension. This means that whereas the horses' *approach* to the jump is similar to that of the trot, the added element of the moment of suspension greatly aids the horse in lifting its forehand. Thus we have a moment of suspension (all the legs are off the ground) with the forehand rising. The hindquarters coming forward and under the horse haven't yet met the ground but as they do so they propel the horse both upward and forward (see drawings no. 28 a & b & plate iii). This action is not that different to the moment of suspension experienced during a normal canter except that the inside foreleg throws the horses body much higher and with more energy and is further assisted by the raising of the head. The hindquarters are *lowered* placing the body at a suitable angle for negotiating the jump, which is enhanced by the powerful muscles of the loins. This state of affairs will not be achieved unless the canter has a marked degree of collection and impulsion.

Some reflections on the bascule.

This is the term used to describe the parabola performed by the horse during a jump. Some suggest that the horse actually *rounds* his back. Now I would take issue with this description because it does tend to create, in the mind of the rider, the idea that the horse jumps in a manner similar to that of members of the cat family. This is not true. There is no doubt that the horse does use a considerable bend in his neck during the jump (Plate iii). He also flexes the posterior part of his spine (i.e. the lumber section) from the region of the pelvic girdle to the tail, he gives the *impression* of flexing his spine but I do not think that, in reality, there is very much bend *throughout* the back. The horse's confirmation simply does not allow for it.

How does a rider jump?

If taught in-correctly, usually not very well. The reason for this is that whereas riders may have no particular pre-set views on riding in general, when it comes to jumping they certainly do! The idea is engendered as a result of watching show jumping, cross country jumping, Cowboys and Indians. You name they've seen it, at agricultural shows, racing, on television, in the cinema, Oh yes they know what jumping is all about. It's to do with sitting on a horse, approaching a jump at high speed and flying through the air with gay abandon. The truth of course is somewhat different.

The first thing that you must do is to disabuse them of the idea that jumping has to do with speed. It should be explained that asking a horse to jump is no different from asking him to trot or to canter. You should point out that there is a considerable energy requirement, in other words as they approach a jump at either trot or canter the horse must have impulsion. ***Impulsion does not necessarily mean speed.***

You must go on to explain that it is necessary for the rider to place himself or herself in a position that will not impede the horse as he tries to obey their will. In other words they must go forward at the moment of the jump. Not only that but they must *not* try to support themselves by hanging on to the reins. If they fail to go forward correctly the very least that they must do is to bend forward at the waist and ensure that their arms follow the extension of the horse's neck as it stretches over the jump. If they fail to do so, then as the reins tighten the reward to the horse, for jumping is a jab in the mouth with the bit biting into his jawbone! Personally I prefer to have the horses tacked up with a neck strap so that this may be used by riders who tend to get '*left behind*' in other words they have ***not gone forward*** at the moment the horse goes over the jump. Another alternative is for the rider to hold the mane.

The first jump.

Before you start, ask everyone to re-check his or her girths. Watch them in turn and if anything seems not to your satisfaction then go and tighten the girth yourself.

Ask the class how they feel about jumping. If anyone expresses fear then tell him or her that they have nothing to worry about but that if they do not wish to jump then they don't have to. Jumping should be no different from going forward to trot or canter. If you feel that that does not mollify them, then offer to *lead them over* the jump. You do this by attaching the clasp of a lead rein to the bit ring, accompanying the rider by trotting with them and hopping over the jump. (Don't forget the horse must go in front of your shoulder) Of course you also continue after the jump because you must not let the lead rein go so loose that the horse trips up over it. Alternatively, should you not have a lead rein to hand then you may take the rider over the jump by simply holding the rein just before the bit. In this case once the jump has been completed you may let the horse go on by itself. With the former method there is less chance of your interfering with the horses' mouth should you miss- time your own jump.

What do you need to tell the rider to do as they approach the jump?

1. Before the rider prepares to approach the jump. You must make sure that they are holding the reins correctly. Pay special attention to slack or dangly reins. If the pupil does not have the correct contact then the horse may decide to do his own thing and that may include a disinclination to put himself

through the effort of having to jump. Of course in these circumstances it is quite possible that the pupil may well be holding on to the reins like 'grim death'. In which case you must try to obtain a happy medium.

2. They must ensure that they approach at a steady trot that has impulsion (power).

3. They must be confident in themselves. If they are not then, unwittingly, this feeling may be transmitted to the horse who in turn will loose confidence and decline to jump.

4. As they make their initial approach turning in towards the jump they must *look* at the *middle* of the jump *the whole time*. It is amazing how many riders are not able to do this. One tells them 'Look at the jump'. They do so but only for a fraction of a second then their heads snap back as though there was elastic attached from chin to shoulder. 'Look at the jump and keep your eyes fixed on it', is what you say. The horse must be looking in the same direction.

5. They must be able to judge the distance from three strides out. To do this they must count out loud 'Three, Two, One' at which point, if they are correct, they will be going over the jump.

6. They should take the forward position from *three strides out,* (ideally towards the end of the lesson they should do this during the last stride, but I believe that to start with, they need to have time to get themselves organised). You may even consider telling them to take the open position as they start the approach curve and then to go to closed position three strides away. It all depends on how well their horses are going. At this time, if they are correctly positioned and the head is held correctly, they should now be *looking ahead of the jump*.

7. As the rider goes over the jump, they *must* allow the hands and arms to stretch forward so that they follow the movement of the horse as it stretches its neck forward and down. If they do 'get left behind' then they *must* let the rein slide through their fingers.

8. Finally the depart from the jump must be ridden in a straight line and to do this the rider must, again, *look where they want to go*. If they do not, then it is quite likely that their horse will try to rejoin its mates as soon as the jump has been completed.

The first round.
I usually start by dismantling the grid, placing all but three poles safely out of harms way. Two poles then have one end (the other end remains on the ground), placed on plastic blocks, which have been turned on their sides thus ensuring the minimum height. The poles are placed so that they cross one another in the centre of the jump. The third pole may be placed on the ground adjacent to and in front of the other two poles (to act as a ground line). This provides a good target towards which the rider should aim (see fig. 108). The ride may either be lined up along a long side of the arena or across the short side, at one end. It does not matter too much so long as they are all clear of any of the jumping activity taking place (it really depends on how many riders you have in your class).

When you line up the class place them in an order where you have a quiet but forward going horse with a confident rider, to start the proceedings and also a 'goodun' to finish. This will give confidence to the more diffident members of the class.

From the halt have the whole ride turn in abreast with the lead file level with say 'E'. If on the left rein then the last rider will be approximately level with the letter 'H'. Start the proceedings by inviting the first rider to go large around the arena; in this case, left-handed at a nice steady trot (as they leave have the whole ride move up one place). Between 'A' and three quarter line, this rider now commences a nice even approach curving inwards until they have a straight line going towards the centre of the jump, which in this case will have been placed level with the 'B' - 'E' line. You may also place the jump either before 'B' or past 'B'. It is up to you. It will depend on whether or not you have horses that tend to rush. If you do then place your jump nearer to the end where the rider is making their approach. By doing this the horse will have less time to get over excited.

Going forward they count 'Three – two – one' - through the air and over the jump.

What do you do should a horse run out or refuse to jump?
Personally I seldom have any problem with matters of this sort. If the preparation has been thorough then everything will proceed smoothly. None-the-less there may be that odd occasion when you do have a bit of a problem, and if you do, then the first thing is to decide where the problem lies. If it lies with the rider and not the horse, by that I mean that the rider is actually wittingly or unwittingly stopping the horse by hanging

326

onto the rein, then the problem is easily solved by your leading the rider over the jump. Have the pupil let the actual rein go a little loose while they hold the neck strap .You guide the horse towards the jump by holding the rein. When the horse is going forward confidently then you let go just before it goes over the jump.

On the other hand it may well be that one of your charges has decided to lark about a bit. In this case use one of the spare poles from the grid. Place one end on the ground while the other is placed on top of the plastic block. This will make a low rail and will help to constrain any desire to exit on the side away from you. You stand on the other side blocking that exit. Should this ploy not work then lead the horse over the jump but have a long whip in your outside hand and, just before the jump, reach behind you and touch the horse just behind the riders leg. All of these suggestions will work well, unless that is, you have a horse that simply does not like jumping or is just being very disobedient. We have discussed such a situation at the beginning of this chapter. – Have it removed from your class!

What do you do if a horse canters at the jump?

If you know your horses then you will take precautions to ensure that this does not happen. It does depend on the temperament of the horse and the manner in which it has been jumped in the past. If the horse has been used in classes where this is the norm or it is a horse that is part liveried then you should not be surprised. Ideally you should have a competent rider on a horse of this type. By that I don't mean that they have had past experience in jumping but that they can be relied upon to have reasonable control. In this case you and your pupil are going to do the horse a bit of good for it is about to learn that it does not have to 'rush its fences'.

Should you not have a rider of sufficient ability to carry out the little exercise described above, then simply lead in the horse at a walk and let it go when three strides out. With a competent rider have them make their approach at a walk. As they do so tell them not even to think about jumping. They are to have a good contact but no tension. They may even sing a little tune. If the horse does not relax and still shows a tendency to start to rush then the rider applies a series of half halts. After each one however there must be a moment when the horse is allowed to show that it is starting to relax. When the rider has placed the horse three strides from the jump then and only then may they ask it to go forward to a trot. The result is immediate, there is no rushing, and the horse goes forward at the trot and goes clear

The second round.

After the cross poles have been jumped at least twice on each rein, you should readjust them slightly. Take one pole and place it with each end on the plastic blocks. Place the other pole on the ground just in front of the jump with the one that it is used to provide a ground line.

Now ask if there is anyone who does not wish to continue with this next stage. If you do have a pupil who expresses the wish not to do so, then do not make fun of them but tell them that they are being very sensible and allow them to jump the first jump again. Now discuss with your class the advantage, from the horses' point of view, of having a ground line. You should mention the fact that though horses are considered, to some degree, to be colour blind, the colour variations of the poles do enable them better to judge the required takeoff point and the height to be jumped.

Jumping with eyes closed.

Proceed as you have for the first round. Still keep to the trot but this time whilst still insisting that everyone count out loud the last three strides allow the riders to go forward at the last stride when they judge that they are correct. Jump once on each rein. As they now continue tell them to close their eyes at the last stride and to open them as their horse lands. It is amazing how an exercise of this sort will cure all those with a tendency to get left behind or to jump in front of the horse. Most people find this great fun.

The final round.

If all has gone well, and you are quite happy with everyone's progress, then you may allow the class, still jumping individually, to have a final round going over the jump at the canter. Don't allow all the earlier work to be spoilt by allowing riders to gallop around the arena. The canter must be steady and collected. Whether or not the riders count out loud is up to you.

If, generally speaking, they have been reasonably accurate in judging the last three strides then my inclination is to dispense with the counting and simply to allow everyone to enjoy the pleasure of a simple unfettered jump. Depending on the time factor you may have a jump at the canter on each rein. But beware this is the time when riders may be getting a little tired – perhaps one jump at this pace is enough?

Reverting to the reasons for jumping on a hot day.

Now having read the above I am sure that you now realise why, for this standard of jumping, you are providing a respite for the horses in hot weather. For after you have spent your time telling your pupils about the basics, have organised the jumps and finally allowed everyone to go round one at a time, you will not have over-stressed your horses one bit!

Continuing the jumping lessons.
The second lesson.

The second, third and fourth lessons should always commence as for the first lesson. Basics must be repeated until they are thoroughly understood and remembered. The pupils will however have become more confident. This means that you may provide a course that is a little more demanding. I usually go about this, by adding an extra jump towards the end of the lesson. Generally the jumps are no higher than they were for the first lesson but with the inclusion of a second jump the pupils have something extra to think about. For the second lesson this jump is usually placed on the other side of the arena. This will serve to ensure that the correct approach is being made. At first the riders will tend to cut the corner after the first jump and they must learn to go straight and then to ride a correct approach as they come up to the second. Sometimes I make the first jump a straight cross pole with a ground pole while the second is a simple cross pole jump.

The third lesson.

This lesson is, again, essentially the same as the first two lessons. By this I mean that you still keep the initial jumping at the trot, but depending on the progress that has been made, I now set up the second jump with a straight cross pole and ground pole. I may also make it *narrower*. This serves very well to teach your pupils to keep their horses straight as they approach, for it is quite likely that any self-respecting horse on seeing a narrow obstacle in front of him and lacking any firm instruction to keep going straight will simply run out. Should this happen, the ratio of distances involved mean that the deviation on the horses' part is not very large. Thus the pupil will not become unbalanced and part company with the horse by going straight on while the horse goes the other way. (Not if they stay at the trot that is!).

You will have noticed that I have not mentioned using uprights. This is not an oversight. When teaching novice jumpers it is not necessary to go higher than that provided by the plastic blocks. If you stand them on their long side you should be able to get a jump about eighteen inches in height. If you do want to provide something more challenging then go for a parallel jump by using two sets of blocks adjacent to each other with a pole straight across each set of blocks (see fig. 109). With its wider width this will provide your pupils with a very satisfying jump and there is less danger of a horses pretending to be over-faced.

If a pupil does become unbalanced and have a fall, then the absence of heavy wooden uprights will avoid them crashing into them.

The fourth lesson.

We should by now have progressed to jumping with uprights and wings if they are available. For this lesson you should set up a figure-of-eight course, that is to say that there are jumps on either side of the arena and also one across the diagonal. Each jump should have a slightly different characteristic. For example the first jump may be a simple upright say about two feet high. The jump across the diagonal may have a little spread and the third jump might be a parallel. You should make the course as you see fit.

Again it does depend on the progress of your pupils. You are the only judge of that. I have given these examples based on four imaginary lessons but you may not get to the stage of lesson four until your pupils have had at least eight jumping sessions.

On the other hand if your pupils have made really excellent progress then perhaps you might include two jumps on one of the long sides but have these placed so that they are not directly in line. This will provide a very good practice for making riders look where they are going.

Though it is great fun I do not advise having any jumping against the clock. If you wish to have some form of competition, then set a bogey time and let it be known that it is not going to be very fast. You may also ask a colleague to attend and give points for style.

Advanced jumping.

As I have said at the beginning of this chapter this book does not encompass the *teaching* of advanced jumping. So what is the difference? Well, the answer is that as a pupils' experience grows they may wish to go over obstacles that are higher and wider. The distances between each jump may be set so that they require finer judgement. The courses become more twisting and thus pupils will have to learn how to ask their horses to change the leading leg while in mid-flight and in order to do this they will be riding horses that, because of their greater expertise and power, will require expert handling.

Teaching children.

Is not so different from teaching adults. One does have to take greater account of their fragile confidence, which if allowed to become dented too frequently, may not recover The majority of youngsters are thrilled by the thought of jumping. Unfortunately the idea that exists in their minds is perhaps not that which they experience in practise. I am frequently asked to produce jumps that are higher than those that they have been jumping very successfully. This is of course a part of human nature. You do not realise the real effect of a flame until you have burned your fingers.

Some children are quite understandably nervous. Signs of this are a suddenly discovered stitch or a stomach-ache. You must assess the degree of this fear. I do not, usually, let anyone off the hook for sudden aches or pains, provided that I am sure that they are only imagined. You must take care. Some children may well indeed have suffered some form of injury, at school earlier in the week and you may have to take this into account. For other children the fear is simply that of the unknown. It is up to you to show them how to deal with this. If you are successful then you may be partially responsible for, eventually, producing a 'new talent' on the jumping circuits – You never know!

Creating a foundation based on confidence.

My technique is to offer to accompany the child over the jump. I promise them that I will not let go of the pony. I also think that it is wise to put down the jump to a minimal height so any the feeling of uncertainty on the child's part will not cause the pony to refuse. You may well be thinking 'He has already got cross poles at a height of no more than fifteen inches, so what is he on about'? What I mean is that you actually place one of the poles on the ground so that on that side there isn't anything to jump at all! Now if you are leading the child in and over the jump you have the option of either going over nothing at all, going over say six inches or jumping near the highest point of the pole. At this stage it ***doesn't matter.*** Your object is to get child and pony over the jump. Once you have achieved that, then you may be a little more ambitious. I repeat the object of the exercise is to demonstrate to the child that they have nothing to fear from going over a jump.

Now for the actual approach. You tell the child to take a firm grip on the mane. This is important because it is essential that they go with the pony should it actually make a little jump. You go along side holding either a lead rein or the ponies' rein just behind the bit. At first you go no faster than a walk. All the while you are having a conversation with the child in a very soft and calm voice. Ask it where it is going for its holidays. Perhaps you are singing a merry little song. If the youngster knows the words you ask them to join in. Three strides from the jump you and the pony go forward to trot. All the time you are both looking at the jump and keeping an eye on the child. We all go over the jump together. On landing you make much and tell the child how brave they have been and that they must give the pony a pat for being so good. I have never had a child refuse to this day (see photo no. 38)

Building on the foundation.

As with all aspects of equitation but perhaps more so when dealing with jumping, it is essential that you try to provide an environment in which 'incidents' of any sort are avoided. With the best will in the world this is not always possible. One cannot always prevent that moment when a youngster gets 'left behind' or that faction of a second when a pony decides to run out while its 'pilot' continues in a straight line. Some might say that if your students never have a bad experience, they will never learn. To some extent this is true but I believe most strongly in postponing that time for as long as possible and from your point of view it means that you must be forever vigilant.

Perhaps one day I will write another book that specialises in jumping. But then again probably not, I am already getting old; in a past generation I should probably have been long gone. And I must say that the precision required to organise my thoughts in order to write these pages is quite enough for me.

Drawings

Drawing 28(a)

A horse preparing to take off at the canter.

The horse is about to take the last stride before taking off.
He is at the moment of suspension in the canter prior to
placing his hind legs well under him. In order to do this and
gain the necessary height he is looking at the jump, tucking
in his chin and gathering himself up with a higher degree of
elevation of his forehand.

Drawing no. 28a. A horse preparing to jump from the canter.

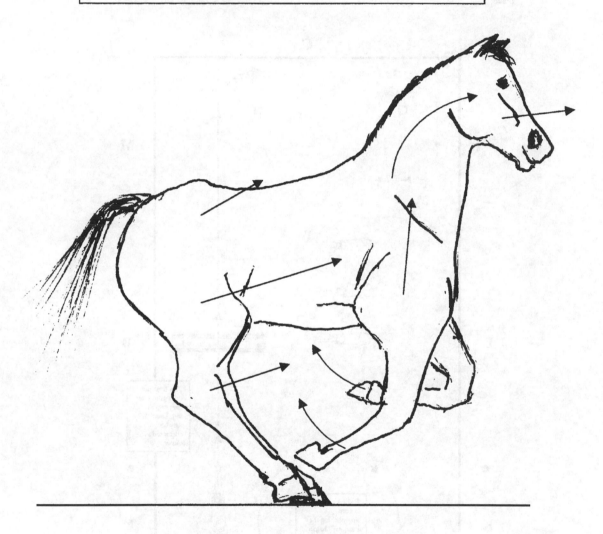

Drawing no. 28b. The moment of take-off.

Diagrams.

Figure 108

Setting up a simple jump.
Horses may be lined up along the centre line or out of the way along a short end of the arena. The way in which you position them depends on the size of the arena and the space that is available to you. Whatever you decide you must make sure that there is sufficient room for riders to leave and rejoin the ride in safety. In the example shown here the rider nearest the 'A' end leaves the ride and having gone over the jump rejoins the ride at the other end. The rest of the class have meanwhile moved up one place.

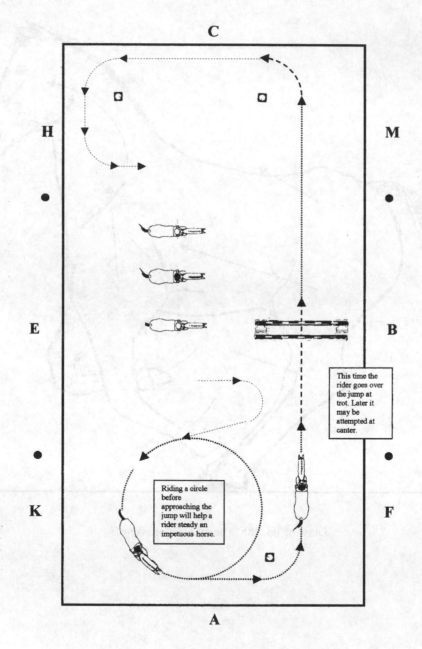

Figure no. 108. Setting up a simple jump.

Setting up a second jump.
Note that at this stage the class has made progress, therfore they may be encouraged to canter over the second jump.
Walk .... Rising trot .... Sitting trot _ _ _ _ Canter _ . . _ . . _ .

Figure 109

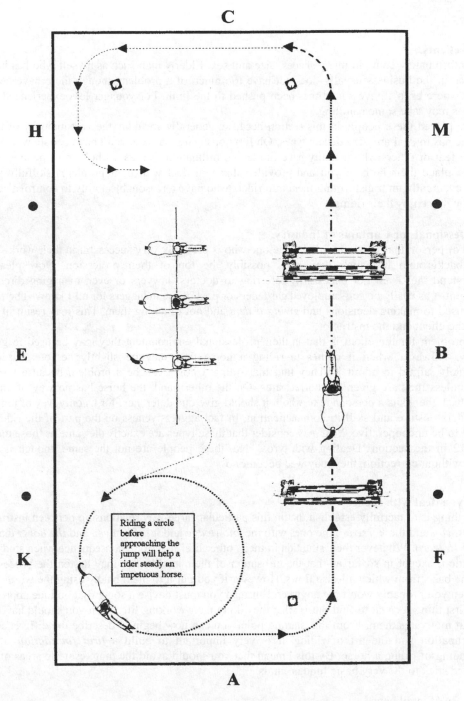

Figure no. 109. Setting up a second jump

333

Chapter 18

Dealing with problems and difficult situations.

People

Difficult clients.

These, unfortunately come in many shapes, size and sex. Elderly man such as myself who has had years of experience in the business usually does not have too much of a problem, though there have been the odd occasion where even I have sometimes been pushed to the limit. For younger less experienced instructors these types may take some handling.

I have placed these people in this section because; generally speaking the vast majority of clients with whom one has to deal are very decent types. Oh I'm not saying that you won't have people who are prone to excessive fear or others who actually have limited co-ordination. But as a whole most people are only too willing to place their faith in you and provided that you deal with their problems skilfully you should succeed, eventually, in transforming them into riders who have a reasonable ability to control a school horse and thoroughly enjoy their riding.

The Professionals or Captains of Industry.

The type of person that I have in mind is the one who is probably very successful in their work. They come from a background in which they may, possibly, be top of their profession. Now please do not misunderstand me, I am not necessarily referring to doctors, lawyers or even managing directors, these types may just as easily be self-employed gardeners or post office managers for all I know. The point is that they are used to making decisions and *giving orders* and not to taking them. This may result in a dilemma both for the client and the instructor.

The problem for the client is that in their professional environment they may be used to getting their own way. However when it comes to riding a horse they may be slightly nervous but even more unfortunately, afraid to admit it. They find that riding a horse can be a problem because horses do not respond unless they are given the correct aids. On the other hand, the horse has no way of knowing that upon its back there sits a personage to whom it should give due deference, for its only way of judging that is by the riders posture and skill in communication. In fact aggressiveness on the part of the rider may well prompt it to be uncooperative. You may consider that these types are exactly the same as those mentioned in chapter 12 in the section 'Dealing with tyros'. No, these people are not the same, though if allowed to continue without correction, they may well become so.

How do you deal with them?

The first thing is to tactfully establish that in this particular three-way relationship between instructor, horse and client, *you* and the *horse* are the ones with the *knowledge* and it is from *you* and *the horse* that the *client* has come to *learn*. Whatever their situation in their 'other life' it is of no consequence when studying the art of equitation, except in so far as that the utilisation of their intelligence may hasten the process, slightly. This is the basis from which all-else flows. However if you put it to them baldly using the words that I have just written you probably won't get anywhere! Instead you must devise a somewhat oblique approach.

The first thing for you to find out is what they do in their working life. Then you should have some idea as to what motivates them. From this starting point you can now begin to describe the differences between their occupation and the art of riding. It is very important to build a ***firm foundation*** of the basic understanding of riding a horse. By this I mean that you should avoid the more esoteric areas of equitation and instead stick to the very basic fundamentals.

1. The use of intelligence.
2. The understanding of the language between horse and rider.
3. The need ***not*** to corrupt this language through poor balance.
4. That most essential requirement to, generously, reward the horse with a kind word ***whenever*** it has performed well.

Most clients, be they absolute novices, or fairly experienced riders bring only the first requirement with them. If they have any of the other abilities then they are quite likely to be flawed or incomplete. Let us take item No. 4 above. The reward. You would think that this was something blindingly obvious to everyone. Frequently I have seen a client pat a horse on the neck subsequent to its having just been a real pain but failing to do so when the animal has just performed a movement to perfection! You see they simply have no idea. They need to be reminded that they have come to the school in order to learn. Unless of course they merely wish to hack out which is an entirely different matter.

Please do not misunderstand me. I am not suggesting that *everyone* who derives from a professional background is going to be difficult. Most of them are absolutely charming. They listen to everything that you say and try very hard to put this into practice. In which case you must take care that in their enthusiasm to make progress, they do not place themselves in situations where things may get a little out of control. What you must watch out for is a tendency to try and take the initiative too early.

What about the 'Quid pro quo'?
Latin is now steadily retreating from our language. What the above phrase means is what do you have to offer in return. The answer to that is that you must know your subject thoroughly. I mean from top to bottom. There should be absolutely no part of general equitation with which you are not familiar.

A little tip.
One way to tell if someone has had previous riding experience. – Look at their boots- are they worn?
Of course it may simply mean that you are dealing with someone who has bought a pair second hand! On the other hand it may be that you have a pupil who has been riding for quite some time. Should this be so, then you do need to make an allowance for that past experience be it either good or bad.

The rider who always complains.
Human nature being what it is, one may have to deal with a quite a large number of clients who, as soon as they experience any difficulty, immediately blame the horse. Listed below are but a few of the comments that I frequently hear.

1. The horse is lazy and will not move.
2. He is dead to the leg.
3. He keeps throwing his head about.
4. He keeps leaning on the bit.
5. He keeps on falling in on corners.
6. He is unable to ride a correct circle.
7. The horse will not perform the movement because he is stiff on that side.
8. The horse will not trot.
9. The horse cannot canter.
10. The horse is downright uncooperative.
11. The horse is obviously very tired. He has already done too many hours.
12. The horse is unwell.
13. The horse is lame.
14. He does not know his work.
15. He obviously finds the saddle – the bit - whatever - uncomfortable.
16. He does not like me.
17. He's known to be quite uncontrollable when ridden out.

I could go on and fill several pages with the various complaints that have either been made to me or else, in my hearing, to other instructors. To some small extend there might have been a germ of truth in some of them. But what these riders do not understand, is that given that all these horses are school horses, who are perfectly capable of doing what is asked of them, the fault, generally, lies with the rider and not the horse.
So how do you deal with this problem? One way is simply for you to get on the horse and demonstrate that there is no ground for the complaint. Of course the client is quite likely to say that that is because you are a brilliant rider and that they are not so skilled, therefore in their case the question still lies with the horse. Alternatively, you need to provide time either during the same lesson or else in a subsequent lesson to take

the client through their particular problem and show them that by the correct application of the aids the horse, will most often do their bidding. Believe me in almost every case that I have ever come across the fault lies with the rider having clumsily applied the aids.

Further on I have gone into greater detail with regard to some common problems.

What about the client who insists on 'doing their own thing'.

In the less advanced classes, you may have clients that *appear* to have an agenda of their own, for the simple reason that they are denied the choice; the horse decides for them. However in an advanced class you may well come across the reverse –the ultimate tyro, who has such a high opinion of their abilities that, during your lesson, they start to ride their own exercises. If you ask them exactly what they think that they are doing, they may well reply that they never ride a movement that they do not ride well. Since their horse does not seem to be obliging (it obviously does not know its business) they have decided to do something that they feel will be more suitable. You must deal with this situation immediately. In the first place you should not have horses in your class that are, completely, unable to perform the movements required, so that argument scarcely applies. Even if you did, you alone decide what the horse will perform at whatever level. Secondly you must point out that it is not acceptable to have any one client going around the arena performing any movement that takes their fancy. Unchecked this could lead to an accident. Ask them to imagine what might happen should they decide to canter in the opposite direction to the rest of the class, catching them unawares? The result does not bear thinking about.

In any case what we are talking about here is the complete disregard of your authority and the consequent interference with your responsibility for the safety of all your pupils. You must maintain discipline and you should explain to the client that if any accident were to occur as a result of their action, the responsibility would lie with you. If a client does not accept your instruction to return to the ride, then ask them to dismount and leave the class. Should they accept what you say, but with bad grace, then report them to the office with your suggestion that they be asked *not to return* for further lessons.

The rider who always has some dubious explanation for a horses' apparent reluctance to do their bidding.

Sometimes a client will offer the most simple or Byzantine reasons for the lack of a horses' inclination to do their bidding. When it refuses to walk on at anything more than a cripples shuffle. They may say 'Ah the poor thing it has already worked for five hours non stop already' You know for fact that it has only done one hour's work a considerable time earlier. On the other hand for a horse, who having decided that it has a plonker on its back and will have some fun as it dashes off with great abandon around the field 'It is obviously overfed'. In these cases as the clients remarks are uttered, I simply reply, 'that is a most interesting observation'. Of course those who know me well realise that what I mean is 'that is the biggest load of rubbish that I have heard for many a year. Uncharitable? Yes indeed even an old hand like me sometimes gets slightly tetchy.

Of course that is not to say that clients do not have many problems. As I have said in the paragraph dealing with complaining riders. ***The most important thing for you is to isolate the fault and help to correct it.***

Just to give one small example. You may have a rider quite incapable of doing a turn on the forehand correctly. For them the horse always seems to turn about its middle. This is not a difficult problem to deal with because the horse is at halt and you have plenty of time both to observe and to instruct your client in the correct manner of going about things. ***What is most important is that you are able to see the fault.*** If you are not able so to do, then you haven't much chance of helping your client. You do need to be meticulous in your observation. Below are a few of the points that you need to look out for.

1. Is the client sitting correctly *on* their seat?
2. Is their position otherwise correct?
3. Are they looking in the direction in which they intend to proceed?
4. Is the horse looking in the same direction?
5. Are they applying the aids correctly?
6. Are they applied in the correct sequence and at the correct tempo?

You may be sure that with careful observation you will find that one or several of these requirements is not being carried out. You may notice the following.

1. The rider is using the wrong leg to give the aid.
2. They are failing to give a half halt.
3. Or if they do, it consists of a very long tug on the rein.

These are just a few difficulties. It is amazing how many, quite experienced riders, are quite incapable of using their legs independently. It is as if they were attached together by a piece of string.

The point is that if you are observant and the client listens to you, then by the end of the lesson the horse will perform the required movement perfectly. That is the time to leave well alone and to celebrate the achievement with the client .

Giving clients problems that are too difficult for them to solve.
Feelings of tension may be induced in your clients for seemingly quite innocuous reasons. Now what am I getting at now? Well – let me put it this way – You may well consider yourself to be the 'Master of the Universe' when it comes to riding a horse. In your own mind you think that the movements that you ask your clients to ride are easy (after all do you not perform them to perfection yourself?). But are you perhaps loosing sight of the fact that this is not the way your pupils see things at all. The actual prospect of performing a movement with which they do not think that they can cope, might well show them up in front of the rest of the ride, and may well induce a feeling of anxiety.

Further more this might also be transmitted to the horse adding to their overall difficulties. Don't forget that the reaction of just one horse alone to a rider's anxiety may be sufficient to start off several of the others, and it is this sort of thing that can lead to accidents. If that were to happen, you may well argue that you really did not have control over the incident – that it was quite unexpected and that therefore you are not responsible. This may well be the case so far as your incident report is concerned but deep down in your heart you should be kicking yourself for not looking sufficiently far ahead to prevent such a thing from happening.

Horses

Reporting odd behaviour.
Should you have a horse in your class that exhibits unusual behaviour, then you must report this to the office. I am not referring to the normal antisocial behaviour towards other horses such as might be displayed by a mare in heat, rather I am thinking about a horse that is normally quiet and who quite suddenly puts in a short burst of bucking. This may not result in the rider being thrown but does need to be mentioned to the office. They must institute an inquiry to try to find the cause. Your client was fortunate but if the matter goes unmentioned that behaviour repeated might cause injury to a subsequent less skilled rider. The reason may be quite transient for example it may be the only animal in the class to have been fully clipped and on a cold day this may well lead to a feeling of disgruntlement. Another reason is that its feed may need to be adjusted. Whatever the reason the matter should be investigated.

Horses that misbehave (see also further down in this chapter).
There are occasions when you may find that you have one or two horses in your class that behave irritably. These may be mares in heat or simply older horses that are getting a bit crotchety. It is obvious that you must look for the warning signs and spot them *early*. Your clients need to be warned to take the appropriate action such as keeping a safe distance from other horses. Both the clients and you need to be constantly vigilant. So far as a client is concerned the responsibility will usually rest with you, for the client may well be concentrating so hard on the exercise that you have given, as to let all other considerations go by the board. Clients have frequently mentioned to me that they have difficulty in concentrating on more than one thing at a time. You must, however, go further. Should you note that you have a horse that is in a bad mood, then, you must adjust the exercises for that client accordingly. For example should you have a client who tends to let the heels come up during canter and thus is likely to lean forward, then I would suggest that it is not a good idea to let them canter on that horse. If the horse has been denied the satisfaction of 'having a go' at the other horses it may well seek satisfaction in dislodging the rider.

Horses proving difficult.

Sometimes one may have to suffer a horse that is consistently uncooperative. This may be due, in part, to the lack of ability, or unsympathetic manner in which the rider gives their aids. The temptation may be to ask the client to dismount and get on oneself. Before doing this be sure that whatever cure you attempt, that there is enough time remaining to ensure that you are able to complete this to your satisfaction. One must, carefully, consider the type of problem that needs to be dealt with. For example, if it is a relatively simple problem of a horse refusing to go 'on the bit' then, the experienced instructor will be able to deal with this very quickly. How can I be sure? Because a good instructor will only have asked the pupil to attempt to get an outline if he knows that the horse is capable of showing same. If it isn't then, it should not have been asked in the first place! On the other hand the problem may be more deep seated than that. Let us suppose that the horse has shown a disinclination to lead with the correct leg. In this case the instructor must be certain that he has enough time available to satisfactorily make the correction. By time available, I mean not only that which remains in the lesson, but also that which can utilised without upsetting the client who, after all has not paid to have a horse schooled during the time he is supposed to be having instruction! Either way it is very unsatisfactory should the instructor attempt the correction and fail to be successful.

Working with young stock.

Now despite my writing earlier about school horses knowing their business, it is quite possible that occasionally you might have a young animal in your class. Should this be the case, then you must inform the client riding it that you are going to make due allowance for this. In fact I would go further. Should you note before you take the class that a young horse has been allocated to a rider who has not had sufficient experience to have developed 'good hands', then I would suggest that you ask for a change to be made.

Why?

Because a young horse may not yet have learned the basics. It may require a little time to understand what is being asked of it. Further it may well not yet have learned to control its limbs adequately and as a result may tend to flounder at the higher paces. The rider must have the *ability* to be able to show due consideration.

This does not mean that you should not ask anything of it at all. Oh no. But what you do ask must be of a limited duration. For example do not encourage prolonged periods of going on the bit. A young horse especially, needs time to relax in between movements. Two minutes continuously on the bit is more than enough. Should you neglect this aspect, you will probably be partly responsible should the horse become sour to its work. You may not notice anything untoward at the time but it will show up later on! In matters of this sort it is probably intermediate and so called advanced riders who will cause the most damage if you don't watch them carefully. I have watched an instructor dwell upon one member of a class whilst totally ignoring another on a five-year-old who proceeded to ride it on the bit for over twenty minutes without a break! Not only that but the rider finding that the creature was actually quite responsive to the leg, proceeded during that period to put the poor animal through all sorts of difficult manoeuvres. These consisted such as continuously riding five metre circles that ended up as tight turns about I know not where, scrappy and ill thought out legs yields and so on. I wanted to cry out with frustration.

Horses that put in a buck.

Some horses have learned that when a client reprimands them with a touch of the stick, a quick buck will cause this to cease. This is quite a reasonable assumption on their part, since most clients will not use the whip after experiencing such a reaction. Now unless the horse has been getting away with it for some considerable time and the buck is quite enormous, you must ensure that the client is not put off by this behaviour. If they feel at all insecure then tell them to hold the pommel of the saddle but they must repeat the reprimand if it is not to result in the confirmation of a vice. Of course sometimes a client will simply not do as you ask; in which case you get on the horse yourself and administer the correction. Even after you have done so the client may still be unwilling to use the whip behind the leg, in which case have them administer a tap on the shoulder. Most horses do not object to a touch in this area and do not put in an objection.

Of course there may be the odd occasion, where you have a fairly strong rider who, having experienced an objection from the horse, proceeds to give it an almighty thrashing. This form of behaviour is certainly not at all acceptable either. In the first place it is unlikely that the horse has done anything so dreadful as to merit this sort of reaction and secondly it will, in the horses mind, create an impression that may work against the rider at a later time.

Horses that have a problem staling.

Many excellent school horses are quite advanced in years. This may lead, (as it does sometimes, to us all,) to some of them having a problem with the waterworks. Now all horses need to adopt a suitable posture in order to pass water; it involves them coming to a halt. Clients sometimes do not recognise when this is about to happen and they strike the poor animal. You must be vigilant and prevent them from so doing. Further more make sure that as the horse relieves itself that rider stands up in the saddle.

If, having halted, nothing happens even after a minute or two, (this is often the case where the first desire has been interfered with by the rider) the horse should be asked to continue but you must watch very carefully for the next indication.

Of course there are a few horses that have learned that adopting this staling posture will allow them a rest even though they have no intention of doing anything, you must rely on your experience to know when this is happening.

Droppings.

Generally speaking a horse does not have to halt in order to pass its droppings. However many horses prefer to do so. This is a matter about which you should decide. It is my view that a horse should not be allowed to get into the habit of stopping without warning if this is not the wish of the rider. On the other hand if you are working in an arena it does help to have all the droppings in one convenient place.?????

The weather
What to do in high winds

Whether in an indoor arena or outside, you must take special care when there is a wind blowing. You should realise that apart from the physical effect of the wind on such a large area as a horse's body, they may also become disturbed due to their excellent hearing. So whether you are in or out there may well be problems that, with forethought, can be avoided.

The effect of wind on sound and vision.

On a windy day sounds will be created that are outside the norm. Little flutterings as the air makes its way through narrow passages, bangs as wheelbarrows get blown over and forks are toppled off the fixtures on which they have been hung up. In an indoor arena these are things unseen and sounds unexplained. Outside one also has to contend with broken branches of trees flying across the arena and objects stored outside the fences such as the wings for jumps being blown over, unfastened gates banging and so forth. I think that there are very few of us who do not jump when we hear a loud bang? How much more so for the horse with it's large and sensitive ears? How much worse for the client who, as the horse jumps, becomes unbalanced and falls, and other horses take fright and dash off – the whole thing can evolve into a nightmare.

What to do?

The sensible thing is to do everything in your power to ensure that potential sources of trouble are eliminated. This may mean that you have to take a stroll around the immediate precincts of the arena *before the start* of your lesson and satisfy yourself that everything that can be battened down is securely fastened. A word to the grooms to be vigilant would not be out of place.

At the start of the lesson you must explain to clients the possible problems and how everyone is going to minimise them. Your warnings should reassure and not alarm and that in the event of an unusual noise that they are ready to simply have a gentle word with their mounts whilst giving a pat on the neck.

The effect of wind on your voice.

Outside, high winds will carry your voice away. You should be aware of this. It is useless standing in the arena and going on at great length, when your class cannot hear a word you say. What is worse they may be too embarrassed to inform you of the fact.

What to do?

Position yourself with your back to the wind fairly close to the track that is on the windward side of the arena. Have the class come to a halt, near you, before speaking to them. In these circumstances you will have to breathe in deeply and project your voice more than usual, but *do not shout*. Ask your class if they can all hear what you have said. If they have not then repeat everything. It also helps to keep your instructions fairly simple.

Make your comments such that they may be clearly understood before a movement is ridden, then, when you send the class on its way you will not need to speak to them again until they come around to you once more.

The effect of wind on temperature.
This is known as the chill factor. It must be taken into account on a windy day. Wrapped up in your warm fleece jacket may feel nice and snug but not so your horses especially when they have been clipped out. Clients too are often inadequately prepared.

What to do?
The first thing is not to have your horses standing still for too long; hanging around while you go off on a long discourse about what it is that you intend to do. Keep most of the work at a steady trot with short periods at the walk so that the horses do not become sweated up. This is one of those occasions when you need to use your own judgement in assessing the horses that are working for you. Are they thick-coated ponies liable to become wet with sweat or are they clipped out thin-skinned animals?

The effect of wind on balance.
This problem is more likely to occur outside rather than in. I must say that in extremely high winds even I have found myself to be slightly disturbed. I have to balance myself by leaning into the wind in order not to fall over. Of course horses have a similar problem compounded by the fact that they have to support their bodies high above the ground on their four spindly legs. Add to this the weight of their riders. I am, of course referring to quite high blustery winds because with a weight of approx. 500 kilos it will take a quite considerable gust to provide sufficient inertia to actually move a horses' body even when it is in the air. But that is not the point, what we are talking about here is the effect it has on the horse's psyche and as with humans this can be quite considerable.

What to do?
To my mind this means that you avoid gaits that, intrinsically require a high degree of balance. It is sensible to dispense with cantering. This gait has the greatest moment of suspension (when all the legs are in the air) therefore leave it alone. Much better to proceed with exercises based on walk and trot, especially trot. As I have said elsewhere horses do seem to become more settled when asked to do a prolonged period of steady trotting. There are dozens of movements that can be performed at this pace and it also allows the horses to maintain their balance and keep warm. You may well comment that even the trot has a moment of suspension that could unbalance a horse but generally speaking this is so slight that, accept in gale force winds, this may be discounted. Anyway it is up to you to monitor the going of your horses and to adjust your program accordingly. If you do think that the wind has become so strong as to interfere with balance even at the trot, then work at walk. Even at that pace the conditions may become so unpleasant, what with dust blowing into everybody's faces, that you might consider ending the lesson early.

For example you might start by saying 'as there is a high wind today the horses may well feel the wind up their tails. Do not worry; we are going to proceed with such and such movements. We will not be cantering'. Then go on to explain your reasons. Your clients will readily understand and be quite relieved. This is one of those times when, to help in inducing a feeling of calm in both in horse and themselves, it is absolutely essential that your clients talk to their horses, in calm quiet voices throughout the lesson.

What to do when it has snowed.
When working outside snow can be a problem even in an arena provided with the most perfect all-weather surface. These conditions might have reduced the workable area, in which case it may not be practical to carryout your usual regime. The reason for this is that snow tends to ball up under the horse's hooves. You should only engage in exercises that are suitable for these conditions. I think that this is the time for a lesson that combines a very simple element of working as a class but to also include a competition that is performed individually, for example the one suggested in Games list no. 8.
Why?
Because you are faced with two problems the first is that you need to keep horses and clients warm but you

have only a limited area in which to do so. Secondly you need to carefully watch the progress of every horse in order to be ready to pick-out hooves should the need arise due to impacted snow.

How best to go about it.

The problem of keeping everyone warm is quite simple, just have the class going large at a steady trot, utilising as much of the arena as is available. Ride several circuits on each rein. While this is going on very quickly set up your arena with obstacles such as those mentioned in game no. 8. You need to provide only so many as will create a course that has duration when ridden at a trot, to provide a time of 30 seconds. This means that the total elapsed time for a complete round of say six riders (i.e. the time that they are standing still) is no more than around 4 ½ to 5 minutes at the most thus preventing everyone from getting cold.

When every one has warmed up ask the ride to line up along one side of the school and allow each of them to compete against the clock. When the first round is finished, ask the class to go large once again for a short period of trotting so that nobody gets chilled. Repeat for as long as you have time available. You may score each individual race and have a series of winners; alternatively, you may make a note of and add up each competitor's score so that you have an overall winner at the end. I, usually change the course slightly after each round, so that the various skills of each rider and the size and personality of every horse may be accommodated. Changes also provide variety and allay boredom.

If you think that conditions are too cold even for this limited period of standing still then you may ask the rest of the class to go large but only at the walk while each competitor leaves the ride to have their turn.

Now I know that I have already stated elsewhere that this is a good game for playing in *very hot weather*, however it is worthwhile remembering that, with suitable amendments, any game or combination of games may be adapted to allow for changed conditions.

Dealing with very wet and bitterly cold weather.

When you take your exams you should be asked to give a lecture on a particular subject. Its duration will be around 20 minutes. If you are lucky it may be on a subject of your own choosing. You may well ponder as to the necessity for this. After all *when* will you be expected to give your clients *any* lecture no matter what the particular subject? The answer is, quite frequently. In the first place your clients may well wish to take riding tests and part of those tests may include elements on such subjects as stable management. Your thoughts on this matter may well be ' Well I'll worry about that if and when the occasion arises. Whatever the matter I will have time to bone up on the required subject when the time comes'. In practise this may not be the case, you may well be called upon to give an impromptu talk of at least an hour's duration without any warning at all! How will this come about? The heading of this section should have given you a clue.

You may be down to take out a hack or give a lesson in an outdoor arena. As you are about to start, the heavens open and there is the most almighty downpour with absolutely torrential rain. It shows no sign of letting up. Your clients let it be known that they are *all* agreed that they have no wish to get completely soaked and that they would be very happy to have an hours lecture on any subject as a substitute for a lesson in the wet. If the office is agreeable; (and there is no reason why they should not be, since the clients are not asking for their money back,) then it is up to you to stand there in front of them either in a box with a quiet horse or in the lecture room and to entertain and inform them *off the cuff* for a solid hour. This should prove to be no problem for have I not already stated that you should be teaching only the top 10% of your accumulated knowledge! Be prepared it may happen!

Teaching in the rain.

The first thing is to have any standing around kept to an absolute minimum. Obviously you will have to carry out all the required checks. However when you do so make sure that your class is lined up with the horse's hindquarters facing into the wind. This is the position that they would adopt if they were turned out in a field. Provided that you are confident that there will be no thunder and lightening, then also utilise any cover that may be provided by nearby trees.

Before starting your lesson check the surface of the ménage or field in which you are about to work. If you think that the surface is getting rather slippery, don't have any cantering. I think that the best pace for these conditions is probably the trot but you must also check that the ground is not getting boggy. If it is, tell your clients to avoid the heavy ground or, better still, use cones to mark out the areas that should be avoided.

At these times you will have to rethink your programme completely from the start. You should eliminate any movements that are too physically taxing for the horses and riders. Simply give them work that they can perform without too much stress, and be sure that you have made this clear to everyone at the start of the lesson. Don't forget that horses will get tired more quickly in heavy going so allow frequent periods of rest at the walk. In bad conditions it is important to keep everyone cheerful and you should not worry too much about making progress in improving your client's riding technique.

Wet weather clothing.

Now it may seem to be so obvious that waterproof clothing is required during periods of bad weather that discussion in these pages may to be deemed unnecessary. However I do think that it is a good idea to discuss some of the less obvious problems.

The first concerns duration. As a professional you will be likely to be teaching for several hours at a time. Should you be self-employed then you are quite likely to accept as much work as the time that you have available, simply due to the fact that there may be many occasions when you do not have any work offered to you at all. I have in mind, for example during holiday periods when many people are away.

In practise this means that garments that are reasonably adequate for say an hour, may not be good enough to withstand a really prolonged soaking. Even if you are wearing a garment that is 100% waterproof it will not be satisfactory if it does not cover your whole body. I have for example a 'puffer jacket' in mind. These garments are quite fashionable at the time that I write and may also be completely weatherproof but some of them are only cut to the waist, while others being slightly longer come down to the hips. During really nasty weather this is not much use if you are standing in exposed conditions for say three hours at a time. You'd be amazed at how cold you become as your jodhpurs or britches get really soaked.

Long coats.

You should have two sets of either a waxed or 100% waterproof drover style coats (see photo no. 39). If you buy one that is properly styled you should be adequately protected from rain either trickling down your collar or getting underneath on to your legs and into your boots. A really first-class coat should have good ventilation, straps to stop the lower part being blown away from your legs and also adequate pockets and hand warmers. It should also be lined to give an added degree of warmth, though to my mind the waterproof aspect is by far the most important because you can always wear additional clothing underneath. Bearing this in mind buy a coat that is of a generous cut or even a size larger than your actual size. If you can afford it, it is also a good idea to buy one that is made of a breathable material. Now with a somewhat limited budget you may query the necessity for buying two such garments. The reason for this is that even if you have a coat that is constructed out of breathable material after a few hours of constant work they do tend to get rather wet inside. This is simply due to the condensation of your own perspiration, which after a while will lead to your feeling very cold and damp. This means that you really need something to change into so that you are comfortable all the time.

Footwear.

When it has been raining for really long periods everything gets waterlogged. If you do not have good boots these too will let in the water. There is nothing more unpleasant than standing around or hacking in wet boots. I would recommend long riding boots. Rubber ones are usually completely waterproof but you will need to buy a size larger than your normal fit in order to allow for the wearing of an extra pair of socks on very cold days. It is also a good idea to try and get a pair that are made with steel toecaps as these will protect you feet should they get trodden on.

Gloves & Headgear.

All instructors should wear riding gloves as part of the uniform. However it is not always possible to buy those that are thin enough for a sensitive feeling on the reins and are also waterproof. In this case have several pairs available and if you are pushed for time always carry a spare pair in your coat pocket in case one pair gets wet.

Generally speaking riding helmets are waterproof and, whenever you ride or teach, you must wear one. None-the-less there may be those times when you are doing neither and a helmet is not required. In this case make sure that you have a wide brimmed waterproof hat available.

Children.

Parents who push their children.

I believe in encouraging parents to watch their youngsters learning to ride. I have to say that I have never had much of a problem in dealing with parents save for the odd one or two who, having observed their offspring make very good progress remain unaware of just how great it is. They wish to push the children further. 'Is it not time' they say 'for little Bengie to be going to a more advanced class after all he seems to be doing so well?' Since they have not, consistently, watched him work they have no idea as to just how much progress 'Bengie' has actually made. I am not referring to the headway he has made in sitting correctly but to the fact that he and I have put enormous effort into getting him to overcome his natural fears. The last thing that he needs is to be taken out of his familiar environment amongst his friends and sent to another class to ride ponies with which he is unfamiliar. To do this would, quite likely, at a stroke, undo all our work together. I very gently tell them that their child is doing very well and is much better left where he is. I also go on to say that I do make provision in the class to accommodate the increased ability of every rider. That is to say I ask more of those whom I feel have the capability.

Parents who interfere with your instruction.

Again I am pleased to say that I have never had any parents try and tell me how I should conduct my lessons. All very well for me but you may not be so lucky. Since we are working in an age when one may well be sued for negligence, it is a matter that one should take most seriously. The child is in your care and you are responsible for its safety. As a competent instructor you will not put this in jeopardy. However do not loose sight of the fact that it is always possible for something entirely *unforeseen* to happen. A car back firing, for example, the result of which is that a pony shies and the child falls off and is hurt! If you have already been criticised by a parent then no matter what the reason for the fall, things may become rather tricky. My advice is; do not let things reach that stage, by then it is too late. If a parent passes a disparaging comment on your work, ask the office to place the child in another class. However it is worthwhile your asking yourself as to whether or not they may have a point and that there is in fact some part of your tuition upon which you need to tighten up?

On the other hand it may well be that you are taking a lesson in which a fall is always a possibility. Jumping is a good case in point. In these circumstances it is my view that if parents express concern then take the child out of the ride and have it standing by you. Either hold the pony yourself or get a helper to do so for you. At the end of the lesson, without getting uptight, go to the office; explain the circumstances and request if it is possible that the child be put in another class in which jumping is not part of the curriculum. Should the parents then approach you and complain about your response, you, in turn, must explain to them that you are not able to work with a burden of responsibility that is outside reasonable expectation.

The social ladder.

This is not, strictly speaking, an instructor's problem. Rather it is one for the school. It is more prevalent in the junior school, though you may, occasionally, come up against it amongst adults as well.

What I am talking about here is the desire by youngsters to be with those that they consider are their social peers. To go to a class that is actually above their ability simply because they have made friends with someone, or have a schoolmate who is in that higher class. Children may well talk their way, willy nilly, via their parents and the office, into a class where things may get beyond their control? Of course with a good instructor in the other class this will not happen, but sudden changes can be very disruptive for everyone.

Why do I bother to mention this? 'Surely' you may be thinking. 'Any riding school worth its salt will not allow this to happen?' I allude to it because it is one of those things that depend to a great extent on the good will and desire to help by those in the office allocating classes. What happens is this:
A youngster is attending a course such as an 'Own a pony week'. During that time they rub shoulders with or befriend a child in a higher class. This personage says to the other 'I have been watching you ride and I think that you are good enough to be in my class'. Now if that child or its parent goes to the office and simply asks for a change they will probably be refused. What they do is, tell the office that it has become extremely difficult to bring the child at the time that they normally ride and could they ride an hour later – which so happens to coincide with the more advanced class! With strict conditions as to the child's' ability to cope the change is agreed. No sooner has this happened then the same child goes and boasts to its mates in the old class as to how they have been put into a higher class and not surprisingly their old friends, who

are probably better riders than they, are also asking to be changed. I need hardly go further to point out the great difficulties that this imposes on everyone as the office tries to fill in the gaps and continuity completely breaks down.

Now it may be that as a young instructor you do have some sympathy for this sort of problem. It is possible that it was not so long ago that you did the same thing yourselves? What you should not forget is that riding establishments are very labour intensive and at the time that I write it is quite difficult to keep fees within reasonable limits. Without an adequate income your jobs are placed in jeopardy, so it is up to you to ensure that all classes are maintained at their correct size. If the scenario that I have described above is permitted then *you* may well end up with a class that has shrunk from 8 riders to only 2! That is not an economical way to run a business and teaching riding is both a vocation and a business.

So you may well be thinking 'should change never be permitted?' The answer is of course it should but at the proper time and that is before the beginning of the new term. At this point the office have the time to discuss all changes and thus to ensure that all youngsters are placed according to their ability, ride at a time that is convenient and are in classes maintained at optimum size.

Safety (again).

Now I have made many references with regard to the need to maintain stringent standards of safety. Such matters as securing doors that may bang in a stiff breeze, ensuring that plastic bags left lying around are put in a rubbish receptacle and so on. However in a busy yard there is quite likely to be a fair degree of bustle going on. For example a tractor may be doing the rounds taking hay bales from the store to boxes, A huge lorry has arrived and is proceeding to remove the contents of the muckheap and so on. Most horses will take these happenings in their stride but you must make sure that you know for certain if any of them are likely to be sensitive and take exception to loud goings on, or to take fright on seeing some huge and unfamiliar machine approaching, as well one might during haymaking. This is particularly the case where you are teaching a fairly inexperienced rider or one of a nervous disposition.

In these circumstances it is advisable for you to, temporally, halt the lesson and take hold of the bridle, (you shouldn't take more than two such horses at any one time in your class. If you do, have a groom or helper come and assist you and if there is no one available then have the riders dismount and take the reins over the horses heads themselves). Turn the horse or horses away from the source of the problem and stroke them quietly on the neck whilst speaking in a calming manner. Wait until the difficult moment has passed or if it seems to be going on for a prolonged period have someone go and point out that you are in the middle of a lesson and would like to be getting on with it.

Fear – dealing with it.

Now it as has often been said that anyone who does not suffer fear is either a fool or an idiot. This is particularly so when it comes to riding horses. The question that arises is not so much, is a client nervous or fearful, but how do they cope with it? I expect that there are very few amongst us who, after having had a goodly battle with a misbehaving horse, have not felt, at the very least, emotionally charged up. We should not be surprised therefore to encounter this emotion when, on the odd occasion, it arises in our clients. The truth of the matter is that, for them, it constantly lies just beneath the surface for much of the time when they are on horseback.

In the past the prevailing attitude towards anyone suffering from a 'fit of the collywobbles' was to say 'pull yourself together and jolly well get on with it!' These days though we may, ourselves, actually harbour such thoughts deep down in our Id; it is not an acceptable attitude. For we are now teaching in an environment where the accent is, quite properly, always on safety and the overruling of a clients fears with simple short sharp commands may, ultimately, result in being sued for negligence and in lawyers booking their next very expensive holiday. In any case as I have already said fear is not so much the problem but how to cope with it.

What is the cause?

The first thing to consider is the causal effect. In other words what has happened to bring this emotion to the surface? Generally it will have resulted from an action by either a horse that the client is riding or that of an animal ridden by someone else. There may have been, without warning, a short argument with bearing of teeth and squealing say between two mares who both take up attitudes and dance about each other. Other reasons may be that a horse has heard a stable door banging shut or has seen something unfamiliar in the yard. Alternatively a horse that is fresh has put in several quite sharp bucks. Any of these may have resulted in a client being caught by surprise and being thrown forward out of the saddle (they may not actually have fallen off). The effect may be at the least, embarrassment or at the worst, a complete loss of confidence. Now I have mentioned these problems elsewhere in this book but here we are going to deal with the effect that this has had on our clients and how we are going to deal with them.

Now what do you do?

The most important thing is to ensure that everything is brought under control. That means that no matter what exercises are being ridden, everything stops. The next thing is for you to speak calmly to everyone in the class and tell them all to sit tall and relax. You must also ensure that this state of affairs is maintained and this will mean that your pupils must soften the grip that they have on the reins. For you may be sure that the majority have got the reins in vicelike hands and are actually causing their horses a fair degree of discomfiture. Now walk slowly to the person who seems to be having the problem and, taking hold of the rein near the bit start to talk to them. You will ask them the following questions: -

a   How do they feel?

b   Are they happy in continuing to ride the horse?

c   Would they like to swap with another rider?

d   Are they prepared to continue with the lesson?

Now you are going to have to make your decision, which is based not only upon the answers that you have received but also upon your knowledge of the riders' personality and whether or not you think that they can cope. For indeed you may have a rider who does not want to be shown up in front of the other class members but who, in reality may not have the ability to continue without some fundamental change taking place.

What do you do?
You must make your assessment?

Now the first thing is to decide on the overall situation. For example if the problem arose out of two mares having a go at one another, the simple answer is to make sure that they are parted. There will usually be one dominant female who has really caused the trouble and the answer is to place her at the back of the ride. In these circumstances your client will quite likely be prepared to continue on the horse that they are already riding. They may have had a slightly unpleasant experience but the fact that you have provided an answer to the problem is usually quite sufficient for them to continue.

On the other hand you may decide that the client is quite shaken up and you may have to consider the possible deleterious effect that this may have on the horse's behaviour (horses smell fear and may take advantage of it). If this is the case then do not hesitate to put the client up on another, much quieter, horse, provided that that rider (the one on the quiet horse) is willing to swap and also has the ability to cope with their new mount. You do this whether or not the rider with the problem wishes to change. Similar decisions will also extend to horses that shied because of a loud noise and so on. It is interesting to note that when making such a change the rider with greater ability will have practically no difficulty whatsoever in getting the horse that originally caused the problem to go about its work in a quiet manner. The rider who was unnerved is also able to carry on and, usually, finish the lesson in a much more confident manner.

Clients who have completely lost confidence.

If you are really skilled you may well have clients come to you who simply wish to regain their lost confidence. In order to be of a help in this matter you should proceed as though they had never been on the back of a horse before. By that I mean start with the lunge and then proceed only slowly. Do not try to make a session interesting by including movements that may, of themselves, provide extra tension for the client through their very difficulty. For example if you ask a client to ride, say natural and reverse circles (even at the walk) as per figure 3 chapter 9 and they have a difficulty with spatial concepts, this alone will induce a state of anxiety. The reason for this is simply because they do not wish to be shown up. This is the opposite of what you are trying to achieve. When you feel that the client *is* sufficiently confident to go large by himself or herself, simply keep it at that – going large. Let them enjoy themselves and have a pleasurable, and perhaps slightly boring (to you) session During this period all lessons should take place in an enclosed arena, in order that the client gain the confidence derived from being thus enclosed.

More problems with horses.
Next we come to the problem of horses that are a little bit full of themselves. This is a slightly more complicated matter. In an ideal world problems resulting from horses being fresh should not arise. The reason being that all horses will have been either ridden or lunged before starting class work with clients. Unfortunately there are many reasons why it is not always possible for this regime to be applied to *every* horse used for schoolwork in the yard. Illness amongst staff, especially during the winter months, may be one of them. And it is during the winter when horses have been standing in their boxes for many hours that this preparatory work is most needed.

What do you do?
I have stated in chapter 22 (liveried horses) that where one has an ongoing problem with a horse that continually misbehaves, then that animal should be removed from the class. Now I can well imagine some readers not so quietly snorting with disgust at that remark. 'Surely he knows' they will say 'That if a horse learns that all it has to do is to play up and it will no longer have to do its work, then that is what it will do' This is a very valid point. But the point that I am making is that one must deal with this situation from a safety point of view. It is absolutely no use in trying to get a rider to control an animal that knows that he has jolly well got the better of them. (In the case of a livery owner riding their own horse, they should be able to take the animal to another arena and get it to work quietly on its own). If they do not have sufficient ability to so do, then they should either review the whole situation with regard to their keeping a horse or, alternatively, make arrangements for someone else to school the animal for them. The same applies to a school horse but it will simply have to be ridden by another member of staff). What you should *not allow* is for *any animal to interfere with the calm that is required for continuing your lesson*. Having made that point we must now review the options to hand. These may be as follows: -

a You ask another rider in the class whom you know is able to cope, to change with the one having a problem (this may in fact result in making more than one change because the rider who has lost confidence may have to be given a *really* quiet horse and the one with whom you first change may not be riding such an animal).

b Sometimes there may be no one amongst your other class members whom you feel can really cope. In which case the next option is to summon help from outside i.e. you send word to ask for an experienced member of staff to come and take over.

c So now we have reached a stage where we (hopefully) have a capable rider on the horse that is causing a bit of a rumpus. Is this sufficient? The answer is that it is not For that horse may still dance about a bit and even though the rider quickly brings it to hand, its continuing refusal to settle, may result in the other horses and riders loosing their concentration.

So what do you do?
The answer, to my mind is to take a leaf out of Reiner Klimke's videotapes on dressage (see chapter 13). Have the whole ride turn in and line up well out of harms way (the positioning will depend on how many riders you have in your class and the size of the arena). Have the troublemaker alone come out onto the track and ask its rider to *quietly canter* it around the arena until such time as you tell them to stop. Watch the partnership very carefully. Every time that you notice that the horse shows an inclination to break to trot instruct the rider to keep cantering. If the rider is caught out then they must establish canter immediately no rising trot for the canter must be re-established immediately (That means that they may not acquiesce to the transition by rising). After several circumnavigations of the arena and well before the animal gets sweated up, you may tell the rider to go forward to trot and walk and return to the ride (do this on both reins).

The *whole* class is now asked to continue with the lesson and I have found that, invariably, this does the trick. Having been allowed to 'let off a bit of steam' the problem horse gets on with its work quietly.

Now you may query the amount of time that this involves. 'Surely' you may say 'Doesn't the rest of the class get a bit fed up with having to stand around for about two to three minutes and what about the horses that are standing still? Well all that I can say is that I have never had a problem with this approach. I start off by explaining to the class that it is a complete waste of time if one tries to give a lesson when everyone is in a state of apprehension because they imagine that one of the horses may start playing up again without warning. So far as the other horses are concerned, I have yet to meet an experienced school horse who doesn't enjoy having to do no more than standing around for a few minutes doing absolutely nothing whilst watching one of its mates working hard! In bad weather simply make sure that the horses are allowed to stand with their rear quarters to the bad weather.

Of course a die-hard critic may well say 'Surely if you keep the rest of the class standing while you work out the problem, then this will result in both riders and horses getting cold?' My reply would be that, as I have continually stated in this book, safety is paramount. You must use your common sense and work according to the conditions. If for example it is very cold then simply change your plan and work at the walk at one end of the arena and have the miscreant cantered at the other.

The other side of the coin!
Now some of you may have got the impression that I am in fact a bit of a wimp and that the moment that a client complains that I, in the pursuit of safety, will always try to accommodate them. Well I have to say that this is by no means the case. It is of course a matter of knowing your clients for indeed you will come across clients who, just like horses, will endeavour to exploit a situation to their own advantage. Some of them only like to ride their favourites and they will do everything in their power to ensure that they so do. This will involve slandering any other horse that they do not like and you may be sure that one of the accusations that they will make, in order to back up their point of view, is to insist that they have been told by some other rider that the animal allocated to them for that lesson misbehaves and is difficult to control. What they are suggesting is that if you do not let them change then you will be responsible for whatever may happen. Well you are responsible anyway, so you must make a decision based on your experience and knowledge, particularly of the horse in question.

What about those *who start* by professing fear?
Now let us be quite clear about this matter. Most people who ride *do* suffer from some degree of apprehension and this is perfectly natural. But the situation to which I am now going to refer is one where you may consider this fear to be absolutely without any justifiable reason whatsoever. The following example concerned one of my long established regular clients whom I had taught for many years. This lady had always suffered from a nervous disposition. Gradually I had brought her on until, eventually, she rode with great confidence and had become an accomplished horsewoman. But she did like to ride only the horses of her choice.

On one particular morning I, having, just finished giving a lesson and hearing a bit of a commotion, looked across the manége, to the mounting area to see this lady sitting on a grey mare with hands high in the air pulling the poor horse's mouth about whilst, at the same time, carrying on at great length about the animals supposed deficiencies. The groom had caught hold of the bridle and the poor horse was showing signs of distress. I quickly summed up the situation and called out to the groom to let go. The horse immediately quieted down and I asked the woman to ride the horse to me in the ménage. She did as she was asked all the while commenting vocally about the animals' supposed shortcomings and how she wasn't going to remain on its back for a moment longer!

I stood in front of her and said to her 'Have you or have you not passed the ABRS level 9 riding test?' She quietly nodded her head in assent. 'Then would you mind please getting on with it and start riding this horse quietly around the arena?' She did as she was bid. The lesson continued through quiet walk and trot until, later, we went on to do some more advanced work such as turn on the haunches. During one of these turns, which were extremely accurate, the horse appeared to anticipate the rider. The client commented on this. 'No', I said, 'she did not anticipate, you touched her with your leg but you did not realise that you had done so. Now, perhaps you will reflect on the fact that you are riding a very willing and sensitive mare whose sole aim is to do your bidding. And perhaps you will also consider the distinct possibility that when you mounted her earlier you, accidentally, touched her with your leg or with that ridiculously long schooling whip that you are carrying?' 'Yes I suppose I did'. She replied. 'Are we still friends?' 'Of course' I replied mellowing a mite.

Now I have no doubt that the office will, generally, try and provide a client with a mount that is to their liking. But this is not always practical. In the first place this approach may result in the same few horses always doing most of the work. Then one must take into account the fact that the favourites may not be able to work, lameness for example. Another factor is that their temporary masters may subject these 'favourites' to an hour of appalling riding and for them to suffer this week after week is not fair. Finally a pupil must learn to ride horses that are not always so obliging. I do not mean that they will place the rider in any danger by, for example, dashing off around the arena. On the contrary their 'disobedience' is subtler, and they may start by falling in as they are asked to go through a corner. If uncorrected this may develop into a reluctance to give a transition say from trot to canter. All these little things while not in anyway dangerous do serve to dent the pride of the rider, who whilst being more or less obeyed on other horses now find that they are not sufficiently skilled to get this horse to listen to them. Your part in all of this is to ensure that they are tactfully made to realise this and that, by the end of the lesson, they have actually improved to the extent of getting the horse to obey them. Satisfaction all round!

Dealing with illness.
Generally speaking you should have no problems arising from clients who join your classes. The office should have dealt with these matters well before any rider is sent on to receive tuition. In any case illness alone should not bar people who wish to enjoy the art of equitation unless that is that the ailments from which they suffer may threaten their safety. In this respect I am not only referring to those who may have a chronic illness but also anyone who may have a passing virus.

Nonetheless when you meet a client for the first time in your class it is your duty to ask if they are fit and well. Should you receive a reply in the negative then you must interrogate further and decide for yourself whether or not you should allow that client to continue. Furthermore even if you are dealing with someone whom you know very well and they *tell* you that they are, say, suffering from a cold or even flue then you must ask them if they do *really* feel able to ride. And even then should they tell you that they are quite able to cope, do not let the matter lie there but make sure that for that client the difficulty of exercises is reduced. Throughout the duration of the lesson you must every so often ask them if they feel able to continue.

You may have someone attend a class who for example suffers from a quite serious disease such as Diabetes. Again this should not be a problem because drugs now quite easily control a disorder of that kind. But you do need to ensure that the treatment is effective and be aware of the condition in order to be able to react quickly enough should the client's blood/sugar level suddenly drop.

However there are some conditions that may not be declared to the office when the client signs on simply because the client is not aware that they have a problem. One such is Dyspraxia. This condition has only recently been recognised and understood by the medical profession. It is an illness associated with poor co-ordination. The sufferers thus have difficulty in successfully taking part in certain sports or doing specific dance steps. Apparently they have no left or right hand dominance. It may not always be easy to spot this lack of co-ordination. In equitation it may manifest itself as a simple inability to combine leg and hands aids for certain movements. But there may be other concomitant symptoms that are, quite often, more revealing, for many clients have poor co-ordination or a lack of spatial awareness without, necessarily suffering from Dyspraxia. One example is that the client becomes quite depressed by their lack of success and their remarks often show that they hold themselves in very low esteem. So what may well appear, to you the instructor, as a rider who simply does not have a sufficiently developed talent for riding, advanced movements is in fact quite simply Dyspraxic.

So we have now reached a situation where you think that you may have a client suffering with this problem. What are you going to do about it? **Well the one thing that you do not do is say to your pupil 'I think that you are Dyspraxic'.** In the first place you are engaged to teach riding and not to practise clinical psychology. On the other hand you do not want to loose a client because they become so frustrated that they quit. My suggestion is that you try to help them in an unobtrusive way. Thus if you suspect that a client is unable to obtain canter because they have difficulty in giving the aids with fluency and in the correct order, arrange for them to ride a really willing schoolmaster. When mounted on this obliging horse tell them to shorten the aid sequence by simply sitting still, bracing the back and touching the horse with the outside leg. Forget about giving the correct half halt or obtaining the correct bend. A really good schoolmaster will canter and continue to so do, at least for a sufficient time, for you to tell your pupil when touch the horse with the inside leg simply to keep the canter going. This more simplified sequence of aids will be sufficient for the client to achieve their ends and will give them the satisfaction that they so badly need. Of course from your point of view what is paramount in all of this is patience!

In a delicate condition!
Some years ago I had a lady continue to hack with me who was so far advanced in her pregnancy that I really feared that she might possibly go into labour while we were out in the countryside (of course I agree that that was not an illness!). If memory serves me correctly she was about seven months gone! Eventually I simply had to refuse to allow her to accompany me any longer. This was her third child who is now happily taking riding lessons with me as did her brother and sister before her.

Popularity.
Sometimes ones very popularity may cause a slight problem. Word spreads around that you are a good teacher. This may mean that you have new clients asking to join a class that is above their ability either because they have a friend already in that class or simply because that is the only one in which there is a vacancy. If this should happen, in other words the office allows them join, then you will have to adjust your lesson in order to accommodate these clients. This is not a satisfactory state of affairs because it will affect the progress of those who have already been attending that class. I suggest that, after the lesson has finished, you ask the office to place them elsewhere.

Sitting with a stiff back.
In chapter 9 - **Points to watch continuously.** I make mention of the need to ensure that the rider always allows flexion in the lower part of the spine in the region of the lumbar bones (also known as the lordosis or the small of the back). See drawing no 20. I wish to mention this again in greater detail because I have found that quite a number of riders find this a bit of a problem. The flexion of this part of the spine is essential to the development of a 'good seat'. In other words a position in which the rider is able to maintain perfect balance together with a soft suppleness.

Generally speaking many people do not have too much of a problem during the walk. If one observes them carefully one can see the flexion of the spine working quite correctly and thus maintaining a stillness of the whole upper torso, arms and head. However that seems to change as soon as they are asked to ride a sitting trot and becomes even more pronounced if canter is to follow. The reason for this has, of course, to do with the moment of suspension that precedes each trot and canter stride. The rider being thrown forward tries to counter this by gripping with the legs against the horse's sides and generally becomes very stiff through the whole body. This actually has the very opposite effect to that which they desire. In fact it is fair to say that the situation steadily deteriorates and if left uncorrected (especially in canter) may result in the rider departing the horse! Before this state of affairs is arrived at it is essential that you have the rider go forward to halt and explain the problem to them.

At this time the rider, despite your earlier explanations will often reveal that they hadn't the slightest idea what you were talking about. If you ask them to flex their backbone they will try and thrust it out in a backward curve so that they begin to look like the Hunchback of Notre Dame. Alternatively it will be thrust all too far forward and remain in that fixed and rigid position.

You must now take great care to ensure that they really *do* understand what you wish them to do. I, usually manage this by touching them either using the tips of my fingers (If I have received permission from the rider to do so) or else by using the handle of my whip. Very often the first reaction that I get is that the whole upper body starts to sway back and forth. I tell the rider that this must not happen and that what is required is that the spine *and* hipbones shall move forward and back staying in touch with my fingers. Even though you may be dismounted a demonstration also helps. Eventually they get the idea and their position will improve accordingly.

Flies.
During hot and humid conditions flies may plague horses. Inexperienced riders can be quite discomforted by their horse throwing its head about trying to dislodge these tormenting creatures. The rider, due to their profound ignorance, thinks that the poor horse is about to do *them* some mischief. They try to restrain the poor animal by pulling on the reins, or verbally castigating it. To avoid this type of problem, minimise it in the first place. During those periods when you think that you are likely to have trouble, make sure that the grooms have treated all the horses that you are going to use, with fly repellent.

349

Further thoughts on really heavy rain.

Sometimes, when teaching outside, the rain may be so bad that one needs to devise exercises that will help to minimise a horse's discomfiture. By that I mean that horses living out will stand with their hindquarters to wind and rain. Now they may also try to do this when in a class, especially when less than accomplished riders are riding them. In order to minimise such problems one should introduce such exercises that actually enable to horse to move with his hindquarters facing towards the worst of the weather. I have in mind such exercises as, say, shoulder-in and counter shoulder-in. If you ask the class to perform these movements along those sides of the arena where they may obtain the greatest benefit, then, you will find that you are able to deliver a lesson that is both interesting and with a minimum of fuss. Of course I hear you say, 'What if your clients are not really up to riding such movements?' My answer is 'Does it really matter so long as they have a go and you encourage them?'

Sound (i.e. unusually loud noises)

Horses have large and highly mobile ears. These form part of their defence mechanism and, especially out in the wild, they may be inclined, (as I have mentioned else where in this book), to flee first and ask questions afterwards, if they *think* that they detect danger. I have left this problem to the end of this chapter because, generally speaking, noise as such should not be too much of a problem. The reason being, that, in most cases, the noises that horses hear are part of the hustle and bustle of machinery used about the riding school and to which they have become accustomed. Of course there may be the odd occasion, where an animal already in a state of anxiety, perhaps, say, due to the unsympathetic use of a novices hands may seize upon an unseen sound as an excuse for throwing a bit of a wobbly. I have in mind something as simple as the sound of a cars tyres crunching over gravel, as might be the case where an outdoor arena is situated close to a car park.

However there are occasions where the sound may be truly quite unnerving. I have in mind the quite terrifying noise (to me any way) made by a helicopter or low flying fighter. I have actually had experience of both these happenings. The first when a huge machine with twin rotors passed overhead at tree top level, presumably on its way with 'bigwigs' to a nearby RAF station (not a flying one). It was literally only fifty feet above my client and me. I could actually see the pilot looking down at us and I shook my fist at him. Fortunately I had located the source of the sound quite early and was able to tell the client what to expect and he was sufficiently experienced to listen to me telling him to close his fingers on the reins, his legs gently against the horses' sides, whilst, at the same time, speaking kindly to the animal and touching its neck. On the second occasion I was denied the advantage of sight only hearing the extraordinary banshee shriek of a fighter as it passed over the roof of the indoor arena literally shaking the roof. On both occasions these events passed without any serious results but it is the sort of thing that you may have to deal with, once in a while. This may be quite difficult if you have a class of several riders and all that you can do is to give the advice that I have already mentioned. Do bear in mind that you must have *calming authority* in your own voice as you give your advice because the apprehension arising in the rider may add to the horse's alarm.

Chapter 19

New technology.

All technological advances may be used for both good and evil. What we might consider as evil today may, in the long run, prove not to be without any redeeming features. The horse is one such example. As I have mentioned elsewhere, when the Spaniards first landed in America the horse had, on that continent, already become extinct for some considerable time. So for that matter had several other mammalian species. This was probably due to a combination of climate change and over-hunting. The fact is that though simple hunter-gatherer societies may be regarded with a fond nostalgia by the mainly urban people of today, in practise these simple people were not very good at maintaining a balance that preserved the many life forms upon which their very lives depended. During the good years tribal populations with an abundant food supply, expanded exponentially. However when faced with a sudden adverse climate change they were left with no option but to over-hunt or move on. They usually chose the former seeing no reason to move elsewhere until they were forced to do so. Eventually all those creatures that had sustained them were all gone and, failing to adapt, the hunters themselves frequently perished.

With the introduction of agriculture populations became more stable and though they continued to expand new technologies such as the tilling of the soil with ploughs pulled by bullocks, enabled the food supply to keep pace with the growing population.

I am sure that you will therefore understand me when I say that I do not go along with those who hold an over-romantic view when it comes to using modern technology in dealing with horses. To ignore modern inventions, for example the use of electronics, in what may today be regarded essentially as an art form, is to my mind extremely blinkered. If mankind had taken that attitude, then it is quite probable that horses would also have become extinct in Europe as well as America. Going back 6,000 years, the saddle, bridle and stirrups were all 'technological' inventions in their time. They enabled man to use the horse as an ever more efficient weapon. It is true that for hundreds of years some of those 'inventions' were quite barbaric in their design. Fortunately for us in European society men became sufficiently confident and secure in themselves to allow the catalyst of change to encourage new ideas to spring forth. This could not be said of the Chinese whose population had to endure a lower standard of living as a result of rigid centralist control with its concomitant loss of technical knowledge.

In the case of the horse this process started during the Renaissance. High School riding was considered to be an essential part of a young gentleman's' education. Gradually this gave rise to greater thought about the best way of obtaining an ever-higher performance. This eventually evolved into a way of treating horses that was considerably more humane than it had been in the past, though I hasten to add they were still not spared death as a weapon of war.

Today we have new inventions many of which I fully embrace when it comes to teaching people to ride. These are examples of what I would call technology put to good use.

The video camera.

I don't need to be so pedantic as to explain what this is because most people these days own one. I think that it can be very useful when used by an instructor in order to show clients, subsequent to the lesson, exactly what they have been doing - right or wrong. It really is quite amusing to watch the faces of some clients who have a very high opinion of their ability when they see themselves on the small screen. However in order to be effective in the short term it is a good idea to have a camera that has a small viewing screen that unfolds from the side so that you may run the tape back quickly after the lesson has ended. It may also help to arrange a special viewing lesson and then after the review you can follow this with a period during which errors are corrected.

The mechanical horse.

These have been around for quite sometime. In America they are used as bucking Broncos and feature in competitions where members of the public try to stay on as long as they can. Here in the U.K. Bill Greenwood has devised a machine, which I am told on very good authority reproduces all the gaits and further more with the feeling of collection or extension if required. Some people say, 'well this isn't really riding is it?' This may be true to a great extent. Horses are not machines, they are unpredictable, but I have no doubt that even a degree of capriciousness will be encoded in the software of later models.

In the meantime I think that this is an excellent way in which novices may start to get their muscles 'in tune' as it were with the motion of a horse, without the concomitant danger of becoming unbalanced and suffering a heavy fall. Do not misunderstand me. I don't mean that they will not fall off, it's simply that if they do they will land on a nice soft mat instead of a hard arena. Further more it wont be at 15 to 20 mph and there will be no danger of their being accidentally trampled on .

The mobile phone.

I mentioned the use of this item in the chapter dealing with hacking out. I do not think that I need say any more save that you do need to ensure that *your clients are not carrying them* when they ride with you. They are one of those items together with sharp pointed biros and dangling earrings that could cause a problem at any time. Just imagine the possible effect of a loud a chorus of Beethoven's ninth or Mission Impossible, suddenly busting forth on your unsuspecting horses and clients as a mobile starts to ring.

The tension or positional alarm.

This is a little device which I invented and patented some years ago. The patent has now lapsed but you may feel free to try and have one made if you are able so to do. In the meantime the patent licence provides a rather attractive decoration for the wall of my study!

In essence this a little electronic device which is either operated by a spring mechanism or a positional switch such as mercury contact. In its first form it consists of two parts, which are hooked across a small loop in the reins. The parts have a sliding action and a spring, which keeps them joined together. The pressure of the spring may be varied. Thus the two parts slide when a light or a heavy touch pulls them apart. When the two parts have travelled a certain distance they activate a switch. The pulling is done as the rein is taken up. Inside there is a little chip with an electronic voice message. There is also a time delay resistor. The device is pre-set to a particular time, say about 15 seconds. If the rider grabs hold of the reins with fixed hands for longer than that period, keeping the two sections apart, then a little voice cries out of a tiny loudspeaker in the device 'Ouch your hurting my mouth!' The whole point about the device is that it doesn't go off if the rider gives a simple, quick half halt. It only does so if the rider hangs on past the pre-set elapsed time. The object is for you to set the device to go off over ever shorter periods with a lighter and lighter setting to the spring and thus for the rider to learn to develop 'good hands'.

The other form of the device (with the mercury switch) is that it may be attached to riders' helmet. In this form the object is to allow a rider to glance down – briefly- but should they remain looking down past a pre-set time, then the device will give a different message such as 'For heavens sake look up before you bang into something!'

The plastic horseshoe.

This device has nothing to do with teaching equitation and I simply mention it because it is my invention and I am proud of it and it is an example of lateral thinking. I have this patent also on the wall by me in my study. The number is 1512983. I was prompted to try and invent an alternative method of shoeing after hearing a young girl being told by a farrier that he would not have time to re-shoe her horse for an event that weekend. 'Surely' I thought 'There must be someway in which a shoe may be fixed on in a temporary manner, apart from nailing on which requires great skill'. I started to investigate the possibility of using cyanoacrylic adhesives (these were supplied to me by my father-in-law who was a chemical manufacturer) only to make two discoveries. The first was that though these adhesives were immensely strong when it came to a constant force being applied to them, they only had fracture strength of 6lbs. That is to say that a light blow would break the seal and since a horse weighs around 1000 lbs. and that force hits the ground on one leg only during each stride of the canter, there was no way that the adhesive would stand up to a continuous pounding. Secondly someone else had started down this road before me.

So I had to think of an alternative way of attaching a shoe. I started to look more closely at the structure of the foot. The one part that seemed to offer an alternative was the heel. Up to that time (1974/5 or thereabouts) it had always been considered that the nailing on should never proceed towards the back of the foot past a point two thirds of the way along from the toe. The reason being that the horn at the heel is very thin and will not take a nail. Of course one may place a nail in that area but only to prevent over-expansion of the heel. I started to obtain dozens of feet from the knacker's yard and proceeded to dissect them. I noticed two things, the first was that there was a reasonable thickness of quite soft tissue from the wall extending to the bars; secondly there were no nerves in that area. It therefore seemed to me that there was a possibility of using that part of the hoof if one were to attach horizontally and the best means of doing this was to use a pop rivet. The Dunlop Rubber Company very kindly produced moulded plastic shoes made to my specification and I bought a box of roofing pop rivets and a tool with which to fix them and set about 'shoeing' my first horse. My dear friend Sheila Freeman kindly provided this. The horse was in use with the shoes until its foot growth necessitated their removal.

I only invented this method of shoeing to prove a point, namely that there were other ways of putting shoes on horses. After successful trials, I then went on to other things. However it is worthwhile remembering that I used the crudest of materials. With rivets made of steel and of a minimal diameter, this would be a very good method for prophylactic shoeing for those horses with hoof walls that have become rather friable and need a period of re-growth before re-shoeing in the traditional manner.

The horse walker.
This is a machine that may be especially seen in racing yards. It is consists of a circular wire cage approximately 15 metres in diameter. The inside is divided into equally sized sections that pivot around a central vertical arm. This arm is driven, at a pre-set speed by an electric motor, which causes the sections to revolve inside the cage. There is a gate large enough to admit a horse into each section.

When horses have become familiar with its operation it may be used to provide them with a degree of exercise with fairly minimal supervision. It is especial useful for large yards during the winter when it is not possible to turn horses out to pasture.

Note all drawings and illustrations for this chapter are now shown at the end of the book after the coloured photographs.

Chapter 20

Hacking Out.

Introduction

Do bear in mind when reading this chapter that this is simply the inclusion of my previously booklet on Safe and Interesting Hacking published in 1995. I have made very few amendments to that which I had written previously. However the form of expression may seem slightly out of context due to the fact that the original was written as a stand-alone guide. I occasionally refer to the 'instructor' and sometimes to the 'escort'. This is simply because though a hack must be in the charge of someone both qualified and experienced it does not automatically follow that this person is necessarily engaged regularly in the occupation of teaching people to ride.

Since the middle of the 18th century there has been much debate, especially in France, as to the different techniques required for what was then known as equitation d'interieur (school riding) and equitation d'exterieur (outdoor riding). Many military academies would have nothing to do with the restrained systems of schools teaching 'Haut Ecóle', for it was believed that this interfered with a horses' ability to go forward *38. Nowadays horses are trained, very successfully, in both disciplines, though there is no doubt that they do behave differently outside and this can prove to be a problem for less experienced riders.

In the past any riding establishment engaged in the hiring of horses to the general public would display a notice in the yard office stating, *'You Ride At Your Own Risk'*. Provided reasonable precautions were taken to establish the level of competence of clients and to ensure that they were not allocated a horse that was completely unmanageable, then the notice was considered sufficient protection against litigation should any person sustain an injury whilst under instruction at the establishment. It was the accepted wisdom in those days that if you went 'horse back riding' (to use the American parlance) then at some point you would probably depart your mount — and after seven such descents to earth you might consider yourself a 'rider'.

Today, however, that is no longer the case. There are some that wish to emulate the American tendency to resort to litigation whenever the opportunity presents itself. In fact, it might be said that they, perhaps, go so far as to help create 'incidents' in which the legal fraternity is given an opportunity to become involved.

The adjective most frequently used in these incidents is *'negligent'* and the one to whom it is usually directed is the person in charge of the lesson or the ride, be they qualified with papers to prove it, simply someone with years of experience, or perhaps a young person just embarking on a career as a riding instructor. It may well be that in the end no blame attaches itself to the person held to be responsible, but in the meantime for both the individual and the employer there may be periods of great stress and worry.

In the end, it is extremely probable that there will be a degree of financial expenditure. Even if the establishment involved in the litigation has adequate insurance, it may provide insufficient protection if certain formalities are not observed. In any case there will be statements to be taken and, in the worst-case scenario, even the trauma of an appearance in court.

It seems to me that a riding instructor is most vulnerable when escorting horses and riders out into the countryside, where they (the horses) may be subject to fears, real or imagined, and which may cause them to behave in an unpredictable manner. It is in circumstances such as these that an 'incident' is most likely to happen.

In this chapter I may not by any means offer a complete answer to the many problems that may arise but it should help, if the advice in these pages is followed correctly, to minimise the difficulties that can ensue should an accident occur.

The instructor.

The dictionary definition of a hack is 'to ride a hired horse from place to place'. We are now concerned with the management of such a ride, ensuring it is carried out in safety and, hopefully, with all the participants enjoying the experience. In this chapter the advice and information given is that considered applicable to an instructor or for that matter a student working towards a teaching qualification, who is considered competent to carry out the responsibility of acting as an escort. However these fundamental rules apply whenever members of the public are involved in any form of equitation. The instructor or escort involved in taking clients out on a hack has *extra* responsibilities and must be aware of these rules, with safety being paramount. Therefore, *before* a hack starts, the instructor must always ensure that:

1. No activity of any sort whatsoever should be commenced unless the instructor is satisfied that all-reasonable precautions have been taken to avoid accidents. Never proceed at a gait or speed beyond the control of your least experienced rider, i.e. for beginners – **WALK**. For others according to their experience and skills. It is now my considered view that a rider, who has not yet learned to sit to the canter for at least half a dozen strides, should not hack out (see addendum at the end of this chapter).
2. The result of the hack will be that Clients are mentally stimulated through taking part and will have enjoyed their ride.
3. All those participating will learn more of the fundamentals of good horsemanship.

The order in which I have placed these three rules should be noted. The first rule needs no further comment; however, the juxtaposition of second and third is interesting. I have placed enjoyment second and learning to ride third, because without the second element, it is unlikely that clients will return with sufficient regularity to benefit from the third.

The instructor's equipment

Needless to say, as an instructor your own equipment and general appearance must be immaculate. Leather boots, highly polished, rubber ones clean. Gloves should be worn. All other garments should be suitable and in keeping with the requirements of the establishment for whom you are working.

In addition, on a hack you should always carry with you:
> A first-aid kit (and be familiar with basic first-aid procedures).
> A leading rein.
> A folding hoof pick.
> A notebook and safe writing instrument.
> A map of the route you plan to take and, in ideal circumstances, a mobile telephone.

Furthermore, you should always make certain that you carry a length of string (bailing twine is ideal); this may be used either to provide 'grass reins' that may be required should a bad-mannered horse continually put its head down and eat grass despite the best efforts of the client (even after he or she has been advised as to how to 'make a bridge'), to prevent the horse from so doing, and also to provide emergency repairs.

The horses

It is extremely important that an instructor, especially a freelance, makes use of all the information that can be obtained from the riding establishment's management as to the temperament and ability of the horses provided. This is especially important when the instructor is working for a particular employer for the first time. It is possible that the owner, yard manager or head groom may rather tartly point out that 'only *suitable* horses are ever used', the inference being that you have a bit of a nerve to ask otherwise. Nonetheless, if the question is not put to the management, you have not done your job as an instructor properly.

A well-run yard will have no problem in giving advice as to the personality traits of each animal employed. Based on this information, you can then plan the order in which the horses will be placed during the hack. Not only temperament should be taken into account but also the age and ability of an individual horse to perform the work required. This obviously means that you should visit all the horses in their boxes before they are tacked up. At this time you can then make your own assessment of each animal.

In making up your own mind you will include a judgement of your own horse. In an ideal world the instructor's horse will be of a quiet temperament as it is something of a nuisance to be mounted on an animal that is continually misbehaving. In the first place such behaviour does tend to distract your attention from the job in hand — that is, observing your clients. Secondly, there are occasions when a client's horse may start to play up and become too much for that person to handle. If this happens, and when there is no animal in the group of a similar type with whom a change can be arranged, then you should offer your own horse if it is suitable.

For other problems, such as a bridle breaking beyond even emergency repair, or a horse going lame, the same rule applies. Do not forget, however, that an instructor should be a good enough horseman to ride any horse quietly; this same animal may behave entirely differently with a novice on its back! Therefore, you must judge the situation very carefully.

Readers may well query whether or not all this advice is practical when out in the country. This is where good planning comes into effect, which we shall discuss in a moment. However, you should remember that the client has paid to ride and, if there is any walking to be done, then it is the instructor who does it!

The riders

Assessments of clients are important and part of being an instructor, especially when you are working for an employer on a regular basis. Matching the client to the horse and managing the employer's interests is something you will become familiar with. But, again, safety is paramount. Although you will have become familiar with most of the horses in the yard, you still do need to check in advance the list of those horses chosen for the hack. The selection of particular animals will most likely have been arranged several days before your particular outing is due, because a well-run yard with a regular clientele will not allow the running of the business in a haphazard manner.

Therefore, if you notice that a client has been assigned a horse that you consider is beyond his or her ability to handle, then, you should say so and ask for a change. This may not be possible due to the fact that the client may, for example, be a heavyweight and all the other weight-carrying horses may be booked up; or, it may well be that there is no other suitable horse available due to lameness or illness. You must put your point of view to the management and abide by their decision but be ready to make a change of riders whilst out on the hack, should you consider it imperative so to do.

A check with the yard management as to the ability and temperament of all the riders who are going to take part in the hack is always a sensible precaution.

Planning the route

As you are the escort to the hack it is essential that you should familiarise yourself, preparatory to taking clients out, as to the exact route to be followed and to also assess, by asking other instructors or the management for whom you are working, if trouble is likely to arise at any particular point.

For example, find out at which part of the route canter usually takes place. The reason for so doing is that very often staff will allow horses to start cantering at the same place every time they go out. This is an undesirable state of affairs since the animals become used to this pace at a particular point and may therefore be inclined to take the initiative; in so doing they can inculcate in less experienced riders a certain nervousness. If this happens, the riders' uneasiness will register with their horses and could possibly lead to a dangerous situation.

Ideally you should ride or walk the course before ever taking out a hack in order to be quite familiar with the suitability of the going and also be able to plan the hack in such a way that, using our earlier example again, canters are initiated over parts of the route where this does not normally happen. I suggest that for those stretches where cantering has become a habit, a walk is the ideal pace. This will give the clients plenty of time to get their horses under control and allow the hack to progress without incident. Bearing this in mind you should also take note of any steep downhill stretches, which may cause a rider to become unbalanced, enabling the horse to take advantage. Also *avoid* any route that takes your ride through excessively boggy ground — this going, more than any other; can cause horses to go lame.

The effect of ground on both horses' and riders' physical wellbeing is something to keep in mind; for example, take into account the amount of roadwork involved on any route and also any rough terrain where a horse may stumble.

Finally, you must calculate accurately the time element. This is absolutely essential. You can't be bringing back your ride late so that the next group to go out are delayed and thus do not 'get their monies worth'.

Emergency meeting points

On any route you take, decide beforehand on suitable places to establish, if not already done so, emergency meeting points. Ideally, these will be near a telephone, either a phone box or a building known to be connected. Each of the emergency meeting points should be clearly marked on a map, a copy of which you should carry with you.

Above all be sure to learn the names of roads or fields *en route*. In the event of an accident where help might be required, you must be able to direct the emergency services (for example, an ambulance) to the exact spot where the incident has occurred. The same applies, for whatever reason, if you need to contact the yard office.

The clients

The instructor must allow a few minutes before the hack starts in order to get to know the class and to carry out certain procedures. Over time, individual instructors develop their own tried and trusted procedures, but those listed below are essential before any hack proceeds.

1. Introduce yourself by name and state your function. Ask each person his or her name. You should also ask them how they wish you to address them; in other words, whether they prefer the use of Christian name or a more formal title, such as 'Mr.' or 'Mrs.' and so on. Establish with each rider how much riding experience they have had. Take some answers with a 'pinch of salt'; some clients have a very inflated idea as to their own abilities. Use your eyes and judge for yourself. Try to remember the name of each client; if you are not very good at doing this, write the names down in your notebook for occasional reference. (I have heard instructors giving advice by using the name of the horse a client is riding. This is very bad form, apart from being a poor way of advising anyone.)

2. Your earlier questioning will have established whether or not a client has actually been out on a hack before. This is a very important point and one that should not be overlooked. Some horses, that clients may have ridden quietly enough in the ménage, might tend to behave slightly differently when outdoors. All this is, of course, especially dependent on the time of the year. During spring for example, horses congregating together try to establish their position in the pecking order of relationships, both with other horses and with their riders. This behaviour may manifest itself in attempts to bite other horses, positioning of the hindquarters in a threatening way, making faces at other horses, or attempting to kick out. Indulging in racing is another way in which a horse tries to establish superiority; but a demonstration by a horse that it is faster than another can lead to trouble for an inexperienced rider. This is true in winter when the horses, newly clipped out and in a cold wind, may be very anxious to get going. With inexperienced riders on board a dangerous state of affairs exists which can lead to possible injury to both rider and horse. Therefore, the instructor needs to be able to assess how clients and horses react to each other.

3. At the same time as you introduce yourself to the class, you should inspect the horses carefully to ensure that they have been tacked up correctly. That is to say, bridles have been properly fitted, all loose straps are retained and, where a numnah is used, examined to make certain that the numnah reflects the same channel as that provided by the saddle, thereby preventing pressure on the horse's spine. (A numnah placed flat on the spine can do as much damage as a badly fitting saddle.)

4. Ideally, on this first meeting between instructor and clients, the instructor should check the headgear of each client —*before they mount.* Ask each client to undo the chinstrap of their riding hat and then to bend at the waist so that their head is pointing almost vertically toward the ground. A helmet that does not fit correctly will fall off at this point; if this does happen ask the client to go to the yard office and obtain a riding hat that is of the correct size. The reason for this is, of course, quite obvious: should the rider forget to do up the chinstrap or if for any other reason it comes undone during the ride, then in the event of a fall the hat will remain in place on the rider's head and so provide the required protection. One other important point that should not be overlooked concerns the hoods of anoraks. Where stitching or even open-ended zips affix these, then, when they are not being worn over a rider's helmet, they must be either tucked out of the way inside the garment itself or completely removed and placed in a pocket. If they are allowed to hang down the rider's back, they may catch in a branch and, possibly, pull the rider off the horse.

5. Another question that needs to be asked is whether the clients are carrying any sharp objects. *Most important of all,* however, is to look and see if *any jewellery, in particular earrings or sleepers are being worn.* On no account should an instructor allow a client to proceed on the hack until the offending articles are removed. Also check footwear for a smooth sole and sensible heels that will not become wedged or allow the client's foot to slip through his or her stirrup: trainers are not acceptable.

6. Before riders mount, the instructor must ask them to check their horses' girths. That is to say, you will ask the clients to make certain that the girth is tight enough. You should also ask them how they are going to do this and make sure they are aware that if they have any doubt at all as to whether or not the girth is correctly tightened they can ask you to check. The instructor should not be satisfied with this procedure alone. In the final analysis the responsibility is the instructors. So, if you have any doubt, walk along the ride and check the girths yourself. *Any girth which, after tightening, has been done up near the top holes of the girth straps on both sides of the saddle must be changed for girth that allows further subsequent adjustment.* And don't forget the stirrup leathers. You should ensure that clients check to make certain that they are not about to ride with uneven leathers. On many occasions clients are not even aware of the problems, which usually occur when a stirrup is lengthened prior to mounting and then is forgotten about.

7. Before proceeding further, *ensure that all riders are mounted on the horses allocated to them* in your checklist. Be alert to the fact that new clients may not know the animals and might therefore make a mistake. Other clients may try to change with friends because they prefer one horse to another. No client should be permitted to change without your permission.

8. As an instructor you must remember that at all times you are 'On parade'. In other words your own riding position should be correct. Do not allow yourself to slouch in the saddle just because you are only on escort duty.

The hack
At this stage the instructor will be familiar with the horses, with the route to be taken, and with participants in the hack. Once all are assembled and in good order the hack can begin.

Types of hack
There are, to my mind, generally five types of hack:

      1.   Adults, who are reasonably, experienced riders and simple wish to traverse the countryside at a good pace.

      2.   Semi-experienced riders, who are taking part in an instructional hack.

      3.   A hack for novices. This does *not* include children for whom the instructor should make special provision.

      4.   The private hack.

      5.   A special hack for a nervous rider.

Each of these five types of hack has specific elements that need to be taken into account. Consideration should be given to: -

The energy available to the horse. Bear in mind that the horses on your hack will have a work programme already planned for them by the yard office, it is likely, therefore, that they will probably still have further work to do after you return with your party;

The paces at which you choose to proceed. It is essential that your horses return to the stable cool. You must never lose sight of the fact that you are dealing with working horses and their well-being must always be foremost in your mind.

The time of year. If you are taking out animals during the autumn, when winter coats are growing through but horses have yet to be clipped out, then only proceed at such a pace as is compatible with the animals not getting sweated up. The same applies when the weather is very warm irrespective of the state of the animals' coats. *During prolonged dry spells when the going is hard do not allow any cantering whatsoever*. The only exception to this would be if you had access to a specially prepared all-weather surface.

When heavy going is encountered you will have another factor to consider. This is muscle fatigue in so far as it effects a horses' mental disposition. By that I mean that it is unlikely that your riders will have the ability to listen to what their horses are telling them. They may fail to realise that as with human beings horses do suffer the pain that arises as a result of prolonged physical effort, (try to imagine yourself running a considerable distance through heavy mud. Or of exercising in a gym and pushing yourself through the pain barrier). You must therefore do this thinking for them. If you allow your riders to push their horses at canter or even a fast trot through heavy mud then do not be surprised if, when the opportunity occurs, the horses in their turn put in a hefty buck.

During the hack
As the escort to the hack you should beware of appearing to remain aloof from the clients.

Do not ride ahead all of the time and, when you do, make sure that you continuously look behind to ensure that all is well. When the opportunity occurs, ride alongside people and engage them in conversation (asking them their occupation is always a good starting point). As conversation proceeds, you will probably notice that those individuals who were originally rather tense begin to relax and this, in turn, has a beneficial effect upon their horses. At the same time you may tactfully correct their positions and also give them some helpful hints. This will, again, elicit a positive response from their horses and thus the riders will obtain more enjoyment from the outing. When giving instructions always speak quietly. Do not yell as though you were an army drill sergeant. Always keep the conversation general and do not become involved in discussions about politics or religion and *never, ever,* discuss or comment upon the business of your employer.

Placing yourself in this position will enable you to view each rider and horse individually and thus you will be able to accurately assess both rider and horse.

Giving commands
Always give your instructions in a quiet but firm voice, the tone of which should indicate that you expect your instructions to be followed. There are occasions when a client will want to argue with you. Listen to what they have to say and, if you consider their remarks unreasonable, repeat what you have already said. Always explain your reasons and if necessary point out how the element of safety has played its part in any decision you have made. Should the client subsequently disobey your instructions, you should inform him or her that you intend to report the matter to the yard office on your return to the stables. Do just that and be sure that your comments are entered in whatever record book is kept by the yard. Also make an entry in your own note-hook for future reference.

Avoiding difficult situations
You can preempt difficult situations developing if, before the ride departs (and, as you should do in any case) you organise the horses according to the terrain to be covered. For example, if the hack is to start with an element of roadwork, then the horses that get on well with one another should be placed in pairs, the quietest horses to the outside. (But do be very particular about this because some drivers of motor vehicles are very inconsiderate and tend to pass extremely close to horses, making no allowance for the fact that they may shy or kick out.)

Occasionally, there may be a horse that is completely anti—social; in this case, it is recommended that the horse proceeds unaccompanied being placed either at the back of the hack or between pairs of quiet horses in front and behind (see drawing no. 29).

Riders should be reminded as to what is entailed in riding in pairs. In other words, their horses should be shoulder-to-shoulder with the riders close enough together to touch stirrups. Where an individual horse in a pair is inclined to make faces at its partner, the rider should be advised to turn its face slightly away from the other.

If the hack includes any roadwork it is advisable to have an experienced assistant as part of the hack escort. The assistant takes up a position to the rear of the ride and should be thoroughly familiar with the requirements of road safety. Experienced riders should also be placed in the first and last files. Clients should also be informed as to what is expected of them in this respect. For example, a client should be reminded to keep the distance between horses at one horse's length away from the horse in front. You cannot of course assume that a client experienced or otherwise already knows, this or indeed, how to gauge the distance. You will therefore have to define it exactly: a length can be judged by the rider seeing half the tail of the horse in front — the whole tail, they are too far away; less than a half, they are too close (see drawing no. 30).

The reason for being so particular about this matter of distances should be explained to the client, If too far away, the ride will become straggly; if too close, the horse in front may kick out, especially a mare coming into season. It is my view that roadwork should, on the way out, be ridden at a nice steady trot. The rhythm seems to keep the horses occupied and the period for which one is on the road is shortened.

Leaving the road

Ideally, the hack should leave the road at a point where there is room for it to reorganise and for riders to re-check the horses' girths.

The instructor should be very particular about this check because some horses may have been 'blown out' when they were first tacked up and girths that appeared tight may have become quite loose.

Even now you will need to pay attention again to those horses whose girths might be done up near the top holes. It may well be that such horses have lost condition or the wrong girth has been used and, even when the girth is done up to the top hole on both sides, it may still not be tight enough. If you spot any horses in this situation, dismount and ask those clients whose horses need attention to do likewise. Look for a horse whose girth is short enough to enable you to carry out a change. Do not allow the hack to move off until the change has been completed, and the riders involved remounted and their girths re-checked.

Proceeding across country

I mentioned above the manner of proceeding on a hack where there is a degree of roadwork involved, pointing out the desirability of initiating a steady trot. In ideal circumstances, if the hack is able to leave the road and proceed across country through bridle ways or paths that are traffic-free, then of course the initial half-mile to a mile should be ridden at no faster pace than a walk. The horses should be allowed to go forward on a long rein so that they may stretch their necks and at the same time engage their hindquarters correctly. However, the instructor needs to make clear to his or her clients that there is a difference between a long rein and a loose rein. The long rein indicates that although the rein allows the horse to stretch, contact between the bit and the rider's hand is maintained. In the case of the loose rein, the rider holds the rein only by its buckle and there is no contact whatsoever.

Before starting *any* cross-country hack.

It is very important to point out, to your clients, that at *any gait*, for example, when passing along the side of a field an horse may pick up a scent, believe that it sees something lurking in a hedge or be startled by a bird flying out and shy. It is very important that the rider be warned to be prepared for this by being ready to bring their inside leg (i.e. the one away from the hedge) against the horse's side thus keeping it going straight. The odd calming, word or two from the rider will also not go amiss! If the rider does not react quickly enough it is all too likely that the horse will swerve away from the imagined danger, while the rider continues in a strait line!

In any case you need to think ahead. Which in modern politically correct parlance is referred to as 'assessing the risk'. For example, are you likely to pass by a field in which sheep are grazing, who upon hearing a horses' approach, especially in canter, may start to panic. This may cause some horses to wonder what the fuss is all about and increase their pace, considerably. Another possible problem is the scent left by a fox when it marks out its territory. I have found that some horses find this very disturbing and they start to become quite nappy. What is more this is quite often passed on to the other horses in the ride. Before you know where you are you have suddenly got a number of horses all dancing about and the riders are also starting to panic.

Thus it is incumbent on you as the escort to the hack to be sure that you change the gait to one that is suitable for any possible set of circumstances. This will go some way to enable clients to maintain their balance should something unusual occur. In other words when you ride past a high dense hedge do so at the walk.

This may lead you to conclude that if you are able to ride across the wide-open space of a field you may relax somewhat. Do not be so foolish, for this brings me to a point that I have made in an earlier chapter (chapter 11) about confidence being quite fragile. In that chapter I was referring to children, but experience has taught me that even though you may be escorting adult clients who *seem* to be very confident riders when things start to go wrong they simply fall apart. In this case I am referring to the lure of the 'wide open spaces'. In this situation we have apparently confident riders and in most cases they remain so. But, ride across a field and those horses that have been used to hunting will recall their past life and quite suddenly open up and go forward at a good gallop. Many clients will enjoy this and so they should, provided that they do not allow their mounts to overtake you! For others the experience may be quite unnerving and they will give a little shriek and bale out. I have to tell you that this may take some explaining when you come to fill out the accident form!

The experienced hack

It is not reasonable for an instructor to take out people who are competent riders and expect them to spend the whole hour (or whatever) simply walking and trotting. There are those riders who should be encouraged to enjoy a fast ride, provided that the going and conditions are suitable. When deciding who these riders are and what qualifies as 'suitable', you have to bear in mind a number of factors, some of which we now discuss.

Provided all conditions are within the parameters set out above, I am inclined to let clients in the category of 'experienced rider' have a really good canter fairly early on. In the first place this frequently allows the horses to 'let off steam'. Secondly, from my experience, most clients are not very fit and after a longish canter are quite content to proceed at nothing faster than a walk; this will also give them the opportunity for a quiet gossip. For a hack of one hour's duration I usually allow three canters, each progressively over a shorter distance. If this arrangement is adopted, it will provide sufficient time towards the end of the period to allow horses to cool off.

Under no circumstances should you allow any members of the ride to race one against the other. Clients may try all sorts of tricks in order to pretend that what appeared as a race, was simply that they lost control and were 'carted'. You should be sufficiently observant to know whether or not this is true — if you think that there is some element of truth in the claim, then the client must pay the price of not being allowed to proceed at a faster pace than a walk for the rest of the ride! If, however, you know perfectly well that the riders concerned are too experienced for this 'carting' not to have been premeditated, don't lose your temper. Simply tell the culprits (in an icy tone) that, if they ever do that sort of thing on your hack again, you will report them to the yard office and have them banned. I've never known this threat to fail! (Though I must say that I have only ever had to use it once!).

It may be that you have to arrange the manner of going in such a way as to accommodate horses whose coats are in greater or lesser stages of growth. In other words, you may permit some clients to have longer periods at the faster paces than others. Most people understand the reasons for this and will co-operate; some will not and will try to persuade you to allow them to canter when you know that this is not in the best interests of the horse. Whatever you decide, *do not weaken!*

The instructional hack

If the hack is travelling over land, riders should be encouraged to check that their horses are tracking up, especially during an instructional hack. Some riders will need the term 'tracking up' explained to them and an instructional hack is a good place to do so. You should tell them that what is meant is that the imprint of the horse's hind leg is made in front of that of the foreleg on the same side. With a horse that is moving freely, this should be a distance of at least 5 or 6 inches.

During an instructional hack the instructor is dependent on the area in which it is taking place as to when he or she can send on the riders. If, for example, the hack has come to an enclosed field, this is an ideal opportunity to send the riders off one at a time in order to assess how well they cope. A large enough gap should be left before the departure of each rider so that the horses do not get the idea that they are simply following the horse in front. Horses that may be frisky or inclined to fidget should proceed first; those that are nappy should be encouraged to follow the horses that have already gone. In this way they will cause less of a problem.

When you really know all the horses in your charge, you may refine the matter even further. As a rule of thumb you should send off your riders so that the distance between each of them is sufficient to give them the feeling that they are riding alone. It is of course only a 'feeling' for the whole ride is contained in the field and you are watching everyone very closely. Sometimes you must make adjustments. You may have a horse who, should the distance between itself and the horse preceding it become too extended, will loose interest completely and generally try to muck its rider about. Such an animal should be sent off fairly soon after the one that it follows. On the other hand you may have a horse that, as soon as it comes into a close proximity with the one in front, immediately tries to initiate a race.

It therefore follows that every member of your hack must keep a lookout for the rider in front. If they see that someone is having a problem they should slowdown or even stop. Sometimes this is sufficient to allow the rider with problems to sort him or herself out. On other occasions you may have to ride up yourself and give instructions for a rider following to quietly trot past and give a lead.

The instructional hack provides the opportunity for several schooling elements to be included at selected spots along the route. For example, you can ask each rider to leave the ride and, at some point in his or her circuit of the field, ride a large circle. Clearly indicate for them the size of the circle you want; either give them the measurement in feet or metres or use a prominent landmark as a guide (see drawing no. 31).

This sort of exercise is very suitable for encouraging riders to use their own initiative. The horse, too, can learn that it does not always have to follow the established path, which it has done so often before. Remember, however, to check beforehand because these exercises may only be carried out where you have the permission of the landowner to leave the track. Also remember that you as *instructor must keep the ride in sight at all times.*

It is during this part of the hack that you may assure yourself that all is well and that your clients are not going to have any problems. Pay particular attention to the action of each horse as it moves away; what you are looking for is that none of the horses are lame. This is the point, too, where possible changes in horse and rider should be made. If for any reason you need to dismount, then your pre-planning will pay off now. You should always have made an allowance for a possible change of route that will enable you to send the ride away from you whilst still keeping it in sight. For example, if you are in a field you should ask the ride to proceed all the way around its borders and then return to you. Before sending them away be sure to stress the need for them to make their return approach at a pace that will not upset the horses waiting. On the other hand, if you have to make progress along your chosen route then ask the clients to ride the three sides of a field and to wait for you at the end while you walk along the fourth side to meet them (see drawing no. 32).

The instructor must always make it quite clear as to where the clients are to walk, trot and canter. Indeed, it may be sensible to tailor these paces to the ability of each client. Also remind them to take extra care that they do not allow their horses to become bunched up as they wait for you to join them and that they must follow the basic rules of safety at all times.

Other exercises

Another feature of the instructional hack is that there are a number of other exercises, which can be tried out. These are all designed to improve horsemanship.
Some are discussed below.

1.   Ask the riders to leave the ride in pairs. Make sure that the horses sent away are compatible with one another.

2.   Another exercise that members of an instructional hack can practice is to go away from you and, at certain points as they go around a field, execute a series of transitions such as walk to trot, trot to canter and the reverse. This exercise will give riders the opportunity to develop their ability in obtaining their horses' obedience.

3.   That segment of the ride at which individuals are going to be sent off one at a time at the canter can also be utilised to illustrate one of the most important elements in equitation — one that is constantly overlooked. *The art of riding involves giving signals to the horse rather than trying to impose one's will by the application of brute strength* — for example, trying to stop the horse going forward by heaving on the reins is pointless as, after all, horses are much stronger than humans and will, generally, win such contests in the end. There are some horses that as soon as they see another horse depart desire to do the same. It has probably become a habit with them. What usually happens is that the rider, if he or she is experienced, will turn the horse around so

that it is looking the other way (Horses usually submit to being turned.) However, as soon as the horse turns back, it again will show an inclination to follow on at a great pace. In many cases this is sufficient for the rider who will now allow the horse to depart. The instructor must at this stage point out that this is not good enough. Explain to the rider that not only should it be unnecessary to have the horse turned away but that the horse must not even be allowed to compromise by standing sideways (which many horses tend to do). The rider must be told not to pull on the rein with all their strength but to sit tall and deep and give a series of half-halts. Whenever the horse starts to move forward without instruction from the rider, then, immediately, it should be turned away and then gently moved back, using the half-halt until such time as the horse is standing straight along the indicated path. Once this is achieved, the rider is able to completely relax the tension on the rein and at the same time touch the animal gently on the neck in order to reward it for its obedience. This exercise demonstrates to the rider the need for a speedy reflex, and also to allow an instant of relaxation to follow the moment of tension created by a half-halt. To my mind, it is one of the most valuable exercises that a rider can learn because once the rider has mastered the art he or she will seldom find himself or herself out of control. Above all, be sure at this moment that the client *gives the horse a kind word immediately it obeys*. Riders so often overlook this important matter.

4.   One of the best exercises is that of opening and closing gates. No matter what standard a rider has reached, be they expert or novice, this is an exercise all should practice. The movements involved can be quite complicated, since there may be an element of lateral movement as well as rein back — hence its value as a very good instructional lesson. Furthermore, the client asked to carry out this exercise may also have to learn to instil a degree of obedience in the horse since the animal will certainly be required to stand still as the rider operates the gate latch. The instructor should be very careful not to allow riders to undertake this task if they are riding horses known to he extremely bad-mannered; such a horse may, with a small buck, try to dump its rider as soon as it feels the weight on its back shift as its rider leans over to unfasten the gate. My own preference in this situation is to call for a rider to volunteer his or her horse. I then choose from several suitable applicants. By this I mean always select a horse that you know will be reasonably co-operative. If you do choose an animal that has never had to stand and wait as a gate is opened you are quite likely to have insufficient time at your disposal for the exercise to be completed correctly. This could possibly have a derogatory effect on that particular horse's future behaviour. While the client is carrying out the task never be sarcastic should they get into difficulties. Make quiet but positive suggestions: advise them to start by aiming for the gate hinge so that they have time to get the horse in hand and come up, quietly, alongside the gate. Make sure, too, that they understand the importance of correctly positioning the horse so that its quarters are tucked out of the way. This to ensure that the horse is not tempted to kick out as the rest of the ride goes through the gate. If a client really does have a problem then don't hesitate to take over yourself (see drawing no. 33a, b, c & d).

5.   Finally, there is no reason why an instructional hack should not practice some simple dressage movements at suitable points during the ride. For example, riding a counter shoulder-in, as a ride, parallel with a hedgerow, along the side of a field. After all, high-school movements do not need to be always reserved for the ménage!

Special points
The instructor must watch for the unusual or for the client who may not be managing the ride as well as the rest of the hack. For example, should a client express fear or uncertainty and ask not to canter, do not insist that they do so. Instead, seek to reassure them and allow them to proceed at a steady trot.
The danger here, if you do insist that one of your party canter when they have declined to do so, is that they might subsequently sustain a fall. (They may even be purposely falling off simply through fear, known as 'bailing out'.) If this happens, you may well he held responsible for any injuries sustained.
    It is one matter for a horse to behave in an uncharacteristic manner or to be frightened by something unusual and entirely another for a set of circumstances to be created as a result of the instructions you have given.

The most satisfactory way of dealing with a problem is not to allow it to arise in the first place.
When sending riders off one at a time it is essential to have an overall view of the terrain that will be covered. One needs to be sure that, having sent your riders away, there is no likely-hood of a change in circumstances that could cause problems. Let me give an example. I have seen an instructor out with two riders on a private hack. They had come to a field, which had two gates adjacent to one another in one corner. One gate was that which they have just entered and the other, a short distance away, was the one that they would use to exit the field as they made their way home. The time was 12.50 p.m. And lunch was but ten minutes away. Now don't forget that this was a busy, well-established riding school and it is the weekend. There were several hacks going around tracks that they were using. However in that field there was no one around so the instructor had no need to make inquiries as to what another instructor had asked their pupils to do. He sent his clients cantering around three sides of the field telling them to stop at the end of the third side. He did this because that third side had an incline and was the highest point in the field and he didn't want to risk the horses stumbling as they might if they cantered down the hill on the fourth side. He asked them to halt and then, to walk quietly back along the forth side to return to him. They carried out his instructions and halted at the top of the small hill. However as they were about to start their return another ride entered through the same gate that they had used, they were simply making their way straight back home and immediately exit through the second gate. One of the client's horses seeing the other ride going away and thought to itself 'Ah ha time for lunch' and immediately dashed off *down* the hill to join his friends. The rider, caught unawares was thrown - hit the ground and was rendered unconscious. I think that I have made my point? In case you don't know what it is, the point being that you need to be ***looking not one but always two steps ahead.*** The above scenario actually happened but, fortunately, I was riding nearby and able to summon help with my mobile phone.

It is quite natural for any client to have some residual fear of being 'carted'. I usually deal with this problem by pointing out that should anyone feel that they have exhausted all the options available for exercising control (that is, a half-halt, riding a large circle, and so on) then the best thing to do is simply to place the reins in one hand and with the other hand take a firm hold of the saddle pommel (the arch just in front of the rider). In this way riders can then concentrate on simply pulling themselves down into the saddle and thus remain secure. 'Always remember,' I tell my clients, 'that one thing is for certain, all horses will get tired and eventually stop.' Therefore, it is unlikely that any harm will befall a client if they simply concentrate on sitting still, deeply, and above all quietly!

The instructor must make it clear that the most serious problems only occur when clients try to stand up in the stirrups and hang on to the reins to support themselves while (at the same time very often) screaming. What these clients do not realise is that it may be the continual pulling on the reins that makes the horse go off in the first place and the screaming certainly doesn't help either.

As I write, my barely five year old mare needs only a breathed word such as 'don't even think about it' to be encouraged to stand absolutely still, on a long rein, while a ride is cantering past under her nose. My daughter, Emma, mentioned this, the other day. She then went on to say ' I'm glad she did, (stand still) for if she had decided to dash off, there wouldn't have been very much that I could have done about it'. In this particular case she was wrong and in this respect typifies many riders. There is usually *something* that can be done to insist that a horse obey ones will. In general the major problem lies in the rider's own perception and surrender.

The novice hack (see also addendum at the end of this chapter)
For those clients who have had little experience in hacking out, the manner of going must always be very quiet. An instructor should not send riders away from his or her control. Horses know full well when they are reasonably beyond an instructor's control and some will not hesitate to take advantage of a novice rider. (They feel the lack of balance and smell the nervousness.) Only proceed at paces that you are quite confident your clients can manage. Leave cantering alone if at all unsure. Don't forget to ask clients if they are happy with a chosen pace.

The private hack.
The instructor taking out a private hack will usually be dealing with a smaller number of participants than is the case with a group or class hack. Furthermore, the riders taking part may very well be of varying ability. The *standard* of each rider *must be established* in the first place by asking the yard office. (A well-run business will *never* allow any client to go out until their level of experience has been assessed; the client

will be asked to have a lesson with a senior instructor in an enclosed ménage.) You are still responsible for making sure, so far as you are able, that clients about to go out for a hack will be placed on horses that they are able to manage. Furthermore you must assess whether or not this is so in a defined space such as an enclosed field, before allowing anyone to take part in a canter as a ride.

As an instructor, and whether or not an assessment has been made, you must come to your own conclusion as to a client's ability. Simple observation and casual questioning can do this. For example, always, before embarking on an upward transition, ask clients if they have ridden at that pace before. *If they are uncertain then keep going at paces that you feel confident they will be able to manage.* If you receive complaints from them that, for example, there isn't any cantering, explain that in the interests of safety you consider it inadvisable to proceed at that pace.

Where you do have clients of differing ability and you feel confident that *some* of them can proceed at faster paces, then there is no reason why they should not be allowed to do so. They can either go away from you (around a field, for example), provided you feel that those riders remaining behind will be able to control their horses or that you will be able to do so for them (using a lead rein), or, alternatively, if you are riding along a straight path, then the thing to do is to ask the experienced riders to remain and await for your signal while you go on ahead with the rest of the hack. It is obvious that this way you will have those left behind in view the whole time.

When taking out a private hack, the instructor is obliged to act even more as 'the escort and companion' since the clients will probably regard this as a special outing. Therefore, do not simply ride silently in front with occasional barked instructions. Instead, be ready to dispense kindly advice and engage in light-hearted conversation.

A special hack for a nervous rider.

Sometimes one may be asked to escort a rider whom for one reason or another may be quite nervous. This fear may have absolutely nothing to do either with riding out or ability. It may have arisen as a result of an entirely different experience. For example you might be asked to escort a client who is quite an accomplished rider. They own a horse liveried at another yard and this animal is proving too much for them. This has resulted in a loss of nerve. By quietly hacking out with you they hope to regain this lost confidence. In these circumstances you must proceed slowly. Start by simply taking the client out for say twenty minutes around a nearby field at nothing more than a walk. If you think that it will help then by all means use a lead rein. As the outings continue so you both extend the duration and also introduce a higher gait – if the client is willing – but do not push them. As soon as they regain some degree of equanimity ask them if they are happy to proceed without the lead rein.

On each occasion present your client with your proposed itinerary and explain your reasoning. Ask them if they are comfortable with it. If you are truly skilled then before long the client will be quite willing to go on hacks of quite extended duration. Eventually you will ask them if they wish to canter and if they reply in the affirmative be sure that you only start with a very short one. Very soon the rider will have overcome their fears and it is you who will have played a significant part in this.

Returning from a hack

The return from a hack should be made in the same manner, as was the start. In ideal conditions the ride should encourage their horses to go forward on a long rein. At this time do be alert to those riders (frequently men) who decide that now the hack is more or less over it is quite safe for them to ride without stirrups. In the first place, no member of the hack should undertake any particular manner of going without your express permission. Secondly, you need to explain to the client that, at the end of the hack, horses should be encouraged to rest and that this can be enhanced by riding with the weight spread evenly over the saddle, which requires the rider to keep feet in stirrups where they belong. Easing of girths should NOT be allowed until after riders have dismounted

It is quite a good idea to explain to riders that horses should return to the stable quietly. You may choose to mention why this is, for the following reasons:

> The need to ensure that horses are brought back cool and should always return to their stables in a quiet mental state.

You may go on to explain that when a horse moves at a faster pace the release of adrenalin into its bloodstream increases. If this state of affairs exists at the end of the ride, especially before the horse is due to feed, then it is possible that its digestive system will be upset.

The reader will note here, however, I have not suggested you further explain to clients that horses, normally being quiet grazing creatures moving slowly only to crop new areas of grass, take to flight involving faster paces only when they are afraid. (Unless they are showing off.) I do not favour this explanation since it may possibly create in a client's mind a fear forever to be associated with the faster paces; obviously, this is not desirable.

The time at which the hack returns to the yard should be taken into consideration. If the hack is the last of a session before a feed is due, it is probably a good idea to encourage horses to drink if the ride is passing a water trough. If horses are prevented from drinking at this point, they may not necessarily be inclined to do so immediately they are back in their boxes because it is quite likely that their feed will be ready on their return. It may not actually have been placed in the box, but the time of day and the smell of the food will be sufficient to cause some horses to think of the feed alone and they may not take a drink until after they have fed. This is particularly true of horses described as 'good doers'. Having eaten their meal with great relish the horses may then turn their attention to the water bucket; this is an undesirable state of affairs since it goes against the basic rule of watering before feeding. This rule has evolved over time to avoid horses from first bolting back their food and then drinking immediately afterwards; a horse that drinks after a meal may wash through the contents of its stomach before digestion has properly taken place. In some animals, this can lead to colic. It is obvious, therefore, that, if one encourages the horse to drink at the end of the last ride, before a meal, the problem can be avoided.

If you do allow clients to take their horses to the water trough, you must make sure that each horse proceeds in turn and that the others do not crowd in too close behind. When horses are drinking they tend to kick out if they feel other animals approaching them before they have finished.

Further thoughts on hacking out.
It is not only an absolute requirement for an instructor or escort to bring the horses back to the stable cool but also to try and ensure that during the hack a horse is not subject to undue stress. This is not necessarily the result of galloping about here and there. In fact stress can be induced in a horse without any fast movement whatsoever. For example an inexperienced rider mounted on a horse that continually wants to get going may induce stress in that horse simply because they do not have the skill to control the horse in a quiet manner. Continuously heaving on the reins, never letting the horse have a long rein because the rider is afraid and imagines (maybe with good reason) that the horse will dash off as soon as they ease the rein. All these things will induce in the horse a feeling of stress. The escort must try to remedy the situation. This might involve changing the rider for another horse, down grading the overall pace of the hack or even, should the client have good enough balance allowing the horse, at the correct moment, to have a good canter and let some of the steam escape. An escort should report these sorts of happenings to the office. It may well be that it is decided, perhaps for a period, that the horse should not hack out.

What to do - if...
In any occupation things do go wrong from time to time. Teaching riding is no exception to this. Prevention is possible if proper precautions are taken, but there are always situations, which cannot be foreseen.

To end this booklet, therefore, I have described below some of the common situations the riding instructor has to face and how they should be dealt with.

1. *The horse continually attempts to eat grass*
Riders out hacking should not be allowed to let horses get their heads down to eat grass. Any self-respecting horse may succumb to this temptation, especially in the spring, but provided the rider is not casual about the matter then he or she can prevent a passing desire from becoming a bad habit. Where the impulse is already established and the rider is becoming tired of continually trying to pull the horse's head up, then advise the use of a 'bridge'. This is made by the rider holding both reins as a double loop in both hands and then pressing the hands down against the horse's neck; if the horse then pulls, it pulls against itself. If this fails, dismount and make use of the string you have brought with you. Attach one end of the string to a secure ring on either side of the client's saddle. The other end of the string is then fastened to the bit ring. Always use a slipknot for easy release in case of an emergency. These arrangements are known as 'grass reins'.

2. Another client has told a rider that a horse is known to be 'a bit of a handful'.

If the instructor has prepared correctly, there should be no truth whatsoever in comments of this sort. However, such situations do arise, sometimes with a depressing frequency. I have known many perfectly respectable horses acquire a spurious reputation without any justification at all. I remember one occasion where a rider, leaning over to open a gate with his horse remaining motionless, accidentally lost his balance and fell off. For months afterwards the poor horse was banned from being asked to open gates because it was deemed to be 'unreliable'. In these circumstances, the only course of action is to quash such rumours firmly but quietly.

3. A rider suddenly panics

Sometimes a rider, for no accountable reason or simply because he or she has been 'carted', will suffer a complete loss of confidence. Should this occur when you are out in the countryside, immediately approach the client and speak to them very quietly'. Be calm, and try to calm them; use such phrases as, 'There is nothing to be afraid of, I am here to help you,' or, 'Sit tall, try to relax and think of something that gives you pleasure and has nothing to do with horses.'

As soon as you *are* close enough, attach your own lead rein to the client's offside bit *ring*. (Offside so that the client is positioned on your near side for any roadwork.)

Do *not;* under any circumstances, engage the rider in any pace faster than a trot. This decision will mean that you now have to make use of your pre-planned route if you intend to allow the rest of the ride to cover any further part of the hack at the canter. Should this not be possible, then, the rest of the ride will have to forego any more cantering. They may not be best pleased about this. Too bad: it is always a case of *safety first.*

4. There is a thunderstorm

At the first crack of thunder reassure the ride that there is nothing to worry about. Tell them to gently stroke their horses' necks so that all will remain calm. You must then immediately assess the situation and decide whether or not the storm is coming your way and, if so, how far away it is. The general rule is to count the seconds between the flash of lightning and the sound of thunder. Count steadily, 'One and two and three.' The general rule is that you allow one second for each mile: that is to say, 10 seconds equals 10 miles distance. Check the wind direction. If the storm is downwind, then you should be in no danger. If, however, the storm seems to be approaching and you believe that it might pass overhead, then a decision must be taken. Ideally, the best option is to find a barn or some similar building nearby, one large enough to accommodate all the horses. You and your party can then shelter until the storm has passed from the immediate vicinity. In the main, this will probably be an unlikely scenario. If, therefore, there is no alternative, the best course of action is to return to base, maintaining a steady trot all the way.

Under no circumstances should you ever ask the ride to take shelter under individual trees. To do so would be extremely dangerous because lightning always seeks the shortest path to earth and frequently strikes a freestanding tree.

5. A horse goes lame

This is the reason you carry a folding hoof pick. Dismount, cross your stirrups and carry your reins over your horse's head and then hand the horse over to a responsible person.

Start by picking up and examining each foot of the lame horse in turn. (Don't forget to calm the horse by running your hand gently, first from the neck then down to its foot.) Using the hoof pick, check to see if there are any stones lodged in the sole of the horse's foot. (Always work from heel to toe.) Should your examination not provide the answer, continue to examine the feet and tendons for heat, which may give-you an idea on which leg the horse is lame. This is, of course, purely academic, since the horse may no longer be ridden. This may result in having to rearrange the route, riders and horses and that you end up walking.

6. A client is taken ill

This situation, hopefully, is a very unlikely event. However, if a client does complain of illness, then it is a matter that cannot be ignored. What you must do is to try and find out the extent of the problem. You must also take into account your distance from base, and the nearest emergency meeting point.

Start by asking the client for a description of the symptoms. Should the reply be that they feel rather dizzy, or are in pain, they should not remain mounted. Arrange for the client to dismount and hand over their horse to a reliable rider who has a quiet horse. Suggest to the client that they should sit down. Next, contact the yard office and explain where you are located. (Your mobile phone is an invaluable aid in this situation.) If you have no means of contacting base, ask the client if they are sufficiently recovered enough to be able to walk. Explain that this walk is only as far as the nearest point where contact can be made and vehicular transport able to gain access.

Whatever the given situation, when a client complains of illness the instructor must set in motion the necessary action to ensure that the person concerned is safely returned to base. This will apply even if it means the hack has to be cut short.

7. *There is an accident*

I have often been asked what I think about as I return from a hack. Quite frankly, I have two thoughts uppermost in my mind as I complete the last few strides into the stable premises. The first is to 'Thank the Almighty' that all participants have returned safely. The second is that the clients should have derived pleasure from the time that they have been in my company.

An instructor will soon learn to gauge if the clients have enjoyed themselves. As you open the last gate, or simply stand aside to allow the ride to pass by you into the yard, the riders will indicate to you their feelings. This may show itself as their thanking you for a pleasant hack, or by their relaxed bearing and constant gossip. (There is nothing like a bit of chatter to reveal a client's mental state. When they are tensed up they say nothing!)

Unfortunately, until someone invents an anti-gravity belt or a similar device, there is no way of preventing a client from descending to the ground should, for example, a horse put in a little buck catching the client unawares and unbalanced.

Should this occur then everything stops. It is not within the remit of this book to describe first-aid treatment in detail though a brief résumé is given in the section on first aid. However, you must first turn your attention to the client. Do not worry about the horse; it will probably have its head down and be quietly munching grass.

First, ask the rest of the ride to stand quietly nearby, but not on top of the unfortunate soul on the ground. This is the time when the correct use of your voice becomes paramount. No matter how you feel you must *speak in a very calm and authoritative voice that indicates you have everything under control.* (This may be a very difficult thing for an inexperienced instructor to do. Nonetheless it is essential.)

Hand your horse over to a reliable and competent person, then approach the prostrate figure. In a quiet but very calm voice ask the client if they are hurt and, if so, is there severe pain. If they reply in the affirmative then ask where the pain is felt. *Under no circumstances move the casualty if they are unconscious or if serious injury is suspected.* Simply cover the casualty with a coat or anorak to ensure they are kept warm. Make sure that their air passages are clear, summon help and wait until it arrives.

If the client has simply sustained superficial cuts, then deal with these according to your first-aid knowledge. Very often the client is no worse than bruised and winded. If this is the case, ask the person to *first try* to move their fingers and toes. If they are able to do so without pain then repeat the enquiry for arms and legs and, finally, the whole body. However, if the person complains that their head hurts they may be suffering from concussion. You must, therefore, arrange, *through the yard office,* for transport. The latter may involve private assistance or an ambulance.

However, if none of this proves necessary and out in the countryside all goes well, the client should be invited to remount. This is an important decision for both instructor and client, especially the latter if they are not to lose their nerve. If the client declines to get back on the horse, accept the decision and make suitable arrangements for their return to the yard.

As soon as you have dealt with the immediate emergency, then, at once record the circumstances in your notepad. (Don't forget to note the date and time.)

In all cases and without exception, whether there has been an injury or not, an accident report *must be filled in* on your return to the yard office. Ensure that the client concerned is present when this report is made out.

What do you do if the horse declines to be caught?

Sometimes this can be a problem. As I have already said your first duty is to satisfy yourself as to the well-being of your client. When you have established that all is well you should then turn your attention to the recapture of the horse. If another member of staff (the one who takes up position at the rear) has accompanied you, then you may have already given the responsibility to that person who will have attended to the matter.

However there is the odd occasion when a horse decides to have a 'bit of fun' and to remain elusive. This may be especially so where an inexpert rider has simply been pulled down the horse's neck as it decides to have a mouthful of grass. Should this happen then as the rider slides down the neck it is possible that they will try to grab the bridle in order to slow their descent. As they do so they actually pull it off the horse's head. This may completely change the status quo, for the horse suddenly realizing that it is now bridleless will quite likely decide to be off, this is especially so when you are riding through fields that have other horses grazing there.

Now you must make a decision.
Obviously the first rule should be to try and catch the recalcitrant horse and you do this by offering a tit bit that you should have taken with you in your utility pack.

If you are already in a field, then walk towards the gate but to do not go through it. The horse will probably follow, for horses do not like the idea of being left behind.

Should this attempt fail (you must not forget that you are working to a schedule and therefore do not have unlimited time at your disposal), you must make an alternative plan. A horse that has decided to lark about will quite likely make life difficult for you and further more the other horses in the ride may well pick up on this and also start to give some problems.

Survey the area and decide whether or not the horse is going to be in danger if left alone. Should you be riding along a road then obviously the horse must not be left to wander about unattended. This being the case ask your helper to undertake the task of trying to catch the horse.

Use your mobile to contact the office and tell them of the situation. They must make the decision as to what they wish you to do. Between you a plan should be worked out.

If for some reason this does not prove to be possible, then try and find a *nearby* meadow that you have had permission to use and take your whole ride back into it. As you do so have your helper get behind the errant horse so that it is encouraged to follow. When you are all in the field, should it still refuse to be caught, then simply leave it there securely locked in and return for it later. I have never known a horse that was not willing to be caught after being left alone for half an hour or so.

Conclusion to the Hacking chapter.
As you will by now have noted this chapter was originally produced as a stand-alone booklet and its purpose is to highlight the very different situations that may prevail when going across country.

It may be that the additional responsibilities I have described will cause some apprehension. This should not be the case. Remember that riding horses is an exhilarating and enjoyable pastime and the advice in this chapter is merely intended to give the reader confidence to enjoy it to the full and in safety. With such confidence, you will be able to communicate your enjoyment to other people.

I began escorting people on hacks in my early twenties, nearly forty years ago! As a result, I have learned from experience; the number of 'incidents' that have occurred during these years has been minimal and none have resulted in any serious injury to riders or horses.

The key phrase is - always 'take care'. If that is your watchword then all will be well.

Addendum.
Shortly after the publication of my booklet 'The instructors' Guide to Safe and Interesting Hacking', I received a charming letter from Mr. Charles Harris FIH FABRS FBHS. He thanked me for writing the booklet and told me that he found it 'Excellent material for those to whom it is addressed'. He made two suggestions one of which was 'Never proceed at a gait beyond the control of you least experienced rider, i.e. for beginners – WALK'. I took heed of his comments and have amended the text accordingly (see page 353). However it did start me thinking about an apparent omission on my part and that was to make the assumption that a yard would not allow a client to go on a hack unless they had first reached a minimal standard. Today this is not necessarily the case. There may be the odd *trekking* centre that does not carry

out an assessment for any of its customers, some of whom appear without prior appointment and ask if they may go for an hours ride trekking through the surrounding countryside. Please do not misunderstand me. I realize that a small establishment may not be able to afford the time to appraise these clients. They have a living to earn and in any case what would the basis of that test be? I have heard of a case recently where a riding establishment being sued by a client and was asked by lawyers if they had carried out an assessment. 'Yes' they answered. 'We look at the rider as they approach the pony and decide whether or not they show any signs of apprehension or fear!' Well that is one way of doing it, but is it sufficient and if not then what is?

After having given the matter much further thought it is my view that so far as *hacking* out is concerned **no client should be allowed to undertake this form of recreational riding unless they have first learned to sit to several strides of canter**. The reason for this is that, as mentioned earlier in this chapter, horses do behave differently when proceeding across the countryside than when they are in an enclosed arena. It is in a horse's nature to flee from what, in a misunderstood instant, they perceive as danger. It might be a car backfiring, a piece of plastic blowing in the wind. These events and several dozen more may cause an animal to dance about a bit for just a few seconds even when on a lead rein. This unaccustomed motion may cause a client to become unbalanced and fall. However if they have actually experienced the canter gait (even if they are unable to sustain it) then they should have developed a reflex that will react sufficiently quickly to, at least, grab hold of the pommel of the saddle and support themselves. Now I have no doubt that there will be many readers who will immediately ask the question. 'Aren't things of this sort just as likely to happen in an arena'. The answer is 'Yes of course they are, but in the more controlled situation of an arena they are easier to avoid especially if you follow the advice given at the end of chapter 18'.

Now please do not misunderstand me. I am not trying to be a 'killjoy'. I am merely pointing out that these possibilities exist and it is up to the instructor to be able to show that every reasonable precaution has been taken, especially so when facing a battery of lawyers! In the case of those running a trekking yard, or come to that any riding establishment, it might help to mitigate matters if the clients (no matter what their level of skill) were made to sign a carefully worded contract before being allowed to go out. Apart from the need to preserve life and limb of the clients the other matter is, what is in the small print of the insurance policy?

In these days of ever increasing claims for negligence I think that it is essential that a *contract* should always be signed before any client goes anywhere near a horse. It might be worded along the following outline.

I understand that riding is a risk sport and that horses are unpredictable. They may loose their balance and thus there is no way in which their actions can be completely controlled. I understand that in wishing to ride a horse I do so in the clear knowledge that I cannot be protected from falling off and, possibly, getting hurt. Therefore I undertake the sport in the clear knowledge that whatever injury I suffer, including death, I have no claim against the establishment where I ride or the instructor teaching me. *

1.

So we start at the very beginning where the client states that they have no experience whatsoever.

If this is the case then it is up to the establishment to take every, reasonable, precaution to avoid them sustaining injury. One then progresses.

2.

I can get a horse to walk around the outside track of a 20m. arena without allowing the horse to turn in or stop

3.

I can go large at a walk all the way around the arena on both reins with a change across the diagonal of a 20m. arena without the horse coming to a halt or wandering off the track.

4.

I can ride around a 20m. arena, on one rein, at a trot once only without the horse changing gait to walk, turning in or going forward to a halt. (But I am not yet able to do a rising trot).

5.

I can trot around the arena in a rising trot on both reins in a 20m. arena with a diagonal change without the horse changing gait to walk, or turning in and stopping.

6.

I can canter but can only maintain this pace for 5 or 6 strides. (I'm not very good at maintaining directional control).

7.

I can canter all the way around a 20m. arena on the outside track on one rein, without the horse changing gait to trot or walk, turning in or halting.

8.

I can canter, continuously, all the way around a 20m. arena on both reins, riding the change of direction across the long diagonal at trot.

9.

I can walk, trot and canter both in an arena and out hacking.

10.

I can walk, trot and canter both in an arena and out hacking. I am able to maintain a 'forward' position. I can also jump obstacles not higher than 2 ft. 6" with a spread of 1 ft 6" be they show jumps or natural obstacles. I can maintain control at all times.

11.

I am able to quietly ride **all** well schooled horses in an arena or out hacking and I can also jump over show jumps or natural obstacles that are over 3 ft in height with a spread of 2 ft 6". I can maintain control at all times.

I confirm that the last time that I rode a horse for 1 hour a week for 6 consecutive weeks was ……….Day ……… Month ……… Year.

I have read and fully understand *all* the terms used in this document which I consider to be a binding contract between myself and this Riding School.

Signed…………………….. Date…………….. Witnessed by…………………
Print name in capitals…………………….

Now this is suggested only as the basic contract and it may be that the client should have a period of time to reflect before it becomes binding. Any other rules or conditions e.g. cancellation times, payments for lessons where the client did not turn up, cancellation, change, or renewal of the contract, charges, rules concerning dress code etc. etc should also be included. Further more the document MUST be scrutinised by a solicitor.

Now it may be argued that this may put off some clients if they are required to commit themselves in this way. My answer would be 'Good'. If they are the sort of people who will sue for the slightest problem such as 'sore bums' or 'losing their nerve', then the industry can do without them.

On the other hand it does open the way for Trekking Centres to encourage holiday makers to make their first contact with a horse without the Centre fearing that they may be sued for no good reason. Subsequently these new customers may then go on to learn the real Art of Equitation at a riding school. Believe me that is where it starts.

* Now it may be argued that the Unfair Contracts Act of 1977 would make this contract void. Well there are two points that I would make and they are firstly, that the Insurance Industry were exempt from this act when it was passed through Parliament therefore it could be amended to include the Horse Industry. Secondly, riding a horse must be designated a risk sport and the public must be made aware of this fact. None-the-less should a client sustain a fall if a stirrup leather broke because the stitching was rotten, the establishment would still be considered negligent and thus liable for damages.

Chapter 21

Playing games.

Games are a means of providing both interest and an element of entertainment whilst at the same time improving rider's skills (you of course help in this by giving constant advice). I never cease to be amazed at how well young riders manage to control their ponies. Turning first this way and that, as they try to evade capture in a game such as Cowboys and Indians and at the same time maintaining the gait that has been set for them. They really work hard, and very often make great advances in their riding skills. They learn without realising that they are doing so. This may be summed up by the remark made by a little lad that I taught many years ago called Adam. As we returned from a field where we had spent the lesson 'playing games' in which he had performed extremely well, he remarked to me 'that was great fun' but when are we going to start learning to ride!

It may be considered that these games only appertain to children but this may not necessarily be so. Adults, just as much as children, may enjoy the clock game (see chapter 25 'Games List'), but since they are more likely to be played by young people than adults, for this chapter I shall continue to refer to ponies instead of horses.

Some of the games mentioned below are suitable for indoors whilst others may be better played outside, where there is more room. Most of these are team games. There are one or two that an individual may play solo. In the list shown below I have marked them accordingly.

A suitable type of pony.

Any form of exercise that does not involve the strict control imposed by school riding single file, demands ponies that are reasonably well behaved and of suitable social disposition. Do not use a pony for games of any sort that is known to kick out as soon as another pony comes anywhere near. When your attention is momentarily diverted, from an overall view, that is the very moment when a nasty fellow will have a go. Usually most ponies do not actually try and make contact, but you can't be too careful. I say again 'When in doubt – don't'

Sharing an area.

I have already mentioned that when you are required to share an arena you should eschew team games. They may cause a problem for the instructor or clients with whom you are sharing.

Working out in a field.

When you are working outside it is very important to make it quite clear where the ponies may be ridden. Use cones, if you have them to hand. If not, then explain to everyone where the boundaries are drawn using focal points such as trees or any other landmarks. The skill of the riders and character of the ponies dictate the size of area that you use and the type of game that you play.

Maintaining control by reducing the area of play.

Even if you are alone in an arena it is not always a good idea simply to use the whole of it just because it's there. Sometimes it is better to have your charges restricted to an area that does not involve them having to move too far away from you. In this case place cones at suitable points to help delineate the area you wish to use. ***Make it clear to everyone that they may not go outside this space.***

Using the gaits to maintain control and to accommodate varying conditions.

A simple way of ensuring that control is maintained may be by establishing the gait at which a game may be played. Thus – where one has fairly inexperienced youngsters a game may be played *only* at the walk. It is surprising just how much enthusiasm will be generated even at this pace. The walk is a pace that will encourage children who may be rather timid to take part with gusto. Further more at the walk they have time to think and in turn communicate their thoughts to their ponies. For your part, you must be very strict and take the required action for any infringement of the rules. That is to say that anyone trotting during a walking game is eliminated. That said there is no reason why the more experienced should not play games at the trot or even the canter. So long as you maintain control and you do not let things get out of hand, an enjoyable and exciting time may be had by all.

Setting the rules

Before commencing any game you must establish the rules of play. Further more you *must* ensure that everyone understands exactly what those rules are. If you have any players that ask for you to repeat the rules, then do so. Team members must not be allowed to proceed until some form of exchange between the returning player and the next to go has taken place. Touching hands palm to palm is a very good way. Handing over a baton is another. For obvious reasons do not permit any exchange to take place by one rider touching another with a whip; a pony may well take exception to seeing a whip being brandished in its face.

I have found that a very practical and popular way of initiating the departure of the next team member is to have the returning rider halt in front of their team and say a short poem or rhyme. Each team member must say a complete verse of whatever rhyme they have chosen and no other team member may repeat the same rhyme.

Since in this age of television and 'modern education' things may have reached a stage where, by the time that you read this book, children may be no longer familiar with these little ditties. I therefore take the liberty of reminding you of some rhymes from my youth.

Georgy Porgy pudding and pie,
Kissed the girls and made them cry,
When the boys came out to play,
Georgy Porgy ran away.

Humpty Dumpty sat on a wall,
Humpty Dumpty had a great fall,
All the Kings horses,
And all the King's men,
Couldn't put Humpty together again.

The Grand old duke of York,
He had ten thousand men,
He marched them up to the top of the hill,
And marched them down again.

Little Miss Muffet sat on her tuffet,
Eating her curds and whey,
Along came a spider and sat down beside her,
And frightened Miss Muffet away.

Jack and Jill went up the hill,
To fetch a pail of water,
Jack fell down and broke his crown,
And Gill came tumbling after.

Mary, Mary quite contrary,
How does your garden grow?
With cockle shells and little bells,
And pretty maids all in a row.

It may surprise you to know that when they were originally written all the above were really caustic political comment. Georgy Porgy for example is a rhyme about poor George III who, suffering from a quite rare illness, would quite suddenly chase after some of the ladies in his court.

Setting the parameters for all gaits.
The walk

Obviously the walk is a gait that does not consume the pony's energy as fast as the higher gaits. When playing a game at the walk you may be more generous as to the duration of play. This gait is the only acceptable one in extremely wet conditions, when the ground has been badly poached and the going very heavy with the possibility of a pony slipping.

The trot.

A strict time limit should be placed on games at the trot. You must remember that most participants are going to be playing as hard as they can. Therefore you must make the games of such duration as will allow your ponies not to get too hot and sweaty. Restrict the trot if the going is soft but do use it if the going is too hard for cantering. At the end of a game ensure that all participants allow their ponies to walk on a long rein. Do not allow the warm ponies to stand around; otherwise they may get a chill.

The canter.
With experienced riders you may have a game that includes this gait as a part of the action. As mentioned above you should only do so when the going is good. When the ground is very heavy or very hard then do not use it. Your decision may result in howls of dismay since, so far as children are concerned, cantering is synonymous with fun. Stick to your guns and do not be swayed. It would be unforgivable if you suffered a lame pony as a result of a wrong decision on your part.

Games that involve combinations of gaits with the accent on safety again.
A sensible way of proceeding is to have some games that include a combination of gaits. For example, you may devise a game that contains the elements of walk, trot and canter. Whatever gaits you decide to use; one rule is fundamental. **The faster gaits should always be ridden when the riders are going away from their teams** and the slower ones when they return. Thus you would organise a game with the canter element as each team member rides away from his or her own team but as they return they are only allowed to walk or trot. The reason for this is obvious; it is not a good idea to have riders approaching others at speed.

Downward transitions before the competitor starts to turn back.
You control the pace of the game by varying the gait; since ponies are frequently reluctant to *leave* their mates the rider has to exercise their ability in getting the pony to go into a canter. However on the return that same skill must be used to engage a downward transition and yet create impulsion. Some times a pony will try and 'take the law into its own hands' and canter back to its friends anyway. In order to avoid this a lower gait must be ridden *before* the child turns to ride back. I usually insist that this be at the walk. This has a twofold benefit since it will avoid a pony falling over through too tight a turn and it will also be robbed of the initiative of a fast return. With a lower gait this speed will depend more on the skill of the riders and less upon the disposition and character of the ponies. If the rider breaks the rules by cantering, when they should not, then they must be made to ride a circle. It is amazing how hard youngsters will try both to get the best out of their ponies and yet ensure that they stay at the prescribed gait.

What do the riders get out of these games?
They get used to making their ponies go away from the others.
They learn to maintain a gait when they have asked for it.
They learn to ride in a straight line.
They learn to become part of a team.
They enjoy themselves.

Maintaining discipline and safety.
For reasons of safety, as much as for any other reason, it is essential that you maintain strict discipline. Before you start any type of game you must assess the prevailing conditions both with regard to your location and also the weather. Not only will you be considering the safety of your pupils but also you should never forget the well-being of your horses or ponies.

It is quite likely that youthful enthusiasm will lead to some excitement. You must ensure that this is kept within reasonable bounds. If not then the ponies may get overenthusiastic themselves and go dashing off with possibly harmful results.

Team games and choosing team leaders.
So far as teams are concerned it is a good idea to have a leader, for each team. I usually select these as a result of a 'race', walking, or trotting if you like. The riders must proceed in straight lines and touch the wall at one end of the arena and then return and pass you or touch the wall or fence at the other end. You decide according to the suitability of the location.

Alternatively, if you are out in a field, then have everyone ride towards a hedge and pick a twig before returning. Do bear in mind that this 'selective race' needs not be restricted to simply one lap. It all depends on the time available and the extent to which you wish to work in your ponies. You may decide that you would like six laps. Whichever is the case be sure that your competitors pass given points before being allowed to continue, otherwise you may get a degree of cheating. I have found that children are very observant when it comes to ensuring that the rules are obeyed. If you are not meticulous in your maintenance of fair play they will feel a grave sense of injustice. However do not forget your word must be final.

Choosing the teams.
The team leaders are responsible for choosing their teams. They are asked to come out in front of the rest of the ride who should line up facing them. The team leaders stand opposite one another at each side of the arena. They then choose their teams alternatively. The winner of the 'race' has first choice. As they are chosen, the team members walk out and join the team leader. You may find that one rider is consistently left until last, either because they are riding a pony that does not go as well as the others or because they are not that skilled. You should not let that child feel that they are suffering any form of discrimination. I always say something like 'Last but not least' or 'I don't know why they left you until the end when you are much better than the others'. In this way you help to maintain a child's' self-esteem.

Uneven numbers.
Where you have uneven numbers, you obviously allow one member of the smaller team to go twice. They may start and finish or go at some other time but they may not ride consecutively. The team leaders should be allowed to decide in what order the team members are to go.

Having helpers.
While you alone may control the action, as it were, all the games that I describe in chapter 25 'Games List', should be played by riders with sufficient experience. However it is essential that you have helpers for very young children. *For really little ones you must have a helper for each pony*. In some cases it is important to have leading reins attached to each bridle. Where this is the case you must ensure that the helpers be constantly aware of the fact that it is their job *to look after the rider*.

It is also a good idea to take a helper or two if you have included in your class ponies that may be excitable or nappy. So far as the latter are concerned, a helper at first should assist the rider only to a limited extent in getting the reluctant pony to do what is expected of it. For example in going away from the rest of the team. By that, I mean that they should first give the child a chance to try and get the pony to obey their will. Where the pony is very obstinate, the child should not be left alone to struggle in vain and suffer extreme frustration. The helper assists but at the same time urges the rider to also do their utmost to get the pony to go forward. After all we are playing games and these should be fun for *all* the participants.

A helper must also be on hand to give assistance at the end of the arena or area, when the child is about to return to their team. It is at this point that some ponies that have previously been very reluctant to go away, wish to return with all speed! This is why I advocate a speedy depart but a slow return. These combinations exercise the skills of young riders to the maximum. A helper at the far end can also be used as a judge to ensure that all riders ride the course correctly (boys are notorious at trying to cheat!).

Cheering on their team.
I do believe in encouraging everyone to help and cheer on each rider as they go away. But the encouragement must be kept within reasonable bounds; otherwise the ponies may get over excited. It has been my experience that children can assist one another in very practical ways. Many are the times that I have heard them calling out such helpful hints as 'Look where you want to go' and 'Sit before asking for canter', 'prepare for the walk' and so on. What is more, that team member listens to the advice!

Dealing with cheats!
It has been my experience that, generally boys try to cheat more than girls. Not that girls are such angels. None-the-less you must deal with cheating whenever it occurs. This should be done with a sense of humour. Allow the rest of the players to shame anyone trying to get away with such things as, not crossing the line or not touching the palm of the next one to go. Take care however, if you do not have eyes in the back of your head, then one team may well, wrongly, accuse the other of cheating. What is more, as they make the accusation, they will look at you wide eyed as though anything other than the absolute truth could not pass their lips! As you momentarily turn to help someone, you hear the words 'I saw James trot when he should have been walking and what is more he did not ride a circle'. The other team will vehemently insist that this

is not true. You will require the judgement of Solomon. I deal with such matters by saying 'Since this is a democratic society, I have the sole final decision and I decide as follows....'. There will be an immediate wail from whosoever feels that they have been hard-done-by. 'You said this is a democratic society why are you making the decisions? It's not fair?' I reply something like 'I know it simply goes to show that life is very unfair!' Good fun is had by all.

You're especial contribution.
There is one further thing that you alone will add to these activities and that is your commentary. For while the game is being played you do not simply stand still and observe the progress of the game, finally announcing who has won or lost. It is your job to keep up a constant stream of comment rather like a race reader. This will include advice to the competitors as to what they need to be doing in order to make satisfactory progress. You should be ready to correct any fault that you observe. These may be such matters as 'Sarah, shorten your rein'. Or 'James, sitting trot if you wish to ride a really small circle'. You may include the rest of the team with such a comment as. ' Why isn't he getting to the target at the end?' Reply shouted with much gusto by the rest of the team. 'Because he isn't looking where he is going. John look where you want to go and not down at your pony'.

What you are doing and you are involving everyone else as well, is providing instruction so that your pupils end up both having fun and improving their skills.

Riding and leading races.
A race of this type can be utilised as a team game or as a race in which everyone takes part at the same time. When playing team games I do like to insert the occasional race of this type. When one has a large class, it serves to prevent too long a period when ponies are standing still and also to avoid participants loosing concentration as they wait for their turn during a team race where each competitor goes in turn.

Learning a lot.
All games are designed to demand a high degree of riding skill in order that they are carried out successfully. A leading race has even more demanding components.

Dismounting and leading (for detail see chapter 8).
1. In the first place you should ask for a volunteer to come out and demonstrate. Ask the rest of the class to observe and make comments. What you are looking for is the correct dismounting procedure. The placing of the hand through the rein and sliding it up the arm so that it is secured at the riders' elbow. The correct running up of the stirrups and the taking of the rein over the pony's head. The whip to be held correctly.

2. When the securing procedure has been carried out the volunteer should then be asked to 'walk on'. Ask the class to check that the riders' position is correct in relation to the pony and to shout out when it is not. The rider should then turn the pony so that they are reversing their track. What every one should be looking for at this time is the rider remembering to *turn the pony away* from themselves so that they are on the outside of the turn.

3. Finally you should stress the importance of the pony going slightly in front of the rider at all times. There should be no turning around and trying to pull the pony forward. This is likely to result in complete failure for ponies do not like being stared at in the eye.

The components of the 'leading race'.
I usually make this a race in which the first component is moving away while mounted; say to the end of the arena to be followed by a quick dismount and preparation to lead back. The winner is the first to *remount correctly*. Before the race starts I always ask 'What to you do before remounting?' All answer with a roar *'Check the girth'*.

Riding without stirrups.
As with all other exercises the gait chosen should be the most suitable for the level of expertise that has been achieved by *all* the class members. Thus you may choose walk, trot or canter. However you should

take extreme care should you decide to give the competitors the option of 'making up ground' as it were. By that I mean that since a *quick dismount* and the securing of the irons can be an important part of the race, you could suggest that in order to save time there is no reason why the competitors should not quit and cross their stirrups before the race starts. This is obviously an encouragement to those who may be a little frightened of riding without stirrups. I never pressure anyone into doing this but it is surprising that in the prevailing competitive atmosphere many youngsters will do so. You should only allow this where you know that the riders do have reasonably secure seats.

Games for bad weather.

In an outdoor ménage when the weather is really bad, it is a good idea to forgo the more formal types of exercise and instead to play some simple games that will none-the-less involve a high degree of control.

Bad weather can come on quite suddenly and when it does, think in terms first of making use of any shelter that is available. By that I mean use a side of the arena that affords some protection because it is backed by a wall or hedge. It is quite surprising how an unpleasant situation may be made more comfortable on a very cold, windy and wet day, by simply having the class stand out of the wind. As soon as everyone is sheltered the weather does not seem nearly so bad.

In these circumstances you will have to think quickly in order to find the materials for some very interesting games. For example four plastic or rubber buckets can be sufficient to provide two teams with an endless variety of competitions. One should however take note of the numbers in the class for it is important not to have members of the class standing around for too long while the others try to do their tasks. This can be easily achieved by simply having three teams instead of two.

To illustrate my meaning let us assume that you have, say six riders; split these into two teams of three and each rider has a go every third time. Not too long to have to wait? With nine riders then you will have somewhat unwieldy teams if you split them into two teams. One will have four riders and the other five. The odd numbers are not very important because someone can always go twice, but even waiting for four riders to take part might involve everyone waiting for a period that *is* too long, therefore split them into three teams of three.

Choose the team leaders in the manner already described. The basic rules of safety still apply. For less than expert riders there should be no cantering back to the ride.

An alternative.

If you are dealing with little ones or even a class of mixed ages, then it is useful to have some ' races' in which the pony does not take part at all. All that you do is to arrange for the teams to be divided according to the size of those participating and then, having the ponies held either by the older members of each team or else by helpers, you have races on foot only.

Children riding as part of a holiday camp.

Using magic!

Occasionally one may have to deal with children whose parents have decided to have riding included as an option during a stay at a holiday camp. It is quite likely that there will be quite large numbers in the class and the chances are that they have had no previous riding experience whatsoever. Further more they may not really be very interested in riding at all! In which case the first thing, obviously, is to have a leader for each pony and to keep things at a slow pace. However there is no reason why they should not have an exciting hour with you. I, quite often, utilise the sense of wonder that children, fortunately still posses even in this age of television. I tell them that I too am on holiday and that, in real life, I am a wizard! I go on to give some background as to my status as such and that I am the possessor of powerful spells. Now if I have previous knowledge that these youngsters are coming for a lesson then I come prepared with spells already printed. (see drawing 36). If the surface of the arena is suitable then I sometimes conceal them, before the class arrive, under the surface, adjacent to cones or the arena letters . I then ask my charges if they are able to spot where the owl (whom I have previously sent to get these spells) has put them. Dismounting and leading their ponies (supervised by the helpers) a merry time ensues until the spells have been found. They then are told that, in order to activate the spells, they have to get the, invisible, magic powder. This can be obtained by riding around the arena and touching as many letters as possible.

THIS IS TO CERTIFY

THAT

....

HAS STARTED TO LEARN THE ANCIENT ART
OF HORSEBACK RIDING.

UNDER THE TUITION OF THE GREAT WIZARD
(U.K.)

THE MAGNIFICENT TONE.

THE MAGIC SPELLS INCLUDED FOR THE SAME PRICE: -

LEVITATION (i.e. anti gravity – how not to fall off)
HYPNOSIS (i.e. How to persuade your pony to go where you wish him to go)
**THE CREATION OF MAGIC POWDER (For use in persuading parents to let
you stay up and watch television especially those programmes that have
absolutely no educational value whatsoever).**

Signed.

Maglone –

Wizard extraordinary. In this year of 1979

**To activate the spells or to obtain invisible magic powder simply ride around the
arena and touch each letter. The powder must be placed in a pocket in order to
prevent any loss of strength. At a later time it may be sprinkled over a parent.**

**This is only a magic certificate and is not a qualification in terms of riding
instruction.**

Wizard's Certificate

Chapter 22

Liveried and part liveried horses.

This is a book about teaching people to ride. *It is not about training horses.* If you wish to know about that aspect of equitation then there are many many books written by truly great experts who, if read properly, will be able to guide you along the right path. I frequently repair to the books 'Equitation' and 'Dressage' written by Henry Wynmalen. Though there are some that may have quarrelled with his views – no matter – for me, his mastery of the written word and his logical and loving approach surmount any criticism of technique: for indeed technique is not necessarily writ in stone. *Read the words. Absorb them. Learn and come to your own conclusion!*

In the past chapters I have made the point that the horses used in classes are riding school horses and should know their job. In fact I have gone so far as to say that, in such circumstances, I do not believe that instructors should give lessons in which the accent is on 'schooling your horse'. I have made it plain that I consider that, in a well run stable, with horses of a suitably developed musculature, it is the object of the instructor to teach the client to 'unlock' the potential that has already been stored in the horse's memory through its earlier training. This is achieved by learning to be thoughtful, to sit correctly and be sufficiently determined and tactful to achieve this end. *But you may find that you have horses in the class either ridden by their owners or having them used as part liveries and it is incumbent upon you to take account of this.*

However it does not automatically follow that the moment you are invited to accept a livery that you will have problems, there are thousands of owners who ride competently and have well-mannered horses. When you have them riding their own horses in your class all that you have to do is to teach them in the same manner that you would teach any other pupil.

If you are a good instructor and respected by all the horses that serve you, then you are unlikely to have any difficulties with liveries. I make this point specifically because one instructors' inability to manage a horse will spread around the yard like a bush fire. Before you know it a horse may be placed in your class with the pre-conceived notion that that horse is a 'bad un' when in fact it isn't. Only react when you need to and not before. *Beware of any tendency to prejudge.*

Why should a livery owner have problems?

Ideally they shouldn't. In fact there are large numbers of people who own their own horses who do not have any problems at all. In fact, given that an owner has received adequate instruction and possesses a nice quite forward going horse, then this should be a unique opportunity for you, the instructor. *You are in the position to endow the owner with the means to establish that particular bond that can only exist in a truly symbiotic partnership of horse and rider.* However one must be prepared for those, unfortunate, occasions, where problems do occur and we do need to discuss them in some detail. We need to learn how to, quickly, deal with them, should they arise in a class that we are taking.

In the first place it is necessary to draw some parameters. You might well be speculating as to why I have put this chapter on its own towards the end of this book. The reason for this is that it is my view that, until they have reached a reasonable level of competence, *no novice should own a horse* unless they are under *constant supervision by someone qualified.* I have seen so many *good* horses spoiled by riders who not only have a low level of riding ability but also do not *understand the need to impose simple, basic, discipline.* The times I have seen horses and ponies dump their owners on the floor and then go hareing off around an arena refusing to be caught until such a time as suits them, is without number. Not only that but one must not overlook the *owners* with quite reasonable horses who persist in asking their animals to perform in a manner for which they are neither physically nor mentally prepared!

So what is one to do in these circumstances? Should one simply refuse to have such creatures in ones class at all? The answer is that you should *not exclude* them, provided that they are not so young and silly as to cause a rumpus. If you do find that you have included a horse that starts to 'play up' seriously, then ask the rider to take it out of the arena. The horse that dumps and then goes dashing off, during a lesson, can have unpleasant results for the rest of the class. The other horses, no matter how well behaved generally, may well decide that 'the revolution' has arrived and that all horses deserve to be 'free'! I've seen it happen.

Dumped riders all over the floor: not in my own classes I'm thankful to say.

When this happens, it is my view that the situation should be dealt with on a permanent basis. You must remember, you **should not compromise the safety of anyone** even when you teach a class consisting **entirely of livery owners, .** In order to prevent a re-occurrence, you should suggest to the office that the owner and horse subscribe to a series of private lessons which as a result both would hopefully be sorted out. If both horse and rider improve then they should be allowed to return to the class but the private lessons must continue in parallel. None-the-less what I would consider to be ideal and what takes place in real life is an entirely different matter! Anyway this may not be practical, further more the client may carry weight (*influence* not handicap as per poor John Gilpin!) with the management and it may be *suggested* that an instructor of your calibre can well manage. Despite the fact that this book is not about *training* horses but riders, then if the client is to remain in your classes you will have to devise a suitable strategy.

Providing simple answers for simple problems.

Whether one has a person riding their liveried horse as a member of a class or one has simply been summoned privately to try and put to rights a situation that is becoming untenable for the poor owner, you have to start with basic essentials. The most important of these is the *obedience* of the animal. In order to instil this you must first decide where the problem lies.

Considering those areas where problems may occur through simple incorrect choice.

There is a saying that 'No one sells a good horse'. This would seem to indicate that only bad horses are sold. Sometimes this is true. The animal is sold because it has been allowed to develop bad habits; these are carefully concealed at the time of the sale. If this is the case a would-be owner may well end up with a difficult animal unless they have the advice, before buying, of someone with experience. This person will insist on certain safeguards being built into the selling contract that will allow for the animal to be returned within an agreed period. You must understand that I am writing here of matters within the context of behaviour and not health. The health aspect should be very adequately dealt with through an inspection by the would be new owners' *own* vet.

Over horsed and under used.

But let us assume that the buyer has not had the misfortune to buy a 'bad un'.   It may be that they have been offered a lovely family owned animal only being sold because their children have outgrown it. The new owner gets the horse home and to their chagrin they find that the animal, which they saw with their own eyes, behaving perfectly, seems to have turned into an uncontrollable beast (Or at least that is what they believe). On another occasion they may have bought a horse from a dealer – same result. Puzzling in the first instance and in the second 'Well - we all know about horse dealers don't we!' But the fault will, usually, lie with the new owner. The horse being sold by the family is probably a brilliant riding horse *in the right hands*. The one bought from the dealer – probably not the horse that the dealer had originally offered but a different one that took the buyers' fancy. Of course the dealer would offer a horse that he wanted to sell but if he is well known in the district, he will also want to protect his reputation and having sized up the potential buyer in casual conversation, he will offer a horse that suites. The buyer, on the other hand, has his or her own self-image. They do not see themselves sitting on an unassuming but extremely willing and manageable creature. Oh no! They wish to be seen, by their friends, on a high stepping and supercharged animal that will impress everyone. The result is that you may simply be asked to take into your class someone who is over-horsed.

Need things be as dramatic? Not necessarily, even a very quiet animal will suffer some degree of disorientation for the first two to three months after its transfer from one yard to another. This will require tactful and skilful handling, but if it is allowed to get away with bad behaviour, then this too will lead to a downward path.

Standing for many hours on end.

The regime for a liveried horse is sometimes deficient in regular exercise. Unlike their counterpart the school horse that has to work for a living and will therefore be used uniformly. The owner with a horse at livery sometimes forgets that they have a living creature that needs constant work both to keep it fit and happy. More often than not they think of it as a lawn mower, to be put in the garage until required again, sometime in the future! I'm afraid that things do not work that way with horses. Of course I am not referring to a properly run stables where I am certain that any livery agreement would make provision for horses to have a proper routine. But there are more and more DIY yards opening up where provision for correct exercise in the owners' absence, is lacking.

Horses that will not stand still.

The fact is that most riders - owners or otherwise, allow their horses to take little liberties without realising it. The effect is to hand over an ever-greater degree of initiative to the horse, which if left unchecked, can grow into a problem. I have in mind something as simple for the horse as standing still while the rider mounts. Having been mounted, many horses then start to walk on. This is not a fundamental form of disobedience. It occurs through the rider's neglect, not of the horse's physical well-being but of its mental one. To insist on this very basic but most profound form of obedience – standing still until asked to move - is the fault of the rider The moment the horse does move it should be halted and made to stand still for the count of five. Only when it has stood motionless for this time should it be asked to walk on.

Sometimes it is not only a simple matter of stepping forward unasked. A horse may swing its quarters away from the mounting block, simply to adjust its weight or just for a bit of a lark. It moves because nobody, instructor, owner or rider has bothered to take the trouble to ensure that this very basic form of obedience is also insisted upon.

Affecting a cure.

Prevention is of course better than cure for habits can become ingrained. If this is the case they must be corrected. One way of doing this is to place the horse along side a wall, preferably one that has a side projecting forward at 90 degrees, in other words it is part of a corner. The horse is stood with its side against the wall opposite that from which the rider will mount. Its nose faces the corner. If there is no corner, then have an assistant stand in front. The rider mounts in the normal manner. Any attempt by the horse to move or fidget should be countered with the response 'Stand still'. If the owner proceeds in this manner, then, after a while the horse will listen and stand still even when mounted in the open.

When owners are responsible for bad habits.

There are some occasions when the horses' manner of going is entirely the fault of the owner, in spite of the fact that the rider may be very experienced. For example the owner enjoys cantering and never stops. This is his preferred way of riding. The unfortunate result is that the horse, mild mannered though he may be, always expects everyone who rides him to behave in the same manner. He therefore earns an undeserved reputation for carting people.

When you come across problems such as those mentioned above, you must change tactics immediately. The question of paramount concern is not to get the horse to carry out the movement that has been asked of it, but to try to return control to the rider. As soon as you become aware of a problem you must do something about it. Of course this type of behaviour may also be found in school horses but in my experience they more frequently occur in privately owned animals

Starting remedial action.

Some may suggest that what you should do is to get up on the horse and ride it yourself. Whereas I am entirely in favour of instructors giving demonstrations that will show to perfection a particular movement, or to get a recalcitrant animal to move correctly, I do not believe that it is useful to ride a horse simply to demonstrate your dominance over the animal. It may well obey *you* but as soon as the owner remounts the creature will return to its former state of intransigence. The owner has to re-establish their authority albeit at a slower gait. It may help if the horse has a period of solo schooling in the hands of a professional but in the end it is the horse that has to be schooled with the owner mounted.

This being the case you are going to have to return to basics, as far as both *horse and rider* are concerned. However you may be able to arrange matters so that when you do have the horse in your class it has become reasonably amenable to the idea of being taught its job.

First instil disciplined thought in the rider!

In the main, the forms of discipline are those that you are trying to get *all* your clients to develop in themselves. They must learn not to be casual or sloppy. Thus every *transition should be from an exact spot e.g. a letter in the arena,* and then riding accurately from one letter to another either through diagonals, down the centre line or on circles. All the forgoing is in fact a form of schooling not only for the horse, but also for the rider! A specific exercise will help. Therefore if you have asked for an individual canter away from the front of the ride to the back, this must not be asked of a horse inclined to dash off madly. Instead you must ensure that that horse is only allowed to proceed at a pace at which it is under control. This may mean that whereas the rest of the class are, say cantering from front of the ride to the rear, you should ask the owner to go large around the arena at either trot or walk. (You use whichever pace results in the horse yielding to the riders' wishes without any tension in either party). The rider may think that they are being hard done by, but this is the discipline that you imbue in them and which they, in turn, are instilling in their horses! The same rules apply to other problems. The object is to be sure that the horse begins to understand that it must be obedient. In this way you are getting this co-operation but doing so without curtailing the instruction of the remainder of your clients.

Horses that are fresh.
Since the owner probably has access to the horse at a time of his own choosing, then he should do that which is practised by Dr. Reiner Klimke *16. The horse should first be ridden out for a short period. During this time it should be allowed to engage in short canters, through which it may 'let off steam'. Then on returning the owner will have helped to remove one of the reasons for playing up.

Young horses.
You must use your experience in understanding the limits of young unschooled horses. You must know when a horse is reaching the limit of its as yet, undeveloped musculature and you must also know when it is approaching the end of its ability to wrestle with the mental problems set for it.

Obviously all of that which we have been discussing in earlier chapters applies just as much to livery owners as to clients who do not possess a horse. So what is there that applies more to the client riding their own horse? Obviously it is the *riders'* development of greater obedience in that horse and, building of the bond between them. This is the foundation that will lead to preparation physically and mentally for more advanced work.

When dealing with a liveried horse one must not make the supposition that the horse knows anything at all! It is up to the owner, through your guidance to find out! In this 'voyage of discovery' the principal of 'little and often' must prevail. If for example you are teaching shoulder-in then you must help the owner to prepare the horse for the movement – give it time to understand what is required – and ***above all not to get angry when the movement fails to materialise correctly***.

If the horse is a youngster and has attempted the movement once or twice excuse the owner from asking for more. In a mixed class the others may continue with the exercise. If you are asking for movements at walk or trot, then let the owner remain with the ride. If you are performing exercises at canter, then ask for a young horse to be brought in to the centre of the arena. It's all a matter of common sense. The one thing that you should not allow is for any movement to be performed for too long so that the animal becomes stressed.

Provide a higher target for the owner of a liveried horse.
I have placed this paragraph in this section because though it is a target for *all* riders, it is more fairly applied to owners riding horses at livery. Whereas we are striving to obtain relaxation and correct application of the aids from weekend riders and obedience from the horses that they ride, for an owner we do need to go a step farther.

The contract between owner and horse will be such that the horse is schooled to the point that it will not change its way of going until it is told to do so. The obligation for the owner is that having once given an aid and been obeyed, ***will not give the aid again*** until they wish to institute a change or that they *anticipate that moment* when the horse is going to disobey them. In other words at all other times they must sit ***absolutely still.*** All too often, especially in competitions I see riders continually ***nagging*** at the horse *every stride*. When cantering and questioned about it, they will say ' I'm afraid that he is going to break to the trot', I am not surprised. If they ride like that all the time the probability is that the horse has long ago learned not to take any notice of their meaningless signals.

Dressage or jumping?
Some clients, especially livery owners, may challenge you about the usefulness of dressage. I would suggest that you point out, most firmly, that dressage teaches the horse obedience. It also develops the horses'

382

musculature throughout its whole body. This is the foundation that should be developed *before* the horse is taught to jump. Since jumping depends to a great degree on balance *and* obedience there is no argument.

General schooling.

All owners are to be encouraged to carry out schooling on their own, after all is not the essential distillation of good equitation, the union of rider and horse? An owner wishing to bring on their horse should prepare a program of exercises ***before the start*** of the schooling period in exactly the same way as an instructor would so do for a class. The essence of this program should be to ***keep*** the horse ***interested***. No movement should be maintained for so long that the horse, through fatigue, as much as for any other reason, should feel compelled to disobey. If this does happen, then it is the rider who is solely responsible for this first step on the downward path to being nappy.

Jumping for liveries.

One of the opportunities most available to livery owners is the freedom to jump their horses when they so choose. In your approach to teaching owners to jump their horses, there is no great difference from the lessons given to weekend riders, except to bear in mind that the livery owner will very likely jump their horses at times when they are not receiving instruction or under supervision. This is quite understandable and as it should be. However it is important to stress to the owner that when in search of pleasure or trying to impress ones friends, matters should not be allowed to get out of hand. The horse must neither be pushed too far nor driven out of its mind through boredom.

Do try and impress on owners that the ***essence of success lies in width before height***. It is through jumping wider obstacles that a horse gains the confidence to jump higher. In fact many owners do not realise that in schooling their horses over jumps that have width, they are actually also gaining height.

Final thoughts on instructing livery owners.

In discussing my views with other instructors I may say that there are many that disagree with me. I am not so rigid in my opinions that I am incapable of listening to what they have to say. I have written this book from the point of view of someone who is working in the environment of a riding school. Under these conditions it is necessary that free licence to experiment at will, is somewhat restricted. However so far as freelance private instruction is concerned, that is entirely another matter. For me to argue that only experienced riders should own a horse is to go against what actually happens in real life. It is an attitude akin to King Canute commanding the tide not to come in. So I am prepared unbend and to acknowledge that it is up to you. Quickly, assess any new client and undertake their teaching in such a way that whatever problems you encounter, they do not escalate while horse and rider is in your care. In fact I would go further> If the period were sufficient, during which a horse is under your tuition, then you will have the opportunity to contribute considerably to its growing maturity.

Experimentation.

I might go even further and say that, provided the owner has learned the basics to some degree and the horse is reasonably well behaved, there is no reason why a degree of experimentation should not be tried out. By that I mean that without pushing the horse so far in schooling that it becomes stressed and uncooperative, the livery owner should take the opportunity to devise their own private language with their horses. This may well lead on to levels of co-operation that they had, previously, only dreamed of.

Working liveries.

I must make quite clear what this means. These are horses that are privately owned but earn part of their keep by spending some time working with school clients. The owner and the school come to an agreement that certain specified hours are to be reserved for the owner's use. The rest of the time the horse is available to the school. Actually I think that it is not a bad idea to keep a horse in this way. In the first place it should receive sufficient work to prevent it getting bored out of its life. Regular work also helps to keep it fit and allow its musculature to develop. Secondly if the owner is lucky the horse may be used in an advanced class where it may learn a thing or two.

Some people may have read my words with absolute horror. 'What'? They will say. 'Have my horse used by ignorant riders. The poor creature will be ruined'. In fact it is usually the other way round, for the damage is done not by the non-horse owning clients who come for lessons but during the time when the owners ride by themselves. The reason for this is quite obvious. While the horse is in the school and being used by school clients it is under the control of an experienced instructor. In the process of getting their clients to ride correctly there will be the by-product - that the horse learns his business. I am, of course, making the assumption that the instructor is up to standard. If they are not then not only will this be detrimental to the working livery but also to all the horses that have the misfortune to be in that class.

Is there anything that we, as instructors need to worry about? The answer is 'yes' we do need to be watchful. For a working livery may well cause *disruption* in a class *subsequent* to the *owner having ridden it.* If, during that time, the horse has been allowed to get its own way, then you may have a problem in re-imposing discipline. If it is an animal that does not respond quickly to your treatment, send it out of the class. If the client riding is able to obtain another mount, well and good. If not, then ask the office to arrange for a partial refund.

 I know I am repeating myself again! Why? Because I have seen the problems that can arise as a result of having such a horse in ones class. It will start with a small buck or a dashing off at the canter. The client may well get everything under control, but the horse waits for its moment. At a point when every one is engaged in working through a movement; and it may be only at the walk, the livery will suddenly start an almighty rumpus and before you know it the whole class is dashing off right, left and centre.

Should this happen, then if you are lucky the class will have suffered no injury. However after the miscreant has departed you will need to scale everything back for a short while because even if your clients have coped well with the situation, they may well be a bit shaken up and the horses will know it! Some people may argue that this is a marvellous 'get out' for the horse. 'It learns' they will say 'that all it has to do is to cause a rumpus and its work is finished'. There is a lot of truth in this if the matter is allowed to remain unresolved. Some may say' Why don't you get up and sort it out?' I have mentioned this problem before but I will repeat, you ride the horse it goes well for you, but its resentment still remains and it takes it out on your client as soon as they remount. Not only that but an 'atmosphere' will still lie over the rest of the class. It is important that this 'atmosphere' is dispelled. If you are not successful *and a similar incident is repeated, your clients may well suffer a fall.* If they do so and are then trodden on by horses careering around the arena, you may well wish that you had proceeded otherwise. Your duty is to the safety of *all* your clients. If the livery is to remain a useful member of the schools' retinue of horses then it should be 'sorted out' in a class where there are only members of staff riding, all able to deal with their own horses competently and especially able to deal with the hooligan. In that environment it will learn the lesson that being in a class means getting on with the job and no mucking about.

Dealing with private clients.
I would not be surprised if the above heading raises an eyebrow or two. ' Surely', you may think 'Hasn't the fellow already been talking about *private* clients in the many paragraphs that I have just read?' Well the answer is that I am now going to help you to deal not with riders and their horses in a well-organised yard, but how to go about establishing good ongoing relations with clients whose horses haven't ever been within shouting distance of a school. *I am talking about DIY yards*. Yes, people who keep horses without anyone else at all to help them. *They have to do everything* and it does not necessarily follow that these people keep their horses in dirty conditions or that their horses are hard done by.

So above all, the first thing that you must have is tact. You may come across owners who have established a very good relationship with their horses but whose position, for example, is less than perfect. After all there is no immutable law that says that every aid must be subject to a fixed criterion! Of course the owner has asked you to come and instruct them because they may wish to improve their standard of riding or they may be having some problems that they find difficult to solve. Therefore the first thing that I do *not* do is to steam in and give them a jolly good telling off because their position is poor.

I first accompany the owner to the box before they tack up. There I give their horse a quick 'once over', talking to it quietly as I examine its back, feet and mouth. I then watch the rider tacking up. If I do see something being carried out incorrectly, I immediately, quietly, point this out.

Owner and horse then proceed to the arena or whatever area they have to work in and of course I look around to ensure that all jumps and any other equipment have been stored safely out of harms way. Having made sure that all the usual safety checks have been carried out (Oh yes you must proceed in exactly the same manner as you would if you were working in a regular riding establishment) I then give them five to fifteen minutes to work in by themselves during that time I seldom say anything, unless that is I see that they are about to do something that might place themselves or their horse in danger. During that time I study them carefully, sometimes making notes, and after the warm up period is over I then start to talk to them and tell them what I have noticed and how they may go about improving matters.

Giving a demonstration.

In these circumstances I have found that many clients *do* benefit from my getting up on their horses and showing them how they may make progress. I do try not to this on the very first meeting; instead I prefer that the horse and I get to know one another better. I do this by always accompanying the owner back to the box where there is an exchange of carrots between the horse and myself. I do this for at least four or five sessions. Then should the occasion arise where I feel that it would be beneficial for me to ride the horse, the poor thing is not frightened out of its wits as it feels this alien being upon its back and what is more one whose very position would seem to indicate that some very precise signals are about to be given.

Usually the horses that I see are well cared for, and I must say that I have a soft spot for DIY horse owners, and very often reduce my fees if I think that it is really hard for them to make ends meet.

Teaching how to develop creativity.

One of the most frequent problems facings owners is that they have no imagination whatsoever. The result of this is that when schooling their horses the programme usually consists of continuously riding large around the arena with an occasional change of rein. Sometimes they may add a few circles. This frequently results in their horses getting bored to death. Quite often they simply doze off. In many circumstance there is very little being done that will contribute to an improvement in the manner of the horse's going.

With private clients I try to overcome this by creating a series of exercises that I prepare and type out *before* going to see them. I do usually start this routine around the third or fourth lesson. By that time both horse and client have got to know me quite well and I have also been able to assess what needs to be done and thus prepare a sequence of movements that will help. These are also designed to make up for that lack of imagination to which so many clients are prone and impart a degree of creativity.

When you do this, base your exercises on the movements that you have already been teaching but also try to provide a variety of changes that result in the horse being unlikely to anticipate what the rider is going to ask of them. On your next appointment ask the client to show you what they have been doing.

Checking tack.

Do remember when checking tack to take great care over detail. Livery owners usually tack up themselves and I have found that many of them do not know how to do this correctly. Take care to check the noseband, especially a dropped noseband. I have noticed that owners do tend to do these up much too tightly (the bones of the nasal peak are very delicate) and also to position them so low that they interfere with the horses' breathing. One problem that sometimes occurs is the use of an overly severe bit. When asked, the owner tells you that the tack came with the horse and that they have continued to use it. The problem that arises is that the new owner's hands may be much harsher than those of the person who owned the horse previously. They wonder why the horse, which was so quiet, now seems to get overly excited and dash off madly. The answer, very often, lies in getting them to change the bit for a kinder one. Another problem concerns numnahs, which may be placed flat on the horses back and thus, negate the effect of saddle arch and gullet.

Finally horses that are allowed to get over excited.

One of the problems that can arise may have nothing whatever to do with either the work that you do in your classes or the manner in which horses are livered. I am referring to those times when the owners ride their steeds by themselves. During this time, at many yards, these activities are not supervised. Why should they be? After all the animals belong to the owners and they have agreed times when they will ride. This may lead to some problems. Horses are creatures that have the ability to, quite quickly, fix certain responses in their brains. Once these connections have been established they can become quite difficult to remove. This is usually to our advantage. It is the way in which we establish certain modes of behaviour that enable us to make our animals a joy to ride.

However, an owner left to their own devises may unwittingly *create problems* without really understanding what is happening. For example, an owner has just acquired a new horse. They are very excited about this and ask all their relations down to see and ride the animal. Many of these people may not be very experienced riders. Further more their first desire is to see if they can get the horse to canter. So up they get, one after the other, and belt around the arena at high speed. The horse, which may actually have quite a quiet disposition, gets more and more excited. There is a real possibility of an accident occurring.

If you come across such a state of affairs then, immediately have a quiet word with the owner and explain what is happening. You may well think 'What has this to do with me?' The answer is 'everything'. As a member of staff, whether on duty or not, it is your job to ensure that no unfortunate 'incidents' occur. Further more, should the animal be part liveried, the effect of such goings on will certainly affect its work when it is used for lessons. In fact its behaviour may become so bad that the school may no longer be prepared to use it in this way and the owner will be placed in a position where they are unable to afford to keep it.

Chapter 23

The reasons why.

Leading leg - cantering with the correct.

A horse is said to be cantering with the correct lead either around a corner or on a circle when the inside foreleg, appearing last in the sequence of the three beats of the canter, is thrust forward so that the shoulder on that side appears to be slightly ahead of the other. The rider should always check this ideally by feel, but if the skill to do this is lacking, then the rider should glance down and make sure that it is correct.

As Instructor you must check *every* canter depart and should you spot a horse with the incorrect lead, then you must ask the rider to go forward to trot and ask for canter again.

Why is it important?

The reason is a similar one to that of sitting on the correct diagonal when rising to the trot. The horse is pivoting about his *inside hind* leg. Just to remind ourselves of the sequence, the rider asks with their outside leg for the horse to lead with its inside foreleg. When the horse, obeying this aid, goes forward to canter the first thing that it does is to slightly lift its' body into the air by throwing the forehand upwards with the inside foreleg. As it does so it strikes off with its outside hind leg; (coming underneath and thrusting its body foreword) followed by the inside hind leg and outside foreleg together, finally the inside foreleg comes under the horse thrusting itself up in the air again and the legs are now all, momentarily folded underneath it. (The moment of suspension see drawing no. 7). To look at the movement from a slightly different angle, the canter depart from the trot results in a split of one pair of diagonals. These now become the leading leg - the one in front and the strike off leg - the diagonal behind. The other pair of legs still move together. The horse needs to pivot on the inside hind leg of this pair. It makes him feel more secure and better able to balance both his own bodyweight and that of the rider and helps to avoid him falling over.* (see end of chapter).

Again Why?

Let us apply a pivoting motion to ourselves. You wish to twirl to the right. Well then, arms held out horizontally to get a good swing and… which leg do we *naturally* tend to pivot on? Why the right leg. Oh yes, I know that there will be some that purposely swing about the left leg. You can do this if you have a degree of athletic ability, so far as a *natural tendency* is concerned, you will use the leg closer to your centre of gravity brought about by the direction of swing.

Is the incorrect lead dangerous?

Is a horse immediately in danger if it strikes off with the incorrect lead? The answer is usually no it is not; unless it goes off at an almighty pace. Generally most horses are capable of performing what is known as a *counter canter*. That is to say they can canter with the outside foreleg (relative to bend) leading.

Keeping the body still as one asks for canter.

Sometimes it does help to give clients a graphic description in the form of an analogy so that they may more easily understand why they should do certain things. To see things from a horse's point of view as it were.

I ask my clients to imagine that they are rock climbing. They are not actually heaving themselves up the rock face with ropes; instead they are climbing from one rocky projection to another. Upon their backs they are carrying all their equipment. It is quite a heavy load. At one point they come to a spot where they have both feet placed on one small outcrop. The next step is going to require them to step across to another, it is not too far away, but it is only wide enough to step up to with one leg. What is more the distance is such that this cannot be the achieved with a simple stride. By that I mean that they cannot simply stretch a leg across secure their footing and then follow with the other leg. They actually have to hop so that for a split second they are 'in the air' and when they land they do so on only one foot.

As they are about to do so, the backpack slips and it falls over one shoulder. Now are they going to complete the stride or are they going to try and step back to the rock where there was room for a secure stance on both feet? Do I need to translate this into the canter situation?

'Near side and off side - what is meant by?

The near side of a horse is the left side and the offside is the right side (from the horses back looking forward). The reason for this is that riding a horse and indeed driving a car on the left (as we still do, in the

387

U.K. at the time I write) means that the pavement where one would mount is on the left side of the horse. Providing one is proceeding in the same direction as the traffic on a road.

Sitting on a particular diagonal (at rising trot).

A rider is said to be on the 'correct' diagonal, when their seat is *in* the saddle as the horses' outside foreleg is coming under it.

Why?

The reason for this is due to the fact that the trot is a two-time movement in which the horse 'hops' as it were from one pair of diagonals to the other. As it moves through a corner or goes on a circle then the pivoting action takes place as the *inside hind* leg comes underneath it. The horse may tend to feel slightly unbalanced at this time, therefore the rider needs to help the horse by making sure that their body weight is securely in place (i.e. they are sitting down) as the pivot is taking place. Ideally this should be done by feel. Many novice riders do not have this ability, therefore if they look down at the outside foreleg and ensure that they are sitting as this is passing under them, then they will also be sitting as the inside hind leg does so, since both legs are moving simultaneously.

If they find that they are on the *incorrect* diagonal they should be instructed to sit for two strides to make the correction.

Spare rein loop - what is the correct position?

Carried *under* the reins to avoid any erroneous signal caused by its weight on the reins themselves. It should lie across the withers on the riders' *right* hand side.

The custom derives from the fact that a rider, in past times, would have his sword hanging down his *left* side. By placing the loop out of the way on the other side there would be no danger of this getting caught up in the sword hilt, should he wish to draw it in a hurry.

Weighting the inside hip.

An aid that sometimes causes much confusion. It is one that should have been taught right at the beginning of a pupil's education. We have touched upon it early on in this book where I have talked about the rider 'bringing forward, and stretching down, *almost* on the girth, the *inside* leg as a rider goes into and out of a corner.

This is in effect a 'weighting' of the hip for as the leg is stretched down so this has the effect of bringing more pressure from the hipbone on that side. In more advanced movements and in particular lateral work it is useful in so far as that it gives the horse a feeling of support. This is due to the fact that a horse will respond to a steady pressure against its side by leaning into it. You may try this yourself from the ground. Place your hand gently against a horse's shoulder and apply a gentle but steady pressure. You will find the horse tending to lean towards your hand and should you remove this suddenly then you will quite clearly see the animal move towards you. Of course the pressure must be steady and gentle, if it is too strong then the horse will simply move away.

The reason for working- in for an adequate period.

Unlike human athletes (who are able to run at quite high speed with only a relatively short limbering-up period), horses require somewhat longer before their energy utilisation becomes efficient. Bearing in mind that they have evolved without any of the built-in defensive weaponry (horns) of some other prey species, and have as the only real means of defence a blow (albeit a powerful one) with a hoof, it was necessary to also develop a type of musculature that would provide for instant flight.

What evolved was the storage of a molecule in the muscles of the leg containing the chemical phosphocreatine (PC). Almost the very second that a horses sees something, or believes that it sees something, that it feels will be a danger to it, a reflex reaction takes place turning this molecule into a chemical called adenosine triphosphate (ATP). This reaction, together with the very small reserves of residual ATP in the muscles provide about 10 seconds of swift flight, after which those stocks run out. A second chemical mechanism then comes into play utilising the energy stored in fat molecules called glycogen. This is also converted into ATP giving a further energy source for about 60 seconds. Both these forms of energy utilisation, which are known as anaerobic reactions (they don't utilise oxygen), are extremely inefficient. The energy conversion is particularly low (about 13% of the total available) and the production of waste by-products (pyruvic acid to lactic acid) builds up extremely quickly. These cause extreme muscle fatigue. Of course this is only a means to an end. It may give the animal sufficient time to leap out of harms way, or at the very least place itself so that it can lash out with a goodly kick from the hindquarters. During this period adrenaline has caused the heart to beat faster and the lungs to fill with air more quickly so that oxygen may be pumped through the arteries to provide a more sustainable and efficient form of energy transfer. This is known as aerobic metabolism, which, not only through several combined chemical reactions, provides more ATP but also breaks down the waste products more quickly into carbon dioxide and water. The aerobic reaction is slower to get going than the anaerobic one. (*33 Stephen Budiansky. The Nature of Horses).

Thus we have the answer to several questions when working with horses. It explains a young horse suddenly shying when there is, apparently, nothing to be seen. And we also have the answer as to why one needs to work- in for a reasonable period before subjecting the horse to exercises that involve a high expenditure of energy (embarking on a flat out gallop or jumping high jumps). We may also understand why a normally quiet animal may quite suddenly put in an enormous buck.

You may well query why the horse has developed in such a manner that escape may engender quite severe muscular pain. I daresay that the horse considers a short period of discomfort a small price to pay for prolonging its life. In any case, out in the wild, a horse will only take such action for as long as it deems it *strictly necessary*.

This will of course bring us to quite an interesting discussion point and that concerns the actual need to 'work in' at the walk in an arena when one is only going to subject the animal to quite light work with say a novice rider. In other words the horse isn't going to do much more than walk combined with very short periods of trot. The simple answer is that it isn't strictly necessary in order to get the muscles and tendons working properly but it is important to allow the horse time to ensure that, as it makes it's way around the arena, everything is as it should be. By that I mean that the visual appearance of the arena compares with that already recorded in the horse's brain. As I have said in an earlier chapter, I am convinced that horses tend to think, mainly, in visual terms whereas we tend to think in terms of sound and word. Thus if a horse enters an arena in which something has changed, then it is quite likely to stop and have a really good look at whatever it thinks is different. I have noticed this time and time again. Small things such as the advertising board of a firm put up against a wall after they have renewed the working surface. A jump upright not put away properly. Any of these things may cause many horses to suddenly stop and have a good look! And it is possible that one of these un-scheduled stops may cause a rider to loose balance and fall off! It is worthwhile bearing in mind that some people also have the ability to think completely visually. Here I am referring to those who have a 'photographic memory'. If shown a page in a book they only have to glance at it for a few seconds and can then remember that page in perfect detail. Many people regard this as a sign of high intelligence but that does not necessarily follow. For though the page may be recalled verbatim, it cannot be taken for granted that the contents will be understood.

* Do bear in mind that a horse that is 'rassembler' i.e.- collected to perfection - should be able to strike off without necessarily needing to use the leading leg first in the sequence.

Chapter 24

Care of the arena.

Just a page about taking care of the tools with which you work. – Yes an arena is a tool and all arenas whether a simple field or an all-weather prepared surface need be looked after. The sum that has to be allocated for the maintenance of artificial surfaces is, at the time I write, about £10.00 per square/metre/year. If you consider the large areas that make up the surface of many modern riding schools this comes to a tidy sum.

Degradation, from which arises the need for the surface maintenance, depends, mainly, on three basic factors.

The weather.

Extremes of climate do not help in preserving the integrity of a surface. Excessively wet weather may produce areas of very boggy ground. Should this be the case, then it is up to you to help to ameliorate the problem by having your students avoid that area. Easier said than done. You may well tell your class to circumvent a certain part of the arena but they may be relatively unsuccessful in so doing. The simple reason being that what with trying to concentrate on the lesson they forget to do that which you have asked. Never mind about avoiding certain areas in the arena, sometimes, even asking clients to take an inside track is more than they can manage after a circuit or two. In order to help them out you should mark designated points with cones. This, at least, will give a visual target for them to bear in mind.

In exceedingly dry weather, the outside track is very likely to become compacted. Here again it will help if you ensure that all riding activity – going large – is conducted on the inside track. This will help to avoid the complete break-up of the fibres on the outside track until such time as the surface is harrowed.

The amount of work to which the surfaces are subject.

This heading really speaks for itself but you may be able to extend the life of a surface by arranging your exercises intelligently so that your clients utilise a greater area of the school, rather than simply pounding round the outside all of the time. Apart from utilising the inside track there are also the three-quarter lines. Or you can be quite radical and ask your class to ride from major letter to letter i.e. A – E - C – B. (see fig. 112).

Keeping the arena clean.

One of the main factors that contribute more than anything else to the degradation of the surface are horse droppings. These need to be picked up the moment that they fall. It is so easy to fail to do so because the class is in the middle of a movement. As soon as you see a horse giving you ' a little present' instruct the class to try to avoid it, if they are likely to tread on it the next time around. Once a horse has trodden on excrement it is much harder to remove from the surface. In fact, there is always likely to be a small residual amount and as time passes this devolves into a fine powder. Not only does this clog the drain holes in the subsurface but in dry weather it is lifted into the air by the action of the horses' feet and everyone present breaths it in.

So take your time and be meticulous when it comes to picking up droppings. *Do not leave the job until the end of the lesson. Do it right away (having had the class go forward to walk).* My clients have always been most understanding about this. If I have been concentrating on one particular client and did not notice they call out immediately a motion has been passed. I have a little joke with them as I move around the arena while I clean up. Pretending to moan that a senior instructor like myself should be reduced to such circumstances. Please bear in mind it is unforgivable for you to hand over your arena to another instructor when it is covered with of droppings deposited by your horses.

Diagrams.

Figure 112.

Utilising inside tracks and changing the reference points. (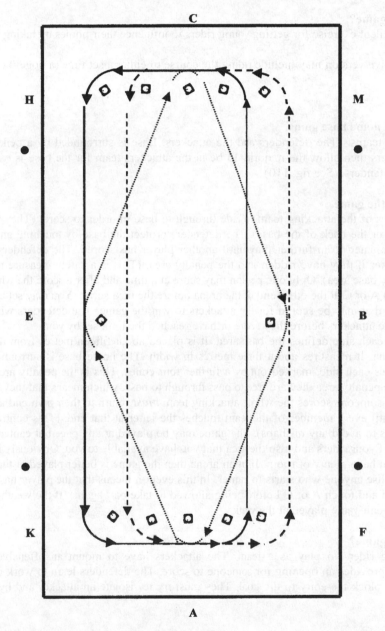 = Cone)

Figure no. 112. Utilising the inside tracks or three-quarter line and changing the reference points.

Chapter 25

Games list (See also playing games).

1.
Navigation game.
Riders are numbered 1 to …. A course is set up and riders are called in by number to ride the course whilst the rest of the class go large. They have to navigate a number of obstacles, which may include a jump or jumps (provided that the class is up to jumping standard). They then have to return to their correct position in the ride.

Object of the game?
This is an excellent exercise for getting young riders to influence their ponies by taking them away from the rest of the ride.

An alternative version may include riding the course to either a set time (a bogey) or maybe against the clock.

2.
The getting to home base game.
There are two teams. The defenders and the attackers. Base is surrounded by a penalty area. If you are short of numbers then allow the majority to be in the attackers team for the base is easily defended by as few as three defenders. (See fig. 110)

The object of the game.
Is for a member of the attacking team to ride through to base in order to score. (They may do so riding in from the front or the back of the base). The defenders protect the base by touching an attacker, who once touched is eliminated from further play until another player has scored. The defenders are not allowed to touch an attacker if they have ridden into the penalty area. (This is a safety measure to prevent too much crowding in the base area). Only one person may score at a time and after a score the whole team has to ride back and touch A or C at the other end of the arena before the next sortie. You may set a limit to the number of home bases that may be scored for the attackers to win the game. The defenders win if they are able to eliminate all the attackers before they score or have reached the limit set by you.

A cone on each side defines the base area. It is placed about fifteen metres from the side of one short end of the arena. It measures about three metres in width. The home base is surrounded by a square, of about six metres each side, marked out by a further four cones. This is the penalty area. Once an attacker has entered the penalty area they are free to pass through to base, which means that they have scored.

As soon as someone scores the whole attacking team *must* return to their own end and the game cannot be restarted until every member of the team touches the letter at that end. (This controls the speed of the game and helps to avoid any mishaps). The game may be played at any pace but cantering depends strictly on the ability of your riders and also the area that you have available to you. Obviously if you are playing in a field then you have plenty of room. If in an arena then the game is better played at the trot. (You must be strict and penalise anyone who starts to canter. In this event it means that the player has to walk back to his or her own end and touch A or C before being allowed to take part again). If the weather is warm, then the game is just as enjoyable played at the walk.

Object of the game?
Teaches young riders to play as a team. The attackers have to mount an offensive that splits up the defenders and provides an opening for someone to score. The defenders learn to work in co-operation with one another to block the entry to the goal. They must try to isolate an attacker and by touching eliminate them quickly.

3.
A 2nd variation of base game, but with Ping-Pong balls.
Similar rules to that mentioned above except that the attackers have several Ping-Pong balls in a box at their end. They have to take one at a time from their end, and by passing it to one another, drop or throw it in a box or rubber tyre placed between the cones in the base area.

Another Ping-Pong ball game.
Two equal teams play this game. The teams are each lined up at the same end of the arena. Each member of the team is given a Ping-Pong ball. The teams are provided with a cardboard cone (that you will have made up previously). There is only *one* cone for each team. Riders use this in turn to carry their ball balanced on top of the cone to the other end of the arena where it is dropped into a box. Each team has their own box (to avoid kicking).

The riders must carry the reins in one hand and are not allowed to cover the ball with; say their thumbs or fingers. If they drop the ball then they must dismount and pick it up (Have helpers available for each team to hold ponies while this takes place). The competitors are permitted to hold the ball only while they are mounting. They may not move off until the ball is placed in the cup.

If the ball bounces out of the box then the rider must dismount and place it back in the box if it is to count. On return the next rider cannot go until the cone has been passed to them. First team to place all their balls in their box wins.

Object of the game?
To encourage riders to keep their hands still.

4

Cowboys and Indians.
This is a very traditional team game. The majority of the class is designated as 'Indians' they have to be caught by others who are the 'Cowboys'. The manner of its playing depends on the number of riders in the class. If there are, say, eight in all, then the Indians will number say six with the other two riders being the Cowboys.

Suggested gaits.
Since this is a game that involves a great deal of twisting and turning, I would suggest that it be played only at the walk or trot.

Choosing the Cowboys.
For this type of game, I usually look for volunteers. However I do direct things somewhat and ensure that, for the first round anyway, the Cowboys selected are those with ponies that go well

The rules of the game.
Obviously the Cowboys have to catch the Indians, they do so by riding along side and touching them. They may only do this with their hands and not with the whip. They are not allowed to approach any pony from behind. When a rider has been caught they become part of the cowboy's team. If anyone rides outside the prescribed area or proceeds at a faster gait than that permitted, then, they are immediately designated as caught. Continue either until all the Indians have been captured or until the time for the games' duration has run out. If anyone evades capture right through the game, then, they should be congratulated. **When you have a child riding a pony that will not move give them a hand.**

Object of the game?
The players learn to maintain a given gait.
They also learn to turn their ponies around in tight circles using their bodies.

Stuck in the mud.
Similar to the game above. Riders split into two groups the smaller one to catch, the others to evade. This time, if a rider is caught, they may not move until one of their team-mates touches them. Should they be caught three times, then they are designated a catcher.
Suggested gaits.
As for Cowboys and Indians.

Object of the game?
As for Cowboys and Indians but also develops a team spirit, since the Indians can prevent their eventual, complete, capture by freeing their compatriots.

393

Walking, leading, trotting and cantering races.
The above title is self-descriptive. Having selected two teams, you may make up any combination of the above. Once again have faster paces as the riders go away and slower paces as they return. During extremes of either very hot or cold weather a race that has a riding and leading element is to be recommended. These races may be done as a ride i.e. everyone competing against everyone else, or else in teams. You should always try to alternate team races with those that involve the whole class together. This will avoid both ponies and riders getting too cold in poor weather, also a class race will probably make it easier for those riding ponies that do not like going away from the others.

Before embarking on a leading race, use this as an opportunity to instruct children in the correct manner of leading, and mounting. Have someone come forward as a guinea pig. Ask them to demonstrate the correct way to go about these matters. Have the rest ready to comment as to whether or not they are proceeding correctly. Use this as an opportunity to remind them about leading the pony away from oneself when turning, *rechecking the girth before mounting* and so on.

A race that involves leading back may be made up as follows. Have the first ridden section as a trot. Point out that crossing the stirrups will save time if this is done before the rider dismounts or better still even before they start. In other words you are giving those prepared to ride without stirrups an advantage, which most children will readily seize. Of course only permit this for those children who you know have the ability to do this whilst riding unaided. For the others it is acceptable providing you have a helper who will assist them in staying on. Otherwise tell them to keep the stirrups until dismounting. The return is through leading back and the winner the first person to remount.

Obstacle course against the clock. (The clock game)*
This is an excellent game for playing in hot weather, since the participants go one at a time and there is plenty of time for ponies to rest. From my experience this is a game in which all youngsters are keen to take part. No matter in what order they finish, they will try and improve on their times in subsequent rounds. (actually it is also very much enjoyed by adults).

The requirements.
A stopwatch and a selection of cones and trotting poles.

Essentially you make up a course using a combination of cones and trotting poles. The combinations are endless. However once again you must play the game at gaits that are concomitant with safety. Suggested courses (See fig. 111 a & b)

The course should start with walk and trot only and, if conditions are reasonable may be developed to have a short canter element later on.

The course should be able to be ridden at the correct gait so that the duration is not more than say around 30 to 50 seconds on average. In this way should you have say 6 riders in the class then the total length of standing around for every rider should be no more than 6 minutes; presuming that you allow say 15 seconds for each change-over.

Grandmother's footsteps.
Same as you would have played at school except that, in this case, it is mounted. A very good game for a hot day. To refresh your memory: -

A volunteer rides about 25/50 yards away from the ride. (You may adjust the distance according to your preference). They stand facing away from the rest of the ride who have formed a straight line. The object of the game is that, riding as individuals, they try to get as near 'Grandma' as is possible without being seen to move. This game may be played at any pace. If Grandma turns her head and sees anyone moving then those players have to return to the starting line and try all over again.

Advice to Grandma.
Not to turn ones head too soon early on in the game otherwise it is difficult for the players to make any progress and the game looses some of its excitement.

Advice to the rest.
Make your moves quickly and for a short duration, then halt in order to avoid being caught out.

The numbers game.
This is a game that I literally dreamed up. I awoke in the early hours one morning and wrote it down so that I would not forget.

The equipment.
Cut out ten squares of card or plasterboard approx. 30cms square. The quality of board should be fairly heavy so that it will not easily be blown away in a slight breeze. Mark each one with numbers from 1 to 10. You may also draw a circle of around 10cms diameter (for a variation of the game).

Approximately 40 to 50 paper cups. I do not find plastic cups satisfactory, as they tend to split very easily). Paint the underneath of half the quantity; say Red and the other half Green (or whatever colours you like so long as they are different).

Setting up the game.
Divide the ponies into two teams. Do this by whatever means you wish i.e. select two teams leaders by age or through a race and allow them to choose whom they will – divide the class by age- boys and girls – its up to you.

Have the teams line up. Place the cards in front of the teams with the numbers facing upwards, lowest denominations nearest the teams and the highest further away. Always make sure that every number is placed far enough away from any other so that riders may approach different numbers at the same time without fear of ponies kicking out.

Give a specific number of red painted cups to one team and the same number of green to the other. Decide on the total per team according to the number of riders. If you have say five riders in each team then I would think that 15 cups per team is sufficient for the first game (every team member has three goes).

One person is designated the ***custodian of the cups for the other team*** (They may hand them over to someone else when their turn to play comes up). Each member of the other team has to approach the custodian of his or her teams' cups. (This prevents cheating through team members giving their own team more than one cup at a time).

They ride out at whatever pace you have decided upon (I usually allow canter away for those so able ***but always trotting back***). They place the cup upon a numbered card. If they miss then they must dismount and replace the cup accurately. Obviously the further they are prepared to ride away the greater the numerical reward, provided they place the cup correctly. The disadvantage is that it takes longer. As soon as they have returned across the line the next team member is allowed to go.
Safety rules.
No two players are allowed to approach the same number at the same time. The game ends when one of the teams has used up all its cups. (If it goes on too long then place a time limit).

At the end of the game all players approach each number in turn and add up the points scored by multiplying the value of the card by the number of cups in their own colour. All scores for each card are then added together. The highest total wins.

Variations of the rules.
These are endless
Players may place their cups on top of those already put down.
You may decide that only the topmost cup will win points on any card thus you encourage each team to try and gazzump the other. You may utilise the circle drawn under each number and give double the points if a cup if placed accurately in the circle.

Object of the game?
Encourages the riders to make their ponies stand still. Also at the end of the game, as the scores are added up, it is a very good exercise in mental arithmetic.

The cup game. *
Place paper cups around the arena, either on the uprights supporting the fence or, if none available, on top of poles such as those used for bending (with poles place on every other pole). They should be positioned about 5 metres apart. The object is for each rider to ride by a cup, lift it and put it down on the free upright which has been placed before the next cup which, in turn, is lifted and so on. The game should at first be played at the walk, then the trot and, individually, with a skilled rider even at the canter.

Version 1.
Have the ride going large around the arena. Each rider has to pick up a cup and ride with it to the place

where the next cup has been placed. They then put down the cup that they are carrying and have to pick up the next cup. If a rider drops a cup then they are considered 'out' and have to leave the ride and stand on the centre line. The game continues until only one rider remains. This version should be played at walk or trot.

Version 2.
For this game the riders pick up a cup but they have to place it on top of or inside the next cup that they come to.

Obviously these cup games may be played with teams.

The object of the game.
The object of the game is to place each cup accurately before lifting the next one.
This teaches the rider to be able to concentrate on more than one thing at a time. In this case they have to keep the horse going straight along the sides of the arena and at the same time judge the correct point as to when to lift and replace each cup.

Variations.
The cups may be partially filled with water and the object is to avoid spilling any.

The reservoir cup game.
The riders place the reins in their outside hand and have to hold a cup filled with water with the inside hand. The game may be played at any pace that is *within the capability of all the riders*. The players simply proceed around the arena for a specified time, after which the remaining water in each cup is checked. The winner is the person who lost least water.

The Points of the Horse game.
Preparing the hardware.
Requirements.
1. A sheet of stiff board. (Measuring approx. 1m by 1.5m)
2. A piece of cartridge or drafting paper to fit.
3. A sheet of clear acrylic to fit.
4. 50 plant tags. (The stick in the ground variety. See drawing no. 34).
5. Blue tack or Velcro.
6. A Prittstick.
7. Two cotton bags with a large opening along one side. Or if all else fails then a couple of empty sweet boxes.
8. Drawing pins and a few nails.

On the cartridge paper draw the diagrammatic outline of a horse and mark 50 different points as black dots, (see drawing no. 35 & 35a.).
Paste or pin the outline drawing of the horse to stiff the board.
The sheet of clear acetate plastic covers the drawing. Each dot is then covered by a small glob of Blue tack or Velcro placed on the plastic.
   You now need to prepare the names of fifty different points of the horse on a sheet of A4 paper. You can write these free hand or prepare them on your computer. Half the names should be in red and the other half in green. Try to be even handed when dividing the names between red and green so that you do not have too many difficult names in one group. These should be cut into strips that will fit the plastic plant markers, (see drawing no. 36). Stick the names onto the plant markers with the Prit. Place all the green names in one of your cotton bags and the reds in the other. You are now ready to set up the game.
   Nail or pin the board to a wall or rail at one end of the arena. It should be placed at such a height that a youngster can reach any part of the drawing from their pony. At the other end of the arena pin each side of the back and the bottom of each bag to a rail or wall. This is important to prevent the bags flapping about if it is windy.

Playing the game.
Select team leaders in the usual manner, and then have them choose their teams. Odd numbers do not matter.

The teams are lined up along opposite sides of the arena. Players depart in an order chosen by the team leader. They proceed, one at a time and ride to the bag on their side and, *without looking*, pick out a plastic tag. They then ride up as fast as they can and stick the point of the tag firmly on the Blue tack dot or Velcro strip, which they believe correctly corresponds to the name shown on the tag. They trot back and touch the next member who then proceeds in the same manner. The game ends when one team has allocated all their tags or after a pre-set time.

(An option is to allow a team to remove and keep another players tag if they believe that it has been placed on the wrong point).

Scoring.
At the end of the game both teams ride, quietly up to the board where they form a half circle. You then take one team at a time (Don't forget that each team has their own colour) and add up their score of *correct* tags allowing one point for each correct one. If you have allowed the removal option, then examine the tags that have been removed by each team. If their decision was correct, they get extra five points (per tag) but if they removed a tag incorrectly then they loose five points from their total.

Make sure that you have everyone return the tags that have been removed and don't forget to pick up any that have fallen on the ground.

Object of the game?
Well obviously it teaches youngsters the points of the horse. (Incidentally, I usually give out a sketch correctly marked up a week or so before playing this game. It works better if everyone has, at least, some knowledge of the points of the horse. It also teaches riders to make their ponies go way from the others and also to stand still.

Musical horses.
This is a very simple game and one that can be played in a quite restricted area. You place a number of empty feedbags or sacks on the ground in a circle. There should be one less than the number of riders taking part. It is very similar to musical chairs except that when the music stops (or if you haven't any music you simply call out 'go'). The ride dismounts and leads their horses as quickly as they can to try and find a bag to stand on. The one left out looses that round. The game continues with one sack being removed each round until there is only one rider left. They win.

Equipment.
Feedbags placed in a circle. The minimum circle should be large enough to accommodate all the riders around the circumference with at least a horse's length between each rider and a bit to spare. The bags should be placed on the ground with the edges dug slightly into the surface of the arena. This is in order to stop them moving should there be a bit of a breeze and also when a rider steps on to them

The rules.
The game is simple, when the music starts the ride proceed around the circle either walking or trotting. Everyone must be on the move and the gait must be the same for all competitors. If the game is played at the trot, anyone walking at that time are disqualified.

Riders must not get too close to the pony in front.

Anyone failing to check the girth before remounting each time is disqualified.

Touching a letter team competition.
With competent riders on well behaved ponies, I sometimes like to end a formal lesson with a team competition. The class are divided into two teams. Each team is lined up at the end of a long side of the arena on the outside track but facing across towards the other long side. Say one team from the corner to 'K' looking across at 'F'. While the other is placed at the other corner lined up towards the letter 'H'

looking across at 'M'. If there are several members in each team then they may extend past these letters in order to maintain a safety distance between them. The advantage of lining everybody up in this way is that the two teams are well separated from one another being placed at opposite ends of the school.

You may decide the exact form that the competition will take but, basically it involves each team member leaving their team and riding around two sides of the arena touching the furthest letter on the opposite long side as they pass it by. Having done so they then return to their team but must touch the centreline letter in front of their team before the next member of the team can start. Doing this will avoid the possibility of unsociable ponies having a go at each other as might happen if the returning rider were, for example, to have to ride close enough to touch the next competitor. Team leaders decide in which order members of a team will proceed.

You decide the gait at which the contest will be ridden. I usually start the first round at walk requiring anyone who trots to ride a small circle before they are allowed to continue. I then have the next round at a trot and, possibly, (if the riders are sufficiently skilled) a part of the following round at canter.

Very often I add a cone at either corner and have the riders riding a circle around one or both cones. The riders of each team will be passing one another but since they have been very firmly told to **always** pass 'left hand to left hand' and to allow a generous distance between them as they pass, there is little danger of a anyone being kicked. Further more I am continually watching them and have placed myself in such a position that I can quickly take hold of a rein should anyone have a problem. I also give a commentary which adds a certain *frisson* to the proceedings.

If you let it be known that a 'race' of this sort *might* take place at the end of the proceedings, and the previous exercises have been well ridden, this usually means that you will have great attention and effort put in by your pupils at the beginning of the lesson.

Traditional games for really little ones.

All these games must only be performed with the reins knotted over the pony's neck and an experienced helper holding the pony. Further more the helper must ensure that *they watch the child* at all times and steady him or her should the child show any tendency to become unbalanced. It is also a good idea to have one child who has done the movement before, demonstrate to the rest of the class.

Round the world.

Round the world. In this game the rider is encouraged to place one leg first over the pommel twisting their bodies around until they have completed a complete circuit of the saddle.

Half scissors.

For this game the youngster is asked to again place one leg across the pommel so that they are sitting with both legs on the same side of the pony. They must then twist their bodies so that they now have the tummy across the saddle with the legs hanging down on the same side. After which they then swing one leg around so that they are able to return to a normal sitting position.

Full scissors.

This is a much more complicated movement and I do not recommend it for a very young child and certainly not when riding a pony that has a sensitive back.

For this movement the child throws its torso forward and as it does so the body and legs are twisted around so that momentarily the child is facing backwards. This is followed by leaning back against the pony's neck and as they do so the legs are crossed again as the child twists round once more to return to the original correct position.

These games may be performed individually or as a race to see who can finish first. They are extremely popular, once children clearly understand what they have to do. But I repeat that they should never be played without an assistant for each pony and a good safe distance between everyone.

More involved basics.

These may be built upon to include a dismounting on the wrong side and re-mounting on the correct side once, twice or thrice, (or any other combination that you may choose). You must be very strict to ensure that no child dismounts or mounts on a side that you have not specified. It is also useful for instilling safety rules, e.g. Not to let go of the reins, *Never to go behind the back of a pony* as they run from one side to the other for re-mounting. Always check the girth before re-mounting

Before I start a game I always have the class recount these rules. I ask 'What must you *never* do when moving around a pony'? Reply to be shouted out by everyone '*Never go behind*'. 'What must you *always* do before you mount'? Reply '*Always check the girth*'. In this way, if repeated often enough, the rules are learnt, never to be forgotten.

Games to be played away from the stables.

A written competition.

This is something to give the class while they are away from the riding school. You give everyone a copy of say, William Cowper's John Gilpin poem and ask everyone to write a script from the point of view of a newsreader. I suggest something along the following lines.

'In the next four weeks, if you have time, please write a script as though you were a television newsreader about to give the evening news describing this 'exciting' event of John Gilpin being carted by his horse all the way from Islington to Ware and back again. Please include interviews with the wife and any other members of the family whom you think may have anything useful say in order to 'spice up' the event.

Also you may include, during your newscast, the view of an 'expert' (say who they are and what qualifications they have) who may deliberate and pontificate on the whys and wherefores of the event. He or she might have some view as to whether Parliament should pass legislation in order to prevent such a thing happening in the future'.

Everyone is encouraged to take part by receiving a prize. The most popular ones, I have found, are to do with grooming kit and they are quite reasonably priced.

I have to say I have some hilarious 'scripts' residing in my files, and when I read them again I still burst out laughing.

The Points of the Pony competition.

This is another way of encouraging youngsters to learn more about their ponies. Have an outline of a horse photocopied with all the 'points' indicated only by numbers. Give one sheet to each member of the class and ask them to take it away and to return with the correct points listed against each number. I also suggest that colouring the sheet could win extra points.

* Suitable for playing solo.

N.B. In any game where a rider has to touch another in order that they may have their turn. *This must be done with the hand and not the whip.*

Drawings.

Drawing 34.

Plastic plant name tag.

Drawing 36.

This is a suggested list of points of the horse. These have been divided in to two colours, one for each of two teams. Should you have more then you must split them up further and allocate more colours. In this case I have tried to divide the 'points' into equal degrees of difficulty.

Cut out each one along the dotted lines shown and stick to the plastic nametag. Place each group in a different bag.

Print in Red	Print in Green
DOCK	POINT OF CROUP
LOINS	BACK
WITHERS	CREST
POLL	FORELOCK
CHEEK	NOSTRIL
ERGOT	ZYGOMATIC RIDGE
JUGULAR GROOVE	SUPRA ORBITAL FOSSA
POINT OF SHOULDER	THROAT
STIFLE	SHEATH
FROG	CHIN GROOVE
POINT OF ELBOW	FOREARM
KNEE	CANNON BONE
FETLOCK	PASTERN
CORONET	WALL OF HOOF
HEEL	HOCK
POINT OF HOCK	GASKIN
TAIL	BREAST
THIGH	FLANK
8 TRUE	10 FALSE
BELLY	CHESTNUT
EARS	EYE
MANE	MUZZLE

Drawing no. 34 Preparing plastic plant name tags.

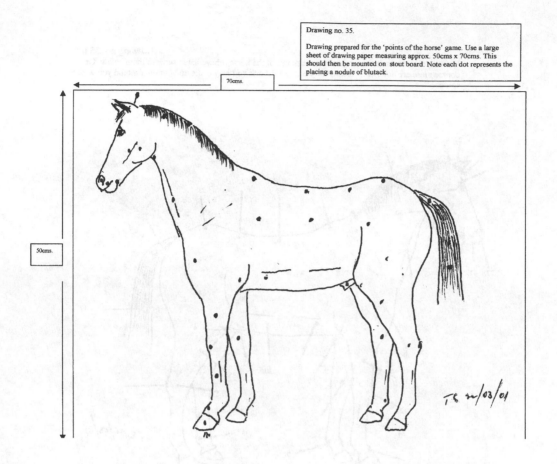

Drawing no. 35.

Drawing prepared for the 'points of the horse' game. Use a large sheet of drawing paper measuring approx. 50cms x 70cms. This should then be mounted on stout board. Note each dot represents the placing a nodule of blutack.

70cms.

50cms.

In case you are a little rusty regarding the points of the horse, I have listed some of them below. Of course these are not by any means the complete list and you may make up your own should you wish to so do.

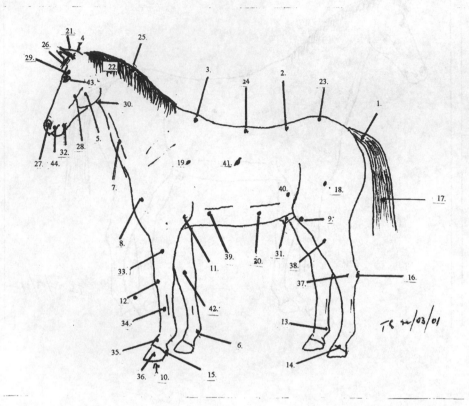

1. Dock	23. Point of croup
2. Loins	24 Back
3. Withers	25. Crest
4. Poll	26. Forelock
5. Cheek	27. Nostril
6. Ergot	28. Zygomatic ridge
7. Jugular groove	29. Supra orbital fossa
8. Point of shoulder	30. Throat
9. Stifle	31. Sheath
10. Frog	32. Chin groove
11. Point of elbow	33. Forearm
12. Knee	34. Cannon bone
13. Fetlock	35. Pastern
14. Coronet	36. Wall of hoof
15. Heel	37. Hock
16. Point of hock	38. Gaskin
17. Tail	39. Breast
18. Thigh	40. Flank
19. 8 true	41. 10 false
20. Belly	42. Chestnut
21. Ears	43. Eye
22. Mane	44. Muzzle

35 Drawing prepared for the 'points of the horse' game. and
35a. Drawing showing the 'points of the horse'.

Diagrams.

The getting home to base game.   Figure. 110

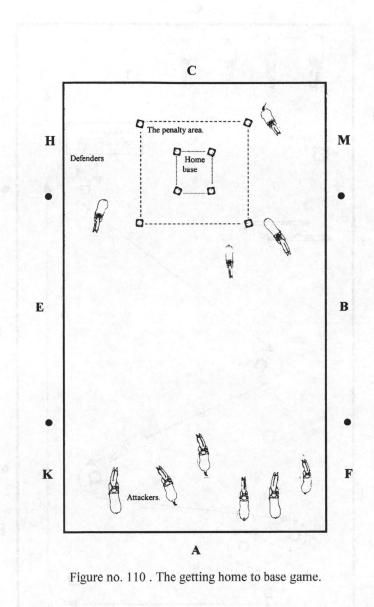

Figure no. 110 . The getting home to base game.

Figure 111 (a).

Obstacle course against the clock. (Early rounds).
Horses may be lined up out of the way along a short end of the arena. The way in which you position them depends on the size of the arena and the space that is available to you. Whatever you decide you must make sure that there is sufficient room for riders to leave and rejoin the ride in safety.

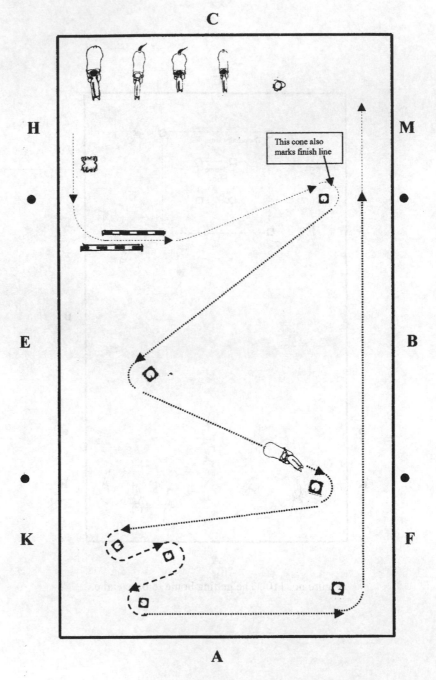

This cone also marks finish line

Figure no. 111a. Obstacle course against the clock (early rounds).

Obstacle course against the clock. (Later rounds).
Where the higher gaits are involved it is a good idea to have the ride lined up around a corner of the arena. This will provide more space for those completing the course.
Walk.......... Rising trot .... Sitting trot _ _ _ _ _ Canter — ··· — ·· — ··

Figure 111 (b).

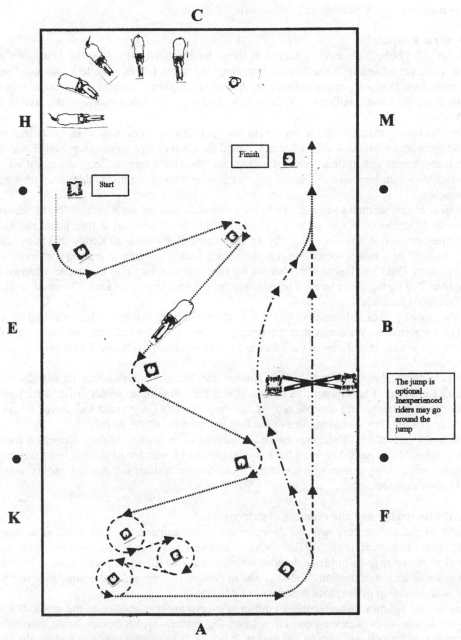

Figure no. 111b. Obstacle course against the clock (later rounds).

405

Chapter 26

Stories to entertain

This chapter is all about having something 'up your sleeve' which you may use on those days when it is very hot. Your horses and probably your clients have been working very hard and all would appreciate a rest. Rather than have them walking around doing nothing you may tell them one of the following tales. My clients seem to find them both entertaining and informative and they do help to pass the time during which the horses may rest before starting on another series of exercises.

The racehorse Eclipse. *1

In 1764, on All Fools Day, a mare named Spilleta, having been served by the Duke of Cumberland's' stallion Marske gave birth to a foal, which was given the name Eclipse. Spilleta had raced only once and was beaten but she was a great granddaughter of Lord Godolphin's Arabian. (The Godolphin Arabian was one of the three founding Stallions in Weatherby's studbook. The other two were the Byerly Turk and the Darley Arabian).

At first Eclipse proved to be a very fiery and perhaps to some extent an uncontrollable horse. A Smithfield meat trader called William Wildman, paid for seventy-five guineas for him. Since the horse was so difficult and horses at that time were not trained until they were four or five years old, it was decided that instead of gelding him he would be loaned to a roughrider who rode him at all hours. The man was a well-known poacher.

The effect of this seemed to change the horse's character and on the 3rd May 1769 he was entered in the Noblemen and Gentlemen's £50 plate at Doncaster. This event was run in four heats and Eclipse having well won the first heat it was announced by an Irishman called Dennis O'Kelley that he would predict the order in which *all* the runners would finish in the second heat. This bet was greeted with much hilarity by all the other punters. But O'Kelley won his bet for the race was won by Eclipse by what is known as a distance i.e. more than 240 yards. Therefore the other horses were considered unplaced. The result being declared as Eclipse first the rest *nowhere.*

O'Kelley having already bought a half share in the horse from Wildman, then acquired the other half for £1000. He suggested to Wildman that the price be either £1000 or £2000. He took three £1000 notes, placed two in one pocket and one in the other and asked Wildman to choose. Unfortunately Wildman chose the wrong one!

Lord Grosvenor, later, offered 11,000 guineas for Eclipse but this was turned down. On another occasion O'Kelley let it be known that he would sell for £20,000, an annuity of £500 a year for life and three brood mares. In the end Eclipse retired, unbeaten, to O'Kelleys' stud and served mares for a fee of fifty guineas. His progeny included three of the first five winners of the Derby.

Towards the end of his life he was moved to Canons (in Edgware, Middx. The estate on which I live) where he died aged 25. After his death he was dissected and it was found that his heart weighed 14lbs! His carcass was buried in the garden of a house in Dukes Avenue and his skeleton can still be seen today in the Natural History museum.

Eadweard Muybridge and the moment of suspension. *2

The middle of the 19th century saw the development of the camera. This has resulted in many significant historical events being captured 'on film'. The American Civil War is one such example. As the century progressed so men strove to improve the tool which had at first merely allowed them to record a scene but with out any suggestion of motion. The idea was to capture this motion and in time they had progressed to the point of the creation of the motion picture i.e. 'Movies'

As instructors we may consider that we observe everything that goes on in the arena. We spend such a goodly part of our lives watching our clients and the manner of our horses going that we come to the conclusion that not much will escape our notice. It is true to say that, despite this view, the fact is that our eyes are actually quite inferior instruments for exact observation. What you may think has this to do with equitation? This failure to see with precision has resulted in an error that has persisted for thousands of years and that concerns the motion of the horse canter and gallop.

Edward James Muggeridge was born in Kingston, Surrey in the U.K. in 1830. Towards the end of the 19th century he left England for the State of California in the USA. For some reason he considered that he would make a better impression if he called himself Eadweard Muybridge (pronounced Mybridge). an Anglo- Saxon rendering of his name. Despite working as a cartographer he continued his intense interest in photography. In 1869 he invented one of the first shutters for the camera. He certainly came to the attention of Leland Stanford an ex-governor of the State. Stanford had a string of racehorses and was very proud of one in particular his trotter, "Occident". He wished to be able to share, with his friends, the ability to contemplate the horse "in action". In 1873 Muybridge was called in to photograph the animal trotting. Motion at this speed had never before been achieved, but Muybridge was suggested as someone who could solve this dilemma. He considered the matter most gravely. Bed sheets were hung up all along the track in order that an outstanding image might be captured (the horse having been familiarised with this arrangement, so that it did not take fright). A new shutter was devised, consisting of *two* leaves operated by a spring thus giving an opening of an eighth of an inch for a five-hundredth of a second. "Occident" in motion was, indeed, clearly captured on film.

Unfortunately Muybridges' work was interrupted by his being tried for the murder of his wife's' lover. Though acquitted he left the country and did not return to resume his work until 1877. The speed of his shutter had by now increased 1/1000 part of a second. Eventually he took a photograph that he thought was good enough for publication. Unfortunately he explained in his letter, which accompanied the photograph sent to the newspaper the San Francisco *Alta* that the picture had been 'retouched as is customary at this time with all first class photographic work'. The authenticity of the photograph was immediately questioned. So he started all over again, this time using twelve cameras spaced apart with the shutters operated by an electric solenoid switch, which were activated by a strings running across the track. The shutter speed was now claimed to be less than the two-thousandth part of a second. The horses, at a gallop, breasted the strings breaking them in sequence and thus allowing, for the first time ever, a series of negatives being made that clearly showed the action of the canter – with the legs all off the ground and *bunched* under the horse's' belly. No more rocking horses with the legs flying out in front and behind as they had been painted for so many centuries! The photographs were regarded as absurd!

Antoine de Pluvinel (1555 to 1620) and Louis XIII. *8

These stories are to be found in Misconceptions and Simple Truths in Dressage by Dr. H.L.M van Schaik and Masters of Equitation by W. Sydney Felton. (I have made slight adaptations for dramatic purposes).

Louis XIII started to learn the art of equitation with Antoine de Pluvinel when he was still Dauphin (the French 16th century equivalent of the English Prince of Wales). In fact it is my belief that it was he who features in the old English folk song 'A frog who would a wooing go', for it has been said that he came over to England to seek the hand of Queen Elizabeth I - who sent him packing. This story would, to my mind fit in with his personality, though I am told that in fact the suitor was the Duke of Alençon.

However to the tale. When Louis became King he got a bit full of himself, spending vast sums of money putting on elaborate fancy dress parties. So it should not be surprising that one day in the Royal Ménage, crowded, as it probably was, by courtiers all dressed in their swanky elegant clothes with large hats decorated by Ostrich feathers, that he should try to catch out his instructor Antoine de Pluvinel. He asked Pluvinel what he looked for first of his pupil. His riding master replied, "That he be an elegant rider" ('Qu'il soit bel homme de cheval'). "There! You are always on about being a good horseman but when you get down to it you are, simply, looking for elegance ! What is the difference?" said the King turning to all the assembled courtiers who proceeded to smirk at what they thought would be Pluvinel's discomfort. However Pluvinel, bowing low and doffing his hat with great elegance, replied. 'It would be very embarrassing if a good rider was not also elegant but there are many elegant riders who are not good riders'!

L'Instuction du Roi.
*11

It is interesting to note that Louis XIII told Pluvinel to make a note of their conversations during the king's riding lessons. Pluvinel died, in 1620, just before he had finished the manuscript. He had made arrangements with a talented Dutch artist, Crispin de Pas a drawing instructor at Pluvinel's academy to produce engravings for the book. The manuscript for the book, though not completed, was entrusted to a friend of Pluvinel's, Rene Menou de Charniray. After Pluvinel's death, Crispin de Pas finding himself in financial difficulties approached a servant of Pluvinel named Peyrol in order to obtain an earlier but discarded draft of the manuscript. In 1623 he used this together with his engravings to publish a book with the title 'Manege Royale'. When Charniray found out he was most upset by the publication of such an obviously bad text. He then undertook a revision of the text that he had been given and in so doing completely rewrote the manuscript, eventually publishing it in 1625 with the title 'L'Instruction de Roi en l'exercise de monte a cheval'. What we now call 'L'Instruction du Roi'. The original edition did not have Crispin de Pas' superb engravings but the two were brought together in latter editions. This is very fortunate for us for it is the beautiful engravings that make the book exceptional.

François Robichon de La Guérinière (1688 – 1751).

Born in Essay a small town near Aleçon in France. He was much troubled by the lack of scientific understanding when training the horse. In 1731 he published his book *École de cavalrie* and this demonstrates his clarity of thought. In the first paragraph of chapter one, part two of the School of Horsemanship he says, ' All science and arts have their principals and rules, by means of which one makes discoveries leading to their perfection. Horsemanship it seems is the one art for which one needs only practise. He goes on to discus, in great detail, the movement for which he is famous, the shoulder-in.

The correct position.

This is quite an interesting subject for discussion, especially after having mentioned Pluvinel above. What exactly is the *correct* position? van Schaik having talked about Pluvinel's remarks to the king goes on to say 'that this conversation took place in the 17th century when nobody had ever heard of dressage competitions. Unfortunately, today it is fact that elegant riders are seen, rarely, and that good riders are not at all embarrassed by the fact that they are very often not elegant riders'. However he then finishes by saying that he is convinced that the functionally correct position is an elegant position.

But let us now consider Wilhelm Müseler in Riding Logic. *10 What does he have to say of the 'Correct Seat'? He provides no illustration of the position. Instead his remarks are set within the black outline of a rectangle. And he says "In order to emphasise the danger which lies in the over-valuation of a 'prototype' no *picture* is shown of the 'correct seat! BALANCE – LOOSENESS- and FOLLOWING THE MOVEMENT OF THE HORSE can hardly be shown graphically. Nor can 'feel' be depicted. By omitting a picture, however the importance of a good seat is not belittled, but particular attention is drawn to those elements, which really matter".

And thus we come full circle to the following remarks of van Schaik *8. 'The position is functionally correct when the rider does not disturb the horse, and when he is able to give the aids in a discreet but emphatic way, at the correct moment to the correct spot, at the correct strength. The rider will not disturb the horse when he has an independent seat. He does not have to use the reins to stay on the horse; his hands are totally independent of the movements of the horse; he never has 'dancing hands' and he never yanks the horse in the mouth because of an unexpected movement.' Having an independent seat means also that the rider is able to move in unison with the movement of the horse, and to keep his centre of gravity as much in line as possible with the horse's centre of gravity. The rider sits at all times as lightly as possible on the horse, for it is evident that the less of a burden a rider is for the horse, the better the horse can perform.' These are the remarks of a world-class *dressage* judge and for me his remarks apply equally to *all* riders, be they dressage competitors, jockeys or weekend riders.

The Olecranon process.

This joint is well described in the 'Horse in Action' By R.H. Smythe. *9. It consists of the Ulna and Fossa. Briefly it is the locking joint in the elbow of the horses' foreleg. In the wild it is not part of a horse's nature to sleep lying down. The reason for this is obvious if one observes in its box the bit of a struggle and the length of time and that it takes a horse to rise. When attacked by a predator out in the wild it could be the difference between life and death. Lying down is something that is encouraged by man. By nature the horse dozes, standing up. But what is it that prevents a horse from falling over as it does so? It is this elbow joint. We have one in our own elbows. Observe a competitor lifting weights in the Olympics. The lift is not considered good until the competitor has locked the joint (the ulna) in his elbow. In other words stretched the arm to its full height.

When the horse stands squarely on all four limbs most of its weight is distributed over the forelimbs. The locking joint means that it may stand and actually relax a hind limb without falling over. The joint does not unlock, unless it either flexes its hock or moves a hind leg forward. As the weight is transferred to the hindquarters so the Olecranon process unlocks and this enables a horse to take a step forward with the forelimb. I have actually read in another book that this mechanism is in the hind limb. I have also heard one eminent 'expert' say the same thing on a television programme. Well the patella (knee bone) of the hind limb does indicate the *possibility* of locking (there is a groove in the femur into which it can slide). But it seems to me that this can only be really effective if the leg is fully extended behind (as one might see when a horse, being shown in hand, stands before the judge). I have never seen a horse doze when standing in this manner. Further more I have carried out dissections on the carcasses of several horses and having separated the lower end of the humerus and the upper end of the radius together have actually locked the forelimb. It goes together with a loud sucking noise and it is then quite difficult to flex. I have never managed the same effect with the hind limb.

Another result of this locking mechanism may be observed during jumping. It is essential that a horse, landing after a jump, does so with its weight on only *one* of its forelegs. Should it land with *both* forelegs touching the ground at the same time, then it will not be able to unlock the olecranon thus enabling it to move one leg forward to accommodate the rest of its body following behind. The result is that it will have no option but to cartwheel and ultimately end up on its nose or neck. This is what is known as a 'peck'

The origin of the word canter.
This description of the three-time gait arose as a result of travellers making their pilgrimage to Canterbury. They realised that with this nice steady lolloping pace the horse could make good progress for quite long periods without getting tired (some suggest around three hours at a steady 20mph. A maximising of energy consumption, something that your clients might care to think about. Further more it was a more comfortable pace, for the rider, than trotting.

The forward seat.
Originally derived through the English love of horse racing. This spilled over into France towards the end of the 18th century causing much concern to those French Masters who believed that the 'classical' way was the only way. The Napoleonic wars however brought about much anti-English feeling and the idea that this could be incorporated as part of a general system of equitation, lapsed for many years to come.

Federico Caprilli. *14
The general acceptance of the forward position, as a part of combined training, could be said to have taken place in 1904. The famous horseman, the Italian, Captain Federico Caprilli, developed it. Born in Leghorn 1868 he ultimately became a cavalry officer. While a student of equitation his professors described his abilities as a 'less than moderate horseman'! This view lasted but a short while, sent for a second term to Pinerolo Cavalry School he passed second out of the whole class.

At Tor di Quinto, a 'finishing school' for military students of equitation, where he went, firstly as a student and then, in 1894, as an instructor, he became convinced that the classical position was totally un-suited to cross country riding. Returning to Pinerolo in 1895 he introduced the *Scivolo* (slide) and demonstrated the advantage of going forward as against the accepted form of sitting well backwards as his horse negotiated this very steep hazard.

For many years Caprilli's views were fiercely opposed by most of the riding world. It was not until 1904 due to the success he had achieved in show jumping, racing and cross-country riding, that this brilliant man was allowed to teach his method to students. Barely had this revolution in style got underway, when its creator died. In 1907 while out riding his horse, at the walk, he was seen to sway in the saddle and fall to the ground, he never recovered consciousness and died from injuries to his skull.

This is what he had to say (in so many words) regarding the rider's hands (any rider!).
*41. 'Thus relieved of all other preoccupations the horse pays undivided attention to the work in hand, and gradually learns how to employ his strength to the best advantage and to the improvement of his action and condition. Let us remember that the horse submits of his own free will, without the necessity of forcing him into any attitude or balance. On the other hand when a horse is ***over-ruled by his rider, who by so doing causes him pain***, he will naturally enough, be continually on the ***alert for pretexts and occasions to avoid this control,*** dedicating his every thought to this purpose. Let us, also, never forget that when a horse defends himself, is restless, bolts, baulks or in any other way opposes our demands, he does so almost invariably to escape pain inflicted on him, or out of fear and anticipation of pain. This pain, or recollection of pain, is often the cause of violent reactions or, at best, even when submitting, of a horse not employing

409

his strength naturally, thereby wearing himself out in superfluous and harmful efforts'.

He goes on to say, talking about his principles and method, that their defective application defeats the very purpose aimed at, namely that of bringing the horse to hand and of always beings its master, a result impossible of attainment if the riders actions are rigid, causing the horse to *lean on the hand,* to stiffen and frequently to react.

Now I wonder how many of our clients with 'dancing' hands and involuntary movements that are often interpreted by the horse as incomprehensible aids, realise that when their horses start to 'play up', they and they alone are responsible for these reactions?

Captain V.S. Littauer.
I mention Captain Littauer as an example of those who take a method to their hearts and advocate its use for everything. This gentleman, originally an officer in the Russian Imperial Cavalry, escaped to the USA after the Russian revolution. Setting up a riding school, in New York, under the name 'Boots and Saddles' with two of his fellow officers, he then started to teach the forward principals in earnest. In his first book 'The Forward Seat' he goes to great lengths to put forward the Italian principals which now not only involved going forward but also did away with classical exercises substituting instead movement over difficult terrain for improving a horses balance. In 1939 he published another book titled 'More about the Forward Seat' *35, in which he explained that he had come round to the view that it was not advisable to do away completely with classical principals but that a combination of the two methods was advisable.

Tongue Twisters.
The following are useful for a nervous client to try and recite whilst performing any movement. The effect is that in order to say the tongue twister correctly they must take in a good lungful of air and also exhale it. This helps with those who hold their breath. Furthermore in so doing they become so involved in what they are about that they loose a great deal of their tension.

If Moses supposes his toeses are posies of roses
Then Moses supposes erroneously,
For Moses' toeses aren't posies of roses,
As Moses supposes his toeses to be!

Peter Piper picked a peck of pickled peppers,
If Peter Piper picked a peck of pickled peppers,
Where is the peck of pickled peppers?
That Peter Piper picked?

William Cavendish the first Duke of Newcastle (1592-1676)
Though a wealthy man he was a staunch supporter of Charles I. Thus when Charles was executed, he had to flee and ended up in Antwerp, where, in order to make ends meet, he opened a riding school. That he was already an excellent horseman (before his exile) is not in doubt but I am sure that in turn his European contemporaries influenced him. In 1658 he published his first book 'La Methode et Invention Nouvelle de Dresser les Chevaux' later translated into English (after his return to England upon the Restoration) under the title 'A General system of Horsemanship'. As one might imagine his views did differ from those of the French. For example he did not recommend the use of pillars in training the horse. He was a very independent thinker of great intelligence and he did share common ground with his European counterparts in so far as he truly believed in abolition of force in the training of the horse.

His logic is quite impeccable. He writes in his second book 'A New Method to Dress Horses' (published in 1667). 'It is a long time before a boy knows his alphabet, longer before he has learned to spell and several years before he can read distinctly. And yet there are some people who, as soon as they have got up upon a young horse, entirely undressed or untaught, fancy that by beating and spurring they will make him a dressed horse in one morning only! I would fain ask such stupid people, whether by beating a boy, they could teach him to read, without first shewing him his alphabet, sure they would beat the boy to death before they would teach him to read. Don't then expect more understanding from a horse than a man.

Now these views are particularly apt for livery owners. An intelligent owner can actually turn these words about as it were. Indeed they do have to teach their horses the alphabet (the basic aids) but having done so they may then use that alphabet to create words and indeed a whole language that are personal to themselves and their horse alone. That can be real magic.

Bibliography.

*1.

A History of Flat Racing. Edition 1978. Edited and part written by Michael Seth-Smith. Chapter 6 - Eclipse page 24.

*2.

The History of Photography. Beaumont Newhall. Fourth edition 1964 second printing 1971. Chapter 7. Page 84.

*3

The Manual of Horsemanship. The Official Manual of the Pony Club. 11th edition 1970. Chapter 27. Pages 312 –316.

*4.

The Manual of Horsemanship. The Official Manual of the Pony Club. 11th edition 1970. Chapter 6. Pages 48 – 58.

*5

François Robichon de la Guérinière. School of Horsemanship. English trans. 1994 Tracy Boucher. Pt. Two. Chapter 1. Page 75

*6

Waldemar Seunig. Horsemanship. 3rd edition 1956 translated by Leonard Mins. Pt. One. Chapter 1. Page 25.

*7

Wynmalen. Horse Breeding and Stud Management. 1950. Pages 177-179

*8

Dr. H.L.M van Schaik. Misconceptions and Simple Truths in Dressage. 1st edition 1986 Chapter 1. Page 19.

*9

R.H. Smythe. MRCVS Horses in Action. 1963. Chapter 1. The origins of the horse, page 19.

*10

Wilhelm Müseler. Riding Logic. First published in English in 1937. Chapter 1. The training of the rider. Page 4. Fig 1.

*11

W. Sidney Felton. Masters of Equitation 1962. Chapter 4. Page 30.

*12.

The Manual of Horsemanship. The Official Manual of the Pony Club. 11th edition 1970. Chapter 27. Pages 301 - 302

*13.

Lt.-Col. M.F.McTaggart DSO the Art of Riding. First published 1931. My edition 8th 1951. Dust Cover illustration.

*14.

The Caprilli Papers translated and edited by Major Piero Santini. Published by J.A.Allen 1967.

*15.

The Manual of Horsemanship. The Official Manual of the Pony Club. 11th edition 1970. Chapter 27. Pages 204 – 325.

*16

Dr. Reiner Klimke. Video - The Dressage Training. Pts. 1 and 2.

*17

Stephen Budiansky. The Nature of Horses. 1st edition 1997. Sociology page 85.

*18

The Association of British Riding Schools – Drills and Formation Riding Compiled by Shirley Renowden F.A.B.R.S.

*19

The British Horse Society and Pony Club Instructors, Hand Book 4th edition 1968.

*20

The B.H.S. Instructors' handbook 4th edition 1968. Pages 20 - 51.

*21

Stephen Budiansky. The Nature of Horses. 1st edition 1997. Chapter 2.

*22

Henry Wynmalen. Equitation. Second edition 1952 – reprinted 1963. Epilogue – The True Secrets Of The Art Of Riding, pages 193-194.

*23

Charles Harris. FIH FABRS FBHS. The Fundamentals of Riding. 1st Edition 1985. Part four. Lunging the rider page 98.

*24

Sydney Galvayne. The XXth Century Book of the Horse. 1st edition page 23, The Art of 'Galvayning'.

*25

Charles M Holmes F.W.C.F. The Principles and Practise of Horse- Shoeing 1928 published by the Farriers' Journal Publishing Co. Ltd. 1949. 'The White Line' page 56.

*26

Henry Wynmalen. Equitation. Second edition 1952 – reprinted 1963. Chapter XII Exercises from the Halt pages 89 -91.

*27

R.H. Smythe. MRCVS Horses in Action. 1963. Chapters 4 and 5.

*28

The Manual of Horsemanship. The Official Manual of the Pony Club. 11th edition 1970. Chapter 11. Pages 94 – 101.

*29

Margot Lawrence. Flyers and Stayers. 1980. Chapter 1. Great rides of long ago. Pages 17 – 20.

*30

Stephen Budiansky. The Nature of Horses. 1st edition 1997. Chapter 4 Socioecology page 95.

*31

Stephen Budiansky. The Nature of Horses. 1st edition 1997. Chapter 4 . Socioecology page 87.

*32

Henry Wynmalen. Dressage. Chapter 7. The seat.

*33
Stephen Budiansky. The Nature of Horses. 1st edition 1997. Chapter 9 assume a spherical horse page 217 - Mobilising energy.
*34
V. S. Littauer. The Forward Seat. (Modern Horsemanship for beginners).
*35
Captain V. S. Littauer. More about the Forward Seat. First published November 1939. My copy reprinted in 1947 from the reset edition published in October 1945.
*36
W. Sidney Felton. Masters of Equitation 1962. Chapter 4. Page 38.
*37
W. Sidney Felton. Masters of Equitation 1962. Chapter 1. Page 13.
*38
W. Sidney Felton. Masters of Equitation 1962. Chapter 4. Pages 34 and 35.
*39
Lockie Richards. Dressage. 5th impression 1984. Chapter 3. Pages 22 and 23.
*40
Jennie Loriston-Clarke and Carol Wicken. An Illustrated Guide to Dressage. 1st edition 1987.
*41
The Caprilli Papers translated and edited by Major Piero Santini. Published by J.A.Allen 1967.
Chapter 1. Page 19. Para 2 and page 21.
*42
Brig. Gen. Harry D. Chamberlin. Training Hunters Jumpers and Hacks. 2nd edition 1976. Chapter III. Page 105.
*43 British Dressage Rules 1998. Notes on the interpretation of Dressage Test Sheets. Page. 48
*44 Black's Veterinary Dictionary. 6th edition 1962. Page 560.

Recommended Reading
Henry Wynmalen. Horse Breeding and Stud management.
Henry Wynmalen. Dressage.
Henry Wynmalen. Equitation.
Henry Wynmalen. The Horses Paces.
Charles Harris. FIH FABRS FBHS. The Fundamentals of Riding.
Gunnar Hedlund. This is Riding.
The Manual of Horsemanship. The Official Manual of the Pony Club.
The Great Horse Omnibus. Edited by Thurston Macauley. 1957 page 322 William Cowper. – The Diverting History of John Gilpin. I heartily recommend that all who teach and those that ride should read this narrative poem. For in its highly amusing verses one comes across so many of the problems that are suffered by the weekend rider.
Silvia Stanier. The art of Lunging.

Definitions and an explanation of terms used.
ABRS. Stands for - The Association of British Riding Schools.

Across the arena.
Means riding across the width of the arena. You will need to specify exactly where you wish this to be. If it is to be the centre, then you must say 'From 'E' to 'B'.

An Aid. - A means of passing a signal to a horse.

Bailing out.
The act of a rider purposely falling off a horse in order to avoid what they consider to be a dangerous situation.

Behind the bit.
A horse that for some reason or other does not like the pressure of the bit on the bars of its mouth (in this context perhaps because the rider is continually pulling on the reins). It therefore shakes its head or the bit and tries to evade it. Sometimes it does so by tucking its head right in to its chest so that the rider believes he has the horse 'collected and on the bit'.

Bend.
The curve of a horse throughout its body from head to tail. Very few horses are able to provide a great deal of bend throughout the spine in the rib area and many riders end up simply asking for bend from the neck.

Bit.
A device usually made of steel but at other times of rubber or other materials and placed in the horse's mouth to assist with control (there are dozens of different designs).

BHS. Stands for - The British Horse Society.

Bracing the back.
I have, sometimes, found that pupils do not understand exactly what this means. The expression is, simply, a tightening of the back muscles in the small of the back in conjunction with the abdominal muscles as a *part* of the aid given to go forward. This would apply, for example, during an upward transition from halt to walk, trot or canter. Once the aid has been obeyed these same muscles then flex very slightly following and encouraging the movement. Similarly this same 'bracing' will also take place when the rider asks for a downward transition. It will, of course, cease as soon as the rider appreciates that the horse is about to obey. The effect of this action causes the hips to be thrust forward *very slightly*. It is the basic foundation of every aid.

Bridge – making one.
A useful method for riders, especially children, who do not have much physical strength when riding horses that persist in putting their heads down in order to eat grass. This is simply a way of holding the reins with both hands at the same time. It is achieved by making a double loop. In other words the loop of each separate rein is placed one inside the other. This double loop is then held in both hands with each thumb pointing at the other. At the very first sign of the horse putting its head down, the rider simply presses both hands down against the withers. Thus the horse is using its strength against itself.

Bridle. - A system of straps put together, usually in order to hold a bit in place.

Boots (for horses).
Coverings made out of a variety of materials, which are used to protect the horses' legs in order to protect it from striking itself.

Canter -the.
The canter is a three-time movement.
The legs move diagonally consecutively and then diagonally simultaneously.
(I.e. the inside foreleg – the leading leg – followed by the outside hind leg – the strike off leg – followed by the inside hind leg and outside foreleg together).
When the regular three-time rhythm is established, the leading leg is the last in the sequence and is followed by a half-beat – the moment of suspension – when all the legs are in the air.

Carted – being.
The act of being taken from one place to another, by a horse that is in a direction or at a gait that is against your will. Or to put it more kindly. A term used to indicate that the horse has departed at whatever pace it fancies (usually canter) without first asking the permission of the rider.

Circle in the centre of the arena.
One that has its centre at 'X'. In a standard arena this will have a diameter of 20m. and its tangential points will be 'E' and 'B'. The circumference will also cross the centre line at points situated exactly half way across the quarter and three-quarter lines This means that a rider will ride exactly one stride only on the track at all these points.
Do bear in mind that the size of any circle is what you make it. Thus if you are working in an arena that is smaller than standard and you give the command to ride a circle of half the arena, then this will obviously be less than 20m. diameter.

Changing the rein.
Going around an arena, first in one direction and then in another.

Circle of half the arena.
A circle at either end of the area with points at either '**A**', **Black dot**, '**X**', **Black dot**, returning to '**A**'. In a standard dressage arena as mentioned above this will obviously have a diameter of 20m.

Client (see also student).
Someone who attends a riding school either to learn to ride or to improve their riding skills.

Collected.
A horse ridden so that the hocks come well under it thus enabling it to flex at the poll whilst carrying the bit in a relaxed jaw. It is thus able to respond to the lightest of aids given by the rider.

Collection.
A horse responding with a shortening of his stride in answer to the light application of the fingers on the rein as pressure from the riders' seat and leg asks the horse to engage his hindquarters under him. The containment of that power.

Conformation.
Horses' make or shape. In other words the relative proportions, angle and position of its limbs and body to each other and its overall size Also the musculature and internal organs that it has in order to perform well the job that it is doing.

Counter canter – the.
Same as canter except that the outside foreleg leads. (Relative to the direction in which it moving that is). The horse is not bent in the direction that it is going and the pivoting leg is the outside hind leg instead of the inside hind. This is an exercise that should only be undertaken when the horse has developed a reasonable degree of balance. (See fig 31)

Counter shoulder-in.
A horse moving on three tracks with his quarters to the inside of the arena but not looking in the direction in which he is proceeding.

Demonstration. - A display by either Instructor or student of a particular movement or gait.

Diagonal. - From the hindquarters on one side to the forehand on the other.

Disunited canter – the.
A disunited canter is one where the sequence of the horses legs move laterally instead of diagonally. The horse will be said to be disunited behind if it appears to be leading with the correct leg and disunited in front if it leads with the outside foreleg (Again that is relative to the direction in which it is proceeding). Since the horse is balanced on two legs on the *same side* for one part of the sequence of the movement, it is possible for it to fall over.

Dressage.
To describe this term one can do no better than to resort to Henry Wynmalen. In his book 'Dressage' Wynmalen devotes his first chapter to the meaning alone.

He tells us that it means to train a horse past the point of simple usefulness. It is an ever-evolving harmony between rider and horse that is expressed in a 'lightness' that includes balance, grace and action.

Dressage test
Sometimes part of a formal examination or else a competition in which rider and horse perform a series of prescribed movements. During this time the rider may not communicate verbally with the horse. Horse and rider are judged on both fluency and accuracy.

Drill ride.
Any movement where each member of the ride moves in strict and constant relationship to all the other members, irrespective of any changes taking place.

Double bridle.
A bridle with two bits and two sets of reins.

Down the centre line.
Proceeding down the middle of the long part of the arena from either or to 'A' or 'C'

Down a quarter line.
Riding down the line that is a quarter of the distance along the short side of the arena away from the track down the long side that is already being ridden. (See fig. 49)

Down a three-quarter line.
Riding down a line parallel to the side of the arena down which the ride has just ridden but three-quarters of the way across the short side. (See fig. 49)

415

'Eyes up'.

An expression used by a rider as a warning when in class and about to embark on a particular movement. For example one may have a series of jumps set up for riders to go over individually, when they consider that they are correctly placed. Thus as they decide to go over the jump they call out 'Eyes up' as a warning to everyone else.

Exercise.

A movement or series of movements to be performed by horse and rider.

Flexing the back muscles.

The 'follow on' as it were, to the bracing of the back, mentioned above, subsequent to the horse having obeyed the aid and gone forward or halted according at the rider's request. Some riders have a problem in understanding what this means in practice. I try to make it clear by touching the rider in the small of the back with the handle of my whip in order to indicate the direction (away from my touch) that the bones and muscles should move. Occasionally the pupil, who is very stiff in the back, will either completely resist my touch or, alternatively will cause the spine to curve backwards in a hunchbacked shape, at the same time pushing the seat bones back towards the cantle of the saddle. This is not what is required at all and you must make sure that the correct movement inducing only a *very slight* forward thrust of the seat is understood and takes place. However under no circumstances should this become so exaggerated that the back becomes 'hollow'.

Flexion.

The bend of a horses' head at the poll.

Flying Change.

The change of leading leg at the canter during the moment of suspension. (The change must be in both front and hind legs).

Focused.

I feel that this use of this word requires a short explanation when used in the context of equitation. I have used it to explain the degree of mental concentration required by a *rider* not only in order to set the standard of performance that they require of the horse, but also of their own awareness as, for example, to their own correct position. I have not used it in the chapters dealing with beginners and novices (though in truth it might well be applied to the simple act of getting a horse to go from one point in the arena to another) because I do not think that it is appropriate in those circumstances where the horses' deviation from a proscribed path is probably the product of so many different factors over which, as yet, the rider has no control (poor balance and posture etc.).However when it comes to advanced riders, it is, perhaps, the single most important factor.

Gelding.

A horse that has been castrated.

Girth.

A strap running under the horse and attached by buckles to the saddle to keep it in place.

Give with the hand.

The opening of the riders' fingers, thus removing any tension on the rein, but without necessarily letting the rein go completely slack.

Going large.

This simply means sending your ride all the way round the outside track of the arena.

Good hands.

A rider who is has sufficient equine education to be able to open and close the fingers precisely so that they are able to give and take at the exact moment required and no more.

Ground line.

The placing of a pole on the ground across the base of a jump. This will help a horse judge to the height that it has to jump.

Half halt.

A, momentary, giving and taking signal with the rein (usually the outside one relative to the horse's bend).

Half Pass.

The horse moves both forwards and sideways laterally. He is looking in the direction in which he is going. The movement is carried out, across the arena, diagonally at an angle of 50°. His forehand must always lead and that means that the horse must be positioned at an angle of 37° to his line of progress. It is a movement on two tracks.

Halt the.

The horse stands foursquare and motionless

Hand - a.

A measure of a horse's height in units of four inches (10cms.).

Harrods' parcel.
This is a term that I use to describe a client who is accoutred in the most expensive riding gear imaginable. However once mounted they reveal that so far as riding a horse is concerned they are incapable of influencing the horse at all. They are simply carted around the arena as their animal follows the horse in front. Rather like an expensive object which having been purchased and deliciously wrapped, is placed in a bag to be carried around by the shopper.

Impulsion.
The term used to define the creation of energy or power, arising from the engagement of the horse's hindquarters. We tend to say 'Use your leg to create energy'. *What we mean is that your leg signals the horse to do this.*

Inside track.
Riding a good 1.5m. away from the outside track thus leaving plenty of room for another rider to pass by on the outside.

Irons.
Stirrups.

Lateral.
On the same side.

Laterally. Sideways.

Leading away.
This is a movement of the rein where the rider simple moves the hand horizontally away from the horse's neck by about two to three inches. It is useful as an added aid to direction, without necessarily changing the bend.

Leading leg.
The leg that the horse uses to initiate the canter as it creates a moment of suspension. After the first stride the leading leg appears to be the last in the sequence that again culminates in the moment of suspension.

Lead rein.
A short leather or canvas strap with a buckle at one end and a loop at the other. It is led to one side of a snaffle bit ring and then fed through to the other side running under the horse's chin and down to the leader's hand.

Leathers.
Straps used for attaching the stirrups to the saddle.

Lightening the forehand.
The action of the rider's seat and leg which cause the horse (by engaging its hind quarters further underneath its body) to move its centre of gravity further to the rear.

Livery.
A horse that is privately owned and which may be kept at the yard where you are giving instruction.

Log. - A written record.

Loop.
A movement in which a horse is asked to move away from its designated track for a prescribed number of steps and then to return once again.

Lunging cavesson. - Special bridle used for lunging.

Lunging rein.
A long line (approx. 10m. in length) usually made out of canvas or rope with a clasp at one end.

Lunging whip.
A long whip with an even longer lash, used together with a lunging rein.

Long diagonal.
Means crossing the arena from either the letters 'F' to 'H' or 'K' to 'M'. (See fig. 53).

Long rein and loose rein.
Please note a *long* rein is not a loose rein the former maintains contact but allows the horse to stretch the neck and with the rider's encouragement, start to track up. The latter means that the rider holds the rein by the buckle only.

Manége. An enclosed rectangular area used for schooling, and generally marked out with letters.

Mare. - An adult female horse.

Martingales.
Additional straps of various designs attached between the girth and either rein or noseband.

Medium circle.
In a standard dressage arena, one that measures 10m. in diameter. If ridden from an outside track, down a long side, its extreme point must be the centre line.

Moment of suspension.
A point when the horse's legs are 'in the air'.

Mounting Block. A platform soundly constructed out of either wood or plastic (portable) or stone (fixed) about 30 –40cm in high. Utilised as an aid to mounting a horse. This may incorporate steps on either side to gain easy access to a section that is high enough for a rider to mount without having to raise a leg too high. It is a good idea to use this whenever possible as it helps to lessen the strain across the horses back caused by the weight of the rider's body as they lift themselves when mounting. It is especially useful for short people mounting large horses or those who through age are somewhat infirm

Neck strap.
A wide leather loop led around the horse's neck so that it rests loosely in front of the chest. Clients should use this to hold on to whenever they feel insecure. The use of this strap will help to prevent a client using the rein to either support themselves or as a psychological prop and thus avoiding much discomfiture for the horse.

Numnah
A pad placed across the horses back and underneath the saddle.

On the bit.
When a horse takes a light but temperate feel on the reins and begins to flex at the poll.

Part Livery.
A horse that is privately owned but whose owner allows it to be kept out in a field at certain agreed times.

Pacing or Ambling trot - the alternative to the diagonal.
In chapter 6, I mentioned that one should explain the rising trot – the trot – In medieval times horses were frequently trained to be 'pacers' or 'amblers'. This is a lateral movement that is unnatural to the horse for it moves it's legs simultaneously and laterally in other words 'pairs' but on the same side.

One may still come across such horses today. I believe that they are used in some forms of trotting races in both the USA and Australia. The reason for this is that these races involve pulling a jockey on a form of two wheeled cart called a Sulky and the movement is not so conducive to a horse under such pressure breaking into a canter, which it may well so do when trotting with diagonal pairs. However to revert to our medieval riders, the pacer does provide a very comfortable form of progression, since the rider instead of 'posting' – going up and down – simply sways from side to side. Unfortunately there is a tendency to an inherent instability in this form of motion since the horse is continuously suspended first on one pair of legs *laterally* with no support from the other side. Should it stumble on an uneven surface, it would have no option but to fall over. The English devised the method of rising and sitting, known as posting or the trot a' l'Anglaise and thus restored a measure of equilibrium without too much discomfort.

Passada.
A lateral movement in which the horse, being extremely collected, moves laterally (both forward and sideways on a curve) looking in the direction in which it is going.

Pirouette.
A circular movement performed by a horse, at either walk or canter, in which its forehand describes a large circle about its hindquarters while these describe only a very small circle (the horse is looking where it is going).

Poll.
The area of the horses' head between the ears.

Pony.
A horse less than 14 hands (14.2 hands for showing purposes).

Positioning the horse to the right or left.
This simply means that the horse's head is bent in one or other direction. The bend should be only sufficient for the rider to be able to see the 'shimmer' of the horse's eye. In other words one can just see the corner of the eye.

RIDDOR
Form (Reporting of Injuries, Diseases and Dangerous Occurrence Regulations).

Reflex. - An involuntary action.

Reins.
Straps usually made out of leather that connect the bit to the rider's hands.

Rein back.
A movement in which the horse steps smartly backwards in diagonal two-time (there is no moment of suspension).

Renvers (Tail to the wall).
A horse moving on two tracks laterally, looking in the direction in which he is going and with his tail to the wall of the arena.

Riding Boots.
Strong shoes with a good heal and with extensions reaching up to just below the knee. They are usually made out of leather or rubber.

Rising trot.
When the rider allows the motion of the horse, at the trot, to move the hips forward and backwards in accordance with the two-time motion. The rider will be said to be sitting on the 'correct' diagonal when the seat returns to the saddle as the outside foreleg is coming under the horse.

School.
In this case a place where riding lessons are given. You will note that I refer to the 'junior school' and the 'senior school'. That is because the riding school where I have given many years of service has two 'schools'. The former is for children from 6 years old until they are too big for the ponies, whereupon they transfer to the 'senior school' and carry on their riding education.

Short diagonal.
Changing the rein from either 'F' or 'M' to 'E', alternatively 'K' or 'H' to 'B'. (See fig 54).

Saddle.
A seat usually made of leather (though nowadays sometimes of plastic) and fastened across the back of a horse in order to allow a rider to sit more comfortably.

Serpentine.
As the name implies a series of snakelike joined curved loops. The horse changes direction with each curve

Shimmer of the eye.
The bending of the horses' head through its neck so that the rider can just see the corner of the eye on that side.

Shoulder-in.
A horse moving on three tracks with his quarters to the outside of the arena but not looking in the direction in which he is proceeding.

Sitting tall.
Simply means holding ones body erect so that it is correctly lined up with the rider's own centre of gravity. (Also sitting arrogantly). This must be achieved without any tension in the rider's body.

Sitting trot.
Ceasing to rise to the trot. This will involve a *very slight* forward movement of the hip as the spine absorbs the upward force emanating from the moment of suspension. Care should be taken that this does not become too exaggerated resulting in a hollowing of the small of the back. This is less likely to happen if the heels and ankles also play their part remaining springy and flexing.

Size of an arena. A standard dressage arena measures 40m. by 20m. (See fig 1.).

Small circle.
In a standard dressage arena, one that measures 5m. in diameter. If ridden from an outside track its extreme point is the quarter line.

Spurs.
Metal contraptions attached by leather straps to riders' boots to show them off (used by some riders as an additional means of control).

Stallion.
An adult male horse, uncastrated, over 4 years old (also known as an 'Entire').

Stiff on one rein.
The revealing of stiffness by a horse on one particular side of its body. This may be indicated by a reluctance to go deeply into a corner or to go around in a circle on one particular rein.

Student.
A person attending a course, of which riding is a part, in order to gain a qualification that will enable them to follow a career as an Instructor.

Tack.
Means all the equipment (e.g. saddle bridle etc) required for a horse to be ridden safely.

Take with the hand.
To close the fingers sufficiently in order to increase the degree of tension on the rein and thus the pressure on the bit.

Torso.
The upper part of the riders' body. This is kept in place by the abdominal muscles.

Tracking up.
Where the hoof print of a hind leg comes in front of that made by the foreleg on the same side.

Travers (head to the wall).
A horse moving on two tracks laterally, looking in the direction in which he is going and with his head to the wall of the arena.

Trot - the.
The trot is a two-time movement. The legs move diagonally and simultaneously (i.e. opposite pairs together).

Turn on the forehand.
A movement performed at the halt when a horse moves its hindquarters with clear and precise steps around its inside foreleg, which simply marks time (the horse is bent in the direction of the turn).

Turn on the haunches.
A movement performed at the halt when a horse moves its forehand with clear and precise steps around its inside hind leg, which only describes the smallest of circles (the horse is looking where it is going).

Walk - the.
The walk is a four- time movement.
The legs move consecutively and laterally (i.e. one after the other on the same side).

Widow Twankies.
You will forgive me for mentioning one or two of my own rather eccentric descriptions. I use this term when taking children's classes. Picture if you will the opening scene from the pantomime Aladdin. On stage his mother the Widow Twankie, a washerwoman. There is a washing line stretching across the whole stage. She is hanging up cloths to dry. The line *droops* under the weight of the washing. Thus with loose reins. 'Widow Twankies'! I exclaim. The class knows that I am referring to a lack of contact.

Where are?
A' & 'C'
Opposite one another in the middle of the short ends of the arena.
'B' & 'E'
Opposite one another in the middle of a long sides of the arena.

Where are 'D' and 'G'?
'D' is a point down the centre line 'A' – 'C' that is level with 'F' and 'K'.
'G' is the point down that line that is level with 'H' and 'M'.

Where is 'X'?
This is a point in the centre of the arena exactly halfway between 'A' and 'C' and 'E' and 'B'.

Whip.
Sticklike and made of materials such as flexible carbon fibre, leather, cane etc and used as a means of reminding a horse to pay attention to an aid. A standard whip measures about half a metre, a schooling whip about one metre. Then there are dressage canes, which are simply part of the dress of a rider taking part in a dressage competition. These measure about half a metre and are sometimes also covered with leather. A really long schooling whip may be sued to *touch* (but only that) a horse on a particular limb.

Working in.
A period of time, before any proper work commences, during which a horse is allowed warm up.

Working livery.
A privately owned horse that the owner has agreed to it being used in the riding school for an agreed number of hours each week.

Yielding the jaw.
The horse taking hold of the bit gently and unresistingly in the mouth as it flexes its head at the poll (this will only be deemed do be satisfactory if the horse first engages its hindquarters under its body).

Glossary of preliminary and executive commands.

Formality and informality.

If you are giving a private lesson, it is my view that you should always start with a more formal approach, use whatever is appropriate. Mr….. Mrs…. Or Ms….. If your client then invites you to use their first name, then do so. Always explain first what it is that you require. Thus using the client's name, explain what you wish them to do. Thus 'Emma' (the personal). From the halt, I would like you to prepare to ride a turn on the forehand to the right through 90°. Are you clear as to what is required?' This allows the client time to query your instruction should it not be clear. This is followed by the preliminary command –'Preparing to turn on the forehand to the right through 90°'.Then a few seconds later the Executive command – 'March'. The executive word of command as suggested in the B.H.S Instructors handbook for commands from the halt. *20 is '**March**'. I sometimes use this word as an executive command for other movements. The reason for this is that I have found that if I use a word such as Ter-rot, as the executive command for going forward to trot, then the horses listen to me and not their riders. It is really up to you. Should you be preparing for an exam then I suggest that you use that which the Board examining you prescribes. You are not entitled to take any liberties with prescribed doctrine until you have been teaching for as many years as I have!

Always make sure that your clients understand your commands. If, for any reason, you are doubtful then ask the class to go forward to halt and find out where the misunderstanding lies.

The giving of commands

I have included a glossary of commands because everyone should have knowledge of the accepted form of giving commands. I do not use these all the time, especially when teaching absolute beginners, who have a lot to think about. It may help to dispense with the accepted form and to use words that do not have to be translated into everyday parlance. In the first lesson or three, I prefer to use language that they can immediately be understood. For example. Instead of 'going large' I would say 'Please go along the outer track of the arena. To help you do so please look towards the next corner, keep looking at it. Make your horse look where you are looking and ride towards it keeping your horse as much on the track as you can'. A trifle wordy you may think but my contention is that one is giving the rider information in small doses in a language that they understand, therefore all they have to do is to try to put this into practice.

After the third lesson or so you should start to use the standard words of command. It is important that you explain exactly what each command means. (See Explanation of terms used.) I mention but a few words of command. If you wish to learn more of them then read The BHS. Instructor's Hand Book. *20

It is important that the class have a means of reference as to when a movement shall be performed. It helps them to move in unison with one another and avoids a dangerous situation as might occur when the class all move at different times. This is the operative word of command. The one that I use frequently is 'March'. Of course one should not forget that as riders improve so they should be encouraged to work-in their horses individually. In which case you do not have to give them any instruction, until the working-in period is over or you have to diffuse a potential problem before it builds up.

The word 'prepare'.

You may have noticed that throughout this book I always use the word '*prepare'*. This is an essential word for any Instructor to include in any command. The reason for this is that this word tells the rider that they are about to give an aid (a combination of signals). For the novice rider and perhaps we may even include the intermediate rider, these are not going to happen by reflex, the rider is going to have to think about what they are going to do if the aid is to be given clearly and correctly. The matter does not end there. Even an expert rider is who simply thinks their way into the movement so that a change appears to flow, must still *allow the horse time to think* about what is being asked of it.

The command for the walk.

You say '**The Ride, prepare to go forward to walk, - walk, <u>March</u>.**' Note the use of the word *prepare* (This means that the rider should initiate the aids for walk) – *Go forward*. All commands should include the words *'go forward'*. The implication being that when working a horse one always starts or ends a transition in such a manner that it is always collected, that is always ready to do the riders bidding for whatever follows next. It also implies no loss of impulsion. Even at the halt the horse remains *at attention*. After go 'forward to walk' there is a slight pause during which the rider has gained the horses attention and gives the aid. 'Walk, March' follow one another swiftly. 'March' is the executive word of command. The point when the rider's fingers open and the horse obeys (we hope). I use the word 'March' because that is the word that I was taught to use. You may use any other executive word of command that you choose. Generally speaking an instruction for an upward transition should be sharp, whilst that of a downward transition be soft. The exception being the transition to halt, which, in my view, should also be sharp, since it involves a cessation of movement, and does need to have an element that lends itself to the storing of impulsion. Of course having asked for a halt or walk the rider should be instructed to give the horse a long rein if it is due for a rest.

The importance of the position of the class in relation to a given command.
Now it must be obvious that commands cannot simply be given in isolation. For example, if you have your class lined up along the centre line and ask them to go forward to walk in line abreast to an outside track of the arena, it is necessary to give them their next instruction before they move off. If you do not do so then there may not be sufficient time for them to react correctly when they get there. Thus from the centre line the class must know that when they reach the track they are to then proceed on either the right or left rein in single file around the arena. Therefore your commands must be clear and precise.

Your command '**As the ride reaches the track prepare to turn to the right and go large single file**'. '**Watch your distances**' (a simple element of a drill ride). So it is obvious that you must keep thinking ahead all the time. This is where your preparation is important. If you have not previously prepared your lesson, then you may well find yourself floundering. Oh you may be able to cover this up but in so doing you will probably find, if your are honest with yourself, that you have strayed far off the subject that you had in mind to teach.

The commands for upward transitions for trot and canter.
The same as for the command for the walk except that one uses the appropriate word. And so one continues. From transitions through to circles.

However when one comes to circles one must add a further dimension and that is the size of the circle and where it will be ridden. Thus: -

Your command "**Prepare to ride a circle of half the arena at 'A'**". Is this sufficient? Answer is no it is not. Before the class reach 'A' they must have been informed what riding a circle involves (see riding circles chapter 8). If you leave your instruction until they are already on the circle or what they think passes for one, it is too late!

Giving the horse a long rein.
This is a command that frequently causes confusion. A long rein allows the horse to stretch its neck and thus to have a period of relaxation. However it should be clearly understood that even with a long rein the rider still has an elastic contact with the horses' mouth. A loose rein is where the rider has no contact whatsoever and simply holds the rein by the buckle.

Giving commands to a ride.
When you are taking a class always prefix you command with the word '**The Ride**'.

Refining this command.
As your lesson progresses you may need to be specific. Thus: -
1. The ride – In single file. Meaning that they all proceed one after the other.

2. The ride – In succession. Meaning individually.

3.   Proceed in Rides……... This will apply should you have split a class of say 8 riders into two groups of four.
4. The whole ride. This means everyone riding a movement simultaneously (i.e. all together at the same time).

5. Both rides….. Is my command where I have two rides and I wish them to perform the same movement.

Open order.

This is simply a command for the class to increase the distance between each rider. In effect it means that every rider should have not less than three horses distance between themselves and the rider in front. In practise you may, if you wish, utilise the whole area of the arena by simply asking the class to increase the distance until they are all spread out evenly around the arena. It is useful for performing such movements as rein back and turns on the forehand where you wish your riders to have plenty of room so that they may walk on as soon as the movement is complete.

Commands for canter.

This is one of the first commands for a novice ride about to try to canter.

'The leading file only prepare to go forward to a working trot, rising. The remainder of the class continue at walk' 'Leading file trrrrrrot – **March**'. When you consider that the time is right. 'Prepare to canter to the rear of the ride – canter **march'**. Note that the instructions are quite specific.

As the class makes progress you may ask them, one at a time, to canter past the ride. Thus 'Leading file only - prepare to canter large around the arena and continue past the ride for one circuit only, then join the rear with a downward transition through trot'. (This last part is dependent on whether you have the rest of the ride at walk or trot. If the former then 'Through trot to walk'.

Macro command - a.

This is a term that I have coined. As with computing, it is a command, this consists of several sub-commands, which are activated by an executive command consisting of only one or two words. The class previously been explained the sub-commands, upon hearing the executive command, proceed with this series of different movements.

Asking the ride to number.

Very simply ask the ride to number from 1 to … depending on how many riders you have. *The lead file calls out 'One' as they do so they turn their head to and face the rider behind them*. The next rider does the same calling out 'Two' and so the numbering continues to the last rider.

Question.

Why turning the head?

Answer.

So that the rider behind can clearly see from whence the number has arisen. If you have a large ride then a rider towards the rear may suffer from confusion as to whether or not the previous caller was the rider in front of them or one nearer the front.

Asking the ride to number in pairs.

As for simple numbering but on this occasion the riders only call out 'One', 'Two', 'One', 'Two'. When pairs numbering has been completed you ask the ride to 'prove'. Your command is 'Number twos prove'. All the twos place the reins in the outside hand and turn the inside one palm upwards towards you.

Index

Index (cont.)

Index (cont.)

Index (cont.)

Index (cont.)

Index (cont.)

Coloured Illustrations

Photographs & Illustrations

Chapter 2

Photo no. 2. The correct dress.

Chapter 6

Photo no. 3. Standing with presence.

Chapter 6

Chapter 6

Photo no. 4. Ensuring the integrity of the arena.

Photo no. 5. Approaching a class to carry out checks.

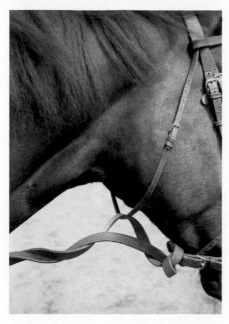

Photo no. 6. Securing the reins prior to lunging.

Photo no. 7. Checking the saddle arch.

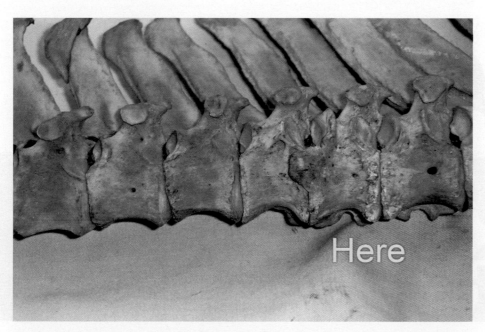

Photo no. 8. Sections of the backbone showing a build up of bony deposit around the joints.

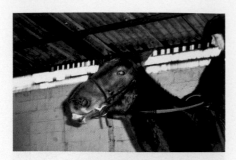

Chapter 7

Photo no. 9. (Top) A horse resisting for all its worth.
Photo no. 10. (Below) Crossing a hand over the neck

Photo no. 11. Using a short whip. Note the reins have been placed in one hand to prevent giving two opposing signals.

Photo no. 12a. Changing a short whip from hand to hand, (commencing).

Photo no. 12b. Changing a short whip from hand to hand, (and proceeding).

Photo no. 13(a). Changing a long whip from hand to hand, (commencing).

Photo no. 13(b). Changing a long whip from hand to hand, (continuing).

Photo no. 13(c). Changing a long whip from hand to hand, (completing).

Photo no. 14. A rider trotting with good balance and no grip

437

Chapter 8

Photo no. 15. Checking the stirrups for correct length before mounting.

Photo no. 16(a). Mounting sequence from the ground. (Note rider's right hand placed on the pommel).

Photo no. 16(b). Mounting sequence from the ground cont. (Rider's left hand placed on the withers).

Photo no. 16(c). Giving a leg-up.

Photo no. 16(d). Using a portable mounting block.

Photo no. 16(e). Mounting from a fixed block.

Photo no. 16(f). Nearly there.

Photo no. 16(g). Up and over (Note that the rider's leg is lifted well clear of the horse's back and the saddle.

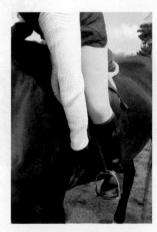

Photo no. 17. A rider re-checking the girth.

Photo no. 18. Un-even stirrup leathers.

439

Photo no. 18(b). A twisted stirrup leather..

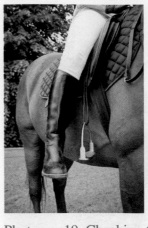

Photo no. 19. Checking the length of the stirrup while mounted.

Photo no. 20. A slightly greater bend in the knee may provide better support in the beginning.

Photo no. 20(a). Making adjustments to the stirrup length while mounted (note that the rider does not take the foot right out of the stirrup, they un-weight it).

Photo no. 21. Putting a knot in the reins for work at the halt.

Photo no. 22. An exercise to induce relaxation, each arm rotated high in the air.

Photo no. 23. Arms folded in the small of the back.

Photo no. 23(a). The rotated arm descending to meet the raised heel.

Photo no. 23(b). Raising the leg upwards and outward away from the horse's side.

Photo no. 24. Marching movement using hands and legs together.

Photo no. 25. Carrying the spare loop of the rein under the bit rein.

Chapter 9

Photo no. 27. Some common faults.

Photo no. 28. Leading a horse correctly.

Photo no. 29. Sitting and holding the reins correctly, as one prepares to ride without stirrups.

Photo no. 30. The beginning of going on the bit. The horse has yielded its jaw but the rider has not asked it to raise its neck and provide a proper outline. Thus there is a danger that the horse will very soon start to 'lean on the bit' and to cease using the hindquarters.

Photo no. 31. Shoulder-in at the walk.

Photo no. 32. Traverse at the walk.

Photo no. 33(a). A long rein (note that the horse is allowed to stretch and relax but the rider still maintains contact.

Photo no. 33(b). A loose rein (there is no contact).

Photo no. 34. Incorrect position for a leg yield. (note particularly the rider's inside leg and hand, which is crossing over the horse's neck).

Photo no. 35. A better position but the horse's quarters are still trailing.

Photo no. 36. Taking the open position (note that the rider is not using the rein for support).

Photo no. 37. The closed position keeping the back straight.

Photo no. 38. Sara's first jump.

Plate iii Chapter 17.
A horse in full flight and a perfect jumping position.
Charlie Swan jumping Istabraq. A superb photograph taken by Caroline Norris and reproduced here with her permission. Note that the rider is speaking to the horse, in mid flight, and the cocking of the horse's ears shows that he is listening.

Chapter 18

Photo no. 39. A long style drover's coat.

Drawings.

Chapter 7

Drawing no. 12.

The sequence of footfalls of the walk from halt.

The horse is shown initially at the halt. Red represents the near hind, Blue the near fore, Green the off hind and Purple the off fore.

Where the foot is raised and thrust forwards it has not been shown because it is in the air. As it lands it is shown at the top of the rectangle. As the horses' body moves forward over the foot so the hoof print is shown as having moved towards the centre of the rectangle (i.e. coming under the horse). Finally as it passes behind and into the air preparatory to being thrust forward again so it is simply shown as a series of arrows in the rectangle lying below those showing the footfalls.

An ordinary walk has been illustrated. At this moment we see alternate suspension on two legs either laterally or diagonally. However it should be born in mind that, dependent on the degree of collection or otherwise, so there may be a fraction of a second where the support is provided first by two legs and then on three.

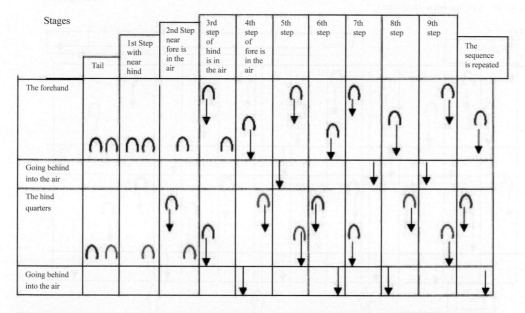

Note that after stage 9 when the sequence is repeated the horse, now being in motion, so the footfalls are now fluid and continuous.

Drawing no. 12. The sequence of footfalls at the walk

Chapter 13

The exact moment to initiate a trot from walk with a desired diagonal

The hores is shown walking, Red represents the near hind, Blue the near fore, Green the off hind and Purple the off fore.

Where the foot is raised and thrust forwards it has not been shown because it is in the air. As it lands it is shown at the top of the rectangle. As the horses' body moves forward over the foot so the hoof print is shown as having moved towards the centre of the rectangle (i.e. coming under the horse). Finally as it passes behind and into the air preparatory to being thrust forward again so it is simply shown as a series of arrows in the rectangle lying below those showing the footfalls.

Knowing exactly when to give an aid is extremely useful. For example if one is riding a horse which tends to pace, then, by giving the aid as it about to place its weight on a pair of diagonals, will encourage it to trot normally.

An ordinary walk has been illustrated.

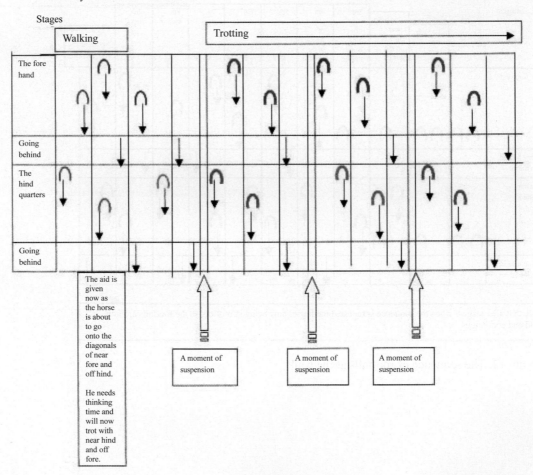

Drawing no. 27. The exact moment to initiate, a trot from the walk, with a desired diagonal.

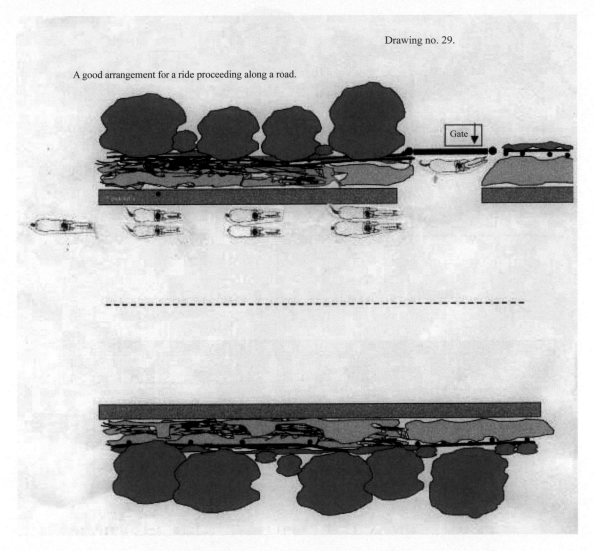

Chapter 20

Drawing no. 29. A good arrangement for horses proceeding on the road.

Drawing no. 30.

A badly arranged ride

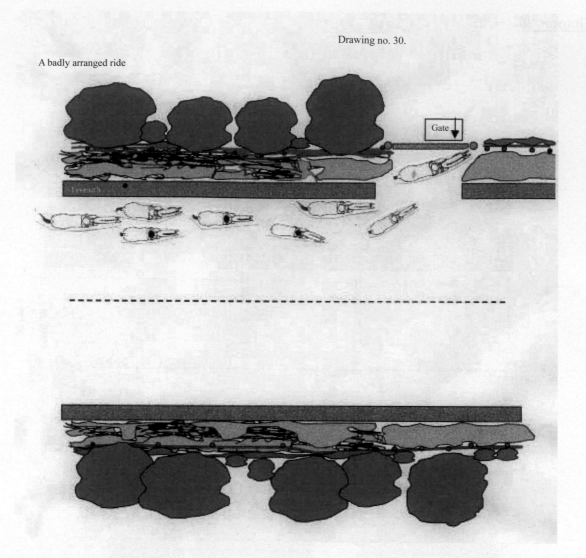

Drawing no. 30. A badly arranged ride.

Opening a gate correctly - The approach (2nd stage).
The rider now has time to position the horse correctly as they walk towards the gate latch.

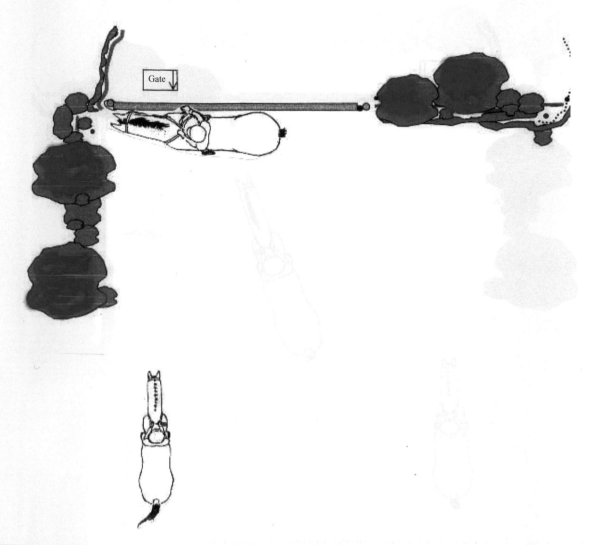

Drawing no. 33b. Approaching the gate latch.

Pointing out landmarks as a guide to riding figures in
In this particular case you might ask a rider to go larg
their attention to the second oak tree from the far righ
ask them to ride a perfect circle the tangential points
left.

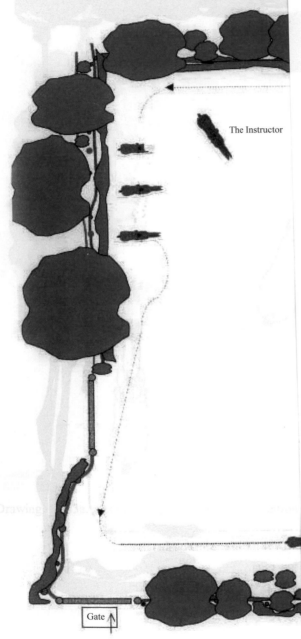

The Instructor

Gate ↑

Drawing no. 31. Pointing out landmarks as a guide to ric

Drawing no. 32.

Opening a gate correctly - (3rd stage).
Having opened the gate latch. The rider now places their hand on the top bar of the gate and starts to open it. As they do so, they ask the horse to step both backward and sideways thus assisting the process.

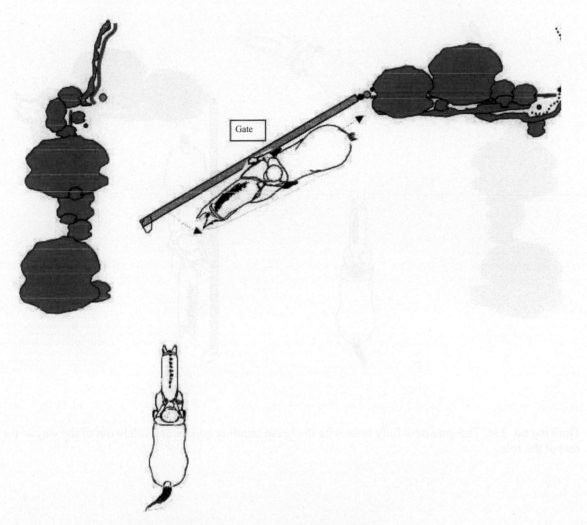

Drawing no. 33c. Proceeding to open the gate with a turn about the hindquarters.

Opening a gate correctly - (4th stage).
Having opened the gate, the rider waits for the ride to pass through (note that the horse's hindquarters are tucked well out of the way of the other horses).
When the ride is well clear, the rider goes to the other side of the gate and repeats the proccess to close it

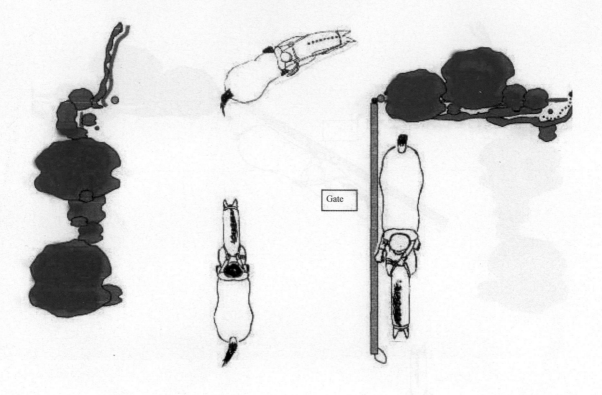

Drawing no. 33d. The gate now fully open with the horse standing quietly and safely out of the way of the rest of the ride.